Perspectives from *Historical Archaeology*

The Archaeology of Spanish Missions and Colonies in the New World

Compiled by
Steve A. Tomka and Timothy K. Perttula

No. 6

SOCIETY *for*
HISTORICAL
ARCHAEOLOGY

Compiled by: Steve A. Tomka and Timothy K. Perttula

Contact Information:
Steve A. Tomka
Center for Archaeological Research
The University of Texas at San Antonio
One UTSA Circle
San Antonio, TX 78249

Timothy K. Perttula
Archeological & Environmental Consultants, LLC
10101 Woodhaven Drive
Austin, Texast 78753

Cover: Unknown Photographer. Mission Concepción, ca. 1880.

Perspectives from Historical Archaeology is a reader series providing collected articles from the journal of the Society for Historical Archaeology (SHA). Published since 1967, <u>Historical Archaeology</u> is the oldest North American scholarly publication on the archaeology of sites and materials from the historic past, and one of the world's premier publications on this subject. Each volume in the *Perspectives* series is developed on either a subject or regional basis by a compiler, who selects the articles for inclusion and their order. The compilers also provide an introduction that presents an overview of the substantive work on that topic. *Perspectives* volumes offer non-archaeologists a convenient source for important publications on a subject or a region; an excellent resource for students interested in developing a specialization in a specific topic or area; as well as a convenient reference for archaeologists with an interest in the material.

The *Perspectives* series is managed by the SHA's Journal Editor and Co-Publications Editor and is published through the SHA's Print-On-Demand Press. Individuals interested in compiling a volume for publication through this series are encouraged to contact the Series Editors:

J. W. Joseph, PhD, RPA
Journal Editor, SHA
New South Associates, Inc.
6150 East Ponce de Leon Avenue
Stone Mountain, GA 30083
jwjoseph@newsouthassoc.com

Annalies Corbin, PhD
Co-Publications Editor, SHA
The PAST Foundation
1929 Kenny Road, Suite 200
Columbus, OH 43210
annalies@pastfoundation.org

Formed in 1967, the SHA is the largest scholarly group concerned with the archaeology of the modern world (A.D. 1400-present). The main focus of the society is the era since the beginning of European exploration. SHA promotes scholarly research and the dissemination of knowledge concerning historical archaeology. The society is specifically concerned with the identification, excavation, interpretation, and conservation of sites and materials on land and underwater. Geographically the society emphasizes the New World, but also includes European exploration and settlement in Africa, Asia, and Oceania. To learn more about the SHA and historical archaeology, visit www.sha.org.

Contents

Part I. Introduction

1. *Perspectives on the Archaeology of Spanish Missions and Colonies*
   Steve A. Tomka and Timothy K. Perttula... 1

Part II. Theoretical Perspectives and Approaches

2. *Archaeology and 19th Century Missions* (HA 1967 1(1):57-59)
   David H. Snow 26

3. *A Unified Approach to the Anthropology of Hispanic Northern New Mexico: Historical Archaeology, Ethnohistory, and Ethnography* (HA 1976 10(1):1-16)
   Paul Kutsche, John R. Van Ness, and Andrew T. Smith... 29

4. *Archaeology and History on Historic Hispanic Sites: Impediments and Solutions* (HA 1985 19(1):32-37)
   Kathleen Deagan and Michael Scardaville.. 45

5. *Some Models for Spanish Colonial Archaeology in California* (HA 1992 26(1):37-44)
   Robert L. Hoover... 51

Part III. Studies of Material Culture – Context and Process

6. *The Role of Ceramics in Spain and Spanish America during the 16th Century* (HA 1992 26(1):92-108)
   Bonnie G. McEwan 59

7. *The Archaeology of Women in the Spanish New World* (HA 1991 25(4):33-41)
   Bonnie G. McEwan 76

8. *The Ties That Bind: Economic and Social Interactions in Early-Colonial New Mexico, A.D. 1598-1680* (HA 2003 37(2):65-84)
   Heather B.Trigg 85

Part IV. Studies of Material Culture – Reflections on Identity, Status, and Culture Change

9. *An X-ray Fluorescence-Pattern Recognition Analysis of Pottery from an Early Historic Hispanic Settlement Near Santa Fe, New Mexico* (HA 1992 26(2):24-36)
   William J. Thomas, Nathan W. Bower, John W. Kantner,
   Marianne L. Stoller, and David H. Snow 105

10. *Ceramic Variability in 17th Century St. Augustine, Florida* (HA 1984 18(2):75-82)
    Julia King.. 118

11. *The Importance of the Community Study Approach in Historical Archaeology, with an Example from Late Colonial St. Augustine* (HA 1995 29(4):59-83)
    James G. Cusick 126

12. *Material Culture and Colonial Indian Society in Southern Mesoamerica: The View from Coastal Chiapas, Mexico* (HA 1992 26(1):67-74)
    Janine Gasco 151

13. *Empire and Ceramics: The Changing Role of Illicit Trade in Spanish America* (HA 1992 26(1):109-118)
    Russell K. Skowronek 159

14. *Eliciting Contraband through Archaeology: Illicit Trade in Eighteenth-Century St. Augustine* (HA 2007 41(4):98-116)
    Kathleen Deagan 169

15. *Purchasing Patterns of the California Missions in ca. 1805* (HA 1992 26(1):59-66)
    Julia G. Costello 188

Part V. Subsistence Change

16. *Historic Subsistence Practices: Synthesis and Conclusions* (HA, SP 3 1992, pp. 92-99)
    Elizabeth J. Reitz and C. Margaret Scarry 196

17. *The Spanish Colonial Experience and Domestic Animals* (HA 1992 26(1):84-91)
    Elizabeth J. Reitz 204

18. *Oranges and Wheat: Spanish Attempts at Agriculture in La Florida* (HA 1997 31(1):36-45)
    Donna L. Ruhl 212

19. *Iberian Foodways in the Moquegua and Torata Valleys of southern Peru* (HA 1996 30(3):20-48)
    Susan D. DeFrance 222

20. *The Market for Meat in Colonial Cuenca: A Seventeenth-Century Urban Faunal Assemblage from the Southern Highlands of Ecuador* (HA 2008 42(4):21-37)
    Ross W. Jamieson 251

Part VI. Site Structure and Mission Layout

21. *Mission-Period Settlement Structure: A Test of the Model at San Martin de Timucua* (HA 1996 30(4):24-36)
    Rebecca Saunders 268

22. *Rethinking Mission Land Use and the Archaeological Record in California: An Example from Santa Clara* (HA 2010 44(2):72-96)
    Rebecca Allen 281

Steve A. Tomka and Timothy K. Perttula

Perspectives on the Archaeology of Spanish Missions and Colonies

ABSTRACT

This introductory essay provides an overview of the contents of the selected articles included in this reader and contextualizes them within the voluminous body of literature written on the archaeology of Spanish missions and colonialism over the past decades.

Introduction to the Volume

The Spanish presence in La Florida began with intermittent coastal explorations during the early 1500s and the establishment of a modest encampment by Menendez de Aviles in 1565, an encampment that was to become the capital of La Florida (Milanich 1990). Over the next 200 years more than 150 missions were established by Jesuit and Franciscan friars in La Florida. In Texas, following Cabeza de Vaca's shipwreck and eventual return to Spain in the 1530s, intermittent *visitas* and *entradas* were made north of the Rio Grande beginning in the late 17th century that culminated in the establishment of missions among the Hasinai Caddo in East Texas in 1691 (Perttula 1992). The first mission in the San Antonio River valley, Mission San Antonio de Bexar, was established in 1718, and by 1731, the number of missions grew to five as a new mission (Mission San José y San Miguel de Aguayo) was established in 1720 and three East Texas missions (San Juan Capistrano; San Francisco de la Espada; and Nuestra Señora de la Concepción de Acuña) were abandoned and re-established in the San Antonio River valley. In the Southwest, the first Jesuit mission was established in 1590 while the Franciscan mission program began in the 17th century and resulted in the construction of 40 missions in New Mexico (Cordell 1989:27-28). Exploration of *Las Californias* began in the 1500s, and after two failed attempts at establishing mission in 1683, successful settlement of Baja California finally occurred in 1697 (Mathes 1989). By the time they were expelled in 1767, the Jesuits had established 17 missions in Baja California. The colonization of Alta California began in 1769 and resulted in the establishment of 21 missions by the Franciscan order (Costello and Hornbeck 1989).

At least in North America, the factors spurring the founding of the Spanish missions, presidios, and colonies were two-fold: first, the political impetus to claim ownership of the new territories in advance of competing geo-political interests, and second, the desire of the church to convert native groups (Wade 2008:3-19). The colonization of Florida, Texas, and California was driven primarily by geopolitical factors, while the colonization of the Southwest falls under the second impetus.

The native groups that were the targets of the Spanish efforts ranged from agricultural chiefdoms such as the Guale of the Georgia coast and the Timucua of the Florida Panhandle, to the more socio-politically complex Apalachee of northwestern Florida (Thomas 1990). Texas native groups were primarily nomadic hunter-gatherers, although the first missions were established among the Caddo farmers of East Texas (Chipman and Joseph 2010:83-147). Coastal hunter-gatherers and highly nomadic hunter-gatherers in South Texas made up the bulk of the groups impacted by the missions. The Spanish venture in Texas produced 38 missions, 15 towns, and 10 presidios by the early 1830s, when the decree for secularization was finally implemented (Habig 1990). In the Southwest, the first missions and colonies were established among agricultural groups such as the Hopi and the Zuni. In contrast, the earliest missions in Baja California were founded among nomadic hunter-gatherers, while in Alta California the native groups were complex hunter-gathers (Bean 1978:681).

These variable circumstances provide a veritable laboratory for social scientists, archaeologists and anthropologists included, to study many themes significant to the social sciences in general, including culture change, ethnicity, identify formation, and technological change, to name just a few. The earliest interest in the missions dates back to around the turn of the 19th century when Bancroft (1884-1890) published his *History of California* and described the unfavorable conditions experienced by the missions' Indian populations. In 1915, Bolton published a compilation of documents depicting the Spanish missionary activities in Texas during the mid-18th century. Only six years later, his compendium on the Spanish Borderlands (1921) from Florida to the Southwest was published and fueled interest in the

Spanish Colonial period. While these initial works were primarily historical documentaries, they also helped fire up the imagination of the general public, and to some degree this interest fueled a desire to relocate many of these lost missions and presidios.

Some of the earliest work at these missions dates back to the efforts of the Work Progress Administration and the Civilian Conservation Corps era when large labor pools were used to expose partially visible ruins and reconstruct missions and presidios (i.e., the 1932 work by Architect H. P. Smith at Mission San José y San Miguel de Aguayo in San Antonio). Sadly, the goal of this work was to reconstruct ruined missions to their former glory to provide a source of tourism traffic, and therefore, no archaeological investigations accompanied these efforts. Later efforts tended to focus on rediscovering missions based on written documentary information (see Cordell 1989:31-34; Costello and Hornbeck 1989:321-323; Milanich 2006:5-13). More focused research into Spanish missions, presidios, and colonies, was spurred by the Columbian Quincentenary. Since the early 1990s, interest in the Spanish Colonial period and mission research virtually exploded, beginning with the three volume *Columbian Consequences* series edited by David H. Thomas (1989, 1990, 1991) and the Society's own Guide to the Archaeological Literature of the Immigrant Experience in America (Ayres 1995). Recent publications include Jackson and Castillo (1995), Hass (1995), Allen (1998), Lightfoot (2005), Hackel (2005), and Voss (.2008), on California; McEwan (2000); Saunders (2000), Bense (2003), Blanton and King (2004), Milanich (2006), and Stojanowski (2010) on the Southeast; Rothschild (2003) on the Southwest; and Wade (2008) on both Texas and Florida.

By the 1980s, a number of archaeologists had begun research to document and understand the processes and patterns that result from cultures in contact (cf. Deagan 1983). Nonetheless, the publication of *Columbian Consequences* represented a true watershed in approaches to mission archaeology by calling for the study of the processes and dynamics that operated both within the Spanish colonial and Native American communities and resulted in a variety of outcomes on both sides (Thomas 1989:11). The call to conduct particularistic case studies was issued to build a comparative database that would then help in defining broad patterns and outcomes of Spanish-Native American interactions (Thomas 1989:11). This shift in theoretical orientation ushered in a new era in historical archaeology focused on culture contact studies (Cusick 1998; Murray 2004). Contact studies soon resulted in the realization that not all contact has the same driving forces and outcomes and that there is a dramatic difference when it comes to colonization (Silliman 2005). While some researchers had already adopted the colonization framework for their studies by the time of the *Columbian Consequences* volumes (Adams 1989; Castillo 1989), the archaeology of colonialism has advanced considerably during the past decade with publication by Lyons and Papadopoulos (2002), Gosden (2004), Given (2004, Stein (2005), and Hurst and Owen (2005). The most recent analytical emphasis in the archaeology of colonialism focuses on the forms of resistance of native populations to colonial pressures (Liebmann and Murphy 2011). Naturally, the Society for Historical Archaeology's (SHA) interest in the archaeology of the Spanish missions and colonial frontier/borderlands dates to its inception in 1967 (Snow 1967). Since then, *Historical Archaeology* (HA) has published a large number of articles and several special and edited volumes relevant to the subject of colonial archaeology, including a recent volume of compiled papers dedicated to the archaeology of Native American-European culture contact (Perttula 2011).

While such selected volumes typically are formulated around a theme, this volume is centered on two of the three most visible products of the Spanish Colonial presence in the New World, missions and colonies. While presidios often accompanied the establishment of missions in the New World, given the recent publication of a dedicated volume of *Historical Archaeology* on presidio archaeology (Bense 2004), the Spanish forts are not considered in this volume. Two principal criteria were applied in choosing the selections incorporated herein. First, there was a concern to provide a chronological sequence representative of the theoretical developments in mission archaeology and, second there was a desire to ensure that all of the research themes currently being pursued are represented in the selections. In addition, an effort was made to select not only examples from North America but to look more broadly to case studies representative of Cental and South America.

II. Theoretical Perspectives and Approaches

The four contributions to this section of the reader represent a collection of papers that provide a review of the theoretical perspectives that have developed over a 30-year period beginning with the establishment of the Society for Historical Archaeology in 1967. The approaches are reflective of the theoretical paradigms of the times. **Chapter 2**, written by Snow (1967), is the first call for a focus on mission archaeology to appear in the Society's journal. Writing one year before the publication of Binford and Binford's *New Perspectives* (1968), Snow proposes two aspects of mission sites that may be of interest to culture historians, anthropologists, and historiographers alike. Specifically, he suggests that mission research has a unique potential to contribute to the study of how the missionaries that were responsible for the construction and daily operation of the missions were changed by their endeavors and how their activities in turn impacted the culture of the indigenous groups that were residing at the missions. There is clear recognition that the process of acculturation is a double-edged sword that left deep scars not only on the native populations it touched but also changed the lives of many of the friars, soldiers, administrators, and colonists that ventured into the New World. This emphasis foreshadows contemporary studies of ethnogenesis that focus on the birth of new identities out of the clash of Hispanic and aboriginal cultures (Powers 1995; Deagan 1996, 1998; Anderson 1999; Mullins and Paynter 2000; Haley and Wilcoxon 2005; Hanson and Kurtz 2007; Voss 2008) Finally, advocating for the integration of historical documents into historical archaeological research, Snow calls for problem-oriented research, regardless of the origin of the problems to be solved.

Kutsche et al.'s contribution in **Chapter 3** comes some nine years after Snow and during the early days of the new archaeology paradigm shift. They advocate for a close relationship between archaeology, ethnohistory, and ethnography to serve as testing grounds for the methods and approaches of new archaeology. They particularly emphasize the need to rely on the historical record as a source of analogies to explain the archaeological record, particularly in cases where there is a demonstrated historical linkage between living groups and their presumed prehistoric antecedents.

To spur research in Hispanic Northern New Mexico, Kutsche et al. (1976) propose a series of testable hypotheses grouped into three broad categories: ecology, social organization, and trade. The hypotheses focus on broadly relevant research issues such as the search for evidence of community-level specialization between Hispanic settlers and Pueblo Indians, and expected patterns of settlement expansion with increases in Hispanic populations. The spatial organization of the settlement and the factors that may condition it is also suggested as a worthy avenue of inquiry. Several topics associated with social organization are also proposed, including the study of the relationship between different family structures, wealth, and characteristics of domestic architecture. Kutsche et al. also see a great opportunity to investigate community organization as reflected in social stratification, the inter-relationship between irrigation and organization of labor, the ethnic composition of villages, and the process of assimilation of ethnically diverse groups. They also suggest that various scales of trade can be studied in historical archaeology, among them international trade, trade between New Mexico and Mexico, and trade between Hispanic settlements and indigenous groups. Finally, Kutsche et al. point out that life on the frontier was not as strictly controlled and regulated as it would appear from the multitude of decrees issued by the King of Spain. Despite the numerous governmental and church orders issued to control aspects of life on the frontier, daily life, "real life," was different than the "ideal" laid out in the decrees. Kutsche et al. (1976) suggest that the collaboration between archaeology, ethnohistory, and ethnography should provide the means to elucidate the degree of fit between ideal and real life conditions. The expressed purpose of presenting these testable hypotheses is to create a rich dataset that can be used by ethnologists to refine their understanding of broad processes and principles such as rates and directions of cultural development, selective borrowing of cultural traits, and persistence of certain traits even in the face of severe pressures to change. It is the combination of the methodological approach—focused on the definition of testable hypotheses—in combination with the desire to define common processes and principles, that explains why the study of culture change is strongly tied to the processual paradigm (Watson 2008). While this proposition is based on strong linkages between the social sciences, history, anthropology, and archaeology, the study of culture change using this broad integrated approach is rarely attempted, even after calls for similar united approaches to historical archaeology (Leonard and Jones 1987).

In **Chapter 4**, Deagan and Scardaville discuss the difficulties associated with designing and implementing a truly multi-disciplinary approach to historical archaeology. They particularly focus on the need for meaningful collaboration between historians and archaeologists, and on a broader level, all researchers associated with multi-disciplinary projects (Deagan and Scardaville 1985). Due to their specialized training, historians and archaeologists typically posses skills and expertise that do not allow them to do each other's research in an effective manner. Archaeologists cannot adequately assess the internal and external validity of historic documents, nor their accuracy and completeness, particularly when relying on fragmentary translations rather than complete original sources. Also, from such fragmentary sources they cannot provide proper context to specific facts that may be relevant to their archaeological research interests. On the other hand, historians often tend to conduct research that is too event-specific and descriptive in nature to be relevant to the broader anthropological research issues that are at the center of much archaeological research, such as documenting social variability, reconstructing variability in production, distribution and exchange of goods, and defining the factors that may affect the archaeological record. Deagan and Scardaville strongly recommend that for a truly multidisciplinary approach to be effective in historical archaeology, the representatives of each sub-discipline need to be brought in at the stage of research design development and close communications needs to be maintained throughout the project to ensure flow of relevant information between the specialists. The methodological difficulties highlighted by them are not uncommon to the practice of archaeology in general, given the need to incorporate a multi-disciplinary team of specialists (e.g., geomorphologists, enthobotanists, faunal analysts, malacologists, etc) in many projects. However, given the fact that information derived from written records may often serve as the source of testable hypotheses and typically contributes a great deal of rich and significant complementary detail to historical archaeology projects, it becomes even more paramount that there is a close research relationship between historians and archaeologists. We would also sug-

gest that historical archaeologists would benefit from discussions with prehistoric archaeologists. Such exchanges would ensure that research problems and hypotheses are defined and articulated in such a manner that they are applicable to understanding human behavior in its broadest context. All too often, conclusions and interpretations of patterns derived from archaeological data are discussed solely within the context of historical or prehistoric archaeology, but not within both, as if dietary practices, trade dynamics, the expression of status and wealth, and other characteristics of the archaeological record are the domains of only one of these time frames.

Hoover's contribution in **Chapter 5** follows in the path of the scientific search for general laws and patterns of behavior by suggesting that various aspects of Spanish Colonial missions in California may be understood by reliance on models generated by social scientists. He suggests that ecological principles such as the process of simplification and competitive exclusion may be applied to the California missions to explain the early forms of social, political, and economic systems documented in them. In turn, the insular and cosmopolitan frontier models of Steffen (1980) appear to fit well with the shift in settlement patterns and economic roles of California missions between the first two decades of the 19th century and following 1821. The economic basis of the missions moved from a diversified economy geared to maintain self-sufficiency to a ranching economy that was tied to the economy of the homeland and indirectly to international markets. Hoover (1992) also highlights the potential that Wallerstein's world-system theory may contribute to explaining economic dynamics across the California missions. For instance, there is a change in trading patterns between the late 18th century and the early 19th century at Mission San Antonio de Padua that may fit well with expectations derived from world system theory. Specifically, the preponderance of Hispanic pottery in early components of the site is replaced by British ceramics between 1802-1834. At the same time, the mission becomes a ceramic manufacture and distribution center despite the fact that the indigenous population did not manufacture ceramics prior to missionization. This shift from an economy focused on self-sufficiency to one that is on the periphery but tied to broader economic spheres is characteristic of the core-periphery systems highlighted by Wallerstein (1974, 1980). Hoover, however, is cautious about uncritically applying World Systems Theory to explain all aspects of the economy of California missions, principally because it is an explanatory model developed for capitalist rather than pre-capitalist economies. Finally, Hoover suggests that mission research can make significant contributions to our understanding of acculturation processes. Specifically, he cites three distinct approaches (Deetz 1963; Hoover and Costello 1985; Farnsworth 1986) that attempt to measure the types and direction of acculturation.

III. Studies of Material Culture – Context and Process

The challenge of developing analytical approaches and methods that accurately measure or gauge changes in human behavior over time is constant in archaeological research. Studies of acculturation dominated much of the anthropological discourse throughout the 1950 and 1960s (Broom et al. 1954; Spicer 1961) and the concept continued to be a viable tool for viewing culture change in contact situations well into the 1980s (Farnsworth 1989). Due to its primarily unidirectional framing, the concept of acculturation has been abandoned in favor of more dynamic and multi-dimensional reformulations (see Cusick 1998; Deagan 1998:26-28). This reformulation, whether it is defined as transculturation (Garcia-Arevalo 1989; Deagan 1998); culture contact studies (Schortman and Urban 1998); mestizaje (Deagan 1973); or creolization (Dawdy 2000), faces the same challenge of how to define material correlates that track, reflect, or correlate with changes in ethnicity and identity over time. The challenge has become even more formidable as anthropologists and archaeologists have given more weight to the possibility that participants in cultures in contact were actively manipulating the interactions they participated in as well as the identities they chose to portray (Dobres 2000; Gardner 2008). Each action has a social context and actors and observers interpret one's actions within socially prescribed frames of reference. Therefore, the meaning of one's actions and the semiotic representations of one's worldly possessions provide symbolic meaning that is often consciously manipulated to result in desired outcomes. This more nuanced perspective on material possessions makes it even more difficult to assign "meaning" to artifacts and correlate them with specific immutable human actions, behaviors, or symbols (Rothschild 2003).

While historical archaeology and prehistoric archaeology are clearly related by an interest in understanding and explaining variability in human behavior, the former has access to a dataset not available to most prehistoric archaeologists, the written record. The text-aided (Beaudry 1988; Little 1992a) nature of historical archaeology offers us the riches of social context and process that we often seek to learn about in prehistoric research. However, recognition of the potential biases in this record is critical if we are to take advantage of the richness of the historical narrative and truly investigate the historical past rather than reaffirm the written record (Little 1992b). The three papers in this section of the reader present aspects of the social context of one class of material possessions, ceramics, within traditional Iberian society and in New World colonial contexts. They provide the background for the case studies presented in the following section.

The first paper in Part III of this compilation, **Chapter 6**, by Bonnie G. McEwan, helps contextualize the role of ceramics in Spanish America during the 16th century by examining the functions of ceramics in Spain and comparing them to assemblages from the New World. In Spain, ceramics played a significant role as architectural elements (e.g., ornamental tiles, wells), household furnishings (e.g., chamber pots, wash basins) and of course as food preparation, serving, and storage vessels. Often even religious artifacts were manufactured of ceramics. And these ceramic artifacts were regularly publicly displayed. The bulk of the ceramics that showed up in the New World came through the port of Seville. Even thousands of miles from Seville, ceramics played an important role in the Spanish colonies. Tablewares and tiles continued to play a significant role in the colonies and maintained their role as one form of signaling of status, wealth, and ethnicity, and also seemed to serve as a thread of connectedness to Old World etiquette and roots. In contrast to tablewares, food preparation vessels are under-represented in colonial ceramic assemblages. This may be due to the availability of suitable replacements, the less public nature of food preparation compared to serving, the relatively low number of female Spanish colonists, and the frequency of either inter-marriages between Spanish males and native females or the use of native females as household help. The overall implication of this pattern is that women were likely to be the main agents of Spanish acculturation in the New World. McEwan's (1992) chapter is a good example of the indispensable contribution that historic research provides to historical archaeology. It provides the kind of rich historical context that grounds the search for process and material correlates in documented social practices contemporaneous with the archaeological remains. It is a luxury not afforded to prehistoric archaeology but one that should be used as a source of testable hypotheses rather than fixed truth. After all, cultural norms are often ideals, and actual human behavior is flexible, adaptable, and malleable to many contexts and conditions.

Until recently (Hays-Gilpin 2008), gender has not been a focus of colonial research, however, in **Chapter 7**, McEwan explores the role of women in Spanish colonial society and summarizes the contribution of Spanish, Native American, and African women to aspects of colonial society that have the potential of leaving signatures in the archaeological material record. The demographic makeup of the majority of the early colonies was dominated by men. This imbalance was so dramatic that in the 16th century, the Crown began mandating that married men living in the colonies had to send for their wives within three years (Boxer 1975:38; Pescatello 1976:132). Spanish women in the New World colonies played a critical role in the maintenance of traditional cultural standards by adhering to strict Spanish customs and educated the household servants in proper food preparation and the appropriate rules of etiquette. From an archaeological perspective, the presence of Spanish women in a household would have been signaled by the presence of Spanish cooking pots and tablewares as well as personal items such as jewelry. There is a strong correlation between the archaeological visibility of Spanish women with family status, since in general, the wealthiest and most influential men in the New World colonies were able to and/or focused on recreating the accoutrements of wealth and status in the New World. In contrast to these individuals, many soldiers could not afford to bring wives from Spain and instead married Native American women, a practice that was encouraged by the government from the first days of colonization in the New World (Deagan 1985). Sauer (1966:199-200) estimates that one out of every three Spanish husbands had a native wife. The native American women that married Spanish soldiers inherited the duties and responsibilities typically allocated to Spanish women. As

such, their roles were primarily focused on domestic activities but they also played an important role in supplying the household with ceramics, and also participated in commerce. Given these roles, native wives tended to be at the forefront of the process of culture change in the colonies. They were the agents of culture change that helped adjust what was permissible in the New World Spain and they also were the key interlocutors between the Spanish colonizing population and the native population.

Archaeologically, the presence of native women is most visible in the domestic sphere through native pottery and colono wares, food preparation artifacts, and storage vessels. There is no doubt, however, that dietary costumes also were influenced by native women, leading to a reconfiguration of diets in the New World. While the Crown frowned upon Spanish men marrying black and mulatta women (Boxer 1975:37), some households maintained domestic servants, slaves, and concubines of African origin. Because very few African goods were brought to the New World, the archaeological visibility of the presence of African women in the colonies is very low. This contribution by McEwan (1991) documents that not only were women key players in the domestic spheres of Iberian society but also held the role of keepers of traditional cultural values and symbolisms in the New World colonial society. The presence of Spanish, Native, and African women as heads of household, servants, and concubines demonstrates how complex and multi-dimensional the archaeological record may be as one searches to distinguish between the correlates of gender, ethnicity, and wealth (see also Voss 2008:100-116).

Chapter 8 by Heather B. Trigg presents a detailed discussion of the web of economic and social ties that bound different segments of early colonial New Mexico into an effective regional economy. Trigg (2003) focuses on mid-level economic transactions that move commodities among people within the colony and identifies a rich network of interactions between members of the colonies that are critical in understanding how, when, and where goods move and what commodities are incorporated into these networks. The regional economy of New Mexico was anchored by four major participants: Pueblo peoples, colonists, the church, and the governor. While *encomenderos* received tribute in the form of goods from the Pueblos, there were few tangible benefits received in return. Outside of the *encomien-*

da system, colonists depended on native peoples for household labor and commodities such as foodstuffs and ceramics obtained through barter. The Pueblo peoples may have received metal tools, seed stock, fruits, and other goods in return. The Governor of the Province also interacted with native peoples, although these interactions were hardly reciprocal but rather exploitative. Clergy representatives also interacted with native peoples, receiving from them various goods including ceramics, foodstuffs, and even labor.

In addition to interactions with native groups, colonists also interacted with other colonists to meet both social and subsistence needs. Often, economic interactions were conducted imbedded in social interactions (e.g., exchanges of presents such as the trousseau and dowry as part of marriages and transfers of goods between households as part of gifting during baptisms). The clergy and the governor also played important roles in the movement of goods (e.g., tithes and operation of stores). The inter-relationships between Pueblo peoples, colonists, the governor, and the church provided a variety of avenues for goods to be transferred between peoples and institutions in colonial New Mexico. These predominantly social interactions also influenced the pace of culture change among both native and colonist groups and left different material imprints within the archaeological record. Trigg's analysis is useful in demonstrating the complexity of interactions and the potential social and economic avenues through which the material culture of native groups and colonists may have come to contain goods from extra-cultural contexts. As in the case of the two prior contributions to this section, this article highlights the complex web of interactions that can occur in the context of colonization between natives, government and church officials, and colonists. Having clearly definable archaeological correlates of these interactions is critical to be able to study the movement of goods in such contexts. However, without this rich contextual information little could be done to reconstruct the avenue of movement of goods. The case study illustrates that the rich contextual information is case-study specific; enriches archaeological research within its particular temporal-regional framework; but the case study has limitations due to its particularistic nature.

IV. Studies of Material Culture–Reflections on Identity, Status, and Culture Change

Identity is a social construct that is both ascribed and prescribed and therefore one's identity is dependent on the social domain in which he or she operates (Meskell and Preucel 2004; Voss 2005). Social domains that tend to play a major role in defining identities include family, religion, status, and ethnicity, to name just a few. Furthermore, identity is constructed, manipulated, and negotiated both by its bearers as well as by those who interact with them (Nagel 1994). Social psychologists have developed a number of theoretical approaches to the analysis of identity, including identity formation theory, social identity theory, and acculturation theory (Yeh and Huang 1996), and have studied identity formation within culture contact settings (Gedmintas 1982; Sutton 2005; Brown 2007). Historical archaeology has a great deal to offer to our understanding of identity formation through its time depth and focus on the materiality of identity (Jones 1997:119-127; White and Beaudry 2009:219-222).

Perhaps the most well studied domain of identity is ethnicity. Ethnicity is a culturally ascribed group identity and represents real or assumed shared characteristics such as country of origin, language, and religion (Jones 1997). It is contextual and situational, since it is the result of social negotiations. Due to the historical development of the field, the archaeological study of ethnicity is closely linked to the study of culture (Jones 1997, 2008). Because the construction of identity relies heavily on the material world, the study of identity falls squarely within the domain of archaeology and is one of the principal aspects of culture contact studies (White and Beaudry 2009).

Wealth and status are socially ascribed identities that also find their reflections in material possessions. Although in some instances material evidence of wealth and status coincides with that of ethnic identity, in many cases ethnic identity and its material definition may actually work in opposite directions, particularly in cases of colonial contact. For instance, in colonization contexts, wealth may be in the hands of the colonizer and may be reflected by goods from the Old World that reflect connectedness to home-country values and ideals. In contrast, the material culture of the colonized may be geared toward reflecting ethnic values and traditions that are being eroded in the face of the conquest. However, influential aboriginal families within the social reality of a particular colony or community may in turn want to demonstrate their allegiance to the new order by imitating the symbolic accoutrements of wealth.

This section of the reader begins with a case study that attempts to track the movement of ceramics between early historic Hispanic sites. As such, it is conceptually related to Chapter 8, which defined the mechanism and patterns of the movement of material goods between elements of Spanish Colonial society. The remaining chapters in this section consist of selections that exemplify the manner in which wealth, status, and ethnic identity are reflected, reinforced, and intertwined in material possessions.

In **Chapter 9**, Thomas and colleagues utilize x-ray fluorescence (XRF) analysis of pottery to explore patterns of pottery movement between colonists and Pueblo peoples. The historic ceramics come from a Spanish colonial site, LA 20,000, located in the lower La Cienega valley in north-central New Mexico that was occupied between 1620 and 1680, the year of the Pueblo Revolt (see Wilcox 2009). The colonial domestic *estancia* is close to a nearby pueblo site (Pueblo de la Cienega), although its exact location has not been determined. Typically, ceramics are the most common artifact recovered from colonial sites and Pueblo ceramics tend to be the most common types at colonial sites. The goal of the analysis by Thomas et al. (1992) was to define the network of economic relationships between Spanish colonies and pueblos by tracing the movement of ceramics. XRF analysis was done on 99 sherd samples from decorated vessels so that they could be assigned to typological groupings. The analysis defined two major groups of sherds, each with three subgroups of their own. By virtue of the fact that the well characterized subgroups can all be assigned to distant pueblo sources means that none of the six subgroups derive from the nearby Pueblo de la Cienega. Additionally, comparison with the ceramics from a nearby Hispanic settlement (LA 16,768) shows that the two sites had very different trading partners. The findings challenge the assumption that Spanish colonial sites tend to obtain their aboriginal ceramic wares from nearby pueblos and suggests that ceramic goods had a much more complex derivation than originally assumed. Socio-economic factors that may have been responsible for the distribution of ceramics defined through XRF could not be defined; however, it is likely that the distribution represents a pattern of interaction between the women potters of distinct Puebloan communities who were typically responsible for the manufacture of ceramic wares. The mechanisms that would have accounted for their transfer to Hispanic households could include those outlined by Trigg in Chapter 8, as well as intermarriage. The *encomienda* system may also have played a role, although ceramics are not listed as being part of commodities traditionally transferred as tribute. This may be a result of the fact that women were typically responsible for the manufacture of pottery and often their economic roles were entirely ignored by the Spanish record keepers.

This XRF analysis case study represents a long line of ceramic provenience studies using the elemental composition of ceramic sherds. Typically, the technique is used to reconstruct ceramic manufacture and distribution, and the existence of trade networks during prehistoric times (Pillay 2001; Neitzel et al. 2002). The use of the technique to test the hypothesis that the ceramic assemblage from the Spanish colonial site of LA 20,000 derive from the nearest Pueblo, in light of expectations derived from the fall-off model of artifact frequency with distance, ended up proving the hypothesis incorrect. This is a significant contribution nevertheless, since it demonstrates that such simplifications of human behavior do not always apply. Defining the social and economic circumstances under which this pattern emerges is an important next step and some of the answers may lie in the complex web of social interactions summarized by Trigg (Chapter 8).

The second article in this section, **Chapter 10**, is by Julia King and examines ceramic variability in the assemblages derived from three 17th century house sites in St. Augustine. During the 17th century, St. Augustine experienced slow population growth and it was relatively isolated from other Spanish colonies in the New World. The settlement relied heavily on the annual subsidy (*situado*) of rations, salaries, and military hardware received from Mexico City. These supplies, as with those shipped across much of the Spanish colonial empire, were very unpredictable, often arriving late and with a partial cargo. As a result, the residents of St. Augustine supplemented their needs with indigenous resources and foods. The increased interaction with aboriginal populations also led to Spanish-Indian intermarriages, which in turn led to the introduction of aboriginal ceramics into the community. King (1984) describes this as a period of cultural crystallization during which the foundations of the Hispanic-Florida tradition of today was developed. The ceramic assemblages from the three sites offer an opportunity to investigate the manner in which the greater reliance on localized resources is manifested in the archaeological assemblages, and how households of different social and economic status may have responded to these shifts in dependence. King divides the ceramic assemblages into those that date to either the early and late 17th century and notes that in two of the three sites, aboriginal coarse earthenwares dominate the assemblages. Furthermore, these wares increase in frequency over time at all three sites. The aboriginal wares consist of the Timucua-made St. Johns series and the Guale-made San Marcos series. The percentage of St. Johns wares remains virtually the same between the early and late 17th century assemblages whereas the San Marcos wares nearly triple in abundance over the same period. The San Marcos wares appear to have been used as replacements for cooking and storage vessels. Olive Jar fragments decrease between the early and late 17th century at the three sites, and majolica earthenware tablewares remain roughly the same over time; Hispanic utilitarian coarse earthenwares decrease in overall frequency. Because no suitable replacement wares were available for the majolica and utilitarian coarse earthenwares, such wares represented a consistent but low proportion of the 17th century assemblages. In contrast, when suitable aboriginal replacements were available for certain functional categories of ceramic vessels, Spanish households often adopted them. King's case study documents the fact that the content of artifact assemblages from Hispanic households may be conditioned by three inter-related factors: functional needs (e.g., adequacy in performing a function), symbolic communication (e.g., status, wealth or ethnicity), and access (e.g., availability and affordability).

Cusick's contribution in **Chapter 11** elaborates on these themes within the context of a community studies approach. He uses case studies from Late Colonial 18th century San Augustine to demonstrate the potential of the approach. The first part of the paper lays the groundwork for community studies while the second half uses the historical and archaeological record of six households from San Augustine to ascertain whether aspects of wealth and ethnicity that distinguish the case study households are revealed by their respective archaeological records. Cusick (1995:59) defines community studies as the study of a town or other small settlement at the household level and defines community as a locale whose residents and participants are linked by social interactions. The unit of analysis is the individual household, but the goal of the comparative analyses is to address issues of adaptation, culture change, ethnicity, and identity formation at the household level but also within the context of the community, the supra-household entity that allows and demands inter-dependence between otherwise isolated households.

The six case studies used to demonstrate the potential of community studies consist of two wealthy Spanish families, two wealthy Minorcan families, and two Minorcan families of lesser social and economic means. Probate records are extensively inspected to define a picture of the material wealth and social context of the case studies and to contrast aspects of material culture that would not be expected to preserve adequately in the archaeological record. These data are compared with aspects of ceramic assemblages and faunal remains from the households to characterize the ethnicity and economic wealth of the families and their food consumption patterns. The analyses indicate that wealthy Minorcans, minorities in the community, tended to imitate Spanish middle class families in terms of material possessions, and there was very little difference between wealthy Spanish and Minorcan families in terms of ceramic assemblage content. Profession or occupation appears to have influenced access to goods and purchasing choices. The material culture of poor households was distinct from those of wealthy households but showed no strong ethnic differences. The faunal assemblages showed little evidence of ethnicity among the wealthy families. However, the less fortunate families exhibited a dietary intake pattern that was most reminiscent of traditional Minorcan culture. The influence of wealth and ethnicity on material possessions is at the center of this chapter. In this case study, it appears that wealth and ethnicity tend to correlate with each other in terms of material possessions, so that wealthy households have a distinct ceramic assemblage compared to less well-to-do households. To a large extent, wealth seems to lessen ethnic differentiation since wealthy Minorcans tend to exhibit their wealth through the acquisition of Spanish tablewares. Less wealthy families tend to incorporate more traditional ceramic wares into their assemblages, although these additions occur in the less visible and non-displayed components of their assemblages.

The signaling of wealth and identity was critical in Hispanic colonial society and most artifacts that reflected both aspects of Iberian society were derived from the Iberian peninsula. It appears that wealth facilitated access to Old World goods and these artifacts were in turn used to symbolically reinforce status. Given that the keepers of the Iberian norms in the New World were Spanish women, it is not a surprise that well-to-do households that were effectively run by women most closely adhered to and reflect this relationship between material possessions and identity. However, as access was reduced, either due to availability or wealth, symbolism become secondary, while practicality became predominant in terms of the composition of ceramic assemblages; thus, functional replacements were readily employed by less fortunate families. In addition, intermarriages between Spanish males and native women introduces a participant in the household with distinctive values and world views that do not emphasize a symbolic connection with Iberian culture, or a tradition that links kitchen wares with the signaling of wealth or ethnicity. Quite to the contrary, in such cases, access to resources produced by native groups may be employed consciously to signal connectedness to one's ethnic roots. At the same time, economic or social pressures on native communities of potters to compete with other potters, or furnish pottery to colonies and towns, may contribute to alterations in traditional vessel forms and decoration. Such pressures may also have been imposed by the Spanish missionaries since the missions were to become largely self-sufficient and therefore had strong reasons to rely on native technologies and craftsmen. The colonowares noted among the Guale (Saunders 2000) and Timucua (Rolland and Ashley 2000) may be reflections of these forces on native potters.

In contrast to the social dynamics present in Spanish colonies, identity signaling may work in reverse in mission settings where the neophytes may be under very different pressures to signal their native or Spanish identity and have a less diverse inventory of material possessions through which to do so. Missionaries would typically appoint the chiefs of the most numerous ethnic groups that resided in the mission to serve as *governadore, alcalde, mayordomo,* and *fiscal* (Leutenegger 1991). These families would have some impetus to conform to Spanish rules, and perhaps even emulate Spanish customs, as some of the positions were endowed with Spanish symbolism: the staff given to the *gobernador* in the name of the King, and a quirt, provided to the *fiscal* (Leutenegger 1991:81-82). In contrast, members of other families may be resistant to the colonial presence and would demonstrate their resistance by incorporating as little as possible of the non-native material inventory (Deagan 2011). Yet others may seek to define a new singular identity symbolic of the native mission-bound community even when it was composed of scores of groups (Goodby 1998).

The next chapter **(Chapter 12)** is by Gasco and it is the first of only three case studies of colonialism outside of the boundaries of the continental U.S. included in this reader. Additional case studies in colonialism in Southern Mesoamerica and Central America are provided in Gasco et al. (1997) and Thomas (1991). The latter includes an overview paper by Jones and Pendergast (1991), and case studies from El Salvador (Fowler (1991), Honduras (Davidson 1991; Laral Pinto 1991), Guatemala and Costa Rica (Carmack 1991). In the case study included here, Gasco (1992) looks at the participation of native populations of Ocelocalco situated on the coast of Chiapas, Mexico, in the colonial economic system. Specifically, she is interested in documenting the impact of their participation in the cacao trade on settlement pattern, house construction, and artifact assemblages (material culture). In an elegant strategy, she takes the late 15th century Late Postclassic archaeological record as the pre-contact baseline and compares it to the colonial town of Ocelocalco founded after 1572 when the Spanish conquered the region and moved the town site a short distance east of its Aztec location. The re-founding of the community gave the Spanish a chance to implement their own sense of town planning, and this is clearly reflected in the center of town where the church and the structures closest to it are aligned to magnetic north. Further from the center of town, fewer of the structures conform to this model, suggesting limited control or oversight of town planning towards the periphery of the town. There appeared to be a strong degree of continuity in house construction methods and house form between the late Postclassic and the Spanish colonial period. The construction of intramural and outdoor features associated with food preparation also appeared to remain relatively consistent between the Late Postclassic and Colonial periods. Much of the ceramic assemblage dating to the early colonial period was identical to Late Postclassic wares. However, as the colonial period progressed, new pottery types replaced the old ones but the functional forms remained the same. The large numbers of Spanish majolica that are part of the assemblages of some sites have replaced polychrome vessels that existed in the Late Postclassic, and the increased use of *comales* reflects the technological role of these artifacts in cacao processing. New artifacts were introduced and adopted, but within an aboriginal milieu that is consistent with pre-colonial practices. In terms of the material culture, there is only one artifact category, horse-related artifacts that have no precedents in the Late Postclassic.

One of the more recent themes to emerge out of material culture studies is that of illicit trade or contraband during the Spanish colonial period. In **Chapter 13**, Skowronek examines the ceramic assemblages derived from Santa Elena and St. Augustine and merchant shipwreck sites to discern patterns of illicit trade between Spanish colonies and European powers competing with them in the New World. Sites in Hispaniola (Puerto Real, Santo Domingo) and Spanish Florida (Santa Elena, St. Augustine) consistently yielded small quantities of German, Italian, and French-made tablewares. Illicit trade conducted by foreign powers or their representatives was widespread during the 17th and 18th century but Spain had a virtual monopoly on trade until the Thirty Year War (1618-1648. Therefore, it had been suggested that increases in illicit trade items should have occurred only after the 1630s. The analysis of the ceramic assemblages from the four sites by Skowronek (1992) showed that non-Spanish goods dating to the 16th century ranged from as low as 0.3 percent to 1.2 percent at Hispaniola and Puerto Real, respectively, but as high as 2.2-17.4 percent at Santa Elena and Spanish Florida, respectively. In contrast, the proportion of non-Spanish ceramic tablewares swells to 32 percent by the early 18th century. Within its proper context, the shifts in the relative frequencies of non-Spanish ceramics on Spanish colonial sites reflect changes in Spain's commercial strength and the operation of global forces. In this respect, it is significant that ceramic analysis can make contributions at this level of understanding.

Deagan's contribution in **Chapter 14** takes a more detailed look at the patterns of illicit trade during the 18th century as reflected at the community and household-scales within St. Augustine. It begins with a consideration of the methodological challenges posed by researching illicit trade. Two particular challenges are highlighted: difference in the scale of the documentary text-based record referring to contraband and the archaeological record's' reflection of illicit trade, and the basic recognition of what contraband looks like in the archaeological record. Text-based records are much more finer-grained than the archaeological record, being well anchored in time and connected to specific persons, while the latter represents simplified and rather generalized sets of behaviors. With few exceptions, Deagan (2007) concludes that this disjunction between the nature of the two datasets will remain for the near future. The second issue of recognition of contraband is just as challenging in that under a given context the same set of artifacts may represent the products of illicit trade while under different socioeconomic contexts they will reflect legal trade. Thus, the context of their circulation defines their role rather than certain formal or stylistic characteristics correlating with the nature of trade. Any goods that were traded by merchants or ships without the authorization of Seville or Cadiz were considered contraband. The purchase of goods from English, Dutch and French ships was not prohibited, as long as they were brought into the Spanish colonies on Spanish-licensed ships. Due to this underlying contextual necessity, it is critical to understand the socioeconomic background of trade to establish the conditions under which artifacts may have been obtained through legal or illicit means.

Deagan summarizes the avenues through which foreign goods could arrive to the Spanish colonies through legal means, and also discusses the periodicity of trade. The time frames during which trade was legal or illegal varied between individual colonies. For instance, at St. Augustine, British goods could have entered legally between 1713 and 1762 while French goods could have been brought in legally between 1702 and 1713. Therefore, any English goods that entered prior to approximately 1713 and French goods brought in prior to 1702 would have represented contraband.

The materials used to investigate trade patterns derived from 124 features recorded at six household sites. The focus of the research was on tablewares since there were no locally available substitutes in the colonies, yet they were the principal means by which Spanish signaled status, wealth, and origin. At the community-wide level, English wares climbed in frequency from less than 1 percent between 1675-1680 to 20 percent by 1700. The proportion of English wares stayed above 20 percent after the War of Spanish Succession ended in 1713 but after this time they were obtained through legal means. After 1739, privateering of English ships increased, as did the proportion of foreign goods that arrived in St. Augustine. At the household level, there was considerable variability in terms of access to contraband goods. The household sample consisted of families of different social and economic means, a mixed Indian-Hispanic household, and a merchant's home. Criollo families connected to the garrison, regardless of marked differences in income, had large proportions of Spanish tradition ceramics and only infrequent pieces of English wares during the early days of the 18th century. However, the proportion of English wares rose to nearly 20 percent by 1735 in these households and some of these wares would have been obtained as contraband. The harbormaster was the one household within which English and French tablewares actually outnumbered Spanish ceramics. Low-income residents of St. Augustine had dramatically distinct ceramic assemblages. Legally and/or illegally obtained English wares represented low proportions within their assemblages. The assemblage derived from a Spanish Canary Islander indicates some participation in illicit trade between 1670 and 1702.

Among households, participation in contraband trade appears to have been contingent not only on economic access to the goods, but also relative positions of social privilege and attitudinal values. Old Criollo families connected to the garrison appeared to discourage participation in contraband. Families not associated with the garrison more readily participated in contraband trade to the point that it became part of their economic strategies to cope with shortages of tablewares. The study suggest that while a community-wide scale of analysis may be appropriate for macro-scale economic questions, the household focus can reveal how actual actors with specific economic, occupational, religious, and ethnic identities engaged in contraband as a strategy for coping with shortages. The study suggests that the household is the proper unit of analysis. Deagan's article illustrates that without written records to document the periodicity of legal versus an illicit flow of mate-

rial goods, such a study would not be possible. Consequently, it challenges archaeologists to develop appropriate methodologies through which such dynamics may be studied in the absence of written records, thus informing researchers about the nature of interactions between complex polities.

In **Chapter 15**, Costello examines how the expansion of the capitalist world economy around the early 19th century and the introduction of new manufactured goods affected the material culture of the California missions, which were secularized circa 1834. By the late 1780s, California missions were systematically provisioning goods and products such as tallow, fat, and hides to Spain and the operation of the missions had become more integrated with international market forces. According to Costello (1992), Alta California was functioning as a peripheral area within the world-system (e.g., Wallerstein 1974) soon after mission secularization.

The beginnings of this transition from a relatively self-sufficient economy to a peripheral area began at the turn of the 19th century. The missions were relatively prosperous, had large populations, the principal building construction activities had ceased, and agricultural production was relatively steady. The missions still received allotments from Mexico City, and exports from the missions could be used to augment needs. The principal exported products were tallow and lard as well as cow hides, sheep skins, and hemp. The primary impediment to mission trade was not a lack of goods but limited means of transportation. Foreign sea-otter hunters filed this need even after royal decrees formally forbade the practice. These Yankee ships would provision the natives with trade goods in exchange for sea otter pelts obtained by the Indians. Two sources, a shipping list associated with a Spanish shipment of resources to Mission Santa Barbara in 1804 and an 1806-1807 account book of the American Mercury sea-otter hunting vessel, provided significant information on the goods that entered the missions during this period from these two sources. With the exception of two types of goods, there appeared to be no major differences in mission purchasing patterns when Spanish and Yankee sources are compared. Religious items tend to be obtained from the Spanish sources while cloth, clothing, and tablewares were obtained from the Yankee supplier. Over time, the proportion of non-Spanish goods increased relative to goods of Spanish origin. The increased production capacity of the missions led them to become more inter-connected with broader regional and international spheres of interaction. The increased purchasing power of the missions allowed them access to material goods that were foreign in terms of origin and symbolic role, yet they were contextually incorporated into the missions.

V. Subsistence Change

Five chapters in the reader reflect research trends related to subsistence changes during the Spanish colonial period. The context and practice of food preparation is embodied with symbolic significance in many cultures (Counihan and Kaplan 1998). Terms such as Hungarian cuisine, or Italian cuisine, embody not only a sense of familiar dishes but also the identity of a people and a geographic place. Similarly, the term Tex-Mex embodies the melding of two cuisines as much as it does the forging of a new cultural identity, otherwise known as ethnogenesis. Previous chapters in this volume have discussed how strongly food preparation and serving can reflect wealth, status, and ethnic identity. For most ethnic groups, the maintenance of traditional food ways is an important symbol and it is often used to maintain social cohesion or build boundaries (Fitts 2002:10).

The arrival of the Spanish colonizers to the New World represented not only a clash of cultures but also food ways. Perhaps the Spanish had the biggest of challenges in having to maintain a dwindling maladapted set of cultigens and domesticated animals in a foreign land (Scarry and Reitz 1990). In contrast, the diet of native populations was centered on local food supplies that were the selective product of centuries of adaptations. In the missions, however, the natives were exposed to new foods (Reitz 1990; Ruhl 1990), although the majority of the Southeastern case studies suggest that native groups maintained significant continuity in diet even once Old World domesticated species appeared on the scene (Reitz et al. 2010). In contrast to the Southeastern patterns, a number of case studies from California missions suggest that in the western missions the neophytes shifted their diet to a heavy dependence on domesticated species, primarily cattle (Farris 1991; Langenwalter and McKee 1985; Romani and Toren 1975). Even under these conditions however, traditional food sources such as fish, shellfish, deer,

and bison do make it into the mission middens, indicating that native groups continued to rely to some degree on traditional food ways, either out of necessity or to demonstrate a continued affiliation to their traditional identities (Rodriguez-Alegria 2005; Mills 2008). In some instances, when domesticated species are incorporated into the native diet the elements are processed by neophytes using aboriginal techniques (e.g., bone grease processing and bone marrow extraction) indicating significant technological continuity in approaches to carcass butchering (Garlinghouse 2009). The articles included in this section of the reader focus on the subsistence challenges faced by Spanish colonists, the manner in which they supplemented their Iberian diet with indigenous food items, and what impact the new food items had on the diet and subsistence of native peoples.

The first contribution, **Chapter 16**, represents the summary chapter of Special Publication Number 3 of the SHA, entitled *Reconstructing Historic Subsistence with an Example from Sixteenth-Century Spanish Florida* (Reitz and Scarry 1992a). It is included here because it not only provides a good summary of subsistence practices in St. Augustine but just as importantly, it provides a series of hypotheses related to expected patters of subsistence in other Spanish colonial sites. Three factors appeared to condition the subsistence practices developed by Spanish colonist in Florida: supplies of Old World basics were unreliable; domesticated plants and animals often did not fare well in the new environments; and locally available foods afforded the option to switch to them to increase security and reduce risk. Household-scale analysis of subsistence variability does show differences in consumption patterns related to socioeconomic status and ethnicity. The higher a household's social status, the more likely it appears that its members will have access to and consume the greatest quantity and variety of imported and luxury foods. The lower a household's social status, however, the more likely that its members will more fully integrate wild foods into their diet in combination with a limited range of domesticated resources.

Reitz and Scarry (1992b) also indicate that subsistence research can provide clues to the pace of culture change and adaptation by colonists. That is, following arrival to the New World, colonists would typically go through a period of experimentation and adjustment to determine how the domesticates in their subsistence arsenal fare under the new ecological conditions. This period of transition results in the elimination of certain dietary items and alterations in the proportion of Old World domesticated foods that are consumed. Finally, as colonists are exposed to new food stuffs through interaction with native populations, they tend to substitute the indigenous crops and resources for their traditional ones. In terms of the periodicity of this change, the period of experimentation appears to have taken place over a 40-year period following which, for the next 200 years, few changes were made in the constellation of food stuffs in Spanish Florida.

In **Chapter 17**, Reitz contrasts the role of Old World domesticates in four 16th century Spanish Colonial settlements characterized by different ecological conditions. The primary domesticated animals brought to the New World from Spain are cattle, pigs, sheep, goats, and chickens. Due to their narrowly adapted physiology, sheep and cattle would have had the most difficult time adapting to the environmental conditions present in the colonies. After summarizing the environmental conditions of Andalucia, from where most domesticated animals would have arrived, Reitz looks at the conditions present in Hispaniola, the island of Cubagua off the coast of Venezuela, and Spanish Florida, the locations of the case studies Reitz (1992) discusses in the second half of the paper. The archaeological data suggests that the abundance of domesticated mammals in the assemblages correlates with the environmental setting of the colony, and the success of the colony is in turn related to how much success the colonists have in maintaining a reliable base of domesticated animals. At Puerto Real, domesticated mammals contributed 43 percent of the individuals and 93 percent of the biomass. Cattle were one of the more successfully adapted domesticated animals on the island. Sea and pond turtles made up 33 percent of the individuals. In the faunal assemblage from the Convento de San Francisco in Santo Domingo, 56 percent of the individuals were domesticated mammals and 32 percent represented wild species, particularly fish, turtles, and manatee. At Nueva Cadiz on the Cubagua Island, only 8 percent of the meat was derived from domesticated mammals, with a heavy reliance on marine resources. Similarly, in Spanish Florida, wild resources represented 85 percent of the identifiable individuals, and pigs, cows, and sheep relatively small percentages (4 percent, 10 percent, and less than 1 percent, respectively). This case study makes it very

clear that the role of these Old World domesticates in colonial subsistence was affected by how favorable environmental conditions were for their survival and reproduction.

In **Chapter 18**, Ruhl considers the role of oranges and wheat cultivation in local and global economies. Oranges and wheat were two of the earliest introduced cultigens into La Florida colonies. The introduction of wheat in the mid-16th century was in part a reaction to shortages of grain in Spain brought on in part by the Crown's focus on wool production. In Spanish Florida some of the earliest agrarian enterprises involved cattle ranching and experimentation with the cultivation of wheat and oranges. Oranges were introduced in Florida around 1565 but the earliest finds of oranges in the archaeological record date to the late 18th century. By the late 17th century St. Augustine became an exporter of oranges. Wheat production began to flourish in Florida by the middle of the 17th century as a result of the establishment of missions and hacienda-like settlements. Archaeological recovery of wheat is common from mid-17th century deposits. Several varieties of wheat may have been cultivated or a new cultivar may have been developed during the 17th century from the original variety brought to La Florida in the 16th century. The case study by Ruhl (1997) notes that oranges experienced a long journey from China, to western Europe and Spain, only to reach the New World before they attained commercial significance. The increased frequency of wheat grains and oranges in archaeological deposits dating to the mid-17th century may be correlated with the rise in commercial importance of these cultigens. Key players in the explosion of wheat cultivation were Native American laborers in the missions.

Chapter 19 is a case study of the Spanish Colonial experience from southern Peru. DeFrance considers two aspects of subsistence and animal use in colonial sites in the Moqegua Valley. She asks whether or not local Andean domesticated resources were incorporated into the diet and whether Spanish colonization had any effect on Andean herding practices. To address these questions, comparisons and contrasts are made between the faunal assemblages derived from four winery (*bodega*) sites with the assemblage from Torata Alta, a site that may have been a colonial *reducción*. While the owners of the bodegas were likely criollo descendants of wealthy families, who resided at and operated the wineries is not known. Similarly, while it is probable that the site's population derived from the *altiplano*, or high altitude plains of the Andes, the actual ethnic identity of the residents of Torata Alta is also not known.

The analysis of the large faunal assemblages indicates that at the wineries most mammals are introduced domesticated species although Andean camelids are also relatively abundant. Chickens represent half of the birds represented and there are at least 10 species of Pacific coast fish. At the higher altitude Torata Alta site, mammalian taxa are heavily skewed toward Andean camelids and guinea pigs. The most common non-native species are caprines, but pigs and chickens are also present. The winery assemblage indicates that few native species of mammals were incorporated into the colonial diet. Nonetheless, Andean camelids did make up the single largest source of animal protein consumed during the earliest occupations. In contrast, the Torata Alta assemblage suggests that the occupants maintained a diet that was very consistent with that of pre-Hispanic times. They relied heavily on Andean camelids and few Old World species were added to the traditional diet. While historical accounts suggest that Andean herding practices were disrupted by the introduction of Old World domesticated species, DeFrance (1996) concludes that the faunal assemblage from Torata Alta shows neither a disruption of traditional herding practices nor a widespread adoption of Old World animals. Instead, the success with which European domesticated animals adapted to and proliferated within the Moquegua valley may have allowed the colonists to maintain a diet that was more Iberian in content than that found in Spanish settlements in the Caribbean and in Florida.

Chapter 20, the last contribution to the subsistence section is by Jamieson (2008), a study of a faunal assemblage recovered in a midden from a 17th-century elite urban residence in Cuenca, Ecuador. It is included here because it represents a dramatic contrast to the dietary patterns noted in the previous case studies. The residence was occupied between 1557 and 1651 and was owned by one of the town's founding families. As if to underscore the status of the family, the lot is situated at one of the corner's overlooking the town's central plaza.

Shovel testing and test excavations in the midden recovered over 3000 pieces of animal bone, with nearly one quarter of the sample consisting of identifiable elements. Domesticated artiodactyls dominate the sample, with sheep and goats being most common, followed by cattle and pigs. Deer were also present but in small quantities (1 percent of the elements). All of the fauna appears to derive from animals butchered on site. Jamieson remarks that the absence of Andean domesticated species, including camelids and guinea pigs, is significant and unique among case studies of food consumption in colonial settings, particularly in the Andes. Given the cultural norms and perceptions of the 16th century, it should actually be the common pattern rather than the exception. Indeed, such refusals to consume the foods of highland native groups persists among mestizo and Spanish families even today. The findings of the study appear to support the expectation that when elite, well-to-do, households have the means to maintain material possessions and food consumption practices that symbolize wealth and status, they will do so.

VI. Site Structure and Mission Layout

There are two contributions included in the final section of the volume. They address aspects of site structure and mission layout. The study of site structure has utility from the perspective of the planning of archaeological investigations because knowledge of the locations of structures, facilities, and features within the mission compound allows one to more efficiently target areas for excavation. In addition, there is a rich body of literature on the analysis of site structure and the organization of activity areas among hunter gatherers (Kent 1985). While some of this literature focuses on site structure within the context of mobile hunter-gatherers, several publications address the effects of how the process of becoming sedentary affects the use of space (Hitchcock 1985; Salzman 1980), and cultural differences in the organization and use of space (Kent 1984; Clark 2005). In choosing or being forced to enter a mission, some hunter-gatherer groups shifted from subsistence strategies based on high degree of mobility to sedentism overnight. No doubt, such a shift necessitated some adjustments in terms of the organization of activity areas and use of space. The mission layout defined new rules of space use based on Iberian preconceptions, and these rules were no doubt distinct from those of nomadic groups with much fewer restrictions on constructed space (Buscaglia et al. 2008). Not only did the clash of cultures follow new rules of engagement and social interaction but the space within which it was taking place also was structured in a new way.

The first of the final contributions (**Chapter 21**) is an assessment by Saunders of a model of mission compound layout defined on the basis of archaeological investigations at Apalachee and western Timucua missions in western Florida (Jones and Shapiro 1990). Jones and Shapiro (1990) note that typically three buildings make up the church complex: the church, the convent, and a smaller square building that likely served as the kitchen. The buildings form a right triangle that encloses a plaza. A cemetery is often located at some distance from the church. It was expected that the church would be the largest structure and would have a rectangular shape while the convent would be roughly square. Together with the courtyard, the compound would have a quadrangular layout. While it was recognized that variability would be expected within this architectural ideal, it was suggested that consistency would be the norm rather than the exception. Based on additional extensive excavations performed at Apalachee, Timucua, and Atlantic Guale missions (see also Saunders 1990), Saunders (1993, 1996) concludes that the treatment of the model as fact rather than a testable hypothesis has been premature. There are at least six factors that can potentially contribute to layout variability, including time period of construction, size of the available labor pool, local and regional economic conditions, political circumstance, architectural and logistical expertise, and whether the mission is being established in an extant town or open space. The spatial layout and content of structures within a mission is also likely to be conditioned by the length of time a mission is in operation, fluctuations in resident population and the periodicity of the shift from less permanent to more permanent buildings. Archaeological work at the Fig Springs site (8CO1), the San Martin de Timucua mission, documents highly complex construction and reconstruction histories that can be ascertained only through long-term and spatially expansive archaeological investigations.

Historic accounts of the building sequences of the San Antonio missions indicate that often the initial buildings constructed following the founding of a mission were made of temporary materials (Habig 1997:45, 85, 165). The church and friary were the first to be built. If during the early years, the location was found to be favorable, the temporary buildings would begin to be replaced by more permanent structures made of either adobe or stone. By this time, irrigation ditches would have been erected to run water to the mission and its agricultural fields. At Mission Concepción in San Antonio, the last configuration of the complex, the friary building, was attached to the church and a kitchen structure adjoined the friary. Attached to one wing of the church was a granary. The four structures formed a cluster of buildings at the southeast corner of the mission compound. Neophyte quarters may have originally been distributed in the center of the compound but eventually came to form the walls that surrounded the entire mission to offer protection from attacks by hostile Indians (Figueroa and Tomka 2009).

In **Chapter 22**, Allen provides a comprehensive review of years of archaeological investigations carried out at Mission Santa Clara in Alta California. The mission was founded in 1777 and was the eighth Franciscan mission founded in Alta California. It was secularized in 1836. The review of the mission's historical record indicates that the mission compound's layout changed often as buildings such as the church were built and rebuilt in different locations over time. Decades of archaeological work on the site, which is on the campus of Santa Clara University, has been able to document numerous features, including the cemetery associated with the fifth mission church, building foundations and tile floors, refuse pits and sheet refuse, and recover a rich assemblage of mission-period artifacts. These investigations by Allen (2010) clearly showed that pockets of intact deposits dating to the colonial period do exist under the parking lots, roads, and other later facilities and they do have a great deal of research potential to address important mission period research issues. One such research theme has been to understand the nature of the use of space within the mission compound, both from the perspective of guiding future campus development as well as in documenting space use by the mission's inhabitants. Recent work within the compound has lead to discovery of a house pit, the outlines of an adobe structure, and the definition of outdoor activity areas used by Native American occupants of the mission. In addition to the circular house pit, there were several pit features, ranging from an adobe borrow pit reused as a trash dump, to pits used to cache food and/or belongings. These finds highlight the fact that the native residents of these missions did not confine their activities to internal spaces but also used the area surrounding their rooms for the performance of a variety of activities. Overall, the rich ethnohistoric record associated with each mission, and the *revisitas* written by representatives of the colleges and crown all provide detailed descriptions of the evolution of mission compounds. And, while they may not always provide sufficient detail to guide archaeological investigations, they do furnish lists of buildings, construction sequences, features, and facilities that existed each time the mission was visited. These descriptions can provide a virtual history of the mission compound and the changes in land use from the very first founding of the mission to its secularization.

Future Prospects

Given the richness of themes being explored in every issue of the journal, and the wealth of professionals involved in historical archaeology across the country, it is difficult to believe that the SHA is a little more than four decades old. Even before the establishment of the society, scholars had been conducting research to relocate lost missions and document the impact of Spanish colonial efforts on the lives of Native Americans. Since those early years, the Southeast, California, and the Southwest have become hotbeds of mission archaeology.

The SHA was not taken over by the "new archaeologists" as forecast in 1967 (Cleland 1993:13) but rather both prehistoric archaeologists and historic archaeologists who found sufficient theoretical common ground to coexist. Over the years, theoretical approaches to mission and colonial archaeology have shifted from acculturation to culture contact studies, colonization research, and more recently to an emphasis on resistance to colonization. Research themes revolve around culture change as manifested in subsistence practices, material possessions, and the conceptualization and use of space. The analytical unit tends to be the household, at least in colonial settings outside missions, but it is recognized that comparative research at the community level is critical to better understand the factors that condition how culture change is reflected in materials possessions. When it comes to archaeology within missions, the unit of analysis is the mission itself. Archaeological investigations are focused on iden-

tifying structures and their use (e.g., churches, friaries, granaries,) defining aboriginal habitation areas, locating cemeteries, and identifying activity areas (Johnson 1993; Thomas 1993; Weisman 1993.) It is noteworthy that while the archaeology of colonies tends to focus on individual house sites, archaeological investigations within missions rarely focus on the same unit of analysis. This is due in part to the fact that the residences of neophytes have rarely been located within the missions. Yet, given that we cannot expect a monolithic response by all neophytes living in a mission to the forces of culture change, there are opportunities to pursue fine-scale research as aboriginal habitations and neophyte-housing quarters are identified and investigated over time.

Methodologically, there is a greater integration of historians and archaeologists in most projects than was the case decades ago, signaling the fact that historic archaeologists have taken to heart the call for true multi-disciplinary research put forth by Deagan and Scardaville (1985) more than 25 years ago. A number of archaeologists are developing and experimenting with new ways to gauge the pace and nature of culture change as reflected in artifacts and material possessions. The field is squarely within the social sciences and the breadth of information it now relies on to interpret the archaeological record is richer and more multi-dimensional than ever.

Yet challenges remain. We highlight four: (1) the lack of integration between archaeologists and social scientists in other fields (e.g. psychologists, sociologists) working on related themes; (2) the absence of approaches that recognize that explanations of cultural/human behavior should form a continuum linking prehistoric, historic, and contemporary processes; (3) the relative lack of inter-regional communication and comparative analysis; and (4) concerns with scales and units of analysis, as well as methodological toolkits, that would permit better and more convincing measurements of culture change.

Sociologist and psychologists, not to mention social anthropologists, are intimately involved in the study of culture change and identity formation. Yet historical archaeologists rarely go outside of our field in search of models and approaches by other social scientists to the same behaviors and processes we seek to explain. To the degree that becoming proficient in another field is more than any professional archaeologist has time for, this is a understandable decision. Yet, in the same manner as historians are better qualified to do documentary research, sociologists and psychologists may have something to offer to the study of culture change and ethnicity. The lack of cross-disciplinary interaction along common themes suggests that we are artificially devising boundaries in the study of human behavior where there should perhaps be none.

Such boundaries are evident even in the discipline of archaeology where prehistoric archaeologists and historic archaeologists rarely broaden their studies of a specific aspect of human behavior to find it necessary to move between the two archaeologies. Even when such phenomena as ethnicity are being studied, rarely (Jones 1997) do archaeologists address the topic by treating it as a continuum from prehistoric to historic and modern times. The study of colonialism provides a positive example of a truly diachronic study, in that archaeologists have been studying its manifestations during prehistoric times (Gosden 2004; Hurst and Owen 2005; Stein 2005) in the historic period, as well as during the recent past. The temporal depth of colonial studies, the multiplicity of case studies, and the variety of conditions under which it occurs should lead to greater understanding of how the cultures and ethnicities of both colonizers and colonized change under colonization, what conditions lead to resistance, and what forms it may take.

It is recognized that Spanish colonization efforts have become distinct across the borderlands although many similarities can also be identified (Wade 2008). While contributions such as *Columbian Consequences* (Thomas, ed. 1989-1991) were able to bring together scholars to discuss case studies from all of the major borderlands, few comparative studies or cross-regional collaborative efforts have followed this commendable effort to depict the effects of Columbus's arrival to the New World. Future symposia bringing together scholars from different regions of North, Middle, and South American are needed to facilitate comparative discourse on colonization processes.

Historical archaeologists studying colonization have made dramatic leaps in theoretical approaches in the past four decades. One of the more dramatic shifts was the abandonment of processual archaeology in favor of approaches that rely on ideology and symbolic structural perspectives to extract meaning from material goods (Shackel and Little 1992:6). There are a number of variants of post-processual

archaeology (Shackel and Little 1992:6), but they accept the perspective that the meaning of material goods is defined by their culturally constructed world (Pendery 1992). This perspective on the meaning of material goods does not explain a more immediate practical problem, what do artifact counts and artifact categories tell us about culture change? Linkages between either artifact counts or variety of artifact types to culture change are rarely defined. Therefore, we are left wondering what differences in artifact numbers and kinds between different mission and colonial contexts represent with respect to culture change. Similarly, are changes in functional artifact categories more indicative of culture change than high numbers of imported artifacts that were simply used to replace traditional wares? Even if the meaning of material goods is culturally constructed, it should be possible to define context-specific linkages between specific artifacts and their meaning to allow comparative analyses.

Finally, it is worth asking what is the appropriate unit of analysis when it comes to the study of the archaeology of missions and colonies? On the one hand, the appropriate analytical unit likely depends on the questions being asked. Without getting into the pitfalls of properly defining the concept (Isbell 2000), a community is an aggregate of people living in a specific space (Yaeger and Canuto 2000). Communities, however, can be composed of a number of ethnic or other socially constructed groups that do not necessarily share a common perspective. Therefore, while community-wide comparisons are desirable, they can only conclude that communities are a varied unit. Is it possible that since the household is the level at which most decisions are made regarding participation in various broader cultural milieus such as religion, profession, and interaction with other households, the locus of culture change is at the household level?

The issues and themes highlighted in this last section of the Introduction are not insurmountable. We anticipate that mission and colonial archaeology will prosper as new theoretical approaches arrive and the full scope of comparative analyses is realized.

References

ADAMS, E. CHARLES
1989   Passive Resistance: Hopi Responses to Spanish Contact and Conquest. In *Columbian Consequences, Volume 1: Archaeological and Historical Perspectives on the Spanish Borderlands West*, edited by David Hurst Thomas, pp. 77-91. Smithsonian Institution Press, Washington D.C.

ALLEN, REBECCA
1998   *Native Americans at Mission Santa Cruz, 1791-1834: Interpreting the Archaeological Record.* Perspectives in California Archaeology, Volume 5. Institute of Archaeology, University of California, Los Angeles.
2010   Rethinking Mission Land Use and the Archaeological Record in California: An Example from Santa Clara. *Historical Archaeology* 44(2):72-96.

ANDERSON, GARY C.
1999   *The Indian Southwest, 1580-1830: Ethnogenesis and Reinvention.* University of Oklahoma Press, Norman.

AYRES, JAMES E. (COMPILER)
1995   *The Archaeology of Spanish and Mexican Colonialism in the American Southwest.* Guides to the Archaeological Literature of the Immigrant Experience in America, Number 3. The Society for Historical Archaeology, Ann Arbor.

BANCROFT, HERBERT H.
1884-1890   *History of California.* Six Volumes. The History Company, San Francisco.

BEAN, LOWELL JOHN
1978   Social Organization. In *California, Handbook of North American Indians, Volume 8*, edited by Robert F. Heizer, pp. 673-682. Smithsonian Institution Press, Washington D.C.

BEAUDRY, MARY C.
1988   *Documentary Archaeology in the New World.* Cambridge University Press, Cambridge.

BENSE, JUDITH A.
2003   *Presidio Santa Maria de Galve: A Struggle for Survival in Colonial Spanish Pensacola.* University Press of Florida, Gainesville.

BENSE, JUDITH A. (EDITOR)
2004   Presidios of the North American Spanish Borderlands. *Historical Archaeology* 38(3):1-153.

BINFORD, SALLY R. AND LEWIS R. BINFORD (EDITORS)
1968   *New Perspectives in Archeology.* Aldine Publishing Company, Chicago.

BLANTON, DENNIS B. AND JULIA A. KING
2004   *Indian and European Contact in Context: The Mid-Atlantic Region.* University Press of Florida, Gainesville.

BOLTON, HERBERT E.
1915   *Texas in the Middle Eighteenth Century Studies in Spanish Colonial History and Administration.* University of California Publications in History, Volume III. University of California Press, Berkeley.
1921   *The Spanish Borderlands: A Chronicle of Old Florida and the Southwest.* Yale University Press, New Haven.

BOXER, CHARLES R.
1975   *Women in Iberian Expansion Overseas, 1415-1815.* Oxford University Press, New York.

BROOM, LEONARD, BERNARD J. SIEGEL, EVON Z. VOGT, AND JAMES B. WATSON
1854   Acculturation: An Explanatory Formula. *American Anthropologist* 56:973-1000.

BROWN, MELISSA J.
2007   Ethnic Identity, Cultural Variation, and Processes of Change. Rethinking the Insights of Standardization and Orthopraxy. *Modern China* 33(1):91-124.

BUSCAGLIA, SILVANA, MARIA X. SENATORE, EUGENIA LASCANO, VICTORIA BONGIOVANNI, MATÍAS DE LA VEGA, AND ANA OSELLA
2008   To Project an Order: Interdisciplinary Perspectives on Spatial Construction in the Spanish Colony of Floridablanca (Patagonia, Eighteenth Century). *Historical Archaeology* 42(4):1-20.

CARMACK, ROBERT M.
1991   The Spanish Conquest of Central America: Comparative Cases from Guatemala and Costa Rica. In *Columbian Consequences, Volume 3: The Spanish Borderlands in Pan-American Perspective*, edited by David Hurst Thomas, pp. 389-410. Smithsonian Institution Press, Washington D.C.

CASTILLO, ED D.
1989   The Native Response to the Colonization of Alta California. In *Columbian Consequences, Volume 1: Archaeological and Historical Perspectives on the Spanish Borderlands West*, edited by David Hurst Thomas, pp. 377-394. Smithsonian Institution Press, Washington D.C.

CHIPMAN, DONALD E. AND HARRIETT D. JOSEPH
2010   *Spanish Texas, 1519-1821.* Revised Edition. University of Texas Press, Austin.

CLARK, BONNIE J.
2005   Lived Ethnicity: Archaeology and Identity in Mexicano America. *World Archaeology* 37(3):440-452.

CLELAND, CHARLES E.
1993   The First Half Decade: The Foundation of the Society for Historical Archaeology, 1967-1972. *Historical Archaeology* 27(1):12-14.

CORDELL, LINDA S.
1989   Durango to Durango: An overview of the Southwest heartland. In *Columbian Consequences, Volume 1: Archaeological and Historical Perspectives on the Spanish Borderlands West*, edited by David Hurst Thomas, pp. 17-40. Smithsonian Institution Press, Washington D.C.

COSTELLO, JULIA G.
1992   Purchasing Patterns of the California Missions in ca. 1805. *Historical Archaeology* 26(1):59-66.

COSTELLO, JULIA G. AND DAVID HORNBECK
1989   Alta California: An Overview. In *Columbian Consequences, Volume 1: Archaeological and Historical Perspectives on the Spanish Borderlands West*, edited by David Hurst Thomas, pp. 303-331. Smithsonian Institution Press, Washington D.C.

COUNIHAN, C.M. AND S.L. KAPLAN (EDITORS)
1998   *Food and Gender: Identity and Power.* Harwood Academic Publishers, Amsterdam.

CUSICK, JAMES G.
1995   The Importance of the Community Study Approach in Historical Archaeology, with an Example from Late Colonial St. Augustine. *Historical Archaeology* 29(4):59-83.

1998   Historiography of Acculturation: An Evaluation of Concepts and Their Application in Archaeology. In *Studies in Culture Contact: Interaction, Culture Change, and Archaeology*, edited by James G. Cusick, pp. 126-145. Occasional Paper No. 25. Center for Archaeological Investigations, Southern Illinois University, Carbondale.

CUSICK, JAMES G. (EDITOR)
1989   *Studies in Culture Contact: Interaction, Culture Change, and Archaeology.* Occasional Paper No. 25. Center for Archaeological Investigations, Southern Illinois University, Carbondale.

DAWDY, SHANNON L.
2000   Preface to Evidence of Creolization in the Consumer Goods of an Enslaved Bahamian Family. *Historical Archaeology* 34(3): 1-4.

DAVIDSON, WILLIAM VAN
1991   Geographical Perspectives on Spanish-Pech (Paya) Indian Relationships, in Sixteenth-Century Northeastern Honduras. In *Columbian Consequences, Volume 3: The Spanish Borderlands in Pan-American Perspective*, edited by David Hurst Thomas, pp. 205-226. Smithsonian Institution Press, Washington D.C.

DEAGAN, KATHLEEN
1973   Mestizaje in Colonial St. Augustine. *Ethnohistory* 20(1):55-65.

1983   *Spanish St. Augustine: The Archaeology of a Colonial Creole Community.* Academic Press, New York.

1985   Spanish-Indian Interaction in Sixteenth-century Florida and Hispaniola. In *Cultures in Contact*, edited by William Fitzhugh, pp. 281-318. Smithsonian Institution Press, Washington D.C.

1996   Colonial Transformation: Euro-American Cultural Genesis in the Early Spanish-American Colonies. *Journal of Anthropological Research* 52:135-160.

1998   Transculturation and Spanish American Ethnogenesis: The Archaeological Legacy of the Quincentenary. In *Studies in Culture Contact: Interaction, Culture Change, and Archaeology*, edited by James G. Cusick, pp. 23-43. Occasional Paper No. 25. Center for Archaeological Investigations, Southern Illinois University, Carbondale.

2007   Eliciting Contraband through Archaeology: Illicit Trade in Eighteenth-Century St. Augustine. *Historical Archaeology* 41(4):98-116.

2011   Native American Resistance to Spanish Presence in Hispaniola and La Florida, 1566-1650. In *Enduring Conquests: Rethinking the Archaeology of Resistance to Spanish Colonialism in the Americas*, edited by Matthew Liebmann and Mellisa S. Murphy, pp. 41-56. School of American Research Press, Santa Fe.

DEAGAN, KATHLEEN AND MICHAEL SCARDAVILLE
1985   Archaeology and History *on* Historic Hispanic Sites: Impediments and Solutions. *Historical Archaeology* 19(1):32-37.

DEETZ, JAMES F.
1963   Archaeological Excavations at La Purisima Mission. *UCLA Archaeological Survey Annual Report* 5:163-208. University of California, Los Angeles.

DEFRANCE, SUSAN D.
1996   Iberian Foodways in the Moquegua and Torata Valleys of southern Peru. *Historical Archaeology* 30(3):20-48.

DOBRES, MARCIA-ANNE
2000   *Technology and Social Agency.* Blackwell Publishers, Malden, Massachusetts.

FARNSWORTH, PAUL
1986   Spanish California: The Final Frontier. *Journal of New World Archaeology* (6)4:35-46.

FARRIS, GLENN J.
1991   *Archeological Testing in the Neophyte Family Housing Area at Mission San Juan Bautista, California.* California Department of Parks and Recreation, Cultural Heritage Section, Sacramento.

FIGUEROA, ANTONIA L. AND STEVE A. TOMKA
2009 *Archaeological Investigations in the Courtyard of Mission Nuestra Señora de la Purisima Concepción Acuña (41BX12).* Archaeological Report No. 403. Center for Archaeological Research, The University of Texas at San Antonio.

FITTS, ROBERT K.
2002 Becoming American: The Archaeology of an Italian Immigrant. *Historical Archaeology* 36(2):1-17.

FOWLER, WILLIAM R. JR.
1991 The Political Economy of Indian Survival in Sixteenth-Century Izalco, El Salvador. In *Columbian Consequences, Volume 3: The Spanish Borderlands in Pan-American Perspective*, edited by David H. Thomas, pp. 187-204. Smithsonian Institution Press, Washington D.C.

GARCIA-AVELARO, MANUEL
1989 Transculturation in Contact Period and Contemporary Hispaniola. In *Columbian Consequences, Volume 2: Archaeological and Historical Perspectives on the Spanish Borderlands East*, edited by David H. Thomas, pp. 269-280. Smithsonian Institution Press, Washington D.C.

GARDNER, ANDREW
2008 Agency. In *Handbook of Archaeological Theories*, edited by R. Alexander Bentley, Herbert D.G. Maschner, and Christopher Chippindale, pp. 95-108. AltaMira Press, Lanham, Maryland.

GARLINGHOUSE, THOMAS S.
2009 Preliminary Analysis of Faunal Remains from Mission Period Features at Santa Clara. *SCA Preceedings* 22:1-5. Society for California Archaeology.

GASCO, JANINE
1992 Material Culture and Colonial Indian Society in Southern Mesoamerica: The View from Coastal Chiapas, Mexico. *Historical Archaeology* 26(1):67-74.

GASCO, JANINE, G. C. SMITH AND PATRICIA FOURNIER-GARCIA (EDITORS)
1997 *Approaches to the Historical Archaeology of Mexico, Central and South America.* Institute of Archaeology, University of California, Los Angeles.

GEDMINTAS, ALEKSANDRAS
1982 The Cultural Components of Ethnic Identity Retention among Binghamton, New York Lithuanians. *Lithuanian Quarterly Journal of Arts and Sciences* 28(3):4-8.

GIVEN, MICHAEL
2004 *The Archaeology of the Colonized.* Routledge, New York.

GOODBY, ROBERT G.
1998 Technological Patterning and Social Boundaries: Ceramic Variability in Southern New England, A.D. 1000-1675. In *The Archaeology of Social Boundaries*, edited by Miriam T. Stark, pp. 161-182. Smithsonian Institution Press, Washington D.C.

GOSDEN, CHRIS
2004 *Archaeology and Colonialism Cultural Contact from 5000 B.C. to the Present.* Cambridge University Press, Cambridge.

HABIG, MARION A.
1990 *Spanish Texas Pilgrimage: The Old Franciscan Missions and Other Spanish Settlements on Texas, 1632-1821.* Franciscan Herald Press, Chicago.
1997 *The Alamo Chain of Missions: A History of San Antonio's Five Old Missions.* Reprinted edition. Pioneer Enterprises, Livingston, Texas.

HACKEL, STEVEN W.
2005 *Children of Coyote, Missionaries of Saint Francis: Indian-Spanish Relations in Colonial California 1769-1850.* The University of North Carolina Press, Chapel Hill.

HALEY, BRIAN D. AND LARRY R. WILCOXON
2005 How Spaniards Became Chumash and other Tales of Ethnogenesis. *American Anthropologist* 107(3):432-445.

HANSON, JERRY AND DONALD V. KURTZ
2007 Ethnogenesis, Imperial Acculturation on the Frontiers, and the Production of Ethnic Identity: The Genízaro of New Mexico and the Red River Métis. *Social Evolution and History* 6(1):3-37.

HASS, LISBETH
1995 *Conquests and Historical Identities in California 1769-1936.* University of California Press, Berkeley.

HAYS-GILPIN, KELLEY ANN
2008 Gender. In *Handbook of Archaeological Theories*, edited by R. Alexander Bentley, Herbert D.G. Maschner, and Christopher Chippindale, pp. 335-350. AltaMira Press, Lanham, Maryland.

HITCHCOCK, ROBERT K.
1985 Sedentism and Site Structure: Organization Changes in Kalahari Basarwa Rresidential Locations. In *Method and Theory for Activity Area Research: An Ethnoarchaeological Approach*, edited by Susan Kent, pp. 374-423. Columbia University Press, New York.

HOOVER, ROBERT L.
1992 Some Models for Spanish Colonial Archaeology in California. *Historical Archaeology* 26(1):37-44.

HOOVER, ROBERT L. AND JULIA G. COSTELLO
 1985   *Excavations at Mission San Antonio, 1976-1978.* Institute of Archaeology Monograph 26. University of California, Los Angeles.

HURST, HENRY AND SARA OWEN (EDITORS)
 2005   *Ancient Colonizations: Analogy, Similarity and Difference.* Duckworth Publishers, London.

ISBELL, WILLIAM H.
 2000   What We Should Be Studying: The "imagined community" and the "natural community." In *The Archaeology of Communities: A New World Perspective*, edited by Marcello A. Canuto and Jason Yaeger, pp. 243-266. Routledge, London.

JACKSON, ROBERT H. AND EDWARD CASTILLO
 1995   *Indians, Franciscans, and Spanish Colonization, The Impact of the Mission System on California Indians.* University of New Mexico Press, Albuquerque.

JAMIESON, ROSS W.
 2008   The Market for Meat in Colonial Cuenca: A Seventeenth-Century Urban Faunal Assemblage from the Southern Highlands of Ecuador. *Historical Archaeology* 42(4):21-37.

JOHNSON, KENNETH W.
 1993   Mission Santa Fé de Toloca. In *The Spanish Missions of La Florida*, edited by Bonnie G. McEwan, pp. 141-164. U. Press of Florida, Gainesville.

JONES, B. CALVIN AND GARY N. SHAPIRO
 1990   Nine Mission sites in Apalachee. In *Columbian Consequences, Volume 2: Archaeological and Historical Perspectives on the Spanish Borderlands East*, edited by David H. Thomas, pp. 491-509. Smithsonian Institution Press, Washington D.C.

JONES, GRANT D. AND DAVID M. PENDERGAST
 1991   The Native Context of Colonialism in Southern Mesoamerica and Central America: An Overview. In *Columbian Consequences, Volume 3: The Spanish Borderlands in Pan-American Perspective*, edited by David H. Thomas, pp. 161-186. Smithsonian Institution Press. Washington D.C.

JONES, SIAN
 1997   *The Archaeology of Ethnicity: Constructing Identities in the Past and Present.* Routledge, London.
 2008   Ethnicity: Theoretical Approaches, Methodological Implications. In *Handbook of Archaeological Theories*, edited by R. Alexander Bentley, Herbert D. G. Maschner, and Christopher Chippindale, pp. 321-334. AltaMira Press, Lanham, Maryland.

KENT, SUSAN
 1984   *Analyzing Activity Areas An Ethnoarchaeological Study of the Use of Space.* University of New Mexico Press, Albuquerque,

KENT, SUSAN (EDITOR)
 1985   *Method and Theory in Activity Area Research: An Ethnoarchaeological Approach.* Columbia University Press, New York.

KING, JULIA
 1984   Ceramic Variability in 17th Century St. Augustine, Florida. *Historical Archaeology* 18(2):75-82.

KUTSCHE, PAUL, JOHN R. VAN NESS, AND ANDREW T. SMITH
 1976   Unified Approach to the Anthropology of Hispanic Northern New Mexico: Historical Archaeology, Ethnohistory, and Ethnography. *Historical Archaeology* 10(1):1-16.

LANGENWALTER, PAUL E. AND LARRY W. MCKEE
 1985   Vertebrate Faunal Remains from the Neophyte Dormitory. In *Excavations at Mission San Antonio, 1976-1978*, by Robert L. Hoover and Julia G. Costello, pp. 94-121. Monograph No. 26. Institute of Archaeology, University of California, Los Angeles.

LARAL PINTO, GLORIA
 1991   Change for Survival: The Case of the Sixteenth-Century Indigenous Populations of Northeastern and Mideast Honduras. In *Columbian Consequences, Volume 3: The Spanish Borderlands in Pan-American Perspective*, edited by David H. Thomas, pp. 227-244. Smithsonian Institution Press, Washington D.C.

LEONARD, ROBERT D. AND GEORGE T. JONES
 1987   Elements of an Inclusive Evolutionary Model for Archaeology. *Journal of Anthropological Archaeology* 6:199-219.

LEUTENEGGER, FR. BENEDICT (TRANSLATOR; REVISED BY CARMELITA CASSO AND MARGARET R. WARBURTON)
 1991   *Guidelines for a Texas Mission Instructions for the Missionary of Mission Concepcion in San Antonio, Texas.* Old Spanish Missions Historical Research Library at Our Lady of the Lake University, San Antonio.

LIEBMANN, MATTHEW AND MELLISA S. MURPHY (EDITORS)
 2011   *Enduring Conquests: Rethinking the Archaeology of Resistance to Spanish Colonialism in the Americas.* School for Advanced Research Press, Santa Fe.

LIGHTFOOT, KENT G.
 2005   *Indians, Missionaries, and Merchants: The Legacy of Colonial Encounters on the California Frontier.* University of California Press, Berkeley.

LITTLE, BARBARA J.
 1992a   Text-aided Archaeology. In *Text-Aided Archaeology*, edited by Barbara J. Little, pp. 1-6. CRC Press, Boca Raton.

LITTLE, BARBARA J. (EDITOR)
    1992b   *Text-Aided Archaeology*. CRC Press, Boca Raton.

LYONS, CLAIRE L. AND JOHN K. PAPADOPOULOS (EDITORS)
    2002   *The Archaeology of Colonialism*. Getty Publications, Los Angeles.

MATHES, W. MICHAEL
    1989   Baja California: A Special Area of Contact and Colonization, 1535-1697. In *Columbian Consequences, Volume 1: Archaeological and Historical Perspectives on the Spanish Borderlands West*, edited by David H. Thomas, pp. 407-422. Smithsonian Institution Press, Washington D.C.

MCEWAN, BONNIE G.
    1991   The Archaeology of Women in the Spanish New World. *Historical Archaeology* 25(4):33-41.
    1992   The Role of Ceramics in Spain and Spanish America during the 16th Century. *Historical Archaeology* 26(1):92-108.

MCEWAN, BONNIE G. (EDITOR)
    2000   *Indians of the Greater Southeast: Historical Archaeology and Ethnohistory*. University of Florida Press, Gainesville.

MESKELL, LYNN AND ROBERT W. PREUCEL
    2004   Identities. In *A Companion to Social Archaeology*, edited by Lynn Meskell and Robert W. Preucel, pp. 121-141. Blackwell Publishing, Malden, Massachusetts.

MILANICH, JERALD T.
    1990   The European Entrada into La Florida: An Overview. In *Columbian Consequences, Volume 2: Archaeological and Historical Perspectives on the Spanish Borderlands East*, edited by David H. Thomas, pp. 3-29. Smithsonian Institution Press, Washington D.C.
    2006   *Laboring in the Fields of the Lord: Spanish Missions and Southeastern Indians*. University Press of Florida, Gainesville.

MILLS, BARBARA
    2008   Colonialism and Cuisine: Cultural Transmission, Agency, and History at Zuni Pueblo. In *Cultural Transmission and Material Culture: Breaking Down Boundaries*, edited by Miriam T. Stark, Brenda J. Bowser, and Lee Horne, pp. 245-262. The University of Arizona Press, Tucson.

MULLINS, PAUL R. AND ROBERT PAYNTER
    2000   Representing Colonizers: An Archaeology of Creolization, Ethnogenesis, and Indigenous Material Culture among the Haida. *Historical Archaeology* 34(3):73-84.

MURRAY, TIM (EDITOR)
    2004   *The Archaeology of Contact in Settler Societies*. Cambridge University Press, Cambridge.

NAGEL, JOANE
    1994   Constructing Ethnicity: Creating and Recreating Ethnic Identity and Culture. *Social Problems* 41(1):152-176.

NEITZEL, JILL E., HECTOR NEFF, MICHAEL D. GLASCOCK, AND RONALD L. BISHOP
    2002   Chaco and the Production and Exchange of Dogoszhi-Style Pottery. In *Ceramic Production and Circulation in the Greater Southwest Source Determination by INAA and Complementary Mineralogical Investigations*, edited by Donna M. Glowacki and Hector Neff, pp. 47-66. The Cotsen Institute of Archaeology, University of California, Los Angeles.

PENDERY, STEVEN R.
    1992   Consumer Behavior in Colonial Charlestown, Massachusetts, 1630-1760. *Historical Archaeology* 26(3):57-72.

PERTTULA, TIMOTHY K.
    1992   *"The Caddo Nation": Archaeological and Ethnohistoric Perspectives*. University of Texas Press, Austin.

PERTTULA, TIMOTHY K. (COMPILER)
    2011   *The Archaeology of Native American-European Culture Contact*. Perspectives from Historical Archaeology No. 3. The Society for Historical Archaeology.

PESCATELLLO, ANN M.
    1976   *Power and Pawn: The Female in Iberian Families, Societies, and Cultures*. Greenwood Press, Westport.

PILLAY, AVIN E.
    2001   Analysis of archaeological artifacts: PIXE, XRF or ICP-MS? *Journal of Radioanalytical and Nuclear Chemistry* 247(3):539-595.

POWERS, KAREN V.
    1995   *Andean Journey: Migration, Ethnogenesis, and the State in Colonial Quito*. University of New Mexico Press, Albuquerque.

REITZ, ELIZABETH J.
    1990   Zooarchaeological Evidence for Subsistence at La Florida Missions. In *Columbian Consequences, Volume 2: Archaeological and Historical Perspectives on the Spanish Borderlands East*, edited by David H. Thomas, pp. 543-554. Smithsonian Institution Press, Washington D.C.
    1992   The Spanish Colonial Experience and Domestic Animals. *Historical Archaeology* 26(1):84-91.

Reitz, Elizabeth J. and C. Margaret Scarry
1992a   (editors) *Reconstructing Historic Subsistence with an Example from Sixteenth-century Spanish Florida.* Special Publication Series Number 3. The Society for Historical Archaeology.
1992b   Historic Subsistence Practices: Synthesis and Conclusions. In *Reconstructing Historic Subsistence with an Example from Sixteenth-century Spanish Florida,* edited by Elizabeth J. Reitz and Margaret Scarry, pp. 92-99. Special Publication Series Number 3. The Society for Historical Archaeology.

Reitz, Elizabeth J., Barnet Pavao-Zuckerman, Daniel C. Weinand, and Gwyneth A. Duncan
2010   *Mission and Pueblo Santa Catalina de Guale, St. Catherines Island, Georgia: A Comparative Zooarchaeological Analysis.* Anthropological Papers No. 91. American Museum of Natural History, New York.

Rodriguez-Alegria, Enrique
2005   Eating Like an Indian. *Current Anthropology* 46(4):551-573.

Rolland, Vicki L. and Keith H. Ashley
2000   Beneath the Bell: A Study of Mission Period Colonoware from Three Spanish Missions in Northeastern Florida. *The Florida Archaeologist* 53(1):37-61.

Romani, John F. and A. George Toren
1975   A Preliminary Analysis of Faunal remains from the VEN-87 Aboriginal and Historic Components: Phase I. In *3500 Years on a City Block: San Buenaventura Mission Plaza Project Archaeology Report,* by Roberta S. Greenwood. Report to the Redevelopment Agency, City of Buenaventura, from Greenwood and Associates, Pacific Palisades, California.

Rothschild, Nan A.
2003   *Colonial Encounters in a Native American Landscape. The Spanish and Dutch in North America.* Smithsonian Books, Washington D.C.

Ruhl, Donna L.
1990   Spanish Mission Paleoethnobotany and Culture Change: A Survey of the Archaeobotanical Data and Some Speculations on Aboriginal and Spanish Agrarian Interactions in La Florida. In *Columbian Consequences, Volume 2: Archaeological and Historical Perspectives on the Spanish Borderlands East,* edited by David H. Thomas, pp. 555-580. Smithsonian Institution Press, Washington D.C.
1997   Oranges and Wheat: Spanish Attempts at Agriculture in La Florida. *Historical Archaeology* 31(1):36-45.

Salzman, Philip C.
1980   *When Nomads Settle: Processes of Sedentarization as Adaptation and Response.* Praeger, New York

Sauer, Carl O.
1966   *The Early Spanish Main.* University of California Press, Berkeley.

Saunders, Rebecca
1990   Ideal and Innovation: Spanish Mission Architecture in the Southeast. In *Columbian Consequences, Volume 2: Archaeological and Historical Perspectives on the Spanish Borderlands East,* edited by David H. Thomas, pp. 527-542. Smithsonian Institution Press, Washington D.C.
1993   Architecture of the Missions Santa Maria and Santa Catalina de Amelia. In *The Spanish Missions of La Florida,* edited by Bonnie G. McEwan, pp. 35-61. University Press of Florida, Gainesville.
1996   Mission-Period Settlement Structure: A Test of the Model at San Martin de Timucua. *Historical Archaeology* 30(4):24-36.
2000   *Stability and Change in Guale Indian Pottery A.D. 1300-1702.* The University of Alabama Press, Tuscaloosa.

Scarry, C. Margaret and Elizabeth J. Reitz
1990   Herbs, Fish, Scum, and Vermin: Subsistence Strategies in Sixteenth-Century Florida. In *Columbian Consequences, Volume 2: Archaeological and Historical Perspectives on the Spanish Borderlands East,* edited by David H. Thomas, pp. 343-354. Smithsonian Institution Press, Washington D.C.

Shackel, Paul A. and Barbara J. Little
1992   Post-Processual Approaches to Meaning and Uses of Material Culture in Historical Archaeology. *Historical Archaeology* 26(3):5-11.

Shortman, Edward M. and Patricia A. Urban
1998   Culture Contact Structure and Process. In *Studies in Culture Contact Interaction, Culture Change, and Archaeology,* edited by James G. Cusick, pp. 102-125. Occasional Paper No. 25. Center for Archaeological Investigations, Southern Illinois University, Carbondale.

Silliman, Stephen W.
2005   Culture Contact or Colonialism? Challenges in the Archaeology of Native North America. *American Antiquity* 70(1):55-74.

Skowronek, Russell K.
1992   Empire and Ceramics: The Changing Role of Illicit Trade in Spanish America. *Historical Archaeology* 26(1):109-118.

Snow, David H.
1967   Archaeology and 19th Century Missions. *Historical Archaeology* 11):57-59.

Spicer, Edward H.
1961   Spanish-Indian Acculturation in the Southwest. *American Anthropologist* 56(4):663-678

STEFFEN, JEROME O.
    1980   *Comparative Frontiers: A Proposal for Studying the American West.* University of Oklahoma Press, Norman.

STEIN, GIL J. (EDITOR)
    2005   *The Archaeology of Colonial Encounters Comparative Perspectives.* School of American Research Press, Santa Fe.

STOJANOWSKI, CHRISTOPHER M.
    2010   *Bioarchaeology of Ethnogenesis in the Colonial Southeast.* University Press of Florida, Gainesville.

SUTTON, DONALD S.
    2005   China's Minorities, Cultural Change, and Ethnic Identity. *History Compass* 3 (AS 109):1-7.

THOMAS, DAVID HURST
    1989   Columbian Consequences: The Spanish Borderlands in Cubist Perspective. In *Columbian Consequences, Volume 1: Archaeological and Historical Perspectives on the Spanish Borderlands West*, edited by David H. Thomas, pp. 1-14. Smithsonian Institution Press, Washington D.C.
    1990   The Spanish Missions of La Florida: An Overview In *Columbian Consequences, Volume 2: Archaeological and Historical Perspectives on the Spanish Borderlands East*, edited by David H. Thomas, pp. 357-398. Smithsonian Institution Press, Washington D.C.
    1993   The Archaeology of Mission Santa Catalina de Guale: Our First 15 Years. In *The Spanish Missions of La Florida*, edited by Bonnie G. McEwan, pp. 1-34. University Press of Florida, Gainesville.

THOMAS, DAVID HURST (EDITOR)
    1989   *Columbian Consequences, Volume 1: Archaeological and Historical Perspectives on the Spanish Borderlands West.* Smithsonian Institution Press, Washington D.C.
    1990   *Columbian Consequences, Volume 2: Archaeological and Historical Perspectives on the Spanish Borderlands East.* Smithsonian Institution Press, Washington D.C.
    1991   *Columbian Consequences, Volume 3: The Spanish Borderlands in Pan-American Perspective.* Smithsonian Institution Press, Washington D.C.

THOMAS, WILLIAM J., NATHAN W. BOWER, JOHN W. KANTNER, MARIANNE L. STOLLER, AND DAVID H. SNOW
    1992   An X-ray Fluorescence-Pattern Recognition Analysis of Pottery from an Early Historic Hispanic Settlement near Santa Fe, New Mexico. *Historical Archaeology* 26(2):24-36.

TRIGG, HEATHER B.
    2003   The Ties That Bind: Economic and Social Interactions in Early-Colonial New Mexico, A.D. 1598-1680. *Historical Archaeology* 37(2):65-84.

VOSS, BARBARA L.
    2005   From Casta to Californio: Social Identity and the Archaeology of Culture Contact. *American Anthropologist* 107(3):461-474.
    2008   *The Archaeology of Ethnogenesis, Race, and Sexuality in Colonial San Francisco.* University of California Press, Berkeley.

WADE, MARIA F.
    2008   *Missions, Missionaries, and Native Americans.* University Press of Florida, Gainesville.

WALLERSTEIN, IMMANUEL
    1974   *The Modern World System, Vol. 1: Capitalistic Agriculture and the Origins of the European World Economy in the Sixteenth Century.* Academic Press, New York.
    1980   *The Modern World System, Vol 2: Mercantilism and the Consolidation of the European World Economy, 1600-1750.* Academic Press, New York.

WATSON, PATTY JO
    2008   Processualism and After. In *Handbook of Archaeological Theories*, edited by R. Alexander Bentley, Herbert D. G. Maschner, and Christopher Chippindale, pp. 29-38. AltaMira Press, Lanham, Maryland.

WEISMAN, BRENT R.
    1993   Archaeology of Fig Springs Mission, Ichetucknee Springs State Park. In *The Spanish Missions of La Florida*, edited by Bonnie G. McEwan, pp. 165-192. University Press of Florida, Gainesville.

WHITE, CAROLYN L. AND MARY C. BEAUDRY
    2009   Artifacts and Personal Identity. In *International Handbook of Historical Archaeology*, edited by Teresita Majewski and David Gaimster, pp. 209-225. Springer, New York.

WILCOX, MICHAEL V.
    2009   *The Pueblo Revolt and the Mythology of Conquest: An Indigenous Archaeology of Contact.* University of California Press, Berkeley.

YAEGER, JASON AND MARCELLO A. CANUTO
    2000   Introducing An Archaeology of Communities. In *The Archaeology of Communities A New World Perspective*, edited by Marcello A. Canuto and Jason Yaeger, pp. 1-15. Routledge, London.

YEH, CHRISTINE J. AND KAREN HUANG
    1996   The Collectivist Nature of Ethnic Identity Development Among Asian-American College Students. *Adolescence* 31:645-661.

ARCHAEOLOGY AND 19th CENTURY MISSIONS

by David H. Snow

The year 1800 heralds the beginning of a new era in North American mission programs. The first Protestant mission boarding school was established in 1804 among the Cherokees (Berkhofer, 1963, p. 179), and the first manual labor boarding school mission was founded immediately thereafter. These were radically new experiments in the Protestant mission program, since previous missionary efforts were limited almost exclusively to itinerant preaching. The boarding school method quickly caught on, and by 1828 there were slightly over forty in operation. As it spread west, however, this mission program failed miserably until the reservations restricted the movements of the nomadic Indians.

Although the Spanish missions in the southwest were secularized in 1834, the Jesuits operated successfully in the northwest interior from 1840 on. The Russian Orthodox Church reached Alaska by 1794, and was later supplemented by the Church of England both before and after the purchase of Alaska in 1867.

One useful approach for the archeologist to post-1800 missions is to outline the development of 19th century missionizing activities from the auspicious beginnings east of the Mississippi River, and to look at some of the major factors which effected these developments. This, in turn, should lead to the designation of appropriate areas of investigation dealing with representative sites according to developmental or other criteria. It is impossible, however, to do justice to such an approach here.

Another way to approach the situation depends on the purpose for which a site is chosen for excavation—and this is precisely the first question that occurred to me on being asked to discuss post-1800 mission site archeology: What expected (or even unexpected) results would justify the excavation of a 19th century mission site?

It occurred to me that students of culture history might be interested in two major aspects of these sites. The first, which has been exploited most often by historians, is concerned with the adjustment of the missionary to his new field of endeavor and the monuments to Christianity and Civilization which he and his followers erected—that is, the mission.

The second, and most obvious aspect of these sites, has not been exploited as it might by archeologists. This concerns the role of missions and missionaries in the development of contemporary Indian culture. The other side of this picture must also take into account the effects—of the Indians who were the subjects of these missions—on the missions themselves.

Neither the work at Whitman Mission, nor at Sonoma Mission in California, for example, took an active interest in this situation. It should be pointed out that this is true also for the work at the 17th century Spanish missions in New Mexico at Abo, Jemez, and the original work at Gran Quivera and Quarai.

These two major aspects of 19th century mission activity in North America—the role of the mission in Manifest Destiny, as well as the role of the American Indian in mission history—are both significant for culture historians. For the archeologist, as field technician, or as anthropologist or historiographer, the important question, however, is just *whose* culture history is concerned—the Indians', or the white mans'. Obviously, both must be considered in any discussion of mission activity; but the emphasis placed on one or the other is a direct consequence of the purpose for which the site will be dug.

The main point of my discussion here concerns the rich potential, for both anthropologist and historiographer, that is present in the spread of the 19th century mission programs in North America. Each of these students—of culture in its broadest sense—brings to the excavation of a mission site his own set of problems, which stem from different purposes. Each will place interpretative emphasis on different aspects of the site and its excavation.

These purposes may have little in common—e.g., the restoration for display of an important historical landmark, such as the Sonoma Mission buildings; or the excavation of a suspected Jesuit "visita" in Idaho as part of a study to determine the range of subsistence activities of the 19th century Nez Perce Indians.

Yet, between these wide contrasts, there is common ground for research and theory. J. C. Harrington pointed out some years ago with regard to historic site archeology, that "acculturation works both ways" (1955: 1123). Mission site archeology is potentially able to exploit this "acculturational feedback" to a greater degree, perhaps, than the other types of historic sites selected for discussion in this symposium.

As an example, perhaps not a valid one because of subsequent work of which I'm not aware, of the common ground for research and theory that I have in mind, I might point to my selection of Sonoma mission in the contrasting situation above. In Treganza's report of the 1954 season at Sonoma, following the initial work of Bennyhoff and Elsasser, is this information: Apparently contrary to usual mission procedure, Sonoma Mission was not located "in near proximity to large Indian villages". "No evidence of Indian occupation was detected—at Sonoma"; and the location of the villages which the mission drew from, is thought to have been at some distance from the mission on Sonoma creek (Treganza, 1956: 12-13).

This situation poses a problem which has implications for both the "Indianist" as well as for the historian interested in Spanish mission development.

For example, a possible re-interpretation of the reason for establishing this mission might be in order—this is at least suggested by the archeological survey. On the other hand, archeological surveys, and limited excavation based on such surveys, might disclose patterns of spatial relationship between missions and local villages (similar to what Kubler found in 17th century missions in New Mexico), which might explain the apparent exception at Sonoma.

The founding of Sonoma mission, according to George Wharton James in 1905

". . . took place in 1823, without any idea of founding a new mission. The change to San Rafael had been so beneficial to the sick Indians that Canon Fernandez, Prefect Payeras, and Governor Arguello decided to transfer bodily the Mission of San Francisco from the peninsula to the mainland north of the bay, and make San Rafael dependent upon it. An exploring expedition . . . finally reported in favor of the Sonoma Valley" (p. 41).

In 1824, a year and a half after the site was chosen, James says that

"The neophytes numbered 693, but many of these were sent from San Francisco, San Jose, and San Rafael. The Indians at this Mission represented thirty-five different tribes, according to the record . . ." (p. 272).

I do not have access to the original report of Bennyhoff and Elsasser, but I assume they were aware of this information. If it is correct, it offers the possibility of new questions and interpretations, that might be tested by archeology.

If the village sites, which were located some distance from the mission (according to Treganza's survey), and the mission occupation, are contemporary, the emplacement of the mission in relation to the villages remains in question. The answer might be indicated by the presence of neophytes from thirty-five different tribes and from different missions— missionizing efforts among the local tribes may not have been overly successful at Sonoma.

What I am driving at, quite obviously, is the need for problem-oriented research in historic site archeology, and I merely repeat the pleas of others in this respect. But this research, and the excavations which might result from it, must, I think, be useful to students of culture, whether they are "Indianists" or not.

A useful definition of a mission will clarify the concept:

> "A mission is an ecclesiastical unit of area of sufficient size, within which all activities (such as construction, farming, handicrafts, herding, recreation, etc.) are administered by a ministry commissioned by, and dependent upon a larger religious organization for direction or financial support".

REFERENCES USED

BERKHOFER, ROBERT

1965 Salvation and The Savage: An Analysis of Protestant Missions and American Indian Response, 1787-1862. University of Kentucky Press.

BURNS, ROBERT IGNATIUS, S.J.

1966 The Jesuits and The Indian Wars of the Northwest. Yale University Press.

HARRINGTON, J. C.

1955 "Archeology as an Auxiliary Science to American History", in American Anthropologist, Vol. 57.

JAMES, GEORGE WHARTON

1905 In and Out of Old Missions of California. Little, Brown and Co. Boston.

KUBLER, GEORGE

1940 Religious Architecture of New Mexico. Colorado Springs. The Taylor Museum.

TREGANZA, ADAN E.

1956 "Sonoma Mission: An Archeological Reconstruction of The Mission San Francisco de Solano Qaudrangle", in Kroeber Anthropological Society Papers, No. 14. Berkeley.

PAUL KUTSCHE, JOHN R. VAN NESS,
AND ANDREW T. SMITH

A Unified Approach to the Anthropology of Hispanic Northern New Mexico: Historical Archæology, Ethnohistory, and Ethnography

ABSTRACT

Archæology, ethnohistory, ethnography—three methodologies within the same body of theory—can be used cooperatively to reconstruct the cultural history of Hispanic Northern New Mexico. The leads suggested for the investigation of Hispanic culture are discussed under the interrelated headings of ecology, social organization, and trade. Other benefits of intensive joint work include distinguishing ideal from real culture and testing theories of culture change. The approach outlined could serve as a model for the investigation of other historical traditions in the same or other parts of the world.

Most archæological investigations of the Hispanic tradition in northern New Mexico to date have concerned themselves with a few important historic sites, like missions and the Palace of Governors in Santa Fe.[1] The purpose of this paper is twofold: first, to suggest the benefits that students of the Hispanic society and culture of New Mexico might realize through undertaking historical archæology on a broad scale, using an anthropological perspective; second, to show that this culture makes a particularly useful type case because of the continuity from past to present—a type case which can become an example for similar approaches to other cultures.

We believe that the "new archæology" is best designed for achieving an anthropological perspective. The "new archæology" views cultures not merely as artifacts to be described, but as human behavior manifested by the tangible remains. Its method consists of formulating hypotheses to test the archæological

record. Further testable deductions and secondary formulations are derived from the successes or failures of the original hypotheses (Binford 1972; Binford and Binford 1968; Hill 1970; Martin 1971). Results are derived in terms of probabilities. Where structural analogies between the archæological record and the ethnohistoric and ethnographic record are greatest, probability for confirmation of hypotheses is greatest. Edward Dozier makes a parallel point concerning time lapse (1970: 203): ". . . the shorter the time gap between a prehistoric site and the living site, the more likely that the inference will be a reliable one." Finally, if some measure can be developed of the conservatism of the cultural tradition from prehistoric to historic times, the reliability of the archæologist's inferences will be further enhanced (Dozier:203–204).

Implications of the "new archæology" should be spelled out as clearly as possible before we proceed. The dichotomy so frequently made between archæology and socio-cultural anthropology is without foundation in theory, because the aims of both are identical—to understand the structures and processes of human culture and society. The real differences between archæology and other aspects of sociocultural anthropology, particularly ethnohistory and ethnography, are methodological. They work with different types of data which must be recorded with different types of tools. But the archæologist, the ethnohistorian and the ethnographer ideally will gather their data with the same theoretical questions in mind.

The archæologist can build up a "data bank" of analogies from ethnography to help him in research design. The ethnographer can record systematically where activities take place, what physical materials are associated with behaviors, roles, etc. (Hill 1970:28–29).[2] He should make his model of a cultural system not only so as to define normative behavior, but also to describe clustering variations of behavior (Hill 1970:18,52; Barth 1969:29).

As Dozier implies in the quote above, the "new archæology" lends itself particularly well to historic periods because of shorter time gap to the present, more nearly similar patterns of culture, and the availability of historic records to check against data from excavations.

Hume (1969) and Schuyler (1970), among others, have argued that this synthetic approach to historical archæology is absolutely imperative. In fact, historical sites may be the best testing grounds for the methods and approaches of the "new archæology". Schuyler (1970:87) states:

> . . . Major problems of social, economic, and ideological interpretation such as are being debated in the "new archæology" can be settled in part by Historical and Historic Sites Archæology. . . . How is social organization or economic structure reflected in the material inventory of a community?

Such structures can be only indirectly inferred at prehistoric sites, but at historic sites they can often be established with considerable accuracy with the help of documentary records on the demographic, social, and ethnic structure, plus extrapolations from ethnographic field data (Schuyler 1970:87).

The temptation is great to oversimplify our models and our analogies, especially pertaining to social structure (cf. Allen and Richardson 1971). Having recourse to ethnohistorical and ethnographic records should help us to avoid this pitfall in the study of Hispanic sites in northern New Mexico. For instance, New Mexican communities have been less conservative socially and economically than their Pueblo Indian neighbors, and ethnohistorical data provide the evidence. Comparative ethnography indicates geographical differences from village to village, family to family, even sometimes individual to individual.

A further caution against oversimplification is that cultural trends are often open to divergent interpretations. For instance, in the nineteenth century a number of Hispanos converted from Roman Catholicism to Presbyterianism, and in the twentieth century others converted to Pentecostal sects. These switches leave evidence for the archæologist in different styles of church buildings (Figures 1 and 2). Some scholars might regard both conversions as of

FIGURE 1. Catholic church of Colonial Spanish style (Museum of New Mexico).

FIGURE 2. Pentecostal church (George McCue).

equal cultural importance, since they both combat Rome; others would regard Pentecostalism as a more radical departure than Presbyterianism; still others, noting that the converts to Pentecostalism had often been the most devout Catholics, see that switch as radical only in the sense of a return to theological roots, and see the Presbyterian conversion as a more fundamental change in cultural identity.

A third caution is that Hispanic culture in New Mexico never existed in isolation, but influenced and was influenced by Pueblo, Athapascan and Plains Indians, and later by Anglo Americans. We shall return to this point below in describing trade.

FIGURE 3. Microbasin with irrigated land below, dry pasture land above.

Having discussed in general terms the relations of three sub-disciplines of anthropology and their potential for aiding each other in particular areas, we shall proceed to pertinent data of Hispanic northern New Mexico under the headings of ecology, social organization and trade. We shall offer some hypotheses derived from ethnohistory and ethnography, which are suitable for testing by the historical archæologist.

Ecology

The most frequent pattern of rural Hispanic settlement from the seventeenth to the nineteenth centuries was for a single village to occupy a single microbasin ringed by mountains.[3] *Placita* (village center) and irrigated fields are in the bottom lands. Above the line of irrigation and into the sierras sheep, goats, cattle and horses of the villagers grazed (Figure 3). Ownership of these basins was granted by the Spanish and Mexican governments to communities or individuals. Individual grants usually came, over time, to be held and used by resident communities.

The subsistence balance between raising plants and animals was closely related to diet and to patterns of life of Hispanic settlers, and sheds light on economic relations between Hispanos and Pueblo Indians. We hypothesize that Hispanos continued the Iberian preference for raising livestock,[4] while Pueblo Indians continued their traditional emphasis on crop-raising (cf. Smith 1976). We should like to see this hypothesis tested by analyses of floral and faunal remains from habitation sites. A series of analyses representing different periods from the seventeenth to the nineteenth centuries would add information on shifts in subsistence balance in either or both cultures over time.

We feel that this hypothesis is particularly worthy of investigation because documentary

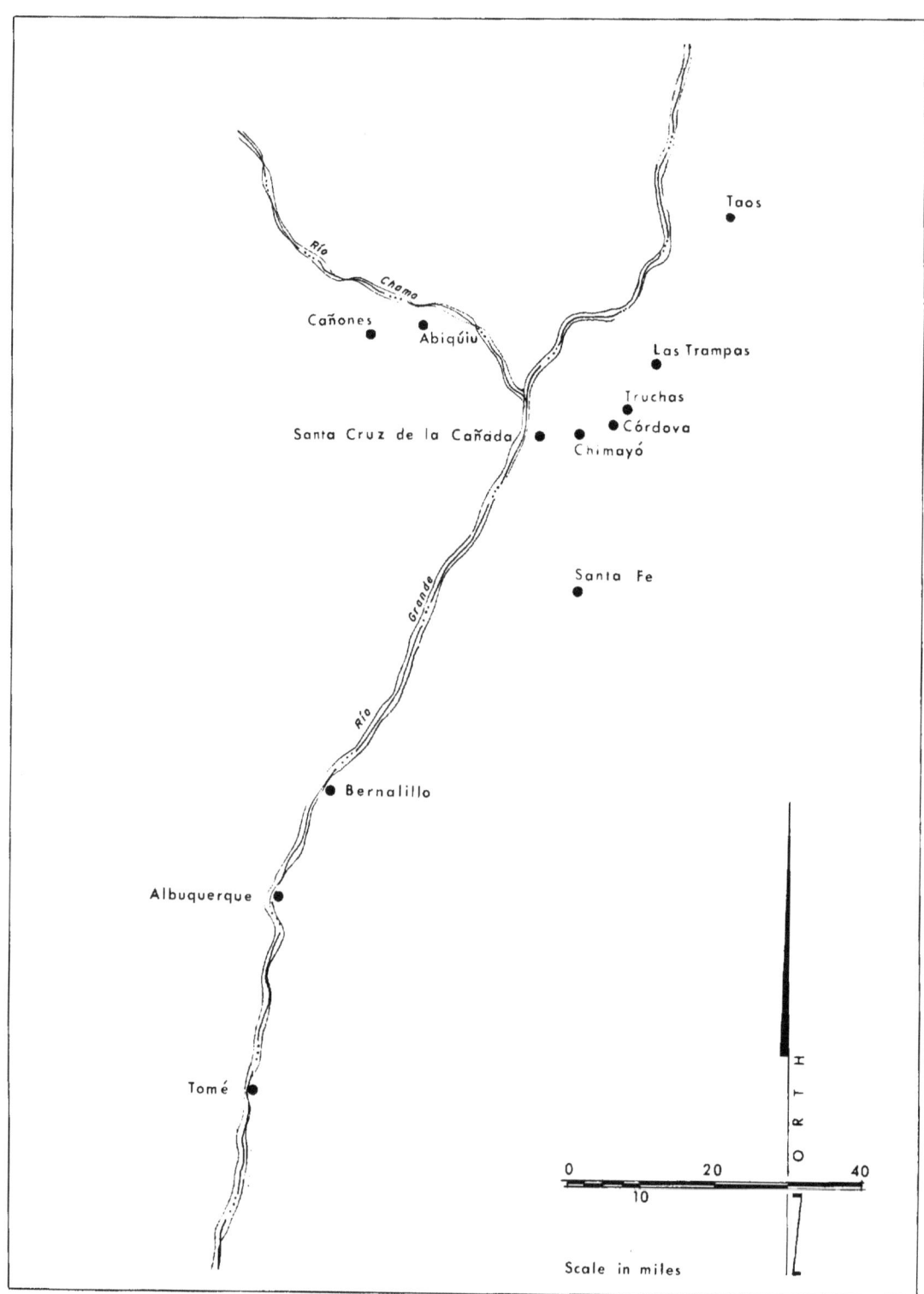

FIGURE 4. North central New Mexico.

research by historians has usually treated Hispanic settlements in Rio Arriba as primarily farming communities, where animal husbandry was a secondary pursuit of limited importance.[5] Archæological evidence should enable us to resolve these conflicting interpretations and lead to new avenues of research.

In addition to the tendency toward specialization between Hispanic and Pueblo villages, there is ethnohistorical record for specialization from one Hispanic village to another, but this record is very fragmentary until well into the present century. We know for instance that Chimayó and Córdova can grow wheat, Truchas cannot. (See location map, Figure 4.) Fruit trees grow better in lower elevations, less well in higher. Certain varieties of chiles are more frequently found in some localities than in others, and so forth for other crops. The implications of this climatically determined special-

ization for trade between subregions is great and will be mentioned again below. The historical record could be enhanced and its complexities better understood through archæological investigation.

We have sufficient ethnohistorical and ethnographic information so that we can offer an archæologically testable hypothesis concerning the extension of Hispanic settlement through time into new areas. We believe that Spanish and Mexican government documents are relatively uninformative, when not outright misleading, regarding the dynamics of growth in this frontier province. The inadequacy of the documentary record in this respect appears to have resulted from the loose adherence by villagers to government regulations in this isolated and poorly administered territory. We term the actual mode of settlement expansion the "budding process". We hypo-

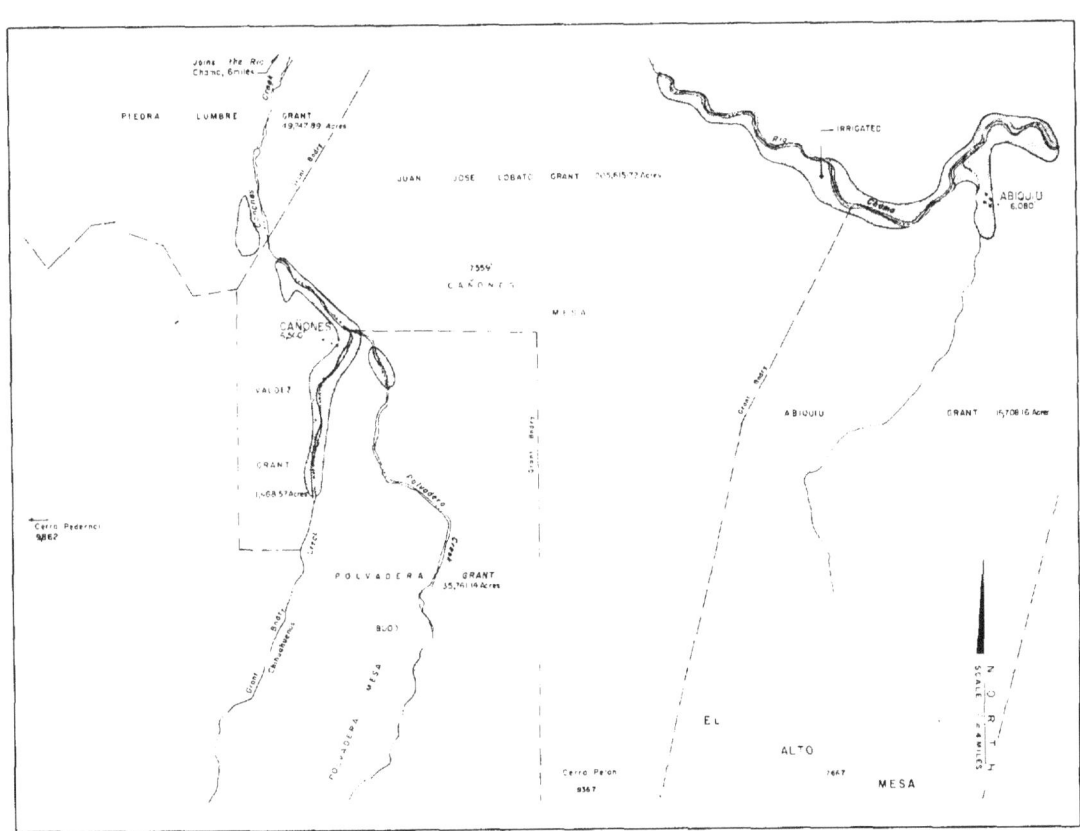

FIGURE 5. Abiquiú and Cañones with intervening mesas.

thesize that as the resources of one microbasin began to be taken up, surplus population spilled over either to adjacent or nearby microbasins. It appears to us that official land grants more often confirmed existing settlement than authorized new settlement. We are at odds with the prevailing historical interpretation of the settlement pattern in New Mexico, as outlined by Marc Simmons (1969). This interpretation utilizes archival records literally, to indicate that settlements date from the date of their grants. An example of the budding process which predates its grant documents is the founding of Cañones from Abiquiú, both of the Chama drainage. A summary of the data follows:

FIGURE 6. Jacal.

Abiquiú was founded beginning about 1730 through a series of grants to Hispanic settlers in the Chama Valley as an outpost against nomadic Ute and Navajo warriors. (In this case the grants indeed preceded settlement.) Indians depredations brought about abandonment in 1747. Resettlement, begun in 1750, included the establishment of a *genizaro* (Hispanicized Indian) village at Abiquiú in 1754. Herding was carried on largely up the mountain to the south, toward Vallecitos, the Mesa de Abiquiú, and El Alto, from which both Abiquiú Creek and Polvadera Creek flow (Figure 5). Abiquiú *placita* consisted of adobe houses closely built, often wall-to-wall, with a church. Away from the *placita,* in the fields or up toward the mountains, summer houses were more casually built of upright sticks or boards in the *jacal* fashion, for occasional use by herders or whole families (Figure 6).[6] It was and is fairly common for a single nuclear family to possess two, three or more houses in various places. Seasonal occupation, begun in this manner, led eventually to new permanent settlements at these outlying points, which in turn led to the formation of new *placitas.* Over El Alto Mesa from Abiquiú we know that as early as 1740 one José Riaño, originally from Santa Fe, had a ranch on Cañones Creek. Between 1740 and 1745 Riaño loaned his ranch house and corrals to the Montoya brothers of Abiquiú, who claimed lands adjacent

to his. About the same time several *ranchos* were established at the head of Polvadera Creek, on El Alto itself. New grants were made for grazing purposes in this vicinity to Juan Pablo Martin and Pedro Martin Serrano in 1766, because the Riaño and Montoya grants had been abandoned due to the Indian threat. More intensive occupation developed as settlers gradually descended Polvadera Creek, asking for a land grant which was made in the name of Juan Bautista Valdez and eight companions in 1807. A *placita* was built, or perhaps a succession of *placitas,* the present one lying just above the confluence of the Polvadera and Cañones Creeks. Thus did Cañones bud off from Abiquiú (Van Ness 1975). We believe that the unit which budded was the patrilaterally extended family which acted as a single farming and herding entity.

Besides Abiquiú, other centers from which villages budded were El Rito, Taos, Santa Cruz de la Cañada, Santa Fe, Bernalillo, and Albuquerque. Area-wide archæological investigation of the process of settlement should prove to be most helpful to all students of Hispanic culture in New Mexico.

We hypothesize that the shape which villages took over time was controlled by an interrelated set of variables. These variables are, in no particular order, (1) the immediacy of the threat of nomadic Indian depredations, (2) subsistence patterns and the related logistical problems, particularly the frequency of illicit

FIGURE 7. Chimayó.

trading activities with the nomadic Indians (which encouraged settlers to locate themselves out of view of too many neighbors or officials), (3) the special characteristics of the local environment (topography, hydrology, climate, etc.), (4) population size and density, (5) the degree of control exercised by government officials, who were required to implement the elaborate legal code established by the Spanish Crown for settling new lands, and (6) the season of the year. Ethnohistorical records indicate that village forms ranged from tightly closed defensive squares (such as Chimayó) (Figure 7) to looser *placitas* strung out along several miles of watercourse, depending upon the relative import of each of the constellation of factors affecting the settlement form. It also appears that the winter style of a village was tighter, its dwellings had larger rooms and they were constructed of more durable materials (principally adobes), while summer residence patterns tended to be much more disbursed, dwellings had fewer and smaller rooms, and construction was flimsier (generally *jacales*).

The archæologist can help us to test our model concerning pattern, density, date of first settlement, and duration of occupation in particular villages, as well as the patterns of land use. In the Cañones microbasin, for example, we suspect considerable over-grazing during the nineteenth century, but we lack precise information. Maps created by an archæological survey could help us to understand a number of other features of early

FIGURE 8. Soterrano, about five feet high (George McCue).

FIGURE 9. Horno under construction (note trapezoidal adobes) (Natalie Owings).

Hispanic settlements by locating roads, trails, farm plot boundaries, and irrigation ditches. For instance, maps of the physical relation of dwellings to irrigation ditches should give us insights into the cooperative use of water. Mapping wider demographic patterns in relation to field systems and grazing lands may tell us a good deal about cooperative and individual patterns of land use. The archæologist can also provide us with more information about what constituted a farmstead. During the 1960's, when Kutsche and Van Ness conducted ethnography, the Cañones farmstead consists of a house, latrine (an innovation from about 1900), and a *soterrano* (a cold storage house, partly underground) used for storing dried and canned vegetables and fruit (Figure 8). It usually contains no other structures, although two or three farmsteads have *hornos* (outdoor ovens) (Figure 9) and farm sheds or barns. There is a community corral, rather than individual facilities. How far back this pattern goes, and whether the earliest houses were of adobes, stone, wood, or *jacales,* we do not know.

Social Organization

Intimately related to ecology is social organization. The traditional village Hispanic family pattern is the patrilaterally extended family. However patrilocal, matrilocal, and neolocal residence were and are practiced,

depending primarily on economic circumstances.

We believe that the size and the arrangement of dwellings offers useful evidence of family size and family structure—whether the household is nuclear or extended. Close dating of the rooms in houses will indicate the dynamics of family size, composition, and growth. As long as villages were growing (until the mobile home changed the style of growth), it was the custom to add rooms to existing houses in gallery or L pattern, as children came along; sometimes rooms were added for married children and their families (Figure 10). Extensive ethnographic data on the domestic cycle in a Hispanic village have been gathered and analyzed by Weaver (1965). So far as we can tell on the basis of historical site excavation to date, the archæologist should usually find seventeenth and eighteenth century houses containing "fair sized, multipurpose rooms," unlike the tiny special rooms of Indian pueblos (Boyd 1974:7).

In the nineteenth century security against Indian attack and wealth both improved, with the result that "in less well-to-do families . . . the average house had three or four rooms, even when there were as many as a dozen members of all ages in the family" (Boyd 1974: 7), while the rich might have many rooms including a *sala* large enough for a whole village to dance in (Jaramillo 1972:17,46,50–51,

FIGURE 10. Gallery house, far end unoccupied.

FIGURE 11. Private family chapel (Museum of New Mexico).

86–87), and a private chapel (Jaramillo 1972: 14; Boyd 1974:30–36; Figure 11). The length of a room varied with function and wealth; width varied little, as evergreen tree trunks for the *vigas* (beams) tended to grow only four to five meters long. A room five meters wide by four to six long is fairly standard for people of moderate means, and we know of none larger in Cañones. In Abiquiú the living room of the Martin Bode home, built originally as the village store, is much larger. One building in the nineteenth century compound of General José María Chávez (now the studio of painter Georgia O'Keeffe) is ten or twelve meters long, but only the usual four or five meters wide. The archæologist will thus find some evidence for social stratification in number and size of rooms. But he must weigh this evidence against the analysis of house contents to decide between wealth, family size, and family composition.

Not only did the composition of households vary greatly, but relations between households took several different forms, some households being economically dependent upon others. This was particularly true with married sons who lived apart from their fathers but farmed and/or ran livestock jointly with them. Among siblings, priority in age-order partly determined the right to direct economic activities while a modified ultimogeniture was often practiced regarding inheritance of the house.

Indian captives placed immediately below the youngest children of the parental household (cf. Swadesh 1974:152–154).

Outside the family, social structure was elaborated to provide for community religious, defensive and subsistence needs, particularly water control for irrigation. During the last few decades educational structures have been added. The physical manifestations of these organizations are fairly straightforward.

Every village had a church or chapel, a few had Protestant churches after about 1870, many villages had *moradas* (chapter house for the penitential *cofradía*). *Moradas* have three rooms, are totally or nearly windowless, and may contain religious paraphernalia (Figure 12). A settlement without a chapel was most likely temporary. We hypothesize that the more spotty distribution of *moradas,* on the other hand, invites inferences about degree of isolation from Santa Fe and the few priests in the province—with conspicuous exceptions such as Santa Cruz de la Cañada, close to priests but a penitente center.[7]

Organization for defense can be inferred to an extent from village and building plans. The enclosed hollow-square village form with windows and doors all facing inward, and *torreones* (defensive towers) (Figure 13), were prescribed by government regulations. Some villages were formed in this fashion—particularly the older ones and those close to the Rio

FIGURE 12. Morada (Museum of New Mexico).

FIGURE 13 Torreón, originally two story (Museum of New Mexico).

Grande. In some instances the siting of settlements (e.g., on promontories) also gives evidence of defensive concerns. Disbursed patterns, more often found in villages on the periphery of settlement (e.g., the Chama Valley), were consistent with mobility as defense. We have ethnohistorical evidence that Hispanic settlers often found a reprisal raid more effective than barricades as defense against nomadic Indians. Guerrilla warfare could be practiced from either tight or disbursed villages, albeit in somewhat different style.[8]

The village schoolhouse dates from the late nineteenth century for Presbyterian schools, and from the 1930's and 1940's for public schools. It disappeared from almost all villages in the 1960's in favor of larger consolidated schools built somewhat apart from village *placitas*.

Irrigation associations may be inferred from the presence of irrigation ditches if they are extensive enough to serve at least five or six fields. Ethnographically, these associations elect *mayordomos* empowered to order construction and maintenance work, to allot water according to custom, and to impose sanctions against those who fail in their obligations. Smaller ditch systems may be handled informally by the two or three families affected.[9] As previously mentioned, interrelationships discovered by the archæologist between ditches, fields and dwelling complexes may be helpful

in reconstructing extended family economic units.

Conspicuously absent from the typical Hispanic village of past or present is formal machinery of government. Hence governmental buildings are absent. Swadesh contends (1974:155–157) that the *patrón-peón* system was seldom present in the Rio Arriba, and consequently could not have been a functional substitute for government. It made an appearance here during the nineteenth century (Jaramillo 1972).[10] During the century the penitente *cofradia* performed some governmental functions, sometimes sitting as judge, jury and executioner in cases of serious malefaction (Woodward 1935:ch. 7; Weigle 1976: ch. 3). Field work of Kutsche and Van Ness in Cañones leads them to hypothesize that flexibility rather than permanence of organization is a key to success of small villages. Cañones united to fight a legal battle against the State Department of Education in 1966 and 1967, in total disregard of intracommunity differences of kinship or religion, then permitted the tight organization to disappear when the battle was over (Kutsche 1967). Flexibility leaves few marks upon the land, so far as we can discover.[11]

Finally, the ethnic composition of villages is an important aspect of social organization along the frontier. Conscious and systematic attempts were made from at least the mid-eighteenth century to assimilate both nomadic and

Pueblo Indians. The term *genizaro,* introduced above, came to be used for Christianized and culturally Hispanicized Indians. Communities of *genizaros* were established at Abiquiú, Tomé, and perhaps elsewhere. Over time this social category lost its identity, gradually merging into the Hispanic population as indicated by analysis of the colonial census records (cf. Swadesh 1974:46). The dynamics of this transformation may be susceptible to archæological investigation and analysis—for instance, in room size, house style, and inventories of material culture. Abiquiú would make a good test case, for the square lower *placita* was built by Hispanos while the less regular *Moki* above is of Indian origin (Figure 14).

Trade

Local trade in the seventeenth and eighteenth centuries was both inter- and intra-ethnic. Long-distance trade with Mexico proper tied into world trade networks.

If the hypothesis we offered above concerning Hispanic versus Pueblo Indian subsistence has merit, then meat and vegetables formed the core of Hispanic-Pueblo trade, especially with those Pueblos which held rich bottom land along the Rio Grande. Indians also traded leather moccasins (called *teguas,* for the Tewa Indians) and the local tobacco called *punche.* Hispanos, in addition to meat, traded metal knives and other tools, and horses. When trading with nomadic Indians, Hispanos offered both animals and crops. Human flesh in the form of captives was traded both ways, particularly with the Navajo and Ute (Swadesh 1974). Many intangibles changed hands in the annual trade fairs at Taos and Abiquiú—gossip about people and events, techniques for manufacture, language, fragments of many other culture traits. To what extent the archæo-

FIGURE 14. Placita of Abiquiú from Moki, ca. 1920 (Museum of New Mexico).

The Archaeology of Spanish Missions and Colonies in the New World

logist will find traces of intangible trade is conjectural.

Trade between Hispanic villages started with the crops mentioned above which are only grown in certain places. To the present day the chile of the Santa Cruz River is considered the best. Landowners of Cañones often go to that region also for onion bulbs and other crops to plant in their own fields. There was and is a good deal of specialization in hand crafts as well. Conspicuous examples are Chimayó and Cundiyó, which began to specialize heavily in weaving in the nineteenth century, although villages elsewhere continued to weave. Córdova more recently has specialized in woodcarving (Briggs 1974).[12] Grist mills had a spotty distribution. Such specialization generated an extensive regional trade network. This record could be much enhanced and its complexities better understood through archæological investigation.

Trade with Mexico sent hides down and luxury goods up. Articles of Mexican manufacture found in New Mexican sites indicate at least a moderate degree of wealth for the owner. Those originating in Europe or the Orient, traded along the Chihuahua Trail from Gulf or Pacific ports, were owned exclusively by the rich, and are very rare in New Mexico. Away from the arterial highway of the Rio Grande they are almost non-existent.

Within the last century, continuing to our certain knowledge until the late 1960's, the itinerant peddler from Mexico made his periodic rounds of even remote New Mexican villages. His stock in trade consisted primarily of cheap plastic, paper or metal religious objects, plus a few herbs. He was welcomed by villagers—whether for the nature of his goods, for the contact he brought from a mother culture, or for more personal qualities, we do not know. Itinerant peddlers from Eastern Mediterranean countries are occasionally mentioned in historical sources.

Trade with Anglos became overwhelming in volume after the Santa Fe Trail was opened in the 1820's. As New Mexico was drawn into the Anglo sphere of economic influence, a new trading institution developed. This was the mercantile store, locally referred to as the *tienda*, its proprietor the *tiendero*. Most of the important *tienderos* in the north were foreigners—the earliest often French, then either Yankee Anglos, Jews or other Eastern Mediterraneans. They served as brokers between the villages and the Anglo economic and governmental institutions, bringing in Anglo-made goods and channelling lumber, hides, wool, and other village products into the market. Through archæological investigations of the sites of mercantile stores it may be possible to chart the spread of Anglo goods that entered New Mexico over the Santa Fe Trail. More broadly, this will enable us to determine the course of Hispanic adoption of Anglo patterns.

Once major highways were paved—1930's and 1940's for the Chama Valley—and the use

FIGURE 15. Shrine inside home (George McCue).

of automobiles became general, Anglo material objects came to swamp those of all other origins. At the present time weekly shopping is usually done in a regional center such as Española, and almost nothing is made at home. A superficial glance inside or outside a Hispanic rural home would not reveal much beyond the adobes themselves that distinguish it from an Anglo residence. And a fairly large number of village Hispanos now build of cement blocks or buy mobile homes, since the wage laborer is neither poor enough to afford the time to make his own adobes nor rich enough to hire someone else to make them for him. Probably the religious shrine in a corner of the living room (Figure 15) and the phenotypes in the many framed family photographs are the chief remaining differences between the Hispanic and the Anglo home.

Photographs of the inside of village homes dating from the early twentieth century are available in numerous regional archives and in some publications. A series of archæological investigations might be useful in adding to our knowledge of the rate and direction of the shift from native homemade to Anglo factory-made house furnishings.

Conclusion

We have spoken of a number of ways in which three subdisciplines of anthropology can aid one another in analyzing and understanding Hispanic culture in northern New Mexico by making use of the approaches of the "new archæology". We add one more which we have touched on only by inference. The documentary record, emphasizing governmental and church orders to be carried out uniformly by the populace, tells us a great deal about the ideal culture, but little about the real culture. In fact, New Mexico offers many parallels to the reply which Viceroys of New Spain sometimes sent to their monarchs, when the latter made impossible demands across the ocean—"*Obedezco pero no cumplo*" (I obey, but I do not fulfill) (Herring 1968:94). The skillful archæologist can help the ethnohistorian and the ethnographer to delineate the real Hispanic culture of New Mexico. The latter two can help the archæologist by describing as concretely and exactly as possible the material context of social activities.

If the three methodologies can succeed in providing a truly rich reconstruction of the development of Hispanic culture then, as we said above, this research can become a model for similar reconstruction elsewhere. Perhaps the first such product can be the extrapolation back to prehistoric Pueblo Indian social and cultural patterns in the immediate area. The useful evidence is both archival and ecological. Historical records, although of varying richness, extend back to Coronado's exploration of the region in 1540. They include government and church documents, chronicles, and folklore. To an extent they go beyond Hispanic events to describe Indians and the relations between ethnic groups. The less direct ecological evidence is derived from the similarity of the microbasin environmental niches still occupied by many Hispanic settlers to the microbasins occupied by many Indians pueblos before the retreat to the banks of the Rio Grande shortly before Spanish conquest in the sixteenth century. In most cases the basins are not merely similar but are the identical locations of Indian Pueblos, particularly of the thirteenth and fourteenth centuries. Up until the nineteenth century, adaption to environment and other aspects of Indian and Hispanic pueblos were becoming more and more similar, due to exchange of culture and genes (Dozier 1964). It was only the special status accorded to Indians by the United States which pulled the paths of these two cultural traditions apart again. With care and due caution, therefore, the better documented Hispanic tradition can be used as a basis for improving archæological hypotheses which aim at understanding the less documented Indian tradition.

We put forth one final advantage in advocating intensive cooperative research on Hispanic northern New Mexico between archæology, ethnohistory, and ethnography. This is testing theory, particularly in culture change. We believe that working together we can achieve an intimately detailed reconstruction of change in the Hispanic tradition, and of the influence of the region's several cultures on each other (Hispanic, Pueblo, Athapascan, Ute, other nomadic Indians, Anglo). As the results of that reconstruction become available, ethnology can refine its concepts of rate and direction of cultural development, of selective borrowing, of persistence in the face of pressure. It is of theoretical and perhaps also of practical importance for us to enrich our knowledge about a geographical area in which several societies have lived in intimate association for several centuries without attempting to exterminate each other.

Notes

[1] This paper is revised from one presented at a joint meeting of the Southwestern Anthropological Association and the Sociedad Mejicana de Antropología, Santa Fe, in 1975. The authors wish to acknowledge the encouragement and guidance of David Snow, Museum of New Mexico, who arranged the original symposium, and of Frances Swadesh, general program chairman. For permission to use photographs we thank George McCue, Bainbridge Bunting, Natalie Owings, the Museum of New Mexico. The authors' fieldwork in New Mexico was supported at various times by grants from the National Science Foundation, the University of Pennsylvania, and Colorado College.

[2] For the ethnographer to ask questions of use to the archæologist will not always come naturally. Archæologist John Atherton, who generously read a draft of this paper, recommended that we ask our oldest informants where their great grandparents dug their latrines, whether they dumped garbage as well as human wastes in them, what kinds of evidence might indicate subsistence agriculture versus ranching versus wage labor. The Cañones field team of Kutsche and Van Ness asked none of these questions, and we should guess that few of our colleagues in ethnography do either.

[3] See the ideal type description of such microbasins in van Dresser (1972:90–105).

[4] See Merriman's *The Rise of the Spanish Empire* (1918:262–263 and elsewhere) for a discussion of the origin of the Spanish preference for ranching over farming. Merriman blames both the difficulty of farming in the arid climate of Castile

and the political turmoil of the Reconquest centuries. Comparative data suggest that pastoralism is more practical on an uncertain frontier where frequent hostilities occur, for one can pick up and move animals to a safer location, unlike farm plots. With low population densities on the frontier, extensive use of land through pastoral pursuits is more common than intensive use of land in agricultural plots, irrigation systems, etc. Today most Hispanic villagers in New Mexico, if asked their occupation, will reply *ranchero* rather than *agricultor,* however few head of cattle they may possess.

[5] This interpretation is in part responsible for the loss of village communal grazing lands since the advent of U.S. control, and thus has practical importance to those attempting to seek restitution of alienated lands.

[6] *Fuertes* (log cabins, built in the same style as those of the Eastern Woodlands, but plastered over in the same manner as *jacales*) were also sometimes built (Figure 16). Since this technique of house construction was introduced into the Western Hemisphere by Scandinavians, it presumably came to New Mexico only after Anglo contact in the early nineteenth century.

[7] Weigle (1976) is the definitive account of penitentes; Boyd (1974:440–466) and Ahlborn (1968) contain the best description of *moradas* and their contents.

[8] Simmons (1971) contains accounts of Seboyeta, which used both the defensive square and reprisal raid.

[9] Simmons (1972) summarizes the historic evidence for Hispanic and for some Pueblo Indian ditch construction and use. Several of these ditches were shared by Indians and Hispanos.

[10] *Patrón-peón* economic relations were more developed in the Rio Abajo (roughly, from Bernalillo downstream) than in the Rio Arriba, starting in the Mexican and continuing in the Territorial period. In the Rio Arriba, the *patrón* was often a non-Hispano storekeeper.

[11] The Cañones school battle resulted in widening the access road from N. M. 96 to the village, and the construction of two bridges. Excavation would discover the road with its bridges, but without documentation would not show their relation to political pressure.

[12] A wealth of information to assist the historical archæologist regarding the provenience and distribution of Hispanic material culture—architectural styles, painting, textiles, woodworking, metal smithing, the making of santos—is contained in E. Boyd's magnificent *Popular Arts of Spanish New Mexico* (1974).

FIGURE 16. Fuerte with mud plaster still adhering (Natalie Owings).

REFERENCES

AHLBORN, RICHARD E.
  1968 The Penitente Moradas of Abiquiú.
       *Contibutions from the Museum of History
       and Technology, Paper 63.* Washington:
       Smithsonian Institution Press.
ALLEN, WILLIAM L. AND JAMES B. RICHARDSON, III
  1971 The reconstruction of kinship from archæo-
       logical data: the concepts, the methods,
       and the feasibility. *American Antiquity,*
       Vol. 36, No. 1, pp. 41–53.
BARTH, FREDRIK
  1969 Introduction. In Fredrik Barth (ed.), *Ethnic
       groups and boundaries,* pp. 9–38. Little,
       Brown, Boston.
BINFORD, LEWIS R.
  1972 *An Archeological Perspective.* Seminar
       Press, New York.
BINFORD, SALLY R. AND LEWIS R. (EDS.).
  1968 *New Perspectives in Archeology.* Aldine,
       Chicago.
BOYD, E.
  1974 *Popular Arts of Spanish New Mexico.*
       Museum of New Mexico Press, Santa Fe.

BRIGGS, CHARLES L.
  1974 An ethnographic study of wood carving
       in Córdova, New Mexico. MS, senior
       thesis, Colorado College.
DOZIER, EDWARD P.
  1964 The Pueblo Indians of the Southwest.
       Current Anthropology, Vol. 5, No. 2, pp.
       79–97.
  1970 Making inferences from the present to the
       past. In W. A. Longacre (ed.), *Reconstruct-
       ing prehistoric Pueblo societies,* pp. 202–
       213. University of New Mexico, Press,
       Albuquerque.
HERRING, HUBERT
  1968 *A History of Latin America* (3rd edition).
       Knopf, New York.
HILL, JAMES N.
  1970 Prehistoric social organization in the
       American Southwest: theory and method.
       In W. A. Longacre (ed.), *Reconstructing
       prehistoric Pueblo societies,* pp. 11–58. Uni-
       versity of New Mexico Press, Albuquerque.
HUME, IVOR NOËL
  1969 *Historical Archæology.* Knopf, New York.

JARAMILLO, CLEOFAS M.
1972 *Shadows of the Past.* Ancient City Press, Santa Fe.

KUTSCHE, PAUL
1967 Ethnographic ethics in the glare of publicity. Paper delivered at annual meeting, American Anthropological Association, Washington.

MARTIN, PAUL S.
1971 The revolution in archæology. *American Antiquity,* Vol. 36, No. 1, pp. 1–8.

MERRIMAN, ROGER BIGELOW
1918 *The Rise of the Spanish Empire.* Vol. 1, The Middle Ages. MacMillan, New York.

SCHUYLER, ROBERT L.
1970 Historical and historic sites, archæology as anthropology: basic definitions and relationships. *Historical Archæology,* Vol. 4, pp. 83–89.

SIMMONS, MARC
1969 Settlement patterns and village plans in colonial New Mexico. *Journal of the West,* Vol. 8, No. 1, pp. 7–21.
1971 *The Fighting Settlers of Seboyeta.* San Marcos Press, Cerrillos, N.M.
1972 Spanish irrigation practices in New Mexico. *New Mexico Historical Review,* Vol. 47, No. 2, pp. 135–150.

SMITH, ANDREW T.
1976 The founding of the San Antonio de las Huertas grant. *Social Science Journal,* Vol. 13, No. 3, pp. 35–43.

SWADESH, FRANCES LEÓN
1974 *Los Primeros Pobladores.* University of Notre Dame Press, Notre Dame, Ind.

VAN DRESSER, PETER
1972 *A Landscape for Humans.* Biotechnic Press, Albuquerque.

VAN NESS, JOHN R.
1975 The Polvadera grant: a history of chicanery and fraud. Paper delivered at annual meeting, Western Social Science Association, Denver.

WEAVER, THOMAS
1965 Social structure, change and conflict in a New Mexico village. MS, doctoral dissertation, University of California, Berkeley.

WEIGLE, MARTA
1976 *Brothers of Light, Brothers of Blood.* University of New Mexico Press, Albuquerque.

WOODWARD, DOROTHY
1935 The Penitentes of New Mexico. MS, doctoral dissertation, Yale.

COLORADO COLLEGE
COLORADO SPRINGS, COLORADO

FORT LEWIS COLLEGE
DURANGO, COLORADO

SANTA FE, NEW MEXICO

KATHLEEN DEAGAN
MICHAEL SCARDAVILLE

Archaeology and History on Historic Hispanic Sites: Impediments and Solutions

The relationship between history and archaeology in the process of studying past societies has been a matter of concern and debate since the beginnings of historical archaeology as a formal discipline. This debate has not always been amicable or productive, particularly in that period when historical archaeology emerged as a discipline in its own right, independently of its early role as a "handmaiden to history" (Harrington 1955; Noël Hume 1964). Nevertheless, because of the existence of both written and buried evidence bearing upon the same processes and events of the past, historical archaeologists must necessarily take into account documentary evidence and, in the process, deal with history and with historians.

As historical archaeology became formalized, many of its scholars rejected an alignment with history. They tended to see history as a particularizing discipline with only limited application in the search for general laws of cultural systemics (Cleland and Fitting 1968; Schuyler 1979:201–02; South 1977:5–13). Historians, on the other hand, frequently characterized archaeology not as a discipline, but rather as a set of techniques that could be used to recover information that could then be synthesized by historians (Dollar 1968; Walker 1973; Frost 1970; Wilderson 1975). Even today no general consensus about the procedures, structure, or norms for the actual integration of historical and archaeological data have emerged in either field. In very recent years, nevertheless, a more productive interaction between archaeologists and historians has begun to take place, particularly in research areas for which primary materials are not in English (e.g., Spanish borderlands). This interaction is based on the necessity of access to documentary materials for all archaeologists, since

documents provide various kinds of controls in archaeological studies, including information about economic networks, demography, cartographic sources, and earth-impacting events. In the Spanish colonial areas such information is in archaic Spanish, and this sets archaeologists working in those areas apart from their colleagues with anglo-american interests. Most Spanish colonial archaeologists who have attempted to locate, transcribe, and translate relevant documents have emerged from the experience with the fervent belief that graduate training in history is a necessary prerequisite for such a task. In non-English speaking areas, in effect, archaeologists and historians have on occasion been forced into collaborative associations for research, a situation not as frequently faced by other historical archaeologists and one that has made evident certain problems and benefits that otherwise might not have been realized as quickly.

It is the intent of this paper to discuss some of the specific problems in the integration of the various disciplines involved in historical archaeology, with a particular emphasis on history and archaeology. An attempt will be made to suggest some directions for developing solutions. These are based on the ten-year, ongoing program of historical archaeology in St. Augustine, Florida, in which both authors have been participants, Deagan as archaeologist and Scardaville as historian (Deagan 1983). The guiding orientation of this program has been toward understanding the initial adaptations of the Spaniards to Florida and the subsequent evolution of this adaptive pattern over three centuries. Such a focus is necessarily multidisciplinary, requiring the data of archaeology, history, zooarchaeology, ethnobotany, economics, and architecture. It is evident that no single researcher possesses the necessary technical and theoretical skills in all of these areas.

The first problem that emerged during our multidisciplinary association was the impression among the historians that the archaeologists were, in general, using the documentary data base in an inappropriate manner. There is an unspoken and underlying attitude in some archaeological quarters that if one can read documents, one can do history.

This assumption is equally distressing to historians as the assumption that "if one can use a shovel, one can do archaeology" is to archaeologists.

In the non-anglo areas particularly, scholars without sufficient language and paleographical skills too often rely uncritically on translations or on a narrow set of documents which relate directly to the research problem. Unfortunately, many translations have been done by local amateur historians or language specialists (including native speakers) who do not necessarily understand either the implications or the precise meanings of colonial terminology. Numerous calendars of documents or other locational aids have been prepared in this country, or are in the process of being prepared for document collections, and too many researchers are using the English summaries of the documents in lieu of reading the entire original document. Moreover, a number of these documentary collections were artificially created in that they represent only fraction of a larger collection in archives outside of this country. They therefore comprise only a portion—and in many cases a nons-ystematically sampled portion—of the entire documentary collection. Because of their lack of professional training in archival work, most archaeologists do not recognize or account for this and often base premises on an incomplete documentary base.

There two potential solutions to this problem—one is that historical archaeologists receive rigorous graduate training in historical research methods (something that the profession as a whole might well consider), and the other more practical solution is that historical research necessary for archaeology be conducted by a professional historian with the requisite linguistic and archival skills. Professionally trained historians know the appropriate questions to ask in order to determine the internal and external validity of the documents which archaeologists use, and they should possess the ability to recognize when the readily available sources are incomplete and limited. They should also know where to go for—and how to retrieve—the necessary materials to ensure that the data base is as complete and accurate as possible. Furthermore, the professionally trained historian should be able to assess and develop the information contained in documents within the political, economic, and social contexts that produced it (a task that most archaeologists could undoubtedly also complete eventually, but almost certainly at greater cost to the project and with far less efficiency than a trained historian). The archaeological programs in St. Augustine and in other hispanic areas have adopted the practice of working cooperatively with Spanish colonial historians, or sending American historians to hispanic archives—approaches believed to have great benefits for the overall program.

Many archaeologists who are responsible for developing budgets for historical archaeological research projects are not fully aware that history—like archaeology—is a labor intensive and time-consuming activity. The time necessary to retrieve from archives that information needed for archaeology is often not accurately estimated. Consequently, the historical research aspects of their projects are inadequately funded and only partially complete. Directors of colonial site research programs should be aware of the occasional necessity to undertake historical research outside of the country unless they are prepared to accept an incomplete and limited local resource.

The cooperative interaction between Spanish colonial archaeologists and historians in St. Augustine also revealed a second problem inherent in this interdisciplinary effort. A phenomenon that became evident in the integration of historical and archaeological data was the frequently encountered insensitivity—or lack of awareness—among historians to the anthropological orientations and needs of archaeologists. This can also extend to a surprising obliviousness among many historians to the actual and potential contributions of archaeological research to the study of the past. Many historians, including those in the Spanish borderlands, are not involved in ongoing, problem-oriented research, and they often do not appear to approach history as a process. A disproportionate amount of traditional Spanish borderlands history, for example, deals with military, political, and diplomatic topics and is far too descriptive and event-specific to be directly central to studies oriented toward anthropological issues (such as frontier adaptation, ethnicity and household level activity and variability). This is being somewhat reconciled by a new generation of historians who have been more strongly influenced in the past decade by the social sciences and the French "Annales" school of social history (Annales). These scholars are more attracted to problem-solving and non-event related research. In the Spanish borderlands particularly, such work is increasingly oriented toward more non-institutional social and economic themes (such as Jones 1979; Leitch Wright 1981; Bushnell 1982). In this process historians are finding that much of the information they need can be best recovered and interpreted through archaeology (Cummins 1980; Wilderson 1975; Scardaville 1981). Nevertheless, the approaches to the same problem taken by a historian and by an archaeologist are not always compatible. In the investigation of Spanish colonial Florida, for example, historians traditionally have tended to overlook or not emphasize such issues as the correlates of social stratification; inter-ethnic relations outside of official policy; diet; kinship and marriage patterns; or residential patterning. These issues are of central interest to most archaeologists. One solution to this problem is that historians who wish to be involved in multidisciplinary archaeological projects receive rigorous graduate training in anthropology. Another—perhaps more practical—is that the specific data needs and research interests of archaeologists be communicated more explicitly and in greater detail to historian colleagues.

The kinds of specific information needed prior to archaeological research are not always considered by historians to be appropriate or interesting subjects. These fall into three categories. The first pertains to information relevant to understanding of social variability within the social unit being studied, including demography, income ranges, occupations, ethnic diversity and inter-ethnic relations, residence patterns, and social class structure. The second category includes that information relevant to the material world and economy of the unit being studied, that is, the specific mechanics, manifestations and variability of production, distribution, and exchange in the social unit.

The third general category of information useful to archaeologists is data relevant to the physical formation of the archaeological record, including such alterations to the earth as building construction methods and sequences, cultural and natural disasters, disposal and sanitation practices, and public works. Such information, although frequently overlooked in historical research, often does exist in the documentary record. Historians aware of these needs not only can help provide the cultural parameters that act as controls for specific archaeological prediction and explanation, but they can also add richer dimensions to their own studies of social history.

Working relationships with archaeologists can also reveal to historians the unique contributions of archaeological findings to the study of history. The reliability of documents and maps can often be assessed, the conditions of life for non-elite and disenfranchised groups can be documented archaeologically, and the physical setting of social history can generally be revealed only through archaeology.

A third problem in the integration of archaeological and historical research stems ironically from attempts to actually implement interaction and achieve an ideal situation of mutually compatible goals and interdisciplinary harmony. Many projects are undertaken by archaeologists, historians, zooarchaeologists, ethnobotanists, and architects working in conjunction. Frequently, however, the results of the projects are interdisciplinary in name only. Typically one discipline—usually archaeology since the archaeologist usually raises the funds—tends to dominate all phases of research, with other disciplines brought in temporarily or on an "as need" basis. Discrete segments of the data base of the project are isolated with various specialists and with little intercommunication among them. The ultimate result is more often a report that segregates the various lines of evidence into separate chapters with only superficial synthesis and integration of these data categories.

A compartmentalized working structure cannot take maximum advantage of the distinct perspectives and contributions of each of the disciplines involved in a project. If researchers are brought into a project simply to deal with an isolated segment of data or a narrow set of questions, their contributions will be correspondingly narrow and isolated from general project goals. The frequency with which this occurs is curious, for the majority of both historians and anthropologists would argue that a household, site, or a community is properly examined and understood as part of its larger political, economic, and social settings. For example, a historian included in project specifically to translate and examine a series of shipping records can only provide a list, whereas a study of trade patterns in general could place the lists—and their material correlates in the ground—into their overall economic milieu. A zooarchaeologist or ethnobotanist sent samples and returning a species list is not making his or her potential contribution to a project. Such a specialist, when provided with the physical samples, the archaeological and historical data, and when also involved in the development of guiding problems and sampling strategies, can provide an interpretation of foodways, diet, and economy not obtainable in any other way. The subsistence work of Elizabeth Reitz and Margaret Scarry (Reitz 1979, 1980; Scarry 1981; Reitz and Scarry in press) on 16th century St. Augustine are examples of what can be achieved.

The problem of integrating specialists in a multidisciplinary project might be brought more sharply into focus by considering the parallel case of an archaeologist brought into a project by an architect to "find a dripline" but denied access to refuse areas. All archaeologists can appreciate—and some have probably suffered from—the loss to a project in a situation like this.

One way in which such situations can be avoided is through the organization of a project as a team effort from the proposal writing and research design stage, through the recovery and analysis stages, and into the reporting and interpretive stages. Colleagues doing prehistoric archaeology have recognized and been confronted with problems such as these for some time (MacNeish 1967; Watson, LeBlanc and Redman 1971:154–55; Redman 1973) and have called for just this kind of interdisciplinary organization. Specific information on how a multidisciplinary, holistic final integration of data categories has actually been achieved, however, is rare in the literature.

The St. Augustine project has been fortunate in its experiments with multidisciplinary organization. Research problems, site specific questions, and recovery strategies have been developed with input from historians, archaeologists, zooarchaeologists, and architects. These specialists have provided the project coordinator—in this case the archaeologist—with fresh perspectives and often more knowledgeable assessments of what could and could not be accomplished given the data base and proposed research strategy. A more realistic scheduling and allocation of resources was also made possible in this way as well as the most efficient sampling strategies for all data classes.

Periodic meetings throughout the field and analysis stages of the project have allowed all researchers to review the fieldwork and the results of each others' analyses, assess the overall progress of research, and outline continuing strategy. One of the most rewarding benefits is now becoming evident in the interpretation and reporting stage in which all investigators are involved in a "chain letter" manner. Nothing is reported or synthesized on any portion of the project without the input of all team members.

This structure is somewhat more difficult to achieve and maintain than one in a project with discrete consecutive segments. The key factor in the relative success of St. Augustine's multidisciplinary organization has been the involvement of researchers from various fields who have a common interest in Spanish colonial Florida. This also helps relieve another difficulty in multidisciplinary research—that of funding. Scholars already involved in the same research questions do not always require compensation for each hour spent on the project—they can afford periodically to exchange their time for research data gains—and they occasionally have access to funding sources in their own fields. It is also suspected that funding agencies are more favorably inclined toward historical archaeological projects with a specifically multidisciplinary structure and strategy. The work in St. Augustine, while primarily funded by the National Endowment for the Humanities, has received additional support from a variety of state and local sources.

Benefits from research with consistently multidisciplinary organization include not only more complete and integrated results but also increased awareness among the researchers involved to the limitations, potentials, and needs of other allied disciplines.

It is a responsibility of all scholars studying the past to expand the data base in the most comprehensive manner possible—and that is in cooperation with other fields whose interests overlap those of archaeologists. Although the ultimate concerns of archaeologists and historians in the same areas may differ, each discipline will be left with an incomplete data base without the effective input of the other. Cooperative planning and prediction from the earliest stage of investigation onward can help history extend itself beyond the confines of the written word and can help archaeologists avoid the grievous pitfall of simply verifying or refuting what historians already know.

ACKNOWLEDGEMENTS

Financial support for multidisciplinary research in St. Augustine has been provided by National Endowment for the Humanities grants RO 32437–78–1425 and RS 20293–82; The Florida State University, the St. Augustine Restoration Foundation, Inc.; the Historic St. Augustine Preservation Board; the Colonial Dames of America and the Florida State Museum of the University of Florida.

REFERENCES

ANNALES
1946   *Annales: Economies, Societies, Civilizations.* A. Colin, Paris.

BUSHNELL, AMY
1982   *The King's Coffer.* University Presses of Florida, Gainesville.

CLELAND, CHARLES AND JAMES FITTING
1968   The Crisis in Identity: Theory in Historic Sites Archaeology. *Conference on Historic Sites Archaeology Papers* 2(2):124–38.

CUMMINS, LIGHT T.
1980   Historical Archaeology and the Spanish Borderlands Historian. Paper presented at the Southwestern Social Sciences Association, Houston, Texas. Typescript.

DEAGAN, KATHLEEN
1983   *Spanish St. Augustine: The Archeology of a Colonial Creole Community.* Academic Press, New York.

DOLLAR, CLYDE
1968   Some Thoughts on Method and Theory in Historical Archaeology. Conference on *Historic Sites Archaeology Papers* (2(2):3–30.

FROST, FRANK J.
1970   Science, Archaeology and The Historian. *Journal of Interdisciplinary History* 1(1):317–26.

HARRINGTON, J.C.
1955   Archaeology as an Auxiliary Science to American History. *American Anthropologist* 57(6):1121–4130.

JONES, OAKAH
1979   *Los Paisanos: Spanish Settlers on the Northern Frontiers of New Spain.* University of Oklahoma Press, Norman.

LEITCH WRIGHT, JAMES
1981   *The Only Land They Knew.* The Free Press, New York.

MacNEISH, RICHARD
1967   Chapter 1, Volume 1 in *Prehistory of the Tehuacan Valley,* edited by R. MacNeish. pp. ?. University of Texas Press, Austin.

NOËL-HUME, IVOR
1964   Archaeology: A Handmaiden to History. *North Carolina Historical Review* 41(2):215–25.

REDMAN, CHARLES
1973   Multistage Fieldwork and Analytical Techniques. *American Antiquity* 38:61–79.

REITZ, ELIZABETH
1979   *Spanish and British Subsistence Strategies at St. Augustine, Florida, and Frederica, Georgia, between 1563–1783.* Ph.D. dissertation, University of Florida. University Microfilms, Ann Arbor.
1980   Subsistence Strategies in Sixteenth Century St. Augustine. Consultant report on file, Historic St. Augustine Preservation Board, St. Augustine.

REITZ, ELIZABETH AND MARGARET M. SCARRY
n.d.   *Reconstructing Historic Subsistence: Sixteenth Century St. Augustine.* Unpublished manuscript, Florida State Museum, Gainesville.

SCARDAVILLE, MICHAEL
1983   Approaches to the Study of Southeastern Borderlands. In *Alabama and the Borderlands: From Prehistory to Statehood,* edited by Richard Krause, pp. ?. University of Alabama Press, Tuscaloosa.

SCARRY, MARGARET
1981   Sixteenth Century Spanish Plant Use. Project Con-

sultant report; on file, Historic St. Augustine Preservation Board, St. Augustine.

SCHUYLER, ROBERT
1979   Theoretical Positions. In *Historical Archaeology: A Guide to Substantive and Theoretical Contributions*, edited by R. Schuyler, pp. 201–02. Baywood, Farmingdale.

SOUTH, STANLEY
1977   *Method and Theory in Historical Archaeology*. Academic Press, New York.

WALKER, IAN
1973   Binford, Science and History: The Probalistic Variability of Explicated Epistemology and Nomethetic Paridigm in Historical Archaeology. *Conference on Historic Sites Archaeology* 8(3):159–201.

WATSON, PATTY JO, STEVEN LEBLANC, AND CHARLES REDMAN
1971   *Explanation in Archeology*. Columbia University Press, New York.

WILDERSON, PAUL
1975   Archaeology and the American Historian: An Interdisciplinary Challenge. *American Quarterly* XXVII(2):115–32.

WOOD, PETER
1974   *Black Majority*. W. W. Norton & Co, New York.

KATHLEEN DEAGAN
FLORIDA STATE MUSEUM
GAINESVILLE, FLORIDA 32611

MICHAEL SCARDAVILLE
HISTORY DEPARTMENT
UNIVERSITY OF SOUTH CAROLINA
COLUMBIA, SOUTH CAROLINA 29208

ROBERT L. HOOVER

Some Models for Spanish Colonial Archaeology in California

ABSTRACT

Nomothetics—the scientific search for general laws and patterns of behavior—is the ultimate goal of inductive archaeology. Specific data from numerous sites can now be used to confirm or disconfirm hypotheses as more general laws about cultural processes. Several interesting models have been generated by archaeologists and scholars in related disciplines that can help to explain the colonial phenomenon. Some of these models will be briefly summarized and applied to the situation in Spanish California.

Introduction

Historical archaeologists in North America have traditionally focused their attention on British colonial sites of the eastern seaboard. This trend was magnified by the preparation for and celebration of the bicentennial of the United States. However, there has been a gradual trend in recent years by interdisciplinary teams of scholars also to identify the various economic, political, and social strategies of colonizing powers following the Age of Exploration (Deagan 1983; Chauduri 1985; Hoover 1985, 1989; South 1977; Thomas 1989), including those of the Spanish, French, Dutch, and Portuguese cultures. Much recent attention has been focused on the Spanish colonization of the Americas.

A period of 277 years elapsed between the initial establishment of Spanish settlement in the Americas until 1769, when Spain finally established control over coastal California south of 39 degrees north latitude. Over a period of 52 years, the Spanish government established a chain of Franciscan missions, four military presidios, three towns or pueblos, and a few privately granted cattle ranches. The presidios were located at the major ports and were designed to protect the province from external European threats.

The 21 missions were established between 1769 and 1823, all but three being founded before 1800. These missions, as the primary instruments of the Spanish state in California, were designed to Christianize and Hispanize the native population. Governmental authorities originally believed that the diverse hunting and gathering Indians could be transformed into Spanish-speaking, Catholic, agricultural villagers within a decade. Mission lands would then be divided among the Indians, and the Franciscan friars could move on to new frontiers, to be replaced by secular clergy. This conception was based on an entirely false understanding of the rate of acculturation. However, the missions did provide a Spanish buffer against Russian and British interests in the Pacific Northwest of North America. California missions were generally places where the converted native population was concentrated while undergoing religious instruction and occupational training. This factor removed most of the Indians from outlying areas, freeing them for the award of private land grants of the Mexican period. In 1821, Mexico gained its independence from Spain and ruled California until the 1846 American invasion.

Explanatory Models

Several recent models generated by social scientists can help to explain the colonial phenomenon of Hispanic California. Ecological models, frontier models, economic models, and acculturation studies are discussed below.

Ecological Models

Several ecological principles have been applied by Kenneth Lewis (1984:12–14) to his detailed archaeological study of the colonial frontier of South Carolina. These concepts are in agreement with what was occurring in Spanish colonial and Mexican provincial California. Lewis discusses the processes of simplification, competitive exclusion, environmental diversity, progressive segregation, and systematization.

In a frontier situation, the social, political, and economic systems of the colonizing power become simplified as specialized forms are lost. The degree of cultural impoverishment varies with the distance from the frontier to nearest focal point of political or economic activity. While many practices of the royal court of Spain were maintained in the viceregal palace in Mexico City, this was clearly impractical on the frontier. California was one of the most remote outposts of New Spain, though its maritime contacts with central Mexico put it in a favorable position when compared to New Mexico or Texas. One would expect, and does indeed find, a much simpler material culture in Spanish California than in Spain or central Mexico.

According to the concept of competitive exclusion, cultures using the same resources and occupying the same space cannot co-exist permanently without alteration of the habits and life styles of one or both societies. Various acculturation studies of missionized California Indians point to the validity of this process. The neophytes were congregated at the missions, agriculture replaced hunting and gathering as the dominant subsistence pattern, and the native habitat was destroyed by the introduction of domestic grazing animals (Archibald 1978:159–186).

Environmental stability can be related to the amount of diversity in a frontier community. Greater environmental diversity makes the success of colonizing efforts less predictable. California is noted for its environmental diversity (Hoover 1974:507). To cope with this unpredictable situation, the colonizing elements may increase the scale and complexity of their economic networks to increase their options. They may also modify the frontier habitat by technological means. Both these efforts require adjustments in social and economic life. In California, the Spaniards modified the natural habitat from the very first by means of agricultural and pastoral activities. They also gradually increased international trading networks after 1800 through the hide and tallow trade (Archibald 1978:180–182).

The processes of progressive segregation and systematization are opposing trends that occurred simultaneously in Hispanic California as it evolved toward a greater degree of integration with the world economy. First, an increasing functional differentiation of parts of society existed in Hispanic California. At the same time, the individual parts became more interdependent as they entered the international market in the early 19th century. By the Mexican period (1821–1846), the missions were major suppliers of labor to the pueblos and of goods to the presidios, while the latter were more active in rounding up fugitive neophytes on behalf of the mission.

Frontier Models

Jerome Steffen (1980:xii, xvii–xviii) has proposed two distinct types of frontiers—insular and cosmopolitan—based on the nature and extent of their links with the homeland. Each is distinguished by distinctly different settlement patterns and economic roles. These differences are summarized in Figure 1. Archibald (1978) has clearly documented the shift from insular to cosmopolitan conditions in California during the first two decades of the 19th century. Later Hispanic California most closely conforms to Steffen's idea of a cosmopolitan frontier. While economic ties with the homeland were weak at first and the early missions pursued a diverse economy, the nature of the province changed gradually after 1800. California was finally recognizable as a cosmopolitan frontier that was fully integrated into the world economy through the hide and tallow trade after 1821. More specifically, it became a cosmopolitan ranching frontier. The ranching frontier was an industrial form of agriculture, though requiring a different habitat and exhibiting different features than the exploitative plantation. Livestock raising is a land-extensive activity, as larger land areas are required for fodder than from the same amount for calories produced by domestic crops. Ranching frontiers are found outside or on the fringe of areas of agricultural development. It is an activity that is geared to the world export market and is thus tied

INSULAR FRONTIERS	COSMOPOLITAN FRONTIERS
FEW ECONOMIC TIES WITH HOMELAND	ECONOMY CLOSELY INTEGRATED TO HOMELAND
EXTENSIVE ADAPTATION TO LOCAL CONDITIONS	GREAT EXPENDITURE TO REPRODUCE LIFE OF HOMELAND
DIVERSE ECONOMY FOR LONG-TERM PROFITS	SPECIALIZED ECONOMY FOR SHORT-TERM PROFITS
PERVASIVE INSTITUTIONAL CHANGE	NO FUNDAMENTAL CHANGES IN INSTITUTIONS OR BEHAVIOR
SMALL FARM OR SETTLEMENT PLANTATIONS	FUR TRADING, RANCHING, MINING, TRANSPORTATION, MILITARY, EXPLOITATIVE PLANTATION
GOODS COMPETITIVE WITH HOMELAND (REGULATED)	GOODS NOT COMPETITIVE WITH HOMELAND
FREE LABOR TRANSPLANTED FROM HOMELAND	IMPORTED SLAVE OR COERCED NATIVE LABOR

FIGURE 1. Comparison of insular and cosmopolitan frontiers, after Steffen (1980).

closely to the economy of the homeland or the international market (Lewis 1984:279–281).

California in the later Spanish and especially in the Mexican periods was an excellent example of a cosmopolitan ranching frontier. After the initial years of Spanish settlement, 1769–1800, when the missions were struggling for agricultural self-sufficiency and the establishment of a few basic domestic industries, the province developed all the features of a ranching frontier by 1810. A relatively small number of colonists engaged in the extensive activity of stock raising which required large areas of rangelands. Productive efficiency favored large land holdings. The mission ranchos, and later the private ranchos, were dispersed but linked to several port towns which served as collection points for hide and tallow. These ports were the termini of national and international maritime transport (Figure 1). Hispanic settlement was confined almost entirely to the coast ranges of California, as there were limits to the distance that hides and other products could be transported by ox-cart. Transportation routes were permanent but unimproved. The hide and tallow trade linked California directly with industrial states and was a short-term, high-return investment that required few capital improvements.

Aside from the ranching frontier, California also contained other types of cosmopolitan frontiers in the Hispanic period. The military frontier was represented by the four presidios designed to protect and regulate conditions in the province. These institutions supported the province but were not themselves producers. They were located to control access and transportation routes. Military frontiers are not usually established as a result of the desire for economic resources but rather to protect existing assets—in this case, the wealth of New Spain.

Frontier models of colonization can be greatly expanded through the independent use of archaeological evidence and documentary records. Frontiers were zones of extraction that formed part of the periphery of the world economic system, but all peripheries did not remain frontiers (Lewis 1984: 297). California developed very quickly out of frontier status in the early Anglo period and could certainly no longer be considered a periphery.

Economic Models

Immanuel Wallerstein (1974, 1980) has presented social scientists with a scheme to explain past and present relationships between nations and social classes. As the economic systems of simple horticultural and hunting-gathering societies have gradually disappeared, so has the complex division of labor within a single cultural framework. What was substituted was a world economic system which had a single division of labor in the context of numerous and diverse cultural frameworks. This phenomenon began in the 16th century as the result of the geographical expansion of Europe, the development of various means of labor control for different zones of the world economy, and the growth of strong states as leaders in that economy.

This interdependent division of labor was geographically based. Core states dominated peripheral and semi-peripheral regions by exploiting the labor of the latter groups and receiving a proportionally larger share of the surplus. Core states were characterized by free skilled labor. Peripheral labor was primarily unskilled and often coerced. The semi-peripheral states held an important intermediate position between core and periphery and shared traits of both. Semi-peripheries were both exploiters and exploited, preventing polarization within the system. Some semi-peripheral states, such as Spain and Portugal, were core states of the past. Others had moved up from the periphery. The entire system was maintained by the superior military strength of the core states, feeling of nationalistic and religious commitment by the participants, and a sense that their well-being depended upon the continuation of the system.

In traditional terms, the world economic system seems remarkably like classic mercantilism. Peripheral areas exported raw materials to core states in exchange for manufactured goods. Economic interaction occurred primarily among core states or between core and periphery. Peripheral areas were less likely to trade with one another; each traded primarily with a particular core state in one or a very few commodities. Trading patterns were one mechanism by which core states maintained dominance and benefited most from the system (Figure 2).

Mission San Antonio de Padua in California represents a site of the 1771–1834 period, where world-system theory might be appropriately tested

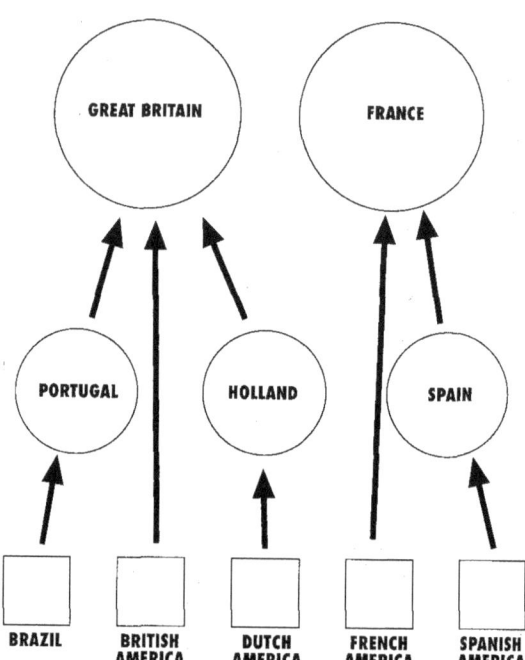

FIGURE 2. The world-system of the 18th century.

(Hoover and Costello 1985). Excavations at the mission's soldiers' barracks over a five-year period revealed two successive components—a structure occupied from 1776–1802 and another superimposed barracks of the 1802–1834 period. Changes in trading patterns in Spanish California were doubtless gradual, but one finds a preponderance of Hispanic pottery (made in Mexico) in the earlier component and a higher percentage of British ceramics in the later component. This change represents a shift in trade from Mexico to Britain during the early decades of the 19th century. One also finds an increase in locally-made pottery over time, as San Antonio became a center for the manufacture and distribution of Mission ware from the 1790s. The local Salinan Indians were a-ceramic in the pre-Spanish period.

World-system theory should be applied to Spanish California sites with caution. It is first important to agree on some of the major features of a world-system as defined by Wallerstein. Before the end of the 19th century, the European world-system was *not* a truly global phenomenon. Wallerstein specifically excludes non-state societies from the system, as well as the French fur empire of North America and the Portuguese trading empire of the Indian Ocean. He bases his division of labor only on staple commodities, denying that trade in "preciosities" played any significant role in the emerging world economy (Wallerstein 1974:41–46). However, a number of archaeologists have taken issue with this very restrictive interpretation. They believe that a world economic system could have been produced by a division of labor based on luxury goods, such as the furs of North America (Schneider 1977; Blanton and Feinman 1984; Peregrine 1988). Peter Peregrine (1988), in particular, notes the possibility that native societies could have supported their own economic systems alongside or prior to the advent of the European world economy.

Hall (1986:391–392) points out that the contribution of world-system theory lies in the de-emphasis of the nation-state as a unit of analysis for a more appropriate economic model of the colonial period. However, the degree of incorporation of non-states by states is obscured by lumping all of the former as peripheries. Some areas of the 18th-century world were external to the world economy. Others were marginal peripheries. Still others were completely dependent peripheries. World-system theory deals with specific events of recent history and glosses over pre-capitalist economies, though it does allow the archaeologist to examine regional relationships beyond the isolated culture (McGuire 1989:40–66).

Acculturation Studies

Several different approaches to material culture studies have been employed to measure the types and direction of acculturation that occurred in California missions. James Deetz (1963) pioneered one approach during his excavations at La Purisima Mission in 1962 and 1963. Dividing the artifact assemblage into traditional classes, such as chipped stone, iron, and copper, he compared quantitative differences between the neophyte dormitory and a nearby historic village midden. The results suggested that greater acculturation occurred among neophyte males than among females.

In retrospect, there are several problems with this comparison. First, two unlike sites—a prehistoric midden and historic dormitory floors—were being compared. Second, the volume of soil excavated to obtain each sample was different. Therefore, absolute numbers of artifacts could be misleading. Finally, artifacts related to the same functions were split into different groups, obscuring the complexity of acculturation (Farnsworth 1986:41).

A second method, employed at Mission San Antonio (Hoover and Costello 1985; Fig. 3), utilized a modified classification system devised by Quimby and Spoehr (1951) for the Great Lakes region. This system has recently been expanded to include 10 groups of artifacts (Farnsworth 1986: 40, 1987:479, 1989:239): (1) imported objects that represent new elements of the culture, e.g., wine bottles; (2) imported objects that directly replace prehistoric forms, e.g., glass beads for shell beads; (3) imported forms made of local materials, e.g., tiles; (4) imported forms, locally made, using local and imported materials, e.g., clothing with metal buttons; (5) imported forms, locally made, using imported materials and techniques, e.g., iron tools; (6) local forms modified by the substitution of imported materials, e.g., porcelain and glass projectile points; (7) local forms modified by the substitution of imported materials and involving a different technological principle to achieve the same end, e.g., ceramic bowls for steatite bowls; (8) local forms with new elements that change the meaning of the artifact, e.g., baskets with Spanish coats-of-arms woven into the design; (9) local forms of the same appearance and meaning, but using an imported technique, e.g., shell beads drilled with iron wire; and (10) prehistoric forms that continue unchanged, e.g., mortars and pestles. This qualitative system can be easily quantified, but it also is not without its drawbacks. In measuring the degree and rate of acculturation, how does one weight the various categories? Is an imported artifact indicative of greater acculturation

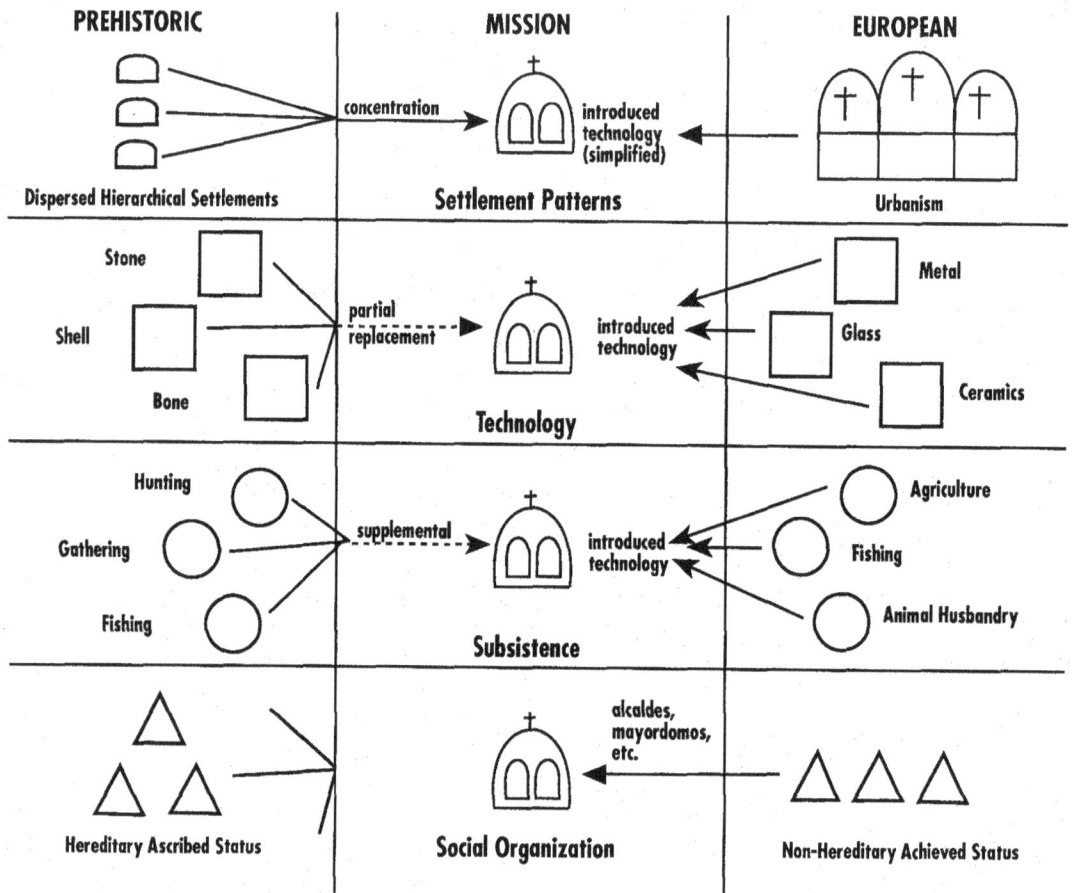

FIGURE 3. Acculturation model for California Missions.

than a native form, however modified (Farnsworth 1986:41)?

Paul Farnsworth (1986), while working at nearby Mission Soledad, developed a third system of comparison based on a modified version of South's (1977) artifact pattern analysis. First used on colonial sites of the Southeast, this system deals with entire assemblages and the functional groups within them. A final group of "other activities" allows the researcher to add artifacts pertaining to additional activities, each as a separate class.

Farnsworth's comparisons of San Antonio, Soledad, and La Purisima show great similarities in artifact patterning, which differ greatly from the patterns on Anglo colonial sites and from the

criollo/mestizo pattern at Spanish St. Augustine. The neophytes at Mission San Antonio appear to have had greater access to, or preference for, imported and locally made pottery and glass bottles than those occupying La Purisima, who used more traditional Indian kitchen items. A higher percentage of European glass beads was used at San Antonio than at La Purisima, where more traditional shell beads were used (Farnsworth, this volume).

Summary

The preceding discussion has shown how the use of different models provides differing perspectives on the archaeology of Hispanic California.

Ecological models such as those of Lewis (1984) explain such general phenomena as the simplification of material culture in the province of California, the acculturation of the native population, and California's integration into the world economy. Lewis' model is not particularly useful for studies of inter-mission comparisons.

Steffen's (1980) frontier models also deal with generalities. They are valuable in understanding the overall processes of economic change in California through time. They define the province's changing role in the world economy. Since Steffen offers a variety of frontier models—ranching, military, transportation, etc., his framework is even useful for comparing settlements of different types. However, the categories of analysis make the detailed comparison of like sites difficult.

Economic models, such as those of Wallerstein (1974, 1980), have proven to be the most controversial. Designed to examine sweeping worldwide trends, world-system theory has been hailed by some as the ultimate in modeling. However, definite problems are associated with applying a model based on the rise of European capitalism to remote areas of the world. A disagreement exists over some of the basic definitions which comprise a "world economic system." It is also clear that not all areas of the world—Asia, for example—had been integrated into a single world economy before the 19th century. Finally, many native societies supported their own more limited "world" economies before the advent of Europeans. On the positive side, the world-system approach de-emphasizes the individual nation-state as a unit of analysis, proving that the economy of Hispanic America was as important to the merchants of Antwerp or London as to the politicians of Madrid.

Acculturation studies such as those of Deetz (1963) were pioneering efforts to measure culture changes between sites in Hispanic California using quantitative differences in traditional classes of artifacts. The usefulness of this technique was limited by samples of unequal size and sampling sites of different character. A second approach (Hoover and Costello 1985; Farnsworth 1986, 1987) using classes of artifacts based on the processes of acculturation is more satisfactory, but problems remain of how to weight each category to measure the degree and rate of acculturation. A third system, developed by Farnsworth (this volume), is a more flexible and sophisticated approach that permits the detailed comparison of similar sites at the same or different periods in time.

As the upcoming Columbian Quincentenary is stimulating an already growing interest in Hispanic archaeology, several models can be drawn from various social sciences to explain cultural change and the processes of economic development. In using these models, one should recognize their limitations. They are convenient frameworks for analysis which may or may not reflect historical reality. However, they should not be ignored. They are powerful tools for an understanding of the processes of comparative colonialism.

ACKNOWLEDGMENTS

I wish to express my appreciation to many individuals who provided ideas and encouragement in the presentation of this research. I wish especially to thank Dr. Harold R. Kerbo, colleague and resident expert in world systems theory, for new sources of ideas. Fellow archaeologists, Jack S. Williams, Anita G. Cohen, and Paul Farnsworth have provided encouragement and constant feedback for the completion of this paper. I would also like to thank Christine L. Hoover, without whose help this paper would not be possible.

REFERENCES

ARCHIBALD, ROBERT
1978   The Economic Aspects of the California Missions. *Academy of American Franciscan History Monograph* 12. Washington, D.C.

BLANTON, RICHARD, AND GARY FEINMAN
1984   The Mesoamerican World System. *American Anthropologist* 86(3):673–682.

CHAUDURI, K.M.
1985   *Trade and Civilization in the Indian Ocean: An Economic History from the Rise of Islam to 1750.* Cambridge University Press, Cambridge, England.

DEAGAN, KATHLEEN
1983   *Spanish St. Augustine: The Archaeology of a Colonial Creole Community.* Academic Press, New York.

DEETZ, JAMES J.F.
1963   Archaeological Excavations at La Purisima Mission. *UCLA Archaeological Survey Annual Report* 5:163–208. University of California, Los Angeles.

FARNSWORTH, PAUL
1986   Spanish California: The Final Frontier. *Journal of New World Archaeology* 6(4):35–46. University of California, Los Angeles.
1987   *The Economies of Acculturation in the California Missions: A Historical and Archaeological Study of Mission Nuestra Senora de la Soledad.* Ph.D. dissertation, Archaeology Program, University of California, Los Angeles. University Microfilms, Ann Arbor.
1989   The Economies of Acculturation in the Spanish Missions of Alta California. *Research in Economic Anthropology* 11(217):249.

HALL, THOMAS D.
1986   Incorporation in the World-System: Toward a Critique. *American Sociological Review* 51(3):390–402.

HOOVER, ROBERT L.
1974   Anthropologische Bemerkungen zur Ethno-Botanik der Indianer Kaliforniens. *Anthropos* 69:505–516. St. Augustin, Germany.
1985   The Archaeology of Spanish Colonial Sites in California. In Comparative Studies in the Archaeology of Colonialism, edited by Stephen L. Dyson. *British Archaeological Reports International Series* 233:93–114. Oxford, England.
1989   Spanish-Native Interaction and Acculturation in the Alta California Missions. In *Columbian Consequences: Archaeological and Historical Perspectives on the Spanish Borderlands West*, edited by David H. Thomas, pp. 395–406. Smithsonian Institution Press, Washington, D.C.

HOOVER, ROBERT L., AND JULIA G. COSTELLO
1985   Excavations at Mission San Antonio, 1976–1978. *Institute of Archaeology Monograph* 26. University of California, Los Angeles.

LEWIS, KENNETH E.
1984   *The American Frontier: An Archaeological Study of Settlement Pattern and Process.* Academic Press, New York.

McGUIRE, RANDALL H.
1989   The Greater Southwest as a Periphery of Mesoamerica. In *Centre and Periphery: Comparative Studies in Archaeology*, edited by Timothy C. Champion, pp. 40–66. Unwin Hyman, London.

PEREGRINE, PETER
1988   The Political Economy of Jesuit Missioning in New France. Paper presented at the Annual Meeting of the American Society for Ethnohistory, Williamsburg, Virginia.

QUIMBY, GEORGE I., AND ALEXANDER SPOEHR
1951   Acculturation and Material Culture—I. *Fieldiana: Anthropology* 3(6):107–147.

SCHNEIDER, JANE
1977   Was There a "Pre-Capitalist" World System? *Peasant Studies* 6(1):20–29. Salt Lake City, Utah.

SOUTH, STANLEY
1977   *Method and Theory in Historical Archeology.* Academic Press, New York.

STEFFEN, JEROME O.
1980   *Comparative Frontiers: A Proposal for Studying the American West.* University of Oklahoma Press, Norman, Oklahoma.

THOMAS, DAVID HURST (EDITOR)
1989   *Columbian Consequences: Archaeological and Historical Perspectives on the Spanish Borderlands West*, Vol. 1. Smithsonian Institution Press, Washington, D.C.

WALLERSTEIN, IMMANUEL
1974   *The Modern World-System.* Vol. 1, *Capitalistic Agriculture and the Origins of the European World-Economy in the Sixteenth Century.* Academic Press, New York.
1980   *The Modern World-System.* Vol. 2, *Mercantilism and the Consolidation of the European World-Economy, 1600–1750.* Academic Press, New York.

ROBERT L. HOOVER
SOCIAL SCIENCES DEPARTMENT
CALIFORNIA POLYTECHNIC STATE UNIVERSITY
SAN LUIS OBISPO, CALIFORNIA 93407

BONNIE G. McEWAN

The Role of Ceramics in Spain and Spanish America during the 16th Century

ABSTRACT

Using archaeological and historical data, this study examines the various functions of ceramics in Spain during the 16th century and compares a ceramic assemblage from Seville to those from several contemporaneous New World Spanish colonies. The patterned differences between the ceramics recovered from the Old and New World sites are thought to reflect differences in the environment, economy, and demography of the various sites.

Introduction

As part and parcel of Iberian life, ceramic objects were integral to most daily activities of Spaniards including sanitation, food preparation, architecture, and religion (Fairbanks 1973; Deagan 1987; Lister and Lister 1987). The development of the ceramic industry in Spain is thought to have been influenced by several factors. Fairbanks (1973:143) suggested that the scarcity of wood in Iberia was a precondition which may have strongly influenced the preference of ceramic vessels over wooden casks. It is also possible that aspects of ceramic technology, such as tin glazing, the use of decorative tiles, and certain vessel forms, became thoroughly ingrained in Spanish culture during the Roman and, more importantly, Islamic occupations. This is supported by the orders of King Alfonso X who declared that no non-Muslim tradition potteries were to be built in Córdoba even after its reconquest (Glick 1979:223).

Although many of the cultural areas first colonized by Spaniards in the Americas had vigorous ceramic traditions, an undeniable demand remained for particular types of Hispanic-tradition ceramics in the colonies. This demand is evidenced by virtually all shipping manifests and Spanish colonial archaeological assemblages.

This discussion is based on historical and archaeological data and is intended to establish patterns of ceramic usage in Spain during the first century of colonization. Changes in these patterns based on data from New World colonies suggest that different social, economic, and demographic variables influenced the types of Hispanic ceramics that remained in demand, as well as those that were readily replaced by aboriginal counterparts.

Historical Background

Demographic research has suggested that the majority of New World immigrants were from Andalusia, and that most of these colonists were from Seville (Boyd-Bowman 1973, 1976). Furthermore, the establishment of the Casa de Contratación, or House of Trade, in 1503 required that all legal cargo to the colonies be registered and taxed in Seville (Elliott 1963:179–183). Although this ruling was gradually relaxed over the subsequent decades, a great economic advantage was felt by local merchants, as well as Andalusian agricultural producers.

Based on these historical circumstances, Seville was selected at the outset of this study as the Spanish city from which most of the cultural and material traditions transferred to the New World probably originated. Consequently, the archaeological and historical data used to develop a profile of Spanish ceramic usage are focused on the city of Seville.

A caveat is in order here. References to "Spanish culture" used in this article are not intended to diminish regional, class, or gender distinctions among Spaniards, since Spanish culture was clearly not a homogeneous or static entity. The term is used here merely as an analytical convenience to underscore the unique social and material characteristics which set Spaniards apart from the cultures of the New World.

With the opening of trans-Atlantic trade, Seville's social hierarchy was transformed. Throughout medieval times, the nobility was associated most closely with the church and the military. However, as fortunes were rapidly amassed, respect for commerce and the social position of the merchant class were quickly elevated. It was not uncommon for the daughters of "old nobility" to marry into families of socially inferior standing. This practice served to enhance the upward mobility of the commercial sector while filling the coffers of often financially waning nobility with substantial dowries (Pike 1972:22). Some documents suggest that, as a result of these changes in the social and economic complexion of Seville, honor or *honra* translated directly into material goods during the 16th century:

> Traditional beliefs emphasizing virtue and valor as a basis for nobility fell into disuse. An acquisitive society was emerging, and a spirit of gain overwhelmed the city [Seville] (Pike 1972:21).

This social phenomenon has been observed in a study of Seville's probate inventories which reveal that material distinctions between social classes became noticeably obscured by the middle of the century (Morell Peguero 1986:140).

Archaeological Background

Sixteenth-century archaeological data from Seville are limited to a single site. The Baños de la Reina Mora site (Figure 1) was established in 1550 as an Augustinian convent known as "Dulce Nombre de Jesús" (Juan Campos Carrasco 1986, pers. comm.; Morgado 1887[1587]). Simultaneously, it served as a home for *mujeres perdidas*, or repentant prostitutes (Pike 1972:210; Morales Padron 1983:254). The site was excavated by Juan Campos Carrasco, Seville's urban archaeologist, under the auspices of the Provincial Archaeological Museum (Fernández Gómez and Campos Carrasco 1985). The materials from the excavation consisted of over 10,000 objects (Table 1) and were analyzed in 1986 (McEwan 1988).

Since all of the deposits were secondary, it was impossible to identify discrete activity areas within the site. Consequently, the assemblage will be considered as a whole. However, the data are valu-able to the extent that this assemblage represents the first systematically analyzed 16th-century archaeological collection from Spain. As such, it provides a foundation from which to examine New World sites with a new perspective.

Architecture

The predominance of Arabic ceramic elements common to 16th-century Spanish architecture persisted after the Almohad occupation which lasted until 1248 in Seville (Jackson 1972:84). Buildings in Spain typically had plastered walls with whitewash and brick flooring (Morell Peguero 1986: 105). Sixteenth-century documents indicate that decorative tiles were in great demand in Seville by residents who could afford them (Sánchez-Pacheco 1981:104). They were often restricted to the lower half of walls, while the upper half was simply whitewashed. *Azulejos* or ornamental tiles included *alicatos* (mosaics in the shapes of diamonds, squares, or stars), *cuerda seca* (lost wax designs), *cuenca* or *arista* (stamped impressions), and *planos* or *pisanos* (painted flat tiles with Renaissance-inspired decorative motifs). Plaster, mortar, and decorative tiles were all recovered from 16th-century contexts at the Baños site, suggesting that the structure was characterized by basic Muslim elements. *Pisano* tiles introduced by the Italian potter Niculoso Pisano in the first decade of the 16th century (Sánchez-Pacheco 1981: 104) were the most common, followed by Arabic-tradition *cuenca* and *cuerda seca* tiles.

Wells (*pozos*) were common in most households, where they were situated in the patio and/or kitchen (Morell Peguero 1986:113). Although some houses had private cisterns (*aljibes*), most used wells with a simple waterwheel (*noria*) (Collantes de Teran 1984:85). The recovery of over 1,000 *arcaduz* or *cangilón* (waterwheel jar) fragments from the Baños site provides evidence that such waterwheels were probably in use at the site (Table 1). These vessels have ribbed necks around which rope was tied for securing them onto waterwheels or for simply lowering them into wells (Figure 2a).

TABLE 1
ARTIFACTS FROM THE BAÑOS SITE BY FUNCTIONAL CATEGORY

Functional Category	Count N	Percentage %
Spanish Tin-Glazed Tablewares		
Andalusia Plain	114	4
Andalusia Polychrome "A"	28	1
Andalusia Polychrome "B"	6	<1
Bisque	2	<1
Caparra Blue	1	<1
Columbia Plain	847	32
Dibujo de Encaje	1	<1
Eroded Tin-Glazed	1	<1
Green Tin-Glazed	89	3
Green and White Tin-Glazed	100	4
Isabela Polychrome	12	<1
Lusterware	2	<1
Melado	38	1
Paterna Tin-Glazed	1	<1
Santa Elena Blue on White Mottled	54	2
Sevilla Blue on Blue	721	28
Santo Domingo Blue on White	84	3
Unclassified Blue on White	238	9
Unclassified Polychrome Majolica	37	1
Yayal Blue on White	242	9
Total	2,618	100
Unglazed Spanish Tablewares		
Bizcocho	1,321	95
Feldspar Inlaid Redware	2	<1
Feldspar Tempered Redware	8	<1
Fine Unglazed Coarse Earthenware	53	4
Orange Micaceous	2	<1
Total	1,386	100
Non-Spanish Tablewares		
Blue on White Delft	1	3
Ligurian Blue on Blue	15	47
Ming Porcelain	3	9
Pisan Slipware	13	41
Total	32	100
Spanish Utilitarian Wares		
Arcaduz	1,003	19
Blue on White Tin-Glazed	74	1
Columbia Plain	91	2
Green Bacín	21	<1
Green Lebrillo	103	2
Green Tin-Glazed	35	<1
Green and White Tin-Glazed	15	<1
Iron Brown Yayal	2	<1
Lead-Glazed Coarse Earthenware	2,578	48
Polychrome Tin-Glazed	4	<1

TABLE 1 (*Continued*)

Functional Category	Count N	Percentage %
Puerto Real Green on Green	11	<1
Santo Domingo Blue on White	21	<1
Unglazed Coarse Earthenware	1,398	26
Yayal Blue on White	41	<1
Total	5,397	100
Indeterminate Ceramics		
Bisque	12	8
Indeterminate Tin-Glazed	145	92
Total	157	100
Glass from the Baños Site		
Green glass	117	43
Clear glass	77	28
Blue glass	16	6
Latticinio glass	15	5
Bottle neck (light green)	14	5
Opaque red glass	10	4
Flat glass (clear)	6	2
Heavily patinated glass	5	2
Mottled glass (red & white on blue)	4	1
Aqua glass	3	1
Amber glass	1	<1
Black glass	1	<1
Bottle base (green)	1	<1
Brown glass	1	<1
White glass	1	<1
Pale yellow glass	1	<1
Total	273	100
Non-Glass Kitchen Artifacts		
Anafe (portable)	46	84
Mortar	9	16
Total	55	100
Clothing and Sewing Items		
Brass straight pins	2	100
Personal Items		
Clay bead	1	50
Iron key	1	50
Total	2	100
Religious Artifacts		
Ceramic Madonna fragment	1	25
Metallic thread (gold)	2	50
Pila de agua bendita	1	25
Total	4	100

(*continued*)

TABLE 1 (*Continued*)

Functional Category	Count N	Percentage %
Activity-Related Items		
Candiles	12	50
Cockspurs	2	8
"Gaming discs"	6	25
Unidentifiable artifacts	4	17
Total	24	100
Furniture Hardware		
Furniture tack (chatone)	1	100
Architectural Items		
Copper wire	1	17
Brass tack	1	17
Wire	1	17
Wrought nail	3	50
Total	6	101
Construction and Masonry Artifacts		
Barrel tile	71	40
Brocal	39	22
Plaster	23	13
Pisano tile	19	11
Cuenca tile	11	6
Unglazed tile	5	3
Marble tile	4	2
Mortar	3	2
Pipe	2	1
Cuerda seca tile	1	<1
Total	178	100
Unidentifiable Metal		
Copper alloy fragments	2	8
Iron fragments	23	92
Total	25	100
Miscellaneous Substances		
Coral	3	10
Fired clay lumps	10	34
Oyster shells	5	17
Quartz fragments	4	14
Rocks	4	14
Slag	2	7
Unidentifiable shell	1	4
Total	29	100

All of the wells at the Baños site were shored with bricks, which was the most common method of well construction in Spain, along with the use of ceramic rings (Lister and Lister 1987:Figure 40). Wellheads or *brocales* were another feature of Spanish wells. They extended from the ground sur-

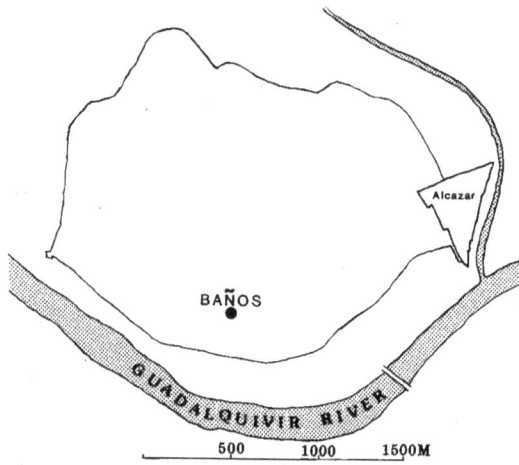

FIGURE 1. Map of Seville indicating the location of the Baños site.

face to approximately 3–4 ft. high, and were commonly decorated with stamped Arabic design elements and covered with green glaze (Sánchez-Pacheco 1981:95–96). *Brocal* fragments were the second most commonly recovered construction/masonry item from the Baños site (Table 1).

Two other types of construction/masonry elements identified from the site were barrel tiles, which were used for roofing, and ceramic pipes or *caños*. Not unlike modern drainage or sewer pipes, 16th-century Spanish versions were unglazed and manufactured so that they could be attached to connecting segments.

Household Furnishings

The most abundant ceramic household furnishings were basins (*lebrillos*) and chamber pots (*bacines*) (Figure 2h, f). While *lebrillos* were multifunctional vessels (Curtis 1962:490), *bacines* were generally used exclusively as chamber pots. Spaniards of the early modern period made virtually no provisions for urban waste disposal (Collantes de Teran 1984:103–106). All forms of excrement and waste were simply dumped out into the street (Pike 1961:14).

The distribution of remains from the Baños site suggests that when wells were abandoned, they were used for dumping debris. However, there was also a great deal of sheet deposit indicating that refuse was regularly thrown in the yard area rather than digging trash pits. The representativeness of this refuse disposal pattern is unknown and will require further testing at additional sites. For example, it is known that, in contrast to the Augustinian nuns, Carthusian monks lived in individual "cells," maintained their own private gardens, and ate alone except on rare religious holidays (Fernando Amores 1989, pers. comm.).

Lebrillo fragments were common from the Baños site, over one-quarter of which were green-glazed (Table 2). *Bacines* were also frequently recovered, the most common being undecorated Columbia Plain fragments.

Although fireplaces and stoves are generally considered architectural in nature, neither was common in Spain until the 17th and 18th centuries. Cooking and heating were both done using portable forms of braziers known as *anafes* (for cooking) and metal *braseros* (for heating).

Food Preparation

While metal pots and pans were not uncommon in Spain as evidenced from early modern paintings and shipwreck assemblages, ceramic cooking vessels were equally widespread. There is no indication that food preparation techniques changed from medieval times to the early modern period. The most common 16th-century meal continued to be liquid-based stews or *gachas* and, as a consequence, hollowware vessel forms prevailed. These vessel forms were generally of lead-glazed coarse red earthenware, the most common ceramic type recovered from the Baños site. Although vessel forms of lead-glazed coarse earthenware included *cazuelas, pucheros, platos,* and *escudillas* (Table 2; Figure 2e,c,g,d), over 50 percent of all *cazuela* and *puchero* fragments were sooted, suggesting that these vessels were made for the express purpose of cooking (McEwan 1988:103).

Ceramic mortars were also identified (Figure 2b). These were either green-glazed or unglazed

FIGURE 2. Various ceramic vessel forms: *a, arcaduz; b, mortero; c, puchero; d, escudilla; e, cazuela; f, bacín; g, plato; h, lebrillo; i, anafe.*

and were presumably used to grind herbs and spices.

As noted above, foods were typically prepared on ceramic braziers or *anafes*. These were two-chambered ceramic vessels with a perforated platform separating the upper and lower sections (Figure 2i). Charcoal was placed in the lower chamber for fuel, while cooking vessels were placed on the upper half. Forty-six *anafe* fragments were recovered from the Baños site. Their rims were frequently inverted and sooted, and the platform separating the two halves was usually broken.

At some point in time, large, permanent *anafes* became a part of kitchen architecture. Although the time of their introduction and rise in popularity is unclear, this style of *anafe* must have been introduced by the 17th century, as indicated by an untitled Velásquez painting (Braudel 1981:231) and by one-half of a marble chamber divider from a permanent *anafe* which was recovered from a 17th- and 18th-century household in Seville (McEwan 1988:Figure 3.16).

Tablewares

The most familiar category of Spanish ceramics is tablewares. While there is no evidence that food preparation techniques changed from medieval times, food service clearly did. These changes, characterized in part by a shift from common to individualized vessels, were firmly in place by the 16th century in urban areas of Spain. Related to Renaissance ideals of individualism, similar shifts are not noted in British and French tablewares until two centuries later (Deetz 1977:59–61; Blanchette 1981:134–135).

The most common ceramic tableware forms were plates and bowls (Table 2), which were accompanied by large platters or *servidores* for serving and small salt cellars or *saleros*, for holding salt or other condiments at each place setting.

Several characteristics of this post-1550 assemblage are of chronological importance. For example, there is an almost equal representation of Morisco-tradition wares and Italian-inspired

Sevilla wares from the Baños site (McEwan 1988: Appendix 1). These results indicate that, in general, the dates suggested for the various ceramic varieties based on Spanish New World sites (Goggin 1968; Deagan 1987) are relatively accurate for Spanish assemblages in the Old World. This argues against a marked time lag for goods to reach the colonies after they were produced.

It is also interesting to note that specific vessel forms from the Baños site were unlike some from nearby colonial sites. For example, at Qsar es-Seghir, which was presumably supplied with ceramics from Seville (Redman 1986:191), Columbia Plain *escudillas* with inverted bases had been completely replaced by those with footrings by the 1530s or 1540s (Boone 1984:Table 6). The same was not true at the Baños site. A full one-third of the Columbia Plain *escudillas* from the site had inverted bases, as did 83 percent of the Yayal Blue on White variety and 71 percent of Melado *escudillas* (McEwan 1988:127–128). This difference suggests that patterns identified in particular colonies may not hold true for mainstream ceramic production and may be more indicative of a particular supplier. These formal traits should therefore only be used with extreme caution for comparison with, or in dating, other sites.

Although very little is known about the relationship between tableware types and socio-economic status among Spaniards, early 17th-century ceramic inventories from Seville indicate that ceramics from China, Talavera de la Reina, and Puente del Arzobispo, in that order, were the most expensive (Sánchez-Pacheco 1981:98). This pattern suggests that Spaniards placed a high value on imported ceramics, as well as those which were good imitations of exotic wares. Although delft and porcelain were both identified from the Baños site, imported ceramics accounted for less than 1 percent of the entire assemblage (Table 1) (McEwan 1988:198).

At the other end of the social ladder were locally produced types which characterized the common household. Undecorated, crude ceramics such as Columbia Plain *escudillas* and *platos* have been described as the working man's ware (Lister and Lister 1974:20). As mentioned earlier, this type,

TABLE 2
IDENTIFIABLE VESSEL FORMS FROM THE BAÑOS SITE

Vessel Form	Count N	Percentage %
Lebrillos		
Unglazed Coarse Earthenware	168	52
Green Lead- and Tin-Glazed	103	32
Yayal Blue on White	32	9
Lead-Glazed Coarse Earthenware	19	6
Eroded Tin-Glazed	2	1
Total	324	100
Bacínes		
Columbia Plain	87	38
Unclassified Blue on White	49	21
Unglazed Coarse Earthenware	33	14
Lead-Glazed Coarse Earthenware	23	10
Green Lead- and Tin-Glazed	21	9
Green & White Tin-Glazed	13	6
Unclassified Polychrome Tin-Glazed	3	1
Feldspar Temp. Red Coarse Earthenware.	1	<1
Yayal Blue on White	1	<1
Eroded Tin-Glazed	1	<1
Total	232	100
Lebrillos/Bacínes		
Unglazed Coarse Earthenware	106	68
Unclassified Blue on White	22	14
Green Lead- and Tin-Glazed	12	8
Lead-Glazed Coarse Earthenware	8	5
Yayal Blue on White	5	3
Columbia Plain	1	1
Polychrome Tin-Glazed	1	1
Total	155	100
Tinajas		
Unglazed Coarse Earthenware	43	64
Lead-Glazed Coarse Earthenware	22	33
Columbia Plain	1	1
Green Tin-Glazed	1	1
Total	67	99
Identifiable Lead-Glazed Coarse Earthenwares		
Cazuela (cooking dish)	252	38
Plato (plate)	150	23
Puchero (globular cooking vessel)	105	16
Escudilla (carinated bowl)	68	10
Bacín (chamber pot)	23	4
Tinaja	22	3
Lebrillo	19	3
Taza	9	1
Lebrillo/Bacín	8	1
Total	656	100

TABLE 2 (*Continued*)

Vessel Form	Count N	Percentage %
Tazas and Everted Rim Bowls		
Yayal Blue on Blue	105	54
Sevilla Blue on Blue	29	15
Unclassified Blue on White	10	5
Lead Glazed Coarse Earthenware	9	5
Columbia Plain	8	4
Pisan Slipware	7	4
Santo Domingo	4	2
Unglazed Coarse Earthenware	4	2
Green Tin-Glazed	3	2
Andalusia Plain	3	1
Bizcocho	2	1
Green and White Tin-Glazed	2	1
Eroded Tin Glazed	2	1
Ligurian Blue on Blue	2	1
Unclassified Polychrome Majolica	2	1
Lusterware	1	1
Total	193	100
Platos		
Sevilla Blue on Blue	510	35
Columbia Plain	396	27
Lead-Glazed Coarse Earthenware	150	10
Unclassified Blue on White	78	5
Yayal Blue on White	77	5
Andalusia Plain	63	4
Eroded Tin-Glazed	44	3
Green and White Tin-Glazed	34	2
Unclassified Polychrome	23	2
Santo Domingo	18	1
Green Tin-Glazed	16	1
Melado	13	1
Isabela Polychrome	12	1
Ligurian Blue on Blue	10	1
Bisque	5	<1
Bizcocho	5	<1
Unglazed Coarse Earthenware	3	<1
Puerto Real Green on Green	2	<1
Andalusia Polychrome "B"	2	<1
Iron Brown Yayal	1	<1
Talavera-tradition Polychrome	1	<1
Andalusia Polychrome "A"	1	<1
Total	1,464	100
Escudillas		
Columbia Plain	367	71
Lead-Glazed Coarse Earthenware	68	13
Yayal Blue on White	43	8
Melado	19	4
Green and White Tin-Glazed	5	1

(*continued*)

TABLE 2 (*Continued*)

Vessel Form	Count N	Percentage %
Eroded Tin-Glazed	3	1
Unclassified Blue on White	3	1
Green Tin-Glazed	2	<1
Bizcocho	1	<1
Santo Domingo Blue on White	1	<1
Unclassified Polychrome	1	<1
Total	513	100
Pocillas		
Sevilla Blue on Blue	108	53
Unclassified Blue on White	42	21
Andalusia Plain	26	13
Andalusia Polychrome "A"	10	5
Columbia Plain	5	2
Unclassified Polychrome	4	2
Yayal Blue on Blue	4	2
Green and White Tin-Glazed	1	<1
Ligurian Blue on Blue	1	<1
Eroded Tin-Glazed	1	<1
Total	202	100
Majolica Jarros		
Santa Elena Mottled	4	21
Andalusia Polychrome "A"	3	16
Unclassified Blue on White	3	16
Yayal Blue on White	3	16
Columbia Plain	2	11
Eroded Tin-Glazed	2	11
Green Tin-Glazed	1	5
Green and White Tin-Glazed	1	5
Total	19	101
Saucers and Saleros		
Bizcocho	68	85
Columbia Plain	7	9
Unglazed Coarse Earthenware	4	5
Green Tin-Glazed	1	1
Total	80	100

along with another locally produced decorated type, Sevilla Blue on Blue, was the most common tableware at the Baños site (Table 1).

Food Storage

Vessels used for transporting and storing food were relatively rare from the Baños site. *Tinajas*, or olive jars (Goggin 1960), which generally are ubiquitous on Spanish colonial sites, were uncommon at the Baños site. This scarcity is undoubtedly due to the fact that foodstuffs did not need to be purchased in large quantities in Seville, which is known to have had numerous public markets (Collantes de Teran 1984:130).

It is also important to emphasize that *tinajas* were truly multi-purpose vessels in Iberia and throughout the Mediterranean world. While there is little doubt that few olive jars were shipped across the Atlantic empty, their presence on Old World Spanish sites is less likely to go hand-in-hand with food storage. As in the New World, tinajas were commonly recycled in Spain where they served a number of architectural functions including roof vaulting and floor fill (Fernando Amores 1989, pers. comm.; Lister and Lister 1981).

Religious Artifacts

Ceramics also played a role in the religious life of Spaniards. However, one of the most interesting results from the Baños site analysis is the small number of religious artifacts recovered from this Augustinian convent. Only three items were identified which were thought to have clear religious significance (Table 1). Pieces of gold thread or *bordado*—presumed to have been used as ornamentation, possibly on an altar mantle—were identified (McEwan 1988:Figure 3.13). Although Spaniards were noted for their highly ostentatious clothing which was often trimmed in gold braid, the Augustinian order had a strict prohibition against personal possessions. Consequently, this piece of *bordado* was more likely to have come from a religious object than a personal one.

A thin, unglazed coarse red earthenware fragment with an incised and molded Madonna head was also recovered (McEwan 1988:Figure 3.13). No other fragments of this ceramic type were identified, making it impossible to suggest what the entire object might have been.

Finally, the upper half of a holy water stoup or *pila de agua benedita* was found (McEwan 1988: Figure 3.13). These small holy water containers were frequently placed at the entrances of Spanish churches.

The sparse number of religious artifacts identified from the Baños assemblage may be the result of a number of factors. There is little doubt that 16th-century Spaniards valued and took great care of their religious possessions. Consequently, religious objects were most likely kept as heirlooms for generations. Also, many objects used in religious services, such as liturgical cruets and ewers (Frothingham 1941:42), were made of glass and probably would not be recognizable as religious objects in the archaeological record. Finally, it has been noted that many of the religious objects from this period were made of wood (Jerald Milanich 1988, pers. comm.), and therefore may not have been preserved archaeologically.

Spain and Its Colonies

One of the most distinguishing characteristics of Spanish colonial sites is their abundant ceramic remains (Deagan 1985:29). Regardless of socio-economic status, ceramic objects played an important role in the material life of virtually every Spaniard. Although the sample from the Baños site in Seville was undoubtedly somewhat skewed by the lack of fine screening, ceramics accounted for 99 percent of the materials recovered.

As noted above, ceramics were not only an integral part of Spanish material life, but Spaniards also had a penchant for public displays of wealth (Vicens Vives 1967:99; Pike 1972:28). This ostentation reached such extremes in Seville during the 16th and 17th centuries that sumptuary laws were passed prohibiting people from ''parading their wealth'' (Perry 1980:220). Although these laws eventually extended to the New World in the 17th century, they appear to have had little impact on material displays (Lavrin 1978:47). As one scholar has observed:

> These colonists clung nostalgically to Spanish ways of life; they wanted the luxuries of the Old World, its textiles, its books, its foodstuffs. Some of these would in time be produced in the New World itself, but meanwhile the ships would leave Seville laden with Castilian or Catalan cloth, and with wine, oil and corn from Andalusia, and would bring back silver and other desirable colonial produce in return (Elliott 1963:182).

Through an examination of 16th-century Spanish colonial assemblages, it is clear that in some respects a very traditional pattern of Spanish material culture was maintained in the New World. This pattern is particularly true in areas of public display such as tablewares and architectural tiles. Assemblages from St. Augustine, Florida; Puerto

Real, Haiti; Nueva Cádiz, Venezuela; and the Convento de San Francisco in the Dominican Republic demonstrate that even in the most remote colonies, food service was characterized by individualized glazed plates, bowls, and glass goblets; and ornamental tiles were frequently used for decoration (Council 1975; Willis 1976; Deagan 1985; McEwan 1986; Ewen 1987). The high proportion of Hispanic tablewares recovered from the New World sites provides strong evidence that the highly visible area of food service was of great importance to Spanish colonists. Since there were no aboriginal counterparts to the glazed, individualized dishes which Spaniards considered an essential component of etiquette and propriety, few alternatives existed but to import these ceramics until Spanish-tradition kilns were established in the New World.

A distinct difference between the material assemblages from Spain and its colonies was the relatively small number of traditional food preparation vessels, and complete absence of cooking braziers or *anafes* in the colonial sites examined. While there were no aboriginal counterparts to glazed cooking pots, there were native vessel forms which could easily substitute in function. Since cooking was primarily a female activity in Spain, it is suggested that the lack of Spanish cooking vessels and braziers from the remote colonies examined in this study is closely linked to the small proportion of female colonists. Exceptions to this pattern would be anticipated in large, cosmopolitan centers such as Lima, Peru, and Santo Domingo, which were populated by Spanish women even in the earliest years of colonization. This situation certainly appears to be the case in Santo Domingo, one of the few Spanish colonial entrepôts for which archaeological data have been published (Ortega 1980, 1982). It is clear that New World Spanish households which included a Spanish wife maintained traditional elements which were not present in homes without Spanish women:

> Rich and poor, concubine and beata, Spanish women made their most basic contribution to the development of the country [Peru] by educating those around them in the ways of the homeland. In their houses Spanish was spoken and learned. They taught their Negro and Indian maids to make beds, sew European clothes, and prepare Spanish foods in Spanish fashion (Lockhart 1968:163).

The paucity of ceramics related to food preparation in predominantly male colonies supports the idea that Indian women were the primary agents of Spanish acculturation in the New World (Deagan 1973, 1974; Burkett 1978). As a result, the most profound changes in traditional Spanish lifeways were in areas related to female tasks.

In relation to architecture, highly visible decorative tiles are among the most common ceramic architectural remains recovered in the colonies. Also, the tradition of recycling *tinajas* and other ceramic vessels as architectural elements was continued in the Caribbean and Central and South America (Lister and Lister 1981). However, there is no evidence in the New World of ceramic drainage pipes or wellheads, or of wells having been shored with bricks or well rings. *Pipas*, or wooden casks, are the most frequently documented substitute for bricks or ceramic rings used in New World well construction (Deagan 1985:13; South et al. 1988:191–199).

As noted earlier, while the olive jar is generally the most common Hispanic ceramic type recovered from the colonies, there were very few *tinajas* recovered from the Baños site. The majority of Spaniards clearly preferred Mediterranean foodstuffs and went to great lengths and expense to obtain them. Records from the Casa de Contratación indicate that agricultural products—particularly wine, oil, and grain—made up the vast majority of the cargo from Spain to the colonies until the 1570s, by which time most of these Iberian staples were being successfully produced in the New World (McAlister 1984:371). Despite the concerted effort to replicate traditional dietary patterns, the historical and zooarchaeological records suggest that, at least in some colonies, the supply was never able to keep up with the demand and that local resources were commonly integrated into Spanish colonial diet (Reitz and Scarry 1985).

The need for large earthenware vessels or olive jars (*tinajas* or *botijas peruleras*) for shipping foodstuffs and other supplies had a tremendous impact on potteries in Seville and perhaps its hinterlands (Lister and Lister 1987:136). After the vessels arrived in the colonies and their contents were emptied, olive jars were resold and/or reused as water and storage containers. As in Spain, there are many New World examples of pots being used for architectural fill (Fairbanks 1973:144; Lister and Lister 1981; Ortega and Fondeur 1982:Figure 37.b).

The importance of Spanish materials in the New World can be substantiated by the inflated prices Spaniards were willing to pay for goods from home. It is interesting to note that prices for goods in Spain are generally recorded in *maravedis*, while in the colonies they are generally reckoned in *reales* (equivalent to 34 *maravedis* [Bushnell 1981:149]). Comparison of prices reveals that empty olive jars were sold in colonies such as St. Augustine in 1572 for 4 *reales* (136 *maravedis*) each (Archivo General de las Indias [AGI] 1572), more than four times their cost in Seville in the mid-16th century, when they cost between 13 and 33 *maravedis* (Wagner 1972:126). Even more marked was the increase in the price of basic tablewares which averaged between 3 and 4 *maravedis* in Seville in 1544–1545 (Wagner 1972:126). Presumably comparable examples were received at Santa Elena from Havana in 1571 for 1.5 *reales* or 51 *maravedis* each (AGI 1571).

Another important point of comparison between the ceramic assemblages from Seville and the American colonies is the role of foreign ceramics in Spain and the trans-Atlantic trade. Despite the fact that Seville was a noted European entrepôt, exotic ceramics comprised less than 1 percent of the ceramic assemblages examined from both the Old World and the Americas. Skowronek (1989: 18) has suggested that the small number of non-Spanish ceramics which have been recovered from 16th-century Spanish colonial sites may well have arrived there through perfectly legitimate trade channels of the extensive Spanish empire.

Spanish Frontier Pattern

The preceding discussion provides baseline data necessary for a tentative definition of a Spanish "frontier pattern" analogous to those defined for British colonial sites (e.g., Lewis 1977; South 1977). Although Spanish sites in the Old and New Worlds are both characterized by a predominance of ceramic remains, most colonial sites appear to contain a much higher proportion of storage vessels. Conversely, colonial sites tend to lack traditional Spanish vessel forms related to female activities (*cazuelas*, *pucheros*, *morteros*, *anafes*, and so forth). Furthermore, ceramic well rings, bricks, and wellheads were not commonly used in New World well construction.

With respect to non-ceramic materials, 16th-century colonial contexts generally had significantly greater proportions of weaponry, sewing objects, nails, and other construction materials (McEwan 1988:222). Trash disposal itself was apparently altered in at least some colonies, such as St. Augustine, where in contrast to the open dumping practiced in Spain, trash was typically deposited in discrete pits and abandoned wells (Deagan 1983:269).

Conclusions

This comparison of Old and New World ceramic assemblages illuminates some of the specific adaptations made by Spanish colonists. Spaniards demonstrated a remarkable degree of adaptability to the social and demographic constraints of the New World. From the very first decades of colonization, the predominantly male settlers are known to have taken Indian servants, concubines, and wives. Their predisposition toward accepting and integrating other ethnic groups into colonial society was undoubtedly tempered by the fact that Spain, and particularly Seville, had an ethnically diverse population (Pike 1972; Glick 1979:175). While rigid ideals of social stratification and the superiority of "pure bloods" was undeniable, inter-ethnic relations, including common-law marriages and miscegenation, were widely accepted within the Spanish social framework (Pike 1961:357).

Spanish colonists appear to have been less flexible when it came to foodstuffs and material goods. The abundance of food storage vessels from every

16th-century Spanish New World assemblage examined provide testimony to a heavy reliance on Mediterranean staples imported from Spain. It was not until the last quarter of the century that Peruvian-grown olives and grapes and Mexican wheat began to meet the heavy colonial demand (Crosby 1972:70–73).

The presence of Spanish tablewares in significant numbers at each of the colonies studied further underscores the importance of certain Hispanic materials in the lives of colonists. Other than olive jars, majolica tablewares were the most commonly recovered Spanish ceramic type. The predominance of majolica in the colonies is thought to be related to two factors. First, as tablewares majolica vessels are highly visible ceramics whose occurrence, at least in some instances, has been demonstrated to be directly related to socio-economic status and may also have served as a form of ethnic identification (Deagan 1983:262). Furthermore, unlike the Baños site, where lead-glazed coarse earthenware cooking vessels were the most common ceramic type, these cookwares were traditionally associated with female activities and, therefore, were probably not in great demand in the colonies where Spanish men far outnumbered Spanish women.

This study has underscored the fact that a broader understanding of Spanish colonial adaptive strategies will require additional comparable and systematic excavations in Spain, as well as in Spanish New World urban centers such as Lima, Havana, and Santo Domingo. Other than the Baños sample, archaeologists have very little additional Old World data (Myers, Amores, Olin, and Pleguezuelo, this volume). While archaeologists have a relatively larger number of New World sites to draw from, the sites are remarkably similar in that they were relatively remote and were occupied predominantly by men. This has undoubtedly skewed researchers' perceptions as to the range of variability within the colonial experience. One result of this bias in the data base is the lack of information regarding the role of Spanish women in the colonization effort. Although their numbers increased steadily through the years, historical archaeologists have little knowledge about how their presence affected Spanish colonial communities or their impact on the local native populations. Spanish colonial archaeology is uniquely well-suited to address this issue, and hopefully researchers will focus more attention in this direction in the near future.

ACKNOWLEDGMENTS

This article summarizes portions of my doctoral research. Funding for various stages of this project was provided by the Instituto de Cooperación Iberoamericana, the Tinker Foundation, the Wentworth Foundation, the St. Augustine Restoration Foundation, Inc., and the Charles H. Fairbanks Scholarship Fund. I want to acknowledge the contributions of Jerald Milanich, Elizabeth Wing, Michael Gannon, Lyle McAlister, James Amelang, and, in particular, Kathleen Deagan for their support and advice over the years. Also, Don Fernando Fernández Gómez, Don Diego Oliva Alonso, and Juan Campos Carrasco greatly facilitated my research in Spain. I have also benefited from conversations with Emlen Myers and Jacqueline Olin of the Smithsonian Institution and Fernando Amores of the University of Seville. Additionally, I am indebted to the thoughtful comments of the reviewers that helped to refine the final version of this manuscript. I also thank Jeffery M. Mitchem who read and commented on an earlier draft of this paper, Charles B. Poe who painstakingly drew the figures, and James J. Miller, Chief of the Florida Bureau of Archaeological Research, who allowed me to take the time from my other job responsibilities at San Luis to write this article.

REFERENCES

Archivo General de las Indias (AGI)
1571 Contaduría 548, No. 8, No. 5, datas, entry 1. Seville, Spain.
1572 Contaduría 548, No. 8, Item 3, without folio. Seville, Spain.

Blanchette, Jean François
1981 The Role of Artifacts in the Study of Foodways in New France, 1720–1760. *History and Archaeology* No. 52. Parks Canada, Ottawa.

Boone, James
1984 Majolica Escudillas of the 15th and 16th Centuries: A Typological Analysis of 55 Examples from Qsar es-Seghir. *Historical Archaeology* 18(1):76–86.

BOYD-BOWMAN, PETER
1973 Patterns of Spanish Emigration to the New World (1493–1580). *Council on International Studies Special Studies* No. 34. State University of New York at Buffalo, Buffalo.
1976 Patterns of Spanish Emigration to the Indies until 1600. *Hispanic American Historical Review* 56: 580–604.

BRAUDEL, FERNAND
1981 *The Structures of Everyday Life*, Vol. 1, translated by Sian Reynolds. Harper and Row, New York.

BURKETT, ELINOR C.
1978 Indian Women and White Society: The Case of Sixteenth Century Peru. In *Latin American Women*, edited by Asunción Lavrin, pp. 101–128. Greenwood Press, Westport, Connecticut.

BUSHNELL, AMY
1981 *The King's Coffer: Proprietors of the Spanish Florida Treasury, 1565–1702*. University Presses of Florida, Gainesville.

COLLANTES DE TERAN, SANCHEZ
1984 *Sevilla en la Baja Edad Media*. Artes Gráficas Salesianas, S. A., Seville, Spain.

COUNCIL, R. BRUCE
1975 Archaeology of the Convento de San Francisco. Unpublished M.A. thesis, Department of Anthropology, University of Florida, Gainesville.

CROSBY, ALFRED
1972 *The Columbian Exchange*. Greenwood Press, Westport, Connecticut.

CURTIS, FREDDIE
1962 The Utility Pottery Industry of Bailén, Southern Spain. *American Anthropologist* 64(6):486–503.

DEAGAN, KATHLEEN
1973 *Mestizaje* in Colonial St. Augustine. *Ethnohistory* 20(1):53–65.
1974 Sex, Status and Role in the Mestizaje of Spanish Colonial Florida. Unpublished Ph.D. dissertation, Department of Anthropology, University of Florida, Gainesville.
1983 *Spanish St. Augustine: The Archaeology of a Colonial Creole Community*. Academic Press, New York.
1985 The Archaeology of Sixteenth Century St. Augustine. *Florida Anthropologist* 38(1-2):6–33.
1987 *Artifacts of the Spanish Colonies of Florida and the Caribbean, 1500–1800*. Smithsonian Institution Press, Washington, D.C.

DEETZ, JAMES
1977 *In Small Things Forgotten*. Anchor/Doubleday, New York.

ELLIOTT, JOHN H.
1963 *Imperial Spain, 1469–1716*. St. Martin's Press, New York.

EWEN, CHARLES R.
1987 From Spaniard to Creole: The Archaeology of Hispanic American Cultural Formation at Puerto Real, Haiti. Unpublished Ph.D. disseration, Department of Anthropology, University of Florida, Gainesville.

FAIRBANKS, CHARLES H.
1973 The Cultural Significance of Spanish Ceramics. In *Ceramics in America*, edited by Ian Quimby, pp. 141–174. The University Press of Virginia, Charlottesville.

FERNÁNDEZ GÓMEZ, FERNANDO, AND JUAN M. CAMPOS CARRASCO
1985 Panorama de la Arqueología Medieval en el Casco Antiguo de Sevilla. In *Resúmenes de las Actas del I Congreso de Arqueología Medieval Española*. Huesca, Spain.

FROTHINGHAM, ALICE
1941 *Hispanic Glass*. Hispanic Society of America, New York.

GLICK, THOMAS
1979 *Islamic and Christian Spain in the Early Middle Ages*. Princeton University Press, Princeton, New Jersey.

GOGGIN, JOHN M.
1960 The Spanish Olive Jar: An Introductory Study. *Yale University Publications in Anthropology* No. 47. New Haven, Connecticut.
1968 Spanish Majolica in the New World. *Yale University Publications in Anthropology* No. 72. New Haven, Connecticut.

JACKSON, GABRIEL
1972 *The Making of Medieval Spain*. Harcourt Brace Jovanovich, New York.

LAVRIN, ASUNCIÓN
1978 In Search of the Colonial Woman in Mexico: The Seventeenth and Eighteenth Centuries. In *Latin American Women*, edited by A. Lavrin, pp. 23–59. Greenwood Press, Westport, Connecticut.

LEWIS, KENNETH
1977 Sampling the Archaeological Frontier: Regional Models and Component Analysis. In *Research Strategies in Historical Archaeology*, edited by Stanley South, pp. 151–201. Academic Press, New York.

LISTER, FLORENCE, AND ROBERT LISTER
1974 Majolica in Spanish Colonial America. *Historical Archaeology* 8:17–52.
1981 The Recycled Pots and Potsherds of Spain. *Historical Archaeology* 15(1):66–78.

1987   *Andalusian Ceramics in Spain and New Spain.* The University of Arizona Press, Tucson.

LOCKHART, JAMES
1968   *Spanish Peru, 1532–1560.* University of Wisconsin Press, Madison.

MCALISTER, LYLE
1984   *Spain and Portugal in the New World, 1492–1700.* University of Minnesota Press, Minneapolis.

MCEWAN, BONNIE G.
1986   Domestic Adaptation at Puerto Real, Haiti. *Historical Archaeology* 20(1):44–49.
1988   An Archaeological Perspective of Sixteenth Century Spanish Life in the Old World and the Americas. Unpublished Ph.D. dissertation, Department of Anthropology, University of Florida, Gainesville.

MORALES PADRON, FRANCISCO
1983   Historia de Sevilla. *Colección de Bolsillo* Número 58. Universidad de Sevilla, Seville, Spain.

MORELL PEGUERO, BLANCA
1986   *Mercaderos y Artesanos en la Sevilla del Descubrimiento.* Diputación Provincial de Sevilla, Sección Historia, Serie 1a, Número 29. Seville, Spain.

MORGADO, ALONSO DE
1887   *Historia de Sevilla.* Reprint of 1587 edition. A. Pescioni y Juan de León, Seville, Spain.

ORTEGA, ELPIDIO
1980   Introducción a la Loza Común o Alfarería en el Período Colonial de Santo Domingo. *Serie Científica* 3. Fundación Ortega Alvárez, Santo Domingo, Dominican Republic.

ORTEGA, ELPIDIO (EDITOR)
1982   *Arqueología Colonial de Santo Domingo,* Vol. 4. Fundación Ortega Alvárez, Santo Domingo, Dominican Republic.

ORTEGA, ELPIDIO, AND CARMEN FONDEUR
1982   Arqueología de los Monumentos Históricos de Santo Domingo. In *Arqueología Colonial de Santo Domingo,* Vol. 4, edited by E. Ortega, pp. 5–241. Fundación Ortega Alvárez, Santo Domingo, Dominican Republic.

PERRY, ELIZABETH
1980   *Crime and Society in Early Modern Seville.* University Press of New England, Hanover, New Hampshire.

PIKE, RUTH
1961   Seville in the Sixteenth Century. *Hispanic American Historical Review* 41(1):1–30.
1972   *Aristocrats and Traders: Sevillian Society in the Sixteenth Century.* Cornell University Press, Ithaca, New York.

REDMAN, CHARLES
1986   *Qsar es-Seghir: An Archaeological View of Medieval Life.* Academic Press, New York.

REITZ, ELIZABETH J., AND C. MARGARET SCARRY
1985   Reconstructing Historic Subsistence with an Example from Sixteenth-Century Spanish Florida. *Special Publication Series* No. 3. Society for Historical Archaeology, California, Pennsylvania.

SÁNCHEZ-PACHECO, TRINIDAD
1981   Sevilla. In *Cerámica Esmaltada Española,* pp. 93–108. Editorial Labor, Barcelona, Spain.

SKOWRONEK, RUSSELL K.
1989   Empire and Ceramics: The Changing Role of Illicit Trade in Spanish America. Paper presented at the Annual Meeting of the Society for Historical Archaeology Conference on Historical and Underwater Archaeology, Baltimore, Maryland.

SOUTH, STANLEY
1977   *Method and Theory in Historical Archeology.* Academic Press, New York.

SOUTH, STANLEY, RUSSELL K. SKOWRONEK, AND RICHARD E. JOHNSON
1988   Spanish Artifacts from Santa Elena. *Anthropological Studies* 7. Occasional Papers of the South Carolina Institute of Archeology and Anthropology. University of South Carolina, Columbia.

VICENS VIVES, JAMIE
1967   *Approaches to the History of Spain.* University of California Press, Berkeley.

WAGNER, KLAUS
1972   Apuntes para el Coste de Vida en Sevilla, Agosto 1544–Febrero 1545. *Archivo Hispalense* 170:119–130.

WILLIS, RAYMOND
1976   The Archeology of Sixteenth Century Nueva Cádiz. Unpublished M.A. thesis, Department of Anthropology, University of Florida, Gainesville.

BONNIE G. MCEWAN
SAN LUIS ARCHAEOLOGICAL AND HISTORIC SITE
2020 MISSION ROAD
TALLAHASSEE, FLORIDA 32304

BONNIE G. McEWAN

The Archaeology of Women in the Spanish New World

ABSTRACT

This paper explores the archaeology of women in Spanish colonial society. While an appreciation of Spanish and Native American women in Hispanic America is gradually emerging, this understanding is still rudimentary and limited almost exclusively to domestic contexts. Similarly, although African women were an important component in many Spanish colonies, their unique contributions are poorly understood.

Introduction

Considerations of gender have rarely been the focus of Spanish colonial archaeology. While there are a few exceptions (Deagan 1973, 1974, 1983), the sexual dynamics of New World communities have typically been discussed as an afterthought. Fortunately, a growing number of scholars are beginning to recognize that traditional approaches have resulted in an imbalanced and inaccurate vision of the Spanish colonial experience.

The Spanish empire was at once the champion of imperialism and a xenophobic nation bent on persecuting heretics wherever they were encountered (Kamen 1965:102). Despite an abhorrence of racial and religious impurity and a preference for Spanish marriage partners, centuries of ethnic admixture in Spanish society promoted an acceptance of intermarriage in the New World that was unparalleled by any other European colonial culture. While heavy physical labor was usually allocated to indigenous and, later, African men, women were more often incorporated into Spanish colonial life where they played an active role as wives, domestics, craft specialists, and, most importantly, cultural brokers.

Spanish Women

Although Christopher Columbus took no women along on his first or second voyages of discovery, provisions for 30 women are listed for the third voyage in 1497–1498 (Boxer 1975:35). From this time forward, Spanish women played an indispensable, albeit proportionately small, role in New World exploration and colonization.

By all accounts, women provided a measure of balance and stability to the colonial enterprises with which they were involved (Lockhart 1968: 163; McAlister 1984:97). Their roles ranged from business entrepreneur to warrior. Among the most courageous Spanish women were Doña Isabel de Guevara of Paraguay and Inéz Suárez of Chile, both of whom bore arms and fought alongside conquistadores (Lockhart and Otte 1976:15; McAlister 1984:97).

These achievements are all the more remarkable when viewed in light of female role definition within the milieu of early modern Spanish society. Although Spanish women engaged in a variety of trades—from folk medicine to textile production, the acceptable professions of women in "polite society" were mostly restricted to homemaker and nun. Among the treatises expounding the place of women was El Jardín de Nobles Donecellas by Fray Martín de Córdoba, who stated that women should be "ordered, restrained, shy, pious, and affable—with chastity and virginity the highest accomplishments" (de Córdoba in Lavrin 1978:25). Similarly, La Perfecta Casada, by Fray Luis de León, was a manual for wives which suggested that "a woman should administer to her husband's estate, love him and help him in times of stress, treat the servants well, nurse her own children, speak little, attend church often, and stay at home as much as possible" (de León in Lavrin 1978:25).

These restrictive views of women grew out of highly conservative social conditions. Seven hundred years of Arabic occupation had encouraged the virtual seclusion of females in Spain (Defourneaux 1979:146). The end of the Reconquest (1492) witnessed a religious fervor epitomized by the formidable Holy Office of the Inquisition. Although in theory the goal of the Holy Office was established to root out heresy, in practice it attempted to impose aristocratic ecclesiastical and lay ideology on the whole of society (Kamen 1965:8).

The family was the most basic institution of Spanish culture (Pescatello 1976:23), and the homemaking duties of women aimed at protecting and perpetuating that institution were reinforced by the Church, government, and society. As a consequence, a great deal of legislative energy was spent trying to reinforce Spanish marriages in the colonies. From the early 16th century, the Spanish Crown passed regulations mandating that married men in the New World must either return to Spain or send for their wives within three years (Boxer 1975:38; Pescatello 1976:132).

While wives and other female relatives were encouraged to emigrate to the colonies with their male sponsors, single women had difficulty obtaining the required royal licenses or raising the substantial amount of money necessary to buy passage to the colonies (Perry 1980:215–216). Peter Boyd-Bowman (1973:8) has noted in his extensive study of Spanish emigration that servants (criadas) were among the most common class of single women to gain passage, although he suggests that the term may also have been used for prostitutes. Despite these exceptions, unattached women of marriageable age were rare and in great demand as indicated by this 1529 letter from a colonial judge in Mexico City to a merchant in Seville:

> Milady María de los Angeles is very well and very beautiful and rich, for women who come here have all that, and property, and much else besides. She sends you a thousand greetings, being here as I write this paragraph. She wants to marry, and will marry very well. So if you are to send any merchandise, let it be women, which is the best business now in this country, and don't worry about her [from Licenciate Diego Delgadillo, judge of the Royal Audiencia of New Spain, in Mexico City, to Juan de la Torre, merchant, in Seville, in 1529] (Delgadillo in Lockhart and Otte 1976: 202).

The shortage of Spanish women in the colonies lent prestige and status to those families with an Iberian female as the legitimate head of household (Boxer 1975:38). The stabilization of many New World colonies and the concomitant desire for female colonists first increased sharply from the periods 1520–1539 to 1540–1559 when Spanish female emigration rose from 6.3 percent to 16.4 percent of the total emigrant population (Boyd-

Bowman 1968:10–11). The advantages for women living in the colonies were both social and financial. They immediately became part of an elite group of individuals whose supremacy was enhanced by the religious purity associated with "Old Christians" (Lavrin 1978:31). Furthermore, the standard of living even among the poorest of New World Spaniards was desirable:

> Even those Spaniards who were poor and plebian could afford things that in Spain were the perquisites of wealth. Most Spanish women dressed in fine stuffs; none were without servants. An artisan's wife could be expected to have a considerable staff, who would call her "señora" and relieve her of most of the burden of daily housekeeping (Lockhart 1968:159).

In most instances, Spanish women in the colonies appear to have worked in the home and maintained traditional standards. Although virtually all households had Native American or African American servants actually to perform most physical tasks, Spanish wives apparently played an active role in ensuring that certain standards were upheld. They generally demanded that Spanish be spoken, that chores such as cooking, making beds, and sewing were all done in the European fashion, and that household servants be encouraged to embrace Christianity and "legitimate" marriage (Lockhart 1968:163). Consequently, Spanish women were important purveyors of Spanish culture among Native American and African American domestics with whom they had sustained daily contact.

The archaeological correlates of Spanish women are associated mostly with their domestic responsibilities. Womens' dowries usually consisted of a share of their fathers' bienes libres or heritable wealth at the time of their marriage (Nader 1977: 417). While the Spanish trousseau or dowry could consist of everything from slaves to pearls, "it is the household equipment, especially the kitchen utensils and other furnishings, which constituted the ajuar of municipal custom" (Dillard 1984:55). These typically included bedding, linens, plates, and cooking pots. Lead-glazed coarse earthenware cooking pots, such as pucheros and cazuelas (Figures 1, 2), were the most common ceramic type from the two colonial-period sites in Spain for

FIGURE 1. Lead-glazed globular cooking pot or *puchero*. (Courtesy of Museo Arqueológico de Sevilla.)

FIGURE 2. Lead-glazed stewpan or *cazuela* sherds. (Courtesy of Museo Arqueológico de Sevilla.)

which there are archaeological data (McEwan 1988, 1989a).

In addition to these basic household goods, the fact that many of the Spanish women in the colonies were married into the upper socioeconomic stratum suggests that they had access to the preferred luxuries of the time, such as jewels and elaborate clothing. These categories of material goods (particularly gems and precious metals) were highly visible, prudent investments, and portable forms of wealth.

Because of the powerful influence Spanish women wielded in their homes, it is reasonable to assume that their presence would be discernible archaeologically. A compelling argument is made by Charles Ewen (1987, 1991) that a Spanish woman was in residence at a particular domestic site (Locus 19) within the 16th-century town of Puerto Real on Hispaniola. It is known from the documentary records that three *vecinos* (heads of household) at Puerto Real had Castilian wives (Sauer 1966:199). Given the economic conditions under which Spanish women travelled to the New World, it is likely that those living at Puerto Real were married to some of the wealthiest colonists. Ewen's excavation revealed a European-style ma-

sonry structure with a high proportion of exotic items. Specifically, the imported goods included a unicorn pendant, a number of beads, a jet ring, and a lace bobbin (Ewen 1987:210). It is worth noting that some of the best examples of identifiable traditional Spanish cooking pots from Puerto Real were also recovered from Ewen's excavation. Although this interpretation is tentative, these objects taken together provide a convincing argument that a Spanish woman resided at this domestic site and engaged in (or supervised) traditional activities including lace making and cooking.

A similar assemblage is presently being analyzed from the 17th-century Spanish mission complex of San Luis de Talimali in Tallahassee, Florida. San Luis was the capital of the western mission chain in *La Florida* and had religious, ad-

Perspectives from *Historical Archaeology*

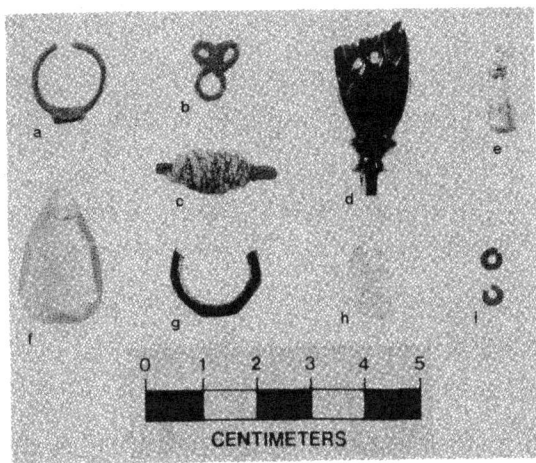

FIGURE 3. Hispanic artifacts possibly associated with a woman: *a*, brass ring; *b*, eye fastener; *c*, silk thread; *d*, jet *higa*; *e, f*, glass pendants; *g*, jet ring; *h*, decorative glass; *i*, silver sequins. (Courtesy of Florida Bureau of Archaeological Research.)

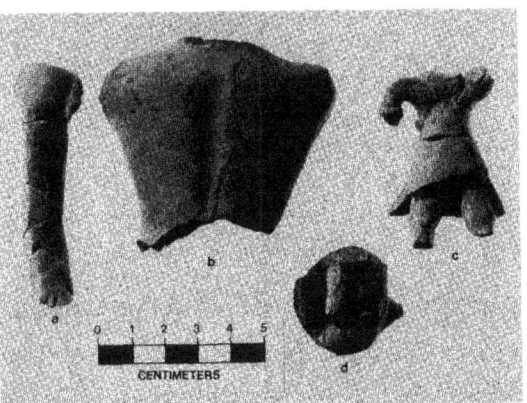

FIGURE 4. Childrens' clay figurines or *juguetes: a*, leg fragment; *b*, back; *c*, torso with partial arms and legs; *d*, genitalia. (Courtesy of Florida Bureau of Archaeological Research.)

ministrative, and military components. It is known that some of the military officials had Spanish wives in residence (Boyd et al. 1951:24–26). Recent examination of the refuse associated with a substantial domestic structure in the Spanish village has revealed a large concentration of exotic ceramics, faceted and incised jet rings, jet *higas* (protective amulets), a group of flat, precious-metal sequins or beads, a quartz teardrop pendant, and a small copper-alloy ring setting which was presumably too small for a man (McEwan 1989b) (Figure 3). A large number and variety of glass and lapidary beads also were recovered from the area. The variety of discarded jewelry and the obvious wealth of the household suggest that a Spanish woman or *mestiza* was in residence. This is further supported by the recovery of a copper-alloy child's ring setting along with small Hispanic-tradition clay figurines (*juguetes*) (Figure 4) which indicate that the children of the house also had European-style objects.

Native American Women

All evidence suggests that Spanish men living in the colonies generally preferred to marry Spanish women. However, the chronic shortage of preferred marriage partners resulted in a regular pattern of intermarriage between Spanish men and Native American women from the earliest years of colonization (Deagan 1985:304). This was not only sanctioned but encouraged, by the Spanish government as a means of stabilizing and converting the native element:

> By a 1501 ruling the Crown explicitly permitted intermarriage, and succeeding instructions—to Governor Ovando of Santo Domingo in 1503, in the royal decree of 1514, and in many later proclamations—noted the necessity of intermarriage as a means of Christianizing Amerindians through female converts. Spanish men and Indian women, living together, were persuaded to marry, although most European males married to Indian women usually were of the lowest social stratum (Pescatello 1976:137).

Two of the earliest records of Spanish–Native American intermarriage are a 1514 *repartimiento* count for the island of Hispaniola and a census of Santo Domingo taken in the same year. Although the *repartimiento* document only includes households that received Native Americans, taken as a microcosm of the population it suggests that approximately one out of every three Spanish husbands had a native wife (Sauer 1966:199–200). Based on the Santo Domingo census, it can be suggested that most, if not all, of these women were probably married to Spaniards of the lowest social strata (Konetzke in Pescatello 1976:139).

The most notable exceptions to poor Spaniards marrying Native Americans were the high-ranking officials who used intermarriage as a form of political alliance. Such marriages took place among Spaniards and Inca *pallas,* Aztec princesses, and Florida *cacicas,* to name a few. Deagan (1985:304–305) has aptly pointed out that while the marriages between Spaniards and Native American elite had the most pronounced impact on the native population through a reorientation of their Native American leadership, those between common Spaniards and Native Americans tended to have a greater impact on Spanish adaptation.

It is assumed that Native American women who had some form of union with Spaniards, whether marital, consensual, or enslavement, inherited the duties and responsibilities traditionally allocated to Spanish women. As discussed above, this included child rearing, food preparation, and home maintenance. However, the influence of Native American women within Spanish colonies extended well beyond the boundaries of the home, as they were often involved in commerce as the primary providers of local foodstuffs to colonial communities. Their inportance may be summarized as follows:

> The activities of these [Native American] women were socially vital on an immediate and material level because indigenous women controlled the preparation and distribution of food to a very large extent. The major exceptions were grain and meat, which were municipal monopolies, and the imported food items found on the shelves of the Spanish-owned stores (Burkett 1978:112).

The material correlates of Native American women on Spanish sites are generally objects associated with household activities and food distribution. The most obvious of these is pottery, since Spaniards often colonized regions with vigorous native ceramic traditions. These would have included ceramic cooking pots, storage vessels, and manioc griddles. Stone implements such as manos, metates, and manioc graters are other aboriginal food-preparation tools typically associated with the presence of Native American women.

Colono-ware (indigenous pottery manufactured in European vessel forms) represents one of the most obvious material adaptations made by native women to accommodate Spaniards. While studies are currently underway to determine the source and distribution of these ceramics among the Florida missions, it is the current working hypothesis that Colono-wares were made by Native American women for use by local Spanish populations (Vernon 1988:76–77). This is based on the fact that, at mission sites such as San Luis, Colono-wares are predominantly found in Spanish contexts (Figure 5).

Although Native American women often strove to be associated with, or married to, Spaniards in order to enhance their social position and that of their children (Burkett 1978:111), it is unclear to what extent their desire to be affiliated with Spaniards may have influenced their taste in personal possessions. Aboriginal burials from several Florida missions clearly indicate the adoption of European material culture in response to religious conversion (Thomas 1988; Vernon and McEwan 1990).

Kathleen Deagan has generated some of the most provocative archaeological evidence of Native American women on Spanish sites. María de la Cruz was a Guale Indian who married Joseph Gallardos, a Spanish (possibly *mestizo*) soldier in St. Augustine in 1728 (Deagan 1983:100). They had three children who were listed on the 1764 property map as the heirs of María de la Cruz. The site was therefore occupied by María de la Cruz and her *mestizo* descendants from 1728 until 1763.

Deagan (1983:123) excavated the de la Cruz site in the early 1970s to understand the process of *mestizaje* (Spanish–Native American intermarriage and descent) and how it influenced material patterning. She found that materials with low visibility related to female tasks, such as food-preparation equipment and basic foodstuffs, were most influenced by Native American culture, while highly visible objects associated with male tasks remained primarily Hispanic. After more than a decade of research on additional sites in St. Augustine, Florida, Deagan has concluded that the material patterning of households inhabited by Native American women and Spanish men is typified by the following characteristics:

FIGURE 5. Colono-ware sherds from Spanish domestic site excavations: *a*, brimmed plate; *b*, bowl with foot ring; *c*, cup or *pocillo* base. (Courtesy of Florida Bureau of Archaeological Research.)

Conservatism in certain areas—most notably, those that were socially visible and associated with male activities— was coupled with Spanish–Indian acculturation and syncretism in other areas, especially those that were less socially visible and female dominated (Deagan 1983:271).

The applicability of this pattern to other domestic sites from Spanish New World colonies has been demonstrated as well (Ewen 1987:231–232). However, researchers are still lacking archaeological data elucidating the role of Native American women in non-domestic settings. The excavation of commercial buildings—stores, markets, and so forth—holds promise as a potentially informative means by which further to understand the various ways Native American women participated in and influenced Spanish colonial society.

African Women

Africans made up a significant servile population in Spain for centuries prior to Columbus' voyages of discovery, and Seville, the city from which all New World trade was regulated, boasted the largest number of slaves in the country (Pike 1967: 345). As a result, Hispanicized African slaves from Seville made up a significant portion of the black slave population during the first decades of New World colonization. In fact, King Ferdinand insisted that slaves being sent to the colonies should be Christian to prevent any "religious taint" (Pike 1967:347). Unlike Native Americans, whom the Spaniards tended to perceive as somewhat naive and childlike (Hann 1988:255), the intellectual prowess of blacks was highly regarded. Some of the first black slaves were actually sent to the colonies as commercial agents for their owners (Pike 1972:184).

However, by the 1530s the native populations of the Caribbean were mostly annihilated, and the increased demand for laborers dictated that slaves be shipped directly from Africa (McAlister 1984: 122). These slaves were gathered from culturally and linguistically diverse regions of West Africa. Consequently, it has been suggested that, at least in some colonial areas, they rapidly became Hispanicized to the extent that Spanish became their common language and they adopted European ways (Lockhart 1968:174).

The role of black women and *mulattas* in the Spanish colonies was probably much like that of Native American women. They were primarily domestic servants, slaves, concubines, and occasionally wives. There is no evidence that free black women were involved in local trade similar to their Native American counterparts. Although African women were far from being the socially preferred companions of male colonists, forced and consensual sexual liaisons as well as intermarriage between Spanish men and African women occurred regularly (Boxer 1975:37). However, this was not completely accepted, as evidenced by a 1678 complaint by the city fathers of Santo Domingo who disapproved that garrison soldiers were marrying black women and *mulattas*. The Crown responded with an order that these soldiers would not be promoted above a particular rank (Boxer 1975:37).

Cultural differences may have been minimal in the earliest decades, since some of these black women were actually born and baptized in Spain. In later decades, slaves imported directly from Africa were preferred over Native American slaves because of their "utter foreignness" which made them dependent and trustworthy in the eyes of their Spanish owners (Lockhart 1968:181).

Despite highly evolved African material traditions, including weaving, basketry, carving, and metallurgy, there was very little, if any, direct importation of African goods to the colonies. However, the recognition that Africans viewed their material traditions as being interconnected with their spiritual world has led many researchers to assume that Africans undoubtedly found ways of perpetuating their belief systems in a variety of social and material expressions in the New World (Herskovits 1966; Bastide 1971). Initial attempts to identify African influences at Spanish colonial settlements are being made at the archaeological investigations at Fort Mose (Marron 1988, 1989). However, African Americanisms that may have survived archaeologically are undeniably difficult to discern.

One study which might shed some light on this issue was undertaken by Greg Smith (1986). Analyzing the non-European ceramics from various contexts at Puerto Real, Smith noted the emergence of a crude ceramic type (Christophe Plain) during the same period that the native population was being decimated and replaced by Africans. He suggested that this new pottery may have been made by Africans (Smith 1986:107). Although it is not known who actually produced Christophe Plain, women were the primary potters in West Africa. As African slaves assumed the place of the Native American population, pottery making may have been one of the few craft specializations that was encouraged by Spaniards to satisfy practical needs and that would have survived under the harshest conditions. It would have been logical to have African women produce pottery, while reserving the men for the most demanding physical tasks.

Conclusions

An examination of women within Spanish colonial society requires a consideration of a number of variables ranging from economics to ethnic affiliation. Spanish women in the New World were often the wives of wealthy men and were mostly restricted to domestic activities. Nonetheless, they had a dynamic impact on their Native American and black domestics—primarily women—whom they integrated into their culture through language instruction, religious indoctrination, and training in European traditions and mores. Spanish women were responsible for maintaining a marked degree of cultural continuity in their homes, and these traditions are thought to be identifiable archaeologically.

For the vast majority of colonial Spanish men, the cost of a Castilian wife was too high, and intermarriage between Spaniards and Native American or black women was not uncommon. In these instances, it appears that these women assumed the roles traditionally held by Spanish women with regard to food preparation, child rearing, and homemaking. Given their active participation in Spanish homes, non-Hispanic women served as the primary agents of acculturation and were mostly responsible for many of the changes identified in Spanish colonial culture. The most common archaeological evidence of intermarriage, concubinage, or servitude often includes the incorporation of large percentages of indigenous foodstuffs and locally produced pottery into households.

Due to the exigencies of Spanish culture, women had a relatively silent place in colonial society. Despite this limitation, they represented a highly influential force. Spanish women lent prestige to their communities, set cultural standards, and, to a lesser degree, exercised financial power. Non-Hispanic women were an equally formidable group. Unlike African and Native American males who generally functioned on the fringes of Spanish society in mining, agricultural, or construction labor gangs, Native American and black women were immediately integrated into Spanish homes. They interacted within the mainstream of colonial society where they adopted and influenced aspects of the world around them. As such, they played an integral role in the development of the colonies and in the formation of Latin American culture.

ACKNOWLEDGMENTS

I would like to thank James J. Miller and the Florida Bureau of Archaeological Research for their continuing support of research at San Luis. Kathleen Deagan, Charles Ewen, Greg Smith, and John Marron generously shared their data from various projects. A special thanks to Robert and Florence Lister for identifying the *juguetes* from San Luis. Finally, I would like to acknowledge Kathleen Deagan, John Hann, Donna Seifert, Richard Vernon, and the *Historical Archaeology* reviewers who read drafts of this paper and offered provocative comments. Although this paper has benefited from the input of many, any errors in interpretation are my own. The research at San Luis has been supported by the State of Florida's Conservation and Recreation Lands (C.A.R.L.) Trust Fund, the Florida Legislature, and by a grant from the National Endowment for the Humanities (RO-21395-87).

REFERENCES

BASTIDE, ROGER
1971 *African Civilisation in the New World,* translated by Peter Green. C. Hurst, London.

BOXER, C. R.
1975 *Women in Iberian Expansion Overseas, 1415–1815.* Oxford University Press, New York.

BOYD, MARK F., HALE G. SMITH, AND JOHN W. GRIFFIN
1951 *Here They Once Stood: The Tragic End of the Apalachee Missions.* University of Florida Press, Gainesville.

BOYD-BOWMAN, PETER
1968 Regional Origins of the Spanish Colonists of America: 1540–1559. *Buffalo Studies* 1968:3–26. State University of New York, Buffalo.
1973 *Patterns of Spanish Emigration to the New World (1493–1580).* Special Studies, Council on International Studies, State University of New York, Buffalo.

BURKETT, ELINOR C.
1978 Indian Women and White Society: The Case of Sixteenth-Century Peru. In *Latin American Women,* edited by Asunción Lavrin, pp. 101–128. Greenwood Press, Westport, Connecticut.

DEAGAN, KATHLEEN
1973 *Mestizaje* in Colonial St. Augustine. *Ethnohistory* 20(1):53–65.
1974 Sex, Status and Role in the *Mestizaje* of Spanish Colonial Florida. Unpublished Ph.D. dissertation, Department of Anthropology, University of Florida, Gainesville.
1983 *Spanish St. Augustine: The Archaeology of a Colonial Creole Community.* Academic Press, New York.
1985 Spanish–Indian Interaction in Sixteenth-Century Florida and Hispaniola. In *Cultures in Contact,* edited by William Fitzhugh, pp. 281–318. Smithsonian Institution Press, Washington, D.C.

DEFOURNEAUX, MARCELIN
1979 *Daily Life in Spain in the Golden Age.* Stanford University Press, Stanford, California.

DILLARD, HEATH
1984 *Daughters of the Reconquest: Women in Castilian Town Society, 1100–1300.* Cambridge University Press, Cambridge.

EWEN, CHARLES R.
1987 From Spaniard to Creole: The Archaeology of Hispanic American Cultural Formation at Puerto Real, Haiti. Unpublished Ph.D. dissertation, Department of Anthropology, University of Florida, Gainesville.
1991 *From Spaniard to Creole: The Archaeology of His-*

panic American Cultural Formation at Puerto Real, Haiti. University of Alabama Press, Tuscaloosa, Alabama.

HANN, JOHN H.
1988   Apalachee: The Land Between the Rivers. University Presses of Florida, Gainesville.

HERSKOVITS, MELVILLE J.
1966   The New World Negro: Selected Papers in Afroamerican Studies, edited by Francis Herskovits. Indiana University Press, Bloomington.

KAMEN, HENRY
1965   The Spanish Inquisition. New American Library, New York.

LAVRIN, ASUNCIÓN
1978   In Search of the Colonial Woman in Mexico: The Seventeenth and Eighteenth Centuries. In Latin American Women, edited by Asunción Lavrin, pp. 23–59. Greenwood Press, Westport, Connecticut.

LOCKHART, JAMES
1968   Spanish Peru, 1532–1560. University of Wisconsin Press, Madison.

LOCKHART, JAMES, AND ENRIQUE OTTE
1976   Letters and People of the Spanish Indies: Sixteenth Century. Cambridge University Press, Cambridge.

MARRON, JOHN
1988   Preliminary Report on Excavations at the Site of Fort Mose, 1987. Ms. on file, Florida Museum of Natural History, Gainesville.
1989   Preliminary Report on Excavations at the Site of Fort Mose, 1988. Ms. on file, Florida Museum of Natural History, Gainesville.

MCALISTER, LYLE
1984   Spain and Portugal in the New World, 1492–1700. University of Minnesota Press, Minneapolis.

MCEWAN, BONNIE G.
1988   An Archaeological Perspective of Sixteenth Century Spanish Life in the Old World and the Americas. Unpublished Ph.D. dissertation, Department of Anthropology, University of Florida, Gainesville.
1989a   Sixteenth Century Spanish Foodways in the Old World and the Americas. In From Chaco to Chaco: Papers in Honor of Robert H. Lister and Florence C. Lister, edited by M. S. Duran and David T. Kirkpatrick. The Archaeological Society of New Mexico No. 15:117–131. Albuquerque.
1989b   Domestic Life at San Luis. Paper presented at the Annual Meeting of the Southeastern Archaeological Conference, Tampa, Florida.

NADER, HELEN
1977   Noble Income in Sixteenth-Century Castile: The Case of the Marquises de Mondéjar, 1480–1580. Economic History Review 30(3):411–428.

PERRY, ELIZABETH
1980   Crime and Society in Early Modern Seville. University Press of New England, Hanover, New Hampshire.

PESCATELLO, ANN M.
1976   Power and Pawn: The Female in Iberian Families, Societies, and Cultures. Greenwood Press, Westport, Connecticut.

PIKE, RUTH
1967   Sevillian Society in the Sixteenth Century: Slaves and Freedmen. Hispanic American Historical Review 47(3):344–359.
1972   Aristocrats and Traders: Sevillian Society in the Sixteenth Century. Cornell University Press, Ithaca, New York.

SAUER, CARL ORTWIN
1966   The Early Spanish Main. University of California Press, Berkeley.

SMITH, GREG C.
1986   A Study of Colono Ware and Non-European Ceramics from Sixteenth-Century Puerto Real, Haiti. Unpublished M.A. thesis, Department of Anthropology, University of Florida, Gainesville.

THOMAS, DAVID HURST
1988   Saints and Soldiers at Santa Catalina: Hispanic Designs for Colonial America. In The Recovery of Meaning in Historical Archaeology, edited by Mark P. Leone and Parker B. Potter, Jr., pp. 73–140. Smithsonian Institution Press, Washington, D.C.

VERNON, RICHARD
1988   17th Century Apalachee Colono-Ware as a Reflection of Demography, Economics, and Acculturation. Historical Archaeology 22(1):76–82.

VERNON, RICHARD, AND BONNIE MCEWAN
1990   Investigations in the Church Complex and Spanish Village at San Luis. Florida Archaeological Reports 18. Bureau of Archaeological Research, Tallahassee.

BONNIE G. MCEWAN
SAN LUIS ARCHAEOLOGICAL AND HISTORIC SITE
2020 MISSION ROAD
TALLAHASSEE, FLORIDA 32304

Heather B. Trigg

The Ties That Bind: Economic and Social Interactions in Early-Colonial New Mexico, A.D. 1598–1680

ABSTRACT

Regional economic transactions in early-colonial New Mexico (1598–1680) have frequently been overlooked as archaeologists and historians focused on large scale, long-distance trade in the imperial economy or smaller scale household production. The few discussions of the regional economy, transactions within the colony, have generally described it as "primitive" and "crude." There was, however, an active regional economy during this period that resulted in movement of goods between colonists' and native peoples' households. The nature of these interactions depended largely on the social identity of the household. In addition, the movement of goods bound households socially as well as economically. Analyzing economic interactions on the regional scale provides a better understanding the colonization process in general because economic restructuring is one way in which empires integrate newly conquered territories. In early-colonial New Mexico, more specifically, economic interactions formed one bridge between the individual household economies and the imperial economy.

Introduction

Early-colonial New Mexico (1598–1680) provides an opportunity for archaeologists to examine contact between cultures. Much of the anthropological research on interactions between the colonized and colonizers has focused on the reactions of the colonized—in the case of New Mexico, the impact of colonization on Pueblo peoples' demography, economies, and social structures. Colonization, nonetheless, is an interaction among different cultures, and investigations of Pueblo cultures reveal only part of a complex system. Examining the culture of Spanish colonists, particularly during the early-colonial period, is, therefore, critical to understanding New Mexico's colonization. Investigations of 17th-century New Mexico have had the benefit of coming from two different disciplines: history and archaeology. Research on this period has been diverse.

Archaeological investigations of the Spanish presence during the early-colonial period have historically emphasized the preservation of Franciscan *conventos* (Bloom 1923; Kidder 1932; Montgomery et al. 1949; Toulouse 1949; Vivian 1964; Smith et al. 1966; Hayes 1974; Hurt 1990), although recent research at the *convento* compound at Pueblo San Marcos has begun to examine more complex issues of social interactions (Thomas 2000). Research into the reaction of native peoples to contact with Europeans has perhaps received the greatest attention in anthropological investigations of the borderlands in general (papers in Thomas 1989, 1991). Nonetheless, there was a substantial population of secular colonists in New Mexico during the early-colonial period.

More recently, the households of these colonists have received attention. Several 17th-century *estancia* (ranch) sites have been excavated (Alexander 1971; D. Snow 1976, 1992b; C. Snow 1977; Scheick 1979; Levine et al. 1985; Pratt and Snow 1988). Frances Levine (1992, 1995) presents a more detailed discussion of excavated early-colonial sites. Since an estimated two-thirds of the 17th-century population of New Mexico lived in rural areas, the character of the rural economy is important, and it has implications for a wide variety of social phenomena, including economic production, social relations, and social organization. Several investigators have developed models of rural household production and relations between colonists' homesteads and Pueblo villages (Simmons 1968; D. Snow 1979, 1983, 1992a; Tainter and Levine 1987; Pratt and Snow 1988; Levine 1992).

During the early-colonial period, Santa Fe was the only *villa* (a settlement with a complete civil government) in the colony. Seventeenth-century deposits from several areas in the *villa* have been identified (C. Snow 1974; Post and Snow 1982; Pratt and Snow 1988; D. Snow 1989, 1990; Tigges 1990, 1992; Willmer 1990; Wiseman 1992; Martinez 1994; Snow and Bowen 1995). These deposits exist primarily under and around the Palace of the Governors (the former *casas reales*), the site of the 17th-century *cienega* to the north and east of the Palace of the Governors, and near the present cathedral. Other locations in Santa Fe have been examined, but these areas revealed scanty evidence of the 17th-century occupation or presented 17th-century deposits that were thoroughly mixed with later 18th- and 19th-century materials (Pratt and Snow 1988). Other research has focused on identifying the location and architecture of various landmarks—the Plaza, Palace of the Governors, and the 17th-century parish church (C. Snow 1974; Ellis 1976). Many of the excavations of early colonial sites have been conducted under limitations imposed by contracts (Levine 1992).

Historians who work specifically on early-colonial New Mexico have almost exclusively dealt with the colonists' activities. Largely due to the scope of information presented in surviving 17th-century documents, many have focused on the political history and the activities of New Mexico's elites, the governors and Franciscan friars, and on long-distance trade (Scholes 1928, 1929, 1930, 1935a, 1935b, 1936, 1937, 1938, 1975; Hackett 1937; Hodge et al. 1945; Hammond and Rey 1953; Cutter 1986; Weber 1992; Ivey 1993). Both historians and anthropologists working on much longer-term trends have also examined other issues such as the relations between native peoples and colonists and the impact of colonization on native peoples (John 1975; Kessell 1979; Spicer 1981; Hall 1989; Gutiérrez 1991; Levine 1999).

Archaeologists and historians have begun to bridge the gap between disciplines, and recent investigations, such as those of the Camino Real (Palmer 1993; Palmer and Fosberg 1999), are providing detailed information about long-distance movement of goods into and out of New Mexico. These data hint at the types of goods, ceramics, textiles, furniture, foods, and luxuries that may have been circulating in the colony's regional economy (Bakker 1999; Fournier 1999; Pierce and Snow 1999; Winter 1999). In the absence of contracts, inventories, and wills, such data may provide our best information on goods such as textiles and chocolate that do not survive in the archaeological record. Nevertheless, the disparity in interests and research agendas has led to gaps in our understanding of the social processes involved in the colonization of New Mexico. With archaeologists looking at Spanish households and Pueblos and historians at elite activities, middle-level economic transactions

consisting of the movement of commodities among people *within* the colony, particularly among the Spanish colonists, have largely been overlooked. Although the term "regional" in the colonial period can be applied to a variety of geographic scales from smaller areas within the colony to the whole of New Spain, "regional economy" is used to denote economic transactions within the colony.

Beginning in the 1920s, France Scholes, known in historical circles as *the* authority for this era, laid the foundation for future historical and archaeological research (Broughton 1993). Scholes wrote that New Mexico during the early-colonial period was "characterized by a roughness, a lack of luxury and refinement, a crudeness, and a striking degree of ignorance" (Scholes 1935a:99; C. Snow [1993] presents an alternative picture). Of the economy, Scholes stated, "economic life of the province was based on agriculture, stock raising, and a primitive commerce," and "was mere barter." "Intra-provincial commerce was necessarily limited to the exchange of a few products" (Scholes 1935a:105, 109). Although the archaeological and documentary evidence do indicate that colonists were not using coins to conduct business and, thus, did exchange only commodities, Scholes's portrayal minimizes the complexity of the social interactions that shaped and were shaped by economic activity during this period. He wrote this in the 1930s, but the characterization continues to influence research today (Simmons 1968; D. Snow 1993). Boyd Pratt and David Snow (1988) have offered one of the few discussions of regional exchange suggesting that Santa Fe was not a market-place for the colony except for goods imported by the governors, and James Ivey (1994) discusses the exchange of goods between *conventos* and Pueblo villages and between colonists and *conventos* during the famines of the late 1660s and 1670s. It is clear, however, that economic transactions involving the transfer of commodities among households in 17th-century New Mexico went beyond mere barter.

One only has to look at the enormous quantity of Pueblo sherds at any Spanish site to get a feel for the importance of native peoples to the colonists' lives and their contribution to the colonial economy. Economic factors within Pueblo villages affecting pottery production also, no doubt, played a role in the interactions between Pueblo people and colonists. The internal economies of New Mexico's native communities played an important part in the relations between native peoples and Spanish colonists. This paper, however, focuses attention on the economic transactions among New Mexico's colonists, particularly those transactions guided by social obligations. The activities of native peoples are discussed only in relation to their direct participation in the economy of Spanish colonists.

Spanish Colonists' Household Economies

Archaeological and documentary evidence indicate that colonists' households during the early-colonial period produced and consumed many of the same items. Corrals have been located on a majority of 17th-century ranch sites, indicating that most households were involved in the production of livestock. Since spindle whorls have been recovered from all Spanish sites, it can also be concluded that at least yarn production, if not textile production, was widespread. Paleoethno-botanical remains from two 17th-century *estancias* and from 17th-century deposits in Santa Fe indicate that colonists were eating wheat and other European crops such as peas, lentils, watermelon, muskmelons, peaches, and apricots (Ford n.d.; Trigg 1999). Although colonists also consumed native foods such as maize and goosefoot seeds (*Chenopodium* sp.), the faunal and botanical remains and documents indicate a strong preference for domestic animal meat and Old World crops (Alexander 1971; Harris 1973; Snow and Bowen 1995).

All households cooked with Pueblo style *comales* (griddles or cooking stones), used predominantly Pueblo pottery, and acquired small amounts of imported goods such as majolica ceramics, metal, and glass (Moore et al. n.d.; Tichy 1939; Alexander 1971; D. Snow 1971, 1973; C. Snow 1977). Documents tell us that colonists acted as guards, blacksmiths, and syndics (Scholes 1935b, 1975; Chávez 1992) and were compensated for their services, although none of these constituted full-time specialization. The broad spectrum of production and lack of occupational specialization suggests that colonists produced many of the subsistence goods they needed. This conclusion has contributed to a false sense of economic isolation evident in many portrayals of early-colonial New Mexico and ulti-

mately, perhaps, the apparent lack of scholarly interest in regional economic activities.

Regional Economic Interactions

Households in early-colonial New Mexico probably bartered freely among each other, perhaps with the nearest neighbor or for the best price or product. Other transactions occurred outside the barter economy but, nevertheless, ensured the movement of commodities among colonists and between colonists and native peoples. Socially mandated exchanges took place, usually among specific social groups. For example, the obligation of tithing required the transfer of commodities from colonists to clergy, but obviously not from clergy to colonists, among colonists, or between colonists and governors. Since the nature of many interactions depended on the social identity of the individuals involved, different rules can be expected to be found acting upon different groups. Social identity is often fluid, particularly so in colonial contexts, but distinct groups, Pueblo or Plains peoples, the clergy, governors, *encomenderos*, and average citizens were identified by 17th-century writers and serve to structure the discussion of the social mechanisms of exchange.

Colonists' Interactions with Native Peoples

Encomenderos' Interactions

Encomenderos were a small group of colonists who were allowed to collect tribute, *encomienda*, from conquered native peoples in exchange for past service, future military support, or protection and conversion of the native peoples "entrusted" to them. It is perhaps the best-studied economic institution in colonial Spanish America and has its roots in the earlier Spanish *Reconquista* when the Moors were driven from Spain. During the early years of New World colonization, abuses of this system occurred—levels of tribute exacted were onerous, and the tribute obligation was at times converted to forced labor (Gibson 1966; Bakewell 1997). Problems in Mexico led to the regulation of this institution, and its implementation in New Mexico concerned the Spanish Crown (D. Snow 1983). In his contract to colonize New Mexico, Governor Juan de

Oñate was specifically instructed to ensure that *encomienda* payments would not be converted to labor service, as they had been earlier (Hammond and Rey 1953:511). Treatment of native peoples continued to worry Spanish government officials, for the viceroy reiterated these warnings to New Mexico's second governor, Peralta, and requested reports from subsequent officials and the clergy (Hackett 1937:119).

As it was implemented in New Mexico, *encomenderos* were appointed at the discretion of the governor, and the *encomienda* was inherited from father to son for "three lives" or three generations (D. Snow 1983). Only villages that had been converted to Christianity could be assigned. In New Mexico, this meant Pueblo peoples but not Apaches or Navajos. The contract between Governor Oñate and the viceroy for the colonization of New Mexico indicated that tribute would be paid in "products of the land" (Hammond and Rey 1953:593), but other documents are more specific. In 1639, former governor Martínez de Baeza in his official report to the viceroy stated, "Each Indian repairs once a year to his *encomendero* with a *fanega* [55.5 liters] of maize, which is worth four *reales* [eight *reales* equal one silver peso], one cotton blanket a *vara* [0.8359 m] and a half square which is valued at one peso, or, in lieu thereof, a raw buffalo hide or deer skin, either of which has the same value" (Hackett 1937:120). Fray Juan de Prada indicated that *encomienda* payments were given as one *fanega* of maize and cotton cloth "six palms square" (Hackett 1937:110). Although in 1639 Governor Baeza indicated that payments were made once a year, by the mid-1600s it may have been collected twice each year (D. Snow 1983).

In return for the tribute payments, the Pueblos were to receive intangible "benefits" from being held in encomienda. For example, encomenderos were obligated to protect the native peoples and to ensure that they were Christianized (Gibson 1966:49; Bakewell 1997:80). The flow of commodities between encomenderos and native peoples, however, was not reciprocal, and, in reality, encomenderos generally received unilateral benefit from this relationship.

It is possible that at first the tribute demands were not onerous, but the encomenderos' demands on individual families become critically burdensome when famines and diseases reduced the Pueblo population and, as a consequence, the

production of maize and cotton cloth (D. Snow 1983). The maize and cloth received from the Pueblos, however, were invaluable to the support of the colony. Encomenderos, by virtue of having a steady supply of commodities, probably attained additional prestige by redistributing subsistence goods to others (D. Snow 1983).

Encomienda was a formal economic institution and was strictly regulated, but it was also modified, both legally and illegally, to adjust to local conditions. In 1639, Fray Juan de Prada indicated that tribute was collected from each household in each village (Hackett 1937:110). In the early 1640s, however, Governor Pacheco attempted to increase the amount of tribute by modifying the tradition and collecting encomienda from each individual rather than each household (Scholes 1937:91). The clergy, who argued that the payments were already onerous, thwarted the governor's efforts.

Throughout the early-colonial period in New Spain, the Spanish government modified earlier laws in an attempt to stem encomenderos' abuses of the system. The government specifically forbade the conversion of encomienda debts to labor obligations, but even in 17th-century New Mexico, such violations did occur. Laws also governed the location of encomenderos' ranches in relation to Pueblo villages to prevent encroachment on Pueblo lands and damage to their fields by colonists' livestock (Ivey 1992). One law forbade encomenderos from building their *estancias* too close to Pueblo villages (Scholes 1935a) or pasturing their herds within three leagues (Bloom 1928; Ivey 1992). While little quantitative data exists, documents indicate that, like other laws regulating encomienda, these laws were also ignored. In some instances these transgressions were addressed. The activities of encomendero Antonio de Salas provide a case in point. Salas was brought to trial both for converting tribute payments to forced labor and for locating his *estancia* too near the Pueblo village of Pojoaque (Scholes 1937). He stated that he "allowed" the people of Pojoaque to provide labor to his household in lieu of their tribute payments, suggesting that such proximity facilitated the interaction between the native peoples who worked for him and his household (Scholes 1937:388). He also argued that the royal laws governing the placement of *estancias* were justifiable in Mexico, but the realities of life in

New Mexico required more flexibility in this regard. The encomendero's behavior, however, generated such complaints that Governor López denied Salas's claim and ordered his *estancia* to be destroyed.

The encomienda system was only one mechanism that facilitated the exchange between colonists and Pueblo peoples. It is unique in that the payments involved only a certain segment of the Spanish population, limited by law to 35 individuals, and a certain segment of native peoples, the Pueblos. Encomienda is different from other economic transactions in that Pueblo peoples had no legal expectation of reciprocity and that the items expected by the Spanish were supposed to be limited to maize, cloth, or hides. Interactions between encomenderos and native peoples, however, were not limited to encomienda but would potentially have included other types of interactions.

Native Peoples' Interactions with Colonists

Since the colonists needed more labor than they controlled within their own households, Pueblo peoples were compelled by law to work for the Spanish. This contributed to the colonists' household production, but it also resulted in the movement of commodities from colonists to native peoples because the colonists were obligated to pay for the labor. Compensation for Pueblo peoples' work and the types of activities that they could be compelled to do were also governed by Spanish laws, but documents suggest that colonists were not scrupulous in paying their native laborers. (Of course, the texts provide only part of the picture, and this problem is particularly acute with documents from this period in New Mexico's history. Since there is generally a lack of diaries, letters, or other personal documents, those items that remain often deal with disagreements between individuals, for example, instances in which agreements were not honored. Primarily, there is evidence of the colonists' unscrupulous behavior toward native peoples, but not examples of those cases in which wages were indeed paid.) Pueblo peoples had recourse to several legal avenues, and some, for example, argued their cases before the governor or *alcaldes mayores* in an attempt to force payment (Scholes 1935a; Cutter 1986). Texts do not specify the commodities colonists paid as wages, but they probably consisted of the colonists' household productions, such as livestock, textiles, or crops, or, during the early years of the colony, of goods specifically brought to New Mexico for trade (Hammond and Rey 1953; C. Snow 1993; Pierce and Snow 1999).

It is known that colonists depended upon native peoples for household labor, but they also procured commodities produced by native peoples outside the context of colonists' households. These included maize, cotton *mantas* (blankets or cloth), ceramics, piñon nuts, salt, as well as bison, antelope, and deer hides (and, perhaps, the meat from these animals).

The precise extent to which colonists depended upon native peoples for labor or commodities is not clear because current archaeological and textual data are insufficient to allow determination of the quantity of most goods exchanged. Wage labor, however, must have been lucrative to some, for one colonist testified that don Pedro Durán y Chávez was "planting and baking for sale ... always having many conveniences and living in ease, being one of those who employed many Indians in his service" (Hackett and Shelby 1942[2]:173).

Currently, ceramics provide the only readily quantifiable indicator of the colonists' dependence on the Pueblos. It is interesting, and perhaps telling, that there is no discussion of ceramic production and exchange in 17th-century New Mexico's documentary record, but archaeological evidence indicates that colonists relied almost exclusively on Pueblo people for domestic pottery. Sherds usually constitute the most numerous class of artifacts recovered from early-colonial sites. From 96% to more than 99% of ceramics recovered from 17th-century Spanish estancias were produced by the Pueblo peoples (Table 1). Likewise, indigenous ceramics were by far (greater than 95%) the most numerous types of pottery recovered from LA 54,000, a 17th-century deposit in historic downtown Santa Fe (Wiseman 1992).

It was probably through barter (or outright theft) that colonists acquired these ceramics, for texts do not specify them as part of encomienda payments. Nor are they items typically used as units of exchange, such as wheat, maize, livestock, and cotton *mantas*. The earliest record of colonists obtaining ceramics from Pueblo peoples is a post-reconquest document stating that native

TABLE 1
CERAMICS FROM RURAL *ESTANCIAS*

Site	Indigenous		Imported		
	Rio Grande % (n)	Hopi/Zuni % (n)	Majolica % (n)	Porcelain % (n)	Native Mexican % (n)
LA 591	99% (8,909)	0.7% (63)	>1%	0	0.4% (39)
LA 34	96% (575)	n.d.	3.4% (20)	0	0.001% (1)
LA 20,000	<99% (3,521)	0.08% (3)	0.3% (9)	0	0
LA 326	n.d.	n.d.	present	n.d.	n.d.
LA 4955	n.d.	present	present	n.d.	n.d.
LA 9142	97% (691)	2.8% (20)	0.3% (2)	.1% (1)	0

Note. Data on LA 591 from D. Snow 1992a; data on LA 34 and LA 9142 from Moore et al. n.d.; data on LA 326 and LA 4955 from D. Snow n.d.; data from LA 20,000 from Trigg 1999.

peoples came to Santa Fe to sell their pottery (D. Snow 1983). In a letter to the viceroy, Fray Pedro Serrano wrote, "These *alcaldes* [probably an *alcalde* mayor, a district judge who also collected encomienda payments] do not visit their pueblos except ... to barter with the Indians, or to gather pots, plates, jars, jugs" (Hackett 1937:486; D. Snow 1983). Although there is not written evidence from the pre-rebellion era, there are indications of exchange of other commodities between colonists and Pueblo peoples for Fray Miguel de Sacristán asserted that Pueblo peoples came to the villa (Hackett 1937: 149). Since Santa Fe was not a strong economic center of the colony (Pratt and Snow 1988) and colonists' estancias were frequently located near Pueblo villages, it is likely that exchange may also have taken place at colonists' households or in the Pueblo villages.

Colonists interacted not only with Pueblo villagers but also with Navajos and especially Plains people. Documents describe some of the colonists' travels to the Plains specifically for trade. In one case before the Holy Inquisition, colonist Nicholas de Aguilar stated that he had, "gone among the heathen Indians to trade" (Hackett 1937:140). In a second document, Captain Diego Romero and other colonists "went to buy antelope skins and buckskins for the governor" (Hackett 1937:156).

The items that colonists used for barter with native peoples are uncertain but may have included Spanish foodstuffs such as livestock, grains, fruits, seed stock, or metal tools. The Ulloa and Salazar inspections of the first coloniz-

ing expeditions indicated that certain items such as combs, knives, sewing equipment, clothing, beads, jewelry, flutes, and mirrors were brought specifically for trade with native peoples (Hammond and Rey 1953:135–136; C. Snow 1993; Pierce and Snow 1999). Foods or the seeds to grow Old World crops may also have been exchanged, and some documents describe instances in which Pueblo people incorporated some introduced foods into their practices. By 1660, Fray García de San Francisco testified, "And the Indians of the neighboring pueblos gathered in the *villa*, and they dressed themselves in their abominable masks in a hall of the palace, and performed the dances, offering to the devil watermelons and other things" (Hackett 1937:156). The speed with which certain Spanish foods such as watermelons and wheat entered the Pueblo peoples' diets also suggests that the fruits or seeds were also desired commodities (Lopinot 1988). It seems clear from both the documents and archaeological data that a substantial amount of commerce occurred between the colonists and the native peoples, and that one mechanism through which the colonists obtained goods was barter or purchase. This mechanism contrasts sharply with encomienda because it is likely that barter or purchase took place as often as desired and with whatever commodities were needed, and, presumably, the exchange was perceived as mutually profitable.

Yet another mechanism allowed the movement of goods between colonists and native peoples. Legal judgments often resulted in the transfer of commodities from colonists to Pueblo peoples because fines were paid in commodities. For example, Nicolás de Aguilar was accused of raping a Pueblo woman, and in compensation, the governor ordered him to pay her a cow (Hackett 1937:185). In a similar ruling, Governor Peralta fined colonist Asencio de Archuleta 50 *mantas* and 50 *fanegas* of maize for his offenses against native peoples (Scholes 1936:48).

Governors' Interactions with Native Peoples

Just as colonists relied upon native labor, New Mexico's governors also hired them to produce and haul commodities. Such activity is suggested in the records of Governor López's *residencia*, the official review of an outgoing governor's tenure. The *protector de indios*, the official charged with handling native peoples' legal affairs, represented hundreds of aggrieved Native Americans who charged that the governor had not paid them for their work or commodities (Cutter 1986). Several native women, both Pueblo and Apache, charged that he owed them for making clothing and needlework. Others alleged that they had not been paid for transporting commodities (piñon nuts, salt, and firewood) or constructing wagons, and the Native Americans, in some cases, demanded compensation, often in the hundreds of pesos. Caution should be used with accepting these allegations wholesale because they were leveled in the course of the governor's *residencia* when many people took the opportunity to avenge perceived insults (Cutter 1986). Nevertheless, clergymen, although not impartial in these proceedings, echoed charges that the governor used native peoples to collect salt and piñon nuts and transport them and other commodities to Parral (Hackett 1937:188).

Other activities had economic consequences for native peoples. As agents of the Spanish Crown, the governors had the power to determine policies, some of which directly regulated economic interactions between native peoples and Spaniards. It was the governor who set the rates that colonists and clergy paid for wages. For example, in 1620, Pueblo laborers were to be paid half a *real* per day and provided with food or one *real* if not provided with food. During his tenure in the 1660s, Governor López raised the wage to one *real* per day and food because Pueblo people were not willing to work. Although wages may not always have been paid, wage labor as a social mechanism was potentially beneficial to both native people and colonists.

Other activities were merely exploitative. Governors López, Eulate, Mora, and Rosas were accused of making expeditions to the Plains solely for the purpose of taking captives for the slave trade (Scholes 1936; Hackett 1937). Slaves were commonly exported to mining towns in northern Mexico (Brugge 1999), but it is known that some captive Apache men and women were sold to New Mexico's colonists in Santa Fe because Apache servants were among those listed as household members in the roll call of survivors of the Pueblo Rebellion (Hackett and Shelby 1942). The magnitude of the slave trade within New Mexico is not known for certain, but it was sufficiently common to cause concern among the leaders of the Pueblo Rebellion in 1680. Among their demands during the siege of Santa Fe was the release of "all Apache men and women whom the Spaniards had captured in war ... as some Apaches who were among them were asking for them" (Hackett and Shelby 1942[1]:99).

As agents of the Crown, governors and *alcaldes mayores* adjudicated complaints among the Pueblo peoples and between the colonists and Pueblo peoples. As some of the examples discussed above illustrate, legal judgments resulted in fines or imprisonment. Although fines were given a monetary value, they were paid in commodities, facilitating the transfer of goods among native peoples and colonists, governors, and clergy. Some judgments did not require the exchange of goods nor were they necessarily beneficial to the native peoples, but they, nonetheless, had economic consequences. In one of the colony's earliest legal judgments, Governor Oñate ordered that the men and women of Acoma serve in colonists' households for 25 years as punishment for their revolt in 1599. The tradition of forced servitude as punishment continued throughout the early-colonial period. In 1659, Juan Zuñi and a compatriot stole goods from the *casas reales*, the government offices and home of the governor, and Governor Manso sentenced Zuñi to 10 years of forced labor for the crime (Cutter 1986).

Clergy's Interactions with Native Peoples

Like the secular colonists, New Mexico's clergy relied heavily on Pueblo peoples for household production, but Pueblo peoples' labor at the *conventos* presents a complex web of interactions that involved the governors, encomenderos, priests, and Pueblo people. Pueblo people who worked for the clergy were exempt from tribute demands and, thus, were not required to make encomienda payments to the encomenderos, which made working for the clergy attractive. The governors not only had the authority to assign encomiendas but also the power to regulate the number of Pueblo people working for the priests. Documents indicate that the number of people serving in *convento* households ranged from 10 to 40 until the mid-1600s when Governor López enacted legislation limiting such labor to 2 individuals. All other Pueblo peoples serving at the mission were subject to tribute demands, and Pueblo people working for the clergy, above the two allotted, were to be paid as wage laborers.

Governor López suggested that prior to 1659 the clergy compensated a day's labor with at most an iron awl, but after his law was enacted, the clergy were required to pay for labor with food, maize, or wool. Just as colonists and governors did not pay wages, documents suggest that the clergy were also less than conscientious about paying their laborers. For example, much to the displeasure of the Franciscans, Governor López ordered Fray Guevara and Fray Moreno to pay the native peoples of Galisteo and Isleta Pueblos the livestock that the villagers claimed were owed them for wages. In testimony before the Inquisition, colonist Miguel de Noriega stated that the governor "ordered Father Fray Miguel de Guevara to pay to certain Indians not only the sheep which they demanded before him, but others as well which he still owed" (Hackett 1937:180).

Texts also recount barter between the friars and native peoples. In their testimony to the Inquisition, the friars stated, "the religious receive a few antelope skins in exchange for sustenance or for the crop" (Hackett 1937: 192). Archaeological evidence also indicates a good deal of commerce between the priests and inhabitants of the Pueblos. Like other early-colonial Spanish sites in New Mexico,

Pueblo ceramics dominate the assemblage at all *convento* sites, and like other Spaniards, the clergy probably obtained them directly by barter or indirectly as containers for bartered goods. Other archaeological data suggest that native peoples provided the clergy with a range of items. Faunal remains from the *conventos* indicate that the friars obtained meat from bison, antelope, deer, and other nondomesticated animals (Toulouse 1949; Snow and Bowen 1995). Documents tell of Plains peoples coming to Pueblo villages such as Pecos and Humanas to trade hides and, in some cases, their children for food. In 1659, the friars proudly stated:

> Some of them [Plains peoples] came with their own children … and offered them to the religious for a little meat or flour. The evangelical ministers, who saw a great opportunity in the temporal and spiritual unhappiness of those souls, did not hesitate to give all they had for the opportunity to catechise them and make them Christians … giving them broken chalices and even richer treasure … . In this manner … the religious rescued some boys and girls from the empire of the devil, and they now have them as gentle, peaceable Christians (Hackett 1937:192).

Pueblo people also gathered piñon nuts for the priests (Hackett 1937:192). Documentary evidence and archaeological data from the Pueblo villages associated with *conventos* suggest some commodities that Pueblo peoples received in exchange. These included majolica and metal (Bloom 1923; Kidder 1932; Hackett 1937:192; Tichy 1939; Wait and McKenna 1990), but perishable goods for which there is no direct evidence, such as textiles and foods, may also have been traded.

The clergy provided subsistence goods, such as food and textiles to native peoples, in particular the poor of the villages (Ivey 1994). Fray Benavides (Hodge et al. 1945:101) stated, "At mealtime, the poor people in the pueblo who are not ill come to the porter's lodge, where the cooks of the convent have sufficient food ready … food for the sick is sent to their homes." In a statement to the Holy Inquisition in 1659, the clergy declared that they supplied large quantities of maize and wheat (Hackett 1937:191). In the late 1660s and 1670s, New Mexico was hit by a series of famines, and during this period the friars provided additional aid to the Pueblo peoples (Ivey 1994). Benavides's statement suggests that the redistribution of goods was commonplace, and Ivey (1994:83) states that during the famines, "the average amounts distributed in each pueblo were approximately 72 bushels of all grains and beans, 3 cows, 10 sheep, and 20 fleeces of wool per month." In addition to donations of food and textiles, the friars also gave Pueblo families who worked on *convento* lands a portion of the harvest they produced (Ivey 1994:83). Although the friars controlled the distribution of food and textiles, the interactions between clergy and Pueblo people involved the colonists because the sources of these goods were tithes that the clergy collected from colonists as well as the *conventos'* own domestic production (Hackett 1937:102).

Economic Interactions among Colonists

Commerce within New Mexico's 17th-century Spanish community has received little attention (Pratt and Snow 1988), but archaeological evidence and textual data provide indications that regional exchange among colonists was important for meeting subsistence needs and as a social necessity. The patchy distribution of natural resources such as arable land, water for irrigation, salt, piñon nuts, and selenite (a mineral used for whitewash, window panes, and to whiten wool) may have made these items unavailable to some colonists. Moreover, the documentary record indicates that some individuals engaged specialized occupations such as the military armorer, blacksmith (or silversmith) working in Santa Fe, the governor's barber, and the baker in Bernalillo (Scholes 1935a, 1975; Hackett 1937: 72; Hackett and Shelby 1942[2]:173; D. Snow 1993). Subsistence goods and services that were controlled by a limited number of people may have made it necessary for households to exchange needed or desired commodities. Goods such as wheat or majolica ceramics specifically were not a physical necessity but were important to the social identity of the Spanish colonists (D. Snow 1993; Trigg 1999) and, thus, would also have been the objects of exchange.

Although the need for critical or desired goods would have encouraged barter, social demands made the circulation of commodities among colonists mandatory. Inheritance allowed for the movement of commodities within extended families. According to the ideal, legitimate children shared equally in the family's wealth (Gutiérrez 1991:230), but the degree to which actual practice fit the ideal depended on the family's standing in the community. In an attempt to keep the wealth concentrated, higher status families with large land holdings allowed the eldest son to inherit the land (Gutiérrez 1991), although lower status families may have more closely followed the law.

Evidence from 18th-century New Mexico indicates that complex social and financial arrangements surrounded betrothals and marriages. These rituals linked households socially but were also economic contracts that provided an opportunity for movement of goods. More specifically, rituals associated with marriage required the bride and groom's families to exchange presents and contribute to the new household.

Although no written information has been found about betrothal ceremonies from 17th-century New Mexico, early 20th-century New Mexican practices are similar to those in Spain, which suggests to folklorist Aurelio Espinosa (1985) that New Mexico's ceremonies are old, dating to the early-colonial period. In some instances, textual sources from 18th-century New Mexico confirm the details (Gutiérrez 1991). Marriage rites consisted of obtaining consent of the parents, making formal agreements before the parish priest, feasting, dancing, and exchanging presents (Espinosa 1985). Although the names are different (betrothals in Spain are called *toma de los dichos* and in New Mexico *prendorios*), they both consist of the *pedir de la novia* (or *pedir de la mano* according to Gutiérrez 1991), a ritualized request for the bride during a meeting between the families. Among elites a formal letter, which outlined the property that the groom would bring to the marriage (Gutiérrez 1991:260), accompanied this visit. If the bride and her family agreed to the marriage, the groom presented the bride with a *donas*, a wooden chest containing the trousseau. Eighteenth-century New Mexican trousseaus consisted of clothing, jewelry, household goods, occasionally money and cloth for the wedding dress. Men of wealthier families traveled to Chihuahua, Mexico, to purchase these goods (Gutiérrez 1991). The value of the trousseau, in theory, mirrored the wealth and status of the bride. As historian Ramon Gutiérrez (1991: 262) wrote, "To contemplate marriage without being able to present the bride with an appropriate trousseau was considered inappropriate and shameless." The transfer of goods was of such importance that, in some cases, the wealth needed created a hardship that delayed some marriages.

After receiving the trousseau, the bride's family reciprocated, presenting the groom with a dowry (Espinosa 1985; Gutiérrez 1991). Although there are no such records for the early-colonial period, dowries in Mexico and post-revolt New Mexico consisted of household products such as linens and tableware or livestock (Gutiérrez 1991). Finally, 18th-century documents also indicate that affluent men would present up to an additional 10% of their wealth (called *arras*) to their wives (Gutiérrez 1991: 263). In less wealthy families, this economic exchange occurred but only in ritualized form. In this case, "the fee an individual paid the local priest for a marriage often included the rental of a small pouch containing thirteen gold or silver coins which were used during the rite to symbolize the bride's endowment with *arras*" (Gutiérrez 1991:263).

Marrying well was of great importance to the colonists for it contributed to a household's standing within the community, particularly among higher status families. Moreover, a woman's dowry was part and parcel of her prospects for marriage. In his exploration of colonial New Mexico's perceptions and mores surrounding sexual activity, Gutiérrez (1991) argued that a woman's chastity was important for finding a suitable husband. A woman who was not a virgin was not highly sought after, but a suitor could be lured by a large dowry. Since providing for such a dowry produced a strain on the family's resources, the male members of Hispanic families closely guarded women's behavior (Gutiérrez 1991).

Baptisms provided another opportunity to link families economically and socially and resulted in the transfer of goods from one household to another. Again, rituals surrounding this rite had economic components.

> The *padrino* and *madrina* (godfather and godmother) take the *ahijado* (god-child-to-be) to church for the religious ceremony. As they leave the church, the children of the village wait outside to receive gifts of small coins. Both in Spain and New Mexico the *padrino* usually is most generous with his money. A *padrino* who does not give anything would disgrace the occasion (Espinosa 1985:73).

Whether these ceremonies accompanied baptisms in 17th-century New Mexico is not known, and it is clear from the archaeological and documentary record that coins were not distributed during this period. Yet there are similarities between peninsular Spanish and New Mexican Spanish ceremonies. In both Spain and New Mexico, the *madrina* sings to the child's mother, "Here I return to you your child. He (or she) was a Moor (meaning pagan) when I took him with me, and now he (or she) is a Christian" (Espinosa 1985:73). The reference to the unbaptized child as a Moor argues for an ancient root for parts of this ritual, and 17th-century New Mexican documents indicate that priests performed baptisms and *padrinos* did participate. Governor Peñalosa wrote to the custodian, "I come for the purpose of having my goddaughter confirmed, and am awaiting the god-parents ...." (Hackett 1937:239), and in a separate case, Governor Juan Manso acted as a godfather (Hackett 1937:195).

Compadrazgo formed a bond between households that included a social and economic relationship between both the *compadres* and the child and between the *compadres* and the child's parents. Through the baptismal ceremony, the parents and godparents are "spiritually related, just like near relatives, and ... bear one another's burdens" (Espinosa 1985:73), and the *padrino* is expected to treat the *ahijado* as his own child. Such obligations may have included economic support and the exchange of commodities.

Clergy's Interactions with Colonists

There was considerable economic interaction between the Franciscan clergy and colonists in early-colonial New Mexico. Colonists (including governors and encomenderos) were expected to tithe, giving the Franciscans a portion of products they produced. In 1638, Fray Juan de Prada indicated that tithes were only paid in grain because the colonists did not have sufficient numbers of cattle (Hackett 1937:112), although New Mexico's Governor Baeza recorded that the clergy were also paid in wheat, maize, livestock, animal hides (deer or bison), or cotton blankets (Hackett 1937:120). Although all colonists were expected to contribute tithes, the Franciscan prelate alone used his discretion in disposing of the goods. According to Fray Prada, tithes were distributed among the *conventos* and to the poor colonists of Santa Fe (Ivey 1994). He stated, "By his order [the prelate's] it is distributed to some convents that are situated in sterile places and lack water—for which reason wheat cannot be sown in their districts" (Hackett 1937:112). In a letter to the Holy Inquisition, other friars asserted that they "succored the Spaniards ... dividing among them over five hundred *fanegas* of wheat and corn which had been received in the tithe" (Hackett 1937:191). During times of famine, colonists gave additional supplies to the priests (Ivey 1994:85). While some goods received in tithe were redistributed among the colonists, it appears that a considerable portion went to support the *conventos*. For example, the priests controlled sufficient quantities of foods—at the same time they distributed the 500 *fanegas* of grain to the Spanish colonists, they had "in the more remote conversions ... of Xongopavi and Oraibi [Hopi villages in Arizona] distributed as many more *fanegas*, the entire pueblos being thus supported in time of famine" (Hackett 1937:191).

There were other mechanisms that allowed the Catholic Church to obtain commodities from the colonists. The church sold indulgences, and bulls issued by the Santa Cruzada, a religious tribunal, ordered colonists to pay alms for the support of the conversion efforts (Hackett 1937: 6-8). The proceeds from these alms were to be collected and returned to Mexico, but in 1639 in its report to the viceroy, the *cabildo* (the town council) of Santa Fe expressed doubts that all of the commodities gathered by the clergy were necessary or were sent to Mexico as ordered (Hackett 1937:68). Nevertheless, if the alms were not paid, the religious exercised powers granted by the Church. Fray Juan de Góngora warned that all colonists who owed the Santa Cruzada had less than a month to pay or they would be excommunicated (Hackett 1937:48–49). While the documents do not indicate whether Fray Góngora made good on his threats of excommunication, the *cabildo* also claimed that the friars confiscated the property, namely the livestock, of several colonists who were in arrears.

There is little mention in the documents to indicate that the clergy were paid for religious services such as officiating at baptisms, marriages, and funerals, although one case suggests that this did happen. In this instance, an adulter-ous affair led to the birth of a child, and Fray Miguel Sacristán was accused of presiding at the burial of a rag doll to hide the existence of the child from the cuckolded husband. Colonists alleged that the child was smuggled into Mexico to be reared there, but the husband believed that a child had indeed been buried. When the case was brought to trial before religious authorities, the friar's superior spoke in the defense of Fray Sacristán and stated, "Why should he have asked for pay, if what he buried was nothing but a lot of rags?" (Hackett 1937:228). This statement suggests that the friars did ask for payment for religious services.

In addition to being paid for officiating at baptisms, marriages, and funerals, the Franciscan Order received goods from colonists for religious services through a *cofradía*. Nuestra Senora del Rosaria La Conquistadora was an association made up of both secular and religious people of the colony, and its sole purpose was the glorification of the Virgin Mary. Dues paid and items donated to the confraternity were not given directly to the Church (Chávez 1950), but the Church did benefit economically because the confraternity paid dues to adorn the figure of the Virgin Mary, to have mass and prayers said for its members, and to support feasts, festivals, and processions in her honor. While there is little reference to the existence of the confraternity before the Pueblo Rebellion, one document from the Holy Inquisition indicates that the *cofradía* was active in the early-colonial period (Chávez 1950). Although this document only indicates that a silk scarf was donated, the *cofradía's* financial ledgers from the late-17th and early-18th centuries indicate that colonists contributed soap, clothing, livestock, wheat, ribbons, exotic cloth, tobacco, and in one instance an Apache child (Chávez 1950). Some of these commodities were used to adorn a statue of the Virgin Mary; others were sold to colonists to raise funds to pay the friars for services.

Texts indicate that Spanish colonists provided the friars with commodities and services and were compensated. For example, because the friars took a vow of poverty, they employed syndics to conduct their economic affairs, and from available documents scholars have identified at least eight individuals acting in this capacity during the early-colonial period (Scholes 1937: 51; Chávez 1950). Although the number of identified individuals is small, the role of syndics contributed to the movement of commodities from the clergy to colonists.

In addition to the formal institutions of tithing and the Santa Cruzada, there were less-regulated economic interactions between the colonists and the friars. Colonists also entertained the friars, cleaned the church in Santa Fe, and engaged in trade. Documents recounting the Inquisition of Governor López provide indirect evidence of such activities. In a letter to the vice-custodian of New Mexico, Fray Sacristán accused the governor of forbidding the colonists to weave cloth for the clergy (Hackett 1937:149). Similarly, in the testimony against the governor's assistant, Nicolás de Aguilar, an unidentified deponent claimed that Aguilar threatened one woman with 200 lashes if she cooked for the clergy (Hackett 1937:145). While the threats may be inaccurate or overstated, these statements indicate that the opportunity existed for informal commerce and, thus, the exchange of goods and services between colonists and the Franciscans.

In 17th-century New Mexico, religion played a critical role in society, and thus colonists probably expected spiritual rewards—salvation—for their support of the Franciscan clergy. Nevertheless, some colonists did accrue material benefits from this relationship. The Franciscans distributed supplies to colonists serving at garrisons, on military campaigns, and as escorts (Ivey 1994). Archaeological evidence suggests other commodities colonists may have obtained. Some scholars have suggested that the average colonist could not afford majolica and that virtually all of it was imported through the mission supply caravans (Lister and Lister 1976), yet majolica is found at virtually every 17th-century Spanish colonial site for which there is data (D. Snow 1993; Trigg 1999). Colonists may have obtained it through exchange for their commodities or payment for services. Indeed, in times of famine, priests did sell goods from the caravan. Ivey (1994:85) indicates that Fray Antonio de Sierra used such items to purchase 34 ewes and 445 bushels of wheat and maize. Many other items were brought into the colony on the mission supply caravans or directly imported by the priests—fine cloth, musical instruments, wine, chocolate, vanilla, medicines, metal tools, and bowls (Ivey 1993). These imported items may also have been the objects of the colonists'

desires and used by the priests as payment for goods or services. Another possibility is that the colonists were paid in commodities produced by the *conventos' estancias* and in their workshops, which would have included livestock, grains, fruits and vegetables, cloth, wooden items, painted hides, piñon nuts and other items.

Finally, the well-documented factional competition between New Mexico's governors and clergy may have influenced commerce between colonists and clergy (Scholes 1937, 1938; Weber 1992:133; Broughton 1993). Faction leaders use a variety of methods to attract supporters, but economic incentives, such as giving gifts, are among the most common (Siegel and Beals 1960; Nicholas 1965; Salisbury and Silverman 1977). In exchange for the colonists' political support in the conflict against the governors, the clergy may have given goods they owned. Imported items, available primarily through elites, may have been greatly desired, and offering such items may have been an effective means of luring supporters.

Some interactions between colonists and clergy, such as tithing and the Santa Cruzada, were highly structured by formal rules regulated by the Catholic Church. These carried the weight of both social and legal sanctions because the church at this time played a significant role in the colonists' social identity. Moreover, through the Holy Inquisition, the church had the power to fine, excommunicate, and imprison individuals who violated religious rules. Other interactions such as barter, faction building, providing hospitality or services were less formal and, therefore, less regulated. All interactions, nevertheless, served to link the colonists and clergy socially and economically.

Governors' Interactions with Colonists

New Mexico's governors interacted with colonists on two levels—as private individuals and as officials of the Spanish government. As individuals, governors owned livestock, imported some goods, exported others to Mexico, and operated stores and textile-producing *obrajes* (workshops). On a second level, governors, as officials of the Spanish Crown, developed and enforced policies that had economic effects on colonists. Much of the information about economic relationships is known only through texts because currently there is little archaeological indication of either of these levels.

Documents suggest that some governors participated in a considerable amount of commerce for personal gain. Governor López brought luxury items from Mexico when he came to New Mexico and imported others later on, all of which he sold to the colonists at reportedly exorbitant prices (Scholes 1937). Among the imports were sugar, chocolate, shoes, hats, ornate saddles, harnesses, silver plate, fine writing desks, beds, bed linens, silver plate, and tobacco boxes adorned with silver and gold. Similarly, Governor Rosas sold wine, chocolate, sugar, spices, and shoes. Both governors sold their goods from a store in the *casas reales*, a situation that distressed some colonists, among them Captain Salazar who asserted that Governor Rosas had turned the *casas reales* into a *taberna pública* (public tavern) and a *zapatería* (shoe store) (Scholes 1937:329). In addition to the highly desired imported goods, colonists also traded with governors for slaves, which the governors or their associates had captured on the Plains (Scholes 1937:75).

It is not known what the colonists used to pay for the imports or slaves, but they probably consisted of the standard goods used for exchange (maize, wheat, cloth, and livestock) and perhaps specialized commodities such as selenite stockpiled at the Sanchez site (D. Snow 1992b). Commodities, such as food, woolen textiles, and livestock, produced in the colonists' homes could have been used to support the governor's household and added to the commodities he exported from the colony. At times, colonists were unable to pay their debts, such as Elena Gómez who died owing Governor López a 100-odd pesos (Hackett 1937:260). Other debtors did not escape, for governors took steps to collect, apparently confiscating encomiendas for what they were owed. One aggrieved colonist testified,

> Don Diego [Governor Peñalosa], without giving any notice or information to the declarant, sent to have the revenues of the encomiendas collected in his own name, and had the proceeds carried away to his own house . . .. Peñalosa told him that he had there the collections for October from the said encomiendas, and that the brother of the declarant, Captain Cristóbal de Anaya … had owed him, the governor, a few pesos; that his father also had owed him three or four pesos, and the declarant still another two pesos; and that he

had ordered the revenues from the encomiendas to be collected in order that he might repay himself (Hackett 1937:248).

Colonists' desires for imported goods drove some of the economic interactions with the governors, but the governors themselves initiated others. For example, one weaver from San Gabriel testified that Governor López commissioned a large carpet from him (Hackett 1937:254).

As agents of the Spanish Crown, the governors were granted broad powers over economic activities in the colony. In their official capacities, governors created and enforced legislation, which, although not necessarily moving commodities between themselves and the colonists, nonetheless affected the colonists' economic activities. Governors were responsible for setting the wages for Pueblo peoples' labor, adjudicating legal proceedings, and levying fines. They also had the power to punish and imprison colonists, which had tremendous economic consequences on prisoners and their households.

One very important economic function served by the governor was the assignment of encomiendas. Beginning with Governor Oñate, the privilege of collecting tribute was conferred on certain men who aided in the colonization of New Mexico. Although the encomiendas were inherited for three generations and, thus, the governors could not reappoint encomenderos at will, trustees were selected to oversee encomiendas that could not be administered by the encomendero. During the Inquisition trial of Governor Peñalosa, Fray Salvador Guerra declared, "When it happens that there is a need to nominate a trustee in case the wife of an encomendero is left a widow, to whom the encomienda legally descends, or where there are children who inherit but are not of sufficient age to hold it, and a trustee is required, the third part of the revenue is assigned to such trustees, or a certain number of houses, as may seem equitable to the owners and to the trustees; so that it is always a moderate compensation which is given them" (Hackett 1937:250).

In other cases, trustees were appointed for encomenderos who were imprisoned. For example, Governor Peñalosa indicated that he had assigned a trustee half of the proceeds of an encomienda held by a prisoner, but the other half was to be used "for the maintenance of [Romero] during his imprisonment" (Hackett 1937:252).

The privilege of collecting encomienda from Pueblo peoples was an important one. As David Snow (1983) has argued, at least during the early years of the colony, the maize and cloth provided by Pueblo people were critical to the colonists' survival and may have served to enhance the prestige of encomienda holders. The ability to control the disbursement of this important source of subsistence goods allowed several unscrupulous governors the opportunity to manipulate them for personal gain. Some colonists and clergy testified that governors illegally appropriated the proceeds from encomiendas or controlled the trusteeships of encomiendas. For example, Governor Pacheco revoked several encomiendas and seized the proceeds before he reassigned them. Governor Peñalosa was particularly notorious. According to Captain Cristóbal Durán y Chávez, the governor collected Diego Romero's encomienda from Zia and Cochiti while the encomendero was imprisoned (Hackett 1937:238, 242). Colonist Anaya Almazán testified that he was assigned the trusteeship of his deceased father's encomienda, but Governor Peñalosa collected it himself (Hackett 1937:248). A third colonist claimed that the governor also collected another encomienda by assigning trusteeship of Francisco Gómez's holdings to one of the governor's dependents (Hackett 1937:249).

Other economic transactions that were probably not sanctioned also facilitated the movement of commodities between colonists and governors. The *audiencia* judging Governor López's *residencia* found the governor guilty of accepting a bribe from a colonist who wanted to avoid punishment (Scholes 1938:74). The *audiencia* also found López guilty of accepting a bribe from the previous governor in return for a favorable *residencia* (Scholes 1938:74). In another incident, Ruiz de Cepeda, the attorney for the Holy Inquisition, indicated that the governor allowed an encomendero to enslave people from Sevilleta Pueblo. The attorney stated, "But for the sake of his own interests, the accused [Governor López] took them to their old pueblo at risk of their continuing their hateful and infamous idolatries .... And all this harm came from the self-interestedness of the accused, he being led to act so unwisely by a gift of some mules which the encomendero of that pueblo had promised him" (Hackett 1937:206). In some cases, the texts specify the items used for bribes, as in the last case where the bribe took the form of livestock. In other instances, it is not known, but bribes may have consisted of items usually used for exchange—textiles, livestock, and grains.

Some governors used their position to thwart the clergy's economic activities, and in doing so, according to reports to the Holy Inquisition, also affected the colonists. Governor López issued orders that restricted colonists from aiding or conducting commerce with the Franciscans. The clergy testified that the governor forbade colonists from baking or cooking, selling them woolen sackcloth, or from entertaining them. Colonist Miguel Noriega stated, "He [the governor] also ordered Luis Martín Serrano ... not to give hospitality to any religious, under penalty of I do not know how many lashes" (Hackett 1937:185).

The Franciscans also complained that governors regularly used their political powers for financial gains. Governor López, in particular, was a frequent target of these accusations. The clergy argued that he limited the export of livestock and silver merely to increase the value of his own products. The governor admitted that he placed some limits but insisted that he did so not for his own financial interests but because he did not want the number of livestock in New Mexico reduced during times of famine (Hackett 1937:211). Although documents describing this affair recount the clergy's concerns and their losses from the restrictions, any individual who wanted to export livestock to Mexico would have been affected.

Trade between the colony and the rest of the empire was dominated by the governors and Franciscans who, largely because of their wealth, controlled the means to participate in an export economy. Wagons and draft animals for shipping goods to Mexico were in short supply and were consequently in great demand. Exporting was thus fertile ground for both actual and imagined abuses of authority. Governor Baeza and others appropriated the livestock and wagons that the Spanish Crown used in the triennial mission caravans, claiming that since they were the property of the Crown, they belonged to the civil authorities. The clergy insisted that these items belonged to the religious authorities, that they had the right to use them, and that the governors abused their position for their own financial gain.

This political wrangling continued in other venues because just as the clergy were concerned with building factions, governors were also interested in obtaining political support from colonists. Since the governors were not permanent members of the colony, nor did they have the administrative network that the clergy had, building factions may have been particularly important to the governors. Like the clergy, the governors may have offered desired imported commodities, chocolate, wine, or cloth, to colonists in exchange for their support.

The Regional Economy in a Larger Context

In examining some of the social mechanisms that influenced economic activity, it is important to note that the choices that individuals made probably had both physical and social aspects and that colonists participated unequally in the economy. A household may have chosen to trade primarily with its nearest neighbor, whereas interactions with more distant households may have been less intense. Economic relations may also have been strongest among households that had social ties, such as those that were related by birth or marriage. Finally, just as people today participate in the economy at different intensities—penny-pinchers as opposed to those who "shop 'til they drop," it can be assumed that some 17th-century Spanish households had more economic connections than others.

Currently, there is not sufficient data to quantify the scope of the regional economy. Nonetheless, the large quantity of Pueblo ceramics on Spanish sites and the wide distribution of majolica ceramics, which some have argued were available only through the Franciscan mission caravans (Lister and Lister 1979), point to an active regional exchange. This network linked native peoples, colonists, and elites in a web of economic relationships (Figure 1). Although the figure depicts the interactions between each segment of New Mexican society as linear, relating only one group with another,

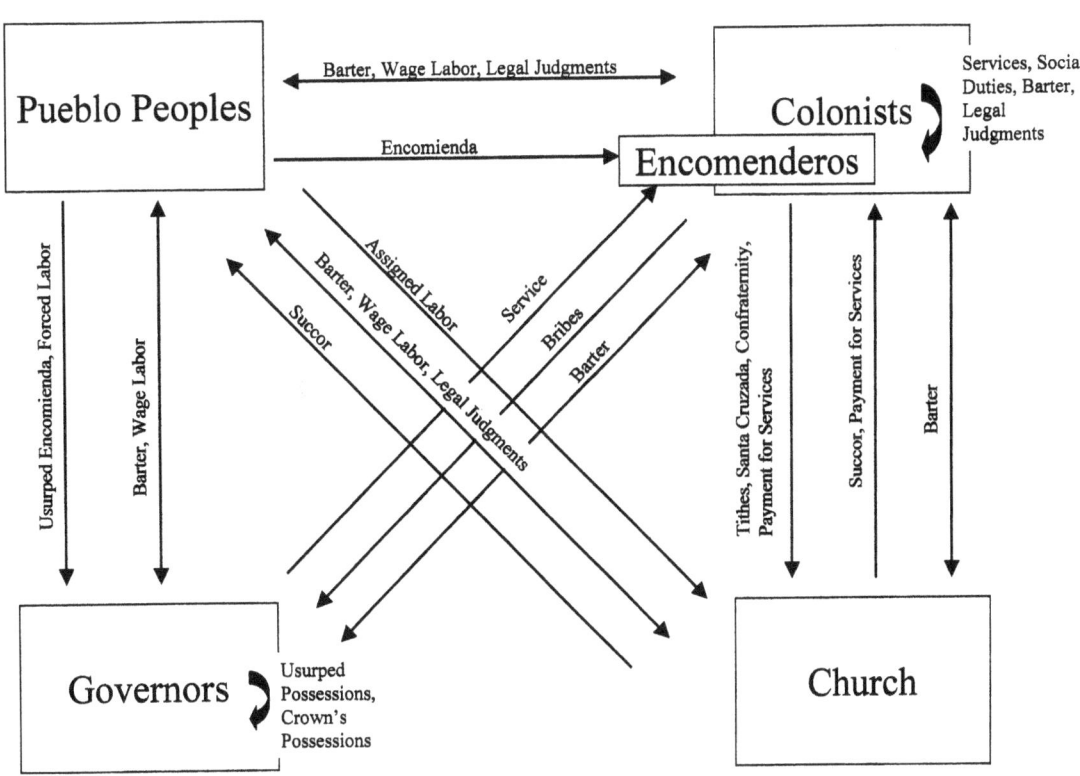

FIGURE 1. Regional economic interactions in early-colonial New Mexico 1598–1680.

economic activities were highly interrelated. Take for example, the encomienda system. An encomendero's income from encomienda depended on the number of Pueblo households and the number of Pueblo people working for the priests. This, in turn, depended both on the priests' wishes and the governor's policies regarding the assignment of laborers. Moreover, governors assigned individuals the right to collect encomienda and appointed trustees. This economic institution, although nominally relating only encomenderos and Pueblo peoples, also connected individuals from other social groups in an intricate system.

Credit and debt were facts of life in 17th-century New Mexico. During the 17th century, merchant bankers in Mexico City became wealthy through a credit system in which they extended money or merchandise to itinerant peddlers who sold commodities in distant reaches of the region (Hoberman 1991). Although it is not known how widespread this practice was in New Mexico, it is known that some governors and itinerant merchants sold items to the colonists on credit. For example, Mexican trader Bernardo Gruber kept a list detailing the amounts colonists in New Mexico owed him (Sanchez 1993), and Governor Peñalosa confiscated encomienda payments for a debt an encomendero owed (Hackett 1937:284). Some governors operated their businesses with the help of agents in Mexico who conducted financial affairs on their behalfs, and documents suggest that Governor Rosas had a formal business relationship with a merchant in Parral, Mexico, who extended the governor credit and sold his New Mexican products (Bloom 1935). It is also likely that the Franciscans operated within this system, and those colonists within New Mexico extended credit to each other.

Regional interactions were important because exchange among households may have helped mitigate the effects of New Mexico's uneven distribution of resources and buffered the risk of famine. Recent research has given a picture of the types of commodities brought into the colony, which colonists, priests, and governors may have exchanged among themselves (C. Snow 1993; Pierce and Snow 1999). These commodities included items specifically for trade with Pueblo peoples, beads, jewelry,

and tools. Others shipped in on the mission supply caravans may not have been intended directly for trade (Ivey 1994) but found their way into the households throughout the colony by means of regional exchange. These studies provide critical information about the items that may have been circulating, but they do not address the types of commodities produced within the colony, textiles, crops, and livestock, which were also exchanged among households. It is the exchange of such basic subsistence items that may have played the largest role in buffering risk.

The regional economy also moved commodities from colonists' households to the elites. This assisted the friars and governors in amassing goods for export because some of the goods that the clergy and governors obtained from colonists, livestock and textiles, were among the same items they exported to the mining communities in northern Mexico. These interactions also moved items in the other direction, from the elites to all colonists' households. As archaeological evidence indicates, some of these goods may have been highly desired as colonists were apparently willing to become indebted to the governors to obtain them. The lure of imported commodities, however, may have gone beyond the desire for luxuries but, instead, were a necessary part of the colonists' ethnic identity (D. Snow 1993). Regional economic transactions not only linked people living in the colony but also provided one bridge between the small-scale household economy and the large-scale colony-empire trade.

ACKNOWLEDGMENTS

This research was supported, in part, by a fellowship from the Clements Center for Southwest Studies at Southern Methodist University. The author would like to thank Richard I. Ford, David Snow, Cordelia Snow, David Weber, James Snead, Frances Levine, and Jake Ivey for their helpful comments on this paper.

REFERENCES

ALEXANDER, ROBERT
    1971 LA 9142: The Signal Site. Manuscript, Laboratory of Anthropology, Museum of New Mexico, Santa Fe.

BAKEWELL, PETER
    1997 *A History of Latin America: Empires and Sequels 1450–1930.* Blackwell, Oxford, England.

BAKKER, KEITH
    1999   New Mexican Spanish Colonial Furniture. In *El Camino Real de Tierra Adentro Volume 2*, Gabriella Palmer and Stephen Fosberg, compilers, pp. 117–132. Bureau of Land Management, New Mexico State Office, Santa Fe.

BLOOM, LANSING B.
    1923   The Jemez Expedition of the School. El Palacio 14: 15–20.
    1928   A Glimpse of New Mexico in 1620. *New Mexico Historical Review* 3:301–323.
    1935   A Trade-Invoice of 1638. *New Mexico Historical Review* 10:242–248.

BROUGHTON, WILLIAM
    1993   The History of Seventeenth-Century New Mexico: Is it time for new interpretations? New Mexico Historical Review, 68:3–12.

BRUGGE, DAVID
    1999   Captives and Slaves on the Camino Real. In *El Camino Real de Tierra Adentro, Volume 2*, Gabrielle Palmer and Stephen Fosberg, compilers, pp. 103–110. Bureau of Land Management, New Mexico State Office, Santa Fe.

CHÁVEZ, FRAY ANGELICO
    1950   La Conquistadora Is a Paisana. *El Palacio*, 57: 299–307.
    1992   *Origins of New Mexico Families: A Genealogy of the Spanish Colonial Period*. Museum of New Mexico Press, Santa Fe.

CUTTER, CHARLES
    1986   *The Protector de Indios in Colonial New Mexico 1659–1821*. University of New Mexico Press, Albuquerque.

ELLIS, BRUCE
    1976   Santa Fe's Seventeenth-Century Plaza, Parish Church, and Convent Reconsidered. In Collected Papers in Honor of Marjorie Ferguson Lambert, Albert Schroeder, editor, pp. 183–198. *Papers of the Archaeological Society of New Mexico*, 3. Albuquerque.

ESPINOSA, AURELIO
    1985   *The Folklore of Spain in the American Southwest: Traditional Spanish Folk Literature in Northern New Mexico and Southern Colorado*. Manuel Espinosa, editor. University of Oklahoma Press, Norman.

FORD, RICHARD
    n.d.   Ethnobotany Lab Report 471. Manuscript, University of Michigan Museum of Anthropology Ethnobotanical Laboratory, Ann Arbor.

FOURNIER, PATRICIA
    1999   Ceramic Production and Trade on the Camino Real. In *El Camino Real de Tierra Adentro Volume 2*, Gabriella Palmer and Stephen Fosberg, compilers, pp. 153–176. Bureau of Land Management, New Mexico State Office, Santa Fe.

GIBSON, CHARLES
    1966   *Spain in America*. Harper & Row, New York, NY.

GUTIÉRREZ, RAMÓN A.
    1991   *When Jesus Came, the Corn Mothers Went Away: Marriage, Sexuality, and Power in New Mexico, 1500–1846*. Stanford University Press, Stanford, CA.

HACKETT, CHARLES
    1937   *Historical Documents Relating to New Mexico, Nueva Vizcaya, and Approaches Thereto, to 1773*, Vol. 3. Carnegie Institution, Washington, DC.

HACKETT, CHARLES, AND CHARMION SHELBY
    1942   *Revolt of the Pueblo Indians of New Mexico and Otermin's Attempted Reconquest 1680–1682*. University of New Mexico Press, Albuquerque.

HALL, THOMAS
    1989   *Social Change in the Southwest*, 1350–1880. University Press of Kansas, Lawrence.

HAMMOND, GEORGE, AND AGAPITO REY
    1953   *Don Juan de Oñate: Colonizer of New Mexico 1595–1628*. University of New Mexico Press, Albuquerque.

HARRIS, ARTHUR H.
    1973   The Vertebrate Fauna from LA 591. In Cochiti Dam Salvage Project, Archaeological Excavation of the Las Majadas Site, LA 591, Cochiti Dam, New Mexico, pp. 38–39. Museum of New Mexico, *Laboratory of Anthropology Note*, 75. Santa Fe.

HAYES, ALDEN
    1974   *The Four Churches Of Pecos*. University of New Mexico Press, Albuquerque.

HOBERMAN, LOUISA SCHELL
    1991   *Mexico's Merchant Elite, 1590–1660*. Duke University Press, Durham, NC.

HODGE, FREDERICK, GEORGE P. HAMMOND, AND AGAPITO REY
    1945   *Fray Alonso de Benavides' Revised Memorial of 1634*. University of New Mexico Press, Albuquerque.

HURT, WESLEY R.
    1990   The 1939–1940 Excavation Project at Quarai Pueblo and Mission Building. *National Park Service Southwest Cultural Resources Center Professional Paper*, 29. Santa Fe, NM.

IVEY, JAMES
    1992   Pueblo and Estancia: The Spanish Presence in the Pueblo, A.D. 1620–1680. In Current Research on the Late Prehistory and Early History of New Mexico, edited by Bradley Vierra, pp. 221–226. New Mexico Archaeological Council, *Special Publication*, 1. Albuquerque.
    1993   Seventeenth-Century Mission Trade on the Camino Real. In *El Camino Real de Tierra Adentro*, Gabrielle Palmer, compiler, pp. 41–67. Bureau of Land Management, New Mexico State Office, Santa Fe.

1994 "The Greatest Misfortune of All." *Journal of the Southwest*, 36:76–100.

JOHN, ELIZABETH
1975 *Storms Brewed in Other Men's Worlds.* Texas A&M University Press, College Station.

KESSELL, JOHN
1979 *Kiva, Cross, and Crown: The Pecos Indians and New Mexico, 1540–1840.* National Park Service, Department of the Interior, Washington, DC.

KIDDER, ALFRED V.
1932 *The Artifacts of Pecos.* Robert S. Peabody Foundation for Archaeology, Phillips Academy, Andover, MA.

LEVINE, FRANCES
1992 Hispanic Household Structure in Colonial New Mexico. In Current Research on the Late Prehistory and Early History of New Mexico, Bradley Vierra, editor, pp. 195–206. New Mexico Archaeological Council, *Special Publication*, 1. Albuquerque.
1995 Guide to the Archaeological Literature of Spanish Colonial New Mexico. In The Archaeology of Spanish and Mexican Colonialism in the American Southwest, James Ayers, compiler, pp. 53–104. Society for *Historical Archaeology, Guides to the Archaeological Literature of the Immigrant Experience in America*, 3. California, PA.
1999 *Our Prayers Are in This Place: Pecos Pueblo Identity over the Centuries.* University of New Mexico Press, Albuquerque.

LEVINE, FRANCES, JOHN ACKLEN, JACK BERTRAM, STEPHEN LENT, AND GALE McPHERSON
1985 Archaeological Test Excavations at LA 16769. Public Service Company of New Mexico, *Report 5*. Albuquerque.

LISTER, FLORENCE, AND ROBERT LISTER
1976 A Descriptive Dictionary for 500 Years of Spanish-Tradition Ceramics. Society for Historical Archaeology. *Special Publication Series*, 1. California, PA.
1979 Distribution of Mexican Maiolica along the Northern Borderlands. *Archaeological Society of New Mexico Papers*, 3. Albuquerque.

LOPINOT, NEAL
1988 Early Spanish Introduction of Cultigens into the Greater Southwest. *Missouri Archaeologist*, 47:61–84.

MARTINEZ, GUADALUPE
1994 Results of the Monitoring of Two Construction Sites along Lincoln Avenue, Santa Fe, New Mexico. Museum of New Mexico, *Laboratory of Anthropology Notes*, 61. Santa Fe.

MONTGOMERY, ROSS, WATSON SMITH, AND JOHN BREW
1949 Franciscan Awatovi: The Excavation and Conjectural Reconstruction of a 17th-Century Spanish Mission Establishment at a Hopi Indian Town in Northeastern Arizona. *Papers of the Peabody Museum of American Archaeology and Ethnology*, 36. Cambridge, MA.

MOORE, JAMES, JOAN GAUNT, DAISY LEVINE, AND LINDA MICK-O'HARA
n.d. Prehistoric and Historic Occupation of Lost Alamos and Guaje Canyons: Data Recovery at Three Sites Near the Pueblo of San Ildefonso. Manuscript, author's personal collection.

NICHOLAS, RALPH
1965 Factions: A Comparative Analysis. In *Political Systems and the Distribution of Power*, pp. 21–61. Association of Social Anthropologists, *Monographs* 2, compiled by Gabrielle Palmer. Tavistock, London, England.
1993 *El Camino Real de Tierra Adentro.* Bureau of Land Management, New Mexico State Office, Santa Fe.

PALMER, GABRIELLE, AND STEPHEN FOSBERG (COMPILERS)
1999 *El Camino Real de Tierra Adentro Volume 2.* Bureau of Land Management, New Mexico State Office, Santa Fe.

PIERCE, DONNA, AND CORDELIA T. SNOW
1999 A Harp for Playing. In *El Camino Real de Tierra Adentro Volume 2*, compiled by Gabriella Palmer and Stephen Fosberg, pp. 71–86. Bureau of Land Management, New Mexico State Office, Santa Fe.

POST, STEPHEN, AND DAVID SNOW
1982 Archaeological Investigations for the Gallery Addition to the Museum of Fine Arts. Museum of New Mexico, *Laboratory of Anthropology Notes*, 282. Santa Fe.

PRATT, BOYD, AND DAVID SNOW
1988 The North Central Regional Overview: Strategies for the Comprehensive Survey of the Architectural and Historic Archaeological Resources of North Central New Mexico, Vol. 1: Historic Overview of North Central New Mexico. New Mexico State Historic Preservation Division, Santa Fe.

SALISBURY, RICHARD, AND MARILYN SILVERMAN
1977 An Introduction: Factions and the Dialectic. In A House Divided: Anthropological Studies of Factionalism, Marilyn Silverman and Richard Salisbury, editors, pp. 1–20. Institute of Social and Economic Research, *Social and Economic Papers*, 9. University of Toronto Press, Toronto, ON.

SANCHEZ, JOSEPH
1993 Bernardo Gruber and the New Mexican Inquisition. In *El Camino Real de Tierra Adentro*, Gabrielle Palmer, compiler, pp. 121–131. Bureau of Land Management, New Mexico State Office, Santa Fe.

SCHEICK, CHERIE
1979 Archaeological Survey near Agua Fria, New Mexico, and Limited Testing of a Seventeenth-Century Spanish Colonial Site, LA 16773. Manuscript, School of American Research, Santa Fe, NM.

SCHOLES, FRANCE
1928 Manuscripts for the History of New Mexican Missions in the Seventeenth Century. *New Mexico Historical Review*, 4:45–58, 195–201.

1929 Documents for the History of the New Mexican Missions in the Seventeenth Century. *New Mexico Historical Review*, 4:45–58, 195–201.

1930 The Supply Service of the New Mexico Missions in the Seventeenth Century. *New Mexico Historical Review*, 5:93–116, 186–210, 386–404.

1935a Civil Government and Society in New Mexico in the Seventeenth Century. *New Mexico Historical Review*, 10:71–111.

1935b The First Decade of the Inquisition in New Mexico. *New Mexico Historical Review*, 10:195–229.

1936 Church and State in New Mexico 1610–1650. *New Mexico Historical Review*, 11:9–76, 145–178, 283–294, 297–349.

1937 Troublous Times in New Mexico, 1659–1670. *New Mexico Historical Review*, 12:134–174, 380–452.

1938 Troublous Times in New Mexico, 1659–1670. *New Mexico Historical Review*, 13:63–84.

1975 Royal Treasury Records Relating to the Province of New Mexico, 1596–1683. *New Mexico Historical Review*, 50:5–23.

SIEGEL, BERNARD, AND ALAN BEALS
1960 Pervasive Factionalism. *American Anthropologist*, 62: 394–417.

SIMMONS, MARC
1968 *Spanish Government in New Mexico.* University of New Mexico Press, Albuquerque.

SMITH, WATSON, RICHARD WOODBURY, AND NATHALIE WOODBURY
1966 *The Excavations of Hawikuh by Frederick Webb Hodge.* Museum of the American Indian, Heye Foundations, New York.

SNOW, CORDELIA THOMAS
1974 A Brief History of the Palace of the Governors and a Preliminary Report on the 1974 Excavation. *El Palacio*, 80 (3):6–21.

1977 The Evolution of a Frontier: An Historical Interpretation of Archaeological Sites. In *Archaeological Investigations in Cochiti Reservoir, New Mexico, Volume 4: Adaptive Change in the Northern Rio Grande Valley*, Jan Biella and Richard Chapman, editors, pp. 217–234. Office of Contract Archeology, Albuquerque, NM.

1993 A Headdress of Pearls: Luxury Goods Imported over the Camino Real during the Seventeenth Century. In *El Camino Real de Tierra Adentro*, Gabrielle Palmer, compiler, pp. 69–76. Bureau of Land Management, New Mexico State Office, Santa Fe.

SNOW, DAVID H.
1971 Excavations at Cochiti Dam, New Mexico, 1964–1966 Seasons: Vol. 1. Museum of New Mexico, *Laboratory of Anthropology Notes*, 79. Santa Fe.

1973 Cochiti Dam Salvage Project: Archeological Excavation of the Las Majadas Site, LA 591, Cochiti Dam, New Mexico. Museum of New Mexico, *Laboratory of Anthropology Notes*, 75. Santa Fe.

1976 Santiago to Guache: Notes for a Tale of Two (or More) Bernalillos. In Collected Papers in Honor of Marjorie Ferguson Lambert, Albert Schroeder, editor, pp. 161–181. *Papers of the Archaeological Society of New Mexico*, 3. Albuquerque.

1979 Rural Hispanic Community Organization in Northern New Mexico: An Historical Perspective. In the Survival of Spanish American Villages, Paul Kutsche, editor, pp. 42–52. *The Colorado College Studies*, 15. Colorado Springs.

1983 A Note on Encomienda Economics in Seventeenth-Century New Mexico. In *Hispanic Arts and Ethnohistory in the Southwest*, Marta Weigle, editor, pp. 347–357. Ancient City Press, Albuquerque, NM.

1989 Report of Preliminary Archaeological Testing: 150 Washington St., Santa Fe, New Mexico.

1990 Report of Archaeological Testing: 113 Washington St., Santa Fe, New Mexico.

1992a Cochiti Dam Salvage Project: Archaeological Excavation of the Las Majadas Site, LA 591, Cochiti Dam, New Mexico. In *The Native American and Spanish Colonial Experience in the Greater Southwest*, David H. Snow, editor, pp. 287–379. Garland, New York, NY.

1992b A Review of Spanish Colonial Archaeology in Northern New Mexico. In Current Research on the Late Prehistory and Early History of New Mexico, Bradley Vierra, editor, pp. 185–206. New Mexico Archaeological Council, *Special Publication*, 1. Albuquerque.

1993 Purchased in Chihuahua for Feasts. In *El Camino Real de Tierra Adentro*, Gabrielle Palmer, compiler, pp. 133–146. Bureau of Land Management, New Mexico State Office, Santa Fe.

n.d. LA 4955. Manuscript, Museum of New Mexico, Laboratory of Anthropology, Santa Fe.

SNOW, DAVID H., AND JOANNE BOWEN
1995 No Scum, No Vermin: Seventeenth-Century Faunal Remains from the Santa Fe, New Mexico Downtown Historic District. Report submitted to the Archaeological Review Committee, Santa Fe, NM.

SPICER, EDWARD
1981 *Cycles of Conquest: The Impact of Spain, Mexico, and the United States on the Indians of the Southwest, 1533–1960.* University of Arizona Press, Tucson.

TAINTER, JOSEPH, AND FRANCES LEVINE
1987 *Cultural Resources Overview: Central New Mexico.* Bureau of Land Management, Santa Fe.

THOMAS, DAVID H.
2000 Excavations at Mission San Marcos, New Mexico, Summer 1999. American Museum of Natural History, New York, NY.

THOMAS, DAVID H. (EDITOR)
1989 *Columbian Consequences Volume 1: Archaeological and Historical Perspectives on the Spanish Borderlands West.* Smithsonian Institution Press, Washington, DC.

1991 *Columbian Consequences Volume 3: The Spanish Borderlands in Pan-American Perspective.* Smithsonian Institution Press, Washington, DC.

TICHY, MARJORIE FERGUSON
1939 The Archaeology of Puaray. *El Palacio,* 47:145–163.

TIGGES, LINDA L. (EDITOR)
1990 Santa Fe Historic Plaza Study 1 with Translations from Spanish Colonial Documents. City Planning Department, Santa Fe, NM.
1992 Santa Fe Historic Plaza Study 2 Plaza Excavation Final Report Fall 1990. Report to the City of Santa Fe, NM, from Cross-Cultural Research Systems, Santa Fe, NM.

TOULOUSE, JOSEPH
1949 The Mission of San Gregorio de Abo. School of American Research, *Monographs of the School of American Research,* 15. Santa Fe, NM.

TRIGG, HEATHER
1999 *The Economy of Early Colonial New Mexico, AD 1598–1680: An Investigation of Social Structure and Human Agency Using Archaeological and Documentary Data.* Doctoral dissertation, Department of Anthropology, University of Michigan, Ann Arbor. University Microfilms International, Ann Arbor, MI.

VIVIAN, GORDON
1964 Excavations in a Seventeenth-Century Jumano Pueblo: *Archaeological Research Series,* 8. National Park Service, Washington DC.

WAIT, WALTER, AND PETER MCKENNA
1990 Quarai Parking Lot Rehabilitation Archaeological Testing Program: Salinas Pueblo Mission National Monument. Branch of Cultural Resources Management, Department of Anthropology, National Park Service, *Southwest Cultural Resources Center Professional Papers,* 27. Santa Fe, NM.

WEBER, DAVID
1992 *The Spanish Frontier in North America.* Yale University Press, New Haven, CT.

WILLMER, ADISA
1990 Archaeological Monitoring along Washington Avenue, Santa Fe, New Mexico. Museum of New Mexico, *Laboratory of Anthropology Notes, 515.* Santa Fe, NM.

WINTER, MARK
1999 Saltillo Sarapes. In *El Camino Real de Tierra Adentro Volume 2,* Gabriella Palmer and Stephen Fosberg, compilers, pp. 133–146. Bureau of Land Management, New Mexico State Office, Santa Fe.

WISEMAN, REGGIE
1992 Early Spanish Colonial Occupation of Santa Fe: Excavations at the La Fonda Parking Lot Site (LA 54000). In Current Research on the Late Prehistory and Early History of New Mexico, Bradley Vierra, editor, pp. 207–214. New Mexico Archaeological Council, *Special Publication,* 1. Albuquerque.

HEATHER B. TRIGG
CENTER FOR CULTURAL AND ENVIRONMENTAL HISTORY
UNIVERSITY OF MASSACHUSETTS, BOSTON
BOSTON, MA 02125

WILLIAM J. THOMAS
NATHAN W. BOWER
JOHN W. KANTNER
MARIANNE L. STOLLER
DAVID H. SNOW

An X-ray Fluorescence-Pattern Recognition Analysis of Pottery from an Early Historic Hispanic Settlement Near Santa Fe, New Mexico

ABSTRACT

The results from a cluster analysis of x-ray fluorescence data on pottery sherds from a rare 17th-century Spanish colonial site are used to make a preliminary identification of the Pueblo origins of these ceramics and to examine the socio-economic interactions between the colonists and the indigenous Pueblo Indians. This work not only provides a needed data base on elemental compositions of Pueblo pottery in the area just to the south of Santa Fe, it also demonstrates that the nearest pueblo was not necessarily the only or even the major source of the pottery present at such sites. Several cultural factors in 17th-century Spanish colonial New Mexico—the tribute (*encomienda*) system, class, status, and gender—are briefly considered for the role they may have played in determining the distribution of pottery sources found at the site, LA 20,000.

Introduction

The interaction of the early Spanish settlers in the American Southwest with the Pueblo Indians is of sustained interest to anthropologists and historians as an archetype for archaeological and ethnohistorical study because of the time depth and high degree of preservation of artifacts and archival documents. It is also of interest because of the continuing impact the interrelationships have between the two ethnic groups in that region even today. The number of identified Spanish colonial settlements/household sites for the earliest period of colonization is necessarily small. Compared to an indigenous population numbering in the tens of thousands, Spanish colonists numbered no more than 2,000–2,500 people by 1680 when the Pueblo Indians revolted against their conquerors and drove the Spanish south to El Paso del Norte. Snow (1983:353) provides population estimates. Colonial settlement sites dating to the 17th century are quite rare since most were reoccupied or disturbed by subsequent generations, and their exact locations are difficult to pinpoint as local records were destroyed in the Revolt (Snow and Stoller 1987:1).

The early Spanish settlement (LA 20,000, 20 km southwest of Santa Fe) under excavation by Snow and Stoller and students from The Colorado College is the focus of this study (Figure 1). It is one of the very few 17th-century sites that has been positively identified and received much archaeological excavation. Discovered on his land by Mr. Alfonso G. Sanchez in 1980, LA 20,000 is one of the largest and least disturbed of these sites, encompassing about 3 acres and consisting of a multiple-room household, sizeable corrals and a possible *torreon*. Cross-dating from the ceramics recovered (over 15,000 sherds) suggests that it was occupied from about 1620 (only two decades after the 1598 colonization by the Spanish in the area) until the Pueblo Revolt in 1680; no artifacts discovered so far postdate that period. Because it was not reoccupied after the reconquest of New Mexico in 1692–1693 and because it has been well preserved by earth washed down from a nearby hillside, it provides an ideal location for a study of the earliest interactions between the two ethnic groups.

This site is located in lower La Cienega valley, a kilometer above the confluence of Cienega and Alamo Creeks with the Santa Fe River. It is assumed to be in close proximity to the Pueblo of La Cienega, although the exact location of that pueblo—occupied in the 1600s but apparently not reoccupied after the reconquest—has yet to be positively determined (Breitbard and Klungness 1987: 8–11). If this assumption is valid, LA 20,000 would follow the general pattern of colonial domestic *ranchos* or *estancias* being located close to Pueblo Indian villages and their Spanish missions that has been identified from references in the published historical documents for the 17th century in

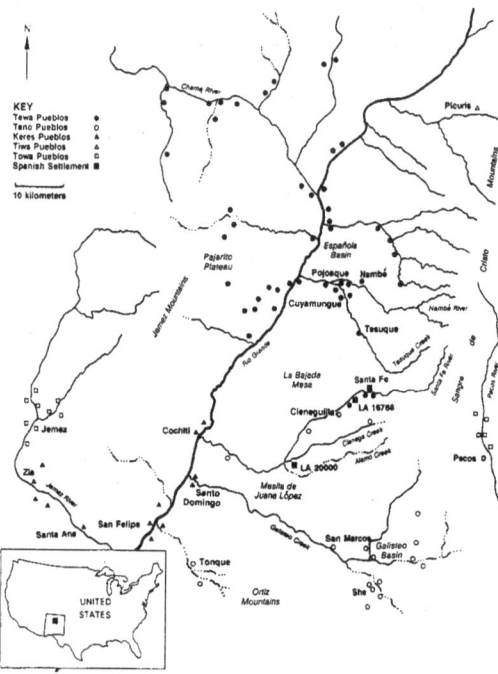

FIGURE 1. Site location and environs of LA 20,000.

New Mexico (Snow and Stoller 1987:6). Archival evidence indicates that the Pueblo of Cienega was held in *encomienda* by Francisco de Anaya Almazan and his sons (Scholes 1942:132), but whether LA 20,000 was his *estancia* is not yet known.

The primary artifactual remains recovered from these early colonial sites are ceramics which, aside from European lead/tin enamels, cannot be distinguished from those found at contemporaneous Pueblo sites. Unless it is assumed that the colonists immediately adopted Pueblo Indian ceramic technology, materials, and designs, the pottery used by them originated among the various Pueblo potters (Snow 1974:56ff.). Basic Pueblo assemblages have been well studied and characterized typologically and petrographically in considerable detail. Ceramic assemblages at Spanish households are identical with those of Pueblo origin in terms of decoration traditions (late glaze- and matte-paint wares, for example), methods and techniques of manufacture, and materials used. Such traditions show little or no significant change from pre-His-

panic times in the region (e.g., Kidder and Shepard 1936:619ff.; Snow 1974:56).

Depending on location, Pueblo ceramics account for better than 95 percent of all sherds recovered from Spanish colonial sites. The locus of manufacture of these ceramics thus becomes a critical question in the study of social and economic contacts and transactions between the two ethnic groups. Earlier studies, making use of typology and statistical incidences, have suggested that, "in general, the Spaniards obtained most of their pottery from pueblos nearest them" (Snow 1974:63; see also Warren 1979:187–193). Thus, while colonial sites south of Santa Fe characteristically contain Pueblo glaze-paint wares as the dominant pottery in use, those north of Santa Fe usually contain a dominance of Tewa style matte-paint wares typical of that area.

LA 20,000 was not represented in these earlier studies as it was only recently discovered and investigation is still in progress. The following preliminary study of ceramics found at this site during the Spring 1990 field season should give clues about the specific pueblos that were involved in a trading pattern or some sort of economic exchange with the colonial residents at LA 20,000. A comparison of these pueblos to the historical records concerning Spanish activities and settlers in the Cienega area should be informative, and should help to identify this *estancia* as excavation continues in the future. The intent of this ceramic analysis is to provide information about the complex network of economic relationships, as represented by this commodity, which prevailed between the Spanish and Pueblo Indians in this period. Comparisons between the origins of the pottery found in this study with those named in the historical records may shed some light on the socioeconomic structures in Spanish colonial society. In particular, the *encomienda* system, class, status, and gender roles as mechanisms effecting interethnic transactions can be examined.

Method

Archaeologists with experience in typological analysis can usually best identify ceramic artifacts using parameters such as the forms and decorations if the sherds are large enough. Petrographic analysis, using a binocular and/or polarizing microscope, of the temper used in the pottery is also very useful for small sherds which cannot be readily identified by shape or decoration, particularly for pottery from this region, as Anna Shepard (1942: 226–232) has demonstrated. A third technique, elemental analysis, provides another method for identification of the ceramic artifacts, as different clays and tempers making up the pottery will have different elemental compositions. The composition of the resulting ceramic ware will reflect these diverse clay and temper sources as well as cultural variability in the preparation of pottery made from them. It may then be possible to determine the origin of the pottery from the elemental profile. Elemental analysis methods are the most adaptable of the three approaches to pattern recognition techniques that use quantitative information. Compared to typology and petrographic analysis, elemental analysis is the least affected by operator bias and training in the data collection stage. Because of these advantages, elemental analysis was selected for this study.

Many elemental analysis methods are available, including instrumental neutron activation analysis (INAA), inductively coupled plasma emission (ICP), and x-ray fluorescence (XRF). INAA is capable of the lowest detection limits for the widest range of elements but is the most expensive in terms of capital and environmental costs, especially in light of growing concern about radioactive waste disposal. ICP typically requires aqueous solutions of the sample, which can be difficult to prepare for the complex ceramic matrix. XRF provides good precision and accuracy for elements present in major quantities with enough sensitivity to provide information on a number of trace elements at an intermediate to low cost compared to other multi-element techniques. Therefore, the quantitative analysis was conducted using XRF on sherds collected from LA 20,000.

Ninety-nine sherds (numbered 1 to 99) from LA 20,000 were selected using a preliminary visual examination of the sherds and their decorations so that a variety of types were included in the analysis. Culinary wares are generally not identifiable by traditional typological methods so the samples selected were weighted more heavily toward the decorated wares in order to assist in identification of the clusters separated by the computer program. However, a random selection of unidentified sherds was also included in order to ensure that a wide range of possible sources were analyzed. The resulting collection had more matte-paint wares (about 30%) and fewer glaze-paint wares (70%) compared to the site as a whole, which has 15 percent matte-paint (primarily Tewa) wares, and 85 percent glaze-paint (primarily Kotyiti) wares. The heavier weighting of matte-paint sherds improves the discrimination of the various Tewa pueblos and does not affect the overall conclusions about the various Kotyiti-producing pueblos. A hierarchical cluster analysis (Aldenderfer and Blashfield 1984:35) was used to separate the sherds into groups, although this approach does not allow a reassignment of a sherd if it is poorly placed in the early stages of the clustering (Everitt 1980:68). These groups were then related to various pueblos using the known sherds in the groups based on typology and a petrographic examination of selected sherds.

Each sherd was cleaned of surface contamination by brushing, washing, and drying the sherd before it was analyzed. A portion of the sherd that was free of surface decoration was selected for analysis by breaking off a small part with clean pliers. A 1–2 g sub-sample was pulverized in a Wig-L-Bug tool steel ball mill to a fine powder smaller than 200 mesh. This sample size was determined by Bromund et al. (1976:218) to be adequate to provide sampling precisions of better than 5 percent with 95 percent confidence for these samples as they have only relatively small inclusions (generally less than 1 mm) in fairly large quantities. However, the variability expected for the wares from the region along the Rio Grande south of Cochiti Pueblo is greater than that for the Española Basin due to the larger sized and more variable tempering used in the wares. For Tewa wares from the Española Basin, the inclusions are primarily from a fine volcanic glass ash added as a temper. Sometimes the pottery contains as much as

50 percent ash temper (Olinger 1988:2), and the ash typically has 4.5–5.5 percent potassium oxide and 5–20 ppm strontium (Goff et al. 1989:387). Quartz sand and mica were also used by these pueblos. For Kotyiti pottery the temper is more variable with potassic and calcic feldspars, quartz sand, mica, and even hornblende for pottery from the Ortiz Mountains (Bower and Snow 1984:292).

A portion of the sample weighing 1.0000± 0.0005 g was mixed with 9.0000 g of lithium tetraborate flux (Spex), and the mixture was fired at 1150°C for 20 minutes in Pt-Au crucibles (Englehardt) while being stirred at 200 rpm on a Junior Orbit Shaker (Labline). The melt was then poured into 3-cm diameter Pt-Au molds kept at 700°C over a bunsen burner, and the molds were promptly cooled by placing them on an aluminum block.

The resulting glass disk was subsequently analyzed with a Rigaku 3070 XRF for 10 major component (sodium–Na, magnesium–Mg, aluminum–Al, silicon–Si, phosphorus–P, potassium–K, calcium–Ca, titanium–Ti, manganese–Mn, and iron–Fe) and 10 minor component (vanadium–V, chromium–Cr, cobalt–Co, zinc–Zn, rubidium–Rb, strontium–Sr, yttrium–Y, zirconium–Zr, niobium–Nb, and barium–Ba) elements. The percent or ppm data were manually transferred to a VAX 750 where Minitab and SPSS (statistical packages) were used to normalize the data and to run the clustering programs. Weighted z-scores were calculated for the normalization, and a correlation matrix of these z-scores was used in the cluster analysis presented here. The relative weighting was dictated by the instrumental precision and accuracy for each of the elements determined. This procedure previously was found to provide the most accurate grouping of the artifacts using this sort of data base (Bower et al. 1988:204). Thus, those elements which cannot be determined as precisely are weighted less heavily. The error-weighted z-scores were calculated using the standard deviations (Table 1) of an analysis of known geochemical reference standards (USGS) rather than the standard deviations calculated from the entire population of sherds, as is usually done when calculating z-scores. The element Zn, however, was left as an unweighted z-score as its concentration varies over many orders of magnitude in a few pottery samples and an error-weighted z-score would give it undue importance relative to the other elements. Using log-normal, error-weighted z-scores might also be useful for Zn and elements which have distributions which are flattened near the detection limit. However, the smaller amount of data manipulation was used in this study as the resulting clusters were satisfactory for addressing the relationships discussed here and because the data base is not yet large enough to statistically justify the extra manipulation.

The SPSS program provides a variety of different clustering schemes, but experience has shown Ward's method works best with error weighted z-scores in this kind of application so it was used for this analysis (Bower et al. 1988:205). The chaining observable with other clustering methods such as single linkage is also reduced with Ward's method as it favors the formation of homogenous clusters. However, purely mathematical considerations sometimes favor single-linkage over Ward's method (Everitt 1980:100).

In addition to the problem of deciding which clustering method to use for the hierarchical clustering, there are questions about how much preprocessing of the data should be done before the clustering analysis is done. Normalization or autoscaling (Sharaf et al. 1986:193) is common to control the weighting of the variables, but the individual clusters may not have normal distributions as a result, even if the data set as a whole has been normalized. This can affect the significance of the separations. First calculating principal components (Sharaf et al. 1986:197–215) should make the distributions more spherical in the variable space, but Baxter (1989:45–46, 1991:29–30) points out that principal component analysis of a correlation matrix of compositional data is biased negatively so that other multivariate approaches may be better used. Even so, cultural variations in the preparation of clays and tempers (Arnold et al. 1991:71) and differences in the temper's composition (Neff et al. 1989:57) will have an impact on the distinctiveness of the ceramics produced irrespective of the analysis method. These complications make

TABLE 1
MEAN ELEMENTAL COMPOSITIONS FOR SUBGROUPS SEPARATED BY CLUSTER ANALYSIS[a]

	A (N=11)	B (N=19)	C (N=14)	D (N=11)	E (N=17)	F (N=27)
				Subgroup		
Na_2O	1.08±0.36	1.35±0.28	1.34±0.55	1.28±0.48	1.60±0.20	1.50±0.29
MgO	2.33±0.37	2.15±0.34	1.62±1.01	2.87±0.87	2.30±0.40	2.76±0.26
Al_2O_3	14.8±0.8	14.7±0.9	17.8±3.1	16.8±2.0	18.3±1.2	18.7±0.8
SiO_2	62.0±1.9	62.7±2.4	64.9±5.8	55.5±5.0	58.2±1.8	55.8±1.7
P_2O_5	0.12±0.02	0.15±0.06	0.08±0.05	0.22±0.09	0.21±0.06	0.20±0.05
K_2O	3.89±0.61	3.96±0.42	2.22±0.41	2.57±0.28	2.86±0.64	2.65±0.15
CaO	4.43±0.22	4.10±1.00	2.75±1.62	7.00±0.29	5.62±0.82	6.18±0.47
TiO_2	0.49±0.11	0.47±0.04	0.71±0.11	0.85±0.20	0.76±0.06	0.90±0.11
MnO	0.15±0.03	0.11±0.03	0.08±0.04	0.11±0.03	0.14±0.03	0.12±0.03
Fe_2O_3	4.74±0.18	4.11±0.63	4.97±0.98	7.85±2.08	7.27±0.71	9.08±1.46
V	65±15	57±10	88±20	169±54	125±18	178±30
Cr	55±62	37±16	134±64	69±17	91±19	90±28
Co	10±3	10±3	13±4	16±4	12±3	15±4
Zn	129±32	94±15	167±145	816±1907	262±267	379±657
Rb	138±15	151±28	105±20	71±20	97±18	79±9
Y	45±3	44±13	23±15	19±13	11±13	18±10
Zr	478±41	200±28	243±43	167±43	186±39	162±18
Nb	31±5	37±12	19±5	13±3	14±4	13±2
Sr	231±39	250±74	133±32	445±96	742±96	602±110
Ba	725±177	824±345	702±225	1347±1553	857±222	762±166

[a]The standard deviations for a typical analysis for the oxides are as follows (in %): Na 0.4, Mg 0.3, Al 0.4, Si 1, P 0.04, K 0.4, Ca 0.4, Ti 0.1, Mn 0.02, and Fe 1. For the trace elements, the standard deviations are (in ppm): V 12, Cr 10, Co 5, Zn 10 (but the population deviation of 630 ppm was used), Rb 5, Y 2, Zr 10, Nb 5, Sr 20, and Ba 200.

any analysis tentative and subject to further investigation (Wilson and Melnick 1990:403). Despite these limitations, hierarchical pattern recognition methods applied to compositional data have proven fruitful for determining sources of ceramics in this region, especially when coupled with verification by methods such as petrographic analysis (Stewart et al. 1990:619).

In addition to the cluster analysis of the sherds to determine their origins, a principal component analysis (Shennan 1988:261) was coupled with an R-mode analysis in which a cluster analysis on the elements rather than the sherds is done after transposing the data matrix (Nie et al. 1975:470). These analyses were used to gain information about which minerals were dominating the clustering process.

Results

Figure 2 presents the dendrogram obtained using Ward's clustering method on a correlation matrix of the error-weighted z-scores. Two major groups (illustrated on the left and right sides of Figure 2) which are completely uncorrelated (Pearsonian r = −0.2) are evident in the pattern obtained. The first of these two groups has three subgroups which are composed primarily of Tewa Red and Polychrome wares from the Española Basin (subgroups A and B) and glaze-paint pottery from Pecos Pueblo (subgroup C). The second major group also has three subgroups (D, E, and F) which are significantly different (95% confidence level based on a Pearsonian correlation coefficient of r = 0.5 for 12 degrees of freedom, estimated from a correla-

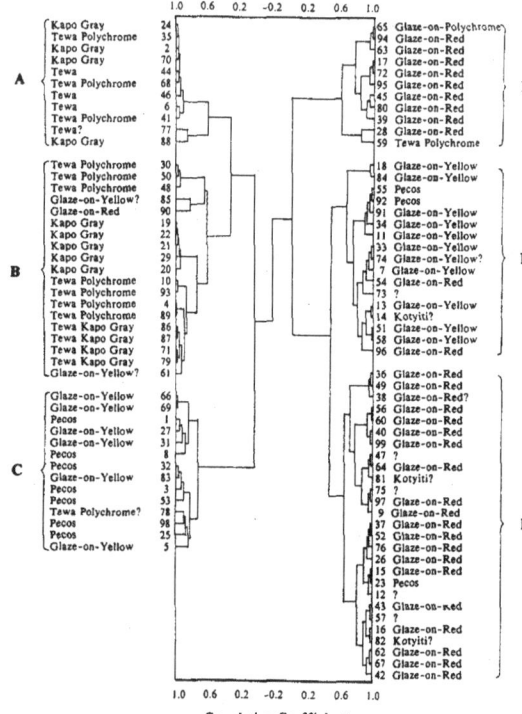

FIGURE 2. Dendrogram, produced by a hierarchical cluster analysis performed on a correlation matrix of error-weighted z-scores of XRF elemental analysis from pottery sherds found at LA 20,000. Groups are tentatively identified as having their origins at the following pueblos: A, Pojoaque; B, Cuyamungue, Tesuque, and/or Nambe; C, Pecos; D, E, and F, exact source unidentified but known to be from one or more of the Kotyiti-producing pueblos.

tion matrix and a factor analysis). The sherds in subgroups D, E, and F are primarily from the Galisteo Basin and the middle Rio Grande (below La Bajada Mesa). Most of these sherds are from glaze-on-red, with some glaze-on-yellow and glaze-on-polychrome, wares. The average compositions and standard deviations for the groups are presented in Table 1, and a tentative identification for the groups based on a visual inspection of the pottery style, temper, and composition is given in the caption to Figure 2.

The principal component and R-mode analysis of the elements were in agreement in showing that three major mineral components were important in forming the clusters in Figure 2. The three mineral components were represented by a group of refractory elements (Fe, V, Ti, Al, Cr, and Co), a group associated with the plagioclase feldspar elements (Ca, Na, Mg, Ba, Mn, Zn, and P), and a group associated with the alkali feldspar elements (K, Rb, Si, Zr, Y, and Nb). Sr was associated with both the refractory group and the plagioclase group, as expected. In fact, the refractory group and the plagioclase group were significantly closer to each other than they were to the alkali feldspar group. These groupings make geologic sense as the eastern Española Basin is dominated by the granitic rocks from the Sangre de Christo range and the volcanic ash from the caldera in the Jemez Mountains, while the Galisteo Basin has a larger percentage of the refractory elements found in the Ortiz Mountains (Figure 1). These patterns are also in general agreement with the major components found by Stewart et al. (1990:619) for Robinson Pueblo, New Mexico, using INAA.

Figure 3 is an example of a two-dimensional scatter plot of a representative element from one of the mineral groups (Sr) versus an element from another one of the mineral groups (K). The letters plotted correspond to the subgroups shown in Figure 2. From plots such as these, it is easy to see whether a given element is particularly diagnostic for a given type of sherd. The same information is inherently contained in the data and dendrogram presented in Table 1 and Figure 2, but a plot such as that shown in Figure 3 can help one to visualize the spatial variation of the elements. Note, for example, the elongation of subgroup F. Taking the logs of the data before normalizing might help make the data more spherical in distribution, but it is also possible subgroup F either belongs with subgroups D and E, or that with more data or processing F would split into further subgroups. For those elements whose concentrations are near the detection limits, using a more sensitive method—such as INAA—may be required. For Sr, this was not the case, but the concentration of some elements, such as Co and Nb, is very near their 10 ppm detection limit, and using a log-normal distribution would increase the noise in the clustering

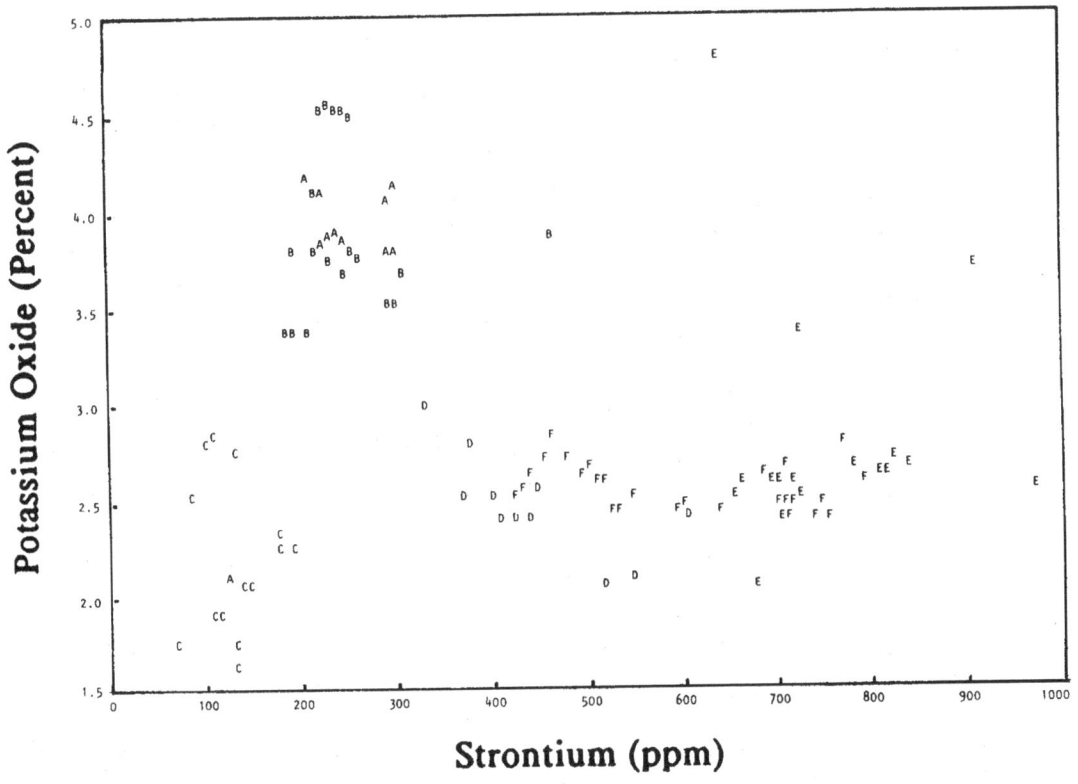

FIGURE 3. Scatter diagram of strontium and potassium data illustrating the separation of pottery groups possible with just two variables. Letters corresponding to the various pueblos are identified in Figure 2.

step unless these elements were first deleted from the data set.

The first cluster or subgroup (A) contains seven sherds tentatively identified as Tewa Polychrome or Red wares (6, 35, 41, 44, 46, 68, and 77). (Tewa Red wares cannot be separated from Tewa Polychromes in a number of instances because of the very small size of these sherds.) There are also four Kapo Gray wares (2, 24, 70, and 88), which usually are indistinguishable from the Tewa Red wares in elemental composition, the difference in color being produced by firing conditions. The loosely associated Tewa sherds (77 and 88) have half as much K and Sr (77), comparable to that found in pottery from Pecos Pueblo, or four times as much Cr (88) as the other members of subgroup A. Cr is usually found in high concentrations in

mineral pigments along with other transition metal elements like Mn. Mineral pigments are not typical of Tewa wares as they used carbon-based pigments for decorating most of their wares. The source of group A is suspected as being Pojoaque Pueblo based on the unique signature of the elements. The ratio of Zr to Sr and K is particularly useful in this identification, as the relatively high K and intermediate to low Sr (230 ppm) locate the sherds as coming from a pueblo in the Española Basin, while the high Zr relative to Sr matches that found by Olinger (1988:2) for Pojoaque. The temper also supports this identification, showing only minute particles of quartz or feldspar sand and mica. A more critical comparison with Olinger's work is unfortunately not possible, as standards that calibrated the XRF were not used in that work, severely restricting the value of the work to other researchers using a different instrument.

The second subgroup (B) also contains Kapo Gray (19, 20, 21, 22, 29, 71, 79, 86, and 87) and Tewa Polychrome (4, 10, 30, 48, 50, 89, and 93) sherds. This subgroup contains a misplaced Kotyiti glaze-on-yellow soup plate (85) and a sherd that appeared at first to be a glaze-on-red (90), but which may be misidentified. A glaze-on-yellow sherd (61) also seems to be misplaced, but the presence of a foot on the sherd indicates that it—like sherd 85—does not follow the typical stylistic traditions for this pottery, and it is possible that the pottery manufactured for the Spanish was not produced in the same place or with the same procedures as the regular Pueblo pottery.

The Kapo Gray and Polychrome wares in subgroup B appear to have been produced by Cuyamungue, Nambé, or Tesuque pueblos. Cuyamungue pottery typically has only a little fine sand and ash temper while Nambé and Tesuque commonly have relatively large quartz sand grains and mica temper. Tesuque's temper seems to be slightly larger than Nambé's, the ratio of Zr to Sr is higher in Tesuque than in Nambe pottery, and Cuyamungue has the lowest ratio. The elemental compositions also get more variable as the temper increases in size. Based on these considerations, the Tewa Polychrome wares (4, 10, 30, 48, 50, 89, and 93) in subgroup B might be assigned to Tesuque while the Kapo Gray wares seem to have originated in Cuyamungue (19, 20, 21, 22, and 29) and Nambé (71, 79, 86, and 87). These assignments are necessarily very tentative on such a small data base for pueblos that are only 10 km apart, but both the typology and temper support the elemental analysis. Although it is tempting to try to extract too much from the cluster analysis, the clues provided even in the fine structure of the patterns imply that using r = 0.5 to separate the various groups should be adequate, at least for the relatively homogeneous pottery from the Española Basin.

The third subgroup (C) of sherds is probably not from the Española Basin. It contains only one sherd that may be a Tewa Polychrome ware (78); the rest appear to be from Pecos Pueblo with some decorative features reminiscent of the Kotyiti pottery. The whole group appears to have a Pecos-like paste with rounded quartz sand grains typical of Pecos pottery, except 78 which has lots of mica. The very low Sr (about 130 ppm) separates this source from the other glaze-paint sources along the Rio Grande and in the Galisteo Basin. If Sr had been weighted as less important, this subgroup would appear with the Kotyiti sources, but this would belie the importance of Sr in identifying a separate source of pottery. Sr and K are very useful for differentiating pottery originating near the Sangre de Cristo Mountains from pottery originating further down the Rio Grande, as the Sr content is higher and the K is lower in the latter.

Subgroup D is the first of the groups which originate in areas south of Santa Fe. This subgroup consists almost entirely of Kotyiti sherds possessing a sandy temper. Most of them are from glaze-on-red wares except for a glaze-on-polychrome sherd (65) and a misplaced Tewa Polychrome sherd (59) which has a large-grained sandy temper. This subgroup's elemental profile is very similar to that for sherds previously analyzed (Bower and Snow 1984:293) from Cochiti Pueblo, although the silicon is about 7 percent lower and the iron 2.5 percent higher than was found there. The two sherds 28 and 59 are only loosely associated with this group. Sherd 59 is probably misplaced, but 28 appears to be separated due to its high Ca content (15.4% compared to the more usual 6%), which may be caused by caliche in the pottery picked up from the soil or simply the natural variation of this relatively diverse group.

Subgroup E is composed almost completely of glaze-on-yellow sherds (7, 11, 13, 18, 33, 34, 51, 58, 74, 84, and 91) with a few glaze-on-red sherds (54 and 96) and Pecos (55 and 92) or indeterminate (14 and 73) sherds. Sherds 14, 54, and 74 have been burned badly enough to make their identification difficult, and 73 was too small a fragment for typological identification. Subgroups E and F are separated from D mostly due to their higher Sr content, while E is separated from F primarily by its lower Fe content, as might be expected for a yellow instead of a red clay body.

The last subgroup, F, is composed of 19 glaze-on-red sherds, a possible Pecos sherd (23), and seven indeterminate sherds (12, 38, 47, 57, 75, 81, and 82), many of which have been burned making identification difficult. This subgroup, like subgroup E, is probably from more than one Kotyiti-producing pueblo, and the relatively high concentrations of Sr, Fe, V, and other refractory elements suggest locations in the Galisteo Basin near the Ortiz Mountains. In order to identify more specifically the origins of the sherds in subgroups E and F, more analytical work will be needed on known sherds to develop an appropriate data base.

Discussion

A comparison of the different sherd origins at LA 20,000 to the origins of the nearby Hispanic settlement LA 16,768 (data not given; see Bower and Snow 1984:293) indicates the two settlements had different trading patterns. Sherds from subgroup C especially were not represented in the earlier study. This subgroup appears to be from Pecos, which is closer to LA 16,768, and therefore its absence was a surprise. Within the glaze-on-yellow and glaze-on-red Kotyiti pottery there may also be a distinct split based on the Sr, Y, and Zn concentrations. Previously, Zn had been identified as a constituent primarily in matte-black pigments, but it may also be associated with a clay component (Bower et al. 1986:313). Future studies will try to determine whether clay sources from the Santa Fe river drainage where LA 20,000 is located and known pottery from nearby pueblos match any of the unidentified sherd profiles. It seems likely that at least one of these groups will be identified as La Cienega Pueblo itself. Its exact location still remains a mystery, but it should be very near the LA 20,000 site. Even if one of these groups is attributed to La Cienega Pueblo, the small percentage of sherds from what is assumed to be the closest pueblo raises some questions. If *none* of the sherds are from the Pueblo of Cienega, the questions of course intensify. Perhaps the inhabitants of Cienega Pueblo were otherwise employed by the Spanish, or were reduced in number for some reason during this period. However, until

and unless this pueblo can be identified archaeologically, attribution remains a moot question.

The multiple origins of the pottery from LA 20,000 call into question the usefulness of the previous generalizations of Snow (1974:63) and Warren (1979:187–193) that ceramic assemblages at Spanish colonial sites are usually characteristic of the nearest pueblo source. The exceptions to this generalization may be even more revealing of trade and socio-economic relationships. In the discussions that follow, it should be noted that the present study used only a selected sample of sherds from one period of excavation, and a few wares (e.g., Tabira, identified by visual typology) were not included in the analysis. One can safely assume, however, that this sample represents a minimum of ceramic sources at the site.

Local glaze-paint wares represent approximately 85 percent of the ceramic assemblages at LA 20,000 (based on Spring and Summer 1990 field seasons), and these wares appear to come from at least three different glaze-producing pueblos located to the south, east, and southwest of the site. Matte-paint wares, which represent approximately 15 percent of the ceramics at the site, appear to originate in four Tewa pueblos to the north. As Bower and Snow (1984:295) have previously shown, XRF analysis makes it possible to tell pueblo sources apart even with a small number of samples due to the large number of elements that are measured. Another x-ray fluorescence analysis of ceramics from LA 20,000 which tackles the more complex problem of culinary wares may help to differentiate and identify better the multiple sources of supply found in this study. It will also be wise to correct the data for the lack of independence that results when multiple sherds from the same pot are analyzed by including the proximity of the sherds when selecting a sample set. Continuing excavation and subsequent statistical analysis of the incidence of the different pottery types and forms will eventually provide a more complete picture of the exchange relationships of this commodity between colonists and Pueblo Indians. Unfortunately, an analysis of the sources of ceramic artifacts cannot in itself identify the exact processes whereby Pueblo ceramics came to Spanish settlements. This type of study must instead be supported with other sources of information, such as oral histories and archival research, in order to determine the processes of interethnic contact which created the artifact assemblages.

Under the Spanish colonial institution known as the *encomienda* some of the Spanish conquerors were entitled to payment of tribute from the local pueblos in return for protection from nomadic tribes and other services (Scholes 1935:78–79). The documentary records offer evidence that these *encomenderos* often maintained *ranchos* or *estancias* close to "their" pueblos, as indeed they would have to in order to exercise their "protective" functions. However, they may not have lived there themselves, and many other colonists also inhabited the countryside amidst the established pueblos. The *encomenderos* with their tribute would have played a key role in the systems of trade and economic relationships among colonists, government officials, missionaries, and Pueblo Indians. According to historical records, this tribute consisted of a specified number of textiles or animal hides and a quantity of foodstuffs (Snow 1983:350). Although ceramics are not listed among the items collected as tribute from the various pueblos, pottery may also have been exchanged in this network, at least as containers for the foodstuffs.

The ubiquitous presence of Pueblo-manufactured pottery at these Spanish colonial sites indicates that this commodity was heavily involved in transactions between the two ethnic groups on a much broader scale than the formal tribute system (Snow 1974:63; Fedor and Lord 1990:39, 74–75). The scarcity (1% or less) of Spanish- or Mexican-manufactured ceramics, and the frequent presence of Spanish forms such as soup plates and candlesticks among the abundant ceramic artifacts recovered from these 17th-century sites together with the lack of evidence of pottery manufacturing at the sites, reiterates the dependence of the colonists on Pueblo potters for their domestic needs. Thus the origins of these ceramics promise information on the network of *informal* transactions of commodities. Whether the transactions occurred under modes of barter, gift, purchase, or seizure, they indicate a system of interethnic and possibly interpersonal relationships.

Despite the admiration that early Spanish explorers recorded for ceramics of Pueblo Indian manufacture (see especially the Gallegos account of the Rodriguez-Chamuscado expedition of 1581; Hammond and Rey 1966:82, 85), researchers are confronted with the fact that pottery is almost never mentioned in the surviving 17th-century documents (nor those of the 18th and 19th centuries). The Spanish colonists apparently attached no "official" economic value to it. Together with other material items in daily use, such as building materials, firewood, and grinding implements, the ceramic vessels used for storage, preparation, and consumption of daily foodstuffs appear to have been taken for granted and deemed unworthy of economic recognition. Snow has argued that pottery was an ethnic boundary marker between the Spanish colonists and indigenous pueblos— "making pottery was the Indian thing to do" (Snow 1974:57), and in the class- and status-conscious Spanish society it would have been therefore devalued.

Another possibility, and one which could be closely tied to status and class structure, is that pottery was the domain not only of the household but also of women and as such was submerged as an economic commodity. Under Spanish colonial law and administration, women had protected property rights and could buy, sell, and manage real property just as men could; they shared equally in inheritance and retained their own names after marriage (Jenkins 1983:335). One woman is even listed as holding an *encomienda* (Snow 1983:354). Nonetheless, the government officials were men and their records contain scant mention of women's roles in economic activities and interethnic contacts, and none at all in trade. Historic and ethnographic accounts identify Pueblo women as the primary potters (Batkin 1987:19); the preparation of daily meals in an Hispanic household traditionally has been the responsibility of women, whether Spanish mistress or Indian servant (Swadesh 1974:178). Thus, the production and use of pottery was strongly gender-specific, and this consideration together with those related to ethnicity and status may help explain the high incidence of ceramic artifacts in Spanish colonial household sites coupled with the paucity of written records pertaining to them. It also underscores the significant insights into 17th-century New Mexican society that may be gained by the identification of sites of origin for these ceramic vessels. Not only can a deeper understanding of the network of relationships between the Spanish and Puebloans be obtained, but it may also modify the male-oriented documentary record to include what is very rare—a context for understanding contacts among women in both ethnic groups and the extent and degree of influence women in a given colonial settlement or household might have over the surrounding pueblos—and vice versa.

The implications of this situation for understanding intra- and inter-district exchange patterns among Pueblo Indian potters and Spanish colonial households and individuals are clearly significant as the conditions and processes of frontier acculturation and enculturation in the 17th-century Rio Grande area are elucidated. The ability to distinguish the Pueblo origins of the pottery destined for colonial use will be a key component in helping to sharpen perspectives on the conditions and patterns of 17th-century Pueblo/Hispanic cultural processes.

ACKNOWLEDGMENTS

The analytical portion of this work was generously supported by the Margaret T. and Otis A. Barnes Trust, which provided a summer stipend as well as necessary equipment for the preparation of the samples. The Rigaku XRF instrument used in the analyses was provided by a grant from the Keck Foundation. Preliminary exploration of the site LA 20,000 was done by The Colorado College in collaboration with the Laboratory of Anthropology, Museum of New Mexico, in 1980 and 1982. The artifacts recovered from LA 20,000 are in the custody of the Museum of New Mexico and are on loan to David H. Snow and The Colorado College for study. Excavation was resumed in 1987 by The Colorado College with support from El Rancho de Las Golindrinas, the New Mexico Endowment for the Humanities, and private grants, and by permission of Alfonso and Cecilia Sanchez and La Cienega Partnership. Our appreciation is extended to all, especially to the students who have worked on the site.

REFERENCES

ALDENDERFER, MARK S., AND ROGER K. BLASHFIELD
1984 *Cluster Analysis.* Sage, Beverly Hills, California.

ARNOLD, DEAN E., HECTOR NEFF, AND RONALD L. BISHOP
1991 Compositional Analysis and Sources of Pottery: An Ethnoarchaeological Approach. *American Anthropologist* 93:70–90.

BATKIN, JONATHAN
1987 *Pottery of the Pueblos of New Mexico 1700–1940.* The Taylor Museum of the Colorado Springs Fine Arts Center, Colorado Springs, Colorado.

BAXTER, M. J.
1989 Multivariate Analysis of Data on Glass Compositions: A Methodological Note. *Archaeometry* 31(1): 45–53.
1991 Principal Component and Correspondence Analyses of Glass Compositions: An Empirical Study. *Archaeometry* 33(1):29–41.

BOWER, NATHAN W., S. FACISZEWSKI, S. RENWICK, AND S. PECKHAM
1986 A Preliminary Analysis of Rio Grande Glazes of the Classic Period Using Scanning Electron Microscopy with X-ray Fluorescence. *Journal of Field Archaeology* 13:307–315.

BOWER, NATHAN W., D. RADAMACHER, T. SHIMOTAKE, T. ANSELMI, AND S. PECKHAM
1988 A Pattern Recognition and Scanning Electron Microscope with X-ray Fluorescence Analysis of Glaze-paint Anasazi Pottery from the American Southwest. In *Proceedings of the 26th International Archaeometry Symposium*, edited by R. M. Farquhar, R. G. Hancock, and L. A. Pavlish, pp. 204–209. Archaeometry Laboratory, University of Toronto, Toronto.

BOWER, NATHAN W., AND DAVID H. SNOW
1984 A Comparative Study of Early Historic "Tewa" Pottery. In *New Mexico Geological Society Guidebook, 35th Field Conference, Rio Grande Rift: Northern New Mexico*, edited by W. S. Baldridge, P. W. Dickerson, R. E. Riecher, and J. Zidek, pp. 291–295. New Mexico Geological Society, Socorro, New Mexico.

BREITBARD, ELISSA, AND KRISTI KLUNGNESS
1987 Analysis of 17th-Century Cienega and Cieneguilla

Pueblos. Ms. on file, Department of Anthropology, The Colorado College, Colorado Springs, Colorado.

BROMUND, RICHARD H., NATHAN W. BOWER, AND ROBERT H. SMITH
1976 Inclusions in Ancient Ceramics: An Approach to the Problem of Sampling for Chemical Analysis. *Archaeometry* 18:218–221.

EVERITT, BRIAN
1980 *Cluster Analysis*. Second edition. Halsted, New York.

FEDOR, LARA, AND SARAH LORD
1990 Seventeenth-Century Spanish Colonial Material Culture. Ms. on file, Department of Anthropology, The Colorado College, Colorado Springs, Colorado.

GOFF, FRAZER, JAMIE N. GARDNER, W. SCOTT BALDRIDGE, JEFFREY B. HULDEN, DENNIS L. NIELSON, DAVID VANIMAN, GRANT HEIKEN, MICHAEL A. DUNGAN, AND DAVID BROXTON
1989 Volcanic and Hydrothermal Evolution of Valles Caldera and Jemez Volcanic Field. *New Mexico Bureau of Mines and Mineral Resources Memoir* 46: 381–434. Charles E. Chapin and Jiri Zidek, editors. New Mexico Bureau of Mines, Socorro, New Mexico.

HAMMOND, GEORGE P., AND AGAPITO REY
1966 *The Rediscovery of New Mexico, 1580–1594*. University of New Mexico Press, Albuquerque.

JENKINS, MYRA ELLEN
1983 Some Eighteenth-Century New Mexico Women of Property. In *Hispanic Arts and Ethnohistory in the Southwest*, edited by Marta Weigle, Samuel Larcombe, and Claudia Larcombe, pp. 335–345. University of New Mexico Press, Albuquerque.

KIDDER, ALFRED V., AND ANNA O. SHEPARD
1936 *The Pottery of Pecos*, Vol. 1. Phillips Academy and Yale University Press, Andover, Massachusetts, and New Haven, Connecticut.

NEFF, HECTOR, RONALD L. BISHOP, AND EDWARD V. SAYRE
1989 More Observations on the Problem of Tempering in Compositional Studies of Archaeological Ceramics. *Journal of Archaeological Science* 16:57–69.

NIE, NORMAN H., C. HADLAI HULL, JEAN G. JENKINS, KARIN STEINBRENNER, AND DALE H. BENT
1975 *Statistical Package for the Social Sciences*. McGraw Hill, New York.

OLINGER, BART
1988 Pottery Studies Using X-ray Fluorescence, Part 3: The Historic Pottery of the Northern Tewa. *Pottery Southwest* 15(4):1–6.

SCHOLES, FRANCE V.
1935 Civil Government and Society in New Mexico in the Seventeenth Century. *New Mexico Historical Review* 10(2):71–111.
1942 Troublous Times in New Mexico 1659–1670. *Historical Society of New Mexico Publications in History* 11. University of New Mexico Press, Albuquerque.

SHARAF, MUHAMMED A., DEBORAH L. ILLMAN, AND BRUCE R. KOWALSKI
1986 *Chemometrics*. John Wiley and Sons, New York.

SHENNAN, STEPHAN
1988 *Quantifying Archaeology*. Edinburgh University Press, Edinburgh.

SHEPARD, ANNA O.
1942 Rio Grande Glaze-Paint Ware; A Study Illustrating the Place of Ceramic Technological Analysis in Archaeological Research. *Carnegie Institution Publication* 7. Washington, D.C.

SNOW, DAVID H.
1974 Some Economic Considerations of Historic Rio Grande Pueblo Pottery. In *El Corral de Santa Fe Brand Book 1973*, edited by Albert H. Schroeber, pp. 55–72. Rio Grande Press, Glorieta, New Mexico.
1983 A Note on Encomienda Economics in Seventeenth-Century New Mexico. In *Hispanic Arts and Ethnohistory in the Southwest*, edited by Marta Weigle, Samuel Larcombe, and Claudia Larcombe, pp. 347–357. University of New Mexico Press, Albuquerque, New Mexico.

SNOW, DAVID H., AND MARIANNE L. STOLLER
1987 Outside Santa Fe in the 17th Century. Paper presented at the Annual Meeting of the American Society for Ethnohistory, Berkeley, California.

STEWART, JOE D., PHILIP FRALICK, RONALD G. V. HANCOCK, JANE H. KELLY, AND ELIZABETH M. GARRET
1990 Petrographic Analysis and INAA Geochemistry of Prehistoric Ceramics from Robinson Pueblo, New Mexico. *Journal of Archaeological Science* 17:601–625.

SWADESH, FRANCES LEON
1974 *Los Primeros Pobladores*. University of Notre Dame Press, Notre Dame, Indiana.

WARREN, A. HELENE
1979 Historic Pottery of the Cochiti Reservoir Area. In *Archeological Investigations in Cochiti Reservoir, New Mexico*, Vol. 4, edited by J. V. Biella and R. C. Chapman, pp. 187–216. University of New Mexico, Office of Contract Archeology, Albuquerque, New Mexico.

Perspectives from *Historical Archaeology*

WILSON, SAMUEL M., AND DON J. MELNICK
  1990 Modelling Randomness in Locational Archaeology.
         Journal of Archaeological Science 17:403–412.

NATHAN W. BOWER
WILLIAM J. THOMAS
DEPARTMENT OF CHEMISTRY
THE COLORADO COLLEGE
COLORADO SPRINGS, COLORADO 80903

MARIANNE L. STOLLER
JOHN W. KANTNER
DEPARTMENT OF ANTHROPOLOGY
THE COLORADO COLLEGE
COLORADO SPRINGS, COLORADO 80903

DAVID H. SNOW
CROSS-CULTURAL RESEARCH SYSTEMS
SANTA FE, NEW MEXICO 87501

JULIA KING

Ceramic Variability in 17th Century St. Augustine, Florida

ABSTRACT

One of the issues central to the archaeological research program in St. Augustine has been the nature of colonial adaptive variability and how it is reflected archaeologically. Early and late 17th century ceramic assemblages from three undocumented sites in the town were analyzed and compared using the chi-square test for significance. Observed differences in the ceramic patterning occurred predominantly among Spanish Olive Jar and aboriginal ware categories. Based on previous research at documented 18th century St. Augustine sites, it is suggested that variation among these categories may be linked to 17th century income and occupational status.

Introduction

St. Augustine, Florida, the nation's oldest continuously occupied city, has been a focus for the archaeological investigation of colonial Hispanic culture in North America. The city was predominantly Spanish for most of its colonial history with the exception of a short period of British occupation following the French and Indian War (1763–1781). Initially, archaeological research in St. Augustine was concentrated on the 18th century first Spanish period (Poe 1979; Deagan 1983). More recently, the 16th century (Deagan 1978a, 1978b, 1980) and 17th century (King 1981) periods have also been investigated.

This paper is intended to provide an analysis of ceramic variability at three 17th century sites in St. Augustine from both early (1600–1650) and late (1650–1700) contexts. Ceramics were chosen for this study because of their importance as part of the Spanish subsistence system and because they have been demonstrated to reflect both social and temporal variability in 18th century St. Augustine. Their analysis may provide suggestions concerning the nature of adaptive variability in 17th century St. Augustine.

Historical Background

St. Augustine was founded in 1565 by Pedro Menéndez de Aviles of Spain in an effort to protect the Spanish claim to the Florida province and to strengthen Spanish control of the treasure fleet route originating in Mexico (Lyon 1976:38–71) (Figure 1). Although the town's importance as a military outpost necessitated permanent settlement in the face of growing international rivalry, St. Augustine remained a "poor and isolated market with little to export" (Bushnell 1982:10). From 1565 until the end of the first Spanish period in 1763, the majority of the population was dependent upon the *situado,* an annual subsidy of rations, salaries and military equipment. Responsibility for the *situado* was with the treasury at Seville and then Veracruz during the late 16th century, and subsequently switched to the treasury at Mexico City by the 17th century (Bushnell 1982).

During the latter part of the 16th century, St. Augustine was plagued with Indian troubles and the threat of French attack. In 1586, the Englishman Sir Francis Drake raided and burned the small *presidio* and, in 1599, a hurricane and subsequent fires destroyed the town. By this time, the indigenous Timucua Indians had been weakened by disease and the threat from the French and English declined as they began colonizing efforts elsewhere in the New World (Arnade 1959). For these and other reasons, hearings were held in the town in 1602 to decide whether to continue settlement at St. Augustine. Despite the generally unenthusiastic testimony, the Spanish colonial agencies decided to maintain the garrison at St. Augustine (Arnade 1959).

Two stages are evident in the colonial development of 17th century St. Augustine. Throughout the 17th century until about 1670, St. Augustine was characterized by an impoverished economy, recurring epidemics, slow population growth, and relative isolation from other European (including Spanish) colonies in the New World. The population remained at approximately 600 individuals from the late 16th century until about 1675. During this period, the *situado* often arrived late and partially spoiled, or not at all (Bushnell 1982).

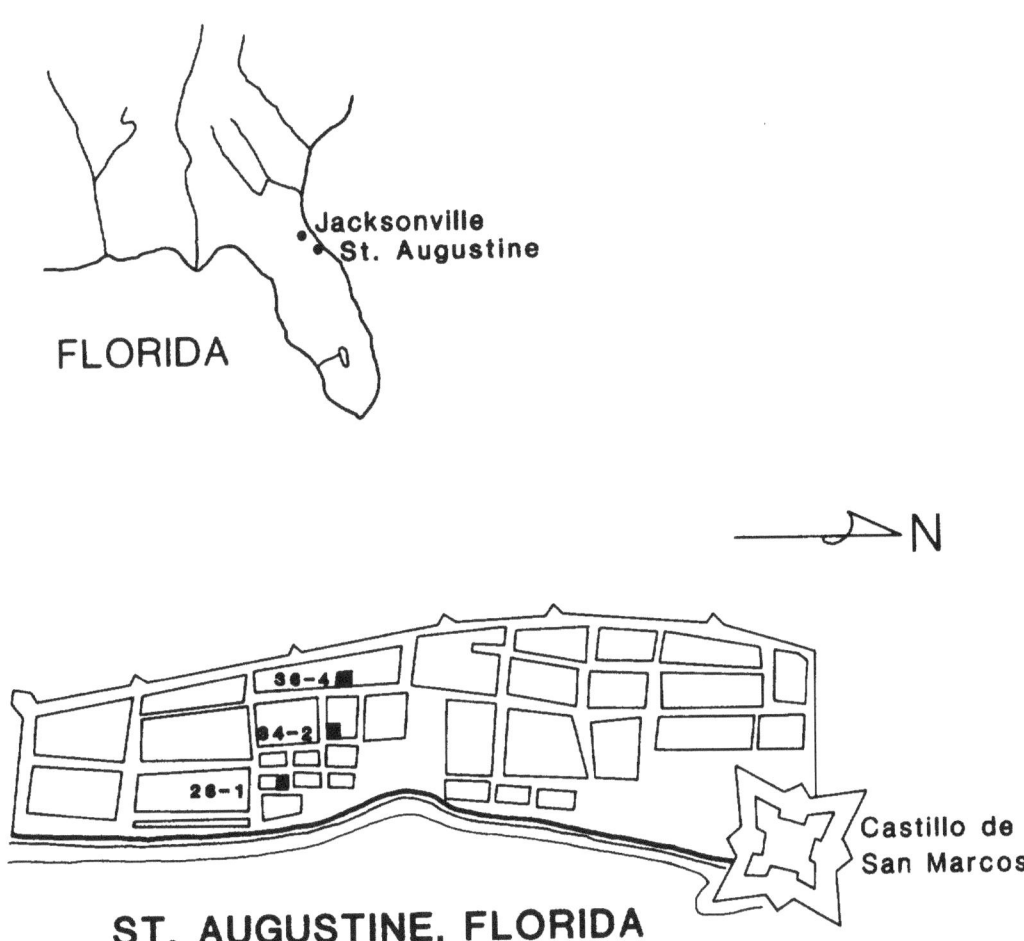

FIGURE 1. Map of St. Augustine, Florida, showing the location of sites SA 34-2, SA 26-1, and SA 36-4.

The last reported 17th century epidemic was in 1672, after which the town population increased to 1,000 persons by 1680 and possibly 1,400 by 1685 (Dunkle 1958:6, 9). The Spanish mission system, which had been established in the late 16th century, reached the peak of its development by 1675, stretching solidly west to the Chattahoochee River and north to present-day Port Royal Sound in South Carolina (Gannon 1967). Spanish cattle ranches had been established in north central Florida by the second half of the 17th century and may have even exported some of their products to New Spain (Bushnell 1978). By the end of the 17th

century, Spaniards, mestizos, Indians, and blacks formed significant components of the town's ethnic composition (King 1981).

At the beginning of the 18th century, Spanish occupation in north Florida was seriously weakened by the raids of Colonel James Moore of South Carolina and his English and Indian allies. Moore captured and destroyed most of the Spanish mission settlements in 1702 and 1703 and laid seige to St. Augustine, burning the town but leaving the majority of the population safe within the stone fortress, Castillo de San Marcos. After Moore's retreat, the colonists rebuilt the town and maintained settlement there until 1763, when Spain ceded Florida to Great Britain following the French and Indian War.

The undependable nature of the *situado* throughout the 17th century forced the St. Augustine residents to rely more on indigenous and aboriginal food sources. Thus, this was a period of cultural crystallization in Spanish Florida during which the Hispanic-Floridian tradition, so visible for 18th century St. Augustine, developed (Shephard 1983).

Data Base and Methods of Analysis

Three sites in St. Augustine with known 17th century occupation were chosen for this study. These include the Ximenez-Fatio House site (SA 34-2), the Josef de Leon site (SA 26-1), and the Palm Row site (SA 36-4) (Figure 1). All three sites fall within both the 16th century and expanded 17th century town boundaries as defined by archaeological investigation (Deagan 1982) and each has been occupied from the late 16th century to the present day. Unfortunately, no documentary evidence pertaining to the occupants of individual 17th century sites is available in this country at the present time.

Archaeological excavation at these sites was carried out by the Florida State University field school between 1976 and 1980 under the direction of Kathleen Deagan. All excavated materials were subsequently cataloged and are curated at the Preservation Board in St. Augustine.

A total of 162 17th century proveniences containing one or more ceramic fragments was recovered from the sites. These proveniences, which include zone or midden deposits, trash pits, well pits and well fill, post holes and post molds, and features of unknown function, were classified as either early or late 17th century. This temporal division was made in an effort to archaeologically approximate the two-period division within the 17th century suggested by the historical evidence. Of these proveniences, 73 dated to the early 17th century and 89 dated to post-1650.

The ceramics were classified into categories based on the presumed ethnic affiliations of their origins. All Hispanic types were further grouped into functional categories, including tablewares (Majolica), storage containers (Olive Jar), and utilitarian wares. The data were analyzed at an IBM computer terminal using both the Statistical Package for the Social Sciences (SPSS) and the Statistical Analysis System (SAS) programs.

17th Century Ceramics And Change Through Time

The 17th century ceramic assemblages from St. Augustine were found to contain Hispanic, Mexican, Timucuan and Guale aboriginal, and other European (primarily English) elements, although in varying proportions. The raw counts and relative frequencies for each ceramic category from early and late contexts are presented in Tables 1 and 2.

Aboriginal coarse earthenwares constituted the largest ceramic group recovered from both early and late proveniences at all sites except the early component at de Leon, and increased in frequency at all sites in the late 17th century. This category consists primarily of the St. Johns and San Marcos Series ceramics, with a small amount of other, non-local aboriginal wares. At sites of the early 17th century, St. Johns ceramics account for 21.2% of the total ceramic assemblage, decreasing slightly to 20.0% of the late 17th century assemblage (Tables 1 and 2). At the .001 level of probability, the St. Johns Series ceramics were found not to be significantly different in frequency between early and late contexts ($x^2 = 1.62$; df $= 1$). (Although the .05 level of probability is often considered standard for statistical tests of significance, the .001 level was preferred in this analysis because of the large amount of ceramic fragments used in this study.) San Marcos ceramics, however, which account for 15.8% of the early 17th century ceramic assemblage, increase to 41.8% of the total late assemblage, a statistically significant increase in proportion ($x^2 = 544.2$; df $= 1$). This trend is apparent at all three sites examined.

The St. Johns Series ceramics, a fine chalky

TABLE 1
PATTERNS OF CERAMIC VARIABILITY FROM EARLY 17TH CENTURY CONTEXTS

CERAMIC GROUP	Fatio (SA 34-2) Count	Fatio (SA 34-2) Percent	De Leon (SA 26-1) Count	De Leon (SA 26-1) Percent	Palm Row (SA 36-4) Count	Palm Row (SA 36-4) Percent	TOTAL Count	Percent
Majolica	18	5.7	184	7.2	10	4.8	212	6.8
Olive Jar	82	25.9	1174	45.6	40	19.2	1296	41.8
Coarse Earthenwares								
Hispanic	9	2.8	198	7.7	2	1.0	209	6.7
Unidentified	5	1.6	69	2.7	10	4.8	84	2.7
Other European								
Ceramics	0	.0	10	.4	0	.0	10	.3
(TOTAL EUROPEAN)	(114)	(36.0)	(1635)	(63.6)	(62)	(29.8)	(1811)	(58.3)
St. Johns	62	19.6	532	20.7	64	30.8	658	21.2
San Marcos	117	36.9	293	11.4	81	38.9	491	15.8
Other Aboriginal								
Ceramics	24	7.6	113	4.4	1	.5	138	4.5
(TOTAL ABORIGINAL)	(203)	(64.1)	(938)	(36.5)	(146)	(70.2)	(1287)	(41.5)
TOTAL CERAMICS	317	100.1	2573	100.1	208	100.1	3098	99.9

TABLE 2
PATTERNS OF CERAMIC VARIABILITY FROM LATE 17TH CENTURY CONTEXTS

CERAMIC GROUP	Fatio (SA 34-2) Count	Fatio (SA 34-2) Percent	De Leon (SA 26-1) Count	De Leon (SA 26-1) Percent	Palm Row (SA 36-4) Count	Palm Row (SA 36-4) Percent	TOTAL Count	Percent
Majolica	43	7.6	206	7.8	36	6.4	285	7.6
Olive Jar	83	14.7	627	23.8	72	12.8	782	20.8
Coarse Earthenwares								
Hispanic	19	3.4	48	1.8	18	3.2	85	2.3
Unidentified	3	.5	49	1.9	18	3.2	70	1.9
Other European								
Ceramics	2	.4	10	.4	11	2.0	23	.6
(TOTAL EUROPEAN)	(150)	(26.6)	(940)	(35.7)	(155)	(27.6)	(1245)	(33.2)
St. Johns	106	18.8	579	22.0	66	11.7	751	20.0
San Marcos	276	48.8	1011	38.4	287	51.1	1574	41.8
Other Aboriginal								
Ceramics	33	5.8	105	4.0	54	9.6	192	5.1
(TOTAL ABORIGINAL)	(415)	(73.4)	(1695)	(64.4)	(407)	(72.4)	(2527)	(66.9)
TOTAL CERAMICS	565	100.0	2635	100.1	562	100.0	3762	100.1

paste pottery usually either left plain or check-stamped, were the characteristic ware of the indigenous Timucua Indians (Goggin 1952). At the time of the 1565 founding of St. Augustine, the Timucuans inhabited the northeast coast of Florida and, in the early years of the settlement, the Spaniards were forced to take shelter in a Timucuan village located adjacent to St. Augustine (Lyon 1976:180). Contact with Europeans resulted in increased tensions, widespread epidemics and, consequently, a breakdown in Timucuan social structure (Deagan 1978c:112–13). The population was rapidly decimated by the end of the 17th century, and the last report of a living Timucua was made in 1733 (Deagan 1978c:115).

The San Marcos Series ceramics, a sand and grit-tempered ware, are believed to originally have been manufactured by the Guale Indians located along the southeast coast of Georgia between St. Andrew and St. Catherines Sounds (Smith 1948; Otto and Lewis 1975). As early as the 16th century, attempts had been made to establish Spanish missions among the Guale, although it was not until the early 17th century with the arrival of the Franciscans that such attempts were successful (Gannon 1967). Guale Indians were often sent to St. Augustine as laborers in the early 17th century and isolated references to intermarriage between Spanish men and Guale women exist (Deagan 1978c:118–19). Beginning about 1670 and continuing into the 18th century, English expansion into the southeast and the opportunities for day laborers in the construction of Castillo de San Marcos encouraged the relocation of the Guale mission Indians to St. Augustine (Bushnell 1982). This population was integrated with and eventually replaced the local Timucuan population.

The San Marcos wares in post-1670 St. Augustine have been demonstrated to have supplemented cooking and storage vessels otherwise not available in European wares (Otto and Lewis 1975). Bostwick (1976:143–45) and Herron (1978) have suggested that the use of St. Johns ceramics by pre-1670 St. Augustine residents paralleled the later function of San Marcos wares.

Non-local aboriginal wares other than San Marcos form a minor but significant component of the 17th century ceramic assemblages, comprising 4.5% and 5.1% of the total early and late ceramics, respectively. This slight increase in the total late 17th century assemblage was not found to be significantly different at the .001 level ($x^2 = 1.43$; $df = 1$). Non-local aboriginal ceramics are predominantly pottery of the Leon-Jefferson period, manufactured by Indians in northwest Florida, and the Lamar, Irene, and Ocmulgee Series wares manufactured by Indians in coastal and central Georgia (cf., Smith 1948; Piatek 1980). During the 17th century, missions located in these areas served as an interface between the settlers at St.

Augustine and the Florida aboriginal population, and evidence for such contact is reflected in the ceramic assemblages.

Olive Jar fragments, which represent the largest Spanish ceramic category at the sites sampled, decrease in overall frequency from 41.8% of the total early 17th century ceramic assemblages to 20.8% of the total late assemblages, significantly different at the .001 level ($x^2 = 355.4$; $df = 1$). This trend is apparent at all three sites. Spanish Olive Jars, which have a sand-tempered, flesh-colored paste with conical bottoms and are sometimes glazed, were used primarily to ship wine and olive oil, and secondarily used as storage vessels during the first Spanish period (Goggin 1960). A strong negative correlation significant at the .0002 level was observed between San Marcos wares and Olive Jar (Correlation coefficient = −.989), suggesting that St. Augustine residents who could not afford the imported wines and olive oil transported to the Florida province in Olive Jars instead purchased the San Marcos wares, which served as cooking vessels as well as storage containers. St. Johns ceramics are not strongly correlated with Olive Jar or San Marcos wares, indicating that St. Johns wares were not competing with either San Marcos pottery or as substitutes for empty Olive Jars. It should also be noted that St. Johns ceramics did not decrease through the 17th century and remained a consistent component of 17th century ceramic assemblages.

Spanish tin-glazed earthenwares, or Majolica, exhibit a slight increase in proportion through the 17th century, from 6.8% of the total early period ceramics to 7.6% of the late period ceramics, although this increase is not significant ($x^2 = 1.25$; $df = 1$). Majolica, often in the form of brightly colored plates and bowls (Goggin 1968), was the major tableware used during the first Spanish period, supplemented by tablewares of English origin in the 18th century. No suitable replacement was available for Majolica at the time of the founding of St. Augustine, nor does the archaeological record suggest that Majolica forms were copied by makers of aboriginal pottery. In addition, Majolica, unlike Olive Jar, was manufactured in Mexico (Goggin 1968; Lister and Lister 1974) and was available for export throughout the 17th century.

Hence, Majolica remained a consistent proportion of the 17th century ceramic complexes.

Hispanic glazed and unglazed utilitarian coarse earthenwares other than Olive Jar decrease in overall frequency from 6.7% in the early period to 2.3% in the late 17th century. The recovery of 133 Spanish storage jar fragments from an early period trash pit at the de Leon site has probably distorted an accurate representation of these earthenwares in early 17th century contexts. At both the Ximenez-Fatio and Palm Row sites, the frequency of Spanish coarse earthenwares does not significantly change from one period to the next (Tables 1 and 2). Many of these vessels were used in food preparation and storage but had forms similar to tinglazed (Majolica and English delft) tablewares, indicating that these items also were not copied by indigenous potters.

The final category of ceramics include those which could be positively identified as European but of non-Spanish origin. These ceramics form a minor part of the assemblages of both the early and late 17th century with no statistically significant change from one period to the next ($x^2 = 2.38$; df = 1). Other European ceramics form less than 1.0% of the total respective ceramic assemblages for both periods (Tables 1 and 2). Despite the undependable nature of the *situado* and the founding of Charleston in 1670, the archaeological evidence suggests that the residents of St. Augustine did not participate in illegal trade with their English neighbors to the north in the 17th century, although this trade flourished in the 18th century (Harman 1969; Deagan 1983). Those non-Hispanic wares recovered from 17th century contexts are predominantly English in origin, although French tin-glazed earthenwares, or faience, and Chinese porcelains have also been found.

Intersite Variability in the 17th Century

The first documentary evidence available for individual sites in St. Augustine is the Puente map of 1763, made prior to the Spanish departure from St. Augustine when Florida was ceded to Great Britain (Puente 1764). The pre-1763 occupants of each site are listed on this map, and the ethnic and occupational identification of these individuals has been provided by archival research. Using these data as controls, research was begun with the 18th century sites of St. Augustine. Three sites known to have been occupied by *criollos* (New World-born Spaniards) and one by a mestizo of varying incomes in 1762 were excavated and the material culture assemblages from each site compared. Although aboriginal pottery constituted the largest proportion of ceramics at each site examined, relatively smaller proportions were evident at sites in which occupants were fully Spanish and whose incomes were higher (Poe 1979; Deagan 1983). Differences in amount and variety of non-ceramic material culture and faunal assemblages were also noted (Poe 1979; Deagan 1983). Unfortunately, similar historical controls are not available for individual 17th century sites in St. Augustine. The ceramic assemblages, however, have been similarly classified and can be compared.

Analysis of intersite variability for early and late proveniences at the Fatio, de Leon and Palm Row sites was done using the chi-square statistic with a significance level of .001. Intersite variation among ceramic categories was found to occur predominantly in relative proportions of Olive Jar and aboriginal ware fragments.

The patterns of ceramic variability for the early 17th century at the Fatio and Palm Row sites are statistically similar with the exception of an increased frequency of non-local aboriginal wares at the Fatio site, suggesting that the occupants at these two sites were probably of similar ethnic background and income level. The early 17th century ceramic assemblage from the de Leon site, however, contains significantly more Olive Jar sherds and less San Marcos ceramics. Based on the research at the 18th century sites of St. Augustine, this difference at de Leon in relative proportion of Hispanic (Olive Jar) and aboriginal (San Marcos) Wares probably reflects a difference in ethnic and/or income status.

Variation among the ceramic assemblages from the late 17th century parallels variation for the early period. Percentages of Majolica do not differ significantly among the three late assemblages. Further, the patterns of ceramic variability at both the Fatio and Palm Row sites are similar for each of the categories except the St. Johns wares, which have a lower relative frequency at the Palm Row site. Again, this would suggest occupants of similar ethnic and income status. The late component at the de Leon site, however, contains a significantly larger proportion of Olive Jar and, conversely, a lesser amount of San Marcos pottery than that found at either the Fatio or Palm Row sites. In addition, the de Leon assemblage has a larger frequency of non-local aboriginal wares and fewer St. Johns ceramics than the Palm row assemblage. The relative proportions of the Olive Jar and San Marcos ceramic categories suggests occupants of different ethnicity and/or higher income at the de Leon site in the second half of the 17th century.

Inferences concerning absolute ethnic affiliation and income level for individual 17th century sites are difficult to make and conclusions must therefore remain tentative. More sites from all locations within the 17th century town boundaries must be investigated to determine what relationships, if any, exist between these socioeconomic variables and material patterning. At present, it appears that the occupants of all three sites for both periods were probably *criollos*, based on the proportion of Majolica recovered from each site (Poe 1979; Deagan 1983). However, the occupant(s) of the de Leon site probably had a relatively higher income.

Individuals with higher incomes had better access to Spanish ceramic forms although suitable replacements were available in aboriginal wares. Olive Jars and their contents were imported to Florida through the *situado*, were almost certainly more expensive than aboriginal forms, and thus were more readily available to individuals with higher incomes. The unreliability of the *situado* and the reality of the economic situation, however, in 17th century St. Augustine eventually forced most, and probably all, residents to depend more on aboriginal ceramic technology.

Conclusion

The comparison of the patterns of ceramic variability from 17th century St. Augustine has revealed processes of both conservatism and acculturation in the Hispanic adaptation to the Florida environment. Interaction with aboriginal peoples, historically and archaeologically evident at the beginning of Spanish colonization in Florida, increased through the 17th century. The isolation of Spanish Florida, the unreliable nature of the *situado*, and Spanish-Indian intermarriage contributed to an increasing dependence of the St. Augustine residents upon aboriginal ceramic technology. Contact with Florida and Georgia aboriginal populations is also archaeologically evident and a Spanish sphere of influence clearly extended into the west Florida and costal Georgia regions.

The increase of San Marcos wares through the 17th century with a corresponding decrease in the presence of Olive Jar and the parallel functions of these two types suggests that when suitable aboriginal forms were available, they were adopted by Spanish households. No suitable aboriginal replacement was available or developed for Majolica or utilitarian coarse earthenwares, vessels which had tableware forms, and these wares remained a consistent component of the 17th century ceramic assemblages. Analysis of intersite variation for both periods has suggested that although the contents of Olive Jars may have been scarce and more expensive than locally produced food supplies, these commodities were preferred by those individuals able to afford them, thus making empty Olive Jars available as storage containers.

The 17th century was a period of cultural crystallization in Spanish Florida. Status distinctions in the small *presidio* were limited by the general poverty of the Florida province, but were not so rigid that, during the 17th century, residents in St. Augustine were unable to adjust to New World conditions in variable ways. The result was a European way of life adapted to southeastern North American conditions.

ACKNOWLEDGEMENTS

Funding for the archaeological research at the Ximenez-Fatio House site (SA 34-2) was provided by the Florida Chapter of the Colonial Dames of America. Excavations at the Josef de Leon site (SA 26-1) were funded by a grant from the National Endowment for the Humanities (RO-32537-78-1425), and at the Palm Row site (SA 36-4) by a grant from the state of Florida.

The Historic St. Augustine Preservation Board permitted access to the archaeological field records and reports from excavations at all three sites. Robert C. Dailey and J. Anthony Paredes (Florida State University) made comments and suggestions during the course of this research. Harold L. Dibble (University of Pennsylvania) provided assistance with the statistical analysis in his course on computers in anthropology.

Finally, I am especially grateful to Kathleen Deagan, who provided invaluable support during the research and writing of this paper.

REFERENCES

ARNADE, CHARLES
1959   *Florida On Trial, 1593–1602*. University of Miami Press, Coral Gables.

BOSTWICK, JOHN A.
1977   Aboriginal Ceramics in Pre-18th Century Colonial St. Augustine: the de Leon Site. *The Conference on Historic Sites Archaeology Papers* 2.

BUSHNELL, AMY
1978   The Menéndez Marquez Cattle Barony at La Chua and the Determinants of Economic Expansion in 17th Century Florida. *Florida Historical Quarterly* 56(4):407–31.
1982   *The King's Coffer*. University Presses of Florida, Gainesville.

DEAGAN, KATHLEEN
1978a   Archaeological Strategy in the Investigation of an Unknown Era: 16th Century St. Augustine. Ms. on file, Historic St. Augustine Preservation Board, St. Augustine.
1978b   The Material Assemblage of 16th Century Spanish Florida. *Historical Archaeology* 12:25–50.
1978c   Cultures in Transition: Fusion and Assimilation Among the Eastern Timucua. In *Tacachale*, edited by J. T. Milanich and S. Proctor. University Presses of Florida, Gainesville.
1980   Spanish St. Augustine: America's First Melting Pot. *Archaeology* 33(5):22–30.
1982   St. Augustine: America's First Urban Enclave. *North American Archaeologist* 3(3).
1983   *Spanish St. Augustine: The Archaeology of a Colonial Creole Community*. Academic Press, New York.

DUNKLE, JOHN
1958   Population Change as an Element in the Historical Geography of St. Augustine, Florida. *Florida Historical Quarterly* 37(1):3–32.

GANNON, MICHAEL V.
1967   *The Cross in the Sand*. University Presses of Florida, Gainesville.

GOGGIN, JOHN M.
1952   Space and Time Perspective in Northern St. Johns Archaeology, Florida. *Yale University Publications in Anthropology* 47.

1960   The Spanish Olive Jar: An Introductory Study. *Yale University Publications in Anthropology* 62.
1968   Spanish Majolica in the New World. *Yale University Publications in Anthropology* 72.

HARMAN, JOYCE
1969   *Trade and Privateering in Spanish Florida, 1732–1763*. St. Augustine Historical Society, St. Augustine.

HERRON, MARY
1978   A Formal and Functional Analysis of St. Johns Series Ceramics from Two Sites in St. Augustine, Florida. Ms. on file, Florida State University, Tallahassee.

KING, JULIA
1981   An Archaeological Investigation of 17th Century St. Augustine, Florida. M.A. Thesis, Florida State University, Tallahassee.

LISTER, ROBERT AND FLORENCE LISTER
1974   Maiolica in Spanish Colonial America. *Historical Archaeology* 8:17–52.

LYON, EUGENE
1976   *The Enterprise of Florida*. University Presses of Florida, Gainesville.

OTTO, JOHN AND R. LEWIS
1975   A Formal and Functional Analysis of San Marcos Ceramics. Florida Department of State, Division of Archives, Bureau of Historic Sites and Properties *Bulletin* 4.

PIATEK, BRUCE J.
1980   Non-Local Aboriginal Ceramics in Early Historic Context: St. Augustine, Florida. Ms. on file, Historic St. Augustine Preservation Board, St. Augustine.

POE, CHARLES B.
1979   Pattern and Status Recognition of 18th Century *Criollos* in St. Augustine, Florida. Paper presented to the Society for Historical Archaeology, January 1979, Nashville.

PUENTE, ELIXIO
1764   Plano de la Real Fuerza, Baluarte, y Linea de la Plaza de Sn. Augustin de la Florida. Buckingham Smith Collection (microfilm reel 2). P. K. Yonge Library, University of Florida.

SHEPHARD, STEVEN J.
1983   The Spanish *Criollo* Majority in Colonial St. Augustine. In *Spanish St. Augustine: The Archaeology of a Colonial Creole Community*, edited by Kathleen Deagan, pp. 65–98. Academic Press, New York.

SMITH, HALE G.
1948   Two Historical Archaeological Periods in Florida. *American Antiquity* 7(4):313–79.

JULIA KING
DEPARTMENT OF AMERICAN CIVILIZATION
UNIVERSITY OF PENNSYLVANIA
PHILADELPHIA, PENNSYLVANIA 19104

JAMES GREGORY CUSICK

The Importance of the Community Study Approach in Historical Archaeology, with an Example from Late Colonial St. Augustine

ABSTRACT

The community study has been one of the most productive but least used approaches to the archaeological study of the past. This situation is especially ironic because community study offers a framework which overcomes many of the problems and fulfills most of the goals of contemporary historical archaeology. It is based in the relationship of people and locale, it is conducive to the synthesis of documentary and archaeological data, it can be used in conjunction with hypothesis testing, and it employs a comparative approach which deals with groups of sites and multiple classes of data. This article reviews the development of community study in sociology, anthropology, and historical archaeology; defines its methods as employed by major practitioners; and shows how the community study approach was applied to the study of ethnicity and class in late colonial St. Augustine.

Introduction

To be both artist and social scientist is by no means an easy task.

—Rutman and Rutman (1984:12)

In recent years, numerous articles and symposia papers have challenged archaeologists to develop research methods that meet the demands of both processual and postprocessual perspectives in archaeology (Cleland 1988:14; Leone 1988:29; Schiffer 1988; Schuyler 1988:37–38; Hill 1991; Wylie 1992, 1993:13–15). One means of meeting the challenge is by renewing historical archaeology's commitment to the community study approach. Community study has been one of the discipline's most successful but least frequently applied methods for integrating documentary and archaeological evidence and interpreting the past. Closely related to historical ethnography, the community study approach has come to mean a study of a town or other small settlement at the household level, comparing numerous household sites, with information on the occupants compiled both from documents and from excavation (Geismar 1982; Deagan 1983). Historic sites, researched in such a manner, provide unique opportunities as social laboratories.

The intent of this article is to review the development of community study, to point out its uses and limitations in ethnographic situations, to demonstrate how historical archaeology often compensates for or overrides those limitations, and to show what community study has, can, and will accomplish, when correctly applied. The benefits and limitations of community study thus form the bulk of discussion. However, method and theory have no practical value without demonstration. For this reason, the article concludes with an abbreviated account of how the community study approach was employed to study questions about ethnic and social class affiliation in late colonial St. Augustine, 1784–1821.

As a research methodology, community study meets many of the demands for proof and synthesis in archaeology that have been at the center of the processual versus postprocessual debate. It shares, with historical ethnography, a concern for the in-depth analysis of people and culture in social context; it deals, like many analyses in historical archaeology, with issues of ethnicity, acculturation, and social structure; and its research strategy requires the comparison of household level data. In these respects, community study is one facet of an enormous literature. For instance, many archaeological investigations of ethnicity, status, acculturation, and consumption, while not specifically formulated as community study, often overlap with its methodology by incorporating comparisons of household level data within delimited geographical areas. Examples include Staski's (1987a) analysis of Mexican- and Anglo-American sites in El Paso, Pyszczyk's (1988, 1989) dissertation and subsequent publications on ethnically distinct fur trading posts in Canada, Greenwood's (1980, 1991) and Maniery's (1994) analysis of Chinese communities, and Kirch's (1992) and Sahlins' (1992) historical ethnography and study of households on Hawaii, as well as many studies concerned with urban archaeology, missions, plantations and African-American settlements, and foodways and consumer behavior (Deetz 1977; South 1977a; Baker 1978; Bowen 1978; Dickens 1982; McGuire 1983; Yentsch 1983; Kelso 1984; Otto 1984; Singleton 1985; Spencer-Wood 1987; Staski 1987b; Bragdon 1988; King 1988; Armstrong 1990; Gasco 1992). The relative success of these studies in historical archaeology indicates the general utility of comparative approaches and multiple source databases.

What distinguishes the community study approach from others is its explicit use of a "community" or "place-oriented" conceptual model. The key element of community study is its ability to position people and their material world in geographical and social space—in their relation to territory and to each other—as a basis for researching the past. Its crucial component is the linkage of people, household, site, place, and time in order to interpret relationships between social and material patterning in the context of localized ethnography. This does not mean its treats place or community as an isolate. Researchers must still deal with the economic and social networks that extend beyond the local. However, by seeking to study the past within a bounded geographical and social space, community study offers numerous advantages to researchers. For instance, it controls for such variables as ecological setting, commodity flow, and market access which need to be considered when studying social process. It also provides a framework for long-term, in-depth research at a locale, with data collection that is cumulative and interpretation that is subject to retesting and verification. As such, it allows for limited generalization or prediction based on the results of case study.

While providing a strong framework for interpretation of the past, the community study approach also has several inherent disadvantages, to which the investigator must acquiesce. Many different applications of the concept of "community" are considered, below. The approach cannot be applied at all archaeological sites, and indeed is difficult to apply at sites with poor or missing archival sources. Archaeological community studies also carry the limitation of all studies of community—that interpretations based on the specific cannot always be applied more generally. Finally, the pursuit of community study is expensive in terms of both time and labor. Most true community studies in historical archaeology are books or book-length monographs.

Despite these limitations, community study has been broadly and successfully applied toward the goals of anthropological archaeology. The development of community study approaches in historical archaeology ranges over concern for many topics and through publications that cover the spectrum from short article to book. The major markers of the tradition are book-length publications that can be identifed with an explicit community study tradition—e.g., Lewis (1976, 1977, 1984) on frontier sites in South Carolina; Geismar (1982) on Skunk Hollow; Deagan (1983) on St. Augustine; and Hardesty (1988) on mining encampments in Nevada. More recently, concepts of "place" have been used to model plantation archaeology (Wilkie 1993; Armstrong 1995) and general interest in "community" research has been reactivated (Ernstein 1994; Kaiser 1994; King and Chaney 1994; Maniery 1994; Seidel 1994; Wilkie 1994).

What Is Community?

Forty years ago, George Hillery (1955) catalogued 94 different definitions of "community" within the field of sociology alone. Since then, innumerable articles on community have been written in sociology, and to them must be added the application of "community" concepts in ecology, social history, and anthropology. The various permutations of community have been the topic of numerous review articles, notably in sociology by David Minar and Scott Greer (1969:1–84), Colin Bell and Howard Newby (1972:14–54), Dennis Poplin (1972:1–28), and Roland Warren (1972:1–51, 1977:1–129); in social history by Darrett Rutman (1973:57–88, 1980:29–32), and Darrett and Anita Rutman (1984:19–35); and in anthropology by Conrad Arensberg and Solon Kimball (1965), and Solon Kimball and William Partridge (1979).

Archaeologists seeking to establish a basis for

community study must therefore choose among the various definitions of the term (Poplin 1979:3–8). Early formulations of the concept incorporated a psychological dimension—that people seek community to fulfill emotional needs (Bell and Newby 1972:24; Warren 1972:13). Within this tradition, community is sometimes said to represent emotive, natural relationships between people, in contrast to more impersonal connections to the marketplace or to society as a whole (Tönnies 1957:33–103; Bell and Newby 1972:25–26; Warren 1977:2–3). By contrast, human ecologists define community in terms of space, territory, or habitat, often with no explicit reference to human social interaction (Park 1936:4). More recently, sociologists have developed formulations of community that see social interaction as the crucial element in community, with common territory being of secondary importance (Kaufman 1959:9–11; Sanders 1960, 1966; Parsons 1960; Warren 1972; Poplin 1972:14–15; Erikson 1976:186–187). This emphasis on social relations and interaction has led to the development of network analysis as an offshoot of community study (Scott 1988; Wellman and Berkowitz 1988).

Within this article, "community" is used in its broad sense as locale linked with social interaction. Such a usage is well-defined in sociology, social history, and anthropology (Redfield 1955; Arensburg 1961:248; Arensburg and Kimball 1965:4; Dean 1967; Lockridge 1970; Kimball and Partridge 1979:235–236; Isaac 1982:5; Rutman and Rutman 1984; Fowler and Hardesty 1994). For example, Roland Warren (1972:6–7) describes community as "a total framework of living—a complex network of people, institutions, shared interests, locality, and psychological 'belonging'." For Bell and Newby (1972:29), communities are territorial units in which a population group regularly interacts. They add the criterion of size—places or social units conceived as communities are usually small. All of these elements are inherent in Brownell's (1950: 198–199) definition of community as "a potential or practically face-to-face group in which a member may be easily in another's presence and where, in the day-to-day comings and goings of life, they may and do run across each other with familiarity and without surprise."

Forms of Community Study

Variations in the definition of community are closely related to different methods of community study. The three major approaches are: 1) studies of the meaning of "community"—what gives people their sense of commonality or belonging; 2) studies of communities as typological categories of human social organization—e.g., what is an urban as opposed to a rural community; and 3) studies of social phenomena within the context of a community or a place defined as a community—e.g., how is social structure, kinship, or ethnicity expressed in a specific locale.

All three of these methods have been employed by anthropologists engaged in ethnography and by sociologists doing community study. In contrast, the archaeological community study has uniformly followed the last method and has focused on issues of social process through intensive case study. The emergence of this approach in archaeology to some extent reflects broader trends in the social sciences. In its classic form, the community study often explored community in the emotive and psychological sense (e.g., Brownell 1950; Nisbet 1953; Isaac 1982). Since the 1960s, however, social scientists have increasingly divorced concerns for spiritual community from those dealing with community as place. More and more, community study has come to mean the study of a locale and people with reference to social relations and the local physical environment.

The anthropologist Conrad Arensberg (1961) was one of the first to advocate this divorce in his article "The Community as Object and Sample," which was later reprinted in his book with Solon Kimball (1965). Arensberg asserted that within studies of community as place, researchers had to choose between two different traditions. On the one hand were social scientists who were interested in studying community as an object—a typological social unit that varied over space and through time. On the other were those who were primarily interested in studying social processes within a community environment (Arensberg 1961:242–243). In this sense, the community became a social lab, case study, or sample used to investigate an issue (Arensberg and Kimball 1965: 12). It served "as a sample or unit of observation for the study of a culture or society, as the locus or local embodiment of a wider or general social problem or phenomenon, as a testing ground for plans of change, amelioration, or development" (Arensberg 1961:241; Arensberg and Kimball 1965:7).

The Development of the Community Study Approach in Archaeology

Community studies in historical archaeology emerged relatively late on the scene and immediately focused on studying social process within a community setting, as stipulated by Arensberg and Kimball. Within this context, towns or settlements became units of study, partially bounded universes in which the habits of a larger society could be observed in detail. Out of this approach emerged the characteristic features of archaeological community study: broad-based data organized at the household level, attention to "backyard" archaeology," use of archives and excavated data to define households within their social context, a comparative framework, and a commitment to addressing issues of general scholarly interest.

The earliest archaeological monograph that can be placed in this community study genre is Kenneth Lewis's (1976) "Camden: A Frontier Town." Although Lewis did not specifically frame this work as a community study, his analysis of Camden featured methods that were firmly within the tradition, as evident in his original and subsequent writings.

Lewis posited Camden as a locus in the geographical landscape with a spatial and social organization that altered over time because of the settlement's relation to a larger society. His approach to interpretation was processualist, based in the assumption that patterns in the archaeological record reflect patterns in human behavior through time. In developing his thesis of frontier settlements, Lewis specifically cast Camden and its immediate hinterland in terms of a community, as defined by Conrad Arensberg:

It may be best to view a frontier town as part of a larger, dispersed social entity. . . . The notion of 'community' in an anthropological sense, defined as the 'basic unit of organization and transmission within a society and its culture' [Arensberg 1961:248], appears to be useful in dealing with a settlement of this type. Arensberg's definition stresses function rather than form and sees the community in an organizational rather than a spatial sense. . . . Thus a community may include more than a single settlement, and its form may even vary periodically according to the adaptive model of the particular society [Trigger 1968:60–61] (Lewis 1976:88, cf. 1977:172–173).

While concern with Camden as a frontier town was the acknowledged focus of Lewis's study, he noted that "our interests need not be confined to this question alone, because the utilization of the model of frontier change permits the use of both documentary and archaeological data to construct a fuller interpretation of the changing role of Camden during the 18th century" (Lewis 1976:16). Lewis was interested in what Camden revealed about development of an entire frontier region. He was able to demonstrate that Camden represented a "part community" in which much of the population was dispersed away from town. Its size, organization, and trade networks were consistent with functional definitions of frontier towns as nodes for trade with the metropolitan and local redistribution.

Lewis expanded his analysis of the frontier in a subsequent work—*The American Frontier*—dealing not only with Camden but with other South Carolina settlements such as Ninety Six, Orangeburg, Long Bluff, and Pickneyville. This work further integrated documentary and archaeological data, producing maps of settlement pattern, charts of trade, and assessments of site organization and function. Analysis of Camden included the geographic extent of its retail trade network and discussions of its military functions (Lewis 1984:77–82). However, Lewis embedded Camden within its region, so that the town became one part of a study on the general evolution of frontier society. Ultimately, Lewis (1984:251–262) demonstrated how sites in South Carolina represented the frontier towns, special-function nucleated settlements, and dispersed settlements predicted by his model of an agrarian insular frontier. He then formulated ways in which archaeologists could model and test the occurrence of other types of frontiers (Lewis 1984: 263–300).

Lewis's work on Camden helped to shape the development of community study in archaeology. It was cited by both Joan Geismar and Kathleen Deagan in archaeological studies that were aligned more directly with the community study approach. Geismar's (1982) analysis of Skunk Hollow focused on the social disintegration and eventual abandonment of a small, African-American community in New Jersey. *Skunk Hollow* drew directly on approaches to community study espoused by Arensberg and Kimball (Geismar 1982:1, 193). Indeed, not only the structure but the goal of Geismar's research followed Arensberg's precept that community study should focus "on testing hypotheses of changing group organization and function" (Geismar 1982:1). For Geismar, Skunk Hollow served as the social laboratory in which to investigate factors regulating social change. Embedded in a processualist tradition, Geismar's interpretation relied on data from numerous sources:

> This archaeological investigation of Skunk Hollow has explored the question of community disintegration. It has suggested a correlation between the community's population rise and the status ascendancy of a community member, and its population decline with his loss in status. While cause and effect in this case cannot be concretely established with either archaeological, or for that matter, historical data, these findings tend to support Homan's hypotheses of cohesiveness and disintegration (Geismar 1982:197).

A related but somewhat different approach informed the work of Deagan on 18th-century Spanish St. Augustine. Like Geismar, Deagan's (1983:6) community study followed Arensberg and Kimball's "social lab" approach. However, Deagan did not focus on studying social organization per se, in the tradition of sociology, but rather on social processes of interest to Spanish colonial studies—the influence of adaptation, traditional culture, and *mestizaje* on material life (Deagan 1983:7). With this focus, Deagan embedded her research in larger questions of acculturation and assimilation in anthropology:

> It is clear . . . that without a long-term research orientation toward the colonial town as unit, rather than toward individual sites, we would not have learned much of what we

know from Saint Augustine that transcends the 18th century and the Spaniards in Florida. The emphasis upon community patterns and variability ultimately led to insights into such issues of general interest as acculturation mechanism, the roles of cultural heritage in adaptation, the emergence of Euro-American cultural traditions, and the manifestation of social variables in the archaeological record (Deagan 1983: xviii).

Because she adopted a comparative framework, and studied households against more encompassing community pattern, Deagan was able to evaluate the material culture of a Spanish-Indian, or *mestizo*, family against that of Spanish creoles of varying levels of income. Her research not only showed clear differences in material life, but demonstrated that some aspects of material life were gender-related. From this, she developed her thesis that in cases of intermarriage between Spanish men and native women, the womens' culture played a profound role in shaping domestic life, introducing many indigenous traditions that were absent or less pronounced in Spanish households.

By appealing to issues of broad concern in the social sciences, Lewis, Geismar, and Deagan also exemplified that tradition in historical archaeology which seeks to make general contributions, not only to the advancement of the discipline, but to history, sociology, and anthropology (Schuyler 1988:37). This perspective on archaeological research was emphasized by each author:

> Because of its regional approach and emphasis on the utility of material culture studies, this book should appeal to scholars in several fields, including history, geography, and anthropology (Lewis 1984:xxiv).

> The study presented here examines social organization and change as they are reflected in the archaeological record. Its focus is the application of a model in historical archaeology, but its ramifications are interdisciplinary . . . it is relevant to anthropologists, sociologists, historians of 19th-century America, and researchers involved in black studies (Geismar 1982:ix).

> Although the research program in St. Augustine has several goal orientations, including public interpretations and education, historic preservation, and cultural resources management, this book is concerned primarily with the studies and results that interest anthropological archaeologists and social historians (Deagan 1983:7).

As part of an overall concern with holistic interpretation of the past, these works also established the methodological procedures for community study in archaeology, which are particularly well-defined in the contributions of Geismar and Deagan. Both their works incorporated a similar corpus of data. They included an analysis of spatial organization, demography, distribution of wealth, and economy for the communities under study (Geismar 1982:7–62; Deagan 1983:9–43). They actively sought to integrate historical and archaeological information into a single unified project (Geismar 1982:193–198; Deagan 1983:3–8). And they focused on the household as unit of analysis, proceeded by comparative analysis of household material culture, and used functional categories of material culture in order to compare artifact assemblages (Geismar 1982:51–63, 105–170, 171–192; Deagan 1983:231–262).

Most importantly, however, both Geismar and Deagan broke with the Arensberg and Kimball method of community study in one crucial dimension. Arensberg and Kimball were advocates of "massive immersion." This technique, directed primarily toward ethnography, asserted that a researcher should become engulfed in the community under study and that both the questions for research and the answers would emerge, of their own accord, during field research (Arensberg and Kimball 1965: 10). Immersion, as a research strategy, has been heavily criticized by both sociologists and social historians, although it continues to be an indelible part of doing ethnography (Fowler and Hardesty 1994:3). While immersion provides scholars with a rich understanding of specific locales, it frequently results in studies that read like novels and have no systematic methodology (Bell and Newby 1972: 14). Kimball, recognizing this problem, later advised anthropologists to develop conceptual models of community prior to undertaking fieldwork; these models could then be revised based on empirical observation (Kimball and Partridge 1979:180, 227–238).

In structuring their community studies, Geismar and Deagan followed the processual school in anthropological archaeology by bringing research questions to the study, formulated as hypotheses that would be tested against observed patterning. In this, they significantly advanced community study as a method. Archaeological community studies offer the social sciences something not generally represented in sociology or social history—an example of uniform use of the community study method, at different communities, directed by shared methods toward a narrow range of research issues. In this way, community studies can provide a core contribution on which to base broader, more regional research. Lewis was interested in Camden, not only as a frontier town, but as a node in an advancing and developing frontier zone in South Carolina. Similarly, Deagan's findings in St. Augustine, rather than being part of an isolated case history, became a basis for investigations into Spain's Caribbean colonies (McEwan 1983; Ewen 1991) and Florida's Spanish missions (McEwan 1991). Thus, community study is one method of building cumulative, regionally-based knowledge about the past (Cleland 1988:14).

Community studies, therefore, have typically developed a database that allows in-depth analysis of community pattern and theories of process without resorting to either particularistic perspectives or reductionist explanations of social change. Indeed, practitioners of community study are too fully aware of the many variables affecting community life to assert reductionist explanations. As an approach, the community study in archaeology belongs equally to two traditions. On the one hand, it evinces the concern with social process, formation of the archaeological record, pattern, and rigorous methodology promoted in South's (1977a, 1977b) *Method and Theory in Historical Archeology* and *Research Strategies in Historical Archeology*. At the same time, its access to wide-ranging sources of information and its long-term research focus give community study the power to evaluate alternative explanations of the past. Such studies are concerned not merely with the generation and testing of hypotheses, but with continual evaluation of hypotheses against an ever-expanding database. In this, they can be said to anticipate and illustrate the type of research strategy recently advocated by Alison Wylie:

Although it can no longer be assumed that there is one set of standards or reference points to which all models, hypotheses, and claims can be referred . . . at any given time, there will be a number of stable, shared evidential reference points that can be exploited piecemeal in the comparison and evaluation of contending claims, and these can sometimes yield 'rationally decisive', if never final, conclusions (Wylie 1992:29).

Indeed, Lewis, in his work on frontiers, made a comparable assessment about verifying interpretation when he wrote:

The procedure followed here involves testing of a historical model through an examination of archaeological hypotheses. It is not intended to establish this model as the best or only explanation of frontier change. To do so would require a comparison of competing frontier theories that represent propositions at the same level of logical inclusiveness. Testing a theory against data produces probabilistic rather than absolute results and thus cannot entirely prove or disprove the former. This type of testing is, however, a necessary first step in measuring the adequacy of a given theory and is especially useful when alternate theories have not yet been formulated (Lewis 1984:101).

Archaeological community studies thus fulfill Arensberg and Kimball's (1965:11) "two imperatives of all science: that hypotheses be built from empirical perception . . . and that generalization be checked by a return to it." Such studies offer a bridge between archaeology in the processualist tradition and much that has emerged within postprocessualism. This may be one reason why community studies have emerged largely unscathed from the processualist–postprocessualist debate. While postmodernism identifies inherent difficulties in constructing definitive knowledge about the past, community study offers a reasonably grounded, rigorous means of investigating the past and gaining relevant understanding of it.

Before leaving the subject of the archaeological community study, it is important to review two additional works. The research of Donald Hardesty on the archaeology of mining settlements, and the work of two social historians, Darrett and Anita Rutman, illustrate important trends in the use of the community study approach, and demonstrate its continuing vitality.

Like "Camden" (Lewis 1976), "The Archae-ology of Mining and Miners" (Hardesty 1988) was not specifically framed as a community study. Hardesty (1988:ix) designed the monograph to be a guide that "lays out for the non-specialist how to approach the documentary and archaeological records of hardrock mining." His principal concerns were to establish research strategies and standards of research in CRM projects, to develop and illustrate methods for fieldwork at mining sites, and to discuss mining from the perspective of "industrial archaeology" Hardesty (1988:ix–xi). However, the section of his book dealing with mining settlements was a comparative study of different households based explicitly on a community concept as defined by Murdock (Hardesty 1988:13). Moreover, his integration of archival resources and archaeological data followed the community study method (Hardesty 1988:5–12, 81–104).

Hardesty's study of two mining encampments, Gold Bar and Shoshone Wells, provides an elegant demonstration of both the strengths and limitations of a community study approach. Gold Bar was a short-lived settlement, occupied between 1905 and 1909 in southern Nevada. Archival material on the settlement proved difficult to locate, and forced Hardesty to wrestle with the difficult problem of studying communities in the face of missing or inadequate documentation. Through analysis of structural foundations and associated assemblages at the site, he was able to functionally differentiate various buildings (Hardesty 1988:75–77). However, he found that "good statistical studies of the correlation between household organization and artifact diversity cannot be done without independent documentary data" (Hardesty 1988:75). The case of Gold Bar exemplifies the fact that community study requires multiple, overlapping, or intersecting sources of data to realize its full potential.

Such an overlap existed for Hardesty's other settlement, Shoshone Wells, which had a longer occupation from the 1860s to the early 20th century. Here, Hardesty (1988:81–82) was able to define clusters of households within the settlement, "including what appear archaeologically to be geographically separate Chinese, Italian, Anglo-European, and possibly Mexican 'neighborhoods'." Census and tax list data were incomplete for Shoshone Wells, but by cross-referencing various archival sources, Hardesty was able to pinpoint the house of one Chinese resident, and from there matched additional residents to household sites. This form of "record-stripping"—reorganizing archival data to develop a community profile—was used by Deagan and Geismar, and is especially associated with the social history of the Rutmans, who constructed more than 10,000 mini-biographies by stripping archival materials for Middlesex County, Virginia, 1650–1750. Hardesty's use of record-stripping is a good example of how people and households can be linked even in the absence of comprehensive censuses. Ultimately, he was able to compare the archaeological remains of numerous, known households in a very small and isolated settlement (Hardesty 1988:96–101). Based on his analysis, he evaluated definitions of mining communities. Economics and ecology were important determinants in the placement of mining settlements, but other factors, including ethnic diversity and fissioning, tended to characterize the social and spatial patterning of such sites (Hardesty 1988:102–103).

Another work which is destined to have a profound influence on future efforts in community study is Darrett and Anita Rutman's (1984) *A Place in Time*. The Rutmans completed their social history of Middlesex County, Virginia, about the same time that Geismar and Deagan were writing their studies in archaeology. Lacking good census records, the Rutmans reorganized all available archival material on residents of Middlesex for the years 1650–1750. By cross-indexing and following the names of residents through thousands of documents, they generated their own census of the county. The Rutmans then wrote an historical ethnography of Middlesex, taking as their metaphor the use of ethnography in anthropology. They rejected a tradition in social history that saw community as a spiritual bond, and instead favored the viewpoint of sociology. For them, the subject of community study is "the people of any particular locale, the pattern of their associations among themselves, and with others beyond the locale, and, over time, the changes in that pattern" (Rutman and Rutman 1984:25). Darrett Rutman has at times suggested that "community study" could also be called "place-oriented research:"

In sum, sociologists and anthropologists are consciously attempting to divorce the concept of community from any and every particular set of values and behavior. Community is being considered simply an inevitable concomitant of the fact that people live and associate territorially; hence the nature of associations within territories, and because no group is ever completely isolated, between those within and without, can be studied at the level of territory (Rutman and Rutman 1984:25).

Like Geismar and Deagan, the Rutmans rejected the notion of "massive immersion," arguing that a researcher must bring questions to his or her study. Their grounding in geography, demography, and economy, their concern for the material, and their interest in pattern and process brings their work into close alignment with anthropological research: "Allow me to suggest that historians' efforts to characterize early American life should not be directed by an assumption about the *mind* of Anglo-America and its small communities but by the broad social processes underway to which those communities—or at least studies of them—testify" (Rutman 1986:172).

A Place in Time was therefore constructed upon four overt assumptions about community study: 1) the social interaction of people is not chaotic but ordered and tends to be channeled through nodal points of contact; 2) social interaction is to some extent related to landform, distance, and technology; 3) just as associations are related to the physical topography of the locale, they are related to the social topography; and 4) interpersonal relationships form networks among people, and are thus subject to network analysis (Rutman and Rutman 1984:31–32).

The Rutmans applied this approach to Middlesex County, and the same approach has subsequently influenced the social history of St. Mary's City and the Chesapeake (Walsh 1988). What is important for archaeologists, however, is that with the addition of only two more assumptions, the Rutmans' framework can also be used in archaeological community studies: 5) that archaeological pattern is also not random, but related to social behavior; and 6) that it is therefore possible to compare the material patterns of life with reference to the social patterns.

Although not yet attempted, such a framework suggests that archaeological patterning can be analyzed with reference to social networks as a means of examining material life within the context of social relations.

Community Study: A Demonstration

A community study approach based on Deagan (1983) and incorporating suggestions from Rutman and Rutman (1984) was applied to the study of ethnic groups and class in late colonial St. Augustine. Unfortunately, to encompass a full exposition of the study in a journal article is impossible. Instead, the remaining portion of this article demonstrates the methods used to set up the study, and gives an abbreviated account of findings. The many theoretical implications and methodological considerations that cannot be engaged fully in the present discussion have been presented in Cusick (1993).

Research on late colonial St. Augustine focused on whether patterns of household material life would show a strong correlation with ethnic and/or class affiliations during the final period of Spanish rule in Florida, 1784–1821. To accomplish this aim, primary and secondary sources were assembled and used to develop an economic and social profile of the town. From the extensive archival material on this period, the study relied principally on the 1784–1814 census returns, East Florida Papers [EFP Census], the 1784–1821 register of shipping arrivals and departures [EFP Register], the 1784–1821 testamentary proceedings [EFP Testamentary Proceedings], and the 1790–1804 oaths of allegiance for new settlers [EFP Oaths]. This profile developed information on the spatial organization of St. Augustine, its trade links, and the demographic, occupational, and social divisions of its residents.

Ongoing work on colonial censuses produced a basic breakdown of the colonial population by place of origin (Table 1). Several recent historical ethnographies, as well as research into the local equivalent of immigration records, provided additional information on how this population was divided in relation to occupational sectors (Landers 1988;

TABLE 1
1786 ST. AUGUSTINE CENSUS DATA[a]

Affiliation	N
Spanish	216
Minorcan	469
Casta/Free Black	33
European	87
Slave	461
Total	1,266

[a]Data exclude the garrison.
Sources: Landers (1988:58), Johnson (1989:38), and Griffin (1990:118).

Griffin 1988, 1990; Cusick 1989, 1994; Johnson 1989; Rasico 1990). These data are presented in Table 2. An analysis of shipping arrivals produced detailed evidence on the nature of commodity flow into St. Augustine, the range of goods available, and their prices (Cusick 1991). This analysis was supplemented by studies of the colonial treasury (Bermúdez 1989) and colonial trade (Tornero Tinajero 1979). Finally, census and tax data, keyed to colonial maps, made it possible to relate specific households to specific archaeological sites. All of these data were used to assess the representativeness of the probate records and sites used in analysis.

Florida, like most Spanish borderlands in the late colonial period, was characterized by an ethnically diverse population of settlers, and this diversity was particularly evident in St. Augustine, the principal town and provincial capital of Spanish East Florida. The 1790s saw an influx of immigrants, due partly to favorable Spanish land grants and partly to social upheaval in the Caribbean and Napoleonic Europe. After 1795, the principally Spanish and Minorcan population was joined by American, English, French, and Irish colonists (Landers 1988; Cusick 1989; Johnson 1989; Griffin 1990). For a while, St. Augustine also contained a growing population of free blacks, but as the plantation economy grew, avenues to freedom for blacks decreased, and by 1800 more than two-thirds of the total colonial population lived in slavery.

The subject of the archaeological community

TABLE 2
OCCUPATIONS IN LATE 18TH-CENTURY ST. AUGUSTINE

Occupation	Spanish	Minorcan	Free Black	French	Irish
Public Employee					
Government Official	15				
Military Commander	3				2
Priest	1	2			2
Physician/Surgeon	2				
Master Artisan	9				
Hospital Staff	15				
Hospital Servant	12				
Farmer		59		15	30
Fisher		14	1		
Mariner		46	1	12	3
Artisan	n/a	42	10	22	40
Physician/Surgeon				3	
Servant/Domestic	n/a		9		
Merchant/Retailer	n/a	11	1	20	16

Sources: Oaths of Allegiance for New Settlers (EFP Oaths 1790–1804), Lockey (1949:198–199, 202–204), Landers (1988:70), Johnson (1989), and Griffin (1990:152).

study was the Minorcan and Spanish population. The Minorcans arrived in Florida when the colony was under British rule, and worked as indentured servants on an indigo plantation. The group consisted principally of people from the island of Minorca, in the Balearics, but also included some Italians, Greeks, and Corsicans. During 10 years of servitude, nearly 1,200 of the group succumbed to disease, impoverishment, and bad treatment, and in 1777 the survivors—between 500 and 600 people—demanded release from their indentures and settled in St. Augustine (Griffin 1990:105; Rasico 1990: 55). There they formed an endogamous ethnic *barrio* in the north part of town. As non-English-speaking Catholics in an English and Protestant territory, the Minorcans were viewed with suspicion by the British. During 16 years of life under the British there is no record of a Minorcan marrying outside of the group (Griffin 1990:110). They did, however, intermarry among themselves, and the Italians and Greeks were gradually linked in kinship with the greater Minorcan community.

In 1783, Spain regained both Florida and Minorca under treaty, and the Minorcans of St. Augustine came under Spanish rule (Lockey 1949:

232–233). In contrast to the rural background of most Minorcans, the incoming Spanish colonists were an urban and urbane group, consisting of peninsular Spaniards serving in Cuba, native Cubans, and descendants of former Spanish settlers in Florida. Comprising only about 200 people, their presence was augmented by their control of government and by the 450 soldiers of the Castillo de San Marcos (Johnson 1989).

The focus on Minorcan and Spanish residents was particularly appropriate to questions of ethnicity and class affiliation. While sharing a general Hispanic culture, the two groups spoke different languages, were further divided by differences in occupation and status, and for much of the late colonial period were associated with separate parishes, militias, and sections of town. Spanish attitudes toward the Minorcans were ambiguous, ranging from praise of their industry to distrust of that same industry as being overly opportunistic (Griffin 1988:69). Social distance between Spanish and Minorcan colonists was also a consequence of concepts about social class. By late colonial times, a person's class and status in Spanish America was predicated on a shifting combination of traditional legal rights claimed through purity of blood, *hidalguía,* and occupation, as well as on considerations of wealth. Despite attempts by the government of Carlos III to ennoble various crafts and professions, manual labor and retail trade were still considered "low" professions in Spain and Spanish America. As most Minorcans fell into either one or the other of these occupational categories, relatively few were accorded high status in the eyes of Spanish residents.

Ethnohistories of the Minorcans indicate that under Spanish rule numerous affluent families did move out of the Minorcan quarter, intermarried with Spanish families, and established close business connections with colonial officials. Yet, on the whole, the Minorcans remained a community apart. By almost any definition of the term, they formed an ethnic group—e.g., Bell (1975:169), Greeley and McCready (1975:210), Parsons (1975:56), Engelbrektsson (1986:148), cf. Kelly and Kelly (1980), McGuire (1982:160), Horvath (1983:23), and Cusick (1993:39–61). This being the case, it raised the question of whether the ethnic boundary between Minorcans and Spaniards so well attested to in the documentary record would be evident in material patterning, and how this patterning would vary across ethnic and class lines. Would a comparison of the material culture of a sample of individuals and households show them to be more similar according to ethnic affiliation or measurements of social rank? And what could be inferred from patterning?

To answer these questions, research focused on two sources of data about Minorcan and Spanish life. All available Minorcan and Spanish probate records, totalling 48, were translated. Of these, 16 contained detailed inventories of clothing and were used to compare colonial costume. In addition, six contemporaneous archaeological sites were compared. Analysis focused on faunal assemblages, as a basis for comparing foodways, and ceramic assemblages, as a well-preserved example of material culture that illustrated household consumer patterns. Each site represented a known colonial household. Four of the six were inventoried in probate records, and a fifth household was inventoried after it had relocated from the site used in this study.

While probate inventories varied in completeness, they provided a means of determining where each household fell in terms of wealth distribution in St. Augustine, and also helped to control for household size. In other respects, archival and archaeological databases were evaluated separately. For instance, most of the data on costume came from probate records other than those associated with the archaeological sites.

The individuals represented in the probate data are listed in Table 3. All data came from probates for adult males, of whom 12 were Spanish and four Minorcan. These individuals are further divided into three groups: Spanish military personnel, other Spanish colonists, and Minorcan colonists. The columns designated "Clothing," "Movables," and "Estate" denote the assessed value of the individual's wardrobe; total movable goods—including jewelry, books, etc.; and major holdings—including land, houses, and slaves.

The households at the six archaeological sites are listed in Table 4. They consist of two affluent Spanish households, two affluent Minorcan households, and two poor Minorcan households. Tax lists and probate information made it possible to provide an economic ranking of these sites. Proveniences for the ceramic and faunal assemblages are given in Table 5. Information about the relative size of each assemblage is presented in Table 6.

The two Spanish sites represented the households of Juan Sánchez, head of the shipyard, and Juan José Bousquet, the surgeon at the hospital. The salaries of Sánchez and Bousquet were above the mean for colonial officials in St. Augustine, putting them in the middle strata of the Spanish colonial bureaucracy. There were four Minorcan sites. The Seguís and the Papys were among the most affluent citizens in St. Augustine. Bernardo Seguí held the bread contact for the garrison, operated a trading business, and held positions as *regidor* and captain of the Minorcan militia. Gaspar Papy was a retail merchant with numerous properties. Since less than 10 percent of Minorcan household heads held occupations as merchants or shopkeepers, the Seguí and Papy households represented the relatively small proportion of Minorcans who achieved affluence through trade. More typical were the households of

TABLE 3
DATA ON INDIVIDUALS REPRESENTED IN COLONIAL PROBATES

Name	Ethnicity	Occupation	Year	C[a]	M[a]	E[a]
Caraballo	Spanish	Officer	1792	44.1	99.1	—
Salcedo	Spanish	Artillery Captain	1796	93.5	—	4,495
Ceballos	Spanish	Infantry Lieutenant	1800	167.8	342.6	1,548
Domingo	Spanish	Soldier	1805	41.5	79.3	—
de la Torre	Spanish	Infantry Commander	1807	190.4	1,035.0	1,470
de la Puente	Spanish	Infantry Captain	1815	65.3	275.0	6,398
Herrera	Spanish	Chief of Public Works	1788	—	—	—
Elisondo	Spanish	Hospital Registrar	1790	—	—	—
Iznardy	Spanish	Merchant	1803	140.8	1,027.4	2,840
García	Spanish		1802	53.0	206.0	5,412
Guadarrama	Spanish	Ship Captain	1804	36.4	83.2	8,424
Bousquet	Spanish	Chief Surgeon	1817	78.3	240.0	4,500
Coll	Minorcan	Trader	1789	21.3	250.5	1,252
Camps	Minorcan	Parish Priest	1790	61.8	295.0	2,112
Usina	Minorcan	Sailor	1794	—	—	—
Casaly	Italian	Artisan	1799	24.3	—	—

[a]C = value of clothing; M = value of movable goods; E = value of lands and properties, in *pesos fuertes*.
Source: Testamentary Proceedings (EFP 1784–1821).

TABLE 4
ARCHIVAL DATA ON HOUSEHOLDS REPRESENTED BY ARCHAEOLOGICAL SITES

Household	Affiliation	Probate (Year)	Household Size	Number of Slaves	1790 Tax List (reales)	Value of Estate (pesos)
Seguí	Minorcan	1813	12	8	n/a	14,049
Papy	Minorcan	1817	7	5	n/a	8,000
Sánchez	Spanish	1803	19	10	n/a	5,815
Bousquet	Spanish	1815	6	9	n/a	4,500
Usina	Minorcan	n/a	5	n/a	633	n/a
Triay	Minorcan	1816	5	2	230	1,215

Sources: Census returns (EFP Census 1784–1814), Historic Records Survey (1939:40, 43), and Testamentary Proceedings (EFP 1784–1821).

Juan Triay and Bartolomé Usina, the poorest households in the sample. They engaged primarily in farming and fishing, as did about 60 percent of all Minorcans in St. Augustine. The differing degree of affluence among the Minorcans in the sample was reflected by geographical distance. The Seguís and Papys lived to the south of the town plaza with other professional and middle-income families. The Triays and Usinas lived in the Minorcan quarter and, for much of the late colonial period, rented their properties from the Spanish Crown (Figure 1).

Background information permitted a critical appraisal of available evidence about expressions of ethnicity and class in St. Augustine. In general, the results of analysis demonstrated that Minorcan traditions in dress and diet were clearly discernible within the less affluent Minorcan community, and that more affluent Minorcan families tended to pos-

TABLE 5
ARCHAEOLOGICAL PROVENIENCES

Household	Site	TPQ	Provenience (Ceramics)	Provenience (Fauna)
Seguí	SA-34–3	1805	Feature 3 (large trash pit)	same
Papy	SA-35–2	1805	Features 2, 4, and 6 (privy, trash pits)	Feature 2 (privy)
Sánchez	SA-7–6	1813	Features 14, 16, 18, and 20	same
			Pits 2, 4, 5, 12, 13, M, and R (trash pits)	
Bousquet	SA-26–1	1795	Features 48 and 54 (wells)	same
Usina	SA-16–23	1813	Features 37 and 38, F.S. 58 and 73 (well, trash pits)	no sample
Triay	SA-12–26			
British period		1784	Well Feature	same
Spanish period		1799	Features 1, 2, 4, and 14	same
			Areas 1, 2, 5, 6, 9, and 24 (trash pits, midden)	

TABLE 6
CERAMIC AND FAUNAL SAMPLE SIZES

Household	Sherd Counts N	Sherd Weights g	Rim Counts N	Fauna NISP N
Seguí	970	2,928	88	411
Papy	541	9,385	154	948
Sánchez	818	1,903	160	473
Bousquet	452	2,567	76	1,087
Usina	880	2,216	58	—
Triay	304	1,665	54	714

sess a material life similar to that of the Spanish middle class in St. Augustine. The analysis of probate records, ceramic assemblages, and foodways contributed to this interpretation.

Probate Records

Probate records contain helpful information. For instance, male costume, as described in available probate records, strongly reflected occupational and traditional aspects of dress. While the sample is small, with a gender bias, it can be assessed critically against historic accounts of late 18th-century costume and against the differing economic and occupational backgrounds of the persons represented.

Traditional attire in Spain varied widely by region and occupation, but by the late 18th century, certain regularities governed the dress of the gentry, urban lower class, and peasant. Male costume consisted of articles of clothing that had been in use, in one form or another, since the 1680s. Garments basic to the male attire of the nobility, military, and middle classes were the shirt (*camisa*), breeches (*calzones*) or pantaloons, stockings (*medias*), and buckled shoes. Shirts were adorned at the cuff and down the breast with ruffles (*bolantes*) and at the collar with a neckcloth or cravat, variously given as *pañuelo, corbata, corbatín* (Köhler 1963:333–340; Laver 1988:113–118).

Spanish terminology for other articles of dress are loosely translatable into English equivalents, but carry connotations of style and cut which escape easy translation. Hence, the Spanish terms are used here. The main outer garments of male dress were the *casaca*, the *chupa*, the *chaleco*, the *capote*, and the *capa*. The *casaca* was a knee-length, skirted coat. The *chupa* was a short, jacket-like coat with skirts and long sleeves. Either could be worn over the *chaleco*, a sleeveless vest. The *capote* was a heavy, collared cape and the *capa* was a cape or cloak (*Diccionario* 1817).

Casacas and *chalecos*, in combination with breeches or pantaloons, stockings, and some form of neckcloth, formed the elements of the *vestir de militar*, a costume modeled on French fashion and worn by the Spanish court, military, and bourgeoisie. In contrast to the *vestir de militar* was the costume of the *majos* and *majas*, the fashionable

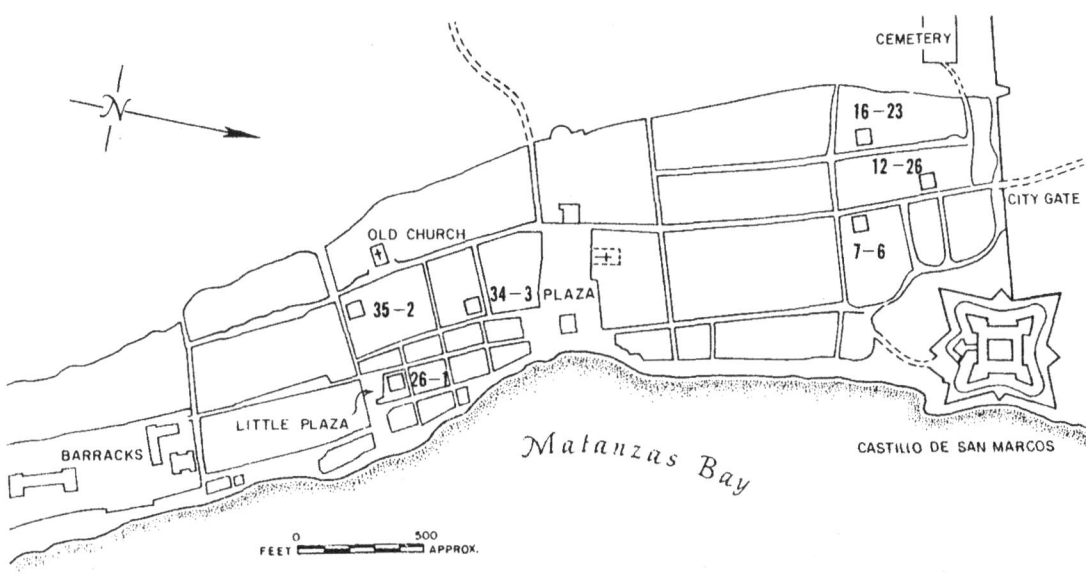

FIGURE 1. Map of St. Augustine ca. 1790 showing the locations of the archaeological sites under consideration: SA-26–1, Bousquet household; SA-35–2, Papy household; SA-7–6, Sánchez household; SA-34–3, Seguí household; SA-16–23, Usina household; SA-12–26, Triay household. The Minorcan quarter centered on the six small blocks to the west of the Castillo de San Marcos.

lower class of Madrid (Kany 1932:37). In male dress, the principal distinctions were in the substitution of a jacket for the *casaca* and in the importance associated with the cape or cloak. Both forms of costume are frequently depicted in the portraiture and scenic art of Francisco Goya.

On Minorca, traditional male costume also featured the short jacket and cloak. According to John Armstrong's (1756) *The History of the Island of Minorca*, "the Dress of the lower Rank of the Men consists of a loose short Coat, a Waistcoat, and a red worsted Girdle going many times round the Belly, or a broad Leather belt; a coarse Shirt, a colored Handkerchief about the Neck, a red Worsted Cap, a Pair of Breeches reaching almost to the Ankles, coarse Stockings and broad flat shoes with no heels, made of white leather, a flapped Hat, and a Cloak." Only the wealthiest men affected the dress of the English gentry. The jacket appears to have been an essential element of traditional dress in the Balearics, for Racinet's *History of Costume* depicts Majorcan males from the 1880s wearing short, waist-length jackets known as *sayos,* and an ac-

count of Minorca in the 1920s still cites the short jacket and cape as part of traditional costume (Racinet 1988[1886]:296–297; Chamberlain 1927: 133–134).

Table 7 presents basic information on male dress for the individuals listed in Table 3. The numbers of shirts, trousers, breeches, and stockings owned varied directly with wealth, and hence are not considered further here (cf. Cusick 1993:96–97). Table 7 gives the number of outer garments inventoried and their relative frequency as a percentage of the total number of outer garments. Variation in wardrobe conforms to differences in occupation and ethnicity. The principal components of Spanish dress were the *casaca* and *chaleco,* often in the form of a matched suit, called a *centro.* Whether civilian or military, Spanish males in St. Augustine tended to dress in the attire of the *vestir de militar.* These articles, especially *chalecos* and *centros,* were comparatively rare in Minorcan inventories (Table 7).

The *chupa,* or jacket-length coat, was most frequently represented in the probates of two groups: Spanish officers and soldiers, and Minorcan civil-

TABLE 7
DISTRIBUTION OF OUTER GARMENTS OF MALE CLOTHING

Name	Ethnicity	Casaca		Chupa		Chaleco		Capa/Capote		Centro		Total
		N	%	N	%	N	%	N	%	N	%	
Spanish Military												
Caraballo	Spanish	1	4.3	4	17.4	15	65.3	1	4.3	2	8.7	23
Salcedo	Spanish	2	11.8	4	23.5	—	—	0	0.0	11	64.7	17
Ceballo	Spanish	10	45.5	4	18.2	—	—	1	4.5	7	31.8	22
Domingo	Spanish	6	23.1	10	38.5	9	34.6	0	0.0	1	3.8	26
de la Torre	Spanish	—[a]	—	2	20.0	6	60.0	2	20.0	—	—	10
de la Puente	Spanish	1	10.0	0	0.0	6	60.0	0	0.0	3	30.0	10
Subtotal		20		24		36		4		24		
Mean ($\bar{x}$)		3.3	15.8	4.0	19.6	6.0	36.6	0.7	4.8	4.0	23.2	
Other Spanish												
Herrera	Spanish	5	15.2	3	9.1	24	72.7	0	0.0	1	3.0	33
Elisondo	Spanish	5	25.0	1	5.0	7	35.0	1	5.0	6	30.0	20
García	Spanish	3	30.0	0	0.0	—	—	1	10.0	6	60.0	10
Iznardy	Spanish	4	16.0	1	4.0	13	52.0	0	0.0	7	28.0	25
Guadarrama	Spanish	2	16.7	2	16.7	8	66.6	0	0.0	—	—	12
Bousquet	Spanish	4	33.4	0	0.0	8	66.6	0	0.0	—	—	12
Subtotal		23		7		60		2		20		
Mean ($\bar{x}$)		3.8	22.7	1.2	5.8	10.0	48.8	0.3	2.5	3.3	20.2	
Minorcan												
Coll	Minorcan	—	—	7	63.6	3	27.3	1	9.1	—	—	11
Camps	Minorcan	—	—	6	46.2	5	38.5	1	7.7	1	7.7	13
Usina	Minorcan	1	14.3	4	57.1	1	14.3	1	14.3	0	0.0	7
Casaly	Italian	1	14.3	3	42.9	3	42.9	0	0.0	0	0.0	7
Subtotal		2		20		12		3		1		
Mean ($\bar{x}$)		0.5	7.2	5.0	52.5	3.0	30.8	0.7	7.8	0.2	1.9	

[a]A dash "—" indicates an item was either not explicitly mentioned or was mentioned as part of a more inclusive category, such as a suit (*centro*). Calculation of means ($\bar{x}$) treated "—" as a value of "0," which minimized the differences between Spanish and Minorcan means ($\bar{x}$).

Source: Testamentary Proceedings (EFP 1784–1821).

ians. The use of the *chupa* in the former case was probably related to profession. Like the *casaca,* shorter jacket-like coats were standard parts of military uniform. The few Minorcans for whom data were available are representative of the less affluent members, and therefore majority, of their group. Father Pedro Camps, although of high status because of his standing as a priest, had a modest estate (Table 3). In addition, his attire was probably influenced by his profession. Lorenzo Coll was a well-to-do trader, but not one of the principal merchants in town. Juan Usina and Pedro Casaly practiced traditional Minorcan trades in sailing and

crafts. Among these Minorcans, the *chupa* appears to have been a substitute for the *casaca.* The use of this garment in St. Augustine was consistent with Old World Minorcan costume, where it was a basic element of clothing.

Unfortunately, the probate records of wealthy Minorcans in St. Augustine, while well-represented, do not provide details on clothing. As has been discussed elsewhere, some evidence exists that upwardly mobile Minorcans adopted more gentrified forms of dress (Cusick [1995]). However, only a more detailed study of the probates, currently underway, can resolve this question.

Data on costume, however, are consistent with other data that all point toward the same conclusion: Old World traditions are most clearly reflected in St. Augustine among less affluent Minorcans. Data on ceramic assemblages and subsistence, as recovered from excavation, provide additional contrast in the habits of poor and wealthy Minorcans in St. Augustine, and also support this conclusion.

Ceramic Assemblages

Ceramics represent one of the mass-produced forms of material culture that were directly tied to changes in trading patterns in late colonial Florida. In St. Augustine, finished products, including earthenwares and glasswares, were mostly imported from Charleston (Cusick 1994). In contrast to early 18th-century assemblages, which consist largely of Mexican- and locally-made earthenwares, late colonial assemblages are dominated by British-made creamwares, edged wares, and hand-painted wares. These assemblages can be quantified according to Miller's (1980, 1991) ware classifications for 18th-century ceramics. Indeed, local Spanish probate records reflect the basic distinction between edged wares, *lozas con orillas verdes o azules,* and plain wares, *lozas ordinarias o blancas,* on which Miller based his system.

Ceramic assemblages proved to be the most difficult database to compare. Cusick (1993:116–165) provides a full exposition on methods. Site assemblages were drawn from tightly dated, closed contexts (Table 5). They were divided into ware categories based on Miller's work and on information about commodity flow and pricing in St. Augustine (Cusick 1993:68–78, 120–126). The relative frequencies, i.e., percents, in each category were quantified in four ways: as sherd counts, sherd weights, rim counts, and estimated vessel counts. These data were then used to assess patterns of consumer behavior with respect to acquisition of ceramics, and to determine whether similarities and differences in the site assemblages correlated with socioeconomic position, ethnic affiliation, or other factors. Following Pyszczyk (1989), the rim count and vessel count data were entered into a cluster analysis program to determine which sites seemed to have the most similar assemblages.

All results of analysis are reported in Cusick (1993:131–165). Quantification of assemblages by both sherd count and sherd weight was demonstrated to be biased due to the differential breakage. All assemblages contained a mixture of near-complete vessels and other fragmentary and partial vessels represented by differing numbers of sherds. Sherd counts tended to bias assemblages toward ware categories in which most vessels were highly fragmented, whereas sherd weights skewed assemblages toward ware categories represented primarily by complete vessels. Counts of cross-mended rims and estimates of the Minimum Number of Vessels tended to minimize the obvious skewing in the count and weight data (Cusick 1993:136, 143–150). Comparison of site assemblages is illustrated here using the rim count data (Table 8).

Analysis of ceramic data indicated two general patterns. Hand-painted wares were common in all assemblages, but better represented in the wealthy households (Table 8), which reflected the association of hand-painted decoration with tea wares. The range of tea wares in each assemblage varied directly with assessments of socioeconomic rank. The most affluent sites had the greatest number and broadest range of tea wares (Cusick 1993:150–154).

The distribution of flatwares and utilitarian wares in assemblages showed considerable variation. In cluster analysis, households were grouped or separated based on what appear to be consumer buying preferences. The assemblage at the Minorcan household of Gaspar Papy showed perhaps the greatest influence of occupation on purchasing choices. Gaspar Papy was a retail merchant and was closely tied, through his business, with suppliers in Charleston. The assemblage of plates from this site conformed generally with fashions that were current in the United States at the beginning of the 19th century. It consisted partly of creamwares but primarily of green- and blue-edged pearlwares. In this respect, the Papy assemblage was the most "Americanized" of the sites. Assemblages at the two Spanish sites and at the most affluent Minorcan site, on the other hand, were noticeably lacking in edge

TABLE 8
SITE ASSEMBLAGES QUANTIFIED BY VESSEL RIM COUNTS

Ceramic Types	Bousquet		Sánchez		Seguí		Papy		Usina		Triay	
	N	%	N	%	N	%	N	%	N	%	N	%
CC	38	50.0	58	36.2	39	44.3	59	38.3	9	15.5	17	31.5
Delft	6	7.9	17	10.6	8	9.1	2	1.3	5	8.6	2	3.7
Dipped	4	5.3	2	1.3	2	2.3	3	2.0	2	3.5	4	7.4
Edged	1	1.3	19	11.9	3	3.4	43	27.9	9	15.5	15	27.8
Ironstone	0	0.0	3	1.9	0	0.0	0	0.0	3	5.2	0	0.0
Majolica	10	13.1	2	1.3	3	3.4	1	0.7	3	5.2	2	3.7
Mexican	0	0.0	1	0.6	2	2.3	0	0.0	0	0.0	0	0.0
Painted	11	14.5	30	18.7	20	22.7	35	22.7	8	13.8	4	7.4
Printed	0	0.0	13	8.1	2	2.3	11	7.1	9	15.5	4	7.4
Slipware	5	6.6	9	5.6	4	4.5	0	0.0	8	13.8	5	9.3
Spanish leadglazed	1	1.3	4	2.5	2	2.3	0	0.0	1	1.7	1	1.8
Stoneware	0	0.0	2	1.3	3	3.4	0	0.0	1	1.7	0	0.0
Total	76	100.0	160	100.0	88	100.0	154	100.0	58	100.0	54	100.0

wares. They consisted of large amounts of creamware, with some delft and majolica, and minor amounts of most other wares. Zierden (1979) has previously characterized such assemblages as "cosmopolitan." The similarity of the Minorcan Seguí assemblage with the Spanish assemblages was consistent with other information about this household. The Seguís were among the wealthiest Minorcan families in St. Augustine and were integrated with local Spanish interests through marriage and business contacts. Their two-and-a-half-story house, built of coquina stone, incorporated all the Spanish elements characteristic of 18th-century domestic architecture in St. Augustine.

The assemblages of the poor Minorcan households resembled neither each other nor the wealthier sites. The Triay assemblage had a pattern similar to that at the Papy site, but with a higher incidence of slipware. The Usina household had a singular pattern, consisting of almost equal percentages of creamware, edge ware, transfer-printed ware, and slipware.

The clustering of assemblages is depicted in Figure 2 (cf. Cusick 1993:137–165). Cluster 1 contained both of the Spanish households and the Minorcan household of the Seguís. The remaining site assemblages, all Minorcan, appear to have been

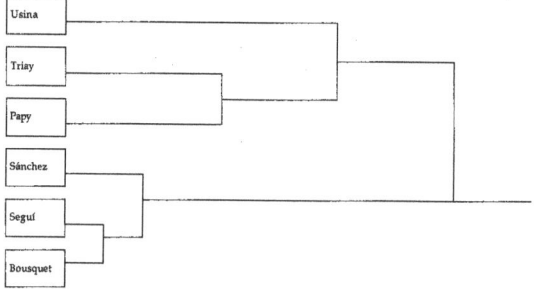

FIGURE 2. A schematic of the cluster hierarchy for similarity of site ceramic assemblages based on rim count data, reproduced from Cusick (1993:138–140). Clustering was based on the Pearson r coefficient. Single linkage, complete linkage, and Ward's minimum variance all produced the same clustering pattern.

grouped together primarily because of their dissimilarity to assemblages in Cluster 1 rather than their similarity to one another. Ceramic assemblages, then, showed no strong ethnic preference in buying patterns, and tended to reflect household status, income, or occupation (Cusick 1993, 1994).

Foodways

Analyses of household faunal assemblages provided one of the most interesting sources of com-

TABLE 9
FAUNAL CATEGORIES BY MNI AND BIOMASS

Sites	Measurement	Domestic Animals %	Wild Terrestrial %	Wild Birds %	Aquatic Reptiles %	Fish and Sharks %	Commensals %	Total %
	MNI							
Bousquet	101	10.5	6.5	4.0	0	75.0	4.0	100
Sánchez	78	20.5	5.1	3.8	2.6	59.0	9.0	100
Seguí	60	11.7	8.3	8.3	5.0	65.0	1.7	100
Papy	99	49.5	2.0	13.1	2.0	24.3	9.1	100
Papy (−chicken)	(55)	(9.2)	(3.6)	(23.6)	(3.6)	(43.6)	(16.4)	(100)
Triay Spanish II	75	5.3	2.7	0	1.3	90.7	0	100
Triay British	48	4.1	2.1	2.1	0	91.7	0	100
Fatio site	152	15.1	5.3	4.0	6.7	59.9	9.0	100
	Biomass (kg)							
Bousquet	35.6	83.9	2.7	0.1	0	13.1	>0.2	100
Sánchez	14.0	83.8	6.1	0.2	1.3	8.1	0.5	100
Seguí	17.7	82.7	7.8	0.7	0.7	7.8	0.3	100
Papy (−chicken)	(9.4)	(85.1)	(1.0)	(3.9)	(0.3)	(9.2)	(0.5)	(100)
Triay Spanish II	3.6	19.0	9.0	0	1.0	71.0	0	100
Triay British	4.0	12.3	1.3	1.6	0	84.8	0	100
Fatio site[a]	54.32	59.1	2.7	0.1	13.6	17.8	4.3	100

[a]Other/unknown = 2.4%.

Source: British-period Triay data from Quitmyer (1988), Fatio site data from Reitz and Brown (1984), and all other data from Cusick (1993).

parative data. The details of analysis have been extensively discussed elsewhere. For information on the faunal samples, methods of analysis and quantification, and measures of diversity, see Cusick (1993:173–183, 202–223, 261–279). Assessments of NISP, MNI, and biomass for each assemblage are given in Tables 6 and 9.

Among the affluent households, subsistence bore a marked similarity to Spanish households of the early 18th century, as reported by Reitz and Cumbaa (1983:166–176) in Deagan's study of the Spanish creole community, 1700–1763. Indeed, these households reflected the localized adaptation noted for the earlier period: "The criollo and peninsular diets also evidence substantial modification from the Old World pattern. The use of pigs and cattle as a primary food source, to the virtual exclusion of sheep, is a notable shift in dietary pattern away from

that found in Spain" (Reitz and Cumbaa 1983: 181–182).

The faunal assemblages from the Spanish sites of Bousquet and Sánchez and the Minorcan sites of Papy and Seguí showed little evidence for ethnic differences in diet. Clear evidence was present for the raising of poultry at the Papy household, and both the Papy and Seguí assemblages had relatively high frequencies of wild bird. Ethnohistories of the Minorcans note the importance of raising and hunting birds both in the Old World and during the plantation days at New Smyrna, Florida. The St. Augustine assemblages may reflect this tradition; however, sample sizes for the sites are small, and sample size could be a factor in assessing MNI at these sites, hence further analysis is needed.

The assemblage of the Triay household, on the other hand, showed a pattern of foodways that varied little from 18th-century accounts of subsistence on Minorca. Faunal materials at the Triay lot were recovered from a well dating to the British period occupation and from trash pits dating to the late Spanish colonial period. Both assemblages indicated a heavy reliance on fish. Fish accounted for more than 90 percent of MNI in both the British- and Spanish-period contexts; biomass data also reflect its importance (Quitmyer 1988; Cusick 1993). While sample size from the well context is extremely small (MNI = 48), two additional analyses of samples from the well produced almost identical results (Fernández-Sardina 1992; Trocolli 1992). A comparison of the Triay site with other site assemblages is presented in Table 9.

Ethnobotanical analysis of materials recovered from the well corroborated the faunal evidence for a traditional diet. Contents of the well included many common garden cultigens that were exploited on Minorca and that formed a major component of diet in both Minorca and Florida (Newsom 1990). Subsistence at the Triay site appears to have been supplemented with seasonal use of shellfish (Quitmyer 1988). In all, the archaeological assemblage from the Triay site conformed with an assessment of traditional Minorcan diet recorded by an 18th-century observer "that scarce a fifth of their whole diet is furnished from the animal kingdom; and of this, fish makes up the considerable portion" (Cleghorn 1779:35).

Discussion

In St. Augustine, the community study approach has proven to be an exceptionally useful tool for studying the social composition and interaction of colonial households. Studies of ethnicity in archaeology have been plagued by difficulties in identifying ethnic groups archaeologically and in relating material culture to the operation of ethnicity. Too often, such studies have sought neat, clean answers to complex situations: either a family assimilated or it did not. In the case of St. Augustine, the availability of documentary evidence about ethnic group formation, of historic records on costume and diet, and of multiple categories of material culture were an advantage in interpretation of data. These permitted questions about ethnicity, assimilation, and class to be addressed within the contexts of community study. Results show that ethnic patterns of behavior were closely associated with economic level, and tended to become less marked in the material record with upward mobility.

In general, the results of analysis support the following conclusions. Evidence for traditional Minorcan culture comes from less affluent individuals and families who, for the most part, were still living within the Minorcan quarter of town. Their adherence to Old World lifeways reflects both their status as first-generation immigrants and a colonial social hierarchy that offered them limited mobility. For those Minorcan families who did achieve upward mobility, material life appears to have reflected affinities of social class and status. Subsistence conformed generally to a pattern established earlier in the century for well-to-do households, and choices in ceramics correlated with status, income, and occupation.

Obviously, this pattern emerges only because numerous sites were included in analysis, and interpreted against other evidence. A second stage of analysis, still underway, involves network analysis of the various families represented in the archaeological sample. This network analysis makes possible a more sophisticated assessment of material life. For instance, even with analysis in a preliminary stage, evidence exists for a disjunction between the material and social life of affluent Minorcans in St. Augustine. While the material world of the Seguís conforms very closely to that of middle-class Spaniards, this family has a social network that is centered primarily on their Minorcan kin group, as well as with a few key Spanish families. In other words, this seems to be a family that openly professes affinity with the Spanish gentry, but actually has its closest social ties with other Minorcans. The family's dual identity may prove to be related to its economic position as a merchant family. Comparisons with the Papy household, another merchant family, are underway. As the network analysis proceeds, it should be possible directly to compare and contrast each family's material world with its social interaction in St. Augustine.

Conclusions

The strengths of community study lie in its focus on locale as a unit of research with social meaning, its unifying framework for integration of multiple sources of data, its utility as a strategy for long-term, ongoing research, and its long history of concern with issues of interdisciplinary interest in the social sciences. Two community studies of St. Augustine have demonstrated that the approach can be applied to the archaeology of a medium-sized colonial town. Lewis's application of the method to frontier settlements and Hardesty's study of mining encampments offer evidence that the scope of community study is potentially broad. It is not hard to visualize ways of studying mission sites or segments of urban cities along the same lines. Through the synthesis of archaeological and documentary material, community studies fulfill one of the basic methodological goals of historical archaeology: to construct a more complete ethnography of the past than can be achieved by emphasizing *only* archival or *only* excavated materials.

ACKNOWLEDGMENTS

Research on late colonial sites in Spanish St. Augustine was made possible by a dissertation improvement grant from the National Science Foundation (#BN-9003961), two grants for fieldwork from the St. Augustine Historical Society, and additional support from the Florida Museum of Natural History and the University of Florida. Identification of faunal material was done by Dr. Patricia Foster-Turley at the Florida Museum of Natural History. I am grateful to the following organizations and people for their assistance in completing this research: Stan Bond, Bruce Piatek, and Susan Parker of the Historic St. Augustine Preservation Board; the St. Augustine Archaeological Association; Carl Halbirt, City Archaeologist; Bruce Chappell, archivist, P. K. Yonge Library of Florida History; Kathleen Deagan and the members of my doctoral research committee, Darrett Rutman, Murdo MacLeod, Elizabeth Wing, and Jerald Milanich; and Elizabeth Reitz, Patricia Griffin, Jane Landers, and the St. Augustine Historical Society. I would also like to thank the property owners of the various sites for their cooperation. The dissertation on which this article was based was awarded the 1994 Jay I. Kislak Foundation Prize for a Dissertation or Monograph in History or Anthropology.

REFERENCES

ARENSBERG, CONRAD M.
1961   The Community as Object and Sample. *American Anthropologist* 63(2):246–264.

ARENSBERG, CONRAD M., AND SOLON T. KIMBALL
1965   *Culture and Community*. Harcourt Brace and World, New York.

ARMSTRONG, DOUGLAS
1990   *The Old Village and the Great House*. University of Illinois Press, Urbana.
1995   African Jamaican Transformation at Seville: Application of a Functional Analysis. Paper presented at the Annual Meeting of the Society for Historical Archaeology Conference on Historical and Underwater Archaeology, Washington, D.C.

ARMSTRONG, JOHN
1756   *The History of the Island of Minorca*. Printers to the Royal Society, London.

BAKER, VERNON G.
1978   Historical Archaeology at Black Lucy's Garden, Andover, Massachusetts: Ceramics from the Site of a Nineteenth-Century Afro-American. *Papers of the Robert S. Peabody Foundation for Archaeology* 8. Phillips Academy, Andover, Massachusetts.

BELL, COLIN, AND HOWARD NEWBY
1972   *Community Studies: An Introduction to the Sociology of the Local Community*. Praeger, New York, and Washington, D.C.

BELL, DANIEL
1975   Ethnicity and Social Change. In *Ethnicity: Theory and Experience,* edited by Nathan Glazer and Daniel P. Moynihan, pp. 141–174. Harvard University Press, Cambridge, Massachusetts.

BERMÚDEZ, LIGIA
1989   The Situado: A Study in the Dynamics of East Florida's Economy, During the Second Spanish Period, 1785–1820. Unpublished M.A. thesis, Department of History, University of Florida, Gainesville.

BOWEN, JOANNE
1978   Probate Inventories: An Evaluation from the Perspective of Zooarchaeology and Agricultural History at Mott Farm. In *Historical Archaeology: A Guide to*

Substantive and Theoretical Contributions, edited by Robert L. Schuyler, pp. 149–159. Baywood, Farmingdale, New York.

BRAGDON, KATHLEEN J.
1988   Occupational Differences in Material Culture. In *Documentary Archaeology in the New World,* edited by Mary C. Beaudry, pp. 83–91. Cambridge University Press, New York.

BROWNELL, BAKER
1950   *The Human Community: Its Philosophy and Practice for a Time of Crisis.* Harper and Row, New York.

CHAMBERLAIN, FREDERICK
1927   *The Balearics and Their Peoples.* Dodd, Mead, New York.

CLEGHORN, GEORGE
1779   *Observations on the Epidemical Diseases in Minorca, from the Year 1744–1749, to Which Is Prefixed a Short Account of the Climate, Productions, and Inhabitants and Endemical Distempers of that Island.* Library East, University of Florida, Gainesville. Microfiche.

CLELAND, CHARLES E.
1988   Questions of Substance, Questions that Count. *Historical Archaeology* 22(1):13–17.

CUSICK, JAMES G.
1989   Residenters with the Spaniards: Demographic and Geographic Data on the Non-Spanish Settlers of Spanish East Florida Who Signed the Oaths of Loyalty, 1790–1804. Manuscript on file, P. K. Yonge Library of Florida History, Library West, University of Florida, Gainesville.
1991   Across the Border: Commodity Flow and Merchants in Spanish St. Augustine. *Florida Historical Quarterly* 69(3):277–299.
1993   Ethnic Groups and Class in an Emerging Market Economy: Spaniards and Minorcans in Late Colonial St. Augustine. Unpublished Ph.D. dissertation, Department of Anthropology, University of Florida, Gainesville.
1994   St. Augustine as a Port Town: Local Response to the Atlantic Economy in the Late Eighteenth Century. Paper presented at the 60th Annual Meeting of the Southern Historical Association, Louisville, Kentucky.
[1995] Archaeological Perspectives on Material Culture and Ethnicity. In *Material Culture: The Shape of the Field,* edited by Ritchie Garrison and Ann Smart Martin. *Winterthur Portfolio,* in press.

DEAGAN, KATHLEEN A.
1983   *Spanish St. Augustine: The Archaeology of a Colonial Creole Community.* Academic Press, New York.

DEAN, LOIS R.
1967   *Five Towns: A Comprehensive Community Study.* Random House, New York.

DEETZ, JAMES
1977   Parting Ways. *In Small Things Forgotten: The Archaeology of Early American Life.* Anchor Press/Doubleday, New York.

DICCIONARIO
1817   *Diccionario de la Lengua Castellana.* Royal Academy, Madrid, Spain.

DICKENS, ROY S. (EDITOR)
1982   *Archaeology of Urban America: The Search for Pattern and Process.* Academic Press, New York.

EAST FLORIDA PAPERS [EFP]
1784– Census Returns [Census], EFP Bundle 323A, Reel
1814   148. P. K. Yonge Library of Florida History, Library West, University of Florida, Gainesville. Microfilm.
1784– Register of Shipping Arrivals and Departures [Reg-
1821   ister], EFP Bundles 214–258, Reels 91–109. P. K. Yonge Library of Florida History, Library West, University of Florida, Gainesville. Microfilm.
1784– Testamentary Proceedings [Testamentary Proceed-
1821   ings], EFP Bundles 301–319, Reels 134–146b. P. K. Yonge Library of Florida History, Library West, University of Florida, Gainesville. Microfilm.
1790– Oaths of Allegiance for New Settlers [Oaths], EFP
1804   Bundle 350, Reel 172. P. K. Yonge Library of Florida History, Library West, University of Florida, Gainesville. Microfilm.

ENGELBREKTSSON, ULLA-BRIT
1986   Ethnicity in the Local Context: Italians and Greeks in a Swedish Town. *Ethnos* 51(3–4):148–172.

ERIKSON, KAI T.
1976   *Everything in Its Path: Destruction of Community in the Buffalo Creek Flood.* Simon and Schuster, New York.

ERNSTEIN, JULIE H.
1994   Land and Community in Prince George's County, Maryland, 1740–1790. Paper presented at the Annual Meeting of the Society for Historical Archaeology Conference on Historical and Underwater Archaeology, Vancouver, British Columbia.

EWEN, CHARLES R.
1991   *From Spaniard to Creole: The Archaeology of Hispanic-American Cultural Transformation.* University of Alabama Press, Birmingham.

FERNÁNDEZ-SARDINA, RICARDO
1992   Analysis of Faunal Remains from Ribera Gardens, St. Augustine, Florida. Manuscript on file, Florida Museum of Natural History, Gainesville.

FOWLER, DON D., AND DONALD L. HARDESTY
1994   Introduction. In *Others Knowing Others: Perspec-*

tives on Ethnographic Careers, edited by Don D. Fowler and Donald L. Hardesty, pp. 1–14. Smithsonian Institution Press, Washington, D.C.

GASCO, JANINE
1992 Documentary and Archaeological Evidence for Household Differentiation in Colonial Soconusco, New Spain. In *Text-Aided Archaeology,* edited by Barbara J. Little, pp. 83–96. CRC Press, Boca Raton, Florida.

GEISMAR, JOAN H.
1982 *The Archaeology of Social Disintegration in Skunk Hollow: A Nineteenth-Century Rural Black Community.* Academic Press, New York.

GREELEY, ANDREW M., AND WILLIAM C. McCREADY
1975 The Transmission of Cultural Heritages: The Case of the Irish and Italians. In *Ethnicity: Theory and Experience,* edited by Nathan Glazer and Daniel P. Moynihan, pp. 209–235. Harvard University Press, Cambridge, Massachusetts.

GREENWOOD, ROBERTA S.
1980 The Chinese on Mainstreet. In *Archaeological Perspectives on Ethnicity in America,* edited by Robert L. Schuyler, pp. 113–123. Baywood, Farmingdale, New York.
1991 Historical Archaeology in California. *Historical Archaeology* 25(3):24–28.

GRIFFIN, PATRICIA
1988 The Minorcans. In *Clash Between Cultures: Spanish East Florida, 1784–1821.* St. Augustine Historical Society, St. Augustine, Florida.
1990 *Mullet on the Beach: The Minorcans of Florida, 1768–1788.* University of Florida Press, Gainesville.

HARDESTY, DONALD L.
1988 The Archaeology of Mining and Miners: A View from the Silver State. *Special Publication Series* 6. Society for Historical Archaeology, California, Pennsylvania.

HILL, JAMES N.
1991 Archaeology and the Accumulation of Knowledge. In Processual and Postprocessual Archaeologies: Multiple Ways of Knowing the Past, edited by Robert W. Preucel. pp. 42–53. *Center for Archaeological Investigations, Occasional Paper* 10:42–53. Southern Illinois University, Carbondale.

HILLERY, GEORGE A.
1955 Definitions of Community: Areas of Agreement. *Rural Sociology* 20(2):111–123.

HISTORIC RECORDS SURVEY
1939 Descriptions of the City of St. Augustine, East Florida, 1788, 1790. Manuscript on file, Historic Records Survey, Works Progress Administration, Jacksonville, Florida.

HORVATH, STEVEN M.
1983 Ethnic Groups as Subjects of Archaeological Inquiry. In Forgotten Places and Things: Archaeological Perspectives on American History, edited by Albert E. Ward. *Contributions to Anthropological Studies* 3:23–25. Center for Anthropological Studies, Albuquerque, New Mexico.

ISAAC, RHYS
1982 *The Transformation of Virginia, 1740–1790.* University of North Carolina Press, Chapel Hill.

JOHNSON, SHERRY
1989 The Spanish St. Augustine Community, 1784–1795: A Reevaluation. *Florida Historical Quarterly* 69(1): 27–54.

KAISER, HANNAH
1994 Class, Race, and Community in Late 19th-Century Annapolis, Maryland. Paper presented at the Annual Meeting of the Society for Historical Archaeology Conference on Historical and Underwater Archaeology, Vancouver, British Columbia.

KANY, CHARLES
1932 *Life and Manners in Madrid, 1750–1800.* University of California Press, Berkeley.

KAUFMAN, HAROLD F.
1959 Toward an Interactional Conception of Community. *Social Forces* 38(1):8–17.

KELLY, MARSHA C. S., AND ROGER E. KELLY
1980 Approaches to Ethnic Identification in Historical Archaeology. In *Archaeological Perspectives on Ethnicity in America,* edited by Robert L. Schuyler, pp. 133–143. Baywood, Farmingdale, New York.

KELSO, WILLIAM M.
1984 *Kingsmill Plantations, 1619–1800: Archaeology of Country Life in Colonial Virginia.* Academic Press, Orlando, Florida.

KIMBALL, SOLON T., AND WILLIAM L. PARTRIDGE
1979 *The Craft of Community Study: Fieldwork Dialogues.* University Presses of Florida, Gainesville.

KING, JULIA A.
1988 A Comparative Midden Analysis of a Household and Inn in St. Mary's City. *Historical Archaeology* 22(2): 17–39.

KING, JULIA A., AND EDWARD E. CHANEY
1994 Community and Boundaries in the 17th-Century Chesapeake. Paper presented at the Annual Meeting of the Society for Historical Archaeology Conference on Historical and Underwater Archaeology, Vancouver, British Columbia.

KIRCH, PATRICK V.
1992 *Anahulu: The Anthropology of History in the Kingdom of Hawaii.* Vol. 2, *The Archaeology of History.* University of Chicago Press, Chicago, Illinois.

KOHLER, CARL
1963   A History of Costume. Dover, New York.

LANDERS, JANE
1988   Black Society in Spanish St. Augustine, 1784–1821. Unpublished Ph.D. dissertation, Department of History, University of Florida, Gainesville.

LAVER, JAMES
1988   Costume and Fashion: A Concise History. Paget Press, New York.

LEONE, MARK
1988   The Relationship Between Archaeological Data and the Documentary Record: 18th-Century Gardens in Annapolis, Maryland. Historical Archaeology 22(1): 29–35.

LEWIS, KENNETH E.
1976   Camden: A Frontier Town. Anthropological Studies 2. Occasional Papers of the Institute of Archeology and Anthropology, University of South Carolina, Columbia.
1977   Sampling the Archeological Frontier: Regional Models and Component Analysis. In Research Strategies in Historical Archeology, edited by Stanley South, pp. 151–202. Academic Press, New York.
1984   The American Frontier: An Archaeological Study of Settlement Pattern and Process. Academic Press, Orlando, Florida.

LOCKEY, JOSEPH BYRNE
1949   East Florida, 1783–1785: A File of Documents Assembled and Many of Them Translated. University of California Press, Berkeley.

LOCKRIDGE, KENNETH A.
1970   A New England Town, the First Hundred Years: Dedham, Massachusetts, 1636–1736. W. W. Norton, New York.

MANIERY, MARY L.
1994   Examining Changes in Feng Shui Through Time: A Study of Three Chinese American Communities in the Sacramento River Delta Region. Paper presented at the Annual Meeting of the Society for Historical Archaeology Conference on Historical and Underwater Archaeology, Vancouver, British Columbia.

McEWAN, BONNIE
1983   Spanish Colonial Adaptation on Hispaniola: The Archaeology of Area 35, Puerto Real, Haiti. Unpublished M.A. thesis, Department of Anthropology, University of Florida, Gainesville.
1991   San Luis de Talimali: The Archaeology of Spanish–Indian Relations at a Florida Mission. Historical Archaeology 25(3):36–60.

McGUIRE, RANDALL T.
1982   The Study of Ethnicity in Historical Archaeology. Journal of Anthropological Archaeology 1:159–178.

1983   Ethnic Group, Status, and Material Culture at Rancho Punto de Agua. In Forgotten Places and Things: Archaeological Perspectives on American History, edited by Albert E. Ward. Contributions to Anthropological Studies 3:193–204. Center for Anthropological Studies, Albuquerque, New Mexico.

MILLER, GEORGE L.
1980   Classification and Economic Scaling of 19th-Century Ceramics. Historical Archaeology 14(1):1–40.
1991   A Revised Set of CC Index Values for Classification and Economic Scaling of English Ceramics from 1787 to 1880. Historical Archaeology 25(1):1–25.

MINAR, DAVID W., AND SCOTT GREER
1969   The Concept of Community: Readings with Interpretations. Aldine, Chicago, Illinois.

NEWSOM, LEE A.
1990   Plant Remains from the Ribera Gardens (SA-26), St. Augustine, Florida. Manuscript on file, Florida Museum of Natural History, Gainesville, Florida.

NISBET, ROBERT A.
1953   The Quest for Community. Oxford University Press, New York.

OTTO, JOHN SOLOMON
1984   Cannon's Point Plantation, 1794–1860: Living Conditions and Status Patterns in the Old South. Academic Press, Orlando, Florida.

PARK, ROBERT E.
1936   Human Ecology. American Journal of Sociology 42(1):1–15.

PARSONS, TALCOTT
1960   Structure and Process in Modern Societies. Free Press, New York.
1975   Some Theoretical Considerations of the Nature and Trends of Change in Ethnicity. In Ethnicity: Theory and Experience, edited by Nathan Glazer and Daniel P. Moynihan, pp. 53–83. Harvard University Press, Cambridge, Massachusetts.

POPLIN, DENNIS E.
1979   Communities: A Survey of Theories and Methods of Research. Second edition. Macmillan, New York.

PYSZCZYK, HEINZ W.
1988   Economic and Social Factors in the Consumption of Material Goods in the Fur Trade of Western Canada. Volumes in Historical Archaeology 6. South Carolina Institute of Archaeology and Anthropology, University of South Carolina, Columbia.
1989   Consumption and Ethnicity: An Example from the Fur Trade in Western Canada. Journal of Anthropological Archaeology 8:213–249.

QUITMYER, IRVY R.
1988   Zooarchaeological Analysis of British Period Food Remains from the Ribera Gardens Well, St. Augustine, Florida. Manuscript on file, Florida Museum of Natural History, Gainesville, Florida.

RACINET, ALBERT
1988   *The Historical Encyclopedia of Costumes.* Reprint of 1886 edition. Facts on File, New York.

RASICO, PHILIP D.
1990   *The Minorcans of Florida: Their History, Language and Culture.* Luthers, New Smyrna, Florida.

REDFIELD, ROBERT
1955   *The Little Community: Viewpoints for a Human Whole.* University of Chicago Press, Chicago, Illinois.

REITZ, ELIZABETH J., AND CATHERINE BROWN
1984   Three Hundred Years of Faunal Use at SA-34–2, St. Augustine, Florida. Report prepared by the authors. Submitted to Florida Museum of Natural History, Gainesville.

REITZ, ELIZABETH J., AND STEPHEN L. CUMBAA
1983   Diet and Foodways of Eighteenth-Century Spanish St. Augustine. In *Spanish St. Augustine: The Archaeology of a Colonial Creole Community,* edited by Kathleen A. Deagan, pp. 151–185. Academic Press, New York.

RUTMAN, DARRETT B.
1973   The Social Web: A Prospectus for the Study of the Early American Community. In *Insights and Parallels: Problems and Issues of American Social History,* edited by William L. O'Neill, pp. 57–88. Burgess, Minneapolis, Minnesota.
1980   Community Study. *Historical Methods* 13(1):29–41.
1986   Assessing the Little Communities of Early America. *William and Mary Quarterly* 43(2):164–178.

RUTMAN, DARRETT B., AND ANITA H. RUTMAN
1984   *A Place in Time: Middlesex County, Virginia, 1650–1750.* W. W. Norton, New York.

SAHLINS, MARSHALL
1992   *Anahulu: The Anthropology of History in the Kingdom of Hawaii.* Vol. 1, *Historical Ethnography.* University of Chicago Press, Chicago, Illinois.

SANDERS, IRWIN
1960   The Community Social Profile. *American Sociological Review* 25(1):75–77.
1966   *The Community: An Introduction to a Social System.* Ronald Press, New York.

SCHIFFER, MICHAEL B.
1988   The Structure of Archaeological Theory. *American Antiquity* 53(2):461–485.

SCHUYLER, ROBERT L.
1988   Archaeological Remains, Documents, and Anthropology: A Call for a New Culture History. *Historical Archaeology* 22(1):36–42.

SCOTT, JOHN
1988   Trend Report: Social Network Analysis. *Sociology* 22(1):109–127.

SEIDEL, JOHN L.
1994   Military Community at a Revolutionary War Military Cantonment at Pluckemin, New Jersey. Paper presented at the Annual Meeting of the Society for Historical Archaeology Conference on Historical and Underwater Archaeology, Vancouver, British Columbia.

SINGLETON, THERESA (EDITOR)
1985   *The Archaeology of Slavery and Plantation Life.* Academic Press, Orlando, Florida.

SOUTH, STANLEY
1977a   *Method and Theory in Historical Archeology.* Academic Press, New York.

SOUTH, STANLEY (EDITOR)
1977b   *Research Strategies in Historical Archeology.* Academic Press, New York.

SPENCER-WOOD, SUZANNE (EDITOR)
1987   *Consumer Choice in Historical Archaeology.* Plenum Press, New York.

STASKI, EDWARD H.
1987a   Border City, Border Culture: Assimilation and Change in Late 19th-Century El Paso. In Living in Cities: Current Research in Urban Archaeology, edited by Edward H. Staski. *Special Publication Series* 5:48–55. Society for Historical Archaeology, California, Pennsylvania.

STASKI, EDWARD H. (EDITOR)
1987b   Living in Cities: Current Research in Urban Archaeology. *Special Publication Series* 5. Society for Historical Archaeology, California, Pennsylvania.

TÖNNIES, FERDINAND
1957   *Community and Society,* translated by Charles P. Loomis. Harper and Row, New York.

TORNERO TINAJERO, PABLO
1979   *Relaciones de dependencia entre Florida y Estados Unidos, 1783–1820.* Ministerios de Asuntos Exteriores, Madrid, Spain.

TROCOLLI, RUTH
1992   The Zooarchaeological Analysis of a Well Sample

from the Ribera Gardens Site (SA-26), St. Augustine, Florida. Manuscript on file, Florida Museum of Natural History, Gainesville, Florida.

WALSH, LORENA S.
1988   Community Networks in the Early Chesapeake. In *Colonial Chesapeake Society,* edited by Lois Green Carr, Philip D. Morgan, and Jean B. Russo, pp. 200–241. University of North Carolina Press, Chapel Hill.

WARREN, ROLAND L.
1972   *The Community in America.* Second edition. Rand McNally, Chicago, Illinois.

WARREN, ROLAND L. (EDITOR)
1977   *New Perspectives on the American Community: A Book of Readings.* Third edition. Rand McNally College Publishing, Chicago, Illinois.

WELLMAN, BARRY, AND S. D. BERKOWITZ
1988   *Social Structures: A Network Approach.* Cambridge University Press, Cambridge, U.K.

WILKIE, LAURIE A.
1993   Plantation as "Place": Reflections of Ethnicity, Race Relations, and Social Space at Oakley Plantation, Louisiana. Paper presented at the Annual Meeting of the Society for Historical Archaeology Conference on Historical and Underwater Archaeology, Kansas City, Missouri.
1994   Coping with Racism: African-American Community in Postbellum Louisiana. Paper presented at the Annual Meeting of the Society for Historical Archaeology Conference on Historical and Underwater Archaeology, Vancouver, British Columbia.

WYLIE, ALISON
1992   The Interplay of Evidential Constraints and Political Interests: Recent Archaeological Research on Gender. *American Antiquity* 57(1):15–35.
1993   Invented Lands/Discovered Pasts: The Westward Expansion Myth and History. *Historical Archaeology* 27(4):1–19.

YENTSCH, ANN
1983   Expressions of Cultural Variation in Seventeenth-Century Maine and Massachusetts. In Forgotten Places and Things: Archaeological Perspectives on American History, edited by Albert E. Ward. *Contributions to Anthropological Studies* 3:72–83. Center for Anthropological Studies, Albuquerque, New Mexico.

ZIERDEN, MARTHA
1979   The Archaeology of the Nineteenth-Century Second Spanish Period in St. Augustine, Florida: Examination of a Peninsulare Household. Unpublished M.A. thesis, Department of Anthropology, Florida State University, Tallahassee.

JAMES GREGORY CUSICK
1253 TANGERINE DRIVE
JACKSONVILLE, FLORIDA 32259

JANINE GASCO

Material Culture and Colonial Indian Society in Southern Mesoamerica: The View from Coastal Chiapas, Mexico

ABSTRACT

The native population of the colonial Province of Soconusco, New Spain, cultivated cacao throughout the Spanish colonial period, which provided the means for acquiring relatively large quantities of Spanish-introduced goods. This paper examines the extent to which other aspects of the archaeological record—the settlement pattern, house construction, and indigenous—tradition artifacts—exhibited change and continuity from the Late Postclassic to Spanish colonial periods.

Introduction

For the past few years documentary and archaeological data have been used to examine how the native population of the colonial Province of Soconusco participated in the Spanish colonial system (Gasco 1987b, 1989a). The Province of Soconusco was located on the hot, humid Pacific coastal plain of what is today Chiapas, Mexico (Figure 1). In the late 15th century the Soconusco region fell under the domination of the Aztec empire. The Aztecs presumably were driven to gain control of the Soconusco by a desire for the cacao and other tropical resources found in the region (Gasco and Voorhies 1989; Voorhies 1989a). Following the Spanish conquest of the region in 1524, the native population suffered a drastic decline because of exposure to Old World diseases to which it had no immunity (MacLeod 1973:68–79; Gerhard 1979:169; Gasco 1987a:78ff.). Cacao continued to be the major product of the region, and although heavy population loss resulted in a sharp decline in the cacao industry, it remained an important crop throughout the Spanish colonial period (Gasco 1987a:149ff.).

Most of the research to date has involved looking at the native participation in the colonial economic system, and a major focus has been on the documentary and archaeological data that provide information directly related to economic links between the people of Soconusco and the larger commercial world (Gasco 1987a, 1987b, 1989a). Briefly, the evidence has shown that the natives of colonial Soconusco were linked to the colonial economy largely through the cacao trade. The Indian residents of Soconusco not only paid their tribute to the Spanish Crown in cacao for much of the Spanish colonial period, but they also were engaged in trade with non-Indian merchants who brought a wide variety of merchandise to the Soconusco in order to obtain the expensive and high-quality Soconusco cacao.

The documentary data indicate that non-Indian itinerant merchants traded directly with individual cacao producers in the Soconusco. Whereas the native cacao producers of Soconusco frequently got the short end of the bargain in that they were either paid low prices for their cacao or were forced to pay high prices for goods, it is also clear from the archaeological record that Soconusco natives were able to acquire high-cost imported goods in greater quantities than seems to have been the case in other colonial Indian communities (Charlton 1979; Lee and Markman 1979; Graham et al. 1985; Jones et al. 1986).

Artifacts recovered during excavations at the colonial townsite of Ocelocalco (Figure 1) included majolica and lead-glazed pottery from central Mexico, Guatemala, Spain, and perhaps other production centers, porcelain from China, and metal and glass goods. Presumably other goods such as textiles that are not preserved in the archaeologicl record also were used by the residents of Ocelocalco.

In sum, the economic participation of native Soconuscans in the colonial economy was somewhat unusual in that they produced a commodity of high value on the world market, and as a result, they had access to relatively large quantities of Spanish-introduced goods.

A new focus of research on the colonial Indian society of Soconusco is the examination of what

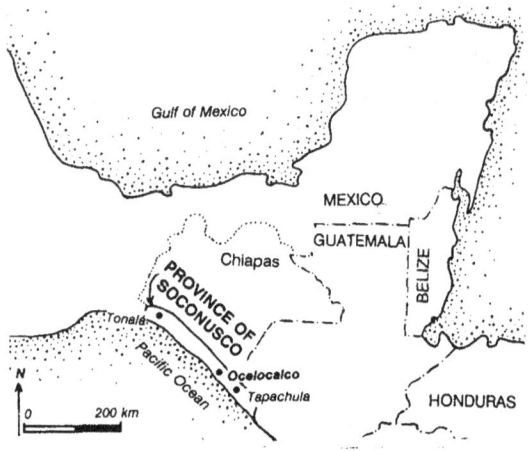

FIGURE 1. Location of the colonial Province of Soconusco in Chiapas, Mexico.

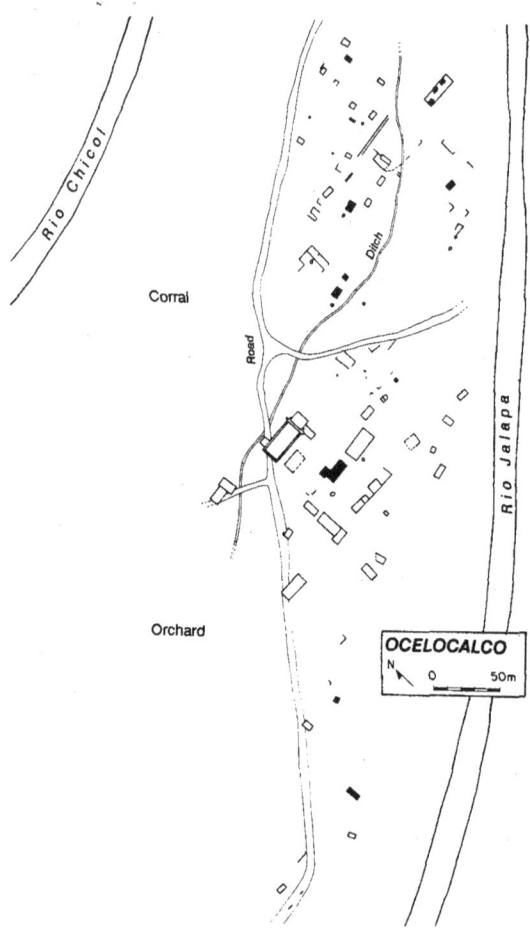

FIGURE 2. Site map of Ocelocalco with excavated structures darkened.

effect this particular form of economic integration had on other aspects of social organization in the native communities of colonial Soconusco. As a first step toward this end, the objective of this study is to evaluate the extent to which there was change and continuity in material culture from Postclassic to Spanish colonial periods in the community of Ocelocalco. Ocelocalco was a predominantly Indian town occupied from approximately 1572 to 1767, at which time it was abandoned by its last three residents (Gasco 1987a:188–195, 1989b).

Several aspects of the archaeological record will be examined including settlement pattern, structures, other features, and indigenous and Spanish tradition artifacts.

Settlement Pattern

The colonial town of Ocelocalco was apparently laid out using basic Spanish notions about town planning (Nuttall 1922), although not without some modifications from the ideal plan. Structures were roughly aligned to north/south, but there is no clear grid with north/south- or east/west-running streets (Figure 2). In fact, only the church and structures closest to the church were aligned per-

fectly to magnetic north. Farther away from the town center, structures were aligned several degrees either east or west of magnetic north. In other ways, however, Ocelocalco did conform to Spanish ideals of town planning. The church is in the center of the community, and the area to the east of the church may have been the town plaza.

To date no specific information regarding the founding of colonial Ocelocalco has been located. The earliest documentary record of its existence is in 1572 (Veblen and Gutiérrez-Witt 1983). Directly to the west of colonial Ocelocalco is a Late Postclassic period site identified by a heavy concentration of Late Postclassic sherds and other materials, but with no visible structures and no colonial ceramics. Presumably, the same people who lived in this community were moved a few meters away to the site of the colonial town that better conformed to Spanish ideals. This move took place sometime between 1524, when the area fell to the Spaniards, and 1572.

Ocelocalco is not mentioned in the Aztec tribute lists that name other Soconusco towns, nor is it mentioned in records of either the Aztec or Spanish conquests of the area. It seems likely that the postclassic community was small and subject to nearby Acapetahua, a regional center (Voorhies 1989b). No documentary evidence has been found to suggest that this short move was part of the *reducción* or *congregación* programs (Cline 1949; MacLeod 1973:120ff.) that saw so many natives moved from their original hamlets or villages into new, larger towns that were easier to control. In Soconusco the Spaniards may have been reluctant to move the natives too far from their established cacao orchards. Cacao orchards take at least five years to produce fruit, so such a move would have been counter-productive. The Spaniards clearly wanted the native Soconuscans to continue producing as much cacao as possible.

Unfortunately, no good information exists regarding intrasite settlement patterns in small communities for the Late Postclassic period in Soconusco, so it is difficult to determine how different the colonial community was from its postclassic counterpart. Voorhies (1989b), however, provides a settlement description of a large, postclassic center.

House Construction

The structures at Ocelocalco appear to be very similar to Late Postclassic period houses as well as modern rural houses. All that remain of the structures at Ocelocalco are foundation stones; superstructures were constructed of perishable materials, most likely pole and thatch. Neither daub nor roof tile fragments were found associated with any of the structures, including the church. The practice of building pole and thatch houses on a cobble foundation has continued to the present (Moore and Gasco 1990).

Most structures at Ocelocalco were isolated rather than being part of a well—defined patio group. In some cases there appeared to be groups of connected rooms (for example, a group of five rooms south of plaza). In the one case where what seemed to be a two-room structure was excavated, the two rooms were found to be *not* contemporary.

Other Features

In addition to structures, other stone features were found whose function is still unknown. Generally, the rock piles are close to and presumably associated with houses (e.g., west of Structure 37). Artifact densities are particularly high within and around the rock features. The features themselves look very much like rocks that are piled up as part of routine yard maintenance around modern-day homes. However, this similarity does not explain the high density of artifacts around these features. In the case of modern rock piles, the area is kept clean rather than being a place of refuse collection.

Hearths were found in several of the structures and were defined by either a simple ring of stones or, in one case, by two adobe bricks lying on their sides. A more common cooking-related feature was the stone-lined pit found on interiors and exteriors of structures. In some cases, the remains of large *ollas* (cooking pots) were still resting in the pits, and in two cases the *ollas* had been burned on the interiors. These may have been ovens for baking *totopos*, the crisp baked tortillas common on the Isthmus of Tehuantepec today. The traditional method of making *totopos* is to build a fire inside a large *olla*, wait until the fire is reduced to coals, and then slap the tortillas on the inner surface of the *olla* and let them bake until they are crisp (Covarrubius 1954:276).

Indigenous and Spanish Tradition Artifacts

The great majority of artifacts found during excavations were potsherds, and most fall into the

TABLE 1

FREQUENCIES OF POTTERY TYPES BY STRUCTURE

Site	Indigenous Tradition Pottery							Spanish Tradition Pottery						Total
	1	2	3	4	5	6	7	8	9	10	11	12	13	
ST 9 (OP 8)	2981	317	297	25	7	39	3	570	89	156	5	1	25	4515
ST 12 (OP 7)	699	228	163	24	3	28	1	405	22	95	4	0	12	1684
ST 37 (OP 1)	636	60	192	5	1	22	0	51	20	5	2	0	0	994
STS 68/83 (OPS 5/6)[a]	1393	45	352	48	0	41	0	143	74	69	7	1	6	2179
ST 73 (OP 3)	53	18	18	1	0	1	0	13	5	0	0	0	0	109
ST 78 (OP 17)	176	4	36	3	0	34	0	25	7	2	1	0	0	288
ST 85 (OP 16)	64	13	30	1	0	8	0	5	0	7	0	0	0	128
ST 89 (OP 12)	330	3	97	3	0	2	0	27	6	2	3	0	1	474
Total	6332	688	1185	110	11	175	4	1239	223	336	22	2	44	10,371

Note. Type 1 = Jalapa Plain, 2 = Acapetahua Coarse, 3 = Fine Gray, 4 = Fine Monochrome, 5 = Fine Bichrome, 6 = Red Hematite Slipped, 7 = Nucatili Polychrome, 8 = Majolica, 9 = Lead-glazed Earthenware, 10 = Olive Jars, 11 = Chinese Porcelain, 12 = Creamware, and 13 = Miscellaneous Spanish-introduced pottery.
[a]It was determined during excavations that Structures 68 and 83 were part of the same residence (Gasco 1987a:254–257).

general category that can be called "indigenous tradition" (Table 1). Indigenous tradition pots are unglazed, they are hand-molded rather than wheel-thrown, and presumably they were fired using open-firing techniques. In other words, they were made in the same ways that pots had been made for over 3,000 years in Mesoamerica. Pots are still made in the area using the same techniques by women potters (Pfeiffer 1989:164ff.).

In the earlier structures at Ocelocalco, much of the pottery was virtually identical to what is found at Postclassic period sites in the area, primarily *ollas, tinajas* (water jars), and *comales* (griddles) that belong to a class of ceramics called Acapetahua Coarse (Voorhies and Gasco 1984). As the Spanish colonial period progressed this pottery was replaced at Ocelocalco by another pottery type, Jalapa Plain, that has a distinctive paste, but occurs mainly in the same three forms (*ollas, tinajas*, and *comales*).

At Ocelocalco fabric-impressed *comales* are the single most common vessel form. These appeared in earlier Postclassic period times, but their numbers increased markedly in the Spanish colonial period. This apparent increase in the use of *comales* may have been related to the cacao trade. Ca-

cao beans were probably roasted on *comales* before they were sold to remove moisture, allowing the cacao to be stored longer without spoiling. Of course, *comales* were used for other purposes as well.

Acapetahua Coarse and Jalapa Plain pottery are the most common indigenous tradition ceramic types at Ocelocalco, and although no physical or chemical tests have been carried out, it is likely that these types were produced locally.

Other indigenous tradition pottery types, however, may have been brought to Ocelocalco from elsewhere. A fine gray paste ceramic type is most frequently found in the *tinaja* form (with strap handles), and it is similar to pottery produced in Oaxaca. Another paste group has volcanic ash temper, so either the temper or the finished pots must have been brought to Ocelocalco from a volcanic region, presumably the nearby Guatemalan highlands.

Finally, there was limited use at colonial Ocelocalco of polychrome plates or shallow bowls, many of which also had hollow supports, that are similar to several Late Postclassic period polychrome types found throughout Mesoamerica.

In a sense, the basic nature of pottery production

TABLE 2
CHIPPED STONE AT OCELOCALCO BY STRUCTURE

Site	Obsidian				Chert			Total
	Flake	Blade	Core	Other	Flake	Blade	Other	
ST 9 (OP 8)	7	13	1	1	11	1	4	38
ST 12 (OP 7)	2	8	1	3	2	0	2	18
ST 37 (OP 1)	0	1	0	0	0	0	0	1
STS 68/83 (OPS 5/6)	5	0	1	1	1	0	0	8
ST 73 (OP 3)	0	0	0	0	0	0	0	0
ST 78 (OP 17)	0	0	0	0	1	0	0	1
ST 85 (OP 16)	3	0	0	1	0	0	0	4
ST 89 (OP 12)	2	1	0	0	1	0	0	4
Total	19	23	3	6	16	1	6	74

and consumption may have changed little from the Postclassic to Spanish colonial periods in Soconusco. Cooking as well as food and water storage vessels at colonial Ocelocalco remained basically the same from the Late Postclassic to Spanish colonial periods in terms of form, function, and methods of production. For the most part, these vessels were produced locally while fancier serving vessels were imported.

Very little of the Spanish tradition pottery—majolica or lead-glazed pottery—was used for either cooking or storage. The exception to this interpretation is olive jars, but presumably they were brought to the province full—they were not imported just for their potential storage capacity. Most of the glazed pots used at Ocelocalco were serving vessels, either plates or bowls, that simply replaced the polychrome serving vessels that had been used in the Late Postclassic period, most of which were probably imported to the Soconusco from elsewhere.

Other ceramic artifacts recovered at Ocelocalco included net weights and spindle whorls. The net weights found in the colonial deposits at Ocelocalco are undistinguishable from net weights found in postclassic sites in the region. The two rivers that border the site would have been, and still are, fertile fishing grounds; fish is sometimes mentioned in colonial documents as an export product of Soconusco.

The spindle whorls found at Ocelocalco presumably were used to spin cotton. They conform most closely to the Late Postclassic period "bead" whorls described by Voorhies (1989c) which are thought to have been used for spinning cotton. What is notable is that no spindle whorls were found in excavated structures that date to the latter period of Ocelocalco's existence, approximately late 17th to early 18th centuries. Soconusco would have been a good place to grow cotton—cotton is grown near Tapachula today, yet cotton cultivation is not mentioned in any of the colonial documents examined. While some spinning must have been done in the early part of the Spanish colonial period, by the 17th and early 18th centuries all textiles may have been imported.

Chipped stone artifacts were found in low quantities at Ocelocalco (Table 2). Flakes, both obsidian and chert, were the most common single chipped stone artifact type, while bifaces and arrow points, common imports in the Late Postclassic period (Clark 1989) were completely absent. Whereas one or more pieces of chipped stone were found in all but one of the excavated structures, only three of the eight structures excavated had more than four pieces of chipped stone. In short, metal tools seem to have replaced chipped stone tools fairly quickly at Ocelocalco (Table 3).

Ground stone continued—and continues—to be a common household item (Table 4). Manos and metates were found in all but one of the excavated structures.

TABLE 3
METAL ARTIFACTS AT OCELOCALCO BY STRUCTURE

Site	Nails	Cutlery/ Machetes	Keys	Horse-shoes	Scissors	Copper Bells	Misc. Copper	Misc. Iron	Total
ST 9 (OP 8)	59	9	1	2	1	0	0	23	95
ST 12 (OP 7)	39	4	0	2	0	1	2	7	55
ST 37 (OP 1)	2	3	1	1	0	0	0	7	14
STS 68/83 (OPS 5/6)	22	6	0	0	1	0	0	5	34
ST 73 (OP 3)	4	1	0	1	0	0	0	0	6
ST 78 (OP 17)	4	3	2	0	0	0	0	3	12
ST 85 (OP 16)	2	2	1	0	0	0	0	0	5
ST 89 (OP 12)	12	10	0	5	0	0	0	3	30
Total	144	38	5	11	2	1	2	48	251

TABLE 4
GROUND STONE AT OCELOCALCO
BY STRUCTURE

Site	Mano	Metate	Other	Total
ST 9 (OP 8)	14	8	0	22
ST 12 (OP 7)	4	4	1	9
ST 37 (OP 1)	3	3	0	6
STS 68/83 (OPS 5/6)	11	2	1	14
ST 73 (OP 3)	0	1	0	1
ST 78 (OP 17)	4	1	0	5
ST 85 (OP 16)	0	0	0	0
ST 89 (OP 12)	6	0	0	6
Total	42	19	2	63

Discussion

In conclusion, what does all this evidence say about culture change within native society in colonial Soconusco? First, it suggests that interpretations of the seemingly high quantities of Spanish-introduced goods found at Ocelocalco should proceed with caution.

Previous work, which was focused on economic links between the natives of Soconusco and the larger colonial economy, has tended to emphasize the uniqueness of the situation; the fact that natives retained control of production of a valuable commodity and consumed large quantities of Spanish-introduced goods.

This unique economic position *did* provide the natives of Soconusco with the means to acquire expensive, imported goods, but it did not bring about a wholesale change in material culture. In terms of the broader process of culture change, the mere presence of large numbers of majolica plates, for example, may be less significant than one might think. Of all the Spanish-introduced material found at Ocelocalco, only the horse-related paraphernalia represents a class of artifacts that is completely new in terms of function. Most of the introduced material simply replaced something else that was already in use.

Despite the presence of high quantities of a few classes of Spanish-introduced goods, the archaeological record as a whole indicates that there was considerable continuity in material culture from the Late Postclassic to Spanish colonial periods in the Soconusco. This apparent continuity does not diminish the extent of social disruption that must have accompanied the imposition of Spanish colonial rule, but it does suggest that upon closer inspection there may be evidence for continuity in certain aspects of indigenous social organization as well.

ACKNOWLEDGMENTS

I would like to thank the Instituto Nacional de Antropología e Historia, Mexico, for granting me permission to conduct excavations at Ocelocalco, as well as the Takemura family who kindly allowed me to excavate on their ranch. Funding for excavations was provided by the National Science Foundation, Grant #BNS82–14029.

REFERENCES

CHARLTON, THOMAS H.
1979 The Aztec–Early Colonial Transition in the Teotihuacán Valley. In *Actes du XLII Congrès International des Américanistes*, Vol. 8, pp. 21–33. Paris.

CLARK, JOHN E.
1989 Obsidian Tool Manufacture. In *Ancient Trade and Tribute: Economies of the Soconusco Region of Mesoamerica*, edited by Barbara Voorhies, pp. 215–228. University of Utah Press, Salt Lake City.

CLINE, HOWARD
1949 Civil Congregations of the Indians in New Spain, 1598–1606. *Hispanic American Historical Review* 39(3):348–369.

COVARRUBIUS, MIGUEL
1954 *Mexico South, the Isthmus of Tehuantepec*. Alfred A. Knopf, New York.

GASCO, JANINE
1987a *Cacao and the Economic Integration of Native Society in Colonial Soconusco, New Spain*. Ph.D. dissertation, Department of Anthropology, University of California, Santa Barbara. University Microfilms, Ann Arbor.
1987b Economic Organization in Colonial Soconusco, New Spain: Local and External Influences. *Research in Economic Anthropology*, Vol. 8, edited by Barry Isaac, pp. 105–137. JAI Press, Greenwich, Connecticut.
1989a The Colonial Economy in the Province of Soconusco. In *Ancient Trade and Tribute: Economies of the Soconusco Region of Mesoamerica*, edited by Barbara Voorhies, pp. 287–303. University of Utah Press, Salt Lake City.
1989b Economic History of Ocelocalco, a Colonial Soconusco Town. In *Ancient Trade and Tribute: Economies of the Soconusco Region of Mesoamerica*, edited by Barbara Voorhies, pp. 304–325. University of Utah Press, Salt Lake City.

GASCO, JANINE, AND BARBARA VOORHIES
1989 The Ultimate Tribute: The Role of the Soconusco as an Aztec Tributary. In *Ancient Trade and Tribute: Economies of the Soconusco Region of Mesoamerica*, edited by Barbara Voorhies, pp. 48–94. University of Utah Press, Salt Lake City.

GERHARD, PETER
1979 *The Southeast Frontier of New Spain*. Princeton University Press, Princeton.

GRAHAM, ELIZABETH A., GRANT D. JONES, AND ROBERT KAUTZ
1985 Archaeology and Ethnohistory on a Spanish Colonial Frontier: An Interim Report on the Macal-Tipu Project in Western Belize. In *The Lowland Maya Postclassic*, edited by Arlen F. Chase and Prudence M. Rice, pp. 206–214. University of Texas Press, Austin.

JONES, GRANT D., ROBERT KAUTZ, AND ELIZABETH A. GRAHAM
1986 Tipu: A Maya Town on the Spanish Colonial Frontier. *Archaeology* 39(1):40–47.

LEE, THOMAS A., AND SYDNEY MARKMAN
1979 Coxoh Maya Acculturation in Colonial Chiapas: A Necrotic Archaeological Ethnohistorical Model. In *Actes du XLII Congrès International des Américanistes*, Vol. 8, pp. 57–66. Paris.

MACLEOD, MURDO J.
1973 *Spanish Central America: A Socioeconomic History, 1520–1720*. University of California Press, Berkeley.

MOORE, JERRY D., AND JANINE GASCO
1990 Perishable Structures and Serial Dwellings from Coastal Chiapas: Implications for the Archaeology of Households. *Ancient Mesoamerica* 1(2):205–212.

NUTTALL, ZELIA
1922 Royal Ordinances Concerning the Laying Out of New Towns. *Hispanic American Historical Review* 5(2):249–254.

PFEIFFER, LINDA
1989 The Evidence for Pottery Production at Rio Arriba. In *Ancient Trade and Tribute: Economies of the Soconusco Region of Mesoamerica*, edited by Barbara Voorhies, pp. 157–174. University of Utah Press, Salt Lake City.

VEBLEN, THOMAS T., AND LAURA GUTIÉRREZ-WITT
1983 Relaciónes de las Cacaiques y Número de Yndios que hay en Guatemala, 21 abril de 1572. *Mesoamérica* 5:212–235.

VOORHIES, BARBARA
1989a An Introduction to the Soconusco and Its Prehistory. In *Ancient Trade and Tribute: Economies of the Soconusco Region of Mesoamerica*, edited by Barbara Voorhies, pp. 1–18. University of Utah Press, Salt Lake City.
1989b A Model of the Pre-Aztec Political System of the Soconusco. In *Ancient Trade and Tribute: Economies of the Soconusco Region of Mesoamerica*, ed-

ited by Barbara Voorhies, pp. 95–129. University of Utah Press, Salt Lake City.

1989c Textile Production. In *Ancient Trade and Tribute: Economies of the Soconusco Region of Mesoamerica*, edited by Barbara Voorhies, pp. 194–214. University of Utah Press, Salt Lake City.

VOORHIES, BARBARA, AND JANINE GASCO
1984 El Período Postclásico Tardío de Acapetahua, Chiapas, México. In *Investigaciones Recientes en el Área Maya*, Tomo I, pp. 431–438. Sociedad Mexicana de Antropología, San Cristóbal de las Casas, Chiapas, México.

JANINE GASCO
INSTITUTE FOR MESOAMERICAN STUDIES
STATE UNIVERSITY OF NEW YORK
ALBANY, NEW YORK 12222

RUSSELL K. SKOWRONEK

Empire and Ceramics: The Changing Role of Illicit Trade in Spanish America

ABSTRACT

Commercial colonial states of the early modern era are noteworthy in their movement of both luxury and bulk goods between the core and the periphery of empires. Frequently, for archaeologists studying the role of trade in the Spanish New World empire, the recovery of imported ceramics of non-Hispanic origins has suggested the presence of foreign interlopers in these closed mercantilist marketplaces. In this study, the ceramic assemblage of colonial Florida is examined against data from the larger Spanish empire to discern more parsimoniously the extent of this perceived illicit trade. Information for this paper is derived from the sites of colonial Santa Elena and St. Augustine in Spanish Florida, as well as from other contemporary Spanish colonial habitation and merchant shipwreck sites in the New World.

Introduction

When historical archaeologists study New World Spanish 16th-century sites, they can frequently forget that the colonies represented not a world unto themselves but rather an extension of the Habsburg Empire and, more importantly, part of the nascent world economic system (Wallerstein 1974). This neglect of the wider world arena within which the colonies were articulated has resulted in somewhat skewed ideas about the commercial position of the Spanish New World empire. For example, the military and commercial weakness that characterized the 17th- and 18th-century Spanish empire has also been applied to the 16th century. This anachronism fails to take into account the realities of 16th-century Spain. The goal of this research is to offer a more accurate interpretation of the role of illicit or contraband trade in the 16th-century Spanish New World. A review of the historical 16th-century expansion and contraction of the Spanish empire is presented. Against this background of Spain and Spanish culture in the New World, an examination of the ceramic evidence for illicit trade in the colonies of Hispaniola and Spanish Florida concludes that it was extremely limited in extent.

Background

The 16th century was a watershed in the development of the modern world economy bringing monumental changes to Spain and Western Europe (Wallerstein 1974). At the time of Columbus' first voyage, Spain consisted of little more than its present Iberian holdings and a few overseas possessions such as the Canary Islands. However, researchers must not forget that at this time Spain was already linked by wide-ranging trade networks to the rest of Europe (Davis 1973:64; Hurst 1977; Croft 1983; Curtin 1984:2). In less than half a century, from 1510 to 1550, alliances, conquests, and dynastic ties via Charles I (or V) to the House of Habsburg would link Spain to the Antilles, New Spain, and *tierra firma* (South America); the Low Countries; Burgundy; Austria; Franche-Comte; parts of Germany; and half of Italy including Naples, Sicily, Milan, Genoa, and Venice (Elliot 1963:165; Tannenbaum 1965:133).

In the latter half of the 16th century, the empire would feel some contraction in Europe due to the split of the House of Habsburg upon the abdication of Charles I and the war with the Netherlands. Still, the additions of the Philippines and the crown of Portugal with its far-flung holdings made 16th-century Spain the most powerful, global European empire of its time (Haring 1947:313; Tannenbaum 1965:99, 133).

It is this burgeoning of Spain in the 16th century and the kingdoms or lands within its sphere of control, influence, and tutelage that many anthropologists and even some historians forget. Although commercial capitalism and mercantilism were in their infancy, raw materials, finished goods, and peoples were moving within the empire and between the nascent nation states, as given in Table 1 (Davis 1973:51, 64; Gerhard 1981:

TABLE 1
SPANISH OLD WORLD POLITICAL AND COMMERCIAL TIES

Area	Dates
England	1558–1625
France	
Alsace/Lorraine	1504–ca. 1680
Burgundy	1504–1678
Franche-Comte	1504–1678
Navarre, Bearn, Rousillon	1504–ca. 1659
Holy Roman Empire	1519–1556
Austria	1519–1521
"Germany"	1519–1531
Rhenish Provinces	1519–1614
Italy	
Florence	1529–1576
Liguria (Genoa)	1528–1684
Lombardy (Milan)	1535–1713
Naples	1516–1707
Sicily	1516–1713
Low Countries	
Belgium	1504–1714
Netherlands	1504–1578
Philippines	1565–1898
Portugal	1580–1640

Sources: Haring (1947), Elliot (1963), Tannenbaum (1965), Wallerstein (1974), Croft (1983), McAlister (1984).

64–65, 89; Lister and Lister 1982:13, 69–71; Lynch 1984:148–155). From Antwerp—the economic capital of Western Europe from the beginning of the 16th century until 1585 (Lynch 1984: 143)—and the rest of the Low Countries, Spain derived over two-fifths of its revenue (Tannenbaum 1965:134; Davis 1973:65). To this region and other Habsburg Old World ports of call, including Seville, sailed Hanseatic, English, Italian, and French ships (Haring 1947:295). This trade was to continue with Holland and England and other such "heretic" nations even during the religious and dynastic schisms of the last third of the century, for war then was not total, and indirect trade could and did take place in ports such as Rouen and Nantes in France (Tanguy 1956; Lynch 1984:145,154).

Trade between Spain and her New World colonies is equally well chronicled. This "Columbian Exchange" (Crosby 1972) brought Spain great wealth from the New World in the form of dyes such as annetto, indigo, and cochineal; hides and other cattle by-products such as tallow; and fish from Labrador. There were tropical luxuries such as cotton, tobacco, medicines, cacao, and sugar for sweets. From the Philippines came silks and porcelains. From Nueva Cádiz there were pearls (Willis 1976), and from Cuba there was copper for bronze guns. Exotic New World ceramics like Mexican Red Painted wares (Smith 1949; Deagan 1987:43–44) were imported and were popular in still-life paintings of the era by such artists as Juan Bautista de Espinosa, Juan Van der Hamen, and Francisco de Palacios (Jordan 1985:93,137,205). Finally, there were the goods that would cause the largest change in the lifeways of Europe: new cultigens, silver from Mexico and Potosi, and, most importantly, gold from the islands and mainland (Haring 1947:293; Crosby 1972:170; Wolf 1982:140; McAlister 1984:364–366; Tuck 1985: 42).

The effect of these new products on the economy and lifeways of Spain and the Old World created great upheavals. This turmoil can be seen not only in soaring rates of inflation (e.g., Hamilton 1934; Lynch 1984:129–136) and population growth (Crosby 1972:165–202) but also in the outward signs of class distinction demonstrated by sumptuous displays of clothing and tablewares and conspicuous consumption of exotic foods (Braudel 1973:125, 137–139). The opulence of this era for the elite is forever captured in portraiture and still-life art that preserves the material markers of this commerce (e.g., Jordan 1985).

Trade between Spain and the New World, which brought these exotica, in the opening and closing 30 years of the 16th century was a monopoly of the city of Seville and its port San Lucar (Haring 1947: 303; Elliott 1963:179). During the intervening 40 years, Coruña, Bayona, Aviles, Laredo, Bilbao, San Sebastian, Barcelona, and Malaga traded directly with the Indies. These latter ports were already part of the extensive intra-continental European trade previously discussed (e.g., Tanguy

1956). No doubt it was a combination of Spain's growing inability to meet the material demands of the colonies with Spanish produce (Haring 1947: 294; Tannenbaum 1965:127), plus the established commercial connections of these ports that made at least one historian comment that by the 1540s trade ceased to be insular and became continental in scale (Lynch 1984:169).

The New World

This mid-16th-century change in the origin of materials exported from the Old to the New World coincides with the end of the initial wave of booty-driven Spanish conquests. By this time colonial maturity—in the form of demographic and economic stability—was in its formative stages (Lockhart and Schwartz 1983:16–180; McAlister 1984). In this emerging colonial society, male and female settlers sought to create "Neo-Europes" furnished with familiar European goods (Crosby 1986; Skowronek 1989). Anthropologists (Foster 1960: 10; Deagan 1985:7–8) have examined these mature manifestations of the Spanish New World and have characterized their adaptation as a "Conquest" or "Criollo Culture" wherein simplified elements of the dominant Spanish culture meld with resident aboriginal cultures or ecological situations. While one researcher (Deagan 1980) has drawn attention to these acculturative and assimilative processes by dubbing St. Augustine, Florida, "America's First Melting Pot," the strength of European ties should not be dismissed.

Historical archaeologists know that immigrants to the colonies were mostly Spanish in background, but they were also joined by Genoese, Germans, Basques, peoples from the Low Countries, and even French, whose homelands were segments of the 16th-century Habsburg domain or had strong commercial ties to it (Elliott 1963:179; Lister and Lister 1982:13, 69–71; McAlister 1984: 113; Manucy 1985:52). Because of this diversity it must be kept in mind that each of these groups represented different elements of "Western European Civilization."

At this time all Western European cultures were more similar than dissimilar (Gerhard 1981:56), sharing common economic, political, and religious philosophies over local ethnic variations. However, like all cultures, once cultural practices become established there is a tendency to conserve them, even when viable alternatives are available (Barrett 1984:99,113). This commitment to customs or cultural persistence means that new adjustments or adaptations are almost always compromises between the limitations imposed by the pre-existing culture and the opportunities offered by new conditions. As Braudel (1973:123) succinctly put it, "man is a creature of desire and not of need." The 16th-century Spanish New World experience, as reflected in its material culture, would prove to be no exception.

Class consciousness was an important aspect of 16th-century Spain. It was said that half the people called themselves *hidalgo* [noble] and that "anyone who could afford the price could dress and live like a noble lady or gentleman" (Tannenbaum 1965:129). This class-conscious, deferential society was part of the colonial world as well, which is well exemplified by court cases in Florida at both Santa Elena and St. Augustine over rights to the honorific titles and privileges of *Doña* and *Caballero* (Lyon 1977:25, 1984:8). The concern over social stratification also was felt by the aboriginal and mixed blood populations. Elite colonists ignored the Spanish government's policy of assimilation. They maintained themselves as a superior race and tried consciously to give the natives a feeling of inferiority while treating *mestizos* as second-class Spaniards (Tannenbaum 1965:119; Gibson 1968:135–136; Reitz and Scarry 1985:30).

Today physical remnants of 16th-century social stratification can be seen in the Mediterranean Urban Complex or grid layout of most New World cities, wherein the elite lived around the central plaza and the indigenous commoners lived on the outskirts of the settlement (Foster 1960:34–49; Lockhart and Schwartz 1983:67; Barrett 1984: 121). It is, however, in the foodways of the 16th-century colonies that archaeologists have one of the best means of physically seeing how, via the networks of trade, the elite displayed their "Spanishness."

Success in the hinterlands of the empire was measured by how well the colonists could Europeanize the New World by replicating the Old World (Skowronek 1989). The Spaniards' staff of life was bread, wine, and oil—all from Old World cultigens (Crosby 1972:67). These and other Old World foodstuffs were heavily imported until the 1540s when olives, grapes, and wheat, among other Old World crops, were finally produced in sufficient quantities in Peru and Mexico to meet the demands of all the colonists (Crosby 1972:79). Indeed, "the Spanish colonist could almost always obtain wheat bread, unless he were very poor or an inhabitant of the hot lowlands—and even the latter could have his wheat if he had the price to import it" (Crosby 1972:71). Even today upper-class Mexicans feel that corn is food for Indians and wheat is reserved for them (Crosby 1972:107). Therefore, it was local and dependable production of familiar Old World foods in the 1540s that helped increase migration and, as mentioned earlier, allowed a change in the nature of commerce from the Old World to greater amounts of finished, status-indicating, material items. These material items, which are archaeologically recoverable and readily identifiable to point of origin, include English pewter (Olds 1976), Venetian glass (Willis 1976), and, most importantly, ceramics.

Ceramics and Status

Research by Kathleen Deagan (1985:23–28) at St. Augustine suggests that the frequency of majolica and other tablewares correlates positively with the status of its users and, as such, shows the Hispanic class-conscious "mind set" as operating even in the furthest hinterlands of the empire. It should be noted that while the frequency of archaeologically-recovered majolica continues to serve as a status indicator throughout the 17th and 18th centuries (Deagan 1983; Skowronek 1984), Old World wares begin to be supplanted by New World production by the end of the 16th century. These New World majolica wares were shipped throughout the New World and to Spain, thus indicating that acculturation was working to realign percep-

tions of what constituted physical manifestations of high status by the end of the 16th century (Goggin 1968:215–216; Skowronek 1987). This shows that the wealthy were no longer obligated to "buy European" to validate their status.

Spanish Ceramics

When the archaeological record relating to status-marking ceramic tablewares is examined it is obvious that Spain produced the lion's share and greatest variety of ceramic types found in 16th-century Hispaniola and the towns of Spanish Florida (Goggin 1968; Council 1975; McEwan 1983; Willis 1984; Deagan 1985; Ewen 1987; South et al. 1988). Recovered lower status tablewares included honey-colored, lead-glazed wares and Columbia Plain majolica (Fairbanks 1973; Deagan 1985, 1987; South et al. 1988). Higher status indicating, decorated majolica wares include Yayal Blue on White, Isabela Polychrome, Santo Domingo Blue on White, Santa Elena Mottled Blue on White, Santa Elena Green and White, Sevilla White, Sevilla Blue on White, and Caparra Blue, among others (Goggin 1968; Council 1975; Lister and Lister 1982; McEwan 1983; Willis 1984; Deagan 1985, 1987; Ewen 1987; South et al. 1988). It would not be until the beginning of the 17th century that Puebla-produced majolicas would be exported from Mexico to the rest of the empire (Goggin 1968:210; Skowronek 1987:106).

Other Ceramic Tablewares

Non-Spanish ceramic tablewares recovered from 16th-century New World sites in Hispaniola and Spanish Florida illustrate by their presence the extent of the Habsburg Empire and its trade connections. Germany and the Low Countries supplied tin-glazed earthenwares and brown "Cologne" stonewares (Deagan 1987:103; Wilcoxen 1987). From northwestern Italy there are majolicas such as Ligurian Blue on Blue, Montelupo Blue on White, and Montelupo Polychrome (Lister and Lister 1982; Deagan 1987:67–71). The Manila Galleon brought Ming porcelain from China via the Philippines and

Mexico (Cervantes 1971). French stonewares and lead and tin-glazed earthenwares assumedly flowed from Nantes and the hinterlands of Brittany and from the southern manufacturing centers of Uzes and Dieulefit to Spain and thence to the New World (Gerard Gussett 1986, 1988, pers. comms.).

It is the recovery of this latter category of non-Hispanic manufactured ceramic tablewares from Spanish 16th-century New World archaeological sites that has lent validity to claims for widespread illicit trade with foreign interlopers (e.g., Council 1975; Willis 1976, 1984; Deagan 1987:20–22; Ewen 1987). Although contraband trade was widespread in the 17th and 18th centuries (e.g., Harman 1969:47–63), some researchers (e.g., Haring 1918:231–257, 1947:308; Elliott 1963:190) have projected the roots of this vast contraband trade and its negative effects on the empire back into the 16th century. Yet, given Spain's 16th-century strength, other researchers have pointed out that the effect of interlopers on legitimate trade represents less than one-twentieth of the total returns (e.g., Lynch 1984:163,172). Importantly, Spain's colonial monopoly remained largely intact until the 1630s at the height of the Thirty Years War (Wolf 1982:152). Given these different historical views it is unclear whether foreign interlopers did or did not make a mockery of Spain's New World mercantile monopoly in the 16th century. To determine the validity of either of these diametrically opposed views requires an objective examination of the material culture from the era.

Illicit Trade—Fact or Fiction?

To accurately ascertain and quantify the role of foreign interlopers in the commerce of colonial Spain requires linking it to archaeologically recoverable materials, such as ceramics, whose points of origin are identifiable. Thus, given that post-1540 Spanish mercantile New World commerce was focused more on the supply of non-food items for the colonial market and that those imported commodities included ceramics, then the frequency of non-Spanish empire produced tablewares should correlate with the role of foreign interlopers in the trade of each colony.

To examine this problem the Spanish 16th-century colonial sites of Puerto Real (McEwan 1983; Willis 1984; Ewen 1987) and Santo Domingo (Goggin 1968; Council 1975) in Hispaniola as well as St. Augustine (Deagan 1985) and Santa Elena (South 1980, 1982, 1983, 1984, 1985) in Florida were considered for their contemporaneity, the presence of archaeological collections, and, in the case of the former colony of Hispaniola, the documented occurrence of contraband trade by foreign interlopers. Additionally, information from the 1554 *flota* (Arnold and Weddle 1978; Skowronek 1987) and the Baños de la Reina site in Seville (McEwan 1986, 1988) is utilized. These latter sites represent contemporary examples of Old World Spanish mercantile trade and settlement and, as such, act as "contraband-free" controls for the study.

The types of ceramic tablewares recovered from these sites have been previously delineated. In Table 2 these tablewares are grouped into Spanish (including colonial-made exports such as Mexican Red Painted) and non-Spanish produced ceramics by count and frequency. Inspection of the frequencies (Figure 1) shows that at four of the sites—Santo Domingo, Puerto Real, Santa Elena, and Baños—so called non-Spanish imports comprised less than 3 percent of the total ceramic assemblage. These non-Spanish imports include Ming porcelain, Cologne stoneware, and Italian majolicas from Liguria, Montelupo, and Faenza, all of which originated in Spanish controlled or monopolized areas. Only at the site of Puerto Real are "French" and "Dutch"-made tin-glazed earthenwares reported (Ewen 1987). While these 39 sherds (representing 0.25% of the total assemblage of 15,604 fragments recovered from the site) may possibly indicate illicit trade, they also may represent aspects of normal commerce from the Spanish Netherlands or Spanish controlled parts of France or Spanish-made imitations ("knock offs") of these wares (Emlen Myers 1990, pers. comm.).

At St. Augustine and the 1554 *flota*, non-Spanish imports make up 17 percent of their respective assemblages. Non-Spanish types represented at these

TABLE 2
SIXTEENTH-CENTURY SPANISH AND
NON-SPANISH TABLEWARES

Location	Count N	Percent %
Hispaniola		
Santo Domingo (*Convento de San Francisco*)[a]		
Spanish	1,016	99.7
Non-Spanish	3	0.3
Total	1,019	100.0
Puerto Real[b]		
Spanish	15,413	98.8
Non-Spanish	191	1.2
Total	15,604	100.0
Spanish Florida		
St. Augustine[c]		
Spanish	614	82.6
Non-Spanish	129	17.4
Total	743	100.0
Santa Elena[d]		
Spanish	9,845	97.85
Non-Spanish	216	2.15
Total	10,061	100.00
The flota and Spain		
1554 *flota*[e]		
Spanish	53	82.8
Non-Spanish	11	17.2
Total	64	100.0
Baños, Seville[f]		
Spanish	1,904	99.4
Non-Spanish	11	0.6
Total	1,915	100.0

[a]Goggin 1968; Council 1975
[b]McEwan 1983; Willis 1984; Ewen 1987
[c]Deagan 1985—excludes Mexican produced Fig Springs Poly., San Luis B/W, Ichtucknee B/W, Mexico City White—post-1590 deposition.
[d]South 1979, 1980, 1982, 1983, 1984, 1985
[e]Skowronek 1987
[f]McEwan 1986, 1988

sites include: Oriental porcelain, Cologne stoneware, and Italian-made Ligurian Blue on Blue, Montelupo Blue on White, and Montelupo Polychrome—all wares made in Spanish controlled lands or carried by the Spanish *carrera* and thus not directly attributable to illicit activities.

Comparison of this 16th-century material with ceramic evidence from the first third of the 18th century provides a scale for interpretive reference. Remains from the 1733 *flota* and 18th-century St. Augustine, Florida, are considered as assemblages that respectively represent the Spanish mercantilist monopoly and a port with documented illicit trade (Harman 1969:47–63; Deagan 1983; Skowronek 1984:182–198). The St. Augustine assemblage represents an economic cross-section of the community. In addition to Spanish empire produced and traded imports such as majolica and porcelain, Rhenish and English white salt-glazed stonewares, French produced faience, and English made delft, Astbury, and other slipwares are present (Skowronek 1984:176–178). Thirty-two percent of St. Augustine's ceramic tablewares are non-Spanish empire in origin while these imports represent less than 2 percent of the 1733 flota's assemblage (Table 3).

These frequencies at 18th-century St. Augustine reflect Spain's economic weakness at this time. The illusion of mercantile monopoly was borne in the highly visible sailings of the *carrera*, but supplying the hinterlands was more difficult for the declining empire to achieve and thus was left increasingly to foreign interlopers. A comparison of the 16th- and 18th-century data (Figure 2) reveals the marked impact of illicit trade in the 18th century in the empire's hinterlands. The 30-fold increase in the frequency of non-Spanish empire produced or traded wares over this 150-year period quantifiably illustrates changes in Spain's commercial strength and helps clarify the limited role of contraband trade in the 16th century.

Summary and Conclusions

The ideas presented here illustrate the need to view research, especially on historical archaeological sites, in the proper holistic cosmopolitan and historical commercial setting. Views of what represents Spain and "Spanishness" in the early modern era and what represents the role of foreign

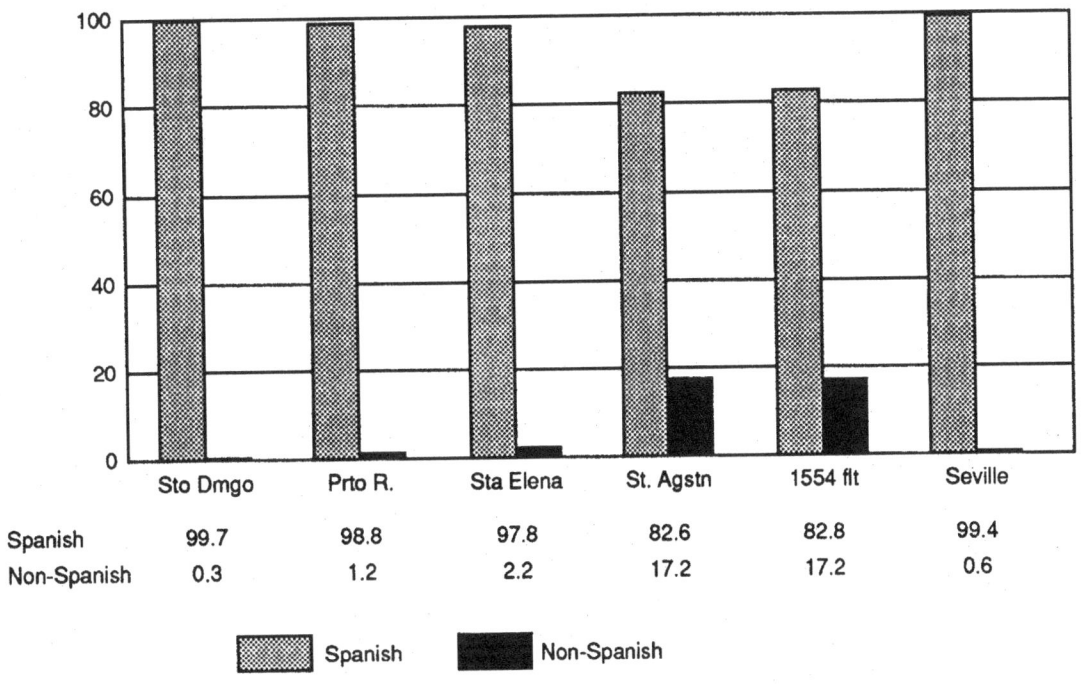

FIGURE 1. Sixteenth-century Spanish and non-Spanish tablewares by frequency.

interlopers in the Spanish colonies requires an historical knowledge of trade networks and patterns—illicit and legal—in both the Old and New Worlds in the 16th through 18th centuries.

Quantification of highly identifiable, as to point of national origin, ceramic tablewares from terrestrial and shipwreck sites in the Old and New World has laid the foundation for an index capable of measuring changes in Spain's commercial strength. It is through changes in the frequency of the presence and absence of Spanish and non-Spanish empire produced or traded wares that a measure for intra-empire commercial, and military, control is discernible. As more work is completed in other parts and periods of the empire, a finer index of these changes will emerge.

Finally, these data also suggest that, given the extent of Spain's political control and trading relations, it is more reasonable for researchers to associate most 16th-century exotic, non-Spanish, Old World materials with legitimate and normal channels of trade, than to consider them the phys-

TABLE 3
EIGHTEENTH-CENTURY SPANISH AND
NON-SPANISH TABLEWARES

Location	Count N	Percent %
1733 *flota*[a]		
Spanish	2,910	98.5
Non-Spanish	45	1.5
Total	2,955	100.0
St. Augustine (SA 7–5, 7–4, 16–23)[b]		
Spanish	1,467	68.0
Non-Spanish	688	32.0
Total	2,155	100.0

[a]Skowronek 1984:176–178
[b]Deagan 1983

ical manifestations of foreign interlopers dealing in contraband. Of course, these exotica need always be considered against the rest of the collections

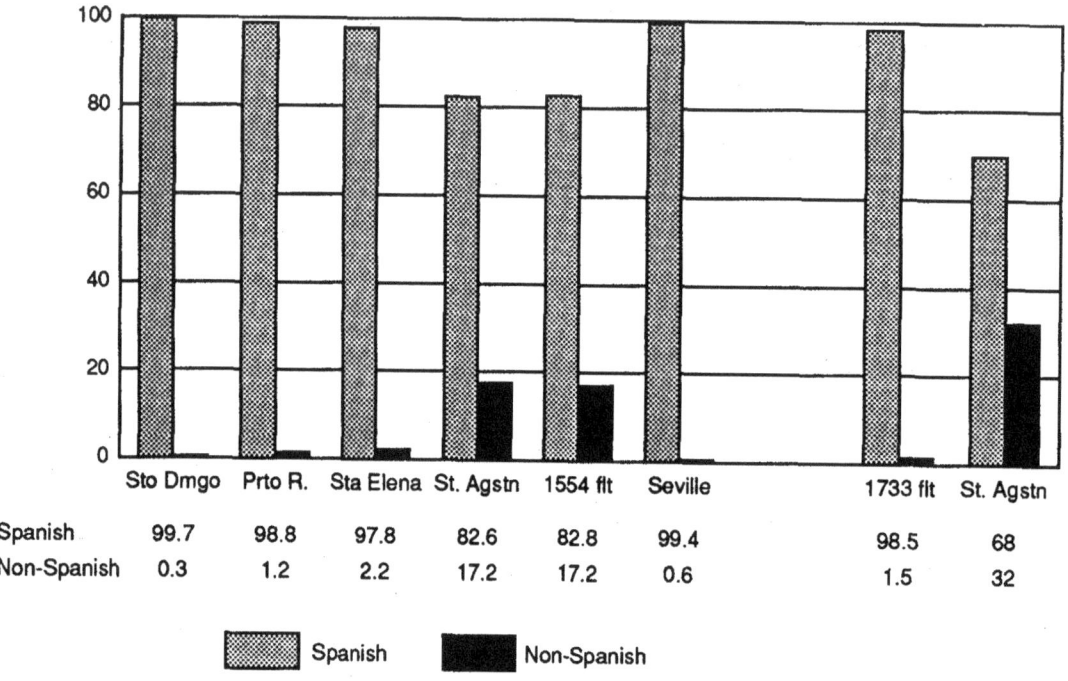

	Sto Dmgo	Prto R.	Sta Elena	St. Agstn	1554 flt	Seville		1733 flt	St. Agstn
Spanish	99.7	98.8	97.8	82.6	82.8	99.4		98.5	68
Non-Spanish	0.3	1.2	2.2	17.2	17.2	0.6		1.5	32

Spanish   Non-Spanish

FIGURE 2. Sixteenth- and 18th-century Spanish and non-Spanish tablewares by frequency.

associated with the site and, more importantly, against the milieu of life in Spain and its colonial expression in the early modern era to understand fully the ramifications of their presence on an archaeological site.

ACKNOWLEDGMENTS

I would like to thank Paul Farnsworth and Jack Williams for creating this forum at the 1989 annual meeting of SHA in Baltimore. Their vision has helped create a dialogue between east and west coast researchers that will transcend the Quincentenary. This paper has immeasurably benefited from the comments and reviews of these individuals and fellow session participants Julia Costello, Bonnie McEwan, and Emlen Myers. Thank you. Earlier drafts of this paper were read and commented on by Michigan State University colleagues Mark Esarey, Margaret Graham, and Ken Lewis whose aid is gratefully acknowledged. Finally, I wish to thank the University of Michigan Museum of Anthropology for their support during the final revisions of this report. I accept sole responsibility for the ideas expressed herein.

REFERENCES

ARNOLD, J. BARTO III, AND ROBERT WEDDLE
1978   *The Nautical Archaeology of Padre Island.* Academic Press, New York.

BARRETT, RICHARD A.
1984   *Culture and Conduct.* Wadsworth, New York.

BRAUDEL, FERNAND
1973   *Capitalism and Material Life, 1400–1800.* Harper and Row, New York.

CERVANTES, GONZALO LÓPEZ
1977   Porcelana Oriental en la Nueva España. *Anales de Antropología e Historia,* Época 8a, 1. Instituto Nacional de Antropología e Historia, México.

COUNCIL, ROBERT BRUCE
1975   Archaeology of the Convento de San Francisco. Unpublished M.A. thesis, Department of Anthropology, University of Florida, Gainesville.

CROFT, PAULINE
1983   English Mariners Trading to Spain and Portugal, 1558–1625. *The Mariner's Mirror—The Journal of the Society for Nautical Research* 69(3):251–266.

CROSBY, ALFRED W.
  1972 *The Columbian Exchange, Biological and Cultural Consequences of 1492*. Greenwood Press, Westport, Connecticut.
  1986 *Ecological Imperialism, the Biological Expansion of Europe 900–1900*. Cambridge University Press, Cambridge, England.

CURTIN, PHILIP D.
  1984 *Cross-Cultural Trade in World History*. Cambridge University Press, Cambridge, England.

DAVIS, RALPH
  1973 *The Rise of the Atlantic Economies*. Weidenfeld and Nicolson, London.

DEAGAN, KATHLEEN
  1980 Spanish St. Augustine: America's First "Melting Pot." *Archaeology* 33(5):22–30.
  1983 *Spanish St. Augustine*. Academic Press, New York.
  1985 The Archaeology of 16th Century St. Augustine. *The Florida Anthropologist* 28(1-2), part 1:6–33.
  1987 *Artifacts of the Spanish Colonies of Florida and the Caribbean, 1500–1800*. Smithsonian Institution Press, Washington, D.C.

ELLIOTT, J.H.
  1963 *Imperial Spain, 1469–1716*. New American Library, New York.

EWEN, CHARLES R.
  1987 From Spaniard to Creole: The Archaeology of Hispanic American Cultural Formation at Puerto Real, Haiti. Unpublished Ph.D. dissertation, Department of Anthropology, University of Florida, Gainesville.

FAIRBANKS, CHARLES H.
  1973 The Cultural Significance of Spanish Ceramics. In *Ceramics in America*, edited by Ian M.G. Quimby, pp. 141–174. The University Press of Virginia, Charlottesville.

FOSTER, GEORGE M.
  1960 Culture and Conquest: America's Spanish Heritage. *Viking Fund Publications in Anthropology* 27. Wenner-Gren Foundation for Anthropological Research, New York.

GERHARD, DIETRICH
  1981 *Old Europe: A Study of Continuity 1000–1800*. Academic Press, New York.

GIBSON, CHARLES
  1968 *The Spanish Tradition in America*. Harper and Row, New York.

GOGGIN, JOHN M.
  1968 Spanish Majolica in the New World. *Yale University Publications in Anthropology* No. 72. New Haven, Connecticut.

HAMILTON, EARL J.
  1934 *American Treasure and the Price Revolution in Spain, 1503–1660*. Harvard University Press, Cambridge, Massachusetts.

HARING, CLARENCE HENRY
  1918 *Trade and Navigation Between Spain and the Indies in the Time of the Habsburgs*. Harvard University Press, Cambridge, Massachusetts.
  1947 *The Spanish Empire in America*. Harcourt, Brace, Jovanovich, New York.

HARMAN, JOYCE ELIZABETH
  1969 *Trade and Privateering in Spanish Florida, 1732–1763*. St. Augustine Historical Society, St. Augustine, Florida.

HURST, J.G.
  1977 Spanish Pottery Imported in Medieval Britain. *Medieval Archaeology* 21:68–109.

JORDAN, WILLIAM B.
  1985 *Spanish Still-Life in the Golden Age 1600–1650*. Kimball Art Museum, Fort Worth, Texas.

LISTER, FLORENCE C., AND ROBERT H. LISTER
  1982 Sixteenth Century Majolica Pottery in the Valley of Mexico. *Anthropological Papers of the University of Arizona* No. 3. University of Arizona Press, Tucson.

LOCKHART, JAMES, AND STUART B. SCHWARTZ
  1983 *Early Latin America, a History of Colonial Spanish America and Brazil*. Cambridge University Press, Cambridge, England.

LYNCH, JOHN
  1984 *Spain Under the Habsburgs*. Vol. 1, *Empire and Absolutism, 1516–1598*. New York University Press, New York.

LYON, EUGENE
  1977 St. Augustine 1580: The Living Community. *El Escribano* 14:20–33. St. Augustine Historical Society, St. Augustine, Florida.
  1984 Santa Elena: A Brief History of the Colony, 1566–1587. *Research Manuscript Series* No. 193. South Carolina Institute of Archeology and Anthropology, University of South Carolina, Columbia.

MANUCY, ALBERT
  1985 The Physical Setting of Sixteenth Century St. Augustine. *The Florida Anthropologist* 38(1-2):34–53.

MCALISTER, LYLE N.
  1984 *Spain and Portugal in the New World, 1492–1700*. University of Minnesota Press, Minneapolis.

MCEWAN, BONNIE G.
  1983 Spanish Colonial Adaptation on Hispaniola: The Archaeology of Area 35 Puerto Real, Haiti. Unpublished M.A. thesis, Department of Anthropology, University of Florida, Gainesville.
  1986 The Historical Archaeology of Seville. Paper pre-

sented at the Sixteenth Century Studies Conference, Concordia Seminary and Center for Reformation Research, St. Louis, Missouri.

1988 An Archaeological Perspective of Sixteenth Century Spanish Life in the Old World and the Americas. Unpublished Ph.D. dissertation, Department of Anthropology, University of Florida, Gainesville.

OLDS, DORRIS L.
1976 *Texas Legacy from the Gulf; A Report on 16th Century Shipwreck Materials Recovered from the Texas Tidelands.* Publication No. 2. Texas Antiquities Committee, Austin.

REITZ, ELIZABETH J., AND C. MARGARET SCARRY
1985 Reconstructing Historic Subsistence with an Example from Sixteenth-Century Spanish Florida. *Special Publication Series* No. 3. Society for Historical Archaeology, California, Pennsylvania.

SKOWRONEK, RUSSELL K.
1984 *Trade Patterns of 18th Century Frontier New Spain, the 1733* flota *and St. Augustine.* Volumes in Historical Archaeology, edited by Stanley South. Conference on Historic Sites Archaeology, South Carolina Institute of Archeology and Anthropology, University of South Carolina, Columbia.
1987 Ceramics and Commerce: The 1554 *flota* Revisited. *Historical Archaeology* 21(2):101–111.
1989 A New Europe in the New World: Hierarcy, Continuity and Change in the Spanish Sixteenth-Century Colonization of Hispaniola and Florida. Unpublished Ph.D. dissertation, Department of Anthropology, Michigan State University, East Lansing, Michigan.

SMITH, HALE G.
1949 Two Archaeological Sites in Brevard County, Florida. *Florida Anthropological Society Publication* No. 1. Gainesville.

SOUTH, STANLEY
1979 The Search for Santa Elena on Parris Island, South Carolina. *Research Manuscript Series* 150. South Carolina Institute of Archeology and Anthropology, University of South Carolina, Columbia.
1980 The Discovery of Santa Elena. *Research Manuscript Series* 165. Institute of Archeology and Anthropology, University of South Carolina, Columbia.
1982 Exploring Santa Elena 1981. *Research Manuscript Series* 184. South Carolina Institute of Archeology and Anthropology, University of South Carolina, Columbia.
1983 Revealing Santa Elena 1982. *Research Manuscript Series* 188. South Carolina Institute of Archeology and Anthropology, University of South Carolina, Columbia.

1984 Testing Archaeological Sampling Methods at Fort San Felipe 1983. *Research Manuscript Series* 190. South Carolina Institute of Archeology and Anthropology, University of South Carolina, Columbia.
1985 Excavation of the Casa Fuerte and Wells at Fort San Felipe 1984. *Research Manuscript Series* 196. South Carolina Institute of Archeology and Anthropology, University of South Carolina, Columbia.

SOUTH, STANLEY, RUSSELL K. SKOWRONEK, AND R. E. JOHNSON
1988 Spanish Artifacts from Santa Elena. *Anthropological Studies* 7. Occasional Papers of the South Carolina Institute of Archeology and Anthropology, University of South Carolina, Columbia.

TANGUY, JEAN
1956 *Le Commerce du Port de Nantes au milieu du XVIe siècle.* École Pratique des Hautes-Études, Paris.

TANNENBAUM, EDWARD R.
1965 *European Civilization Since the Middle Ages.* John Wiley and Sons, New York.

TUCK, JAMES A.
1985 Excavations at Red Bay, Labrador, 1977–1984. In Proceedings of the 16th Conference on Underwater Archaeology, edited by Paul F. Johnston. *Special Publication Series* No. 4: 102–104. Society for Historical Archaeology, California, Pennsylvania.

WALLERSTEIN, IMMANUEL
1974 *The Modern World-System.* Vol. 1, *Capitalist Agriculture and the Origins of the European World-Economy in the Sixteenth Century.* Academic Press, New York.

WILCOXEN, CHARLOTTE
1987 *Dutch Trade and Ceramics in America in the Seventeenth Century.* Albany Institute of History and Art, Albany, New York.

WILLIS, RAYMOND F.
1976 The Archaeology of 16th Century Nueva Cádiz. Unpublished M.A. thesis, Department of Anthropology, University of Florida, Gainesville.
1984 Empire and Architecture at 16th-Century Puerto Real, Hispaniola: An Archaeological Perspective. Unpublished Ph.D. dissertation, Department of Anthropology, University of Florida, Gainesville.

WOLF, ERIC R.
1982 *Europe and the People Without History.* University of California Press, Berkeley.

RUSSELL K. SKOWRONEK
DEPARTMENT OF ANTHROPOLOGY AND SOCIOLOGY
SANTA CLARA UNIVERSITY
SANTA CLARA, CALIFORNIA 95053

Kathleen Deagan

Eliciting Contraband through Archaeology: Illicit Trade in Eighteenth-Century St. Augustine

ABSTRACT

The study of contraband (illicit trade) should offer a uniquely appropriate focus for the multi-evidentiary strengths of historical archaeology, in that it demands the articulation of largely undocumented economic activity (reflected materially in archaeological remains) with legal mandates and formal regulations about commerce. Problematic issues in realizing this are presented by the recognition of contraband goods and activities in the archaeological record and by the difficulties in articulating archaeologically derived periodicity with text-based periodicity of contraband in a given community. With those concerns in mind, the analysis of excavated data from six 18th-century households of St. Augustine is described here with extensive historical documentation of contraband activity in Spanish Florida and the Spanish Americas in general to explore the notion that historical archaeological integration of data about contraband can reveal useful information not knowable from either source alone. Results suggest that at a community-wide scale of analysis, the archaeological data essentially reify and add detail to the already existing documentary accounts of contraband trade. A household scale of analysis and comparison reveals how people with specific economic, occupational, religious, ethnic, and social identities engaged in contraband as a strategy in ways that were not previously known. This helps define the contours of economic possibility and creates a more nuanced understanding of the structure, opportunity, and dynamics of economic choice and agency within a community.

Introduction

Smugglers and pirates have fascinated people for centuries, and stories about them have inspired countless works—ranging from important to awful—in history, literature, art, folklore, music and film. Smuggling and piracy as forms of illicit commerce are concerned with the acquisition and exchange of goods (contraband) through means deemed illegal, such as tax evasion, breaking of economic sanctions, or theft. Contraband, as used here, can refer either to the activities of illicit economic exchange or to the exchanged goods themselves.

Archaeologists have come to the systematic study of contraband relatively recently, working largely from the assertion that an interdisciplinary and multievidentiary approach to the past is an ideal medium by which to reveal the presence of illegal (and presumably undocumented) behavior (Lyon and Purdy 1982; Deagan 1991; Schmidt and Mrozowski 1993; Skowronek and Ewen 2005). Indeed, the question of contraband explicitly juxtaposes well-documented legal economic mandates at a governmental-administrative scale with illicit efforts to circumvent those mandates at the local community scale. As such, its study requires the articulation of textual and material evidence, covert and overt behavior, asserted and lived experience, material and textual representations, and intentional and nonintentional evidence. When Judy Bense invited the author to participate in a session on contraband at The Society for Historical Archaeology annual meeting in 2005, the prospect of putting to the test the notion that the archaeological record could elicit an understanding of illicit trade in a useful and original way was intriguing—that is, could it say something that documentary research alone could not have revealed less destructively or less expensively?

Consideration of contraband in this article is based on information generated by historians and archaeologists working in the Spanish colonial arena and requires a brief methodological caveat. The document-based information about smuggling and contraband is specific, direct, and intentional. It is also generated mostly at a regional or community-wide scale. The text-based information has chronological precision, since it comes from dated legal mandates, political events, and court cases. In other words, this dataset was generated specifically about contraband and its circumstances at specific points in time.

The archaeological data drawn upon here differs as a dataset in almost every way. It is site- rather than community-specific and is based on thousands of observations about excavated deposits and artifacts that have relative and only approximate dates. These deposits and artifacts were not generated directly because of contraband and are not specifically about contraband. They resulted from a complex and diverse set of social behaviors that combined to create archaeological deposits in ways not yet fully understood. In order to elicit information about a specific kind of behavior (such as contraband), researchers have to organize, order, and compress their individual archaeologically derived observations in ways and categories that could reflect the specific question under consideration—in this case, illicit economic behavior.

Such compression and organization necessarily involves quantification and statistical analysis of archaeological observations. It generally results in an approximate, greatly simplified, and probably biased reflection of behavior. This is unlikely to change until understanding of site formation, chronological assignment, and material culture has advanced. While being mindful of these and other more specific methodological shortcomings considered below, this quantification-based approach in the study of contraband is used as one that not only permits articulation of archaeological observations with text-based observations but also places archaeological data (rather than text-based data) at the center of investigations.

This study and many of its methodological concerns are primarily relevant to terrestrial sites. Marine archaeologists have more often been able to elicit smuggling activities successfully, owing to the special circumstances of shipwreck sites, including their ability to confront a single, closely regulated and closed community whose transformation to the archaeological record dates to a moment in time (Lyon and Purdy 1982; Skowronek 1992; Schmidt and Mrozowski 1993).

The Spanish Main

Spain's American colonies have provided a rich focus for those interested in smuggling and piracy. While popular attention has emphasized the treasure fleets of the Spanish Main and those who preyed spectacularly upon them, historical work has shown that Spain's colonial economic policies also rendered illicit commerce a normal part of people's daily life and cultural practice in the Americas.

Principles of mercantilism governed Spain's imperial economic system. Economic strength and self-sufficiency were sought by strictly controlling colonial production and exchange in order to encourage the exportation of raw materials from the colonies to Spain and of manufactured goods from Spain to the colonies. The colonies were not to develop either industries or external exchange networks, and commerce was strictly regulated by a monopoly that restricted trade with the colonies to Spain itself. All goods had to be shipped from Spain, by Spanish-licensed merchants, in Spanish-licensed ships (for comprehensive discussions of Spain's colonial economic policies and problems, see Cohen 2003; also Haring 1966; Lang 1975; Walker 1979; Macleod 1984).

Perhaps the most notable aspect of this system was its failure. Spain was consistently unable to provide the manufactured goods needed by American colonists, so residents of Spanish America turned to illicit trade with foreigners to survive. It has become axiomatic that virtually none of the Spanish colonies in America could adequately subsist by relying on legal supply systems. Historians have shown that illicit trade was an essential part of colonial economic life. They have drawn rich profiles of the timing, contents, flow, and organization of contraband for many communities in Spanish America, suggesting that people developed many kinds of local solutions to coping with the conundrum of an essential but illegal economic mechanism. Historians have also demonstrated that contraband and smuggling can provide a valuable perspective from which to understand agency, resistance, and creative social contracts among inhabitants of colonial America (Cohen 2003).

St. Augustine and Illicit Trade

St. Augustine, Florida, provides an ideal case study through which to understand archaeology's potential role in eliciting useful information about illicit economic activity. St. Augustine is very well documented historically and has a very large, diverse, and temporally controlled body of archaeological data. Established in 1565 to challenge French Huguenot presence in Florida and surviving to guard the route of the homebound Spanish fleets, the settlement remained a subsidized presidio (a fortified military town supported by a government subsidy) until 1763.

On the very fringes of empire, and with no significant natural resources for exploitation or trade, St. Augustine was among the most economically disadvantaged colonies in Spanish America. There was almost no direct trade between Florida and Spain, and few ships other than those of the garrison itself ever called at St. Augustine. As a presidio, Florida was supported by a government subsidy supplied by Crown-mandated fees in Mexico City until 1707, in Puebla from 1707 until 1740, and in Cuba after 1740 (Bushnell 1994; Halbirt 2004; also TePaske 1958; Harman 1969).

For the citizens of St. Augustine, turning to whatever economic opportunities presented themselves—regardless of legality—was only common survival sense. Those opportunities were considerably enhanced after 1670, when the English (enemies of Spain) established Charlestown and provided a potential, if illegal, source of European goods for St. Augustine (for extended discussions of this and other events and ensuing Anglo-Spanish interaction, see Waterbury 1999; also TePaske 1964; Bolton and Ross 1968; Wright 1970; Oatis 2004; Runyon 2005).

The practice of illegal trade between St. Augustine's residents and the English after the 1670 establishment of South Carolina is well documented (TePaske 1958; Gillaspie 1961; Harman 1969). Archaeological evidence has already shown that foreign goods (presumably contraband) were, in fact, used in St. Augustine's households during the period when foreign trade was prohibited by law (Skowronek 1982, 1992; Deagan 1983:236; Halbirt 2004). In a recent analysis of non-Spanish wares (especially English) in household assemblages between 1650 and 1760, Carl Halbirt (2004) demonstrated that there was a steady increase in the use of foreign goods in St. Augustine throughout the 18th century. He was able to correlate this trend with documented increases in exchange (including smuggling) with the English colonies.

Given the clear documentary and archaeological evidence for illicit trade in 18th-century St. Augustine (and probably in most other Spanish colonial communities), the question confronting this project was whether there is anything more that the archaeological record can say about contraband in St. Augustine. This question has implications beyond the Spanish colonial arena, in that it addresses one of the central and longest standing dilemmas of historical archaeology—that of avoiding the role of reifying or simply adding detail to what has already been established through documentary sources. Historical archaeologists can confirm through material analysis, for example, that contraband took place. They can also potentially add interesting detail to documentary accounts by identifying objects that may have been smuggled. Neither of these tasks necessarily provides original insight into the operation or consequences of contraband trade. Nor do these tasks necessarily help historical archaeologists better understand the social fabric and cultural dynamics in communities that engaged in contraband. The challenge is to identify those questions related to illicit trade that can be addressed only through the articulation of multiple categories of material and textual evidence.

Recognizing Contraband

In trying to frame archaeological questions about contraband in St. Augustine, it quickly became apparent that two very basic methodological issues have been generally treated as unproblematic assumptions. One is the question of *recognition*—how can historical archaeologists recognize contraband when encountered? The other is the question of *periodicity*—how can historical archaeologists organize the archaeological record on a temporal scale that is at least roughly equivalent to the temporal scale and periodicity of contraband activity?

One of the great difficulties in studying contraband and smuggling in the Spanish Americas is the identification of smuggled material goods. Contraband goods, according to the Spanish Crown, consisted of anything traded with merchants or ships not authorized by the *Casa de Contratación* in Seville or Cádiz (after 1717). Although Spain prohibited trade between its American colonies and English, Dutch, and French merchant ships, it did not prohibit the purchase of goods manufactured in those countries as long as they arrived on Spanish-licensed ships. In other words, it is generally not the items themselves that indicate smuggling or contraband but how, through whom, and when they got into the community (and ultimately into the archaeological record). English or French items found in the archaeological sites of St. Augustine cannot necessarily be identified as illicit materials unless researchers can demonstrate that these items entered the colony by illegal means. It is critical to consider how goods got to St. Augustine, what was legal, and when.

Legal Sources of Imported Goods in St. Augustine

The Situado

The annual *situado* (a government subsidy of foods and money) was the primary legal source of imported goods in St. Augustine. A single buyer for the colony went each year to collect the subsidy (money, food, and whatever goods were available in Mexico or Cuba) and bring it back to Florida. Once there, the members of the garrison were paid in food rations, supplies, and, if available, cash (for detailed discussions of the organization and problems of Florida's *situado*, see Bushnell 1982:63–90, 1994:43–48; also TePaske 1958, 1964:77–79; Gillaspie 1961). Private merchants were unable to gain a foothold in St. Augustine until the mid-18th century when population and defense-related construction activities dramatically increased in response to military threats from the English colonies. Shop owners during that period acquired commercial goods privately in Mexico, Cuba, or other sources.

Imported goods found in Mexico or Cuba and available for purchase by a either a merchant or a government factor arrived there principally through legal trade with the properly licensed Spanish ships arriving from Seville or Cádiz. From the mid-16th century onward, the majority of manufactured goods arriving on these ships was of non-Spanish origin. Legal Spanish trade with America (particularly during the 18th century) was supplied and controlled by Dutch, English, French, Portuguese, and German merchants resident in Andalusia. This has been documented in detail by numerous historical studies (Chaunu and Chaunu 1957; Haring 1966:286; Vicens Vives 1969:402,434–436; Lang 1975:50–52; Pulido Bueno 1993). For example, each year millions of glass bottles for filling and reshipment to various places were shipped from Bristol, England, and Bayonne, France, to Santander in Spain, including America (Frothingham 1941:125).

Analysis of shipping records for Seville reveals that virtually all classes of nonceramic items found typically on colonial sites (glassware, buttons, pins, scissors, common jewelry, religious items, kitchen implements, tools) were imported to Seville or Cádiz from France, England, Germany, and Holland and re-exported to America throughout the colonial era (Torre Revello 1943; García-Baquero González 1976; Walker 1979: 234–237; Pulido Bueno 1993; for examples of such items on colonial sites, see Deagan 2002). It has been estimated by Spanish economic historians that by 1700 only about 5% of the goods shipped from Cádiz were of Spanish origin, with Spanish contributions consisting principally of wine, oil, some cloth, wax, and iron (Usher 1932:203–205; Walker 1979:15–16).

Foreign Slave Trade Asiento Ships

Another avenue for the entry of legal foreign goods into the Spanish American colonies (and ultimately into Florida) was foreign trade ships permitted by Spain to call annually in Mexico as part of the slave trade *asiento* (contract) to provide slaves to the Spanish colonies. Portugal held the *asiento* until 1640; from 1640 to 1713, the French had the privilege; and from 1713 until 1739, it was held by the English (Haring 1966: 268–269). This was not insignificant for commerce, particularly after 1713, when the English acquired the *asiento*. Two English "trade ships," each permitted 650 tons of merchandise, came yearly to the Indies, whether or not the Spanish trade fleets were dispatched. During several years, the Spanish merchant fleets did not sail at all to America, leaving the English *asiento* ships as the only legal source of new merchandise. In other years, the tonnage of *asiento* ships was only slightly less than that of the entire Spanish merchant fleet (Walker 1979:86–88).

Privateering

Another important way that foreign goods legally entered St. Augustine and many other Spanish settlements in the Americas was through the sale of cargos captured through Spanish

172

privateering, especially after ca.1730. Privateers (privately owned ships licensed by the crown to prey upon and capture enemy vessels) sold the contents of their captured ships as prizes. In 1741, for example, there were 13 English prizes reported in the St. Augustine harbor, with their contents to be sold in the town (Harman 1969:36).

Special Dispensation

Although Spain's restrictive mercantilist policies were system wide, there appears to have been a certain amount of flexibility under conditions of local emergency. Under such circumstances, legal dispensation to trade with foreigners was sometimes granted as relief, such as in the case of Spanish Pensacola and the French at Mobile (Johnson 2003). The governor of St. Augustine requested and was granted permission by the Crown of Spain to trade with English and Dutch merchants in New York in 1683 and 1684 (Bushnell 1982:89). Amy Bushnell (2005, pers. comm.) underscoring some of the taphonomic and sampling problems faced by documentary historians, notes that this event "... should not be considered exceptional. What is unusual is the quantity of paperwork that has survived from the governorship of Márquez Cabrera. If we had that much documentation for every year, we could probably turn up dozens of other cases."

After 1750, the responsibility for provisioning St. Augustine fell to the Royal Havana Company. The company was officially permitted to supply the city directly from English merchants in Charlestown and Savannah, effectively opening St. Augustine to legal English goods (TePaske 1964; Harman 1969).

All these legal measures combined were still not sufficient to meet the needs of the colonies, and, as historians have repeatedly documented, the colonists enthusiastically maintained trade relations with foreigners throughout the colonial era. In St. Augustine the opportunities for this were greatly increased after the establishment of the English settlement of Charlestown in 1670.

Implications for Archaeological Recognition

All of this renders the archaeological investigation of contraband in Spanish Florida problematic.

Given the variety of legal mechanisms by which foreign goods might have entered the colonies, how can researchers distinguish foreign items that arrived illegally from those that arrived legally? The foregoing discussion suggests that this cannot be done at the scale of individual objects or types of objects (except, perhaps, in very rare individual cases). Researchers should be able to suggest illicit origins by careful correlation and articulation of multiple archaeologically connected factors, including

1. artifact origins (where artifacts were produced)
2. artifact periodicity (dates of artifact production and use)
3. trade periodicity (dates during which objects of various national origins should have been available only illegally or, conversely, only legally)
4. archaeological context (when and how artifacts were deposited into the archaeological record)

Methodological Approach

To explore this for St. Augustine, following Halbirt's (2004) initiative, the focus is on tableware ceramics, including in this category vessels used at the table for serving and consuming, as well as the wares and types that occur consistently and principally in tableware forms (Table 1). Because of the very fragmentary nature of most of the ceramic sherds in the sample, the assignment of samples to the tableware category has necessarily been based on ceramic type, organized by sherd count. This is admittedly not the ideal comparative basis, which would, under the best of circumstances, include comparisons by sherd count, sherd weight, and minimum vessel count. This study incorporates data collected and analyzed between 1973 and 1994, a period that witnessed a healthy evolution and increased sophistication in the analytical protocols used by historical archaeologists (including those in St. Augustine). The utility of quantifying sherd weights and vessel counts was recognized and gradually incorporated into ceramic analysis during that time (Rice 1987:290–293). Post-mending sherd count is the only parameter that was applied in a completely consistent manner over

TABLE 1
CERAMICS OCCURRING AS TABLEWARES IN ST. AUGUSTINE HOUSEHOLDS, 1650–1750

	Begin	End
SPANISH-TRADITION ORIGIN		
San Luis Polychrome Majolica	1650	1750
Aranama Polychrome Majolica	1750	1800
Abó Polychrome Majolica	1650	1750
Castillo Polychrome Majolica	1680	1710
Puebla Polychrome Majolica	1650	1725
Puebla Tradition Majolica, White	1700	1800
Puebla Blue on White Majolica	1700	1750
Huejotzingo Blue on White Majolica	1700	1850
Unidentified Puebla Majolica	1650	1800
Aucilla Polychrome Majolica	1650	1700
Mount Royal Polychrome Majolica	1650	1700
San Agustín Blue on White Majolica	1700	1730
El Morro Ware	1550	1750
Rey Ware	1725	1825
Black Lead-Glazed Earthenware	1700	1770
Guadalajara Polychrome	1650	1800
Mexican Red Painted Ware	1550	1750
FRENCH ORIGIN		
Faience, St. Cloud Polychrome	1675	1766
Faience, Provence Blue on White	1725	1765
Faience, Brown Rouen	1740	1790
Faience, Plain	1675	1775
Faience, Brittany Blue on White	1750	1770
Faience, Normandy Blue on White	1690	1775
Faience, Seine Polychrome	1690	1765

	Begin	End
ENGLISH/NORTHERN EUROPEAN ORIGIN		
English Soft Paste Porcelain	1745	1800
Delftware, Blue and White*	1650	1790
Delftware, Plain*	1640	1800
Delftware, Polychrome*	1570	1790
Delftware, Manganese Sponged	1708	1790
Astbury Ware	1725	1750
Agateware	1740	1775
Whieldon Ware	1740	1770
Staffordshire Slipware	1675	1770
Jackfield Ware	1740	1790
Nottingham Stoneware	1700	1810
White Salt-glazed Stoneware, plain	1720	1790
White Salt-glazed Stoneware, molded	1740	1770
Scratch-Blue White Salt-Glazed Stoneware	1735	1775
Rhenish-type Grey Stoneware Mugs**	1700	1775
Elers-Type Ware	1690	1790
ASIAN ORIGIN		
Porcelain, Blue and White Underglaze Ch'ing	1644	1912
Porcelain, "Chinese Imari"	1700	1780
Porcelain, White	1640	1750
Porcelain, Monochrome Brown	1700	1780

* General range: TPQ determined by specific motifs when present

** Stamped or incised

Note: Dates for Spanish-tradition and Asian wares follow the sources provided by FLMNH (2004); dates for French faience follow Waselkov and Walthall (2002); dates for English-tradition wares follow Miller et al. (2000) and Noël Hume (2001).

the 20-year period during which the sites in this sample were analyzed and is used here as the basis for comparative quantification.

Post-mending sherd counts represent, in effect, maximum vessel counts and considerably overestimate the number of vessels. Because this sample (like those from many urban sites) consists overwhelmingly of small body sherds, a minimum vessel analysis tends to considerably underestimate ceramic use. It is of concern that in assemblages with standardized forms and decorative motifs, minimum vessel count using body sherds is likely to compound the underestimation problem. Methods for assessing minimum vessel count over the years (and across the profession) have been inconsistent and somewhat subjective. As in the case of many long-term archaeological programs, a reliable assessment of minimum vessel count will require reanalysis of entire assemblages for this purpose by a single researcher. While this is a strong argument for professional standardization of minimum vessel-form analysis among contemporary archaeologists, it is not an argument for ignoring older existing collections in trying to answer new questions.

Another explanatory caveat that should be applied to this sample has to do with the assignment of sherds to the "tableware" category based on ceramic type. It is possible that a small proportion of the small body sherds may represent vessels used for food storage, food preparation, or domestic furnishing. Nevertheless, this broadly inclusive characterization of tableware ceramics is useful for the questions asked in this study, which focus not on function but rather on access to and acquisition of legal versus illegal imported goods. Tableware ceramics are considered the most appropriate subset of imported goods for this inquiry because

1. all such tableware ceramic types in St. Augustine were imported;
2. tablewares are one of the few artifact categories recovered in substantial numbers for which the country of origin and the dates of manufacture or use can be determined;
3. tablewares were accessible to and used by all people in the colony (although the kinds of tablewares may have varied in cost and quality, the fact of tableware

use does not), presenting a direct representation of both community-wide and household-specific cultural practice and cultural choice.

For purposes of temporal and intersite comparisons related to the question of illicit trade, individual ceramic types were grouped into the following categories (Table 1):

1. Spanish-tradition origin (which includes both Spanish and Mexican-produced tablewares)
2. English/Northern European tradition origin (which includes English and possibly Dutch-produced tablewares and one German stoneware type)
3. French faience
4. Asian porcelain

Trade and Periodicity

Although all of the Spanish colonies were subject to the same economic policies and trade restrictions, the actual periodicity of legal versus illicit trade was specific to individual communities. The legal entry of foreign ceramics into St. Augustine, for example, could have occurred through the legal *asiento* trade ships accompanying the slave traders (France 1702–1713; England 1713–1739), through the sale of English privateering prizes (ca. 1735–1743), and through the legal contracts of the Royal Havana Company (1750–1762). In other words, English goods, including ceramics, could have entered St. Augustine legally almost continuously from 1713 until Spain's entry into the French and Indian War in 1762, just one year before the end of the Spanish occupation in 1763. French goods could have entered legally between 1702 and 1713. Conversely, the highest probability of English goods entering the town illegally would have been before about 1715 and possibly between 1739 and 1750. French goods had few legal mechanisms for entry before 1702 or after 1713 (Figure 1).

Samples

Materials used in this study include the excavated remains from 124 undisturbed, closed context features from six domestic sites that

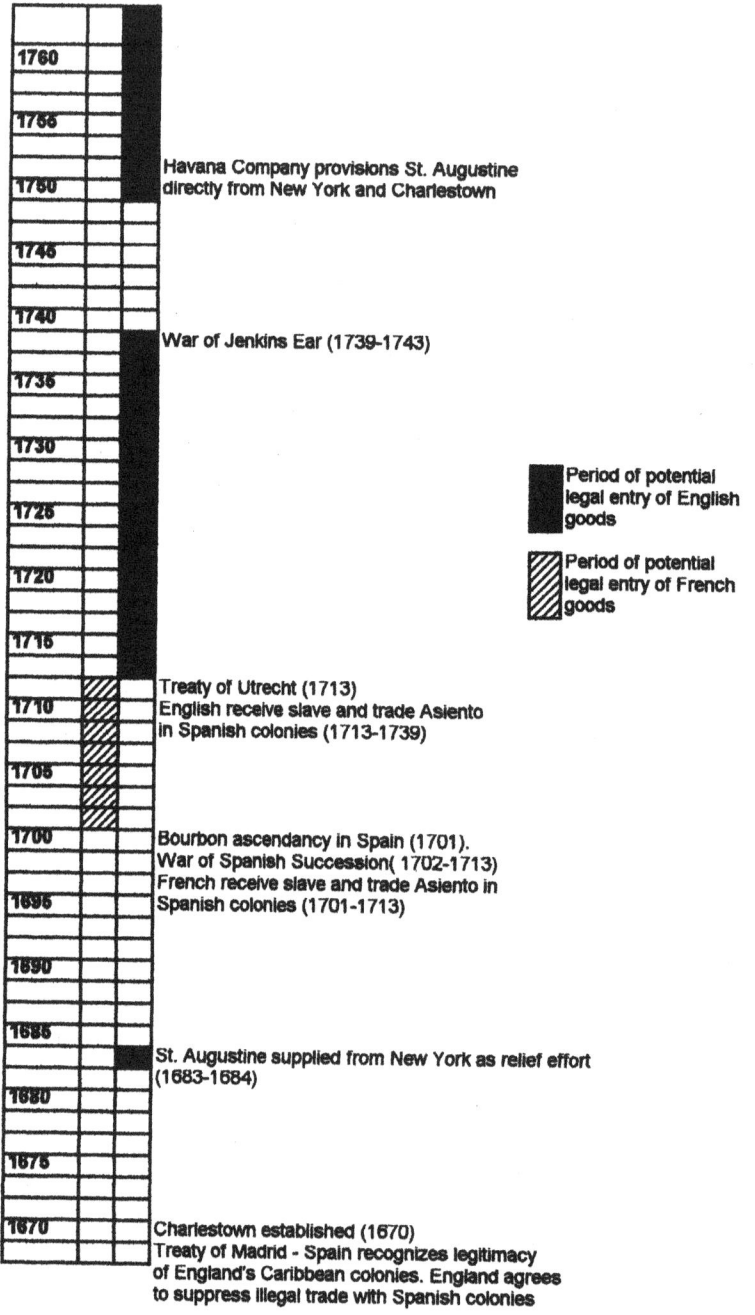

Figure 1. Political events and related time periods for the legal entry of English and French goods into St. Augustine. (Table by author, 2004.)

represent a cross section of St. Augustine's 18th-century households by income, ethnic origin, and occupation. Deposits were all either trash-filled pits or barrel wells, and all were either single-event or very short-term deposits. They were excavated between 1973 and 1994 by the University of Florida field schools and contained 5,051 ceramic tableware artifacts of European or European American origin.

Each feature deposit was assigned a *terminus post quem* (TPQ) based on the latest-dating item in that provenience in combination with stratigraphic associations. In nearly all cases, the TPQ was determined by a ceramic type; in only

Perspectives from *Historical Archaeology*

a few cases did coins or other objects super-cede pottery as the latest-dating item. These dates, based primarily upon what is known about artifact dating, determine the periodicity of the archaeological record and obviously both constrain and bias the ways in which researchers can look at trends through time. TPQ reflects only the date after which a deposit entered the ground (Table 2), and it assumes that ceramics were acquired, used, and deposited shortly after they were first produced. This troubling assumption might be mitigated by calculating a mean ceramic date for each deposit. In this sample many of the deposits lacked a sufficient number of tightly dated ceramic types to make such a determination valid. Dates assigned to the archaeological deposits based on TPQ are probably skewed to slightly earlier than their actual deposit in the ground, something to be mindful of when articulating these data with events dated by documentary sources. In the absence of more refined temporal tools, the TPQ-based chronology does offer a framework (albeit crude in comparison to documentary periodicity) for assessing temporal change.

Deposits incorporated into this study fell into six temporal categories when ordered by their TPQs. Three of the time periods combine deposits with TPQ dates five years apart, to create

temporal intervals and sample sizes that were reasonably even (Table 2).

Community-Scale Trends

Table 3 and Figure 2 show the trend lines for the four production-origin categories of ceramics for the community as a whole between TPQ 1650 and TPQ 1750. Because Asian and French wares each constituted only about 1% of the community assemblage through the entire period of study, the proportions of English-tradition and Spanish-tradition ceramics co-vary (an obvious statistical relationship when there are just two dominant elements in a population). Nevertheless, on a community-wide level, there was a clear general trend for Spanish wares to decline as a part of household ceramic assemblages, and for English tradition wares (as Halbirt suggested) to be incorporated with greater intensity into St. Augustine's households as the 18th century progressed.

Between TPQ 1675 (approximately when Charlestown was established) and TPQ 1700 (approximately when Spain and England went to war over the Spanish succession), there was a dramatic increase in English-tradition ceramics as a proportion of all tablewares. Since there was no legal mechanism during this period for the entry of English goods into Florida, except

TABLE 2

TERMINUS POST QUEM GROUPS FOR ARCHAEOLOGICAL DEPOSITS[a]

TPQ[b]	Determining artifacts
1650	Puebla Polychrome Majolica, San Luis Polychrome Majolica, Abó Polychrome Majolica
1675/1680	St. Cloud Polychrome Faience, Combed Staffordshire Slipware, Castillo Blue on White Majolica, Nottingham Stoneware; Elers-type Red-Bodied Stoneware
1700	Puebla Blue on White Majolica, Huejotzingo Blue on White Majolica, San Agustín Blue on White Majolica, Rhenish-type Grey Stoneware Mugs, Normandy Blue on White Faience, Seine Polychrome Faience
1720/25	Plain White Salt-Glazed Stoneware, Rey Ware, Astbury Ware, Provence Blue on White Faience
1735/40	Molded White Salt-Glazed Stoneware, Whieldon Ware, Brown Rouen Faience; Agate Ware, Jackfield Ware
1745/50	Aranama Polychrome Majolica, English Porcelain, Scratch Blue Salt-Glazed Stoneware

[a]This table does not reflect all dateable ceramic types included in the sample but, rather, those types that occurred as the latest-dating item in a deposit, thereby providing the TPQ date for that deposit.

[b]Dates for Spanish-tradition and Asian wares follow the sources provided by Florida Museum of Natural History (2004); dates for French faience follow Waselkov and Walthall (2002); dates for English-tradition wares follow Miller et al. (2000) and Noël Hume (2001).

TABLE 3
ORIGINS OF EUROPEAN TABLEWARE CERAMICS IN ST. AUGUSTINE, 1650–1750
(Based on imported tableware ceramics from 124 undisturbed deposits in 6 households; see Figure 2)

| | 1650 | | 1675/80 | | 1700 | | 1725 | | 1735/40 | | 1745/50 | | Total |
	No.	%[a]	No.	%[a]	No.	%[a]	No.	%[a]	No.	%[a]	No.	%[a]	No.
Spanish tradition	141	0.92	92	0.92	333	0.77	170	0.80	1,587	0.71	1,363	0.71	3686
English tradition	12	0.08	3	0.03	88	0.20	35	0.16	546	0.24	500	0.26	1184
French faience	0	0.00	3	0.03	3	0.01	2	0.01	73	0.03	24	0.01	105
Asian porcelain	1	0.01	2	0.02	7	0.02	6	0.03	35	0.02	25	0.01	76
Total	154		100		431		213		2,241		1,912		5,051

[a]Percent of all tableware ceramics in time period

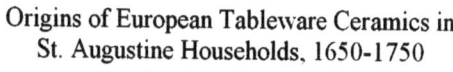

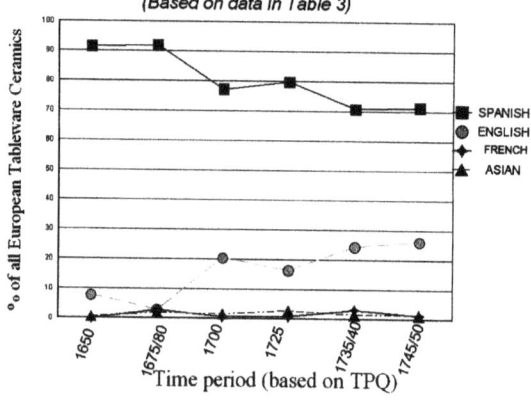

Figure 2. Origins of imported tablewares in St. Augustine households, 1650–1750. (Graph by author, 2004.)

during 1683–1684, the increase in the use of English/Northern European ceramics quite likely reflects a newly established contraband trade network between English merchants in the Carolinas and the citizens of St. Augustine.

This increase in English-tradition wares seems to have stopped shortly after 1700, roughly corresponding to the War of Spanish Succession/Queen Anne's War (1702–1713), in which Spain and France fought against England. Warfare apparently made illicit trade with the enemy not only difficult but also possibly undesirable. The decline in English ceramics continued until about 1725, after which time their numbers increased steadily as a proportion of the tableware ceramics used in the Spanish St. Augustine community.

The treaty of Utrecht in 1713 ended the War of Spanish Succession, and the increased presence of English wares in St. Augustine after TPQ 1725 probably reflects these changed political circumstances. The increase cannot be necessarily attributed to contraband trade, since English goods could also have entered Florida legally after this time, either through the *situado* (via the a*siento* trade) or through the sale of privateers' prizes.

The War of Jenkins' Ear (largely provoked by privateering activity in the Caribbean and Florida colonies) ended the English slave trade *asiento* in 1739. From this period onward, the privateering of English ships and their sale as prizes in St. Augustine reached its zenith, and the proportion of English goods in St. Augustine households continued to rise steadily, presumably until the entry of Spain into war with England in 1762 and the Spanish departure from Florida in 1763.

This exercise reinforces the already established notion that both contraband and legal trade created a steadily greater dependency on or use of foreign goods in the Spanish colonies through the 18th century (Halbirt 2004). It also suggests that the material record of the community as a whole is sensitive to economic fluctuations provoked by political circumstances, such as warfare Although this is gratifying, it is not informative about contraband or economic behavior in Spanish Florida in an original way, since textual evidence had already established both the fact and periodicity of contraband trade at the scale of the community. While a community-scale analysis such as this is demonstrably useful in addressing macroscale economic and political questions, it does not express intracommunity variability at a household scale (at which direct text-based insight is most often lacking).

For instance, did these community-wide temporal trends represent a homogenous economic behavior in St. Augustine with regard to contraband throughout the various social classes, economic levels, and ethnic affiliations reflected in the city? Was the balance of (presumably) legal and (presumably) illegal goods at any given time consistent across all the households in the community? Could anything significant be said about society and economy within colonial St. Augustine? To explore these questions, the consideration of illicit trade was refocused from a community-wide scale to a household scale of analysis.

Household-Focused Insights

Households used in this study include members of the prestigious old criollo families (those of Spanish descent but raised in the Americas), a wealthy government official, low-ranking members of the garrison, a mixed Indian-Hispanic household, and a well-to-do merchant. Income for nearly all of these households is independently documented (Deagan 1983:44; Scardaville and Ganong [1975]). Occupants of specific sites are identified by reference to a property map made in 1764 at the end of the first Spanish occupation (Puente 1764:Fig. 3), and no additional information about potential other, earlier site occupants has yet been located in many cases through

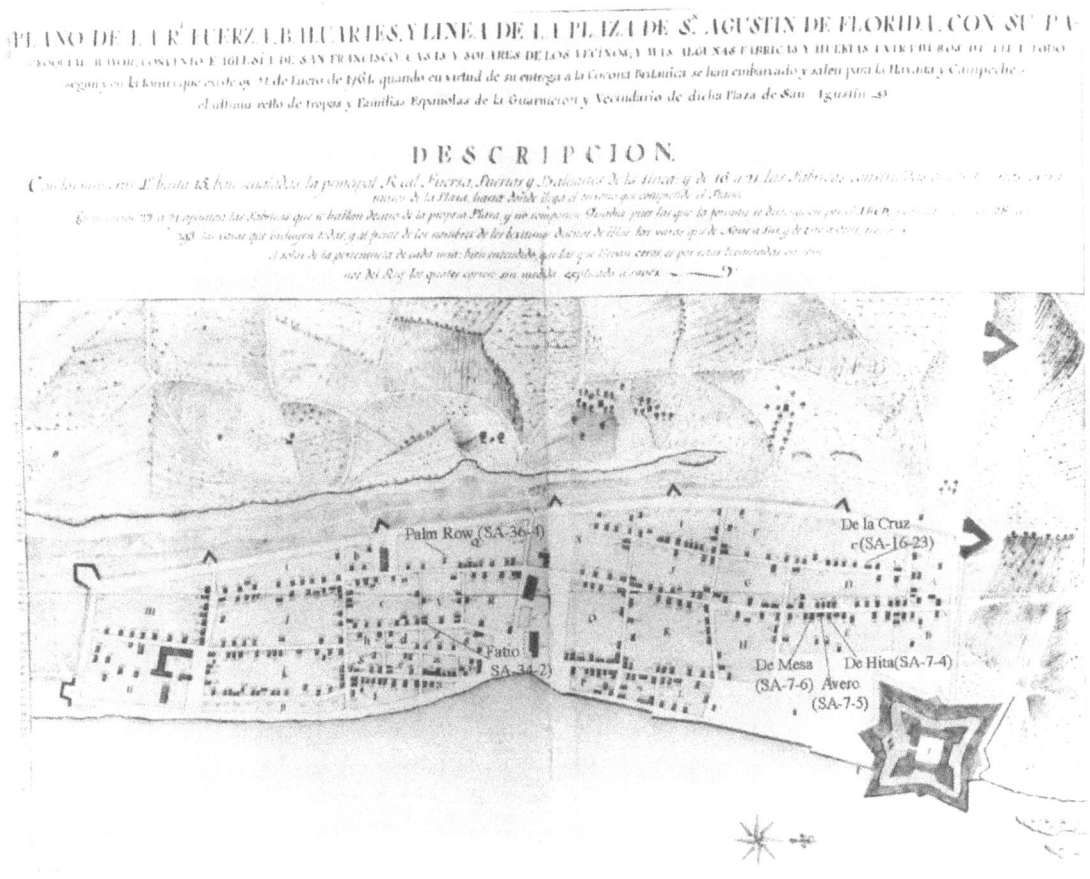

Figure 3. Locations of study household sites on the Puente map (1763). (Courtesy of the P. K. Yonge Library of Florida History, University of Florida, Gainesville.)

documentary research. It is possible that other families occupied some of these sites during the early years of the 18th century.

This possibility is somewhat mitigated among the criollo family households, in that property among this group is well documented to have been held in the family, passed along as dowries for their daughters (Parker 1999). Spanish St. Augustine, like most Spanish towns, is well documented as organizing residential spaces along class and ethnic lines (Deagan 1982; Bond 1995). It is quite likely that if, in fact, some of these sites had earlier household occupants than those documented, those occupants would share economic and class affiliations with later Spanish-period residents.

The Palm Row site (SA-36-4) was occupied during the 18th century by the family of Francisco Ponce de León, who was sergeant major of the Florida garrison. This was one of the elite criollo families of the community, resident in St. Augustine for more than a century. The sergeant major position earned a salary of 960 pesos.

The Avero site (SA-7-5) household was also part of the criollo elite, occupied by the family of Antonia de Avero and her husband Joaquin Blanco (Arnade 1962; Deagan 1976). Blanco was keeper of the Royal Storehouse, which earned an income of 590 pesos (apart from any additional unreported benefits that accrued from this position).

Antonia's sister lived next door at the De Hita site (SA-7-4), and was married to Gerónimo de Hita y Salazar, a cavalryman in the regiment, grandson of a former governor, and a member of the established criollo network (Shepherd 1983). Although Gerónimo never rose above the rank of private, he was commandant of Ft. Mose, which brought an income of 264 pesos

The De Mesa site (SA-7-6) was occupied by the family of Antonio de Mesa, which included six children. De Mesa was a customs harbor guard (*guardia de ribera*) who supplemented his meager income of 180 pesos with fees from incoming ships.

The occupants of the De la Cruz site (SA-16-23) were Mexican garrison soldier Joseph Gallardos, his Indian wife María de la Cruz, and their mestizo children. As a regiment soldier, Gallardos earned between 130 and 170 pesos (depending on his rank). After he died in 1759,

the family income was reduced to 91 pesos, the stipend for widows and orphans (Deagan 1983:44). For comparative purposes, household income is estimated at 150 pesos.

The final household in the sample, that residing at the Fatio site (SA-34-2) is the least well documented for the 18th century. During the last five years of Spanish-period occupation (1758–1763), the site was occupied by the family of Cristóbal de Contreras and Dorotea de Anaya. Contreras was a well-to-do merchant from the Canary Islands and is thought to have had his shop on the site. Neither the date of Contreras's arrival in St. Augustine nor the date of the shop's establishment are known. Contreras himself probably did not live at the site until after 1758 when he married his *criolla* wife, Dorotea. She very likely brought her family's house to the marriage as a dowry in the strong tradition of St. Augustine *criolla* women who married peninsular men (that is, born in Spain) (Arnade 1962; Parker 1999). The archaeological assemblage from this site reflects a criollo family of unknown, but probably well-to-do, station before 1758. After that time, the assemblage presumably reflects what may have been available to private commercial entrepreneurs. Contreras's income is not recorded, although the fact that he was a merchant and slave owner suggests that he probably had a higher-than-average income.

Household Trends

The same methods and data used to construct the community-wide trends in tablewares through time were used to assess the evidence for contraband in individual households. Because only two of the households had 17th-century occupation components, only proveniences of the 18th century were used for comparison among households. Figure 4 and Table 4 show the ceramic trends for each of these households. Those from the criollo sites (Ponce de León, Avero, and De Hita) are very similar throughout the 18th century, despite marked differences in income. The occupants of all these sites were members of old criollo families, and each site was headed by a government official or member of the military garrison. Spanish-tradition ceramics, although declining through the century, consistently made up the majority of tableware ceramics at these

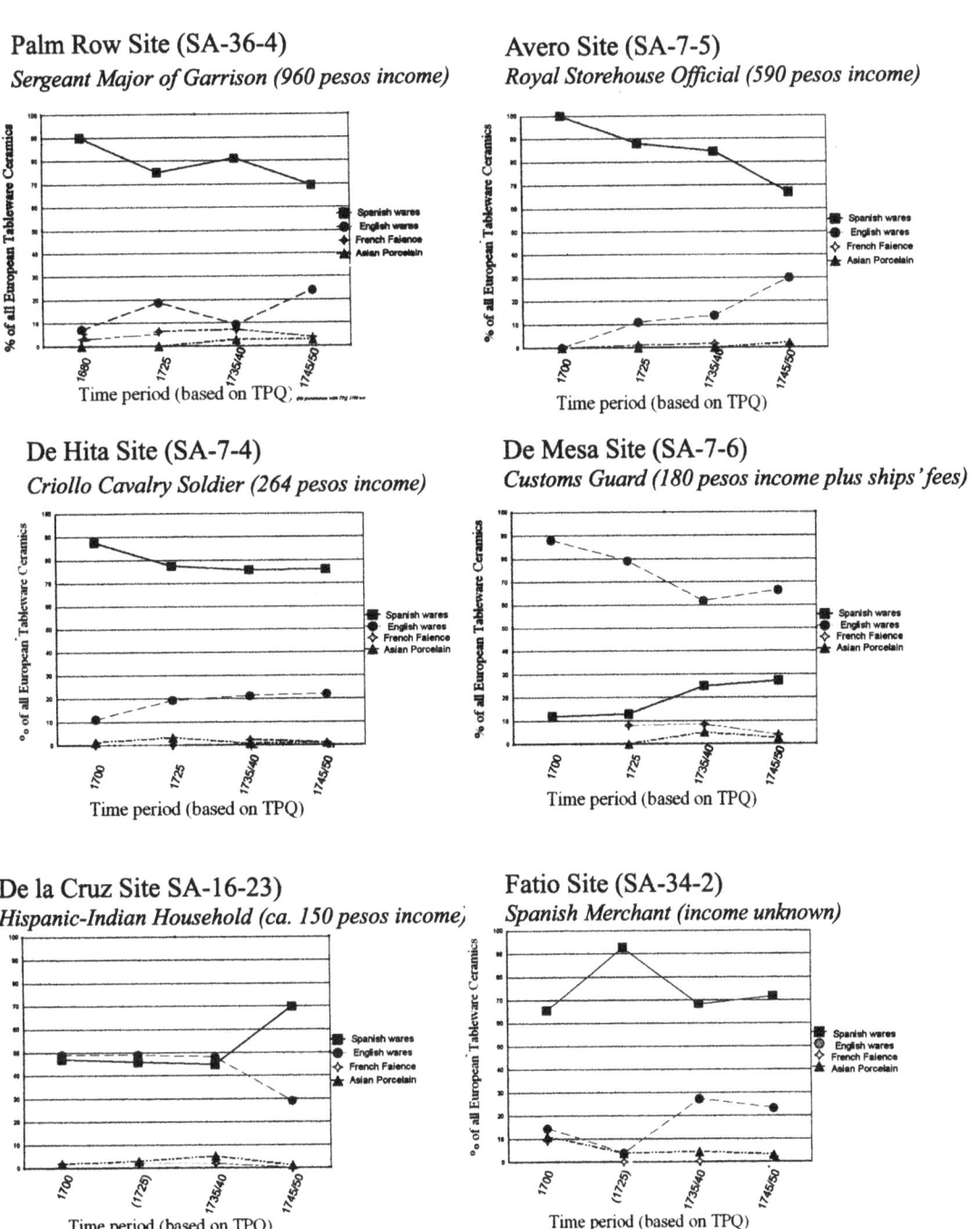

Figure 4. Temporal trends of imported tableware ceramics in St. Augustine households, 1700–1760. (Graph by author, 2004.)

households. Foreign ceramics (predominantly English) were infrequent at the beginning of the century, when it was unlikely that English ceramics were entering the colony legally. By TPQ 1735, the proportion of foreign wares in these households rose to nearly 20% of the ceramic assemblages, corresponding to the peak period of privateering and the legal sale of English prizes (and their cargos) in St. Augustine.

These points of rough convergence in the archaeological and documentary records (that is, consistently low proportions of non-Spanish wares in the household assemblages during periods when non-Spanish wares should have been illegal) may

TABLE 4
IMPORTED EUROPEAN TRADITION TABLEWARES IN 18TH-CENTURY ST. AUGUSTINE HOUSEHOLDS

PALM ROW SITE (SA-36-4) (Sergeant Major of the Garrison, 960 pesos income)

	1680[a]		1725		1735/40		1745/50		TOTAL
	No.	%	No.	%	No.	%	No.	%	No.
Spanish Wares	63	0.9	12	0.75	298	0.81	75	0.69	448
English Wares	5	0.07	3	0.19	34	0.09	26	0.24	68
French Faience	2	0.03	1	0.06	26	0.07	4	0.04	33
Asian Porcelain	0	0	0	0	10	0.03	3	0.03	13
TOTAL	70		16		368		108		562

[a]no proveniences with TPQ 1700 were excavated

AVERO SITE (SA-7-5) (Royal storehouse official, 590 pesos income)

	1700		1725		1735/40		1745/50		TOTAL
	No.	%	No.	%	No.	%	No.	%	No.
Spanish Wares	26	100	80	0.88	207	0.84	67	0.67	380
English Wares	0	0	10	0.11	34	0.14	30	0.30	74
French Faience	0	0	1	0.01	4	0.02	1	0.01	6
Asian Porcelain	0	0	0	0	0	0	2	0.02	2
TOTAL	26		91		245		100		462

DE HITA SITE (SA-7-4) (Criollo cavalry soldier, 240 pesos income)

	1700		1725		1735/40		1745/50		TOTAL
	No.	%	No.	%	No.	%	No.	%	No.
Spanish Wares	274	0.88	48	0.77	621	0.76	1,020	0.76	1,963
English Wares	35	0.11	12	0.19	174	0.21	291	0.22	512
French Faience	0	0	0	0.00	19	0.02	12	0.01	31
Asian Porcelain	4	0.01	2	0.03	6	0.01	11	0.01	23
TOTAL	313		62		820		1,334		2,529

DE MESA SITE (SA-7-6) (Customs guard, 180 pesos income plus ships' fees)

	1700		1725		1735/40		1745/50		TOTAL
	No.	%		%	No.	%	No.	%	No.
Spanish Wares	3	0.12	5	0.13	75	0.25	55	0.27	138
English Wares	22	0.88	31	0.79	185	0.62	134	0.66	372
French Faience	0	0	0	0	25	0.08	8	0.04	33
Asian Porcelain	0	0	3	0.08	15	0.05	5	0.02	23
TOTAL	25		39		300		202		566

DE LA CRUZ SITE (SA-16-23) (Hispanic-Indian family, ca. 150 pesos income)

	1700		1725[a]		1735/40		1745/50		TOTAL
	No.	%		%.	No.	%	No.	%	No.
Spanish Wares	25	0.47		*0.46*	44	0.45	60	0.70	129
English Wares	26	0.49		*0.49*	47	0.48	25	0.29	98
French Faience	1	0.02		*0.02*	2	0.02	0	0	3
Asian Porcelain	1	0.02		*0.03*	5	0.05	1	0.01	7
TOTAL	53				98		86		237

[a]no proveniences with TPQ 1725 were excavated: graph line value extrapolated between 1700 and 1735 percentage values

FATIO SITE (SA-34-2) (Spanish merchant, income unknown)

	1700		1725		1735/40		1745/50		TOTAL
	No.	%	No.	%	No.	%	No.	%	No.
Spanish Wares	36	0.65	25	0.93	254	0.68	71	0.72	386
English Wares	8	0.15	1	0.04	101	0.27	23	0.23	133
French Faience	5	0.09	0	0	1	0.00	2	0.02	8
Asian Porcelain	6	0.11	1	0.04	16	0.04	3	0.03	26
TOTAL	55		27		372		99		553

suggest that the criollo military families did not engage in illicit traffic as a regular and important means of acquiring goods.

This stands in sharp contrast to the household of Antonio de Mesa, the harbor guard with six children. His is the only household in the sample in which non-Spanish wares consistently outnumber Spanish ceramics throughout the century. It is likely that his position as a customs guard afforded ample and enhanced access to goods from both prizes and illicit trade. If so, it was an opportunity of which he took considerable advantage. His household had dramatically high proportions of English and French tableware ceramics through the 18th century, regardless of prevailing regulations about illegal foreign trade. This find is also one of the clearest examples of probable traffic in contraband from St. Augustine's archaeological record.

Low-income occupants of the mestizo De la Cruz site had a notably different ceramic kitchenware assemblage from either the criollo military households or the harbor guard. During the early decades of the 18th century, when English goods were largely illegal, the proportions of English and Spanish pottery were roughly the same. This implies some participation in or access to contraband trade. After TPQ 1735, the proportion of Spanish wares increased quite dramatically, and the English wares decreased equally dramatically. This latter period (post 1735/40) corresponds to the phase of peak legal availability of English goods through sales of privateer prizes. It appears that this family significantly incorporated English ceramics into their household while they were illegal but did not acquire or use nearly as many of the English kitchen wares during the period when they were presumably more available and for sale—whether owing to poverty or preference. Perhaps once goods became legal and entered the commercial marketplace, they were more difficult to obtain for low-income families.

The household assemblage of Spanish Canary Islander Cristóbal Contreras (at the Fatio site) may suggest yet other kinds of engagement with contraband trade. This site sample is somewhat problematic, owing to the presence of both commercial and domestic establishments on the property and the lack of certain identification of the pre-1757 occupants. Archaeological data from the site suggest that the occupants may have engaged in contraband trade—or the acquisition of contraband goods—between the establishment of Charlestown in 1670 and the War of Spanish Succession in 1702. Between those dates, a steady increase in English tablewares and a steady decrease in Spanish tablewares were seen in a period during which there was no legal mechanism for the entry of English goods to the colony. A sharp reversal in this trend occurred between about TPQ 1700 and TPQ 1725, roughly corresponding to the War of Spanish Succession against England.

As was characteristic of the community-wide trend, the very low proportions of English wares during this period suggest that the war inhibited the site's inhabitants from engaging in (or perhaps from wanting to engage in) trade with the English. The household sharply increased its consumption of English ceramics again after TPQ 1725, when English goods became legally available through the sale of English prizes in St. Augustine.

After 1750 the St. Augustine *situado* goods were officially supplied by merchants in Charlestown and New York through arrangement with the Royal Havana Company. When Cristóbal de Contreras established his shop at the Fatio site, English goods were openly and legally available. Despite this post-1750 availability of legal English goods through the *situado*, the assemblage from the Contreras merchant occupation shows a decrease in English wares after 1740 and a concomitant increase in Spanish tablewares. In this, the household departs from the trends shown at all of the other households (except for that of the mestizo De la Cruz site). This may well be a function of Contreras's merchant status. Legal trade with the English was controlled through the Royal Havana Company and arrived in St. Augustine as the *situado*. Private merchants quite likely did not have access to this government-sanctioned and controlled trade. They had to rely on the legal markets of Havana and Mexico where Spanish-tradition wares prevailed.

A number of circumstances can be suggested as influential in the shaping of this assemblage. The fact that Contreras was himself from the Spanish Canary Islands may have encouraged a household preference for and use of Spanish-tradition wares. The presence of a private commercial establishment late in the Spanish occupation may reflect a mercantile rather than a consumer assemblage. Neither documentary nor archaeological sampling error can be ruled out, since the early 18th-century occupants of the site are unknown.

Summary: Household Contraband

Viewing the archaeological assemblages of these individual households through the lens of trade periodicity may suggest how people of diverse origins, occupations, and incomes engaged in contraband trade as part of their household strategies. Contraband played out quite differently among the households. It seems to have been contingent not only on economic access but also on relative positions of social privilege and the attitudinal values that reinforced those positions.

It is possible that members of the old criollo families connected to the garrison may have shared a set of values and practices regarding illicit trade that discouraged their participation in it. This is suggested by the consistently low proportions of non-Spanish wares in their household assemblages during periods when these non-Spanish wares should have been illegal.

Households that differed from the garrison criollo mainstream in economic capacity, cultural origin, or occupation did not conform to criollo patterns of practice or, presumably, criollo values regarding contraband. These households seem to have engaged in contraband trade as a systematic part of their individual economic strategies, according to the degree to which they were presented with or excluded from the opportunity do so. The low-income Hispanic-Indian family, for example, seems to have favored foreign goods when they were illegal and not on the open market, possibly because of restricted access to the mainstream economic life of the town. The harbor guard, in contrast to his criollo neighbors, took full advantage of his position to secure foreign goods—both legal and illegal—throughout his occupation, seemingly unhindered by a value system that emphasized legal mandates.

The predominance of Spanish-tradition goods at the merchant site may reflect a difficulty in participating in illicit trade, possibly because of government-controlled access to English goods after 1750, or the fact that the merchant had to sell his wares publicly.

Conclusions

Illicit economic behavior is a quintessential historical archaeological issue. It requires the articulation of text-generated and archaeologically deposited evidence in order to learn something neither source alone could have revealed. Contraband itself is defined by governmental decrees that asserted the circumstances under which specific exchange mechanisms and goods were legal. This intentional, text-derived macroscale construct provides the context and framework for microscale archaeological investigation of the lived experience of contraband in the places that individual families or households occupied.

It is somewhat disconcerting that this study's effort to engage the question of illicit economic behavior through archaeology has been, by necessity, couched in so many methodological caveats regarding the use of both material and textual information. Many of these are common to all historical archaeological projects and include taphonomic factors operating on sites and document collections, biases in sampling sites and documents, and bias in the compression and quantification of archaeological or documentary observations,

Because the archaeological study of contraband is dependent on close tracking of discrete time intervals, the most problematic methodological issue in its study appears to be periodizing the essentially relative archaeological record in a manner that is complementary to the more detailed and essentially chronometric periodicity of the textual record. The ability to do this archaeologically with confidence is often significantly limited by an ability to organize data and observations temporally. Even when working with undisturbed, single-episode deposits, researchers are usually restricted to such imprecise and relative dating tools as stratigraphy, TPQ, midpoints, and formula dates in establishing the chronology of deposits within a site. The most precise of these tools, such as TPQ, are in turn biased by often imperfect understanding of date ranges for material items as well as by issues of time lag, heirlooming, redeposition, disturbance, and so on. To be able to confidently order deposits even in 10-year increments would indeed be fortunate.

The relatively crude tools of chronology present a critical challenge for any study of temporal change in historical archaeology and particularly for those that rely on analysis of discrete events. A great deal more can be done to achieve an increasingly more refined periodicity, as such examples of rigorous primary research as Karlis Karklins (2000), George Miller and colleagues (2000), Ivor Noël Hume (2001), and Gregory Waselkov and John Walthall 2002 have demonstrated.

That said, the study of illicit commerce in 18th-century St. Augustine suggests that inquiry at the scale of the household may be the most productive approach to the archaeological study of contraband, and that whole-community characterizations, while appropriate for macroscale economic questions, may do little more than verify, refute, or add detail to text-based accounts. A household focus can reveal how people with specific economic, occupational, religious, ethnic, and social identities engaged in contraband as a strategy within the larger system of regulations that defined contraband for the community. This can help establish and inform the shape and limits of economic possibility and lead to a more nuanced understanding of the structure, opportunity, and dynamics of economic practice within a community.

Archaeological studies of household and community practice related to illicit trade also hold an untapped potential for framing comparative studies of colonial economic development related to emergent American identity and, ultimately, the separation of colonies from their imperial centers. Although all of the Spanish colonies were subject to the same economic policies and trade restrictions, the circumstances of individual places shaped the actual configurations of illicit trade in a manner unique to each community. Strategies used in St. Augustine, Pensacola, Hispaniola, Caracas, and Buenos Aires, for example, were highly distinct, despite the fact that they all shared the same set of imperial regulations (Deagan 1995; Schávelzon 2000; Bense 2003; Cohen 2003). Exploration of similarities and differences in how these communities managed the problem of illicit but necessary economic activity has not yet been examined through rigorous comparative archaeological analysis, but it offers a potentially productive focus for historical archaeology throughout the Americas.

Acknowledgments

I wish to acknowledge Carl Halbirt for a number of enlightening discussions and critical evaluations of St. Augustine archaeology and contraband, and for initiating my interest in this topic. Amy Turner Bushnell, Susan Parker, and Jeremy Cohen provided thoughtful and critical assessments of archaeology's potential contributions to (and limitations in) the study of contraband from the perspective of documentary historians. I would also like to acknowledge the very insightful comments of the anonymous readers who reviewed this paper for *Historical Archaeology*, and whose comments resulted in significant revision of this work. Any errors of fact or interpretation remain my own.

References

ARNADE, CHARLES
  1962 The Avero Story: An Early St. Augustine Family with Many Daughters and Many Houses. *Florida Historical Quarterly* 40(1):1–34.

BENSE, JUDITH (EDITOR)
  2003 *Presidio Santa María de Galve: A Struggle for Survival in Colonial Spanish Pensacola*. University Press of Florida, Gainesville.

BOLTON, HERBERT E., AND MARY ROSS
  1968 *The Debatable Land: A Sketch of the Anglo-Spanish Contest for the Georgia Country*. Russell and Russell, New York, NY.

BOND, STANLEY
  1995 *Tradition and Change in First Spanish Period (1565–1763) St. Augustine Architecture: A Search for Colonial Identity*. Doctoral dissertation, Anthropology Department, New York State University at Albany. University Microfilms International, Ann Arbor, MI.

BUSHNELL, AMY T.
  1982 *The King's Coffer: Proprietors of the Spanish Florida Treasury 1565–1702*. University Press of Florida, Gainesville.
  1994 *Situado and Sabana: Spain's Support System for the Presidio and Mission Provinces of Florida*. Anthropological Papers, No. 74, American Museum of Natural History. New York, NY.

CHAUNU, PIERRE, AND HUGUETTE CHAUNU
1957 *Séville et l'Atlantique (1504–1650)*, Vol. 6, *Le movement des navires et des merchandises entre l Éspagne et l'Amérique, de 1504 à 1650* (Seville and the Atlantic [1504–1650], Vol. 6, The Movement of Vessels and Merchandise between Spain and America, 1504–1650). Écoles Practiques de Hautes Études, S.E.P.V.E.N., Paris, France.

COHEN, JEREMY
2003 *Informal Commercial Networks, Social Control, and Political Power in the Province of Venezuela, 1700–1757*. Doctoral dissertation, Department of History, University of Florida, Gainesville. University Microfilms International, Ann Arbor, MI.

DEAGAN, KATHLEEN
1976 *Archaeology at the Greek Orthodox Shrine*. Florida State University Notes in Anthropology, Vol. 16, Tallahassee, FL.
1982 St. Augustine: America's First Urban Enclave. *North American Archaeologist* 3(3):183–205.
1983 *Spanish St. Augustine: The Archaeology of a Colonial Creole Community*. Academic Press, New York, NY.
1991 Historical Archaeology's Contribution to Our Understanding of Early America. In *Historical Archaeology in Global Perspective*, Lisa Falk, editor, pp. 97–112. Smithsonian Institution Press, Washington, DC.
2002 *Artifacts of the Spanish Colonies of Florida and the Caribbean, 1500–1800*, Vol. 2, *Portable, Personal Possessions*. Smithsonian Institution Press, Washington, DC.

DEAGAN, KATHLEEN (EDITOR)
1995 *Puerto Real: The Archaeology of a Sixteenth-Century Spanish Town in Hispaniola*. University Press of Florida, Gainesville.

FLORIDA MUSEUM OF NATURAL HISTORY
2004 Historical Archaeology Digital Type Collection. *Historical Archaeology at the Florida Museum of Natural History*, University of Florida, Gainesville <http://www.flmnh.ufl.edu/histarch/gallery_types>.

FROTHINGHAM, ALICE
1941 *Hispanic Glass*. The Hispanic Society of America, New York, NY.

GARCÍA-BAQUERO GONZÁLEZ, ANTONIO
1976 *Cádiz y El Atlántico (1717–1778): El Comercio Colonial Español Bajo El Monopolio Gaditano* (Cádiz and the Atlantic [1717–1778]: Spain's Colonial Commerce under the Cádiz Monopoly). Escuela De Estudios Hispano-Americanos, CSIC. Excelentísima Diputación Provincial de Cádiz, Cádiz, Spain.

GILLASPIE, WILLIAM ROSCOE
1961 *Juan De Ayala y Escobar, Procurador and Entrepreneur: A Case Study of the Provisioning of Florida 1, 1683–1716*. Doctoral dissertation, Department of History, University of Florida, Gainesville. University Microfilms International, Ann Arbor, MI.

HALBIRT, CARL
2004 La Ciudad De San Agustín: A European Fighting Presidio in Eighteenth-Century La Florida. *Historical Archaeology* 38(3):33–46.

HARING, CLARENCE
1966 *Trade and Navigation between Spain and the Indies*. Peter Smith, Gloucester, MA.

HARMAN, JOYCE
1969 *Trade and Privateering in Spanish Florida, 1762–1763*. St. Augustine Historical Society, St. Augustine, FL.

JOHNSON, SANDRA
2003 External Connections. In *Presidio Santa María De Galve: A Struggle for Survival in Colonial Spanish Pensacola*, Judith Bense, editor, pp. 315–340. University Press of Florida, Gainesville.

KARKLINS, KARLIS (EDITOR)
2000 *Studies in Material Culture Research*. The Society for Historical Archaeology, California, PA.

LANG, JAMES
1975 *Conquest and Commerce: Spain and England in the Americas*. Academic Press, New York, NY.

LYON, EUGENE, AND BARBARA PURDY
1982 Contraband in Spanish Colonial Ships. *Itinerario, Journal of the Institute of European Expansion* 6(2): 91–108. Leyden, Netherlands.

MACLEOD, MURDO
1984 Spain and America: The Atlantic Trade 1492–1720. In *Cambridge History of Latin America*, Vol. 1, *Colonial Latin America*, Leslie Bethell, editor, pp. 341–388. Cambridge University Press, Cambridge, England.

MILLER, GEORGE, PATRICIA SAMFORD, ELLEN SHLASKO, AND ANDREW MADSEN
2000 Telling Time for Archaeologists. *Northeast Historical Archaeology* 29:1–22.

NOËL HUME, IVOR
2001 *If These Pots Could Talk*. Chipstone Foundation, Philadelphia. PA.

OATIS, STEVEN
2004 *A Colonial Complex: South Carolina's Frontiers in the Era of the Yamasee War 1680–1730*. University of Nebraska Press, Lincoln.

PARKER, SUSAN R.
    1999   *The Second Century of Settlement in Spanish St. Augustine, 1670–1763*. Doctoral dissertation, Department of History, University of Florida, Gainesville. University Microfilms International, Ann Arbor, MI.

PUENTE, ELIXIO DE LA
    1764   Plano de la Real Fuerza, Baluarte y Linea de la Plaza de St. Augustin de la Florida (Plan of the Royal Fort, Bastion, and Line of the Town of St. Augustine of Florida). Manuscript, P. K. Yonge Library of Florida History, University of Florida, Gainesville.

PULIDO BUENO, ILDEFONSO
    1993   *Almojarifazgos y Comercio Exterior en Andalucía Durante la Época Mercantilista, 1526–1740* (Tariffs and Foreign Trade in Andalusia during the Mercantile Age, 1526–1740). Contribución al Estudio de la Economía en la España Moderna, Artes Gráficos Andaluzas, Huelva, Spain.

RICE, PRUDENCE
    1987   *Pottery Analysis: A Sourcebook*. University of Chicago Press, Chicago, IL.

RUNYON, SHANE
    2005   *The Founding of Georgia and Spain's Fight for the Frontier 1732–1740*. Doctoral dissertation, Department of History, University of Florida, Gainesville. University Microfilms International, Ann Arbor, MI.

SCARDAVILLE, MICHAEL, AND OVERTON GANONG
    [1975] Historical Report on Block 7, Lot 4, St. Augustine. Manuscript, Historic St. Augustine Preservation Board, St. Augustine, FL.

SCHÁVELZON, DANIEL
    2000   *The Historical Archaeology of Buenos Aires: A City at the End of the World*. Kluwer Academic/Plenum Publishers, New York, NY.

SCHMIDT, PETER R., AND STEPHEN A. MROZOWSKI
    1993   Documentary Insights into the Archaeology of Smuggling. In *Documentary Archaeology in the New World*, Mary C. Beaudry, editor, pp. 32–42. Cambridge University Press, New York.

SHEPHERD, STEPHEN
    1983   The Spanish Criollo Majority in Colonial St. Augustine. In *Spanish St. Augustine: The Archaeology of a Colonial Creole Community*, Kathleen Deagan, editor, pp. 65–97. Academic Press, New York, NY.

SKOWRONEK, RUSSELL K.
    1982   The Patterns of Eighteenth-Century Frontier New Spain: The 1722 Flota and St. Augustine. Master's thesis, Department of Anthropology, Florida State University, Tallahassee.
    1992   Empire and Ceramics: The Changing Role of Illicit Trade in Spanish America. *Historical Archaeology* 26(1):109–118.

SKOWRONEK, RUSSELL K., AND CHARLES R. EWEN (EDITORS)
    2005   *X Marks the Spot: The Archaeology of Piracy*. University Press of Florida, Gainesville.

TEPASKE, JOHN R.
    1958   Economic Problems of the Florida Governors. *Florida Historical Quarterly* 37:42–52.
    1964   *The Governorship of Spanish Florida, 1700–1763*. Duke University Press, Durham, NC.

TORRE REVELLO, JOSÉ
    1943   Merchandise Brought to America by the Spaniards (1534–1586). *Hispanic American Historical Review* 23(4):773–780.

USHER, ABBOTT P.
    1932   Spanish Ships and Shipping in the Sixteenth and Seventeenth Centuries. In *Facts and Factors in Economic History: Articles by Former Students of Edwin Francis Gay*, Edwin Francis Gay, editor, pp. 189–213. Harvard University Press, Cambridge, MA.

VICENS VIVES, JAIME
    1969   *An Economic History of Spain*, translated by Frances M. López Morillas. Princeton University Press, Princeton, NJ.

WALKER, GEOFFREY J.
    1979   *Spanish Politics and Imperial Trade, 1700–1789*. Indiana University Press, Bloomington.

WASELKOV, GREGORY A., AND JOHN A. WALTHALL
    2002   Faience Styles in French North America: A Revised Classification. *Historical Archaeology* 36(1):62–78.

WATERBURY, JEAN P. (EDITOR)
    1999   *Defenses and Defenders at St. Augustine* (A Collection of Writings by Luis Rafael Arana. El Escribano 36). St. Augustine Historical Society, St. Augustine, FL.

WRIGHT, J. LEITCH
    1970   *Anglo-Spanish Rivalry in Eastern North America*. University of Georgia Press, Athens.

KATHLEEN DEAGAN
FLORIDA MUSEUM OF NATURAL HISTORY
MUSEUM DRIVE AND NEWELL ROAD
PO BOX 117800
UNIVERSITY OF FLORIDA
GAINESVILLE, FL 32611

JULIA G. COSTELLO

Purchasing Patterns of the California Missions in ca. 1805

ABSTRACT

During the first decade of the 19th century, Yankee otter-hunters were trading illegally with the California missions, exchanging manufactured goods for pelts. Two documents of this period, an 1804 Spanish *factura* (shipping list) and the 1806–1807 account book of the smuggling ship *Mercury*, reveal differences in the types of items supplied by these two trade networks. Over the next quarter century the Spanish economic system in California would be replaced by the Anglo-based capitalist world economy. The effect of this trend on both Hispanic cultural ties and the material culture of the colony is discernible in these early inventories.

Introduction

Within their short life span of 65 years (1769–1834), the 21 Franciscan missions, as part of Hispanic Alta California (Figure 1), were caught up in a major expansion of the capitalist world economy as described by Immanuel Wallerstein (1974, 1980, 1989). In 1786, Alta California first became an "external area" to Spain with the export of luxury items—sea otter pelts—under private concession. Movement toward the "periphery" of a world-system network is identified by the process of "incorporation": the development of some production process integral to larger commodity chains and responsive to market factors. In Alta California, this process was foreshadowed by the modest exports of hemp and animal fats between 1800–1810. Both production and markets for cattle products began to grow following the 1810 Mexican War of Independence and the relaxation of Spanish control over shipping. Incorporation intensified with the new Mexican government's tolerance of foreign trade after 1821. Alta California became a peripheral area within the economic

world-system once church assets passed into private hands after ca. 1834 (Costello 1990).

This study focuses on the very beginning of this process of incorporation, the period around 1805, and on how the introduction of new sources of manufactured goods affected the material culture of the missions. By this time, the missions were well-established and generally prosperous: populations were large, agricultural production steady and increasing, and construction of major buildings and facilities virtually completed (Costello and Hornbeck 1989). Although the missions were mostly self-sustaining, some manufactured goods and raw materials were regularly imported. Purchases were enabled through the important annual allotments of money to each mission from the Pious Fund, administered by the Franciscan College of San Fernando in Mexico City. This allotment consisted of $800 each year for each mission and about $70 for each missionary, with amounts doubled for the first five years of a mission's life (Archibald 1978:7).

Annual stipends could be augmented by exports from the missions, carried on government ships to the port of San Blas. In this ca. 1805 time period, tallow and lard, packed in bags made of cattle hides, were the primary export commodity. The fats were separated and graded for different purposes: *manteca* for cooking, *sebo* for candle making and other products, and *rinonda* for soap (Ogden 1925; Tays 1941). Mission San Buenaventura's tallow and lard production generated almost $800 in 1806, $660 in 1807, and nearly $2,000 in 1808 (Table 1). Some hides and sheepskins were also exported, and the newly-introduced cash crop of hemp figured prominently in exports from the southern missions by the end of the decade. (Hides would not be the major California export until the early 1820s.)

The missions spent their income on cargos of goods imported on the same Spanish government ships from San Blas that took away the exports—virtually all commerce and communication with Alta California took place by ship. Mission priests sent annual request lists of specific items to San Fernando College where they were filled by the *procurator* (purchasing agent), with costs charged

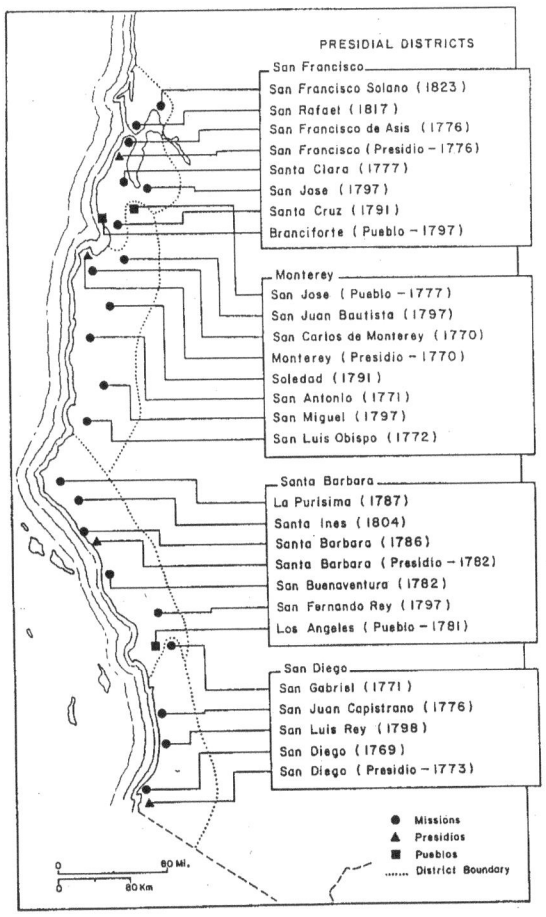

FIGURE 1. Missions, presidios, and pueblos, 1769–1823 (after Costello and Hornbeck 1989).

In the figure, the box lists:

PRESIDIAL DISTRICTS

San Francisco
San Francisco Solano (1823)
San Rafael (1817)
San Francisco de Asis (1776)
San Francisco (Presidio – 1776)
Santa Clara (1777)
San Jose (1797)
Santa Cruz (1791)
Branciforte (Pueblo – 1797)

Monterey
San Jose (Pueblo – 1777)
San Juan Bautista (1797)
San Carlos de Monterey (1770)
Monterey (Presidio – 1770)
Soledad (1791)
San Antonio (1771)
San Miguel (1797)
San Luis Obispo (1772)

Santa Barbara
La Purisima (1787)
Santa Ines (1804)
Santa Barbara (1786)
Santa Barbara (Presidio – 1782)
San Buenaventura (1782)
San Fernando Rey (1797)
Los Angeles (Pueblo – 1781)

San Diego
San Gabriel (1771)
San Juan Capistrano (1776)
San Luis Rey (1798)
San Diego (1769)
San Diego (Presidio – 1773)

● Missions
▲ Presidios
■ Pueblos
······ District Boundary

80 Mi.
80 Km

TABLE 1
EXPORTS FROM MISSION SAN
BUENAVENTURA, 1806–1808

Year	Ship's Port	Commodity	Quantity	Price (pesos)
1806	San Blas	Tallow	132 "skins"[1]	787[2]
		Sheepskins	741 arrobas 64 "skins"	unknown
1807	San Blas	Tallow	103 "skins" 621 arrobas	660[2]
1808	New Spain	Tallow	200 "skins" 1,428 arrobas	1,606[3]
		Lard		361
		Otter Pelts	50 "skins" 321 arrobas 100 pelts	725[4]

[1]Leather bag
[2]1 arroba [25.3 lbs.] = 8.5 reales in 1807 (Señán 1962:30)
[3]1 arroba = 9 reales in 1808 (Señán 1962:34)
[4]Otter pelts at 7–7.5 pesos each in 1808 (Señán 1962:32)
Source: Señán (1962:22,30,32,34,35).

Everything [in the shipment] was in good order except the 24 mattocks. I have never before seen such wretched tools as these. They are small and narrow, and the metal in several is suspiciously corroded and old-looking. The eyes for the handles are badly placed and out of shape. You should be thankful that I warn you of these things, so that you, knowing the poor quality of this consignment, can keep a watch over future shipments. You might also give the artisan who made these mattocks a good scolding (Señán 1962: 49).

Correspondence between missions and the College also documents problems with the *sindac*, damage to or loss of goods in transport, and difficulties in anticipating material needs one year in advance.

If additional items were needed between shipments, they would be purchased from the presidio stores which sold the same inventory of items available from San Blas but at inflated prices. The mission also supplied substantial amounts of agricultural and manufactured items to the presidios (Archibald 1978:92, 100, 104–105) for which they were given credit on government accounts.

Since 1786, legal trade was also carried on with private parties—primarily the Spanish sailors— through special consignments in the government ships' cargos and through goods brought on spec-

to individual mission accounts. The purchased goods were shipped by a *sindac* (secular agent) from San Blas as space was available on the few ships serving Alta California. Finally, one year later at best, the requested items were delivered to specific missions (Señán 1962).

While this system worked well enough, some obvious drawbacks existed. The missions had no direct control over their purchases, either in picking them out or deciding where to cut the request list when wants exceeded the budget. Also, the quality of goods sent did not always meet expectations. Padre José Señán of San Buenaventura wrote to Procurator Guilez on 6 November 1810:

ulation. The only restriction was the standard prohibition against importation of goods from outside
of the Spanish empire (Archibald 1978:119). Padres complained that these imported goods were
not articles needed by the missions but were instead merchandise which fostered "vanity among
our women and intemperance among our men"
(Señán 1962:4). Abuses of the trading privileges
led to a Viceregal decree in 1803 mandating that
cargo space for mission imports and exports could
not be usurped by private trade goods and imposed
freight charges on non-mission shipments.

The primary impediment to mission trade, however, was not a lack of exports or imports but
transport. Augmenting mission revenues was ham-
pered by limited cargo space on the few government ships in service to Alta California. Increasingly abundant tallow, lard, and hemp produced by
the missions overwhelmed available transport and
eventually resulted in substantial economic loss to
the missions.

An illegal alternative was provided by the foreign sea-otter-hunting vessels which worked the
coast, virtually all of which were from the United
States (Table 2), Britain's economic "lieutenant"
(Wallerstein 1989:255). Sea otters, bearing one of
the finest furs in the world, were abundant off the
coasts of Alta and Baja California. Commanding
high prices in China, they were sought after by
European nations seeking to trade with this Asian
empire. A short-lived Spanish experiment in exporting otter pelts from the Californias to China
between 1786 and 1790 (Ogden 1975:15–24)
alerted the missions to the lucrative potential of
this export commodity. In 1796, the first Yankee
sea-otter-hunting ship was recorded in California,
and numbers increased until by 1807 six vessels
were working the coast. Sea otters are difficult to
catch, however, and Yankees soon preferred contracting with the Russians to use Kodiak Islanders
(Aleutians and Koniags) as hunters in exchange for
half of the profits (Archibald 1978:132–134).

Typically working the California coast for one
or two years at a time, these foreign ships regularly
pulled into ports for provisions and were initially
accommodated by the Spanish in compliance with
international maritime policies. The Yankees took

TABLE 2
SHIPS VISITING CALIFORNIA, 1804–1807

Ship	Home Port	Occupation
	1804	
O'Cain	Boston	Otter hunter; Aleut contract
Leila Byrd	Honolulu (USA)	Otter hunter
Hazard	Providence, RI	Otter hunter (two trips)
	1805	
Activo	San Blas	Spanish government
Leila Byrd	Honolulu (USA)	Otter hunter
Princesa	San Blas	Spanish government
	1806	
Eclipse	Boston/Honolulu	Otter hunter
O'Cain	Boston/Honolulu	Otter hunter; Aleut contract
Peacock	Boston/Honolulu	Otter hunter
Tamana	Honolulu (USA)	Otter hunter
Maryland	New York	Otter hunter?
Mercury	Boston/Honolulu	Otter hunter
	1807	
Activo	San Blas	Spanish government
Mercury	Boston	Otter hunter
Derby	Boston	Otter hunter; Aleut contract
Nicholai	Sitka	Otter hunter
O'Cain	Boston/Honolulu	Otter hunter; Aleut contract
Peacock	Boston/Honolulu	Otter hunter; Aleut contract
Princesa	San Blas	Spanish government
Tamana	Honolulu (USA)	Otter hunter

Source: Ogden (1975:158–161).

advantage of this hospitality, however, by illegally
trading goods to the missions for sea otter pelts
collected by Indian neophytes (converts). By
1804, this illegal commerce had become so ram-
pant that a royal order was issued to close all ports
to foreign ships, even for provisioning, a measure
which only resulted in driving the popular smuggling further underground (Archibald 1978:132).

The morality of trading illegally with foreigners
only occasionally seemed to conflict with the commercial spirit of mission padres. Although their
letters often complain about the presence of foreign intruders and profess loyalty to the crown,
diaries of the Yankee captains and their account
books attest to the willingness of the padres to
meet and trade in clandestine locations (*Mercury*
1807; Shaler 1808). The economic advantages of

TABLE 3
TRANSACTIONS[a] BETWEEN MISSIONS AND THE AMERICAN SHIP *MERCURY*, 1806–1807

		Ship Purchases		Ship Payments		
Date	Mission	Otter Pelts N	Provisions $	Cash $	Goods $	Total $
Nov. 2?	Santa Barbara	79	—	400	153	553
	Santa Ines	93	—	449	295	744
Nov. 24	Santa Ines	157	—	1,011	163	1,174
Dec. 12	Santa Ines	50	—	184	272	456
	Santa Barbara	11	150	83	177	260
April 7	San Gabriel	6	—	58	—	58
May 2?	Santa Barbara	—	—	100	—	100
	Santa Ines	44	—	316	82	398
July ?	San Luis Obispo	93	44	253	675	928
July 7	San Luis Obispo	10	34	119	—	119
July 12	San Miguel	7	4	—	54	54
	San Luis Obispo	—	92	40	52	92
Total		550	$324	$3,013	$1,923	$4,936

[a]in pesos

smuggling for the missions are clear: goods could be inspected before purchase, transactions were immediate, and sea otter was relatively abundant. The amount of illegal trade in these early years, however, was relatively small. The American smuggler Shaler (1808) estimated that the total trade from Alta and Baja California totaled only $25,000 annually between 1800 and 1810.

Spanish Shipments and Smugglers: Comparison of Imported Goods

During the first decade of the 19th century, the California colony began to take advantage of an alternative, foreign, trading network. How did this new interaction affect the mission economy and material culture? Were there differences between the types of goods contained in Spanish shipments and those obtained from Yankee smugglers?

Two documents were located that provide some insight into these questions. First is the *factura* or shipping list that accompanied the 1804 Spanish shipment to Mission Santa Barbara—about $2,000 worth of goods (Engelhardt 1908). Second is the account book of the American sea-otter-hunter *Mercury*, on the California Coast from 1806–1807 (*Mercury* 1807). The *Mercury* account book records visits to several small anchorages where transactions were made with the padres of missions Santa Barbara, Santa Ines, San Gabriel, San Luis Obispo, and San Miguel (Table 3). In total, nearly $5,000 worth of sea otter skins and provisions were purchased by the *Mercury*: $3,000 of this amount was paid in cash and $2,000 in goods.

The Santa Barbara *factura* and *Mercury* accounts, containing lists of individual items with quantities and prices, provide a rare and detailed insight into what goods were entering mission life from Spanish and foreign sources ca. 1805. In generalizing from these documents, the goods sent to Santa Barbara Mission in 1804 are assumed similar to cargos sent to other missions at this time. It is understood that each individual mission had unique characteristics that made it unlike the others: Santa Barbara Mission was the most populous and yet the poorest economic producer in this Presidio District (Costello 1990). However, no evidence exists that the types of goods requested from and sent by Mexico each year were not similar between establishments. In a like manner, the goods carried by the *Mercury* are regarded as typical of those carried by other sea-otter-hunting ships from the United States, although there was probably some diversity in trading cargos. Purchases made by California mission padres from the *Mercury* (Table 3) have been combined to represent overall mission buying strategies.

Distribution of Goods by Type

Goods listed in the two documents were identified according to functional categories originally developed by archaeologist Stanley South (1977) for recovered artifacts. An expanded version of these functional categories was previously developed by the author to include more recent time periods (University of California, Santa Barbara 1984); further enlargement was required for this study as fully two-thirds of the items on both the Santa Barbara *factura* and the *Mercury* account book would not survive in an archaeological context (Costello 1990). Standardizing quantities of items for comparative purposes was unfeasible: two-dozen hinges, ½ lb. of buttons, a "piece" of cloth, and a barrel of refined brandy are difficult to compare. Price, however, was a common denominator and also accurately reflected how a finite amount of mission money was apportioned to various categories of items. The total value of various categories of items in pesos (equal to a United States dollar at that time) was therefore used for comparison (Table 4). Only the goods purchased from the *Mercury*, not the cash payments, are included in computations.

Preliminary comparisons reveal that for all but two of the Group categories, there is less than a 3 percent difference in mission purchasing patterns between Spanish and Yankee sources. The major contrast in spending is in the exclusive presence of religious items on the *factura* (35% of the entire inventory) and the preponderance of cloth and clothing on the *Mercury* (67% of the *Mercury*'s sales). The religious items listed on the *factura* include (translations from Engelhardt 1908): decorations for the altar (silk cope with flowers, cornucopias with gold, artificial flowers); silver candlesticks; two carved statues; a tapestry; religious books; vestments; sacramental wine; nearly 300 small crosses; and over 1,700 rosaries. Over half of the items sold from the *Mercury*'s storeroom were bulk cloth which included: blue broadcloth; green, yellow, and red baize; sheeting; coating; flannel; calico; "nankeen" (Chinese silk); blue, red and flowered satin; velvet; chintz; and canvas. Although the *factura* uniquely contained fabric made in Queretaro and French linens, it otherwise carried only blue flannel, calico, and a small quantity of cotton print.

Looking more closely at individual items within Group categories reveals other goods unique to each source. All of the following items were found exclusively in the Spanish shipment (in order of total purchased): iron pots and kettles; chocolate (5% of total shipment; 300 lbs.); farming equipment (hoes, sickles, plow shares); horse tack and gear; hats, shawls, and decorative braid for clothing; medicine; spices and condiments; glass beads; musical instruments; tobacco (snuff and cigars); fireworks; and paper and paint pigments. There are also items that were only found in the smugglers' account book (in order of total purchased): table wares (258 plates, a total of 138 dishes, pitchers, mugs and chafing dishes, 144 tumblers, and 36 decanters); cotton and silk stockings; pen knives, butcher knives, and bone-handled knives; razors; lead shot and powder, powder horns, gun hammers; irons; ivory combs; a watch; buttons; an umbrella; and a cork screw.

Both sources, Spanish and Yankee, had quantities of hardware and an assortment of tools. The smugglers, however, carried a larger variety of these items. In addition to chisels, augers, and axes which appear on both inventories, the Yankees sold: pliers, saw blades, files, hammers, gouges, compasses, gimlets, adzes, hatchets, and drawing knives.

Comparison of prices between Spanish and Anglo sources is difficult as articles identified by the

TABLE 4
PESOS SPENT BY MISSIONS PER FUNCTIONAL CATEGORY

Group/Commodities	1804 Santa Barbara Memoria			1806–1807 *Mercury* Account Book		
	Total	Group Total	Group Percent	Total	Group Total	Group Percent
Kitchen		384	19		311	16
Table	0			164		
Drinking alcohol	34			138		
Kitchenware	219			9		
Spices	27			0		
Chocolate	104			0		
Architecture		35	2		21	1
Hardware	35			21		
Lighting		69	3		12	t[a]
Candles and wicks	69			12		
Clothing		408	20		1,352	67
Buttons	0			8		
Garments	48			166		
Mfg./Maintenance	45			63		
Bulk cloth	315			1,115		
Arms		20	1		73	4
Shot/powder	0			20		
Knives	20			53		
Personal		89	4		51	3
Misc. items	0			51		
Tobacco	20			0		
Medicine	40			0		
Beads	29			0		
Tools and Equipment		210	10		147	7
Horse/Mule tack	67			0		
Shop tools	45			147		
Farming	98			0		
Entertainment		47	2		0	0
Musical Instruments	29			0		
Fireworks	18			0		
Communication		18	1		8	t[a]
Paper/pigments	18			0		
Books	0			8		
Storage		55	3		45	2
Empty cases	55			45		
Religious		710	35		0	0
Unknown		0	0		4	t[a]
Total		2,045	100		2,024	100

[a]t = <0.5%

same name frequently come in a wide range of sizes and quality. The *factura* and *Mercury* accounts contained only seven items that could potentially be identical. Spain apparently charged slightly more for scissors by the dozen and for frying pans while the *Mercury* appears to have asked a higher price for large hinges, augers, and calico cloth. Large knives, by the dozen, and chisels are comparable in cost. Prices could also be increased for resale of goods: the padre at San Luis Obispo nearly doubled the price of Mexican chocolate from what he had paid when he sold over 80 lbs. of it to the *Mercury*.

Conclusion

The new export commodity of sea otter skins increased the purchasing power of the missions and opened up a new, albeit illegal, source of imported goods. It was apparently the process of direct barter for smuggled goods that attracted the padres. Prices of Spanish and Anglo goods were comparable, and most of what the missions purchased from the Yankees was of a practical and utilitarian nature that augmented types of items also available from New Spain. An exception might be found in the comparatively large inventories of British cloth and tablewares, reflecting England's renowned textile and ceramic industries which were capturing markets worldwide. Small quantities of personal goods such as stockings, combs, and razors were also newly available from Anglo traders.

Except for iron kettles and some agricultural equipment, almost all other items coming exclusively from New Spain ca. 1805 fall into the categories of religious items or social amenities: musical instruments, fireworks for feast days, chocolate, Spanish clothing, medicine, paints, church decorations and vestments, sacramental wine, and individual crosses and rosaries. These items can be characterized as being distinctive of Spanish culture: related to social customs, health practices, religion, music, and art. These uniquely Hispanic goods represent the social, spiritual, and aesthetic ties that bound Alta California to Spanish Mexico.

Comparison of the 1804 *factura* and the 1806–1807 *Mercury* account book revealed differences in the two supply networks that would rapidly escalate once regular Spanish shipments from San Blas were interrupted in 1810. In subsequent years, categories of items associated with Yankee sources would increase while those associated with Spanish sources would decline as the hide-and-tallow traders from Boston became California's chief suppliers of imported goods. Ships from former Spanish colonies continued to call in California ports, but between 1822 and 1835 they numbered only 43 against 145 ships from the United States and 70 from England (Costello 1990: Table 3). The declining importation of distinctly Spanish cultural items likely contributed to, as well as chronicled, the transformation of Alta California from a Spanish colony to a peripheral member of the Anglo-oriented world economy.

REFERENCES

ARCHIBALD, ROBERT
1978   *The Economic Aspects of the California Missions.* Academy of American Franciscan History, Washington, D.C.

COSTELLO, JULIA G.
1990   Variability and Economic Change in the California Missions: An Historical and Archaeological Study. Unpublished Ph.D. dissertation, Department of Anthropology, University of California, Santa Barbara.

COSTELLO, JULIA G., AND DAVID HORNBECK
1989   Alta California: An Overview. In *Columbian Consequences.* Vol. 1, *Archaeological and Historical Perspectives on the Spanish Borderlands West,* edited by David Hurst Thomas, pp. 303–332. Smithsonian Institution Press, Washington, D.C.

DAVIS, WILLIAM HEATH
1806–   Account Book of the *Mercury.* De la Guerra Collection, Accounts and Business Papers. Santa Barbara Mission Archives, Santa Barbara, California.
1807

ENGLEHARDT, ZEPHRYN, O.F.M.
1908   Las Memorias, or Invoice of Goods Annually Forwarded to Each Mission. In *Missions and Missionaries of California,* Vol. 4, pp. 647–650. James H. Barry, San Francisco.

MERCURY
1807   Account Book of the American Ship *Mercury,* William Heath Davis, Sr., Captain. De la Guerra Collection, Accounts and Business Papers. Santa Barbara Mission Archives, Santa Barbara, California.

OGDEN, ADELE
1925   McCulloch, Hartnell and Company, English Merchants in the California Hide and Tallow Trade. Unpublished M.A. thesis, Department of History, University of California, Berkeley.

1975   *The California Sea Otter Trade, 1782–1848.* University of California Press, Berkeley.

SEÑÁN, JOSE, O.F.M.
1962   *The Letters of Jose Señán, O.F.M., 1792–1823*, edited by Lesley Byrd Simpson and translated by Paul Nathan. Ventura County Historical Society, San Francisco.

SHALER, WILLIAM
1808   Journal of a Voyage Between China and the Northwest Coast of America Made in 1804. *The American Register: or General Repository of History, Politics, and Science*, Vol. 3, Part 1, for 1808. C. and A. Conrad, Philadelphia.

SOUTH, STANLEY
1977   *Method and Theory in Historical Archeology.* Academic Press, New York.

TAYS, GEORGE
1941   Agriculture in Colonial California; Animal Husbandry in Colonial California. In *California's Colonial Life*, pp. 1–291. Bancroft Library, University of California, Berkeley.

UNIVERSITY OF CALIFORNIA, SANTA BARBARA
1984   Catalogue Code Guide, Version 7. Department of Anthropology, University of California, Santa Barbara.

WALLERSTEIN, IMMANUEL
1974   *The Modern World-System.* Vol. 1, *Capitalist Agriculture and the Origins of the European World-Economy in the Sixteenth Century.* Academic Press, New York.

1980   *The Modern World-System.* Vol. 2, *Mercantilism and the Consolidation of the European World-Economy, 1600–1750.* Academic Press, New York.

1989   *The Modern World-System.* Vol. 3, *The Second Era of Great Expansion of the Capitalist World-Economy, 1730–1840s.* Academic Press, New York.

JULIA G. COSTELLO
FOOTHILL RESOURCE ASSOCIATES
P.O. BOX 288
MOKELUMNE HILL, CALIFORNIA 95245

Chapter 7

HISTORIC SUBSISTENCE PRACTICES: SYNTHESIS AND CONCLUSIONS

Study of documentary and archaeological evidence suggests that Spanish colonists radically altered their foodways to survive in Florida. In doing so, the settlers were forced to compromise or abandon many time-honored practices and foods. The traditional Spanish diet was based on an assemblage of plants and animals which were unsuited to the ecological conditions found in Florida. While some colonists were familiar with the modifications the Iberian diet had undergone in the Caribbean settlements, the Caribbean strategy could not be directly transferred to the Atlantic coastal plain. The Florida environment was sufficiently distinct from the Caribbean one that Old World plants and animals once again had to undergo a period of adaptation. Likewise, many indigenous Caribbean products could not be raised in the new colonies. The distances and difficulties of transportation made it impossible to retain either the customary Iberian diet or the Caribbean diet through food imports.

The archaeological remains and historical records provide two perspectives on the subsistence system of sixteenth-century Florida. When these are combined, the pattern that appears documents the impact of acculturative and adaptive processes on this early colonial effort. The new dietary practices were in many respects similar to aboriginal practices but they were colored by the settlers' Iberian and Caribbean experiences. Moreover, the subsistence system was integrated into an emerging cultural system that placed a distinctive stamp upon its constituent parts.

In this final chapter, the disparate threads of evidence are drawn together and a more complete picture of the subsistence system is woven. This allows attention to be focused on questions that can be answered more accurately by combining ar-

chaeological and historical data. It also suggests that the supply difficulties the Spaniards encountered are common in frontier settings and that other colonial groups may have adopted similar solutions to their subsistence problems. Consideration will be given to variables important in the formation of the subsistence strategy: the frontier setting, socioeconomic status, and ethnicity. Finally, the subsistence strategy will be discussed in terms of subsistence principles, adaptation, and acculturation.

THE FRONTIER SETTING

To some extent the subsistence strategy that developed in Florida reflected the Spaniards' restricted access to markets. The settlements were located at the edge of the Spanish Empire, despite their proximity to the shipping lanes from Cuba to Spain. Supplies arrived sporadically and were an unreliable source of daily nutrition. Unpredictable external supplies encouraged the Florida colonists to depend on resources they could produce for themselves or acquire from the natives. For this reason if for no other, the subsistence base shifted to new foods that were locally available and more dependable. Similar responses by other colonial groups with restricted access to markets should be anticipated.

The stimulus to procure provisions by their own initiatives led the colonists to expand their food base. It has been suggested that wherever security decreases, the subsistence base may be expanded to include taxa that would otherwise be ignored. In frontier settings, access to normal foods is reduced and risk increased. These factors encouraged the settlers to enlarge their food base to include the resources of the local environment.

The local resources were incorporated in the new strategy in two ways. One was to substitute trade with local Indians for trade with New Spain. Spaniards traded extensively with the Indians living on the Atlantic coastal plain. An unknown quantity of trade goods, both edible and non-edible, entered the Spanish system through this exchange. This substitution of an Indian trade network for the one with New Spain had a substantial influence on the Spanish strategy. The second way the colonists acquired local foodstuffs was to produce or capture these resources by their own efforts. The manner in which these new resources were incorporated in a household-level strategy was influenced by several factors, including socioeconomic status and ethnicity.

SOCIOECONOMIC STATUS AND ETHNICITY

Subsistence systems can be viewed from more than one angle. An external perspective considers the general subsistence pattern for a given cultural system. An internal perspective looks for variability within that general pattern. This work has focused on the general pattern of the sixteenth-century Spanish Florida subsistence system. However, individual households exhibit variations on this theme. Some differences can probably be attributed to individual food preferences, but others reflect social status, ethnic affiliation, and the influence of these factors on subsistence decisions.

The proposition that food consumption correlates with socioeconomic status and ethnicity is based on several factors. It appears to be a general phenomenon that differences in social rank are marked by status symbols recognized by the community as a whole (Peebles and Kus 1977:431). Consumption or avoidance of particular foods is often found to be such a status marker (Service 1962:172). Ethnicity and socioeconomic status are frequently tightly intertwined. Wealth and social standing affect an individual's or a household's capacity to acquire valued foodstuffs, but people also make choices based on ethnic traditions.

Social status is not simply a matter of relative wealth or power. It is also delineated by specific behavior patterns. Persons or families of high social status not only have greater access to valued goods but must validate their rank by the sumptuous display or consumption of those goods. On the other hand, their behavior is restricted, since they must appear to conform to social and legal regulations (Homans 1950:287) and to ethnic traditions. Persons or families of low economic

and social status experience restricted access to valued goods. Such restrictions may be economic but may also be socially defined. The Old World hunting laws were examples of this. While the poor may have limited access to valued goods, particularly through legitimate channels, they may be less constrained or inclined to obey laws imposed by the governing classes. Between these two extremes are individuals who have greater access to valued goods than those on the lowest rungs of the social ladder but who adhere more strictly to society's laws because they wish to be considered upstanding members of the community.

Although food consumption patterns undoubtedly correlated with social rank in sixteenth-century Spanish Florida, predicting how they did so is difficult. One problem is that different behaviors might result in similar archaeological deposits. For instance, the governor's household might employ a hunting specialist or have greater access to foods supplied to the town by natives, while a soldier's household that had little capital to purchase supplies might rely heavily on off-duty hunting to provide food for the table. The soldier's household might also include a native woman, through whom the soldier had access to local resources. Both households would produce archaeological deposits containing high quantities of wild resources. A second problem is that differential obedience to social norms might produce patterns opposite to what would be expected. Thus, it might be predicted that high social status would confer greater access to domestic meat sources. However, if the members of the elite felt obliged to follow the dictate that livestock not be consumed so that it could increase and the poor were sufficiently hungry to disregard the regulation, the pattern that would appear in the archaeological record would be the reverse of that which was predicted.

Another interesting aspect of status is the association of diversity and rare goods with higher status households. As Jochim (1976:25–26) has pointed out, high status is frequently associated with items which are rare and energetically expensive to obtain. Trade goods, including foods, fit this category. Access to imported goods increases the diversity of a high-status household deposit by adding rare items to it. These rare items are not found in deposits associated with lower status, which are consequently less diverse. Yet, expanded diversity (expanded niche width in ecological terms) is also a feature of a system which has experienced decreased security. A household which has a diverse food assemblage might either be under stress or upper status. This is not as contradictory as it may appear. It is probably functional in a society to have some members using resources not normally used by the rest of the population.

These problems do not mean that it is impossible to investigate the relationships between food consumption and social status. They do mean that attempts to analyze the relationships must be performed with a full appreciation of the context and subtlety of the archaeological and historical records.

Information from eighteenth-century St. Augustine can be used to make predictions about the patterns that might be found in sixteenth-century deposits. The work of Cumbaa (1975; Reitz and Cumbaa 1983) on the eighteenth-century St. Augustine community exemplifies the subtle interaction of subsistence and status. Cumbaa analyzed patterns of animal use from three households for which the occupants' social standings in the community were known from documents. He found that the diet of one household (SA 16-23) occupied by an Indian woman, María de la Cruz, and her Spanish husband incorporated less domestic meat than the diet of the other two households. This household, of lower social status than the others, made use of more wild resources from the nearby salt marsh (Reitz and Cumbaa 1983:177). Occupying an intermediate social position, the Gertrudis de la Pasqua household (SA 13-5) made use of more domestic individuals than the Cruz household but used fewer such animals than the Cristoval Contreras household (SA 34-2) (Reitz and Cumbaa 1983:177). Contreras was from the Canary Islands (Spanish islands in the Atlantic Ocean off of Africa) and a wealthy man, yet he used wild resources to a greater extent than Cumbaa had expected based on his social status. Cumbaa in-

terpreted this as an indication that Contreras had engaged the services of a hunting specialist (Cumbaa 1975:159). On the other hand, the Cruz household probably secured its wild resources through its own or its kin group's efforts.

In considering the relationship of social rank to food use in early Florida, a distinction should be made between imported and local foodstuffs and between basic provisions and luxury foods. It seems likely that high social status, particularly a position among the administrators of the colony, conferred greater access to imported foods, especially luxury foods. If the basic provisions sent to the colony from Cuba (AGI, *Escribanía de Cámara* 153A; AGI, *Escribanía de Cámara* 1024A) are compared to items shipped from Cádiz for the Governor's household (AGI, *Contaduría* 1174; AGI, *Patronato* 19, R. 15), a disparity in both types and variety of foodstuffs is evident. Provisions shipped from Cuba in 1565 included beans, garbanzos, rice, garlic, lentils, cassava, squash, and maize. In contrast, shipments intended for the Governor's household contained exotic products, such as malaga raisins, figs, Seville olives, capers, quince pulp, anise seed, and marzipan.

How locally procured foodstuffs correlate with social status is more difficult to predict. There may well be differences in the manner in which plant versus animal foods vary with social status. While higher rank might result in consumption of more domestic meat, it has already been noted that the edict that livestock should be left to increase may have produced an opposite effect. In traditional Iberian diets, wild game was used to a limited extent by all social classes, although venison was reserved for the upper class. This society-wide use of wild game may have led to a ready acceptance of these resources by most of the colonists in Spanish Florida. Considering its esteem in the Old World, there would certainly have been no stigma attached to the consumption of venison. Given these factors, it would be expected that wild game consumption in the sixteenth century would follow a similar pattern to that found for the eighteenth century. That is, all levels would use wild game, but the upper and lower echelons would consume more of these meats than would people in the middle.

The locally grown plant staples as well as locally produced fruits and vegetables were probably used by everyone. Cultivated staples may have been available in greater quantity and with more regularity to more well-to-do households, but this would be difficult to detect archaeologically. If each household had a kitchen garden, people on all levels of society had access to fruits and vegetables. The upper echelons may, however, have had a wider variety of such foods. There are two factors which suggest that the use of wild plant foods might have been highest among households of lower social status. First, in the traditional Iberian diet the use of wild plant foods seems to have been relegated to the poor. This being the case, the colonists, particularly the wealthier ones, may have scorned these resources and resisted their use except in times of real food scarcity. Second, some poorer households included Indian women whose familiarity with and lack of scorn for these resources would have led them to more readily exploit wild plant foods than would a person of Spanish heritage.

To summarize the above discussion as it pertains to the consumption of plant and animal foods, the following sketch can be drawn. The more well-to-do households probably consumed the greatest quantity and variety of imported and luxury foods. They may have used the greatest diversity of plant foods but the lowest diversity of wild plant foods. When all foodstuffs are considered together, it is anticipated that the higher ranking households will show the greatest diversity of foods (both domestic and wild). The middle range may exhibit the lowest overall diversity and emphasize domestic over wild resources. Such households may have focused on locally raised domestic plant and animal resources, since they would have had limited access to imported luxury foodstuffs. They may have restricted their use of wild plant foods because of their low esteem for such resources. The lowest ranking households might show a high diversity of wild resources but would be expected to use a limited range of domestic foods. The poor probably had the least access to imported plant foods and may have had no access to luxury foods. Most domestic animals and plants they consumed would have been locally produced and they may have used the greatest quantity and variety of wild plant and animal resources.

Documents from the sixteenth century do not identify status and ethnic affiliations for occupants of the households which have been excavated. Thus, it is not possible to follow Cumbaa's example and test these predictions with data from sites for which the occupants' ethnic and social statuses are known. However, work on eighteenth-century sites has also shown that there are other material correlates of social status which can be found in the archaeological record (Deagan 1975; Cumbaa 1975; Beidleman 1976; Honerkamp 1982; Honerkamp and Reitz 1983; Reitz and Honerkamp 1983). Using the material culture patterns from eighteenth-century St. Augustine as a starting point, Deagan (1985) has had some success in defining material correlates of social status for the sixteenth century. This has allowed her to estimate the social status of four of the sixteenth-century households which have been excavated. Deagan's work suggests that continuing research on the sixteenth-century community will make it possible to deal more adequately with social status and its effects on food consumption.

ACCULTURATION AND ADAPTATION

In colonial situations, it is sometimes difficult to distinguish between the effects of acculturative and adaptive processes. In Spanish Florida, acculturation can be seen in the rapidity with which Native American subsistence items and techniques were incorporated into the settlers' subsistence system. However, many aspects of the new strategy might have developed even in the absence of the models provided by the aboriginal populations. Evidence for this is seen in the similarity of foodways adopted by British and American settlers in this area centuries after the native populations had been disrupted and dispersed (Reitz and Honerkamp 1983; Reitz 1984).

Since raising most Iberian resources in Florida

was not productive, the Spanish settlers had to alter their husbandry techniques to incorporate foods which could be raised in the coastal setting. In the absence of sophisticated ecological knowledge, a period of adjustment and experimentation ensued. Such periods are to be expected when people immigrate to new environments and, in fact, the stages of adjustment have been broadly predicted. According to Bökönyi (1975:4) when people arrive in a new environment, they will try to maintain their original husbandry system under the changed circumstances. They will do this even if it is unproductive, making up losses by increased use of wild foods before incorporating different domestic resources.

At the same time that the colonists were faced with the loss of many traditional resources, they had a good example of a successful strategy close at hand. They lived among aboriginal populations whose subsistence economies were based on a set of cultivated plants adapted to the climate and soils of the area and a complex of wild species easily acquired from nearby habitats. Spaniards purchased or commandeered some foods from their neighbors, and their own subsistence activities were patterned to some extent on the examples offered by their neighbors. Given that *mestizaje* began almost immediately (Deagan 1973), it is also probable that some of the Spanish deposits include foods that were collected and prepared by native women.

Evidence from the sixteenth-century Spanish settlements in Florida attests to a period of experimentation. From the start, though the colonists tried to raise familiar crops dear to their hearts, such as wheat and grapes, they also planted crops that will grow on the coastal plain: maize, beans, and squash. Initial shipments of livestock to the fledgling colonies included animals in proportion to their importance in the Iberian economy. However, the differential abilities of the livestock to adapt to the new environment were soon noted, and the proportions of animals shipped shifted accordingly. Menéndez Marqués said that he had shipped 311 goats, 1,304 hogs, 27 calves, 3,660 chickens, and 87 horses and mares to Florida between 1565 and 1571 (Lyon 1981:286). This is in sharp contrast to the 100 horses and mares, 200 calves, 400 swine, and 400 sheep with which Menéndez de Avilés originally agreed to supply the colony (Solís de Merás 1923:262) and indicates the rapidity with which the new strategy was developed.

Spanish efforts to adapt their diet to the conditions of the new environment conform in part to Bökönyi's (1975:4) predictions. The exploitation of faunal resources fits the suggested pattern. That is, there was an initial attempt to maintain the traditional primacy of mutton over other domestic meats. When this failed, the gap was filled by consuming wild species, especially marine fishes, before pork and beef supplanted mutton as major protein sources.

Bökönyi's model was constructed to explain changes that occurred in faunal exploitation when a population with an established animal husbandry tradition moved to a region to which their livestock were not adapted and where there were no alternative domesticated animals. The case might well be different with plants, if the move was to an area where local domesticated plants were available. In such circumstances one might predict that gaps caused by failures in familiar crops would be filled by adopting the local crops rather than wild plant resources. This seems to be what transpired in Spanish Florida. Wild plants are not abundant in the samples, suggesting they were not intensively utilized. Instead, the colonists seem to have rapidly substituted the indigenous crops for their traditional ones.

Several factors probably affected the speed with which this substitution occurred. First, previous experience in other New World colonies may have led the settlers to be less hopeful and more knowledgable about the chances of successfully raising Old World grains in Florida. Second, while the indigenous cultigens were different varieties or species from those grown elsewhere in the New World Spanish empire, they were nonetheless familiar to some of the colonists and may therefore have been more readily adopted. Third, the indigenous cultigens could be obtained from the local aboriginals and were, thus, in some sense equivalent to wild resources. Finally, once the indigenous cultigens were adopted they were retained in preference to Old World ones because they were more suited to the growing conditions found on the coast.

The subsistence economy that emerged at St. Augustine reflected a pattern of fusion of the various elements available to the colonists. The biological data from the sixteenth-century community indicate that the use of both plants and animals was eclectic. The colonists retained the use of Old World livestock, though the importance of the various animals was significantly altered. They raised some Old World cultigens, but these were largely fruits and vegetables which served to supplement a diet based on New World cultigens. The distinctive aspect of Spanish subsistence, however, was the extensive use of local plants and animals. In many respects the Spanish strategy was largely an aboriginal one with the addition of those European and Caribbean domestic resources which could survive and prosper in the non-Iberian, non-Caribbean Florida environment. Of the fauna identified, 85% of the individuals and 59% of the biomass were from wild species, especially deer, sharks, sea catfishes, drums, and mullet. Though the proportionate use of local floral resources cannot be quantified, it seems clear that the indigenous cultigens, maize, beans, and squash, were the staple plant foods in the colonists' diet.

While the subsistence system was molded in part by the ecological conditions, it was also shaped by interactions between Spaniards and aboriginals. Typical of soldiers in those times, the Spanish settlers relied heavily upon the local aboriginal population for food (Laudonnière 1975:133-134; Diego de Velasco to the King, Havana, Jan. 20, 1577, AGI, *Santo Domingo* 124 In Conner 1930:4/5; Lanning 1935:143; Lyon 1976:140, 1977:23). Indians brought foodstuffs to St. Augustine and Santa Elena or the soldiers went out and commandeered it. The Indians raised some European livestock (Lanning 1935:77), but the large part of the contributed foodstuffs was typical aboriginal fare, primarily fish and maize. The Indians also supplied some wild plant foods, generally fruits and nuts (Solís de Merás 1923:125).

The Spanish and native populations not only shared foods but also employed similar technologies for the acquisition of those foods. Both populations used weirs and nets in their fishing activities (Laudonnière 1975:20; García 1902:202). Consequently, the fish that are found in the Spanish and aboriginal archaeological collections are those species most amenable to mass capture in the estuarine setting. There are no pelagic species, such as were used in Spain in the 1500s, nor are there reef or offshore fishes, such as those used in the Caribbean, although equivalents of both could have been obtained a few miles off the Florida coast, had the Spaniards been willing to expend the effort. Both populations also employed similar practices of field cultivation, using the aboriginally devised techniques appropriate to the indigenous cultigens. The employment of such parallel technologies makes it difficult, if not impossible, to distinguish archaeologically foods procured from the Indians from those acquired using shared techniques. Whatever the case, the role Native Americans played in supplying the towns or in teaching Europeans appropriate subsistence techniques was probably significant in forming new Spanish food patterns during the initial years of European settlement.

It is important to note that although much of the new subsistence system had an aboriginal flavor, it remained distinctly Spanish in many ways. Foremost, of course, was the retention and use of introduced plants and animals, some of which were even transferred to the Indians. Secondly, the slaughter house, the market place, and, possibly, kitchen gardens were characteristically Spanish institutions. Lastly, while the *situado* was an undependable source of provisions, it did serve to interject Iberian, Caribbean, and Mexican items into the colonial diet.

ECOLOGICAL PRINCIPLES

It has been postulated that human populations attempt to follow a subsistence strategy that provides a good return for a minimal effort. While it may occasionally be desirable to shift to a maximizing strategy, taking advantage of seasonal windfalls, the basic desire is to provide steady, reliable sources of food without working too hard. Energetically, it is necessary to expend no more calories in acquiring food than are supplied by the food. In fact, a surplus of calories must be generated by subsistence efforts to support other activities. One subsistence cost is travel to and from the food source. This cost can be reduced by site location and primary exploitation of nearby resources. Technology offers another way to reduce costs. By using devices which require little effort to make or use, it is possible to reduce caloric expenditures. If a device which is costly to make provides a remarkable catch, then the cost is ameliorated. If these devices also capture large quantities of foodstuffs, then their energetic value is enhanced.

The Native American strategy on the Georgia and Florida coasts was to use the nearest possible habitats (Reitz 1985). Estuarine fishes procured using mass capture devices, such as nets and weirs, formed a major portion of the diet and were supplemented by the consumption of nocturnal mammals which could be trapped rather than hunted. Even deer, hunted when they were attracted to agricultural fields, would not have been costly to obtain, although the caloric expenditures might have been greater than those required for fishing. It is unfortunate that data on coastal plant use are not abundant; however, what evidence is available indicates that along with cultivated crops grown in fields near the settlements, locally abundant nuts, fruits, and tubers were gathered.

Given the energetic considerations, the native populations' examples, the available resources, and the supply line difficulties faced by Spaniards in Florida, it is logical that the new dietary complex assumed the form seen in the archaeological and historical record. Because of the use of such devices as nets and weirs—known but not extensively used in Iberia—and the exploitation of the rich estuarine environment, the faunal consumption pattern has an aboriginal flavor modified only to the extent that European livestock were retained in the diet. The employment of these techniques would have produced this effect whether or not the Spaniards were in contact with the native population. The livestock most heavily exploited were not the customary sheep and goats, but rather cattle and hogs, animals better able to fend for themselves and endure on the sub-tropical coastal plain. By emphasizing these hardy, resourceful animals, the colonists reduced the energy they had to expend on husbandry activities. The plant use pattern also reflects energetic and environmental factors. The colonists' subsistence efforts focused on those domestic species which grew best in the sandy soil and hot, humid climate of Florida. Those wild plants which were exploited could all be found in abundance near the settlements. The Native Americans' presence and their role as provisioners for the earliest colonists undoubtedly reinforced the natural direction of the Spanish adaptation and increased its pace. However, the settlers would have been hard pressed to devise any other strategy that would have succeeded in the coastal environment at that time.

DIRECTIONS FOR FUTURE RESEARCH

While much new and interesting information has been assembled on sixteenth-century Spanish subsistence practices in Florida, far more work remains to be done. The research has raised as many questions as it has answered, and many of the apparent trends need to be explored in greater depth. The data base for the sixteenth-century is still small. There is a need not only to expand this base but to add to it data on the subsistence practices of the Indians living in the villages around the settlements and data on the succeeding centuries. These data are needed not only for Indians but also for other ethnic groups, such as blacks living at Fort Moosa, just north of St. Augustine. The floral data base particularly requires expansion, but redundancy could be used in the faunal data as well.

Another direction which needs to be followed is the testing of ideas and hypotheses generated from the Spanish data against data from other colonial and frontier sites. While there has been some interest in historic subsistence information, this is still largely an untapped field. Historical archaeologists are urged to include subsistence studies in their future research designs, following the guidelines offered in the second chapter. While Spanish Florida may be an extreme example, it demonstrates that it is not valid to assume that in the New World Europeans, of whatever national origin, retained their former subsistence strategies. It appears that the new strategies which developed did so following principles which can be made explicit and tested. Only through additional research can the processes involved in colonial adaptations be more thoroughly defined. Only then can it be really known which foods consumed were truly scum and vermin, and for whom.

CONCLUSION

The initial starving time was a period of adjustment for the Spanish settlers in Florida. The 70 years of New World experience before the colonization of Florida may have provided some preparation for the Florida venture, but it was insufficient. The social and natural environments of Florida were not duplicates of either Iberia or the Caribbean Islands. Livestock, crops, and strategies had to be modified yet again. In developing new strategies, the colonists changed their subsistence economy in the following ways: 1) they abandoned traditional resources unsuited to the new environment; 2) they adopted a new constellation of domestic plant resources, the focus of which was the indigenous trinity of maize, beans, and squash;

3) they incorporated aboriginal patterns of wild fauna exploitation; 4) they retained Old World cultigens, primarily fruits, which could be grown locally; 5) they husbanded those Old World domestic animals which could survive with limited attention in humid, forested conditions; 6) they added a few exotic New World cultigens to the locally grown plants; and 7) they relied to a limited extent on imported foodstuffs, especially for luxury items. These modifications were patterned; they are visible not only in the archaeological record at St. Augustine and Santa Elena, but also in the smaller collection from Baptizing Spring. The changes reflect adaptation and acculturation of the Spanish subsistence practices. The new strategies were energy efficient, emphasizing nearby abundant resources which could be attained with a minimum of effort. Variations within this overall theme were apparently correlated with socioeconomic status and ethnic affiliation. This strategy was established during the first 40 years of the colony. Once a balance was achieved, it remained virtually unchanged for the next 200 years.

The data from St. Augustine and Santa Elena provide evidence of the far-reaching changes that transpired on the coastal plain. The conditions that stimulated the colonists to alter their foodways were not unique. The Spaniards developed solutions to their subsistence problems following criteria which would have been applicable in other settings. The reasons for the changes, and the directions they took, go beyond sixteenth-century Spanish Florida. It is anticipated that evidence for changes similar to those found in the Spanish colonies can be found for other colonial groups.

ELIZABETH J. REITZ

The Spanish Colonial Experience and Domestic Animals

ABSTRACT

European colonial efforts were most successful where the plants and animals they brought with them were most successful. This statement makes it appear that European domestic plants and animals either made it or did not. In fact, European animals went through a period of adaptation to their new situations. These in turn influenced the adjustments humans were making to the colonial experience. Examples of the range of animal and European adaptations are taken from 16th-century Spanish colonial efforts on Hispaniola, Cubagua, and Spanish Florida. These examples show that European animals were present in every case, but the suite of animals used and their role in the human diet varied considerably.

Introduction

The impact of Old World animal introductions on native New World fauna is well-known. As Alfred Crosby has demonstrated, many native plants and animals were rapidly replaced by introduced species (Harris 1965; Crosby 1972, 1986; Olson 1982). What is less well-known is the impact of the colonial encounter on domestic animals introduced by colonists. It is often forgotten that domestic animals were not passively transported to new worlds. As biological organisms, they too were colonists faced with adapting to new environmental conditions. The animals brought from Iberia or the Canary Islands to Hispaniola and elsewhere in the New World flourished or languished in their new setting depending on the extent to which their biological requirements were met in the environment to which they were transported. The original animal colonists were adapted to Old World conditions. Success in these areas of origin was in part a reflection of the degree to which the environment satisfied their biological require-

ments. As colonists, domestic animals had to adapt to environmental conditions which might be substantially different from those back home.

The adaptive response of these animals to new environmental conditions was an important factor in subsistence decisions made by human colonists. The success of their animals' adaptations influenced the adjustments Spaniards made to colonial life. Archaeological data provide one of the few avenues through which this aspect of the colonial encounter can be seen. Examples of the range of animal and European adaptations are taken from 16th-century Spanish colonial efforts on Hispaniola, Cubagua, and in Spanish Florida. These examples show that European animals were present in every case, but the suite of animals used and their role in the human diet varied considerably.

The evidence has been assembled using zooarchaeological methods. Animal bones excavated from archaeological settings were compared to modern skeletons in order to identify the taxa recovered from each site. Quantification of the results of these identifications provides an estimate of the relative abundances of animals present at the site. The most standard quantification is an estimate of the Minimum Number of Individuals (MNI) in an assemblage. MNI is estimated by considering the evidence for symmetry, age, and sex for each species identified and calculating the number of individuals necessary to explain the elements identified. The percentage of one group of taxa may then be compared to other taxa in the sample. While there are many factors which can bias the results of this research (Wing and Brown 1979; Grayson 1984), zooarchaeological analysis provides insights into human/animal relationships not found in other ways.

Domestic Animals

Based on archaeological evidence, the primary domestic animals in the New World were cattle, pigs, sheep, goats, and chickens. Of all the Old World domestic mammals transported to the New World, sheep would have been the most difficult to relocate. Sheep (*Ovis aries*) are very sensitive to

TABLE 1
CLIMATIC DATA

Category	Sevilla, Spain	Las Palmas, C.I.	Limonade, Haiti	St. Augustine, FL
Average Temperature	18.8°C		24.8°C	21.2°C
Minimum Mean Daily Temperature	10.5°C (Jan.)	14.4°C (Jan.)	18.8°C (Dec.)	14.3°C (Jan.)
Maximum Mean Daily Temperature	27.8°C (Aug.)	26.1°C (Oct.)	30.8°C (Aug.)	27.3°C (Aug.)
Average Rainfall	534.9 mm	218.4 mm	1399.6 mm	1330.5 mm
Minimum Mean Rainfall	1.0 mm (July)	0 (June–Aug.)	74.0 mm (July)	59.7 mm (Jan.)
Maximum Mean Rainfall	84.0 mm (Dec.)	53.3 mm (Nov.)	257.8 mm (Nov.)	197.4 mm (Sept.)

Note. Data from Bradley 1978; Linés Escardó 1970; OAS 1972; Ruffner and Bair 1977.

heat, humidity, and changes in familiar surroundings. Male sheep are sterile for about a year after being transferred from temperate to tropical settings, and do not breed well thereafter (Williamson and Payne 1978:19). Predators are a problem with sheep, as are epidemics, which spread more rapidly among sheep than in cattle herds (Dahl and Hjort 1976:234). Cattle are also sensitive to environmental stimuli, which influence weight, age at first parturition, frequency of births, and length of pregnancy. However, cattle are less subject to stress caused by high heat and humidity, and are less vulnerable to epidemics and predators (Dahl and Hjort 1976:234). Where diseases are under control, a cattle herd can double in four to six years (Dahl and Hjort 1976:69).

Environmental Variables

It is difficult to summarize the environments from which these domestic mammals would have been transported to the New World since they may have come either from the Iberian peninsula or the Canary Islands. The Iberian peninsula is a diverse geographical area but since all shipping to the Indies was supposed to originate from Seville (Lyon 1976) it is likely that most of the livestock came from the southern Spanish province of Andalucia (Lowery 1959[1905]:106; Foster 1960:31; Rouse 1977:18). The Andalucian climate is Mediterranean with dry summers and humid winters (Landsberg et al. 1965; Linés Escardó 1970). Animals raised there would be adapted to a warm, dry cli-

mate with several months of no rainfall (Table 1). It is more likely that many first colonizing mammals were adapted to the climate of the Canary Islands. The conditions to which livestock had to adapt in the Canary Islands were somewhat more arid than those in Andalucia (Ruffner and Bair 1977; Table 1).

Many of the earliest domestic animals were transported to Hispaniola. On Hispaniola rainfall is abundant, with two wet seasons. During the two dry seasons rainfall abates but does not cease. Temperatures such as those at Limonade, in Haiti, are tropical (Organization of American States [OAS] 1972; Table 1). An important feature of Hispaniola which contrasts sharply with Spain is the depauperate, or impoverished, fauna on the island. The primary mammals were rodents such as hutia, quemi, mohuy, and a mute dog. There were no native ruminants such as deer which could serve as vectors for disease or competitors for food, nor were there non-human predators. The pre-Columbian absence of ruminants was a common phenomenon on the Caribbean islands (Woodring et al. 1924:259; Williamson 1981). Even today, Caribbean islands are notable for their relatively low incidence of cattle diseases and limited parasites, which contrasts sharply with the rest of tropical America (Williamson and Payne 1978: 329).

From Hispaniola, Spanish colonists quickly spread to the rest of the Americas, taking their domestic animals with them. One of the early colonies from which faunal remains are available was on the island of Cubagua, a small, excessively well

TABLE 2
PUERTO REAL: SUMMARY CATEGORIES, MNI

Category	Locus 19		Locus 33/35		Locus 39		Total	
	MNI	%	MNI	%	MNI	%	MNI	%
Old World Domestic Mammals	27	35.5	36	28.6	50	86.2	113	43.5
Old World Domestic Birds	7	9.2	6	4.8	2	3.5	15	5.8
Native Wild Birds	1	1.3			1	1.7	2	0.8
Pond Turtles	16	21.1	66	52.4	1	1.7	83	31.9
Local Marine Animals					2	3.5	2	0.8
Fishes	23	30.3	12	9.5	1	1.7	36	13.8
Commensal Animals	2	2.6	6	4.8	1	1.7	9	3.5
Total	76	100.0	126	100.1	58	100.0	260	100.1

drained island located off the coast of Venezuela. Vegetation is scarce and xerophytic. Native fauna are rare, although neighboring islands and the nearby South American mainland do sustain deer.

Another of the early colonies was Spanish Florida. Here the climate is permanently humid, with warm winters (Mehta and Jones 1977; Bradley 1978). Most precipitation falls in July and September with spring and fall dry spells (Table 1). The two towns in this colony were on low-lying, poorly drained soils overlooking Atlantic coast estuaries. Unlike the Caribbean islands, vertebrate fauna are abundant on the coastal plain. Mammals include carnivores and deer (*Odocoileus virginianus*). Carnivores would have posed a significant problem to introduced herds, especially sheep. The presence of deer raises the possibility that there may have been diseases present which could quickly infect introduced mammals. Today, mineral deficiencies, screwworm, and fever tick are major problems for Florida cattle (Rouse 1973:371).

The Zooarchaeological Evidence

The archaeological evidence suggests that the abundance of domestic mammals in faunal assemblages correlates with the environmental setting of the colony. The first of the Caribbean islands to be colonized by Europeans was Hispaniola. The town of Puerto Real was founded on the north coast of the island between 1502 and 1504. It was abandoned in the 1580s as part of Spain's effort to curtail illegal trading. Although there was some mining near Puerto Real, its main value lay in its port, through which were shipped slaves, hides, and tallow (Sauer 1969:154, 159). Zooarchaeological analysis of animal bones from three 16th-century households at Puerto Real have provided an interesting contrast (Fairbanks and Marrinan 1982; Willis 1982; McEwan 1983; Reitz 1986; Reitz and McEwan 1989; Ewen 1991). Loci 19 and 33/35 were probably high-status residential units and Locus 39 a lower-status residence with perhaps a commercial overlay. Domestic mammals contributed 43 percent of the individuals and 93 percent of the biomass from these loci (Tables 2, 3). Wild noncommensal animals contributed 47 percent of the individuals identified. Commensal animals are those which are commonly found in association with humans but which may or may not have been eaten. Pets are one class of commensal animal. One of the important aspects of this collection is the presence of turkey, indicating that Spaniards quickly adopted one of the few domestic animals offered by the New World. Turkeys would not have been found on the island of Hispaniola, and were probably brought to the island from one of the mainland Spanish colonies. Sea turtles and pond turtles contributed 32 percent of the individuals. Identified fishes were typical Caribbean reef fauna, most of which could have been captured in the near-shore waters. Among the domestic animals identified so far, 45 were pigs, 62 cows, and 6 caprines (Table 4).

TABLE 3
PUERTO REAL: SUMMARY CATEGORIES, BIOMASS, KG

Category	Locus 19		Locus 33/35		Locus 39		Total	
	Biomass	%	Biomass	%	Biomass	%	Biomass	%
Old World Domestic Mammals	163.681	94.6	97.103	75.8	390.29	98.4	651.074	93.3
Old World Domestic Birds	1.132	0.7	0.724	0.6	0.06	0.02	1.916	0.3
Native Wild Birds	0.015	0.01			0.003	tr	0.018	tr
Pond Turtles	7.123	4.1	22.856	17.9	0.66	0.2	30.639	4.4
Local Marine Animals					5.5	1.4	5.5	0.8
Fishes	1.091	0.6	1.093	0.9	0.04	0.01	2.224	0.3
Commensal Animals	0.0244	0.01	6.292	4.9	0.01	tr	6.3264	0.9
Total	173.0664	100.02	128.068	100.1	396.563	100.03	697.6974	100.0

Both zooarchaeological data and historical records indicate that cattle were large and abundant on Hispaniola. Fernandez de Oviedo y Valdéz (1959:79) reported that Hispaniolan cattle were larger and more handsome than cattle in Spain, which he attributed to good pasture, clear water, and temperate climate. If one is to believe Oviedo, many cattle owners had more than 1,000 to 2,000 head, and there were some herds with 3,000 to 4,000 head just a few years after colonization began. Measurements of archaeological cattle bones from Puerto Real suggest that these early New World domesticated colonists were quite large. Some measurements fall within the range of aurochs, the large wild progenitor of domestic cattle (Table 5). In Table 5, the domestic cattle (*Bos taurus*) measurements include early domestic data from Denmark (Degerbol and Fredskild 1970), Iran (Ducos 1968; Hole et al. 1969), and Iraq (Hole et al. 1969) as well as measurements from Neolithic through 18th-century England (Jewell 1963; Maltby 1979).

Stephen Cumbaa's (1975:61–66) analysis of vertebrate fauna from the Convento de San Francisco in Santo Domingo, on the southern coast of Hispaniola, provides data which contrast with those from Puerto Real. The Convento fauna summarized here are associated with a monastery and were deposited during the early 16th century (Goggin 1968). Cumbaa found that 56 percent of the individuals were domestic mammals (Table 6). Turkey was also identified from the Convento de

TABLE 4
SUMMARY OF SELECTED TAXA

Assemblage	Pig		Cow		Caprine	
	MNI	%	MNI	%	MNI	%
Locus 19	14	18.4	11	14.5	2	2.6
Loci 33/35	24	19.0	10	7.9	2	1.6
Locus 39	7	12.1	41	70.6	2	3.5
Puerto Real combined	45	17.3	62	23.8	6	2.3
Convento	4	11.8	4	11.8	11	32.4
Nueva Cádiz	12	5.9	1	0.5	4	2.0
Spanish Florida	68	4.0	17	1.0	1	0.1

Note. Data in the percentage columns are for the individual collections. For example, 18.4% of the individuals from Locus 19 are pigs.

San Francisco. Another 32 percent of the individuals were wild, non-commensal fauna. These were primarily fishes, but also included sea turtles and manatee. The fishes were typical Caribbean reef fauna, most of which could have been captured in the near-shore waters. Sheep or goats comprised 32 percent of the individuals (Table 4).

A third vertebrate fauna from the Caribbean was studied by Elizabeth S. Wing (1961; Cumbaa 1975). Nueva Cádiz was a 16th-century Spanish community on Cubagua Island, just off the coast of Venezuela. The town was primarily a pearl oyster fishing center (Rouse and Cruxent 1963:134; Goggin 1968:42). Cubagua Island had limited resources. Many animal foods and probably most

TABLE 5
MEASUREMENTS OF CATTLE BONES, IN MM

| Element | Dimension | Bos taurus | | | B. primigenius | References |
		Puerto Real	Sp. Florida	Old World	Old World	
Scapula	BG		45.0	40.0–63.0	58.0– 77.0	1
Humerus	Bd	77.5–94.5		47.0–98.3	70.0–116.0	1,4,5,6
Radius	Bp	79.6–87.7		66.0–80.6	91.0–122	1,6
Tibia	Bd	66.0–72.6		48.6–76.0	68.0– 93.0	1,6
Calcaneus	GL	148.0–170.0		138.0–158.0	162.0–192.0	1
Astragalus	Bd	41.3–54.2		46.0–49.0	42.0– 63.0	1
	GLl	67.6–89.6		57.0–78.2	73.2– 97.0	1,2,3,4,5,6

Note. Dimensions follow those of Driesch (1976). References: 1. Degerbol and Fredskild 1970; 2. Ducos 1968:298; 3. Grigson 1969:286; 4. Hole et al. 1969:305; 5. Jewell 1963:84; 6. Maltby 1979:164–166.

TABLE 6
SUMMARY OF FAUNA FROM CONVENTO DE SAN FRANCISCO AND NUEVA CÁDIZ

| Category | Convento | | Nueva Cádiz | |
	MNI	%	MNI	%
Domestic Mammals	19	55.9	17	8.3
Domestic Birds	3	8.8	18	8.8
Wild Mammals	1	2.9	28	13.7
Wild Birds			9	4.4
Turtles	3	8.8	17	8.3
Sharks and Fishes	7	20.6	104	51.0
Commensal Taxa	1	2.9	11	5.4
Total	34	99.9	204	99.9

Note. Data from Cumbaa 1975; Wing 1961.

plant foods were imported from the better-endowed Margarita Island. At Nueva Cádiz about 8 percent of the individuals were domestic mammals (Table 6). Heavy use was made of marine species, 80 percent of which were from the inshore-estuarine area. Sea turtles probably contributed 40 percent of the meat diet. Interestingly, a muscovy duck in the collection indicates that use was quickly made of another native domestic animal. Pigs were the most intensively used of the European domestic livestock (Table 4).

These three examples from the Caribbean basin indicate that the colonial experience was highly varied for Spanish domestic mammals. A fourth example confirms this interpretation. Vertebrate samples from 16th-century Spanish Florida archaeological sites (Deagan 1979) contrast sharply with those from Hispaniola. Wild non-commensal animals, particularly fish, contributed 85 percent of the individuals identified (Table 7). Out of an estimated 1,714 identified vertebrate individuals, there are only 68 pigs, 17 cows, and 1 sheep or goat (Reitz and Scarry 1985:66). Cattle remains are not only rare, but the individuals represented were quite small, falling at the low end of a range formed by Old World pre-modern cattle (Table 5).

Discussion

Even though these archaeological collections all represent 16th-century Spanish colonial economies, the role of domestic mammals was clearly different at the four towns. This variation probably correlates with the local environment and the ability of livestock to adapt. Hispaniola, especially around Puerto Real, offered a congenial setting for cattle. At first there were no indigenous diseases, no ruminant competitors, and no predators except humans. The soils were fertile and savannah grasses extensive. The climate was mild and the growing season long. Cattle quickly became abundant and exceptionally large with minimal care. Hogs also did well. Spanish colonists at Puerto Real consumed beef and pork, ignoring almost all other resources. They also quickly developed an

TABLE 7
SUMMARY OF FAUNA FROM SPANISH FLORIDA

Category	MNI	%	Biomass, kg	%
Domestic Mammals	86	5.0	80.44	36.7
Domestic Birds	86	5.0	7.221	3.3
Wild Mammals	110	6.4	50.425	23.0
Wild Birds	110	6.4	5.115	2.3
Turtles	96	5.6	13.197	6.0
Sharks and Fishes	1142	66.6	61.31	28.0
Commensal Taxa	84	4.9	1.5021	0.7
Total	1714	99.9	219.2101	100.0

Note. Data from Reitz and Scarry 1985.

extensive commerce based on cattle products. Sheep, on the other hand, became a minor resource. Heat and humidity stress, as well as reduced fecundity, resulted in sheep being an unsuccessful animal-colonist. The sheep at Convento de San Francisco probably demonstrate that they were a rare and prized commodity which only people in privileged positions in large urban centers could enjoy.

At Nueva Cádiz and in Spanish Florida the environment was difficult for sheep, cattle, and hogs. The presence of pre-Columbian deer on Cubagua and in Spanish Florida suggests that some ruminant diseases could have been present when European livestock were introduced. At Nueva Cádiz pigs probably survived by foraging in human trash, but the other livestock did poorly. In Spanish Florida livestock not only had to deal with diseases, but also with high humidity, local competition for food, and predators. The soils were leached, low in fertility, acidic, and poorly drained, so graze was less nutritious. All of the domestic mammals did poorly. At Nueva Cádiz and in Spanish Florida cattle and pigs replaced caprines just as they did at Puerto Real but not to the same extent. In place of these domestic mammals, locally abundant wild resources—particularly turtles and fishes—were important in colonial subsistence.

The consequences of the colonial experience of domestic mammals correlates with the success of the colony itself. Hispaniola, where cattle did well, enjoyed an early, active commerce in hides and other cattle products. At Nueva Cádiz domestic livestock of all types apparently never adapted, and there were few local substitutes available. The colony was abandoned in 1545. Spanish Florida, where domestic livestock endured but did not flourish, remained a Spanish colony for 300 years, but experienced a steady loss of territory throughout that time. Ironically, by the late 17th century British colonists newly arrived in North America stole Spanish Florida cattle because the Spanish *criollo* was bigger and more hardy than the newly introduced British cattle (Hann 1986:200).

For a colony to survive depends in part on the ability of its members to obtain food under local conditions, which requires a great deal of adaptability. A colony could not survive if some part of its domestic animal/plant complex did not do so, in spite of political or economic factors operating in a larger sphere. Some colonial adaptations made by Spaniards were more likely to provide an energy base sufficient to support long-term success in the larger economic sphere than others. Spaniards adapted at all four locations, but only at one of these was the adaptation sufficient to permit the colony to be an active player in Caribbean or global affairs.

Conclusion

The zooarchaeological data from these 16th-century Spanish sites provide a new perspective on the colonial experience, suggesting the extent to which the character of a colonial venture depended upon the ability of domestic animals to adapt quickly. Comparing zooarchaeological data from 16th-century Spanish sites offers a new perspective on the colonial experience and domestic animals. These examples suggest that it would be useful to rethink the role of domestic animals in the human colonial experience, looking for other ways in which environmental conditions influenced the style and success of the colonial effort.

ACKNOWLEDGMENTS

I wish to thank the late Charles H. Fairbanks and Kathleen A. Deagan for the opportunity to examine the vertebrate remains from Puerto Real. I am also grateful to Charles R. Ewen and Bonnie G. McEwan for permitting access to their zooarchaeological data from Puerto Real. I appreciate the assistance of Elizabeth S. Wing and the staff of the Florida Museum of Natural History. Charles H. Wood, David W. Hall, Timothy A. Olsen, Lee McDowell, Lawrence D. Harris, Lewis Yarlett, Victor W. Carlisle, and Rochelle Marrinan provided invaluable information. Excavations at Puerto Real were funded by the Florida Museum of Natural History. An earlier version of this paper was presented at the annual meeting of the Society for Historical Archaeology Conference on Historical and Underwater Archaeology, Baltimore, Maryland.

REFERENCES

BRADLEY, JAMES T.
1978 Climates of the States: Florida. In *Climates of the States*, edited by J. A. Ruffner, pp. 211–242. Gale Research, Detroit, Michigan.

CROSBY, ALFRED W.
1972 *The Columbian Exchange*. Greenwood Press, Westport, Connecticut.
1986 *Ecological Imperialism: The Biological Expansion of Europe, 900–1900*. Cambridge University Press, New York.

CUMBAA, STEPHEN L.
1975 *Patterns of Resource Use and Cross-Cultural Dietary Change in the Spanish Colonial Period*. Ph.D. dissertion, Department of Anthropology, University of Florida, Gainesville. University Microfilms, Ann Arbor.

DAHL, GUDRUN, AND ANDERS HJORT
1976 Having Herds: Pastoral Herd Growth and Household Economy. *Stockholm Studies in Social Anthropology* No. 2. Stockholm.

DEAGAN, KATHLEEN A.
1979 The Material Assemblage of 16th Century Spanish Florida. *Historical Archaeology* 12:25–50.

DEGERBOL, MAGNUS, AND BENT FREDSKILD
1970 The Urus (*Bos primigenius* Bojanus) and Neolithic Domesticated Cattle (*Bos taurus domesticus* Linne) in Denmark. *Det Kongelige Danske Videnskabernes Selskab, Biologiske Skrifter* 17(1):1–177. Copenhagen.

DRIESCH, ANGELA VON DEN
1976 A Guide to the Measurements of Animal Bones from Archaeological Sites. *Peabody Museum of Archaeology and Ethnology Bulletin* No. 1. Harvard University, Cambridge, Massachusetts.

DUCOS, PIERRE
1968 The Oriental Institute Excavations at Mureybit, Syria: Preliminary Report on the 1965 Campaign. Part 5, Les Restes de Bovides. *Journal of Near Eastern Studies* 27:295–301.

EWEN, CHARLES R.
1991 *From Spaniard to Creole: The Archaeology of Cultural Formation at Puerto Real, Haiti*. University of Alabama Press, University, Alabama.

FAIRBANKS, CHARLES H., AND ROCHELLE MARRINAN
1982 The Puerto Real Project, Haiti. *Journal of New World Archaeology* 5(2):67–72.

FOSTER, GEORGE M.
1960 *Culture and Conquest*. Quadrangle Books, Chicago.

GOGGIN, JOHN M.
1968 Spanish Majolica in the New World. *Yale University Publications in Anthropology* No. 72. New Haven, Connecticut.

GRAYSON, DONALD K.
1984 *Quantitative Zooarchaeology*. Academic Press, Orlando.

GRIGSON, CAROLINE
1969 The Uses and Limitations of Differences in Absolute Size in the Distinction Between the Bones of Aurochs (*Bos primigenius*) and Domestic Cattle (*Bos taurus*). In *The Domestication and Exploitation of Plants and Animals*, edited by P. J. Ucko and G. W. Dimbleby, pp. 277–294. Duckworth, London.

HANN, JOHN H.
1986 Translation of Alonso de Leturiondo's Memorial to the King of Spain [AGI 58-2-3]. *Florida Archaeology* 2:165–225.

HARRIS, DAVID R.
1965 Plants, Animals, and Man in the Outer Leeward Islands, West Indies. *University of California Publications in Geography* Vol. 18. Berkeley.

HOLE, FRANK, KENT V. FLANNERY, AND JAMES A. NEELY
1969 Prehistory and Human Ecology of the Deh Luran Plain. *Memoirs of the Museum of Anthropology, University of Michigan* No. 1. Ann Arbor.

JEWELL, PETER
1963 Cattle from Archaeological Sites. In Man and Cattle, edited by A. E. Mourant and F. E. Zeuner. *Royal Anthropological Institute Occasional Papers* No. 18: 80–101. London.

LANDSBURG, H. E., J. LIPPMAN, K. H. PAFFEN, AND C. TROLL
1965 *World Maps of Climatology*. Springer-Verlag, Berlin.

LINÉS ESCARDÓ, A.
1970   *World Survey of Climatology*. Vol. 5, *Climates of Northern and Western Europe*, edited by C. C. Wallen, pp. 195–239. Elsevier, Amsterdam.

LOWERY, WOODBURY
1959   *The Spanish Settlements within the Present Limits of the United States: Florida 1562–1568*. Two volumes. Reprint of 1905 edition. Russell and Russell, New York.

LYON, EUGENE
1976   *The Enterprise of Florida*. University Presses of Florida, Gainesville.

MALTBY, MARK
1979   The Animal Bones from Exeter, 1971–1975. *Exeter Archaeological Reports* No. 2. University of Sheffield, Sheffield.

McEWAN, BONNIE G.
1983   Spanish Colonial Adaptation on Hispaniola: The Archaeology of Area 35, Puerto Real. Unpublished M.A. thesis, Department of Anthropology, University of Florida, Gainesville.

MEHTA, A. J., AND C. P. JONES
1977   *Matanzas Inlet, Glossary of Inlets Report* No. 5. Florida Sea Grant Program Report No. 21. Gainesville, Florida.

OLSON, STORRS L.
1982   Biological Archaeology in the West Indies. *The Florida Anthropologist* 35(4):162–168.

ORGANIZATION OF AMERICAN STATES (OAS)
1972   *Haiti: Mission d'Assistance Technique Integrée*. Organization of American States, Washington, D.C.

OVIEDO Y VALDÉZ, GONZALO FERNANDEZ DE
1959   *Historia General y Natural de las Indias, I*. Edición y estudio preliminar de Juan Perez de Tudela Bueso. Ediciones Atlas, Madrid.

REITZ, ELIZABETH J.
1986   Vertebrate Fauna from Locus 39, Puerto Real, Haiti. *Journal of Field Archaeology* 13(3):317–328.

REITZ, ELIZABETH J., AND BONNIE G. MCEWAN
1989   Animals and the Spanish Diet at Puerto Real. In *Puerto Real: The Archaeology of a Sixteenth Century Townsite on Hispaniola*, edited by K. A. Deagan, in preparation.

REITZ, ELIZABETH J., AND C. MARGARET SCARRY
1985   Reconstructing Historic Subsistence with an Example from Sixteenth-Century Spanish Florida. *Special Publication Series* No. 3. Society for Historical Archaeology, California, Pennsylvania.

ROUSE, IRVING, AND JOSE CRUXENT
1963   *Venezuelan Archaeology*. Yale University Press, New Haven, Connecticut.

ROUSE, JOHN E.
1973   *World Cattle: Cattle of North America*, Vol. 3. University of Oklahoma Press, Norman.

1977   *The Criollo*. University of Oklahoma Press, Norman.

RUFFNER, JAMES A., AND FRANK E. BAIR (EDITORS)
1977   *The Weather Almanac*. Gale Research, Detroit, Michigan.

SAUER, CARL ORTWIN
1969   *The Early Spanish Main*. University of California Press, Berkeley.

WILLIAMSON, G., AND W. F. A. PAYNE
1978   *An Introduction to Animal Husbandry in the Tropics*. Longman, London.

WILLAMSON, MARK
1981   *Island Populations*. Oxford University Press, Oxford, England.

WILLIS, RAYMOND F.
1982   Project Puerto Real: Overview 1979 and 1980. Ms. on file, Florida State Museum, University of Florida, Gainesville.

WING, ELIZABETH S.
1961   Animal Remains Excavated at the Spanish Site of Nueva Cádiz on Cubagua Island, Venezuela. *Nieuwe West-Indische Gids* 2:162–165.

WING, ELIZABETH S., AND ANTOINETTE B. BROWN
1979   *Paleonutrition: Method and Theory in Prehistoric Foodways*. Academic Press, New York.

WOODRING, WENDALL P., J. S. BROWN, AND W. S. BURBANK
1924   *Geology of the Republic of Haiti*. Department of Public Works, Port-au-Prince, Haiti.

ELIZABETH J. REITZ
MUSEUM OF NATURAL HISTORY
UNIVERSITY OF GEORGIA
ATHENS, GEORGIA 30602

DONNA L. RUHL

Oranges and Wheat: Spanish Attempts at Agriculture in *La Florida*

Introduction

Historical archaeologists use archaeobotanical data from many perspectives. Primarily, plant remains are treated as subsistence items. Thus, patterns of food consumption have been analyzed to glean insights about class, ethnicity, and interactions between contacting cultures. Unlike other artifacts, plant remains are less often viewed as commodities. However, by analyzing plant remains as artifacts produced for exchange enables us to understand better the role plants played in local and global economies. Consideration of the late 16th- and 17th-century archaeobotanical record along with the historical record regarding imports and exports for *La Florida* can shed light on the impact of colonial plant commerce by Spanish entrepreneurs, Franciscan friars, and caciques in the hinterlands of Spanish Florida.

To date, the synthesis of the analyzed 16th-century remains reflects that both oranges and wheat were limited or absent from most Spanish Florida sites. Yet, these plants were among the earliest known specimens (i.e., seeds and orange saplings) shipped to the New World by Columbus and later exploratory and colonial efforts. Orange seeds are absent from the 16th-century archaeobotanical assemblages. Only occasional mention of these occurs in the next century; yet historical references to their presence and export increase (Harman 1969:12–22; Crosby 1972:68; Lyon 1977:23; Bushnell 1983:36; Waterbury 1983:82). By the 17th century the number of sites containing wheat grains increases as does the quantity of grains recovered (Reitz and Scarry 1985; Scarry 1986, 1987, 1992; Hann 1988; Scarry and Reitz 1990; Newsom and Quitmyer 1992; Ruhl 1993) (Table 1). This "pattern" stimulated questions concerning when

and why these two "Old World" plants became economically, politically, and ecclesiastically significant suggesting some middle-period patterns in *La Florida*. It also revealed how potentially dynamic plants can be, as their use and function may change through time. The recognition of the potentially dynamic nature of certain plants can also help guide archaeobotanical recovery strategies and interpretations.

Increasing Significance of Oranges and Wheat

Often, the uses of plants in the past are mistakenly equated with contemporary uses, which may cause misinterpretations as plants may undergo changes in their use and function through time and from region to region. Cultural and natural conditions impact their ability to grow, their abundance, and peoples' preferences for particular plants—all of which can affect plant use. In some instances, plants initially introduced into cultures in the Americas had medicinal or religious purposes, or both, and not necessarily culinary ones. This was true in *La Florida*, where medical supplies included herbs, spices, fruits, and even almonds (Lyon 1992). The change from a primarily medicinal or religious use to being a part of the daily diet may change the archaeological context in which a plant is found. Consequently, archaeological plant remains used for medicines may not be recovered with other plants because they may have been used, stored, and discarded in a different way or place. Change in use often encourages local production as the plant shifts from being solely an import to becoming a marketable export. It may also result in a shift in agrarian practices from a backyard tree to groves or from an individual plot of wheat to monocropped fields.

In Spanish Florida, oranges and wheat appear to have undergone such a transition during the mid- to late 17th century. During that time the Spaniards in *La Florida* began to shift from their earlier colonial ventures to establishing *haciendas*. The onset of orange and wheat commercial

TABLE 1
PALEOETHNOBOTANICAL EVIDENCE FOR THE 16TH- AND 17TH-CENTURY WHEAT

Site	Provenience	Wheat Count (Grains)	Time Period (Century)	Reference
Fountain of Youth (8SJ31)	well	1	16th	Scarry and Reitz 1990
Nombre de Dios (8SJ34)	unknown	1(?)[2]	16th	Ruhl 1995
Santa Elena (38BU162D)	fort	2	16th	Reitz and Scarry 1985
SCDG[1]-St. Catherines Island, GA	*iglesia* (church), *convento*	over 60,000 (analyzed to date)	16th/17th	Ruhl 1990, 1993, [1990-1997]
SCDG-Amelia Island, FL (8NA41)	*convento*	18	17th	Ruhl 1990, 1993, [1990-1997]
Fig Springs/ San Martin (8C01)	Native American domicile?	5	17th	Newsom and Quitmyer 1992; Ruhl [1990-1997]
Ayubale (8JE2)	*convento*?	43	17th	Scarry 1986
Aspalaga (8JE1)	*convento*?	149	17th	Scarry 1986
San Luis de Talimali (8LE4)	*convento*, council house, chief's house	100+ (analyzed to date)	17th	Scarry 1992

[1] SCDG = Santa Catalina de Guale. Mission was first established on St. Catherines Island, Georgia, and then moved south where it was reestablished in the 1680s.

[2] Preliminary fieldwork uncovered this tentatively identified grain (*cf. Triticum* sp.). Dates are not absolute at this time, and further research in this area is presently ongoing, as of January 1997.

crop production in *La Florida* is suggested to have been influenced by Spain's changing economic policies and practices.

Spain's Potential Impact on *La Florida*

By the 16th century the upland plateaus in Spain were deforested and cleared for grazing pastures to feed sheep and for timber for fuel and transportation (Braudel 1972). Wood was used "on a massive scale, . . .one is simply amazed at the vast quantities that must have travelled along the rivers of Europe" (Braudel 1972:178). The former pro-mesta practice had been enforced for centuries (Klein 1964:297–349; Vicens Vives 1967:303). Ferdinand and Isabella's attempts to establish a monopolistic stronghold on the European wool industry (Klein 1964; Vicens Vives 1967; Lynch 1984) resulted in policies that favored pastoral ventures and worked against arable agriculture. Poor foreign relationships with England further compounded Spain's economic problems.

During the 15th century, the Crown began to rely on its monetary gains from the easy and rapid returns on merino wool, which hindered investments in agricultural ventures. Continuing efforts by the local farmers to maintain orchards, grain fields, vineyards, ox pastures, and mowed fields seemed futile as prohibitive export taxes, fines for violation of pasturage laws, fixed rents, and other pro-mesta policies prevailed. Edict after edict was established to prevent the loss of any local pasturage that was integral to the migratory sheep industry. Severe famines of the 16th and 17th centuries are, in part, attributed to this agrarian shortsightedness: "From the beginning of the 16th century, Spain inevitably began to suffer a serious shortage of grain; in 1506, for the first time, the population had to be fed from large-scale imports of wheat and thereafter became increasingly dependent on foreign supplies"

(Lynch 1984:17). In turn, by the late 16th and early 17th centuries, this had an impact on New World agricultural endeavors (McAlister 1984:462).

The forested areas of Spain were further impacted by the New World silver fleets and the armadas. Wood for the construction of caravels and various supplies (e.g., casks, barrels, planks, wheels, etc.) were an additional factor impacting the limited natural resources of the forested regions of Spain.

By the 16th century Spain was importing not only wheat and other grains but also lumber from Flanders as well as carpenters to work the wood. Yet, although some were recognizing the devastation that was occurring and there were the occasional attempts at establishing forestry reforms (e.g., those edicts of 1518, 1548, and 1567), the local governments were too corrupt and embedded to shift easily from the Mesta policies and practices (Klein 1964:321; Vicens Vives 1967:307). The Hapsburgs' narrow-mindedness in favor of the wool industry and against the productivity of the land played a crucial hand in Castile's overall economic history and what was occurring in the Americas. The Old World pro-mesta policies and practices of Spain were complicated by external sociopolitical and religio-economic problems, as well as by internal conditions such as deforestation resulting from wood exploitation.

Spain's problems were further compounded by the eustatic climatic shifts of this period, which may have had an impact on New World agrarian enterprises. Grain shortages were exacerbated by the adverse climatic conditions of the late 16th and 17th centuries (LeRoy Ladurie 1971; Braudel 1972:574; Lamb 1984). Extended periods of winter floods and summer droughts were detrimental to plant growth and especially troublesome to wheat crops (e.g., Viceroy to the King, quoted in Braudel 1972:574). Wheat cannot tolerate flooded soils, though drought conditions can be equally devastating by scorching crops and preventing proper heading, which results in lower yields.

During the 16th and 17th centuries, Spain, like Portugal, was also attempting to retreat from its

basically unprofitable domestic venture (wheat) and supply itself and the New World with other commodities. With the wealth from the New World they were able to afford foreign grains. Olive oil and wine became more important as domestic commodities and foreign exports, causing the gradual transformation of agricultural fields of grain into orchards and vineyards (Braudel 1972:585–589). For example, by the late 1580s, Seville, Andalusia, and Cádiz became increasingly dependent on foreign grain supplies from Burgundy, Italy, Cracow, Hungary, and the Levant (Braudel 1972:576–604). Gradually, New World colonies became less dependent on Spain's exports as different economic strategies ensued.

This change had an impact upon New World agrarian experiments and agricultural enterprises including those in Spanish Florida (Ross 1975; Bushnell 1978, 1981, 1987; Ruhl 1990, 1993). Agricultural endeavors developed more rapidly and were more successful elsewhere in the Americas stimulating more experimentation than in *La Florida* (Keith 1976:29–30, 55–79; Cushner 1980:56, 58–80, 133; McAlister 1984:310–331). Although farming was planned and practiced from the first colonization of Spanish Florida (Lyon 1976:31), commercial agricultural endeavors do not appear to have been established until the mid- to late 17th century.

Dwindling Supplies and Increasing Self-Sufficiency in Spanish Florida

The parasitic nature of the conquest period facilitated the extraction of goods and services from the Native American populations throughout the Americas, including *La Florida* (Figure 1). But the goods, largely foodstuffs, produced by the Native Americans did not always provide the wealthy Spaniards with what they were accustomed to, desired, or felt they deserved. Consequently, many items needed either to be imported or produced locally. In *La Florida*, the *situado* (annual subsidy) fell behind and the supply shipments that did arrive were often limited, looted, or otherwise compromised (Bushnell 1981, 1983). These irregular shipments created a demand for goods that were obtained through both legal or illicit means (Lyon 1976:27, 1977:23; Bushnell 1981:12, 1983:41; Reitz and Scarry 1985:28, 46–47). By the 1640s, Spain's support of the Americas, including *La Florida*, had been in arrears a number of times. This situation continued throughout the 17th century, leaving many with no monetary stipends for years. Yet, the variability of the *situado* may not be as sporadic as was once proffered (Sluiter 1985); while Spanish Florida had lean periods they were not as bad off as once thought (Lyon 1992:8). The potential for entrepreneurial activities existed.

While part of Spanish Florida's motivation was tied to subsidy problems, others may have arisen from the desire for self-sufficiency or profit. Though St. Augustine never became completely self-sufficient, some entrepreneurial opportunities presented themselves to those Spanish families whose position and fiduciary circumstances permitted such privateering, presumably for profit and fame.

The purchase of European imports required foreign exchange. This could be obtained through investments in commerce (e.g., gold, silver, mercury) or by creating a profitable enterprise (*grangerias*). Even when currency was available and *La Florida* was able to send fleets to Spain or the Canary Islands for supplies, the Iberian taxes and prices for foodstuffs, especially flour, had increased so greatly that colonists increasingly began to seek supplies throughout the American colonies (Connor 1930:274; Klein 1964; Vicens Vives 1967; Bushnell 1981). For example, the wheat experiments that were undertaken in the highlands of Mexico in the 16th century had met with some success. However, Mexican exports were also somewhat irregular, creating periods of hardship on St. Augustine (Sluiter 1985; Lyon 1992). With ever-increasing prices and limited supplies, pirate activity had a major impact on the *situados* St. Augustine received in the 17th century, whether from the parent country or Mexico: "Buccaneers grew so bold in the late 17th century that they sometimes waited at anchor outside the St. Augustine har-

bor. To elude the enemy, Floridians crossed their bar at low tide" (Bushnell 1981:72).

In Spanish Florida it appears that some of the first agrarian enterprises involved the production of wheat and oranges along with cattle ranching. Although Pedro Menéndez de Avilés and the Crown had hoped to establish agrarian pursuits in the New World (Lyon 1976:31), some of these attempts were unsuccessful or limited, in part, because edaphic and climatic conditions were unfavorable. This does not include the many adaptable Old World crops such as cantaloupe and watermelon. Agrarian pursuits were limited also, because the labor that might have been used in such endeavors was commandeered for building fortifications, town construction, and daily subsistence activities. Gradually, however, local and incoming Spaniards saw the continued needs of resident populations. As political and economic situations abroad and at home changed, enterprising and entrepreneurial endeavors began to develop.

Agrarian Endeavors in Spanish Florida

In Spanish Florida it appears that some of the first agrarian enterprises involved cattle ranching and included the production of wheat and/or oranges as well as other subsistence crops. The experimental and integrally linked wheat and cattle haciendas that were developing ca. 1640 in the western provinces of Spanish Florida were such endeavors (e.g., Arnade 1961; Ross 1975; Bushnell 1978; Hann 1988). The complex of interrelated relationships involving cultivating the soil, crop production, and raising livestock was well understood. Thus farming practices in *La Florida*, as in Europe, were not a single activity. The association between the enhancement of barren or lean soil with manure and good crop production was a well-known cycle.

Oranges

Historical research indicates that the modern orange most probably originated in north-central China or was derived from species native to southeastern Asia. It has been suggested that initially they were used medicinally and not as a food source. Eventually, the orange, like many other plant foods, traveled on Arab caravans and was introduced into Spain by the Moors who used it for medicinal purposes and in religious services (Simpson and Conner-Ogorzaly 1986:103, 105, 108).

Before 1500 most of the oranges in Spain and Portugal were the bitter orange, which was used for aesthetic, medicinal, religious, and culinary purposes. Medieval recipes indicate that the orange was used on fish, meats, with other vegetables, as well as cooked with sugar and candied. But it is not until the mid-1600s that the sweet orange was apparently introduced from China (McPhee 1975:70). Shortly thereafter, this became a sought-after commodity throughout Europe and, not surprisingly, in their colonies.

Oranges had been grown in southern Spain near Seville and Cordoba for centuries by the time of the Columbian exchange. They not only were an important crop for preventing scurvy but had transitionally become one of the many plants that had become an important commodity as they became popular in Spanish beverages and cooking. Gradually the sweet oranges (*Citrus sinensis*) became the domain of the affluent (McPhee 1965:61–87). Interest in this fruit and its role as a "status" symbol in many regions of the Americas was to be maintained until almost the onset of the 20th century.

A source of vitamin C, this plant aided in curbing scurvy, which was caused by a deficiency of this vitamin. The disease afflicted many sailors and, untreated, could result in death. In 1535–1536, the French explorer Cartier described the ailments of his dying crew, which today are attributed to scurvy (Sauer 1971:90–91, 302). Fortunately, Columbus knew that this disease could be devastating on long voyages and took the seeds of oranges and other plants with him on his first and second voyages (Morrison in Crosby 1972:66–68). Sailors were required to carry the antiscorbutic citrus fruit, recognizing that eating limes, lemons, or oranges took away the aching muscles, pallid color, sour

breath, swollen legs, bleeding gums, and other ailments commonly associated with scurvy today.

Unfortunately, orange seeds are not long lived and desiccate easily, thereby reducing their survival and subsequent viability and germination possibilities. Early Spanish and Portuguese voyages to the New World, like those around Africa, included seeds and seedling orange trees among the cargo and disseminated thousands of them to ports in Africa, the Madeira and Canary Islands, and eventually North, Central, and South America. Subsequently, Native Americans and Spaniards spread the orange across *La Florida*. As Bushnell (1983:36) notes, a Spanish soldier overseeing St. Augustine from his post at the fort in 1580 "must have found it pleasant to look south across the commons toward the weathered church, and beyond the churchyard to the town with its flowering orange trees."

Although first introduced and grown in Spanish Florida ca. 1565, the orange experienced "ups and downs" as a commercial crop until centuries later when it virtually became a monocrop industry for Florida in the first quarter of the 19th century. It is interesting that 16th-century documents (Connor 1930:274; Lyon 1977:23; Bushnell 1983:36) indicate the presence of oranges in both St. Augustine and Santa Elena, a Spanish colony located in present-day South Carolina. Yet, to date, no evidence of this crop has been recovered from archaeobotanical remains. It is from late-18th-century deposits that orange remains begin to appear in archaeological contexts such as wells. Their absence in the archaeobotanical record may be due to preservation, sociocultural practices, as well as socioeconomic policies and practices, such as being discarded randomly and consumed by free-ranging pigs and chickens (Scarry and Reitz 1990:344–345). The orange rind is highly perishable, and the seeds are intolerant of thermal alteration (charring) because of the oil, pectin, and tannin contained in them. Although these preservation factors may add to its limited record, it is also possible that the absence of orange remains is a function of its possible initial medicinal role, and the possibility that the rind and seed scraps were used as fodder. Other events such as the sacking of St. Augustine by Sir Francis Drake in 1586 destroyed many of those planted in yards during the first two decades of the town's existence.

Valencia and Andalusia were Spain's primary orange lands. This area apparently produced enough to preclude New Spain from growing oranges for export. Nevertheless, they were grown, and according to documentary accounts, orange orchards were again observed around St. Augustine in the late 17th century. For example, Jonathan Dickinson, a shipwrecked Englishman comments upon their presence during his stay in St. Augustine in 1696 (Andrews and Andrews 1985:62–63). Spain's own production, its mercantile policies, and the fact that oranges could be produced in many other New World tropical colonies were among the factors poten-

tially inhibiting any initial industrial plans for this well-acclimated tree in Spanish Florida.

Shipments of oranges from St. Augustine (Table 2) can be traced from the late 17th century into the first few decades of the 1700s (Harman 1969:16–24). Both Spain's and England's relationships at home and abroad were obviously strained during the 17th and early 18th centuries (e.g., trade controversy and claim over Georgia), hampering legal trade between these nations. Nevertheless, during peaceful times between Spain and England their colonies exchanged goods—whether legal or illicit. Treaties such as the "kind entertainment" act of 1670 opened the door for British vessels in "distress" in Spanish-American ports to be repaired and provisioned. This action and the 1713 Treaty of Utrecht, which established an *asiento* (contract) with the British South Sea Company for the sale

TABLE 2
ORANGE EXPORTS FROM BRITISH SHIPPING RECORDS

Vessel	Cargo	Date	Export from/Import to	Home Port
Swan & Eagle	Load of oranges	1717	St. Augustine/Charleston	SC
Prince Frederick	Parcel of oranges	1731	St. Augustine/Charleston	SC
Good Hope	Parcel of fruit*	1732	St. Augustine/Charleston	SC
Orange	Parcel of fruit*	1733	St. Augustine/Providence	RI
Catherine	Oranges	1735	St. Augustine/Charleston	Jamaica
Elizabeth	Oranges	1736	St. Augustine/Charleston	RI
Neptune— 3 voyages, July, Sept., Nov.	Oranges	1735	St. Augustine/Charleston	SC
Edward & Elizabeth	Oranges	1735	St. Augustine/Charleston	SC
Edward & Elizabeth	Oranges Feb.—1,000 Aug.–Sept.—17,700	1736	St. Augustine/Charleston	SC
Rebecca & Mary	Oranges—500	1775	St. Augustine/Charleston	SC
Don Carlos	Sweetmeats of candied fruit*	1738	St. Augustine/New York	NY
Dom Phillip	3 casks of oranges	1738	St. Augustine/New York	NY

References: Great Britain, Public Record Office MSS, Colonial Office, SC (COSC), 5:508, fol. 32 Shipping Returns 1717; COSC 5:509, fols. 79–81, 96, Shipping Returns 1731; COSC, 5:509, fol. 115, Shipping Returns 1732; COSC, 5:509, fol. 113, Shipping Returns 1733; COSC, 5:509, fols. 122, 128, 132, 138, 139, Shipping Returns 1734; COSC, 5:509, fols. 151, 152, 153, Shipping Returns 1735; COSC, 5:509, fols. 152, 153, Shipping Returns 1736; COSC 5:510, fols. 1, 11, Shipping Returns 1736; Colonial Office, NY, 5:1226, fols. 2, 13, Shipping Returns, 1738; Gazette, 27 Jan.–3 Feb., 5–12 May 1733; Gazette, 8–15 Nov., 15–22 Nov. 1735; Gazette, 28 Aug.–4 Sept. 1736 in Harman 1969. (Table compiled from Harman [1969:12–22, 30–31].)

* Although not specific these references indicate a fruit export, which most probably was orange or possibly fig. (Crosby [1972:68] notes that these were typical dessert foods.)

of slaves, provided the opportunity for further trade relations between Spanish and English colonies (Harman 1969:6). Apparently, transactions between Georgia, South Carolina, and other northern ports as well as Jamaica and more southerly ports did occur, however illicit or conspiratorial. Payment in gold or silver by the Spaniards was enticement enough for British merchants. Despite the Spanish trade restrictions, St. Augustine both imported and exported British wares on occasion ignoring "the restrictions against trading with foreign colonies and welcomed the usually cheaper, superior, and available British goods" (Harman 1969:13). Similarly, even though *guardacostas* (Spanish coastguard) privateered Spanish Florida waters, British merchants continued to import the Spanish goods for a number of years (Robinson 1945:59; Harman 1969:12–13).

It is during the mid- to late 17th century and into the 18th century that the incipient stages of an orange industry in Florida emerged, as British colonial interests in this exotic item increased and the New World market interests were stimulated. Shipping records and documents issuing reprimands to governors and other entrepreneurs reflect that St. Augustine, like other Spanish New World towns, took advantage of importing goods from the English colonies as well as exporting colonial products such as oranges.

Among the imports to Charleston and Providence and other Atlantic ports were oranges from St. Augustine (Table 2). Although at present the database is still small, these numbers gradually appear to increase from a brief listing to shipments in excess of 28,000 oranges (Harman 1969:23; Waterbury 1983:82). While the Spanish and British trade laws prohibited such transactions, Florida took advantage of the northern demands for the sought-after oranges. Orangeries, or even the presence of the fruit or an orange tree, was a status symbol to many British colonists (McPhee 1965:71–87; Yentsch 1994:121–122) and would become a major commercial endeavor during the British period, ca.1764–1783 (Davis 1937:233).

Wheat

By the middle of the 17th century expansion westward across the Florida peninsula resulted in the establishment of missions and ranches by Spaniards. They were accompanied by Native Americans, who were laborers for both endeavors. Government officials, wealthy Spaniards, and missionaries sought the rewards of commercial ventures while criticizing the "others'" mistreatment of the Native American populations they all were exploiting (Hann 1988:134, 142, 144, 237–263). Wheat production and cattle herding began to increase, and by the last half of the 17th century hacienda-like ventures were established in the western provinces. These ultimately resulted in exports to Havana from St. Marks, a port and subsequently a fort at the mouth of the St. Marks River on the Gulf of Mexico (Hann 1988:134, 142). This trade, like the orange exports, was against Spanish trade laws and considered a nonsanctioned action by the Crown.

Archaeobotanically, wheat grains are much more abundant in the 17th-century deposits than from the preceding century in either coastal or interior Florida mission sites (Table 1). In general, wheat grains are rare except in contexts that appear to be storage areas associated with or in mission church complexes. For example, at the Spanish mission of Santa Catalina de Guale on St. Catherines Island, Georgia (Figure 1), only a few grains have been recovered from deposits near what may have been the *cocina* (kitchen), while thousands have been recovered from the northwest corner of the church.

A similar pattern is found at the Apalachee missions in western Florida (Figure 1). Hundreds of grains have been recovered from storage areas in the church complexes at San Juan de Aspalaga and Concepcíon de Ayubale, while far fewer grains have been recovered, to date, from the Spanish village and council house at San Luis de Talimali (Scarry 1986, 1987, 1992). This association with church complexes suggests that while it was more abundant in the 17th

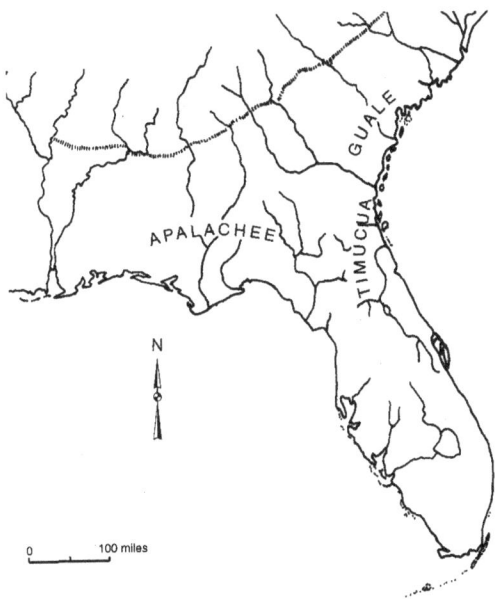

FIGURE 1. General location map of Guale, Timucua, and Apalachee provinces.

century, wheat may have been reserved for sacred purposes such as the Holy Eucharist or wafer consumed during the Catholic ritual of communion. It is also possible that the wealthier Spaniards and friars were consuming the preferred wheat breads instead of the corn tortilla. While some excavations have occurred in high-status houses and the Franciscan friary in St. Augustine, still no archaeobotanical data have been recovered from these sites at this time. Similarly, knowledge of the Native Americans' use of wheat as food or for trade is limited. Some documentary information indicates that it was grown along with other required crops, such as corn, for St. Augustine (Bushnell 1979). The Native American Timucuan and Apalachee people appear to have been the primary laborers in the production and, potentially, distribution of wheat, but appear to have participated minimally in its consumption and economic rewards (Bushnell 1979:17; Scarry 1986, 1992:156–159; Hann 1988:144, 321; Ruhl 1990:369, 1993:271–273, 281).

Interestingly, differences exist between the 16th- and 17th- century wheat grains. Preliminary analyses indicate that 17th-century wheat grains appear to be smaller than the earlier 16th-century coastal grains. Unfortunately, small sample size (to date, less than 200 grains) may be masking the actual size range for grains from interior *La Florida* sites (Table 1). Comparison of these few grains with the thousands of wheat grains recovered from Mission Santa Catalina de Guale on St. Catherines Island, Georgia, may be misleading. If the size difference between the grains from the coastal and interior sites is valid, it may indicate that the assemblages contain different wheat cultivars.

Other morphological differences such as embryo shape and length, apex shape, and caryopsis (grain) length, width, and thickness, also suggest that multiple cultivars may be represented. Variations in size, however, may be the result of shrinkage due to firing conditions. Experiments have indicated that the conditions under which grains become carbonized and are deposited have variable effects upon wheat and other grass grains. If the morphological variability in wheat from different contexts is not a result of firing conditions, then perhaps the larger 16th-century grains reflect the imported Old World stock while the smaller 17th-century grains reflect experimental cultivars grown in *La Florida*.

Wheat was valued highly for food and ritual use, and Spain was experiencing difficult times in domestic agricultural endeavors. Thus, despite the initial failures to grow wheat along the Florida coast in the 16th century, the colonists and incoming Spaniards continued to experiment with this crop as they advanced to new, western locations.

Documents indicate that Governor Benito Ruiz de Salazar y Villecilla attempted to grow wheat at his hacienda-like ranch and farm near the Apalachee-Timucua border in the 1640s (Arnade 1961:116–124; Ross 1975:203–208; Bushnell 1978:407–431, 1981:78, 81–82; Hann 1988:134) (Figure 1). Experiments with wheat were undertaken there, and the governor's foreman planted the selected grains until they produced a reasonable yield (Bushnell 1987:22). Shortly thereafter, Governor Rebolledo ordered that wheat be grown by the Native Americans as part of the tithe that they were to pay the Crown. By the 1680s wheat was reported to be growing in St. Augustine. Governor Juan Marques Cabrera obtained some wheat grains from Apalachee farmers, which yielded thousands of pounds from less than 100 pounds sown (Bushnell 1987:24–25). Apparently, the acclimatized western Apalachee grain fared better than the original Old World grains, which headed poorly and rotted along the coast (Reitz and Scarry 1985). Albeit for sacred and/or secular purposes, the concerted effort by Spaniards to produce a crop not easily grown in this terrain attests to wheat's high desirability and potential commercial applications (Ruhl 1993).

Discussion

To recount briefly, this research has suggested that the ravages on Spain's terrain, in part brought on by a monarchy that promoted short-term agrarian advantages over long-term ventures, impacted Spain's economic history both at home and abroad throughout the 16th century and beyond. The repression of agriculture, sedentary sheep raising, and lack of forestry conservation in Spain inhibited the cultivation of pastures and forest management. Economic changes brought on by the diverse natural and cultural riches of the New World played a hand in the shift from the faltering domestic attempts at wheat production in Spain and Portugal to New World experiments in wheat production in North, Central, and South America, including *La Florida*.

Spanish and New World agrarians were well aware of the demands for more agricultural produce such as wheat, olive oil, and wine. Both domestic and foreign trade were suffering, especially in the Americas where Spain had established various trade restrictions and laws that prohibited the colonists from such production. Despite these constraints, colonial demands for certain commodities as well as foreign inflation contributed to the impetus behind new ventures

and agricultural experimentation in *La Florida* and throughout the Americas. At first, these new ventures concentrated on developing and supplying goods for local markets such as St. Augustine. Through time, orange and wheat were recognized for their commercial significance as foodstuffs, and they, along with other plants and plant products, became somewhat successful. Proceeds from such successful endeavors were used to purchase exotic goods for the church, the home, or the military post. Archaeobotanically, the relative increase in quantities of wheat grains that occurs from the 16th to the 17th century may be one indicator of this agricultural pursuit. The production of wheat and oranges for market was influenced in part by the adaptable New World edaphic conditions and climate, but directed by economic, religious, and political demands and practices of the period. While wheat production may have persisted because of food customs and preferences and religious choices, establishment of orange groves may have been stimulated by the recognition of nonlocal demands and their perceived economic rewards. These findings indicate the progress of the middle-period populations in Spanish Florida towards self sufficiency in the production, distribution, and, to a certain extent, the consumption of locally-raised plant foods.

Because the British colonies wanted oranges, St. Augustine began to export them to Charleston, South Carolina; Providence, Rhode Island; and other North American ports in the late 17th and early 18th century. Wheat went south through the St. Marks port to Havana, Cuba. Both western provinces and eastern markets were producing some of Spanish Florida's first cash crops for the Crown, or more likely for its New World entrepreneurs.

Conclusion

Interestingly, in one instance, the desire for a preferred item advanced the early and continued experimentation that possibly led to a new wheat cultivar. In the other instance, the readily adaptable orange began its long journey toward becoming one of Florida's primary industries. In both instances, these endeavors reflect the interest in local production of plant foods as marketable commodities during the middle period in Spanish Florida. Nevertheless, the onset of such commercial endeavors, agricultural experimentation, and increasing self reliance advanced during this transitional middle period between the first colonial encounters and later amalgamation of cultures as Spanish Florida experienced economic expansion and cultural and biological acclimatization.

ACKNOWLEDGMENTS

Much of the support for the research found in this article came from the American Museum of Natural History and The Florida Museum of Natural History. Special appreciation is extended to David Hurst Thomas and Jerald T. Milanich for their continued support and interest in this research. Bruce Chapel also deserves a special thank you for his assistance with the documents in the P.K. Yonge Library of Florida History on the University of Florida campus. I am grateful to Jerald T. Milanich, Kathleen Deagan, Kathleen Hoffman, Ann S. Cordell, Sylvia Scudder, and an unknown reviewer who read earlier versions of this paper and made excellent suggestions for its improvement.

SUSAN D. deFRANCE

Iberian Foodways in the Moquegua and Torata Valleys of Southern Peru

ABSTRACT

Spanish settlement of the southern Peruvian coastal river valleys and the introduction of new agricultural and industrial enterprises such as wineries and livestock haciendas altered indigenous systems of production and subsistence. A unique pattern of Spanish colonial animal use emerged as a result of introductions of Old World domesticates in combination with the faunal resources of the Central Andes. Zooarchaeological data from four Spanish colonial wineries from the Moquegua valley and the late prehistoric/colonial site of Torata Alta indicate that colonial economy and subsistence combined Old World domestic mammals and South American camelids—llamas, alpacas. In comparison to Spanish settlement in Florida and the Caribbean, the pattern of animal use that developed in the south Central Andes reflects little reliance on local resources. Colonial Andean foodways more closely parallel those of the Iberian peninsula than other areas of Spanish settlement.

Introduction

Colonization of Peru by Spanish settlers during the 16th century brought about dramatic changes in the economic and cultural systems of the indigenous inhabitants. The Spaniards attempted to increase their personal wealth and secure revenue for the Spanish crown by establishing western European economic activities and institutions in the Central Andean region. The interactions between the Spaniards and the indigenous populations of the Central Andes were unrivaled in the Americas because of the combination of unique ecological conditions and the precolumbian expansionistic state level of social organization that characterized the indigenous population.

The environment of the Central Andes, the region roughly from northern Ecuador to northern Chile, bounded by the Pacific Ocean to the west and by the Amazon rain forest to the east (Figure 1), is harsh because of the combined effects of equatorial and altitudinal conditions. The evolution of precolumbian ranked social systems was often contingent upon the development of economic systems that produced abundant foodstuffs. The agricultural food production systems that evolved in the Central Andean region were unique in the New World. The indigenous inhabitants cultivated a diverse inventory of domesticated plants, of which tubers were most important. In addition, this region was the only New World center of large mammal domestication. Domestic llamas and alpacas were the foundation of a multifaceted herding economy. Spanish settlement of this region resulted in the imposition of European practices on very complex social and economic systems.

One consequence of Spanish colonization of the Peruvian Andes was a dynamic change in agro-pastoral production as Old World animal husbandry practices were imposed on the Andean system. The formation of a pastoral economic system that combined European animals with the indigenous faunal resources of Peru is unique in the Americas because the Central Andean region possessed a long-term pastoral tradition dependent on llamas and alpacas. Spanish colonization of new lands was accompanied by the importation of Old World animal resources and institutions for animal management and economic productivity.

Beginning in the 16th century, Spanish colonists introduced a variety of barnyard animals such as cattle, horses, burros, pigs, sheep, goats, and domestic fowl to new settlements (Table 1). These animals served as both subsistence items and for transportation and traction. Several of the taxa provided renewable products, for example wool and milk, or following their death, items such as hides, bone, and tallow were processed. The modern abundance and distribution of nonindigenous fauna in Peru demonstrate the cultural and commercial importance of these animals. The combined use of Andean and Old World animals and their products in both domestic and industrial settings were important components in the formation of Hispanic Andean culture.

This study examines the vital role animals played

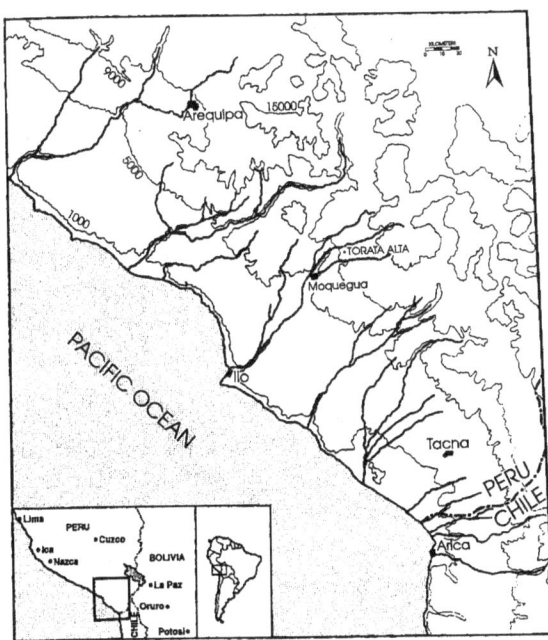

FIGURE 1. Location of the Moquegua wineries and Torata Alta.

TABLE 1
FIRST OBSERVATIONS OF OLD WORLD DOMESTIC SPECIES IN PERU

Species	Common Name	Year
Sus scrofa	Pig	1532
Equus caballus	Horse	1532
Ovis aries	Sheep	1536–1538
Capra hircus	Goat	1536–1538
Bos taurus	Cattle	1539
Bos taurus	Ox	1550
Camelus sp.	Old World Camel	1555–1615
Equus asinus	Donkey	1557

Source: Garcilaso de la Vega (1966[1607]:512–587).

in the colonization and settlement of the Peruvian Andes based on archaeological data from five colonial sites in southern Peru. It explores the role of animals in both the colonial economy and subsistence through an analysis of faunal remains.

Spanish colonial settlement within the Moquegua region of far southern Peru is characterized by two types of occupations (Figure 1). First, a productive wine industry developed in the central portion of the valley near the modern town of Moquegua. Second, a Spanish occupation is documented at the site of Torata Alta located in the northwardly adjacent Torata valley. It remains speculative as to whether Torata Alta was constructed as part of Inca expansion into the Torata valley or whether it was constructed entirely under Spanish decree to serve as a *reducción* where the indigenous population of the valley was ordered to settle. Excavations at both the Moquegua wineries or *bodegas* and Torata Alta produced a substantial quantity of faunal material.

The prolific wine industry established in the Moquegua valley has been the subject of extensive archaeological study. A multiyear program of investigations was conducted in the Moquegua valley from 1985 to 1991 under the auspices of the Moquegua *Bodegas* Project directed by Dr. Prudence Rice. Survey of this short, steep, river valley identified 130 wineries or *bodegas* (Rice and Ruhl 1989). Subsequently, shovel testing and site mapping were completed at 28 of the wineries (Rice and Smith 1989). The shovel-test data, in combination with archival research compiled by López and Huertas (1990), helped to determine the probable location of 16th-century deposits representing the earliest Spanish colonial occupation of the valley. Excavations were conducted at four of the wineries (Figure 2) to locate 16th-century contexts and document colonial lifeways on the wineries (Rice 1990; Smith 1991). Research thus far has focused on Spanish colonial adaptation and acculturation as reflected in the material remains at the *bodegas* (Smith 1991), the production of ceramics within the valley (Van Beck 1991; Rice and Van Beck 1993; Rice 1994), and the botanical remains recovered from the *bodegas* (Jones 1990).

Extensive excavations also were conducted at another colonial community, Torata Alta, located to the north of Moquegua in the Torata valley. During the precolumbian late-intermediate period Torata Alta was either a prehispanic town or a colonial *reducción* where the indigenous population of the surrounding countryside was forced to reside during the early colonial period (Van Buren et al. 1993). Artifacts dating from the mid-16th century to the mid-17th century have been used to identify the

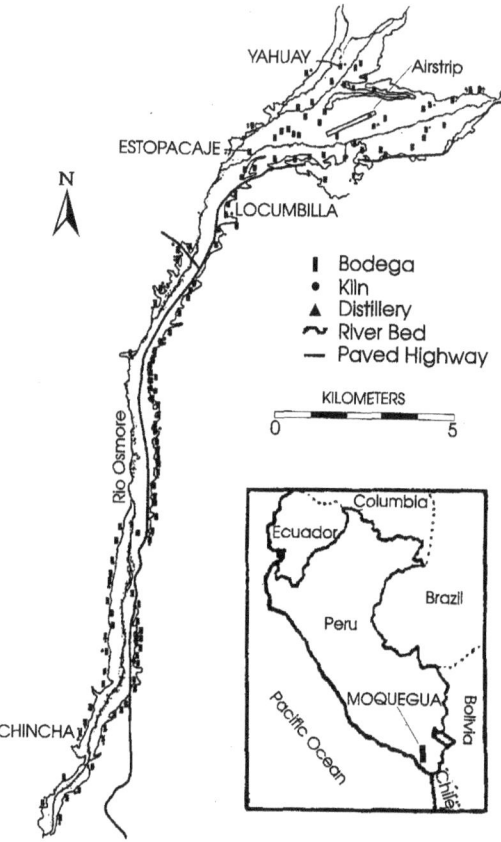

FIGURE 2. Location of identified wineries and four excavated wineries.

ate food items. Food may have been one way that the Peruvian creole populations, i.e., individuals born in Peru of Spanish heritage, distinguished themselves from the Indian population. Therefore, both adaptation and cognitive perceptions may have influenced the faunal materials that were deposited at the wineries and Torata Alta.

The faunal remains recovered during the Moquegua wineries and Torata Alta excavations represent food refuse and remains of animals that served as beasts of burden or provided fiber, hides, bone, and other products. This article identifies and interprets human/animal interactions in the Spanish colonial experience in southern Peru. The research potential of the zooarchaeological record is dependent on the preservation of the faunal material, the historical sources that are available to aid in constructing research questions, and knowledge concerning the physical geography of the Moquegua and Torata valleys.

Research Objectives

This paper addresses two research topics concerning Spanish colonial settlement and lifeways. The first research question examines whether or not local Andean resources were incorporated into the diet. There are no previous zooarchaeological studies of colonial faunal assemblages from the Central Andes that can serve as baseline data. Although faunal data from other areas of Spanish colonial settlement, such as the Caribbean and Spanish Florida, are available, these sites differ significantly from Peru in terms of both the geographical setting and the economic activities of the inhabitants. In the absence of appropriate faunal studies, historical sources and zooarchaeological studies from other geographical areas are used to formulate hypotheses of colonial conditions. Historical accounts indicate that by the late 16th century all of the major Iberian domestic animals were present in Peru. However, colonial histories primarily address the economic uses of animals with little dietary information.

Although Spanish colonial animal use in the Peruvian Andes only recently has been examined using archaeological data, investigations in other ar-

ethnic composition of the site's inhabitants, to examine socioeconomic variability within the site, and to provide material remains for comparison with the 16th-century winery contexts (Van Buren and Bürgi 1990; Van Buren 1993).

The environmental conditions of the study area, most importantly the rugged topography, high aridity, and low atmospheric pressure exerted selective pressures on the introduced Old World domestic animals. The physical adaptability of the imported domesticates determined whether these animals were available for either economic or subsistence uses. However, the acceptance or rejection of food items, particularly meat sources, was influenced by cognitive perceptions of what constitutes appropri-

eas of the New World have permitted more holistic reconstructions of Spanish lifeways. A substantial database has been generated from the Caribbean (McEwan 1986; Reitz 1986; Ewen 1987; Reitz and McEwan 1995), Spanish St. Augustine (Reitz and Cumbaa 1983; Reitz and Scarry 1985; Reitz 1992), and from excavations of Spanish mission sites in the southeastern United States (Reitz 1990, 1991).

The site of Puerto Real, located in modern Haiti, was a 16th-century Spanish town engaged in commerce within the Caribbean and beyond. Most recently, Reitz and McEwan's (1995) synthesis of a number of previous zooarchaeological studies facilitates comparisons with the Peruvian collections. The Indian population of Hispaniola was decimated within a few years of Spanish colonization. Consequently, large herds of cattle rapidly acclimated to the Hispaniola environment because of the absence of both human obstacles to herd growth and large native domestic animals (Reitz 1986). According to Reitz and McEwan (1995), the Puerto Real faunal data suggest that an Iberian diet was maintained with the addition of some new food items, particularly pond turtles and marine fishes.

The zooarchaeology of Spanish St. Augustine also has been the subject of intensive study (Reitz and Cumbaa 1983; Reitz and Scarry 1985; Reitz 1992). These studies span the 16th through 18th centuries, thus representing a greater chronological range than Puerto Real. In contrast to Puerto Real, faunal samples from 16th-century occupations of Spanish St. Augustine consistently indicate that the inhabitants consumed local faunal resources, particularly estuarine fishes and small game animals. The absence of a reliance on Old World domestic mammals has been attributed to two factors: (1) high mortality rates for introduced animals due to poor quality grasslands of the swampy coastal plain of northeast Florida, and (2) irregular shipments of provisions from Caribbean supply centers. Primary historical accounts of the colonists contain frequent complaints that their diet was inadequate because meat was unavailable, despite zooarchaeological evidence that a wide variety of fish and game was consumed (Reitz and Scarry 1985).

Settlement outside of St. Augustine during the 17th century included large cattle ranches and an extensive system of missions, some of which maintained large holdings of domestic animals. Although these enterprises may have been sources of meat for the town, the faunal material from a small sample of 17th-century contexts in St. Augustine indicates that the use of meat from domestic animals did not increase at this time (Reitz 1992:92). Rather, the dietary pattern established in the previous century continued and is characterized by a reliance on wild animals and marine fishes with little use of domestic meat sources. The cattle ranches and missions apparently contributed little in the way of subsistence resources to St. Augustine proper. This conclusion may be revised with the analysis of additional samples from a greater range of 17th-century contexts (Reitz 1992:89).

Studies of faunal samples from excavations at the 17th-century Spanish missions also indicate regional differences in resource use (Reitz 1991). Only at the San Luis de Talimali mission in the western Apalachee province do samples indicate a reliance on domestic mammals. This mission complex is anomalous in terms of its size, the range of personnel who occupied the mission including clerical, military, and indigenous individuals, and the commercial activities that may have taken place at a mission of this size such as tallow, lard, and hide processing (Reitz 1991:296). Therefore, meat from domestic animals may have been readily available at San Luis. In contrast, the basic pattern of faunal use throughout the other mission provinces of north Florida is similar, consisting of a limited use of domestic livestock and extensive use of locally available wild resources (Reitz 1991:301).

The diverse ecological habitats near St. Augustine, including an extensive estuarine system, in combination with low survival rates for introduced domestic mammals, particularly caprines, resulted in unique patterns of adaptation by the St. Augustinians following social class and ethnic divisions (Reitz and Cumbaa 1983:185). Faunal material from 18th-century households suggests that *peninsulares,* recently arrived colonists born in Spain, attempted to maintain an Iberian diet more than did the *criollos,* individuals of Spanish descent born in Florida. Although both the higher status *peninsulares* and the more affluent *criollos* consumed a diverse range of local resources such as wild game and estuarine fishes, *peninsulares* consumed a greater variety of Old World domestic mammals than did the *criollo* households. Lower-class *criollos* had diets dominated by domestic mammals, especially cattle, and little reliance on local game or fish. Reitz and Cumbaa (1983) hypothesized that these lower-class Spanish households may have been unable to afford more diverse foodstuffs that required hiring hunters or fisherfolk.

The exploitation of animal resources in Spanish colonial Mexico, Central America, and other regions of South America has been reviewed by historical scholars (e.g., Poppino 1949; Borah 1954; Gibson 1964; Newson 1987); however, few zooarchaeological investigations have been undertaken (e.g., Emery 1990). Despite the need for zooarchaeological data from other geographical areas, particularly the valley of central Mexico, comparisons can be made of faunal collections from the Moquegua wineries and Torata Alta with those from sites in the Caribbean and the southeastern United States. Comparisons of archaeological patterns among these three areas allow a determination of the degree to which the Peruvian pattern conformed to or differed from Spanish Florida and Caribbean settlements.

The faunal collections of Puerto Real and St. Augustine exhibit variability due to the environmental conditions of these regions and the indigenous populations that were encountered. The three geographic areas to be compared differ in both topography and climate. Nevertheless, the Spanish motives for the colonization of these areas were similar: expansion of the Spanish Empire. Both the role of animal resources in this process and the emergence of mestizo patterns in the Andes have yet to be defined. Considering the zooarchaeological pattern exhibited in Florida and the Caribbean, one can hypothesize that the Spanish settlements in Peru also relied on local resources as either dietary staples or supplements. If this pattern applies to the Moquegua wineries and Torata Alta, the zooarchaeological record should contain the remains of a variety of local faunal resources such as guinea pigs and marine fishes.

The second research question addressed in this paper asks if Andean systems of livestock production were incorporated, disrupted, or replaced by Spanish changes in animal use. The indigenous cultures of the Central Andes possessed the only New World economy focused on large domestic mammals: the llama (*Lama glama*) and alpaca (*Lama pacos*) (Wing 1986). Two species of wild camelids also inhabit the Andes: the large-sized guanaco (*Lama guanicoe*) and the small-sized vicuña (*Vicugna vicugna*). The evolutionary history and relationship between the four species has been the subject of much debate (Franklin 1982; Kent 1982; Browman 1989; Stanley et al. 1994; Wheeler 1995). All four are difficult to distinguish osteologically; however, differences in size and dentition have been used to distinguish species. Collectively the four are referred to as camelids, although historical and ethnohistorical accounts suggest that only the domestic forms were used in colonial Peru.

The Andean pastoral economy had functioned for several thousand years at the time of European contact, thus indicating the evolution of a complex system of human/animal interaction in a region of environmental extremes. The llama and the alpaca were both the foundation of a highland pastoral economy and were valued in religion, ritual, and as wealth and status items (Shimada and Shimada 1985). Today, the llama primarily inhabits high altitude plateaus—*altiplano* or puna—grasslands greater than 3,000 m in elevation. The range of the alpaca is restricted to higher elevations generally greater than 4,000 m (Winterhalder and Thomas 1978). The llama provided a number of products, including meat, sinew, hides, dung, and served as a beast of burden. The smaller alpaca was highly valued for its fine wool, but also provided meat (Orlove 1977; Franklin 1982; Flannery et al. 1989).

Agro-pastoralism was a major component of the Inca-period economy. All of the larger camelid herds were the property of the ruling elite and were maintained by the citizens as part of their *mit'a* or state tax obligations (Garcilaso de la Vega 1966 [1607]; Murra 1965). Individuals would have owned smaller herds, e.g., 10–20 animals, of camelids for their family needs of meat, fiber, and dung for fuel (Murra 1965). Closely related kin living in specific communities often pooled their family herds into one large communal herd that may number in the hundreds (Flannery et al. 1989). The majority of pastoralists today either combine herding with the cultivation of fields for agricultural products or they acquire products through exchange with agriculturalists. This system existed in the past as well. As is the case today, various tasks such as tending herds, transporting animals from corrals to fields, shearing, and butchering animals were divided among family members of all ages.

Interpretations of ethnohistorical accounts indicate that significant changes occurred in the production of agricultural crops and indigenous pastoralism following Spanish conquest and the redistribution of land and indigenous labor under Spanish control (Spaulding 1984). The management of native domestic animals was also altered under Spanish control. Men, who traditionally maintained state llama and alpaca herds, were encouraged to engage in agriculture on land under Spanish control rather than practice free-range camelid herding (Gade and Escobar 1982). Studies also suggest that control of camelid breeding was disrupted and that disease spread within camelid herds during the colonial period. Comparisons of modern coarse-fibered llama fleece with prehistoric llama samples dating approximately 900 to 1,000 years ago suggest that selective breeding of fine-fleeced llamas declined, probably beginning in the colonial era (Wheeler et al. 1992, 1995). Introduced sheep also contributed to the decimation of the native livestock through the introduction of disease, most notably the scab mite (Flannery et al. 1989:103). Not only were the herd sizes reduced from imported pestilence, the distribution of Andean domesticates also contracted following the conquest. The concentration of Spanish agriculture and industry in the coastal valleys forced the native herders to retreat to higher elevations. Archaeological evidence for prehistoric llama breeding on the north coast of Peru (Shimada and Shimada 1985) and for prehistoric llama and alpaca breeding on the south coast (Wheeler et al. 1992) supports the contention that modern herds are much more restricted in their distribution than was the case in prehispanic times. Archaeological data from the colonial wineries provide empirical evidence of the impact of Spanish settlement on indigenous camelid pastoralism.

In addition to the production of wine, the industrial portion of the wineries employed a variety of animals in different capacities. The most common, nonsubsistence, use of animals was for transportation of wine products. Pack animals, either mules or llamas, commonly transported wine or brandy to the highlands (Kuon Cabello 1981:373, 384; Pease 1985:152). Andean pack animals led arduous lives during the colonial era. According to 18th-century accounts such as that of Frazier (in Kuon Cabello 1981:384) in 1713, spare mules were often brought along in the event that an animal would tire along the strenuous routes that lacked both pasture and water. The Andean roads are said to have been strewn with as many mule carcasses as footprints (Kuon Cabello 1981:384). Mule centers located in Chile thrived due to the need for replacement pack animals.

The production of goatskin wine bags, used to transport wine, was one of the most common industrial uses of animals. Heavy clay ceramic jars, or *botijas*, that undoubtedly broke frequently, were used to transport wine until the mid-18th century when goatskin bags, or *odres*, were introduced to Moquegua (Kuon Cabello 1981:366). To prevent leakage, the interiors of the bags were coated with tar, or *brea*. It is unlikely that this treatment enhanced the flavor of the wine and brandy; but rather, it is probable that this process contributed to the disreputable character of Moquegua's wine and brandy throughout Peru (Crosby 1967:331).

In addition to burros and mules, sheep, goats, heifers, and bulls commonly were maintained on the wine haciendas in Moquegua (Kuon Cabello 1981:373) and in other areas of the Peruvian coast (Cushner 1980:71–73). Domestic herds reportedly grazed on the lomas vegetation that bloomed following the austral winter rainy season. The most extensive lomas blooms occurred close to the Pacific Ocean near the modern town of Ilo (Kuon Cabello 1981:373). Horses also were employed for the many trips made between the fields and residences located near the center of Moquegua (Kuon Cabello 1981:373). The introduced Old World livestock apparently came into competition for range space with the domestic camelids, particularly at lower elevations along the north coast (Garcilaso de la Vega in Shimada and Shimada 1985). It is not known if a similar pattern characterized the southern valleys.

Historical sources provide little information on the number of livestock that were present at any particular *bodega* for a specific time. However, one quantified account of livestock holdings is Alonso de Estrada's will, issued in Moquegua in 1610. According to this will, Estrada's estate included seven mules, nine burros, and approximately 250 goats (Kuon Cabello 1981:361). According to Frazier's (in Kuon Cabello 1981:373) 1713 account, some of the wineries possessed alfalfa fields to provide pasturage for horses and cattle. However, large herds may have been maintained on pastures outside of the valley proper, since land within the valley was more valuable for viticulture than as grazelands.

Based on the historical accounts one can hypothesize that European livestock—oxen, horses, and burros—replaced native camelids, especially llamas, as beasts of burden. If a shift to Old World livestock occurred in the Moquegua region, as is suggested by the ethnohistorical and historical record, the zooarchaeological record should contain abundant remains of horses, burros, and oxen, with relatively few remains of the native camelids. This pattern would contrast with the precolonial economic uses of camelids and thereby indicate that Spanish-introduced fauna served nonfood industrial needs related to the production and transport of Moquegua's wine products.

Archaeological Contexts

The western desert slopes of the Andes are transected by a series of river valleys in which agricultural production is achieved through irrigation of arid lands. The central portion of the Moquegua valley is a 1½-km-wide, 28-km-long strip of fertile land ranging in elevation from 1,500 to 2,000 m above sea level. The valley was a major center of wine and brandy production from the 16th to the late 19th century. These products were con-

sumed locally and were traded to other settlements ranging from the Pacific coast to highland industrial locales such as the Potosí silver mine in modern-day Bolivia (Rice and Smith 1989).

The Moquegua *bodegas* are large industrial complexes with facilities to process, ferment, store, and transport wine and brandy (Rice and Smith 1989). They are characterized by multiple cane-roofed adobe structures and open courtyards that presumably served as loading areas for carts and possibly as animal corrals. In addition to structures for wine processing and production, residential areas are present at several of the *bodegas*.

The question of who resided and worked at the wineries is still open to debate. The owners of the *bodegas* are believed to have been *criollo* descendants of wealthy families from the area of Arequipa (Brown 1986). The majority of arable land in the valleys near Arequipa was subdivided among the offspring of early settlers who received sizable land grants during the 16th century (Davies 1984). Subsequent generations were forced to acquire land elsewhere for their livelihoods. Historical studies of labor on the wineries indicate that enslaved blacks replaced Indians as laborers following the decline of the native population in the 16th century; however, once the native population recovered, winery owners commonly employed Indians as seasonal wage laborers beginning in the 17th century (Brown 1986:48). Archaeological contexts representing exclusively indigenous or laborer settlements were not identified in association with the wineries. Today, many *bodega* owners reside in Moquegua or other larger towns for most of the year, with overseers directing daily activities at the wineries. During harvesting and processing season a temporary labor force is employed, and owners are in residence at the wineries. This may have been the pattern in the past as well.

Several field seasons of research consisted of survey, site mapping, shovel testing, and large-scale excavations. Excavations were conducted at four of the wineries: the Yahuay *bodega* in the northern portion of the valley, the central valley sites of Locumbilla and Estopacaje, and the Chincha *bodega* in the southern end of the valley. These sites were selected for excavation based on shovel tests conducted in 1987 and 1989 (Smith 1991) and historical data that suggested 16th-century occupations were present (López and Huertas 1990).

Zooarchaeological materials from excavations at the wineries span the temporal range of *bodega* occupation and include both industrial and domestic contexts. Temporal assignments into early-, middle-, or late-period categories are based on two major chronological markers (Smith 1991:87). All early-period contexts are those below the ash fall from the February 1600 Huaynaputina volcanic eruption. Although the earliest historical references to wineries in the Moquegua valley are from the late 16th century (Smith 1991:chap.2), early-period contexts date from the initial colonial settlement of Moquegua in 1541 to 1600. Middle-period contexts span approximately 1600 to 1775, when European manufactured ceramics with known dates of production came into use. All late-period contexts date from 1775 to the late 19th and early 20th centuries.

Faunal material from contexts dating to the same time period have been analytically combined into units comprising all deposits assigned to a single time period for each excavation unit, block, or trench. For the purposes of this paper, intersite comparisons are made between the three time periods. Additional information on intrasite variability can be obtained from deFrance (1993). The following discussion outlines the winery excavations and information relevant to the faunal samples. For more detailed information on the excavations the reader is referred to Smith (1991).

Locumbilla Bodega

Excavations were conducted at Locumbilla over the course of three field seasons (1987–1989), thereby producing the largest faunal collection from the *bodegas*. Faunal material from a total of 24 excavation units was analyzed (Figure 3). These units include two trenches and a block excavation in an area of dense 16th-century deposits. A total of 43 analytical units (10 early, 24 middle, and 9 late) are present based on the temporal assignments. The faunal analysis includes eight fine-screened samples from features, postholes, and particularly rich midden deposits.

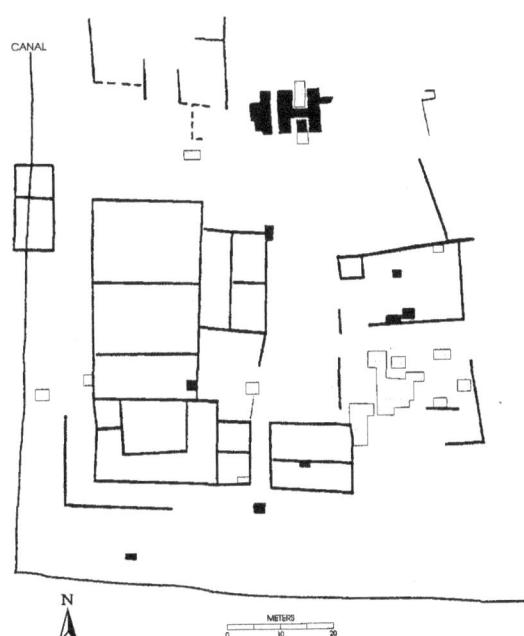

FIGURE 3. Location of faunal samples from Locumbilla winery. Analyzed contexts are shaded. Nonanalyzed contexts are in black.

The excavations were placed in areas of both domestic and industrial activity; however, better-preserved faunal materials were generally found in areas further from the residential structures. This probably relates to the continual occupation of the residential portion of the site by itinerant parties, particularly in recent years, and to patterns of trash disposal. The Locumbilla excavations produced the largest sample of pre-1600 deposits, and include domestic and industrial refuse as well as structural remains (Smith 1991:205). These deposits are concentrated in the southeastern portion of the site. Most of the early-period Locumbilla contexts are from this sector.

Large-scale excavations were also conducted in the northern portion of the site where the ruins of a colonial period kiln were located (Van Beck 1991; Rice and Van Beck 1993; Rice 1994). After the kiln fell into disuse both general debris and refuse from other areas of the site apparently were used as fill.

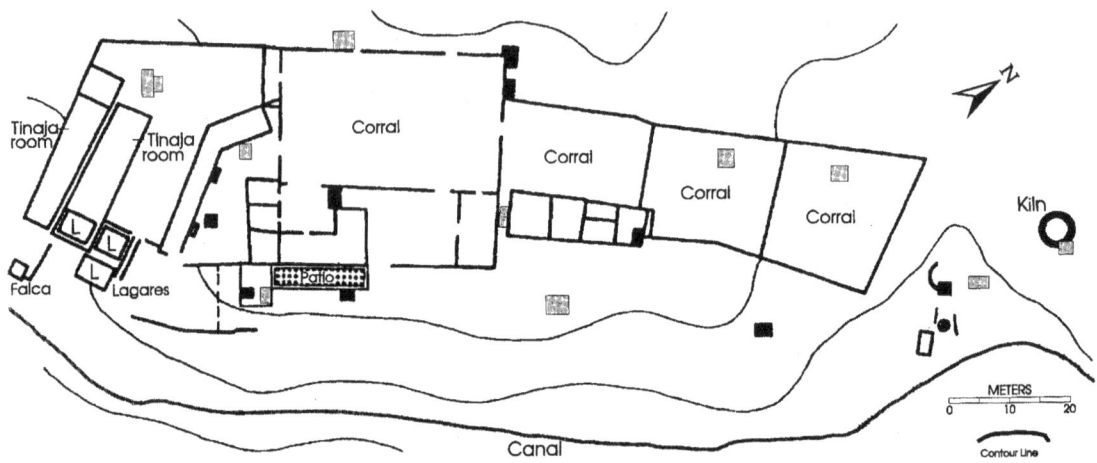

FIGURE 4. Location of faunal samples from Chincha winery. Analyzed contexts are shaded. Nonanalyzed contexts are in black.

A sample of faunal material from this area is included in the analysis.

Chincha Bodega

The Chincha *bodega*, located in the southern portion of the valley, was excavated during the 1988 field season. Faunal material from 11 excavation units representing 20 analytical units was analyzed (Figure 4). Most analytical units are from either middle-period (n = 10) or late-period (n = 9) contexts. Only one early-period context is included in the analysis.

One excavation unit placed in the southern portion of the site produced a substantial deposit of bone refuse. This unit was located in an open industrial area to the west of two *tinaja* rooms. One unit contained a deep lens of bone approximately 60 cm deep and a pit feature containing bone. Post-depositional burning apparently took place in the area, resulting in the presence of a large quantity of burnt bone. In addition to butchered bone refuse, the deposit also contained a large amount of scrap leather such as rawhide straps and hide portions, suggesting that animal and hide processing took place in this area.

Yahuay Bodega

The Yahuay *bodega* is located in the northern portion of the valley where the valley floor rises to form a wide agricultural plain. Structural remains in addition to the wine production facilities include residential areas, a chapel, and a large *tinaja* kiln. Historical data indicate that Yahuay was established by the Dominicans during the 17th century. The purported wealth of the Dominicans apparently lured a number of Moquegua residents to the site in search of buried treasure, thus resulting in a large amount of looting and disturbance to the archaeological deposits.

Although 13 units were excavated, faunal material from only three of these contained sufficient quantities of undisturbed faunal material to warrant analysis (Figure 5). Five analytical units, three middle-period and two late-period, are represented. The densest deposits of faunal materials are from a unit beneath a brick patio adjacent to the presumed residential section of the site.

Estopacaje Bodega

Archival data indicated that Estopacaje was established during the 16th century; however, the

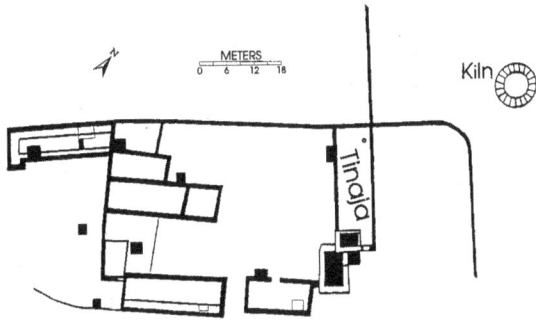

FIGURE 5. Location of faunal samples from Yahuay winery. Analyzed contexts are shaded. Nonanalyzed contexts are in black.

excavations revealed disturbed deposits dating primarily to the late 19th and early 20th centuries. Faunal material from three excavation units representing three analytical contexts are included in the faunal analysis (Figure 6).

Torata Alta

Torata Alta differs from the Moquegua wineries in function, architectural plan, ethnicity of the occupants, and duration of occupation. The site, located approximately 14 km northeast of Moquegua at an elevation of approximately 2,500 m in the dry lower sierra habitat, sits on a hilltop over the Torata River, a tributary of the Osmore River that runs through the Moquegua valley. The architectural plan of the site consists of a gridded layout containing 25 rectangular residential blocks or *kanchas*, each containing a varied number of rooms. The blocks or *kanchas* are separated by a regularly spaced grid of streets (Van Buren and Bürgi 1990: 51; Van Buren et al. 1993:137). The north central portion of the site contains a rectangular plaza, while a church has been identified in the northeast quadrant. The architectural plan and construction techniques contain both Inca and Spanish colonial elements. It remains speculative as to whether the site was constructed as part of Inca expansion into the Torata valley or whether it was constructed entirely under Spanish decree to serve as a *reduc-*

ción where the indigenous population of the valley was ordered to settle (Van Buren 1993).

The recovery of both Late Horizon Chucuito ceramics and European material goods led researchers to postulate that the site was established either under the control of the Lake Titicaca Lupaqa or under Spanish control during the 16th century (Van Buren and Bürgi 1989:80; Van Buren 1993). The historical sources examined and material remains found at Torata Alta suggest the site's population probably derived from the *altiplano*, or high broad plain; however, the precise ethnic identity of the inhabitants remains elusive (Van Buren 1993:235).

Torata Alta may have functioned as a corn-producing center established either in the late horizon or early colonial period based on the identification of several *batanes* or grindstones. Textile production also appears to have been a major economic activity based on the recovery of large numbers of spindle whorls (Van Buren 1993:chap.4) It is not known what other types of economic activities took place at Torata Alta. Beginning in the 17th century the Torata valley became a center of foodstuff cultivation that provisioned both the Moquegua valley and the highlands. Spanish acquisition of cultivable land in the valley may have contributed to the abandonment of Torata Alta. Although it is still open to debate when and by whom Torata Alta was settled, the majority of evidence, both archaeological and historical, indicates the site was occupied by an indigenous population with cultural and economic ties to *altiplano* populations such as the Lake Titicaca Lupaqa.

Torata Alta has been the subject of archaeological study by a number of researchers. Members of Programa Contisuyu, C. Stanish and G. Conrad (Stanish and Pritzker 1983:9), completed the initial survey and mapping of the site. The Moquegua *Bodegas* Project conducted test excavations and completed additional site mapping in 1987. Subsequent surface collection and excavations were conducted by the Moquegua *Bodegas* Project (Van Buren and Bürgi 1990; Van Buren 1993; Van Buren et al. 1993). The most comprehensive report on the archaeological excavations and material culture is provided by Van Buren (1993). Temporal and contextual information for only the Torata Alta archae-

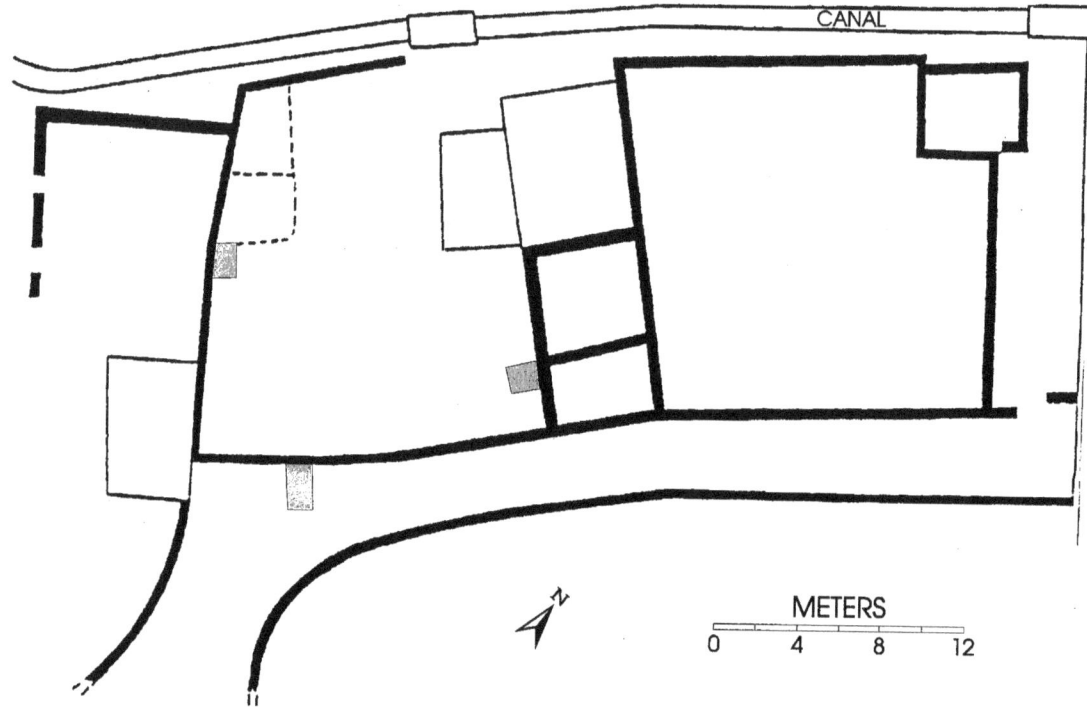

FIGURE 6. Location of faunal samples from Estopacaje winery. Analyzed contexts are shaded. Nonanalyzed contexts are in black.

ological contexts from which faunal materials were selected for analysis are reviewed here.

The greatest concentration of excavations was placed in the southeastern quadrant where the longest occupational history was present. Excavations indicated that the site was occupied during the 16th and 17th centuries. Ash fall from the 1600 eruption of the Huaynaputina volcano suggests that the majority of the site was abandoned by the late 16th century. Occupation in the southeastern quadrant continued into the 17th century, although the entire site was probably abandoned by 1620 when the lower portion of the Torata valley was settled (Van Buren et al. 1993).

Temporal placement of the archaeological deposits at Torata Alta were also based on the presence of ash fall from the 1600 volcanic eruption. Although the temporal range is much less than at the wineries, three time periods are represented: pre-1600, 1600-ash, and post-1600. The Torata Alta occupation was relatively short-lived; therefore, only contexts that contained very clear pre-1600 and post-1600 deposits were chosen for study (Figure 7). Faunal material from two exploratory trenches, Trench M (Block 18) and Trench G (Block 26), were selected. Both trenches contained well-preserved deposits of bone in pre-1600 contexts. The diversity of artifacts found in Trench G suggests that this area of the site or this *kancha*, in particular, was inhabited by wealthier individuals (Van Buren and Bürgi 1990:80). Analytical units totalling nine are represented.

Structure 250 (Block 24) contained the best example of pre- and post-1600 contexts of the excavated structures. Prepared clay floors were identified in both the upper and lower deposits, sug-

Perspectives from *Historical Archaeology*

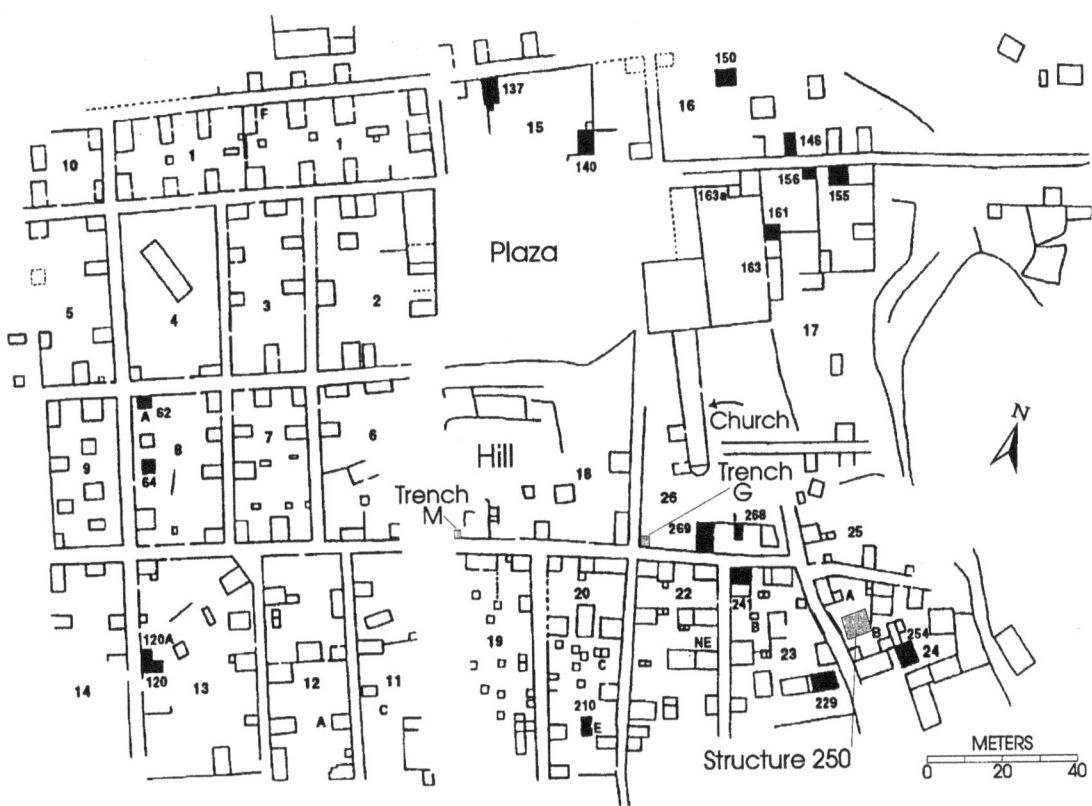

FIGURE 7. Location of faunal samples from Torata Alta. Analyzed contexts are shaded. Nonanalyzed contexts are in black.

gesting a discontinuous, but long-term, occupation of the structure. A large well-preserved deposit of trash was recovered below the ash, suggesting the structure was abandoned for some time prior to reoccupation in the early 17th century (Van Buren and Bürgi 1990:74). Faunal material from the east half of the structure was analyzed.

Soil samples of differing volumes were taken from a number of the units and levels. Twenty-three samples were analyzed for remains of small-sized specimens from Trenches M, G, and Structure 250. The majority of these (74%) are from pre-1600 levels.

Analysis of faunal material from Torata Alta provides baseline data on the use of animal resources by indigenous populations during the early colonial period. Analysis of the recovered zooarchaeological materials also helps determine if Spanish animal resources were present in the earliest occupation of the site and, if so, other potential economic activities that might have taken place at Torata Alta.

Recovery and Analytical Methods

The size of excavation units varied depending on the objectives of the excavation. Units most commonly measured 2 x 2 m in open or unrestricted areas while smaller units measuring 1 x 2 m were more common along standing structures. Large block excavations were employed at the Locumbilla *bodega* to expose buried structural remains. All of

TABLE 2
ALLOMETRIC VALUES AND FORMULA USED IN THIS STUDY

Taxon	Log a	b	r^2	Y	X	Source
Mammals	1.41	.81	.91	EMW	Bone wt.	Quitmyer (1985)
Aves	1.24	.84	.98	EMW	Bone wt.	Quitmyer (1985)
Osteichthyes	1.34	.90	.96	EMW	Bone wt.	Hale and Walker (1986)
Carcharhinidae	.94	1.38	.98	EMW	Bone wt.	Quitmyer (1985)
Gastropoda	-0.16	.92	.89	EMW	Shell wt.	Hale et al. (1987)
Chitons	-0.32	1.08	.84	EMW	Shell wt.	deFrance (1988)
Bivalves	.02	.68	.83	EMW	Shell wt.	Hale et al. (1987)

Allometric Regression Formula: $Y = aX^b$
Transformed: Log Y = Log a + b (Log X)
Where: X = skeletal/shell weight (g)
　　　　Y = edible meat weight (EMW) (g) or total body weight (TBW) (kg)
　　　　a = Y intercept
　　　　b = slope of the line

the excavations followed natural stratigraphic zones. Arbitrary levels were used only in upper levels of disturbed materials or in those instances where natural layers could not be discerned.

Soil samples were collected from features such as hearths, and defined areas of soil disturbance for processing with fine-meshed (1/16-in., 1.70-mm) screens. All other faunal material was recovered with 1/4-in. (6.35-mm) mesh screens. The data, tables, and figures presented here are based on the 1/4-in. fraction. However, reference will be made to significant materials recovered with fine-mesh screens.

Estimates of the Minimum Number of Individuals (MNI) were made using paired elements, age, and sex. Undoubtedly, the meat provided by different animals varied depending on the size of the individuals. Because estimates of MNI do not discriminate between the size of the individuals, edible meat weight (EMW) estimates were determined to help identify the main sources of meat protein. However, MNI is believed to provide the best ordinal ranking of taxa relative abundance, particularly for identifying both the economic uses of animals and the geographical areas from which the faunal resources originated. The allometric formula for calculating edible meat weight is presented in Table 2. Percentages of both MNI and EMW are presented for the various classes and for the wineries and Torata Alta.

Results of Faunal Analysis

When the analyzed faunal samples from both the wineries and Torata Alta are combined the assemblage contains 47,023 specimens representing a minimum of 795 individuals (Table 3). The *bodega* samples constitute a much greater portion of the assemblage, accounting for 62.4 percent (n = 29,323) of the specimens and 77.1 percent (n = 613) of the MNI. The Torata Alta assemblage contains 17,700 fragments (37.6% of total) representing a MNI of 182 (22.9%). For the winery samples the greatest concentration of faunal remains are from middle-period contexts, followed by late-period contexts. The small number of early-period samples produced the lowest quantity of faunal material. In contrast, the pre-1600 samples from Torata Alta constitute the largest portion of the assemblage followed by the 1600 ash contexts and post-1600 deposits. Table 4 presents summary data on Number of Identified Specimens (NISP), MNI, and percentages of EMW by class.

TABLE 3
FREQUENCIES OF FAUNAL REMAINS BY SITE AND TIME PERIOD

Site	Time Period	NISP	MNI	Taxa (N)
Torata Alta	Post-1600	2,287	35	11
	1600-Ash	1,853	39	10
	Pre-1600	13,560	108	26
Locumbilla	Late	4,482	89	20
	Middle	7,630	223	24
	Early	1,140	41	13
Chincha	Late	2,663	80	15
	Middle	6,667	107	26
	Early	16	8	7
Yahuay	Late	4,360	25	7
	Middle	2,144	27	11
Estopacaje	Late	207	12	10
	Middle	14	1	1
Total		47,023	795	(63)

When the *bodega* samples are combined, 41 taxa are represented; however, not more than 13 species are present in any single analytical unit. Table 5 indicates the taxa identified at each site. The identified fauna considered of economic importance consists of 12 species of mammals, at least 7 species of birds, 13 species of bony fishes, at least 2 forms of cartilaginous fishes, 14 species of mollusks, 1 species of crustacean, and sea urchins. The introduced species present in the winery samples consist of 8 mammal and 1 bird species. Species not considered to be of economic importance include bats, rodents, snakes, frogs, barnacles, and small terrestrial gastropods.

In all of the winery samples and in all time periods mammals account for the greatest number of individuals (Figure 8). Most individuals are introduced domestic mammals of economic importance, although Andean camelids are relatively abundant (Figures 9, 10). Also present are introduced species of cats, large dogs, rats, and unidentified small mammals. Half of the birds represented are chickens. Other identified bird taxa include doves, and at least one duck and a hawk. Although fishes account for less than 4 percent of the *bodegas* MNI, there are at least 10 species present, including both bony and cartilaginous fishes. All of these species are

marine forms that would have been transported to Moquegua from the Pacific coast, approximately 75 km to the west. The invertebrate olive snails, false abalone, mussels, arks, oysters, and sea urchins are also marine forms.

The Torata Alta samples contain a slightly more equitable distribution of individuals than do the *bodega* samples (Figure 11). The mammalian taxa are dominated by camelid individuals (Figure 12). Native Andean mammals include guinea pigs and the mountain lion. Dogs are also present and may include introduced breeds based on the large size of the individuals. The most common nonnative species are the caprines, either sheep or goats, as well as pigs and Old World rats. Significantly, both caprines and Old World rodents are present in the basal levels of the deposits, suggesting Spanish resources were present during the initial occupation of Torata Alta.

The identified birds are chickens and doves. The fishes are represented by marine species including silversides, weakfish, seatrout, drum, and bonito. The fine-screened samples from Torata Alta also contained abundant remains of anchovies, primarily vertebrae. Of the 23 fine-screened samples analyzed, only one did not contain anchovy remains. Other marine resources present include a slightly

TABLE 4
RELATIVE ABUNDANCE OF TAXA BY CLASS FOR TORATA
ALTA AND WINERIES[a]

Site	Total		%	
	NISP	MNI	MNI	EMW
Torata Alta				
All Time Periods				
Mammals	17,348	70	38.46	99.62
Birds	74	13	7.14	.27
Fishes	20	8	4.40	.04
Gastropods	13	13	7.14	.01
Bivalves	207	70	38.46	.06
Other Inverts	38	8	4.40	.00
Total	17,700	182	100.00	100.00
Wineries				
Early Contexts				
Mammals	1,130	32	65.31	99.36
Birds	3	3	6.12	0.12
Fishes	3	3	6.12	0.38
Gastropods	5	4	8.16	0.04
Bivalves	13	7	14.29	0.09
Other Inverts	2	0	.00	.00
Total	1,156	49	100.00	100.00
Middle Contexts				
Mammals	16,194	261	72.91	99.90
Birds	62	26	7.26	0.05
Fishes	24	18	5.03	0.04
Gastropods	12	12	3.35	.00
Bivalves	152	34	9.50	0.01
Other Inverts	11	7	1.96	.00
Total	16,455	358	100.00	100.00
Late Contexts				
Mammals	11,603	162	78.64	99.71
Birds	38	16	7.77	0.25
Fishes	5	3	1.46	0.02
Gastropods	4	3	1.46	0.01
Bivalves	30	15	7.28	0.01
Other Inverts	32	7	3.40	.00
Total	11,712	206	100.00	100.00

[a]Using ¼-in. (6.35-mm) mesh

Discussion

greater diversity of gastropods, bivalves, and other invertebrates than were present in the *bodega* samples.

The composition of the faunal assemblages in terms of estimates of the Minimum Number of Individuals (MNI), edible meat weight (EMW), and species diversity allows an assessment to be made of Spanish adaptation and acculturation to the Moquegua region. The first topic addressed by this research concerns whether local faunal resources were incorporated into the diet. It was hypothesized that the colonial inhabitants of the wineries would have incorporated a variety of local resources into their diet. This pattern is consistent with other areas

TABLE 5

TAXA IDENTIFIED FROM THE MOQUEGUA WINERIES AND TORATA ALTA[a]

Taxon	Wineries				
	Torata Alta	Locumbilla	Chincha	Yahuay	Estopacaje
Chiroptera* (bats)	*				
Rodentia unidentified (unidentified rodent)		*	*	*	
Mus musculus (house mouse)			*		*
Rattus spp. (Old World rats)	*				
Muridae (rats, mice)	*				
Phyllotis sp. (leaf-eared mouse)		*			
Sigmodontinae* (New World rodent)	*	*			
Cavia porcellus (guinea pig)	*	*	*	*	*
Felis concolor (mountain lion)	*				
Felis catus (cat)		*	*		
Canis familiaris (dog)	*	*	*	*	
Canidae (dogs, wolves, foxes)	*				
Cervidae (deer)		*			
Sus scrofa (pig)	*	*	*	*	*
Lama spp. (llama, alpaca, guanaco)	*	*	*	*	
Camelidae (New World camels)	*	*	*	*	*
Bos taurus (cow)		*	*	*	*
Ovis aries (sheep)		*	*	*	
Capra hircus (goat)	*	*	*		
Caprini (sheep/goats)	*	*	*	*	*
Equus asinus (burro)		*			
Equus cf. asinus (probable burro)		*			
Equus caballus (horse)		*	*		
Equus spp. (horse, burro, mule)		*		*	
Threskiornithidae (ibis)					*
Anas sp. (duck)		*			
Cairina moschata (muscovy duck)		*			
Psittacidae (parrots, parakeets)	*				
Gallus gallus (chicken)	*	*	*	*	*
Buteo sp. (cf. polysoma) (red-backed hawk)			*		
Columbidae cf. Zenaidura* (doves, pigeons)	*				
Columbidae (doves, pigeons)	*	*	*		
Serpentes* (snakes)	*				
Anura* (frog)	*				
Engraulis ringens* (Peruvian anchovy)	*	*			
Engraulidae* (anchovies)	*	*			
Atherinidae (silversides)	*				
Merluccius sp. (offshore hake)			*		
Hemanthias peruanus (splittail seaperch)			*		
Carangidae (jack)	*				
Anisotremus sp. (grunt)			*		
Cynoscion analis (Peruvian weakfish)	*				
Cynoscion sp. (seatrout)	*				
Sciaena gilberti (corvina drum)		*			
Sciaena sp. (drum)	*				
Trachurus murphyi (southern sack mackerel)		*			
Trachurus sp. (mackerel)		*			
Mugil sp. (mullet)		*			
Bodianus sp. (hogfish)		*			

(continued)

TABLE 5 (*continued*)
TAXA IDENTIFIED FROM THE MOQUEGUA WINERIES AND TORATA ALTA[a]

Taxon	Wineries				
	Torata Alta	Locumbilla	Chincha	Yahuay	Estopacaje
Sarda chiliensis (Pacific bonito)	*				
Carcharhinus spp. (requiem shark)		*	*		
Lamniformes (sharks)		*			
Brachyura (marine crabs)	*	*	*		
Decapoda (swimming crabs)			*		
Crustacea uid (marine arthropods)			*		*
Cirripedia (barnacles)	*				
Chiton *s.l.* (chiton *sensu latu*)	*				
Trochidae (topsnail)		*			
Turritella cingulata (belted turretsnail)	*				
Turritella spp. (turretsnail)	*	*			
Littorinidae (periwinkle)			*		
Crepidula spp. (slippershell)	*		*		
Calyptraeidae (slippershell)	*				
Concholepas concholepas (false abalone)	*	*	*		
Oliva spp. (olive)	*	*			
Hydrobiidae* (hydrobe)			*		
Gastrocopta sp.* (snaggletooth)	*				
Pupoides sp.* (dagger)	*				
Succinea sp.* (ambersnail)	*				
Scutalis sp. (arboreal snail)	*				
Brachidontes purpuratus (purple sea mussel)	*	*			
Choromytilus chorus (choro mussel)	*	*	*		
Mytilidae (mussels)	*	*	*		
Glycymeris sp. (bittersweet)		*			
Anadara sp. (ark)		*			
Ostreidae (oyster)	*	*			
Lucinidae (lucines)		*			
Tellinidae (tellins)	*	*			
Chione sp. (venus)	*				
Veneridae (venus clams)	*	*			
Protothaca spp. (littlenecks)	*	*			
Echinoidea (sea urchins)	*	*	*		

[a]¼-in. (6.35-mm) and ¹⁄₁₆-in. (1.70-mm) mesh
*indicates taxa present only in ¹⁄₁₆-in. (1.70-mm) mesh

of Spanish colonial settlement in Florida and the Caribbean. In contrast to the wineries, the indigenous inhabitants of Torata Alta would have relied on native fauna for most of their needs.

The faunal data demonstrate that animals at the wineries and Torata Alta were employed in different economic and subsistence roles. Torata Alta exhibits a very conservative pattern of faunal use. The late 16th- and early 17th-century occupations demonstrate a continuation of indigenous practices with the occasional use of introduced Old World fauna, most notably caprines, pigs, and chickens. The age profiles of the most common domestic mammals, the camelids, suggest that a breeding population was present (Figure 13). Some juvenile camelid individuals were butchered; however, age profiles indicate that most camelids were adults when butchered. Evidence of bone pathologies,

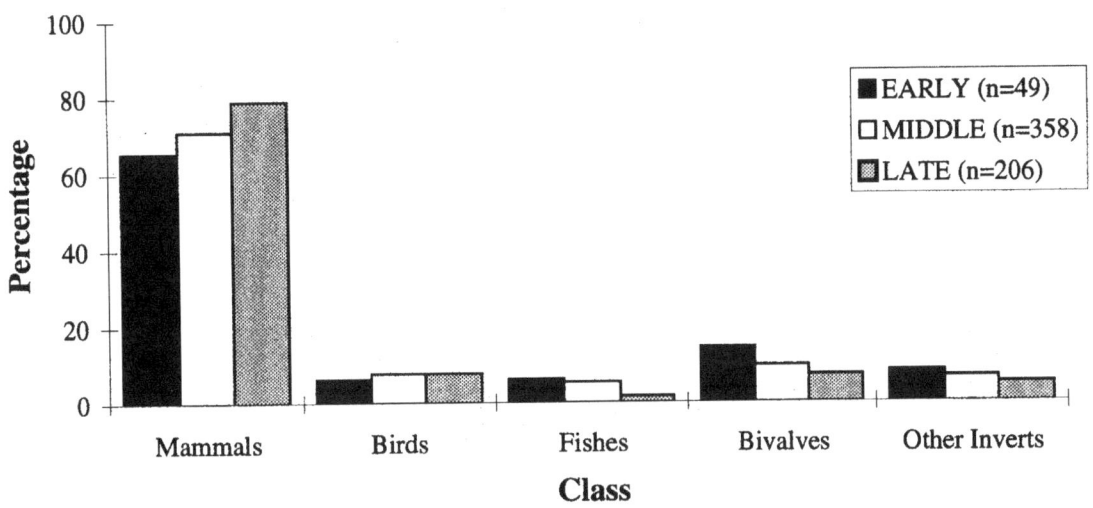

FIGURE 8. Minimum Numbers of Individuals by taxonomic class and time period for the wineries.

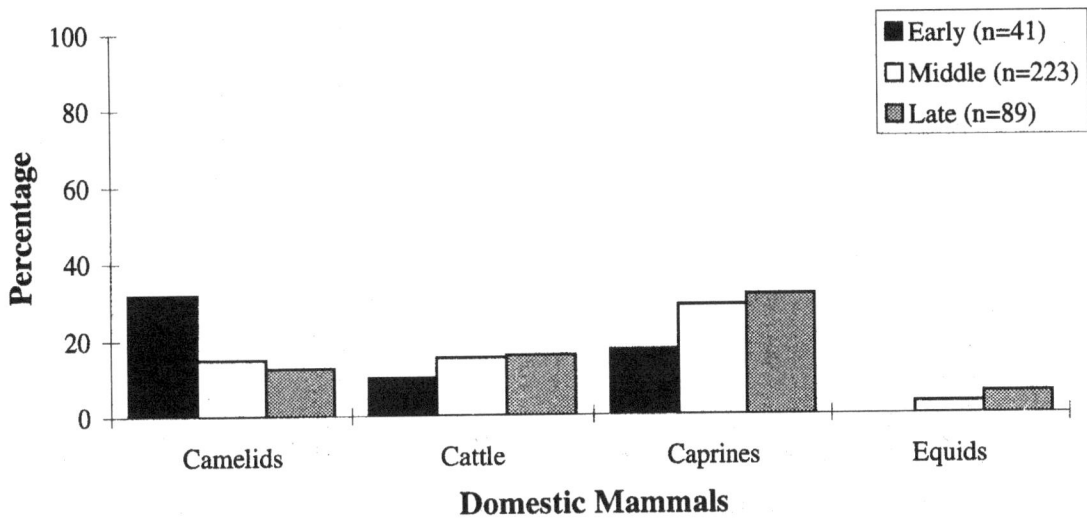

FIGURE 9. Domestic mammal MNI by time period for the Locumbilla winery.

e.g., exostoses and false ring bone, associated with weight-bearing activities suggests that some of these animals were used for transport (Table 6, Figure 14). The large amount of textile-related paraphernalia, e.g., spindle whorls, (Van Buren 1993: Appendix B) present suggests woolen thread was manufactured at the site and used to produce textiles.

The recovery of numerous cranial and other less meaty skeletal portions, such as feet elements (Figure 15), suggests that animals were butchered at Torata Alta; therefore, charqui or dried camelid meat probably was not imported by the inhabitants, a feature present on other prehispanic Andean sites (Miller and Burger 1995). Although camelid meat was not imported, a variety of marine fish and

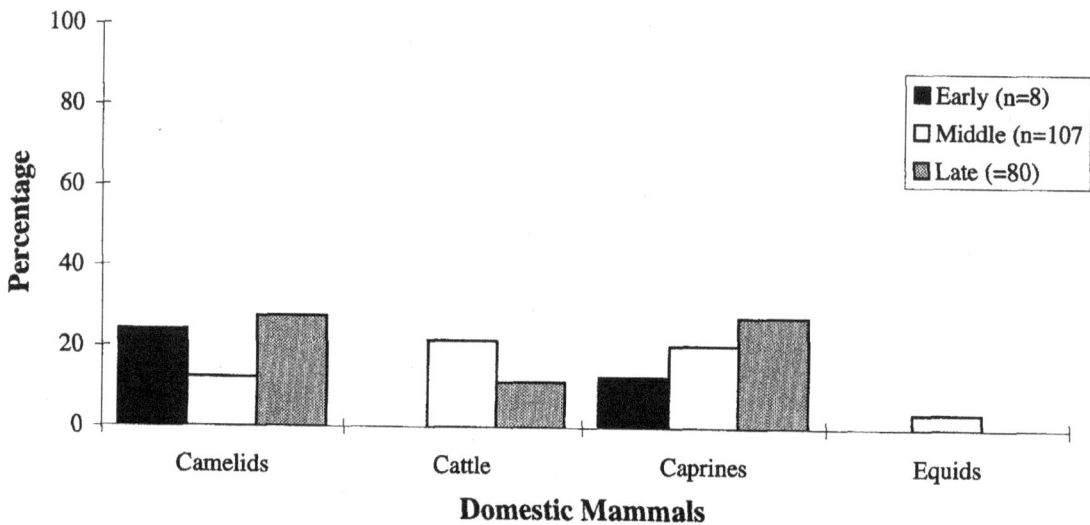

FIGURE 10. Domestic mammal MNI by time period for the Chincha winery.

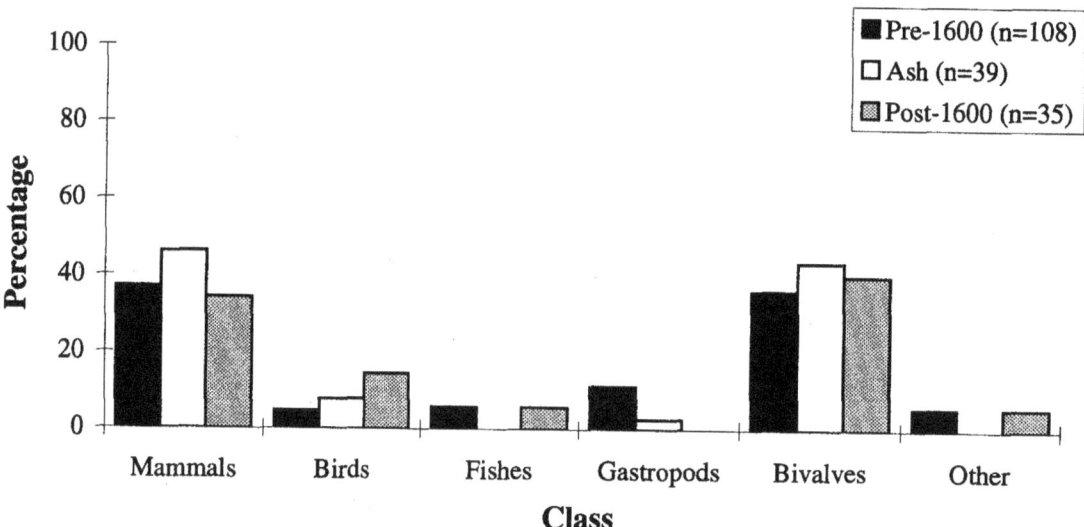

FIGURE 11. Minimum Numbers of Individuals by taxonomic class and time period for Torata Alta.

shellfish were transported to the site, suggesting that exchange routes were used for the movement of food resources during the 16th and early 17th centuries.

The faunal assemblage from Torata Alta provides an indication of the use of animals by an indigenous population during the 16th century. Although Torata Alta represents only one community, some generalizations can be made based on the faunal assemblage pattern. Indigenous populations appear to have been relatively conservative in their adoption of introduced Old World species during the 16th century. Those resources that were used were domesticates represented by smaller-sized individuals, such as caprines and pigs (Table 7, Figures 16, 17). None of the larger-sized introduced species,

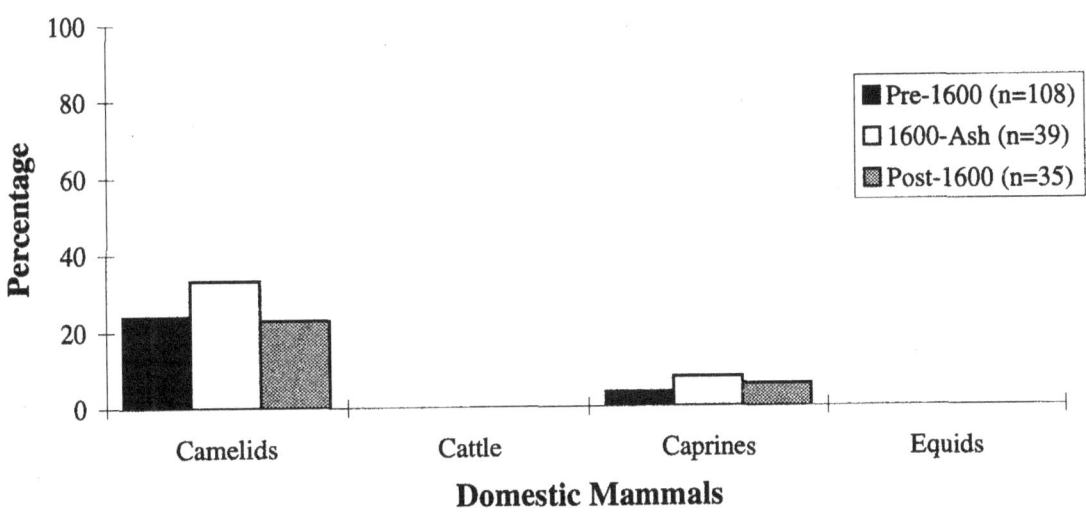

FIGURE 12. Domestic mammal MNI by time period for Torata Alta.

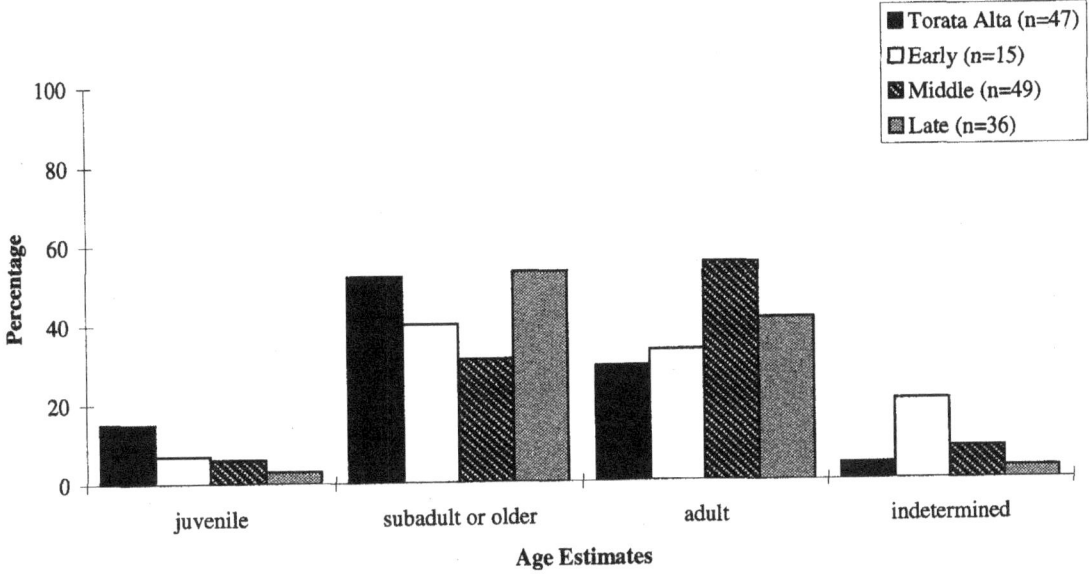

FIGURE 13. Age groups of camelid individuals at Torata Alta and wineries.

that is, cattle or horses, were incorporated into the economy of Torata Alta. The faunal pattern exhibited by the Torata Alta assemblage is a traditional Andean one with little innovation or adoption of new animal resources.

A very different pattern of faunal use characterizes the winery assemblages. The winery samples indicate that few native resources were incorporated into the colonial diet. Marine fish and shellfish were minor components of the diet. Meat from domestic mammals was the main source of animal protein throughout the winery occupation (Figures 16, 17).

At the wineries camelids constitute a large portion of the assemblages in all time periods. Significantly, no other Andean animals were adopted as major economic or subsistence staples at the win-

TABLE 6
BONE PATHOLOGIES FROM TORATA ALTA AND WINERIES

Site	Provenience	F.S. No.	Time	Taxon	Element	Pathology
Locumbilla	984N/1032.5E	1173	Middle	*Lama* sp.	Thoracic vertebra	Osteophytosis
Locumbilla	957.N/1061.5E	1585	Middle	*Lama* sp.	Phalanx 1	False ring bone[a]
Locumbilla	957.5N/1061.5E	1551	Middle	*Bos taurus*	Entocuneiform	Exostosis
Chincha	1017N/1009E	92	Middle	*Bos taurus*	Phalanx 3	Exostosis
Chincha	1034.5N/1044E	80	Late	Camelidae	Rib	Osteophytosis on articular surface
Chincha	1087N/1048E	43	Late	*Lama* sp.	Cervical vertebra	Osteophytosis
Yahuay	990N/958.5E	43	Late	*Bos taurus*	Phalanx 3	Exostosis
Torata Alta	Trench M	740	pre-1600	*Lama* sp.	Phalanx 1	False ring bone[a]
		749	pre-1600	*Lama* sp.	Phalanx 3	Exostosis
Torata Alta	Trench G	581	pre-1600	*Lama* sp.	Thoracic vertebra	Osteophytosis
		581	pre-1600	*Lama* sp.	Thoracic vertebra	Osteophytosis

[a]Bone enlargement of the interphalangeal joints resulting from concussion of the phalanges as the foot is placed on the ground. Consequences for large draught animals range from mild lameness to fusion of the joint, i.e., ankylosis (Baker and Brothwell 1980:120).

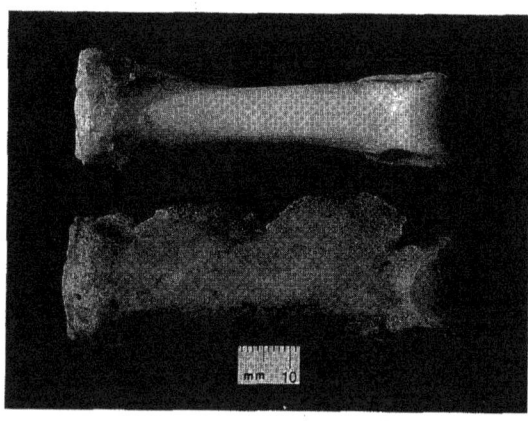

FIGURE 14. Comparison of normal first phalanx of a llama, *top*, with archaeological specimen from Torata Alta exhibiting false ring bone, *bottom*. (Photo by Pat Payne, University of Florida, Gainesville.)

eries. The only other Andean mammal that occurs in the samples is the guinea pig or *cuy*. Infrequent remains of these domesticated animals occur in middle-period (n = 7) and late-period (n = 2) winery deposits. They are also uncommon in the 16th-century Torata Alta samples (n = 3); however, they constitute a greater percentage of the individuals

(Figure 16). Guinea pigs are an adaptable, easily maintained food source that are also used for divinations and sacrifices (Gade 1967; Morales 1995). The popularity of guinea pigs is documented by their remains in other prehispanic archaeological contexts and their consumption today by both indigenous and mestizo populations (Morales 1995).

Two factors probably relate to the low frequencies of guinea pigs in the winery contexts. First, it can be postulated that with the wealth of other meat sources available to the *bodega* inhabitants guinea pigs were not selected for exploitation. Second, the Spanish colonists may have considered these small rodents inappropriate food items that should be excluded from the diet, thereby constituting a cognitive rejection of the guinea pig as a food source. The infrequent consumption of *cuys*, particularly during the earlier years of Spanish settlement, may also have served as a means of distinguishing Spaniards, either creoles or *peninsulares*, from both indigenous and mestizo populations.

The low frequencies of native animal resources in the winery samples also raises some questions concerning the probable diet of indigenous peoples employed on the wineries. An indigenous labor force is described as one of the probable agents of transculturation of Andean material culture to the Spanish colonists (Smith 1991:316–317). How-

TABLE 7

ESTIMATED EDIBLE MEAT WEIGHT FROM ECONOMICALLY IMPORTANT MAMMALS[a]

Mammal	Torata Alta		Early		Middle		Late	
	EMW	%	EMW	%	EMW	%	EMW	%
Guinea Pig	107.4	0.1	—	0.0	4.0	0.0	38.4	0.0
Pig	268.4	0.3	59.2	0.4	4,041.1	1.1	2,180.1	0.9
Camelids	98,901.8	97.1	8,207.3	62.1	55,284.9	14.7	72,550.4	29.7
Cattle	—	0.0	3,629.1	27.5	235,620.3	62.5	109,711.8	44.9
Caprines	2,600.2	2.6	1,323.3	10.0	76,444.9	20.3	55,156.3	22.6
Total	101,877.8	100.0	13,218.9	100.0	377,185.8	100.0	244,362.3	100.0

[a]¼-in. (6.35-mm) mesh

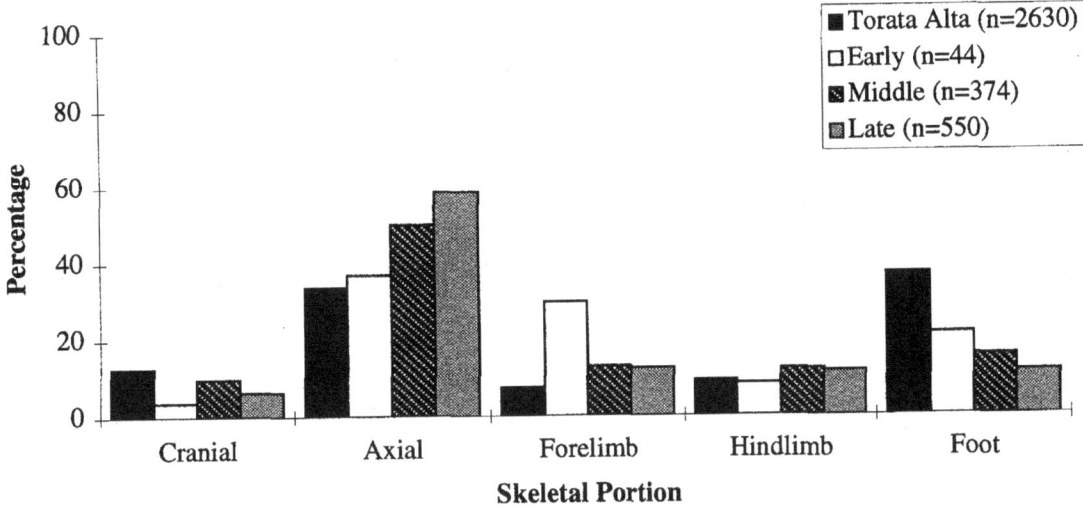

FIGURE 15. Representation of camelid skeletal elements at Torata Alta and wineries.

ever, the paucity of remains from native animals in the samples suggests that Andean dietary items were less frequently incorporated into the colonial culture than were material goods, e.g., ceramics, household, and industrial goods (Smith 1991). It is also possible that indigenous populations attempted to assimilate into the colonial culture by adopting the dietary habits of the dominant culture. Alternatively, these populations maintained very conservative foodways.

Archaeological contexts representing either indigenous laborers or enslaved Africans have not been identified in the Moquegua valley; therefore, the role of these populations in the formation of colonial diet awaits further study.

The second topic this paper examines concerns the effect of Spanish colonization on Andean herding practices. The historical record suggests that Andean pastoral activities were disrupted or replaced by introduced mammalian species as the Spaniards sought to establish rangelands for cattle, sheep, and horses and to control the indigenous population (Orlove 1977; Gade and Escobar 1982). If this scenario holds true for the Moquegua and

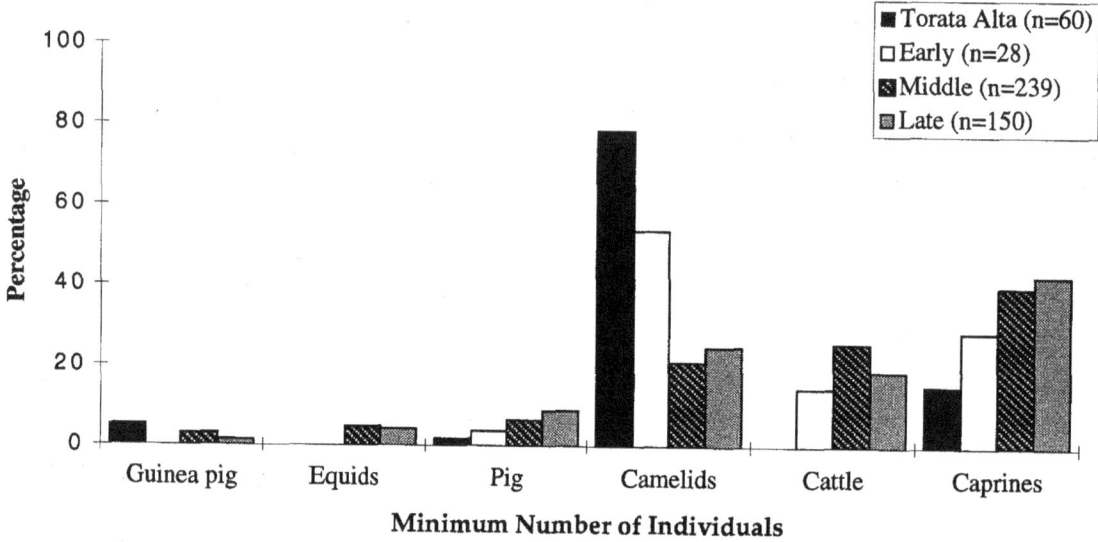

FIGURE 16. MNI of economically important mammals at Torata Alta and wineries.

Torata valleys, one would expect the archaeological record to demonstrate an abundance of introduced utilitarian animals, such as oxen and horses, and little use of domestic camelids.

In contrast to the pattern suggested by historical accounts, the Torata Alta samples indicate neither disruption of traditional herding practices nor widespread adoption of European animals. Although Old World animals were apparently available based on the recovery of caprines, camelids continued to be used almost exclusively into the 17th century. There is no zooarchaeological evidence that cattle, horses, or burros were present at Torata Alta (Figure 16).

In the Moquegua valley, the pattern of animal use at the *bodegas* reflects a blending of Andean utilitarian mammalian resources with Old World fauna. The mammalian component of the winery assemblages indicates that several introduced species thrived in the Moquegua region. Cattle and caprines, of which sheep are more abundant, were the most common introduced animals. Although caprines are generally more common in terms of individuals, particularly in middle- and late-period samples, cattle contributed more meat to the diet

(Table 7, Figure 17). Pigs and equids are least common at all four wineries and in all three time periods. A striking feature of the *bodegas* samples is the abundance of camelids, presumably llamas, at each of the four *bodegas* (Figure 16). This pattern is strikingly evident at both Locumbilla and Chincha, where all three time periods are represented (Figures 10, 11).

The most significant aspect of domestic animal use is that equids, i.e., horses, burros, and mules, are never common in the archaeological collections. Deceased horses may have been disposed of outside of the *bodegas*; however, the low frequency of their remains suggests they were uncommon. Indications that the use of equids was rare is also provided by the scant amount of horse-related hardware, such as shoes, bits, and saddle loops, present in the material remains (Smith 1991:270, 280). Interestingly, both equid remains and horse hardware are very uncommon until the late period, particularly at both Locumbilla and Chincha. Therefore, camelids—llamas in particular—apparently remained the preferred animal for transporting goods, such as Moquegua's wine products, in the mountainous Andean terrain.

The abundance of camelid remains at the win-

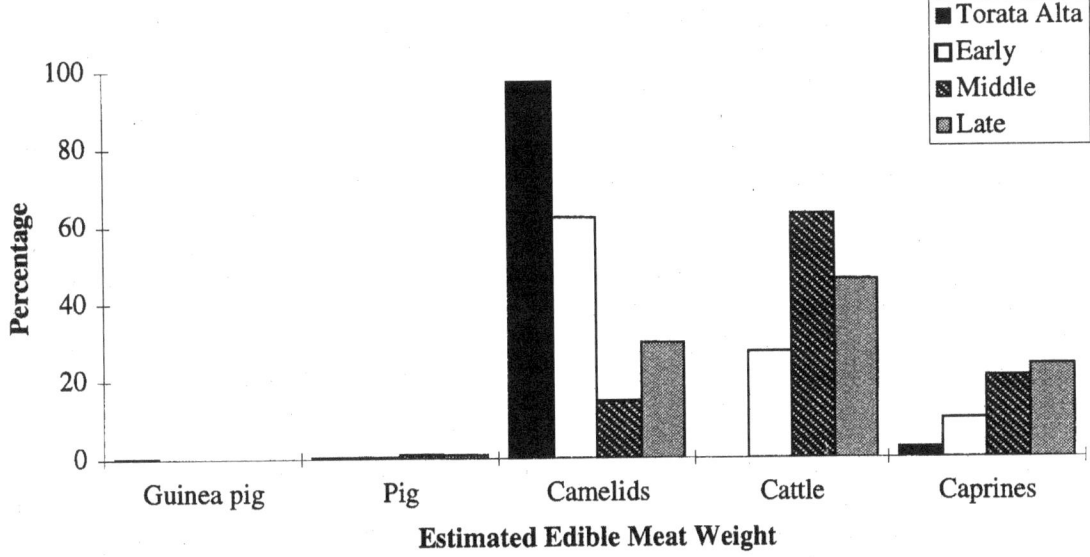

FIGURE 17. EMW of economically important mammals at Torata Alta and wineries.

eries raises some interesting issues concerning diet during the colonial period. There is no indication that an aversion to the consumption of camelid meat developed in the Moquegua region. Camelids were used as beasts of burden and as food. Bone pathologies are common on the camelid remains from the wineries (Table 6), indicating they were used as pack animals. In addition, remains of butchered meaty portions of vertebrae and ribs are common (Figure 15). One can hypothesize that camelids were adopted as food over other Andean resources because they complemented the Iberian herding lifestyle. Herd animals were valued as both a source of income and as food in Spain. The abundant archaeological remains of camelids in colonial contexts indicates that these animals were valued for their multiple economic and dietary roles. Whether or not the pattern of camelid use and consumption exhibited by the wineries is representative of all Andean colonial occupations or only rural ones could be resolved with zooarchaeological data from a greater range of contexts, such as urban house sites and nonindustrial locales.

In contrast to the patterns exhibited in Spanish Florida and the Caribbean, the adaptation and proliferation of domestic Old World mammals in the Moquegua region allowed the colonists to maintain a diet that was more Iberian in character than was found in the Spanish settlements of either the Caribbean or Florida. The pastoral nature of the prehispanic Andean economy in combination with arid, mountainous terrain favorable for the rearing of sheep and goats apparently facilitated the imposition of Spanish livestock practices on the Andean landscape. In no other area of the New World did Spanish colonists encounter either an existing pastoral economy or the environmental conditions favorable for establishing Iberian herd animals. The humid habitats of Florida and the Caribbean were unfavorable for caprines. Although cattle acclimated to the Caribbean, colonists were forced to consume local animals, particularly marine fish and shellfish. The cattle industry that developed at Puerto Real was dramatically different from the traditional economy of Spain. The pastoral economy of the Iberian peninsula flourished, albeit in modified form, in southern Peru.

Conclusions

The repercussions of the early colonial animal importations are important aspects of modern Peruvian diet, economy, and lifeways. This analysis has provided information on the origins and emergence of these patterns. The Moquegua winery and Torata Alta faunal samples have demonstrated patterns of subsistence and economic uses of animals that are thus far unique among Spanish colonial sites.

Torata Alta during the 16th and early 17th centuries appears to have maintained a precolonial pattern of animal use. The inhabitants adopted a very limited number of Old World taxa, primarily smaller-sized domesticates such as caprines, pigs, and chickens. Resources from coastal zones were traded to Torata Alta into the early 17th century. Although the camelid herds may have been obtained from highland populations, age profiles indicate a breeding population was reared near the site. Neither the dietary nor economic uses of animals exhibit much innovation during the colonial era. Although greater time-depth is needed to make definitive statements concerning the use of faunal resources by indigenous communities during the early Spanish colonial period, the Torata Alta sample indicates a conservative pattern of animal use. Traditional Andean sources of animal protein and economic uses of animals were sufficient for the occupants of Torata Alta.

In contrast to Torata Alta, the faunal assemblage from the Moquegua *bodegas* indicates the transference of many Iberian dietary and economic features to the colonial setting. Subsistence resources apparently were either maintained in the Moquegua valley or in an adjacent region, such as the Torata valley (Brown 1986:40). The most consistently used Andean resources were camelids. Age profiles, element distributions, and pathologies of the camelid individuals suggest they were reared outside of the valley, employed as beasts of burden well into adulthood, and butchered after their economic utility had declined. The continued use of camelids contradicts historical sources that indicate equids quickly replaced the sure-footed Andean ships of the desert. Although marine resources were occasionally traded to the wineries and guinea pigs were consumed infrequently, no other Andean resources were used consistently.

The faunal assemblage provides evidence that Old World introductions were integral components of Spanish colonial economy. Caprines and cattle were widely used throughout the occupation of the wineries, and were more widely used than were either pigs or equids, which are relatively uncommon in the samples.

The faunal assemblage indicates that the winery inhabitants were conservative and largely self-sufficient in their use of animal resources, with an obvious preference for Old World taxa. The resources that were adopted, most notably camelids, were important for the movement of Moquegua's wine and brandy products to distant markets. The occupants did not experience subsistence hardships or the need to alter foodways that were considered "Spanish." In comparison to the Iberian model and other areas of Spanish colonial settlement in Spanish Florida and the Caribbean, animal use on the wineries was more similar to Spanish animal husbandry than elsewhere in the New World.

How animals are used in a colonial setting reflects the interplay between the environmental adaptability of animals transported to new settings, the foodways and economic systems that exist in the recently colonized region, and the perceptions of the colonists as to what constitutes appropriate food items and what roles animals should play, e.g., food, beasts of burden, pets. The desire to maintain the foodways or habits of one's homeland would be strongest with the most recent immigrants. However, subsequent generations would be indoctrinated into a dynamic, evolving foodway that contains elements of both the new setting and the homeland. Zooarchaeologists are often faced with the dilemma of determining why certain animal foods appear in a new cuisine at the exclusion of others. In the case of the colonial record from southern Peru, camelids were adopted to serve multiple roles; however, no other Andean animals were incorporated into the diet. The use of camelids for food, fiber, and transport apparently did not affront Spanish perceptions of what constitutes appropriate food items. In addition, the climate of the coastal valleys of southern Peru was conducive to raising caprines. Beef, mutton, and camelid meat were in abundant supply. One can reasonably argue that there was no need for other food items, such as guinea pigs, small Andean game, fish, shellfish, or wild birds.

Despite the abundance of meat from domestic animals in the diet, it remains difficult to explain why other Andean animals are not represented in the archaeological record. Does the absence of certain animals constitute a cognitive rejection of that food or animal? Did the *criollo* populations view some animals as inappropriate or undesirable? Or were some animals deemed inappropriate because of method of preparation, i.e., taste? Alternatively, was there such an abundance of meat from large animals that there was no sense of need for other foodstuffs?

One avenue of research that would help determine if the patterns identified at the wineries are representative of colonial Peru as a whole would be the analysis of faunal collections from house sites of known ethnic affiliation and socioeconomic level. For example, excavation of house sites in the large colonial cities of Arequipa or Lima would expand the understanding of colonial subsistence. If the Moquegua wineries represent rural industrial enterprises that were occupied by individuals of both Andean and Spanish ancestry, then material from urban sites of affluent families would allow insightful comparisons to be made. It would be particularly interesting to see if the use of camelid meat is lower in urban areas where presumably greater social distinctions were maintained between those of Spanish versus Andean descent.

It would also be revealing to examine faunal material from 17th- and 18th-century contexts exclusively associated with indigenous laborers. Presumably, some of the food refuse that accumulated at the wineries was from indigenous laborers or enslaved Africans. Large seasonal labor camps also were established for temporary workers during harvest season, possibly in camps at elevations above the valley. If Torata Alta is an accurate representation of the indigenous diet during the early colonial period, sites associated with laborers should reflect a greater use of native food items and conservatism in the adoption of non-Andean food items.

The environment of southern Peru established the limits of which animals could be raised success-

fully. However, the prehispanic tradition and status of camelid pastoralism facilitated the growth of the colonial pastoral economy. It is evident from the faunal material that the European introductions of both cattle and caprines developed into profitable economies. Cattle ranches were established in many of the Central Andean valleys at lower elevations. Cattle ranching in Peru never achieved the same degree of commercial success that characterized either the Caribbean or Mexico. However, large ranches provided meat, hides, and tallow that was used in the manufacture of candles, an essential item in the deep shaft mines. In contrast to Mexico, where cattle herding was controlled by Spaniards, Gibson (1987:393) argues that Indians participated more in Peruvian cattle ranching because of preconditioning or "psychological preparation" from llama herding. Sheep and goat herding were also adopted by many indigenous populations, including many in the higher elevations, greater than 3,000 m. Today, pastoralism in the Central Andes continues to serve as a symbol of prestige for indigenous populations, regardless of whether the animals are Andean or European (Flannery et al. 1989; Kuznar 1995). Mestizo populations also highly value herd animals. The Andean knowledge of pastoralism was combined with Spanish traditions to create Andean practices that are unique throughout the Americas.

This zooarchaeological analysis has provided a diachronic perspective on the origins of aspects of modern Andean husbandry. The legacy of Spanish colonial animal introductions has endured as a defining feature of modern Andean culture. The pattern of animal use that emerged in southern Peru reflects the interaction of unique Andean and Iberian cultural and historical elements in a complex environmental setting. The colonial diet of the Moquegua valley incorporated more Iberian elements than comparable colonial settlements in Spanish Florida or the Caribbean.

ACKNOWLEDGMENTS

Several individuals contributed to the completion of this research. Elizabeth S. Wing provided access to the zooarchaeological comparative collections of the Florida Museum of Natural History. Prudence Rice provided me with the opportunity to participate in the *bodegas* project and shared excavation information. The field portion of the research was funded mainly by grants from the National Endowment for the Humanities and the National Geographic Society. Relevant temporal and contextual information was provided by Greg Smith and Mary Van Buren. Permission for the export of the faunal material to the Florida Museum was provided by the Peruvian Instituto Nacional de Cultura with the assistance of Omar Benites Delgado. Thanks also go to Luis Watanabe and the Southern Peru Copper Corporation for their help with various aspects of the project. A portion of this analysis was funded by National Science Foundation Dissertation Improvement Grant No. BNS-9020973. Kurt Knowles helped produce the winery figures from originals prepared by Prudence Rice. Pat Payne of the University of Florida provided the photograph for Figure 14. Linda McLean assisted me with the final production of this article. I am grateful to Elizabeth J. Reitz who provided constructive comments both while this analysis was in progress and on this paper.

REFERENCES

BAKER, J., AND DONALD BROTHWELL
1980 *Animal Diseases in Archaeology*. Academic Press, New York.

BORAH, W.
1954 Early Trade and Navigation Between Mexico and Peru. *Ibero-Americana* 38:1–170.

BROWMAN, DAVID L.
1989 Origins and Development of Andean Pastoralism: An Overview of the Past 6,000 Years. In *The Walking Larder: Patterns of Domestication, Pastoralism, and Predation*, edited by Juliet Clutton-Brock, pp. 256–267. Unwin Hyman, London.

BROWN, KENDALL W.
1986 *Bourbons and Brandy: Imperial Reform in Eighteenth-Century Arequipa*. University of New Mexico Press, Albuquerque.

CROSBY, ALFRED W.
1967 Conquistador y Pestilencia: The First New World Pandemic and the Fall of the Great Indian Empires. *Hispanic American Historical Review* 47:321–337.

CUSHNER, NICHOLAS
1980 *Lords of the Land: Sugar, Wine, and Jesuit Estates of Coastal Peru, 1600–1767*. State University of New York Press, Albany.

DAVIES, KEITH A.
1984 *Landowners in Colonial Peru*. University of Texas Press, Austin.

DEFRANCE, SUSAN D.
1988 Zooarchaeological Investigations of Subsistence Strategies at the Maisabel Site, Puerto Rico. Unpublished M.A. Research Project, Department of Anthropology, University of Florida, Gainesville.
1993 *Ecological Imperialism in the South-Central Andes: Faunal Data from Spanish Colonial Settlements in the Moquegua and Torata Valleys*. Ph.D. dissertation, Department of Anthropology, University of Florida, Gainesville. University Microfilms International, Ann Arbor, Michigan.

EMERY, KITTY
1990 Postclassic and Colonial Period Subsistence Strategies in the Southern Maya Lowlands: Faunal Analyses from Lamanai and Tipu Belize. Unpublished M.A. thesis, Department of Anthropology, University of Toronto, Toronto.

EWEN, CHARLES R.
1987 *From Spaniard to Creole: The Archaeology of Hispanic American Cultural Formation at Puerto Real, Haiti*. University Press of Alabama, Tuscaloosa.

FLANNERY, KENT V., JOYCE MARCUS, AND ROBERT G. REYNOLDS
1989 *The Flocks of the Wamani*. Academic Press, New York.

FRANKLIN, W. L.
1982 Biology, Ecology, and Relationship to Man of the South American Camelids. In Mammalian Biology in South America, edited by M. A. Mares and H. H. Genoways. *Special Publication Series* 6:457–489. Pymatuning Laboratory of Ecology, Pittsburgh, Pennsylvania.

GADE, DANIEL V.
1967 The Guinea Pig in Andean Folk Culture. *Geographical Review* 57:213–224.

GADE, DANIEL W., AND MARIO ESCOBAR
1982 Village Settlement and the Colonial Legacy in Southern Peru. *Geographical Review* 72:430–449.

GARCILASO DE LA VEGA, EL INCA
1966 *Royal Commentaries of the Incas and General History of Peru*, translated by Harold V. Livermore. Reprint of 1607 edition. University of Texas Press, Austin.

GIBSON, CHARLES
1964 *The Aztecs Under Spanish Rule*. Stanford University Press, Stanford, California.
1987 Indian Societies Under Spanish Rule. In *Colonial Spanish America*, edited by L. Bethell, pp. 361–399. Cambridge University Press, Cambridge.

HALE, H. STEPHEN, IRVY QUITMYER, AND
SYLVIA SCUDDER
1987 Methods for Estimating Edible Meat Weights for Faunal Remains from Sites in the Southeastern United States. Manuscript on file, Department of Anthropology, Florida Museum of Natural History, Gainesville.

HALE, H. STEPHEN, AND KAREN JO WALKER
1986 Allometric Regression of Osteichthyes Sample. Manuscript on file, Department of Anthropology, Florida Museum of Natural History, Gainesville.

JONES, JOHN G.
1990 Archaeobotanical Analyses. In *Moquegua* Bodegas *Project, Interim Report, Fifth Season, 1989*, edited by Prudence M. Rice, pp. 95–98. Department of Anthropology, University of Florida, Gainesville.

KENT, JONATHAN D.
1982 *The Domestication and Exploitation of the South American Camelids: Methods of Analysis and Their Application to Circum-Lacustrine Archaeological Sites in Bolivia and Peru.* Ph.D. dissertation, Department of Anthropology, Washington University, St. Louis, Missouri. University Microfilms International, Ann Arbor, Michigan.

KUON CABELLO, LUIS
1981 *Retazos de la Historia de Moquegua.* Familias de Kuon Cabello and Kuon Montalvo, Moquegua, Peru.

KUZNAR, LAWRENCE A.
1995 *Awatimarka: The Ethnoarchaeology of an Andean Herding Community.* Harcourt Brace College Publishers, Fort Worth, Texas.

LÓPEZ, L., AND L. HUERTAS
1990 Relación de Viñas y Bodegas de Moquegua, Siglos XVI y XVII. In *Trabajos Arqueológicos en Moquegua, Peru*, Vol. 3, edited by Luis K. Watanabe, M. E. Moseley, and F. Cabieses, pp. 255–258. Museo Peruano de Ciencias de la Salud and Southern Peru Copper Corporation, Lima.

McEWAN, BONNIE G.
1986 Domestic Adaptation at Puerto Real, Haiti. *Historical Archaeology* 20(1):44–49.

MILLER, GEORGE R., AND RICHARD L. BURGER
1995 Our Father the Cayman, Our Dinner the Llama: Animal Utilization at Chavín de Huantar, Peru. *American Antiquity* 60(3):421–458.

MORALES, EDMUNDO
1995 *The Guinea Pig: Healing, Food, and Ritual in the Andes.* University of Arizona Press, Tucson.

MURRA, JOHN V.
1965 Herds and Herders in the Inca State. In Man, Culture and Animals, edited by A. Leeds and A. Vayda. *American Association for the Advancement of Science, Publication* 78:185–215. Washington, D.C.

NEWSON, LINDA
1987 *Indian Survival in Colonial Nicaragua.* University of Oklahoma Press, Norman.

ORLOVE, BENJAMIN S.
1977 *Alpacas, Sheep, and Men: The Wool Export Economy and Regional Society in Southern Peru.* Academic Press, New York.

PEASE, FRANKLIN G. Y.
1985 Cases and Variations of Verticality in the Southern Andes. In *Andean Ecology and Civilization*, edited by S. Masuda, I. Shimada, and C. Morris, pp. 141–160. University of Tokyo Press, Tokyo.

POPPINO, ROLLIE E.
1949 Cattle Industry in Colonial Brazil. *Mid-America: A Historical Review* 31(4):219–247.

QUITMYER, IRVY R.
1985 Zooarchaeological Methods for the Analysis of Shell Middens at Kings Bay. In Aboriginal Subsistence and Settlement Archaeology of the Kings Bay Locality. Vol. 2, Zooarchaeology, edited by W. H. Adams. *Department of Anthropology, Reports of Investigations* 2:33–48. University of Florida, Gainesville.

REITZ, ELIZABETH J.
1986 Vertebrate Fauna from Locus 19, Puerto Real, Haiti. *Journal of Field Archaeology* 13(3):317–328.
1990 Zooarchaeological Evidence for Subsistence at La Florida Missions. In *Columbian Consequences.* Vol. 2, *Archaeology and History of the Spanish Borderlands East*, edited by David Hurst Thomas, pp. 507–516. Smithsonian Institution Press, Washington, D.C.
1991 Evidence of Animal Use at the Missions of Spanish Florida. *Florida Anthropologist* 44:295–306.
1992 Vertebrate Fauna from Seventeenth-Century St. Augustine. *Southeastern Archaeology* 11(2):79–94.

REITZ, ELIZABETH J., AND STEPHEN L. CUMBAA
1983 Diet and Foodways of Eighteenth Century Spanish St. Augustine. In *Spanish St. Augustine: The Archaeology of a Colonial Creole Community*, edited by Kathleen A. Deagan, pp. 147–181. Academic Press, New York.

REITZ, ELIZABETH J., AND BONNIE G. McEWAN
1995 Animals and the Spanish Diet at Puerto Real. In *Puerto Real: The Archaeology of a 16th-Century Townsite on Hispaniola*, edited by Kathleen A. Deagan. University Presses of Florida, Gainesville, in press.

REITZ, ELIZABETH J., AND C. MARGARET SCARRY
1985 Reconstructing Historic Subsistence with an Example from Sixteenth-Century Spanish Florida. *Special Publication Series* 3. Society for Historical Archaeology, California, Pennsylvania.

RICE, PRUDENCE M.
1990 Introduction and Overview. In *Moquegua* Bodegas

Project, Interim Report, Fifth Season, 1989, edited by Prudence M. Rice, pp. 1–8. Department of Anthropology, University of Florida, Gainesville.

1994 The Kilns of Moquegua, Peru: Technology, Excavations, and Functions. *Journal of Field Archaeology* 21(3):325–344.

RICE, PRUDENCE M., AND DONNA L. RUHL
1989 Archaeological Survey of the Moquegua *Bodegas*. In Ecology, Settlement, and History in the Osmore Drainage, edited by Don S. Rice, C. Stanish, and P. Scarr. *BAR International Series* S545:479–501. Oxford.

RICE, PRUDENCE M., AND GREG C. SMITH
1989 The Spanish Colonial Wineries of Moquegua, Peru. *Historical Archaeology* 23(2):41–49.

RICE, PRUDENCE M., AND SARA VAN BECK
1993 The Spanish Colonial Kiln Tradition of Moquegua, Peru. *Historical Archaeology* 27(4):65–81.

SHIMADA, MELODY, AND IZUMI SHIMADA
1985 Prehistoric Llama Breeding and Herding on the North Coast of Peru. *American Antiquity* 50:3–26.

SMITH, GREG C.
1991 *Heard It Through the Grapevine: Andean and European Contributions to Spanish Colonial Culture and Viticulture in Moquegua, Peru*. Ph.D. dissertation, Department of Anthropology, University of Florida, Gainesville. University Microfilms International, Ann Arbor, Michigan.

SPAULDING, KAREN
1984 *Huarochirí: An Andean Society Under Inca and Spanish Rule*. Stanford University Press, Stanford, California.

STANISH, CHARLES, AND IRENE PRITZGER
1983 Archaeological Reconnaissance in Southern Peru. *Field Museum of Natural History Bulletin* 54:6–17.

STANLEY, HELEN F., MIRANDA KADWELL, AND JANE C. WHEELER
1994 Molecular Evolution of the Family Camelidae: A Mitochondrial DNA Study. *Proceedings of the Royal Society of London* 256:1–6.

VAN BECK, SARA
1991 Spanish Colonial Kilns of Moquegua, Peru. Unpublished M.A. thesis, Department of Anthropology, University of Florida, Gainesville.

VAN BUREN, MARY
1993 *Community and Empire in Southern Peru: The Site of Torata Alta Under Spanish Rule*. Ph.D. dissertation, Department of Anthropology, University of Arizona, Tucson. University Microfilms International, Ann Arbor, Michigan.

VAN BUREN, MARY, AND PETER T. BÜRGI
1990 Torata Alta Excavations. In *Moquegua Bodegas Project, Interim Report, Fifth Season, 1989*, edited by P. M. Rice, pp. 51–82. Department of Anthropology, University of Florida, Gainesville.

VAN BUREN, MARY, PETER T. BÜRGI, AND PRUDENCE M. RICE
1993 Torata Alta: A Late Highland Settlement in the Osmore Drainage. In *Domestic Architecture, Ethnicity, and Complementarity in the South-Central Andes*, edited by Mark S. Aldenderfer, pp. 136–146. University of Iowa Press, Iowa City.

WHEELER, JANE C.
1995 Evolution and Present Situation of the South American Camelidae. *Biological Journal of the Linnaean Society* 54:271–295.

WHEELER, JANE C., A. J. F. RUSSEL, AND HILARY REDDEN
1995 Llamas and Alpacas: Pre-conquest Breeds and Post-conquest Hybrids. *Journal of Archaeological Science* 22:833–840.

WHEELER, JANE C., A. J. F. RUSSEL, AND HELEN F. STANLEY
1992 A Measure of Loss: Prehispanic Llama and Alpaca Breeds. *Archivos de Zootecnia* 41(154, extra):467–475.

WING, ELIZABETH S.
1986 Domestication of Andean Mammals. In *High-Altitude Tropical Biogeography*, edited by F. Vuilleumier and M. Monasterio, pp. 246–264. Oxford University Press, New York.

WINTERHALDER, BRUCE, AND R. BROOKE THOMAS
1978 Geoecology of Southern Highland Peru: A Human Adaptation Perspective. *University of Colorado Institute of Arctic and Alpine Research, Occasional Paper 27*. Boulder.

SUSAN D. DEFRANCE
CORPUS CHRISTI MUSEUM OF
SCIENCE AND HISTORY
1900 N. CHAPARRAL STREET
CORPUS CHRISTI, TEXAS 78401-1114

Ross W. Jamieson

The Market for Meat in Colonial Cuenca: A Seventeenth-Century Urban Faunal Assemblage from the Southern Highlands of Ecuador

ABSTRACT

Excavation of a midden in the city of Cuenca, Ecuador, revealed faunal remains from a 17th-century elite urban family residence. This faunal data, combined with archival research on the Peñas/Ruiz family, demonstrates that the family raised sheep, cattle, and pigs for sale to the urban market in Cuenca. The absence of camelid and guinea pig remains in this faunal assemblage demonstrates that Eurasian ungulates were favored meat animals at this urban, Andean colonial-elite site.

Introduction

The introduction of Old World livestock into Latin America by 16th-century Spanish colonists was a process that varied immensely in different regions. The two most important introduced species were sheep and cattle. Cattle did well in the initial Caribbean colonies (Deagan and Reitz 1995), but in the Caribbean and tropical regions of Latin America environmental conditions were not ideal for sheep. In highland Mexico and the Andes the climate favored both cattle and sheep ranching, but major cultural differences existed between the two regions. In highland Mesoamerica no large domestic herbivores were present prior to Spanish contact. Andean South America was the only New World region where Spanish colonists encountered Native peoples who were already engaged in an economy of large-animal pastoralism, based on llamas and alpacas (Wing 1986). Andean cultural attitudes toward raising camelids (llamas and alpacas) had many differences from those of Spanish colonial herders at the time of contact (Haber 1999), but the Andean highlands were unique in combining ideal environmental conditions for Iberian-style stock raising with a Native population already involved in a pastoral economy prior to the arrival of the Spanish.

Since at least Lesley Simpson's (1952) *Exploitation of Land in Central Mexico in the Sixteenth Century*, historians of Latin America have been aware of the key role played by cattle and sheep in the conquest of the highland regions of Latin America, with herding and pastoralism changing both the environmental and political landscape of these regions at the time of the Spanish conquest. Environmental historians have demonstrated that herding and pastoralism were important parts of the highland Spanish colonial economy (Jacobsen 1986; Melville 1994). Sheep and cattle provided meat, hides, tallow, and wool, all key elements of colonial trade. Herds needed large areas of pasturage to survive, and thus large-scale ranching in the colonial period clashed with existing indigenous agricultural systems, whether in the Mesoamerican (Sluyter 1996; Chance 2003; Fournier García and Mondragón 2003) or Andean highlands (Powers 1995; Larson 1998; Stavig 2000). Over the course of the 16th and 17th centuries, many indigenous communities had their land wrested from their control, often at the hands of Spanish elites seeking to expand their livestock operations.

The result could be massive ecological and social disruption, as Elinor Melville has demonstrated in highland Mexico. Melville (1994:6–7) relies heavily on the biological idea of an "ungulate irruption," in which newly introduced ungulates expand population rapidly and reduce the height, density, and species diversity of local vegetation through grazing. This process can be worsened where human pastoralists are controlling the ungulates, in that humans will tend to hold the stock at higher densities than would occur naturally while simultaneously introducing other destabilizing forces such as deforestation, burning of landscapes, and road building (Melville 1994:9). In her study of the Mezquital Valley in Mexico, Melville (1994:19) sees this now largely desert landscape as a construct of the early colonial period, when grazing and other forces destroyed a densely populated prehispanic agricultural mosaic. In Mezquital this process occurred between 1530 and 1600, leaving a much more barren landscape by 1600 (Melville 1994:87–115).

For archaeologists who study Spanish colonialism, the analysis of faunal remains has been tied to wider debates about the nature of colonialism itself. Models based on George Foster's (1960) concept of acculturation were common among North American researchers (Deagan 1983; Smith 1991; Cusick 1998), while Fernando Ortiz's (1995) idea of transculturation was widely advocated by a generation of Latin American scholars (Domínguez 1978; Morresi 1983). This somewhat sterile debate has now given way to a healthy diversity of approaches to issues of identity formation, daily practice, and the negotiation of power relationships in the archaeology of Spanish colonialism (Schávelzon 2002; Deagan 2003; Funari and Zarankin 2004; Domínguez 2005; Jamieson 2005; Funari and Brittez 2006). The simple dichotomy of "Spanish" versus "Indian" in the colonial encounter is essentialist and incorrect, avoiding the great diversity of sociopolitical categories and relationships that existed in colonial contexts. Food remains from domestic contexts cannot simply be quantified to create an index of how European or indigenous a household was. Instead, it is necessary to understand how complex ideas about ethnicity and social class interacted with the availability of different foods at the local level, to create local practices in the production and consumption of faunal resources. The production and consumption of animals is a matter of taste, in which people embody the daily repercussions of the colonial encounter through their choices (Stahl 2002). It is clear from historical sources that cattle and sheep were an important focus of colonial production in the Andes, and that this production was related to the demand for the meat of such animals in the colonial marketplace. Highland regions were ideal for such production, and yet the question remains: were colonists attempting to "reproduce a European lifestyle" in their focus on raising Eurasian livestock (Rodríguez-Alegría 2005:551)?

The Spanish colonial system of animal husbandry and consumption is now fairly well understood archaeologically for the Caribbean and Florida (Reitz and Cumbaa 1983; Reitz and Scarry 1985; Reitz 1991) as well as for

Argentina and the Southern Cone (Romero et al. 2002; Silveira 2003). In the Central Andes, however, the immense economic and ecological diversity of the Spanish colonies is represented by only a few archaeological studies in which faunal analysis has been undertaken (deFrance 1996, 2003; Gutiérrez Usillos and Iglesias Aliaga 1996).

The Midden

The city of Cuenca is a UNESCO World Heritage Site at an elevation of 2,800 m in the southern Andean highlands of Ecuador. Officially founded by the Spanish in A.D. 1557, the city is built on and around the ruins of an important Inka regional center called Tomebamba (Idrovo Urigüen 2000; Jamieson 2000; Poloni Simard 2000). During the colonial period, Cuenca was part of the Audiencia de Quito, an administrative unit roughly similar to Ecuador's modern boundaries. Still a vibrant city with over a half-million inhabitants, today Cuenca is the third largest city in Ecuador. The UNESCO (1999) designation was largely based on the preservation of the colonial "townscape" in the city center, but despite these efforts, historical archaeology in the city core is still only a nascent concept for urban planners and heritage professionals in the region (Buys 1997; Carrillo 1998; Jamieson 2005). From 1990 until 2002 the Cuenca Historical Archaeology Project carried out several seasons of archaeological research focused on the colonial period in Cuenca and its environs, providing some initial forays into the potential for archaeology to contribute to knowledge of daily life in colonial Cuenca (Jamieson 2000, 2001, 2004; Castillo 2003; Nimmo 2003). One result of this project was the discovery of an intact early-colonial midden in the rear yard of what is now a pharmacy (Figure 1) immediately adjacent to the main colonial-period city plaza. Located at 9-20 Calle Bolívar (Figure 2), the midden was initially discovered through shovel tests of the rear yard of the property and confirmed with an excavation unit (1 x 1 m) in 1994 (Jamieson 2000:148–155). Ongoing archival research related to this property and the analysis of the midden materials, which revealed its 16th- or 17th-century date (Jamieson 2000:148–155), led to the excavation of another unit (2 x 2 m) in 1999 (Figure 3).

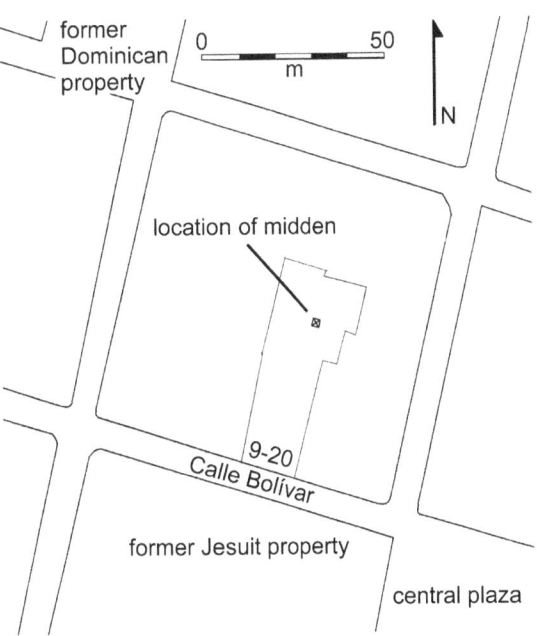

FIGURE 2. Location of the Peñas/Ruiz midden on the block northwest of the central plaza, Cuenca, Ecuador. (Drawing by author, 2006.)

FIGURE 1. The facade of the pharmacy at 9-20 Calle Bolívar, Cuenca, Ecuador. (Photo by author, 1999.)

FIGURE 3. Excavation of the Peñas/Ruiz midden. (Photo by author, 1999.)

Immediately adjacent to the previous unit, this excavation recovered a larger sample from the same deposit.

The context consists of dark organic soil in which distinct lenses represent repeated dumping episodes. The surrounding subsoil indicates that the location was a natural shallow arroyo, or water channel. This property was occupied from the initial founding of the city of Cuenca in 1557, and it appears that sometime over the next 100 years, the arroyo was filled with trash from the surrounding house complex. Artifacts from the midden were mostly locally made, unglazed, coarse earthenware cooking and storage vessels (Jamieson 2000:175–183); *botija* storage vessel fragments imported from Spain (Jamieson 2000:183–185); and majolica tableware, made in Panama. Majolica of the Panama Plain type from the midden has been reported on previously (Jamieson 2001:figs. 3,4) and date to the late-16th through early-17th centuries. The absence of any other chronologically diagnostic materials in the deposit, including anything postdating the 17th century, indicates that this midden was deposited between A.D. 1557 and 1650. Flotation of a 3 liter soil sample from one level of the midden resulted in the identification of a small sample of macrobotanical remains, of which the only clear species identification was for 38 fragments of wheat, either *Triticum durum* (durum wheat) or *T. aestivum* (bread wheat) (D'Andrea 2002). The most interesting aspect of the midden, however, was the dense faunal sample encountered.

Excavated Fauna

The midden at 9-20 Calle Bolívar provides a small faunal sample from the first century of the Spanish occupation in the southern highlands of Ecuador. The feature was associated with an urban house at the time it was deposited, in a location very near the central plaza of this colonial city. It is thus not an example in any way "typical" of life in the colonial Andes but is, instead, a window on the consumption patterns of elite urban households. The context was processed through 1/4 in. mesh screen during excavation. A total of 3,235 bone fragments were recovered from the colonial midden levels, of which 744 were identifiable elements. This is not a large faunal assemblage, representing only

part of a single midden from a single house, but it gives a glimpse into the foodways of urban colonial Cuenca. Analysis of the faunal sample was undertaken by Carmen Tarcan (2005), using comparative collections at Simon Fraser University. The measure of relative abundance employed was the number of identified specimens (NISP), with specimens refitted prior to identification to avoid over-counting.

The resulting distribution of identified faunal remains by taxon (Table 1) reveals that only bird and mammal remains were present in the feature. Mammal remains account for an overwhelming 98% of the assemblage. Domestic artiodactyls dominate the assemblage, with caprines (sheep and goats) by far the most abundant, followed by cattle and pigs. When identifiable, sheep were more common than goats. Deer were also found, but in smaller numbers. The presence of deer is interesting, in that it is proposed that this wild indigenous species was common in Ecuador at the time of the conquest but that overhunting and habitat destruction reduced its numbers greatly in the

TABLE 1
PEÑAS/RUIZ MIDDEN:
IDENTIFIABLE FAUNAL REMAINS

Taxon	Common Name	NISP
Anser spp.	goose	4
Gallus gallus domesticus	chicken	2
Medium birds		8
Lagomorphs	hare/rabbit	1
Small rodents		1
Canis spp.	dog/wolf	2
Small carnivores		1
Medium carnivores		4
Odocoileus spp.	deer	9
Ovis aries	sheep	21
Capra hircus	goat	3
Ovis aries/Capra hircus		150
Sus scrofa	pig	56
Bos taurus	cow	98
Medium artiodactyls		226
Large artiodactyls		30
Small mammals		3
Medium mammals		58
Large mammals		11
Large ungulates		56
Total		744

later colonial period (Gutiérrez Usillos and Iglesias Aliaga 1996:96). Hares or rabbits were recovered in small numbers. Unfortunately, these could not be distinguished as to whether they were Andean or Eurasian species. Identified birds in the midden sample were restricted to duck and chicken (Tarcan 2005).

The vast majority of recovered remains were from artiodactyls. Body-part profiles of the medium and large artiodactyl groups were undertaken, based on standardized body-part profiles. For this purpose, skeletal elements were grouped into head, neck, axial, upper and lower front limbs, upper and lower hind limbs, and feet (Stiner 1994:240,244). The distribution of body parts for the artiodactyls in the sample (Table 2) indicates that complete animals were being slaughtered in this yard and processed there. The body-part representations correlate with those found in living animals. The overall good representation of all portions suggests that the assemblage is the result of primary and secondary butchering of the artiodactyls (Tarcan 2005:13–14).

Owners of the House

This archaeological midden can be tied to particular landowners through urban property transaction records, giving unique insight into the social context that produced the faunal sample (Figure 4). At the founding of the city of Cuenca in 1557, the property was assigned to Gonzalo de las Peñas, one of the most powerful men among Cuenca's founding citizens (González 1991:15). Rather than selling the land, as frequently happened with initial urban property grants in Spanish colonial cities, Peñas resided on the property. He died in 1579 or 1580. In 1583, Ines de Valderrama, his widow, is listed as the owner (Archivo Nacional de Historia [ANH] 1583). This prestigious location on the corner of the main plaza was within easy walking distance of all the main colonial urban institutions, including the city council building across the plaza. Sometime between this date and 1603, the property was passed down through inheritance to Gonzalo and Ines's son, Gil Ruiz de Tapia (ANH 1603). Ruiz's estate sold the property in 1651, several years after his death (ANH 1651). This prestigious corner lot in the core of Cuenca was owned by the same family from the city's founding in 1557 until 1651, a period covering the dates when the archaeological evidence indicates the midden was deposited in the rear yard of the property.

Peñas's powerful position in early Cuenca society is because of his role as a conquistador, not in the region of southern Ecuador but, rather, in New Granada or what was to become southern Colombia. Born in 1499, he came to the New World around 1529. He participated in the conquest of the Cauca River Valley, in what is now southwestern Colombia. This expedition was under the command of Sebastián de Benalcázar, who had conquered the region

TABLE 2
PEÑAS/RUIZ MIDDEN: ARTIODACTYL BODY-PART DISTRIBUTIONS

Body Part	Medium Artiodactyls		Standard		Large Artiodactyls		Standard	
	MNE[a]	%MNE	MNE	%MNE	MNE	%MNE	MNE	%MNE
Head	27	18.49	4	3.38	8	9.63	4	3.17
Neck	3	2.05	2	1.69	1	1.20	2	1.58
Axial	20	13.69	48	40.67	23	27.70	56	44.44
Upper front	11	7.53	4	3.38	8	9.63	4	3.17
Lower front	31	21.23	18	15.25	13	15.66	18	14.28
Upper hind	11	7.53	2	1.69	5	6.02	2	1.58
Lower hind	27	18.49	16	13.55	17	20.48	16	12.69
Foot	16	10.95	24	20.33	8	9.63	24	19.04
Total MNE	146		118		83		126	

[a] MNE = minimum number of elements

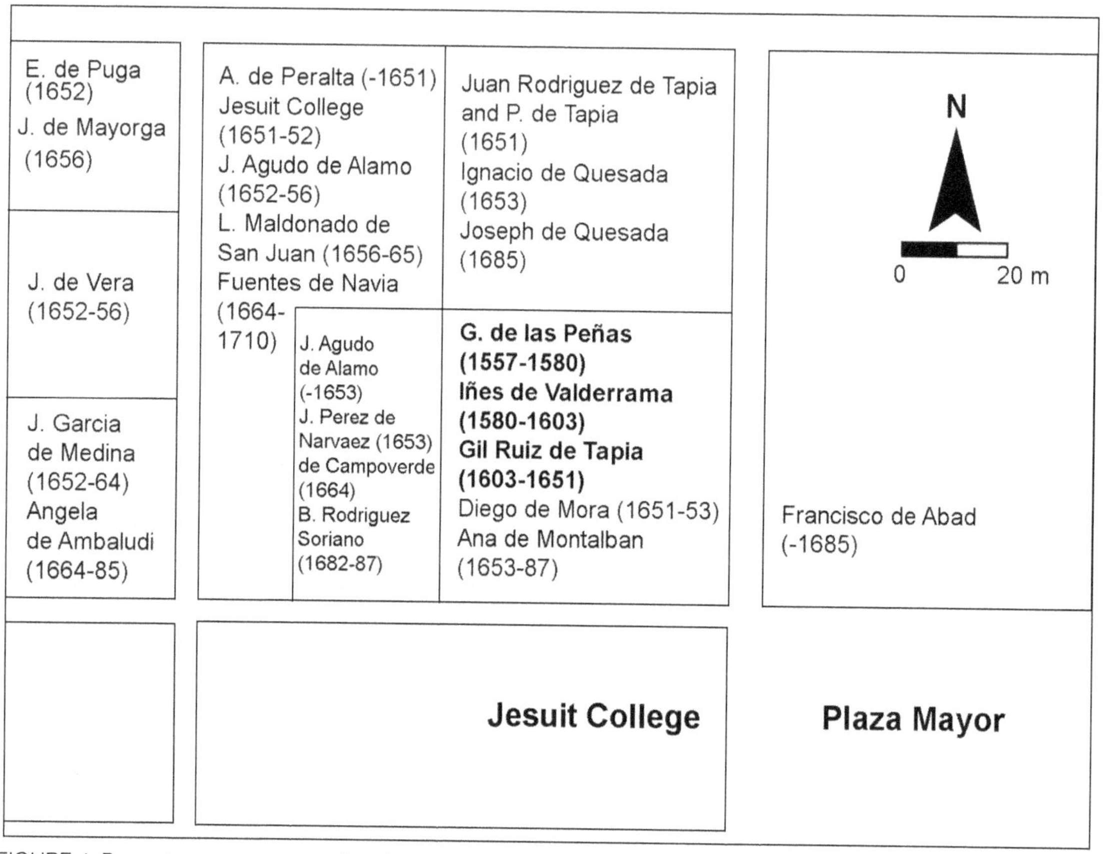

FIGURE 4. Property owners surrounding the excavated property in the 17th century. (Drawing by author, 2006.)

of Quito in 1534 and had then moved on to conquer what is now southwestern Colombia in 1537 and 1538, apparently looking toward a land route from Quito to the Caribbean (Avellaneda Navas 1995:196). Years later, Peñas testified to his participation in this conquest of the Cauca Valley, and witnesses confirmed his story, including the grant of a *repartimiento de indios* (rights to Native Andean labor) in Cali, Colombia. He testified that the area around the city of Cali was very hot, and he became sick there. Peñas eventually decided to give up his grant of *repartimiento* and returned to the city of Quito. It was here that in 1557 Gil Ramírez Dávalos, asked Peñas to participate with him in the task of founding the city of Cuenca in the southern highlands of the Audiencia de Quito (Archivo General de Indias 1569).

In 1557 Peñas was one of 19 founding citizens of the city of Cuenca and apparently one of the most prominent individuals involved in the

enterprise. He was immediately named *alcalde ordinario* (chief councilor) by the municipal council, a post he held again in 1560, 1562, and 1564. This was the highest governmental post in the city, making him chief councilor on the city council as well as the municipal judge, able to arrest and prosecute people on matters related to municipal governance. In 1559 he was named royal treasurer of the city, and he also held various other municipal administrative positions until his death in 1579 or 1580 (Archivo Histórico Municipal, [AHM] 1557–1580). He was survived by his wife, Ines, who lived as a widow in the house from 1580 until her death around 1605 (ANH 1605).

Immediately after the death of Peñas his adult son Gil Ruiz de Tapia attained a similar level of power within the city's economy and politics. Following his father's example, Ruiz served in various municipal administrative posts, including royal treasurer of Cuenca (1588), *alcalde ordi-*

nario (1591), and *alguacil mayor* (chief constable of the city) from 1593 to 1597, in 1606, and from 1610 to 1613 (AHM 1588–1613). Ruiz married Eugenia Bravo, the daughter of Pedro Bravo, another city council member. Bravo and Peñas voted for each other for different offices, and Bravo served as *alcalde ordinario* in 1561 and 1566 (AHM 1561–1566), so the wedding of Ruiz to Eugenia solidified the alliance of two elite Cuenca families in their second generation in the new city. The intertwining of marriage and inheritance patterns with municipal offices and favors gives an idea of the ways in which governmental power and land-based stock-raising operations were intertwined in this time and place. Eugenia died before 1639 (ANH 1639), and Ruiz remained in the house on the corner of the plaza until his own death in 1644, when the house was sold outside the family (ANH 1644).

From its founding in 1557, Cuenca was an important agricultural hub, with meat, hides, tallow, cheese, and preserved hams all being important products. Live animals were sold to Quito, Riobamba, and south into the Viceroyalty of Peru (Chacón Zhapán 1990:127). From the 16th century onward in Cuenca, artisans were active in manufacturing items from hides, including hide workers, saddle makers, furniture makers, and shoemakers (Paniagua Pérez and Truhan 2003:425–460).

Peñas's and Ruiz's ongoing roles in municipal government in Cuenca were an advantage to their ranching interests. The *cabildo* controlled many aspects of the trade in livestock and animal products. A municipal butcher shop was set up in the city center, with prices and weights controlled by a city inspector (Chacón Zhapán 1990:128). Within the first few years of its founding, the city created a municipal slaughterhouse on the road to Quito, one musket-shot length outside the city (Chacón Zhapán 1990:124). By the 1590s, a number of the hide workers had located their shops in the lower part of the Tomebamba River, adjacent to the slaughterhouse (Paniagua Pérez and Truhan 2003:428). With such production came problems in urban regulation of animal nuisances. In the same year that the city was founded, there were complaints to the city council that pigs were wandering freely in the city streets (Chacón Zhapán 1990:123). In 1559 there were

complaints that the number of cattle crossing the city's bridges was doing damage to them (Chacón Zhapán 1990:123).

In the New World colonies, unlike Spain, the municipal city councils took direct governance of issues surrounding livestock without the creation of municipal *mestas* (livestock associations) in most cities (Bishko 1952:505). This was the case in Cuenca, where the city council began recording official brand marks for branding animals in 1559 (Chacón Zhapán 1990:124). In 1560 Peñas was one of the first citizens of the city to be awarded such a brand (AHM 1650).

Urban elites in the Spanish colonies, such as the Peñas/Ruiz family, often invested heavily in livestock and urged municipalities to give them *mercedes* (land grants) for grazing their herds. The first generation of Spanish colonists was eager to solidify their power base in the colony. The acquisition of land and the running of livestock on that land were traditionally very Iberian ways of demonstrating power within the wider society. These families had to make decisions about investing in particular species of livestock. It seems that these choices had surprisingly little to do with the regional livestock traditions of the places that elite colonists came from in Spain. Instead, these choices appear to have had much more to do with a quick, and flexible, adaptation to stock that did better in particular ecological zones surrounding the colonial cities of the New World (Butzer 1988:45). There was also an important, and complex, relationship between local rural indigenous peoples, their landholding in the early colonial period, and the focus of urban elites on particular types of livestock. Peñas and Ruiz were good examples of this, demonstrating the ways in which wealthy urban families in the colonial Andes were heavily tied to the rural economy, particularly in stock raising.

Peñas created an integrated rural and urban set of properties in his first decade in Cuenca (Figure 4). He was awarded 30 *hanegadas* (a surface measurement equivalent to 831 sq. m.) of land in the region of Hatun Cañar in 1561 and a piece of land on the riverside in Cuenca to build a grist mill in 1563 (AHM 1561, 1563; Chacón Zhapán 1990:124). He formed a company with Hernando Marques, a *curtidor* (hide tanner), to cut and tan hides. Peñas put up a piece of land and an enslaved African named Dominguilla as his contributions to the operation, while Marques appears to have been the one actually in charge of the tanning operation, which was located outside of the city center in a neighborhood called the *depósitos* (ANH 1563, 1636). His stock-raising operation must have been fairly large, as shown in a 1565 document for the sale of 1,234 sheep to a market retailer (ANH 1565).

The rural prominence of this elite family continued after Peñas's death. His son Ruiz began to successfully petition for agricultural *mercedes* from the Cuenca city council in the same year that his father died. in 1580, Ruiz received 58 *cuadras* (about 58 hectares) east of Cuenca, between Santa Ana Pichacay and San Juan Paiguara, but this grant proved untenable because "the land belonged to Indians," and so the council granted him an equal amount of land in Ludo, on the Bolo River, in 1586. He was granted another 58-*cuadra* property in 1584 in an unknown location (AHM 1580–1586). When he died in 1644, Ruiz left behind the Cañar ranch with 600 or 700 head of cattle, as well as a mule breeding property with more than 200 head of mules, presumably on the Ludo property (ANH 1644, 1645, 1653).

The scale of the family livestock operations is evident from a 1650 lawsuit (ANH 1650a), brought by Geronimo Muñoz who demanded compensation from the estate of the deceased Ruiz for six years of service to him. Muñoz claimed that around the year 1610 he had served for two years in the slaughterhouse of Ruiz and that he had extensive herding duties, moving livestock for the family between properties. His testimony greatly expands knowledge of the size of the family's rural property holdings. Muñoz claimed to have made two trips to the Ruiz property in Yaguachi to bring back 550 head of cattle, one trip to the Ruiz pig farm in Quingeo, and one to Bolo to the mule breeding area. At the Ruiz Cañaribamba property, Muñoz counted and branded 2,000 head of cattle, which took three or four months. He then transported 30 mules from Cañaribamba to the town of Alausi for sale. Two old letters are included in the court documents for the case. The first is a 1610 sale document in which Alonso Benito of Cuenca sold Ruiz 300 cattle, all between two and four years old, located on a property near

Guayaquil (ANH 1650b). The second was a 1610 letter from Martin de Ocampo, a *corregidor* (city councilor) in Cuenca, demanding that the mayor of the village of Yocón provide three Native Andean laborers to guard some cattle for Ruiz (ANH 1650c). Ruiz's nephew, Lucas de Ortega, responded to Muñoz's claims in court, stating that Muñoz was a poor man who came to Ruiz's house and was given food and lodging. He later worked for the family and married one of the servants in the household. Muñoz was given property and livestock by the family at the time of the marriage, and Ortega claimed that the estate owed Muñoz nothing further. The judge rejected Muñoz's claim, stating that without solid written evidence of any unpaid obligations, Muñoz had no rights to further compensation. This is the end of the file, and, presumably, the suit was dropped.

Environmental Degradation

Livestock operations such as those of Peñas were part of a profound change in the environment of the Ecuadorian Andes in the century following the Spanish conquest. The presence of camelids in Ecuador appears to have steeply declined during the colonial period, to the point of almost disappearing, as was the case in many parts of the Andes (Wheeler et al. 1995; Stahl 2003:471). The end of Inka herd management at the conquest and the very quick adoption of Eurasian ungulates by local populations may be causal factors in this swift transition. By the 1570s, 40 years after the conquest, it would seem that camelids were still common herd animals in some indigenous communities in the region but were absent in many communities (Borchart de Moreno 1995:157). Today in Ecuador there may be fewer than 2,000 llamas, and alpacas have only recently been reintroduced (Stahl 2003:471). This situation is very different from that of the guinea pig, a prehispanic domestic meat animal that is still common in Ecuadorian indigenous households, having apparently been an important staple throughout the colonial period (Stahl 2003:471).

Camelids were quickly replaced with Eurasian sheep on much of the Ecuadorian colonial landscape. Sheep were introduced with the initial conquest of the region and soon became a huge industry, both in woolen textiles and meat, in the northern and central highlands of the country (Tyrer 1988; Soasti 1994; Borchart de Moreno 1995, 1998). This, of course, mirrors the early modern economy in Spain, where Mesta, the livestock owners association, dominated an agricultural economy in which sheep and, to a lesser extent, cattle were lynchpins (Klein 1920; Phillips and Phillips 1997). Wool production did not, however, dominate the landscape of 16th- and 17th-century Cuenca, where regional herding was based on a mixed economy of cattle, sheep, and pigs (Chacón Zhapán 1990). Although dating to the 18th century and much later than the Peñas/Ruiz operation, the records of the Jesuit order in the Audiencia de Quito are one indication of this. The large Jesuit ranching facilities surrounding Cuenca in the 1760s reported herds consisting of 2,257 cattle, 1,318 sheep, and 292 mules. These numbers contrast sharply with other Jesuit operations in the central and northern parts of the Audiencia de Quito, where sheep massively dominated the Jesuit ranching operations and were reported in numbers far higher than cattle or other animals (Cushner 1982:190).

What effect did Spanish colonization have in the 16th-century Andes, when families such as the Peñas family introduced large-scale stock raising throughout many rural zones? The introduction of large numbers of herd animals probably had severe environmental consequences, while at the same time causing a massive 16th- and 17th-century change in colonial Andean land tenure, in which Native Andean communities remained essential parts of the colonial economy but fought long and bitter battles, both legal and social, over the loss of rights to many of their traditionally held lands (Powers 1995; Stavig 2000). The decline in rural indigenous populations would also change the landscape, as irrigation systems and other agricultural maintenance fell into disuse. In the Cuenca area, Native Andean populations declined massively due to disease (Newson 1995:226–236) and out-migration to avoid heavy labor taxes and intimidation (Powers 1995:37–38). This dynamic combined with elite urban Spaniards' expansion of stock raising throughout the zone to create both environmental and social devastation.

Spanish colonial law was an important part of this process. In general, colonial regulations gave rights to pastoralists to graze on any uncultivated lands, including on the stubble of other people's crops. The laws divided land into cultivated plots, held either by traditional cultivation of the plot or by legal right to it, and rangeland, which defined any land not being used for cultivation. The strong legal basis for moving grazing animals into uncultivated land came from the long medieval Christian Reconquista of the Iberian Peninsula from the Moors (Butzer 1988:43–45). In Spain, all parties were generally local agriculturalists, but in the New World these laws tended to favor Spanish ranchers' incursions into indigenous agricultural smallholdings (Melville 1994:116–120). This battle was fought through the basis of *mercedes,* or municipally controlled land grants to pastoralists (Melville 1994:124). It is just these types of land grants that Peñas and Ruiz were adept at getting through their privileged positions on the Cuenca city council from the 1550s to 1640s. The *mercedes* were only one way in which elite urban people maintained control over Native Andean participation in stock raising. Early Cuenca *cabildo* books record an ongoing dispute over the use of branding by Native Andeans. The *cabildo* made ongoing attempts in the 1560s to 1610s to control the use of brands by Native peoples, demanding that local indigenous leaders give up brands they had created and that they, instead, be held either by the Cuenca city council or, for more distant villages, by a local Spaniard or the town priest (Chacón Zhapán 1990:125–126).

The removal of land from Native Andean control and its distribution to large-scale private ranching interests created environmental devastation. There was little contemporary recognition that such practices might be destroying the landscape surrounding the city, although in the 1690s the Cuenca city council did pass a regulation that *ganado menor* (sheep, goats and pigs) could not be pastured in the same field as *ganado mayor* (cattle) because of the damage to the pasture land that this practice caused (Chacón Zhapán 1990:130). In the highlands of the 16th-century Audiencia de Quito (now Ecuador), it would seem that a difficult environmental situation took hold. Spanish elite *encomenderos* took up large land grants, reducing land available to Native Andean rural inhabitants. The movement of Native Andeans in search of agricultural land led to deforestation, slash-and-burn agricultural practices, and large-scale herding of animals in areas not previously exposed to these practices. The erosion of highland areas and reduction in pasture, agricultural land, and forests were recognized by colonial administrations, but there seem to have been few effective attempts to manage land use in the colony (Powers 2000). The *cangahua* or hardened volcanic subsoils of the Ecuadorian Andes are a particularly susceptible geology for degradation by ungulates. Experimental work has shown that once topsoils have eroded, no reasonable amount of manure or crop waste tillage can reconstitute the soils for good agricultural production. These denuded subsoil zones have become permanent scars on the highland Ecuadorian landscape, many of them dating to the early colonial period (Podwojewski and Germain 2005).

Spanish Colonial Faunal Samples

The faunal sample from the Cuenca midden is the end product of an elite private livestock operation and is thus very different from many other Spanish colonial faunal samples in the published literature. The introduction of Old World fauna to Latin America by Spanish colonists was heavily dependent on a series of environmental variables. Sheep were a key resource in stock raising in Spain but do not thrive in tropical climates (Reitz 1992:85), creating a strong contrast between the Caribbean and Florida where Spanish colonial assemblages tend to show almost a complete absence of sheep, as compared to highland Mexico and the Andes where sheep were a key colonial resource (Dusenberry 1963; Jacobsen 1986; Salvucci 1987; Escobari de Querejazu 1995; Miño Grijalva 1998).

In 16th-century St. Augustine, Florida, the faunal samples show colonists consuming a diet dominated by estuarine fish and small game available locally, only supplemented by Old World domesticates. Attributed to the local environment, which was swampy, tropical, and had poor grassland, this situation was not ideal for Spanish stock raising (Reitz and Scarry 1985; Reitz 1992). This pattern is repeated in 17th-century faunal samples from Spanish missions in La Florida that showed extensive use of local wild resources and only limited consumption of livestock at most of the missions (Reitz 1991).

In the Caribbean, research on Hispaniola has revealed a much heavier reliance on pigs and cattle by Spanish colonists than in Florida. These domesticates did well in this hot but dry climate. Fish and turtles were also significant dietary components in 16th-century Hispaniola, which is logical given the easy access to marine resources (Reitz 1992).

The Caribbean archaeological context that is perhaps most comparable to the Cuenca midden is a household from 16th-century Puerto Real, Hispaniola, known as Locus 39. This location had a faunal sample overwhelmingly made up of small fragments of cattle bone and is thought to have been a location where commercial processing of cattle for hides, meat, and tallow took place (Reitz 1986). Both Locus 39 and the Cuenca midden are examples of Spanish colonial domestic contexts in which a commercial level of meat and animal byproduct processing was taking place. In the case of Cuenca, this assemblage was dominated by primary processing of caprines, cattle and pigs, with all body elements represented; while in Locus 39, the economy was much more focused on beef and cattle byproducts, particularly hides for export. The distribution of cattle elements at Locus 39 also showed a below-average distribution of cranial and phalange elements, in contrast to the Cuenca sample, indicating that primary killing and processing of the cattle took place in another location (Deagan and Reitz 1995:278).

In Mexico City, elite households in the colonial urban core have revealed a diet that included mollusks, armadillo, and deer as well as Eurasian ungulates (Montúfar López and Valentín Maldonado 1998; Rodríguez-Alegría 2005:557).

In the foothills of the Argentinean Andes, the city of Mendoza has provided a sample of colonial-period domestic faunal remains in which cattle and sheep are well represented, but fish are also common, and camelids are present (Romero et al. 2002). At the Jesuit Guaraní mission of Itapúa, on the Parana River, a 17th-century shallow midden was dominated by cattle remains with a small sample of caprines. The lack of fish, in particular, was noted from this site that was directly on a good fishing river (Silveira 2002).

The Rio de la Plata region of Argentina and Uruguay is environmentally very different from the Andes, but it is a temperate climate where Eurasian ungulates do well. At the Colonia del Sacramento in Uruguay, an urban colonial household sample was dominated by cattle and sheep but showed a large number of fish and bird remains as well as small samples of deer, pig, and guinea pig (*Cavia aperea*) (Pintos Blanco 1996).

The city of Buenos Aires has had the most extensive analysis of faunal remains from colonial sites in urban South America. Seventeenth-century domestic trash from both the Museo Etnográfico and Coni Press sites show an overwhelming dominance of cattle and sheep remains (Silveira 1995:48; Schávelzon 2000:135). Trash dumped in the second half of the 18th century in a latrine at the Santa Catalina Convent revealed that these cloistered nuns had a diet heavily emphasizing chicken, duck, and turkey, which may have been bred within the convent walls, although beef and mutton were well represented. There were also wild birds (tinamou and dove) and a considerable number of fish bones (Silveira 2003). A similar range of species were consumed by Dominican monks, evident from analysis of a 1790–1823 trash midden from their Buenos Aires monastery. Sheep and cattle are present, but a very large number of fish, along with a lot of chicken, several species of wild tinamous, armadillos, and domestic ducks, geese, and turkeys suggest that religious communities in late colonial Buenos Aires had much less emphasis on red meat in their diet than seen in elite houses and more emphasis on birds and fish (Silveira and Lanza 1998). The question is whether this diverse diet is due to religious adherence to a large number of days when red meat was prohibited or whether it was an economic decision based on the high cost of red meat in feeding the members of religious orders (Silveira and Lanza 1998:543–544).

The excavation of 19th-century elite houses in Buenos Aires shows that in the 1830s to 1870s, beef and mutton dominated the elite urban diet, with chicken, goose, and turkey as supplementary items (Silveira 1996; Silveira and Lanza 1999; Schávelzon 2000:136). This contrasted with late-19th-century remains from the Peña House, after it had been divided into lower-class tenements, which showed much more emphasis

on turkey, guinea pig, duck, geese, vizcacha, and pig (Silveira 1996; Schávelzon 2000:136).

The colonial wine production facilities of the Moquegua Valley, Peru, provide another important comparative data set (Rice 1996; Smith 1997). These facilitites are 1,800 km southeast of Cuenca in a rural coastal valley of Peru. Here camelids formed the most important food source in the 16th century (by MNI), with much of the remaining animal protein coming from (in order): caprines, then cattle, and then pigs. For the period from 1600 to 1775, this ratio shifted, with caprines becoming the largest contributor (by MNI) to the animal protein consumed at the wineries, then cattle, camelids, pigs, and guinea pigs, in that order (deFrance 1996:table 7). Contrary to an image of camelids having been largely extinguished from the colonial landscape, faunal data from the Moquegua wineries show an ongoing, although declining, presence of camelids from the 16th through the 19th centuries, apparently indicating their continued use as beasts of burden for the wineries, integrated with their use as a source of meat (deFrance 1996:44).

At Tarapaya, an elite rural residence and inn outside Potosí, Bolivia, all food was imported from lower elevations during the Spanish colonial mining boom. Excavations at Tarapaya have revealed that caprines (sheep/goat) were the most important food source, followed by cattle, Andean camelids, and pigs. Chickens and a wide variety of fish also contributed to the diet (deFrance 2003). The presence of camelids at Tarapaya, although not overwhelming, provides a contrast to the Cuenca midden. This may be because camelids were still commonly raised in Bolivia and southern Peru and had become very rare in Ecuador during the colonial period. It may also be due to the nature of the Cuenca deposit as an urban butchering site.

In highland Peru, the colonial village of Torata Alta (Van Buren 1993) provides an excellent contrast to the faunal profile in the city of Cuenca. Occupied from the mid-16th to mid-17th centuries, Torata Alta was a small *reducción* village, inhabited by Native Andean peoples. It is, thus far, the only excavation of rural Andean colonial households in which the recovered faunal sample has been analyzed. This analysis has revealed that camelids were the most common domestic mammal in the diet (by MNI), with caprines, guinea pigs, and pigs also present (deFrance 1996:40). A variety of wild resources, including imported marine fish and shellfish, demonstrate the diversity of this Andean Native village diet in the 16th and 17th centuries (deFrance 1996:38–39). In the Puna de Atacama high-desert region of northeast Argentina, the site of Tebenquiche Chico provides an interesting comparative sample. This camelid pastoral village at 3,500 m was occupied from A.D. 350 until the mid-18th century, demonstrating continuity in camelid herding in the region well into the colonial period (Haber 1999). The dominance of camelids in the diet at these rural sites and the absence of cattle is a strong difference from the urban Cuenca materials.

The closest comparable samples to Cuenca, both geographically and culturally, are those of the San Francisco and Santo Domingo monasteries in Quito, Ecuador, 300 km north of Cuenca. In these colonial urban monasteries, located in the capital of the colonial Audiencia de Quito, the three most common species (by NISP) recovered during excavations were caprine, cattle, and pig, in that order. The fourth most common was chicken, which was more prevalent in Quito monasteries (6% and 9% of NISP), than in the Cuenca midden (Gutiérrez Usillos and Iglesias Aliaga 1996:84). The larger proportion of chicken and the presence of turkey (1.2% of Santo Domingo Monastery NISP) are likely due to the nature of these deposits, which represent the end result of food consumption by the monasteries' inhabitants, rather than a commercial butchering operation as seen in the Cuenca midden. Llama is present in the San Francisco sample (1.8% of NISP) but is associated with Native Andean burial offerings rather than with food consumption in the monastery (Gutiérrez Usillos and Iglesias Aliaga 1996:87). Deer are present in very small numbers (1.1% and 0.2% of NISP) in the monasteries and are thought by the excavators to be largely from early colonial contexts (Gutiérrez Usillos and Iglesias Aliaga 1996:96).

Conclusions

Susan deFrance (1996:45) has called for further data on Andean colonial faunal remains, particularly from elite urban contexts, to compare with an emerging range of data from rural sites. The Cuenca materials provide a small window on the diet of elite urban Andeans, showing a complete rejection of camelids and guinea pig and a dominance of caprines and cattle. This seems in no way surprising, given the 16th- and 17th-century dietary and cultural ideals of Andean urban elite people like Ruiz. Far from demonstrating the end of consumption of Native Andean domesticates in the region during the 16th century, however, this sample confirms the diversity of dietary choices and cultural norms present in the colonial Andean faunal record. Dietary choices are about the availability of particular foods in particular environments but are also about the symbolism of these foods in the daily practices of a variety of colonial individuals. A comparison to other Spanish colonial faunal samples raises a series of intriguing questions. Deer appear to form a minor but steady component of elite urban colonial domestic assemblages in Mesoamerica and South America, to the exclusion of other wild species that could have been hunted. Is this because of the association of hunting these animals with the nobility in Europe? The absence of camelids and guinea pig, on the other hand, appears to be a rejection of Native Andean domesticates by the colonial elite in urban settings. This seems different, somehow, from the absence of particular Eurasian domesticates, like pigs, chickens, other fowl, fish, and goats. These are present at sites like the Santa Catalina Convent in Buenos Aires, suggesting that such items may have had associations with poverty and lack of access to high-status beef and mutton in the minds of urban elites.

As members of the early colonial Andean urban elite, the Peñas/Ruiz family participated actively in urban life and urban government, but the family's economic base came from rural livestock operations. A Spanish colonial city like Cuenca was supplied from its local hinterland, and the control and acquisition of the land and labor of Native Andean peoples in the region were key factors in maintaining such urban elite families. This is a fact that Gonzalo de las Peñas and his descendants understood very well and demonstrated through their dietary choices.

Acknowledgments

I thank Carmen Tarcan for her diligent and thorough analysis of the Cuenca fauna and Nancy Saxberg for an initial foray into this type of analysis. This project was carried out with funding from the Social Sciences and Humanities Research Council of Canada. Susana Klinkicht and her family generously granted access to the property where the midden is located. I thank Deborah Truhan for all her work at the archives in Cuenca. Thanks to Judy Tordoff, Andrés Zarankin, and two anonymous reviewers for their excellent suggestions for improvements. Finally, to Laurie Beckwith, I give my thanks for all her support.

References

ARCHIVO GENERAL DE INDIAS
  1569 Méritos. Servicios: Gonzalo de las Peñas: Nuevo Reino Granada. Patronato 158, N3, R6, Archivo General de Indias, Sevilla, Spain.

ARCHIVO HISTÓRICO MUNICIPAL (AHM)
  1557–1580 Minutes of Cuenca Municipal Council. First through Fifth *Libros de Cabildo*, Archivo Histórico Municipal, Cuenca, Ecuador.
  1561 Minutes of Cuenca Municipal Council. First *Libro de Cabildo*, 3 Nov., Archivo Histórico Municipal, Cuenca, Ecuador.
  1561–1566 Minutes of Cuenca Municipal Council. First and Second *Libros de Cabildo*, Archivo Histórico Municipal, Cuenca, Ecuador.
  1563 Minutes of Cuenca Municipal Council. First *Libro de Cabildo*, 22 March, Archivo Histórico Municipal, Cuenca, Ecuador.
  1580–1586 Minutes of Cuenca Municipal Council. Fifth *Libro de Cabildo*, Archivo Histórico Municipal, Cuenca, Ecuador.
  1588–1613 Minutes of Cuenca Municipal Council. Sixth through Eighth *Libros de Cabildo*, Archivo Histórico Municipal, Cuenca, Ecuador.
  1650 Minutes of Cuenca Municipal Council. First *Libro de Cabildo*, 16 Aug., Archivo Histórico Municipal, Cuenca, Ecuador.

ARCHIVO NACIONAL DE HISTORIA (ANH)
  1563 Business contract. *Libro* 487 f1v, Archivo Nacional de Historia, Cuenca, Ecuador.
  1565 Sales receipt. *Libro* 487 f765v, Archivo Nacional de Historia, Cuenca, Ecuador.
  1583 Property sale. *Carpeta* 106.930, Archivo Nacional de Historia, Cuenca, Ecuador.
  1603 Property sale. *Libro* 494 f616v, Archivo Nacional de Historia, Cuenca, Ecuador.
  1605 Property sale. *Carpeta* 140.732, Archivo Nacional de Historia, Cuenca, Ecuador.
  1636 Property sale. *Libro* 530 f568r, 15 July, Archivo Nacional de Historia, Cuenca, Ecuador.
  1639 Last Will and Testament of Gil Ruiz de Tapia. *Libro* 489 f614, Archivo Nacional de Historia, Cuenca, Ecuador.
  1644 Last Will and Testament of Gil Ruiz de Tapia. *Libro* 489 f619r, Archivo Nacional de Historia, Cuenca, Ecuador.
  1645 Property sale. *Libro* 511f363v, Archivo Nacional de Historia, Cuenca, Ecuador.
  1650a Lawsuit (Geronimo Munoz sues estate of Gil Ruiz de Tapia). *Carpeta* 078.58, Archivo Nacional de Historia, Cuenca, Ecuador.
  1650b Lawsuit (Geronimo Munoz sues estate of Gil Ruiz de Tapia). *Carpeta* 078.58 f8, Archivo Nacional de Historia, Cuenca, Ecuador.
  1650c Lawsuit (Geronimo Munoz sues estate of Gil Ruiz de Tapia). *Carpeta* 078.58 f9, Archivo Nacional de Historia, Cuenca, Ecuador.
  1651 Property sale. *Libro* 513 f408, Archivo Nacional de Historia, Cuenca, Ecuador.
  1653 Lawsuit (Gabriel Guena sues estate of Gil Ruiz de Tapia). *Carpeta* 108.512, Archivo Nacional de Historia, Cuenca, Ecuador.

AVELLANEDA NAVAS, JOSÉ IGNACIO
  1995 *The Conquerors of the New Kingdom of Granada.* University of New Mexico Press, Albuquerque.

BISHKO, CHARLES J.
  1952 The Peninsular Background of Latin American Cattle Ranching. *Hispanic American Historical Review* 32(4):491–515.

BORCHART DE MORENO, CHRISTIANA R.
  1995 Llamas y Ovejas: El Desarrollo del Ganado Lanar en la Audiencia de Quito (Llamas and Sheep: The Development of Wool Livestock in the Audiencia de Quito). In *Colonización Agrícola y Ganadera en América, Siglo XVI–XVIII: Su Impacto en la Población Aborigen* (Agricultural Colonization and Livestock in America: Sixteenth to Eighteenth Centuries: Its Impact on Native Populations), L. Escobari de Querejazu, editor, pp. 153–190. Ediciones Abya-Yala, Quito, Ecuador.
  1998 *La Audiencia de Quito. Aspectos Económicos y Sociales (Siglos XVI–XVIII)* (The Audiencia de Quito: Economic and Social Aspects: Sixteenth to Eighteenth Centuries). Banco Central del Ecuador/ Ediciones Abya Yala, Quito, Ecuador.

BUTZER, KARL W.
  1988 Cattle and Sheep from Old to New Spain: Historical Antecedents. *Annals of the Association of American Geographers* 78: 29–56.

BUYS, JOZEF
  1997 Monumentos y Fragmentos: Arqueología Histórica en el Ecuador (Monuments and Fragments: Historical Archaeology in Ecuador). In *Approaches to the Historical Archaeology of Mexico, Central, and South America*, Janine L. Gasco, Greg Charles Smith, and Patricia Fournier García, editors, pp. 111–120. Institute of Archaeology, University of California, Los Angeles.

CARRILLO, ANTONIO
1998 Informe de la Prospección Arqueológica Realizada en la Catedral Vieja de Cuenca, Temporadas: 1996–1997 (Report on Archaeological Excavations in the Catedral Vieja de Cuenca: 1996 and 1997 Seasons). Manuscript, Instituto Nacional del Patrimonio Cultural, Cuenca, Ecuador.

CASTILLO, VICTORIA E.
2003 *Ceramicists at the Convención del 45 Neighbourhood: Contemporary Ecuadorian Artisans and Their Material Culture.* Master's thesis, Department of Archaeology, Simon Fraser University, Burnaby, BC, Canada. University Microfilms International, Ann Arbor, MI.

CHACÓN ZHAPÁN, JUAN
1990 *Historia del Corregimiento de Cuenca, 1557–1777* (History of the Mayorality of Cuenca). Banco Central del Ecuador, Quito, Ecuador.

CHANCE, JOHN K.
2003 Haciendas, Ranchos, and Indian Towns: A Case from the Late Colonial Valley of Puebla. *Ethnohistory* 50(1):15–45.

CUSHNER, NICHOLAS P.
1982 *Farm and Factory: The Jesuits and the Development of Agrarian Capitalism in Colonial Quito, 1600–1767.* State University of New York Press, Albany.

CUSICK, JAMES G.
1998 Historiography of Acculturation: An Evaluation of Concepts and Their Application in Archaeology. In *Studies in Culture Contact: Interaction, Culture Change, and Archaeology,* James G. Cusick, editor, pp. 126–145. Southern Illinois University, Carbondale.

D'ANDREA, A. CATHERINE
2002 Archaeobotanical Samples from Cuenca. Manuscript, Ross W. Jamieson, Department of Archaeology, Simon Fraser University, Burnaby, BC, Canada.

DEAGAN, KATHLEEN A.
1983 *Spanish St. Augustine: The Archaeology of a Colonial Creole Community.* Academic Press, New York, NY.
2003 Colonial Origins and Colonial Transformations in Spanish America. *Historical Archaeology* 37(4):3–13.

DEAGAN, KATHLEEN A., AND ELIZABETH J. REITZ
1995 Merchants and Cattlemen: The Archaeology of a Commercial Structure at Puerto Real. In *Puerto Real: The Archaeology of a Sixteenth-Century Spanish Town in Hispaniola,* Kathleen Deagan, editor, pp. 231–284. University Press of Florida, Gainesville.

DEFRANCE, SUSAN D.
1996 Iberian Foodways in the Moquegua and Torata Valleys of Southern Peru. *Historical Archaeology* 30(3):20–48.

2003 Diet and Provisioning in the High Andes: A Spanish Colonial Settlement on the Outskirts of Potosí, Bolivia. *International Journal of Historical Archaeology* 7(2):99–125.

DOMÍNGUEZ, LOURDES S.
1978 La Transculturación en Cuba (Sigs. 16–17) (Transculturation in Cuba: Sixteenth to Seventeenth Centuries). *Cuba Arqueológica* 1:33–50.
2005 Historical Archaeology in Cuba. In *Dialogues in Cuban Archaeology,* L. Antonio Curet, Shannon Lee Dawdy, and Gabino La Rosa Corzo, editors, pp. 62–71. University of Alabama Press, Tuscaloosa.

DUSENBERRY, WILLIAM HOWARD
1963 *The Mexican Mesta: The Administration of Ranching in Colonial Mexico.* University of Illinois Press, Urbana.

ESCOBARI DE QUEREJAZU, LAURA (EDITOR)
1995 *Colonización Agrícola y Ganadera en América, Siglos XVI–XVIII: Su Impacto En La Población Aborigen* (Agricultural Colonization and Livestock in America, Sixteenth to Eighteenth Centuries: Its Impact on Native Populations). Ediciones Abya-Yala, Quito, Ecuador.

FOSTER, GEORGE M.
1960 *Culture and Conquest: The American Spanish Heritage.* Viking Fund Publications in Anthropology, No. 27. Wenner-Gren Foundation for Anthropological Research, New York, NY.

FOURNIER GARCÍA, PATRICIA, AND LOURDES MONDRAGÓN
2003 Haciendas, Ranchos, and the Otomí Way of Life in the Mezquital Valley, Hidalgo, Mexico. *Ethnohistory* 50(1):47–68.

FUNARI, PEDRO PAULO A., AND FERNANDO R. BRITTEZ (EDITORS)
2006 *Arqueología Histórica en América Latina: Temas y Discusiones Recientes* (Historical Archaeology in South America: Recent Themes and Discussions). Ediciones Suárez, Mar del Plata, Argentina.

FUNARI, PEDRO PAULO A., AND ANDRÉS ZARANKIN (EDITORS)
2004 *Arqueología Histórica en América del Sur: Los Desafíos del Siglo XXI* (Historical Archaeology in South America: Challenges for the Twenty-First Century). Ediciones Uniandes, Bogotá, Colombia.

GONZÁLEZ, IVÁN
1991 *Cuenca: Barrios de Tierra y Fuego (Desintegración de los Barrios Artesanales)* (Cuenca: Neighborhoods of Earth and Fire [Disintegration of Artisans' Neighborhoods]). Fundación Paul Rivet, Cuenca, Ecuador.

Gutiérrez Usillos, Andrés, and José Ramón Iglesias Aliaga

1996 Identificación y Análisis de los Restos de Fauna Recuperados en los Conventos de San Francisco y Santo Domingo de Quito (Siglos XVI–XIX) (Identification and Analysis of Faunal Remains Recovered from the Monasteries of San Francisco and Santo Domingo, Quito: Sixteenth to Nineteenth Centuries). *Revista Española de Antropología Americana* 26:77–100. Madrid, Spain.

Haber, Alejandro F.

1999 Uywaña, the House, and Its Indoor Landscape: Oblique Approaches to, and Beyond, Domestication. In *The Prehistory of Food: Appetites for Change*, Chris Gosden and Jon Hather, editors, pp. 59–82. Routledge, New York, NY.

Idrovo Urigüen, Jaime

2000 *Tomebamba: Arqueología e Historia de una Ciudad Imperial* (Tomebamba: Archaeology and History of an Imperial City). Banco Central del Ecuador, Cuenca, Ecuador.

Jacobsen, Nils

1986 Livestock Complexes in Late Colonial Peru and New Spain: An Attempt at Comparison. In *The Economies of Mexico and Peru during the Late Colonial Period, 1760–1810*, Nils Jacobsen and Hans-Jürgen Puhle, editors, pp. 113–142. Colloquium, Berlin, Germany.

Jamieson, Ross W.

2000 *Domestic Architecture and Power: The Historical Archaeology of Colonial Ecuador*. Kluwer Academic/Plenum Publishers, New York, NY.

2001 Majolica in the Early Colonial Andes: The Role of Panamanian Wares. *Latin American Antiquity* 12(1):45–58.

2004 Bolts of Cloth and Sherds of Pottery: Impressions of Caste in the Material Culture of the Seventeenth-Century Audiencia of Quito. *The Americas* 60(3):431–446.

2005 Colonialism, Social Archaeology, and Lo Andino: Historical Archaeology in the Andes. *World Archaeology* 37(3):352–372.

Klein, Julius

1920 *The Mesta: A Study in Spanish Economic History, 1273–1836*. Harvard University Press, Cambridge, MA.

Larson, Brooke

1998 *Cochabamba, 1550–1900: Colonialism and Agrarian Transformation in Bolivia*. Duke University Press, Durham, NC.

Melville, Elinor G. K.

1994 *A Plague of Sheep: Environmental Consequences of the Conquest of Mexico*. Cambridge University Press, Cambridge, England, UK.

Miño Grijalva, Manuel

1998 *Obrajes y Tejedores de Nueva España, 1700–1810: Industria Urbana y Rural de una Economía Colonial* (Textile Mills and Weavers of New Spain, 1700–1810: Urban and Rural Industries of a Colonial Economy). El Colegio de México, Mexico City, Mexico.

Montúfar López, Aurora, and Norma Valentín Maldonado

1998 Estudio Arqueobiológico de los Sedimentos del Subsuelo en el Edificio Real Seminario de Minas, 1772, México, D.F. (Archaeo-Biological Study of Subsurface Sediments in the Royal Mining School Building, 1772, Mexico City). *Arqueología* 20:97–113. Mexico City.

Morresi, Eldo Serafín

1983 Alternativa y Camino Válido para una Presencia Activa en la Investigación de Arqueología Histórica Argentina (Alternatives and New Directions for an Active Presence in the Investigation of Argentine Historical Archaeology). In *Presencia Hispánica en la Arqueología Argentina, Tomo I* (Spanish Presence in the Archaeology of Argentina, Vol. 1), Eldo Serafín Morresi and Ramón Gutiérrez, editors, pp. 15–27. Universidad Nacional del Nordeste, Resistencia, Argentina.

Newson, Linda A.

1995 *Life and Death in Early Colonial Ecuador*. University of Oklahoma Press, Norman.

Nimmo, Evelyn

2003 *The Concepción Convent of Cuenca, Ecuador: Examining Gender, Class, and Economy in a Latin American Convent*. Master's thesis, Department of Archaeology, Simon Fraser University, Burnaby, BC, Canada. University Microfilms International, Ann Arbor, MI.

Ortiz, Fernando

1995 *Cuban Counterpoint: Tobacco and Sugar*, Harriet de Onís, translator. Duke University Press, Durham, NC. [Originally published in 1947.]

Paniagua Pérez, Jesús, and Deborah L. Truhan

2003 *Oficios y Actividad Paragremial en la Real Audiencia de Quito (1557–1730): El Corregimiento de Cuenca* (Trades and Guild Activity in the Royal Audiencia de Quito (1557–1730): Mayorality of Cuenca). Universidad de León, León, Spain.

Phillips, Carla Rahn, and William D. Phillips

1997 *Spain's Golden Fleece: Wool Production and the Wool Trade from the Middle Ages to the Nineteenth Century*. Johns Hopkins University Press, Baltimore, MD.

Pintos Blanco, Sebastián

1996 Análisis Arqueozoológico del Sitio Casa del Gobernador (Zooarchaeological Analysis of the Governor's House Site). *Historical Archaeology in Latin America* 16:19–26.

PODWOJEWSKI, P., AND N. GERMAIN
2005 Short-Term Effects of Management on the Soil Structure in a Deep Tilled Hardened Volcanic-Ash Soil (Cangahua) in Ecuador. *European Journal of Soil Science* 56(1):39–51.

POLONI SIMARD, JACQUES
2000 *La Mosaïque Indienne: Mobilité, Stratification Sociale et Métissage dans le Corregimiento de Cuenca (Équateur) du 16e au 18e Siècle* (The Indian Mosaic: Mobility, Social Stratification, and Mestizaje in the Mayorality of Cuenca [Ecuador] from the Sixteenth to the Eighteenth Centuries). Éditions de l'École des Hautes Études en Sciences Sociales, Paris, France.

POWERS, KAREN VIEIRA
1995 *Andean Journeys: Migration, Ethnogenesis, and the State in Colonial Quito.* University of New Mexico Press, Albuquerque.
2000 Land Concentration and Environmental Degradation: Town Council Records on Deforestation in Uyumbicho (Quito, 1553–96). In *Colonial Lives: Documents on Latin American History, 1550–1850.* Richard E. Boyer and Geoffrey Spurling, editors, pp. 11–17. Oxford University Press, Oxford, England, UK.

REITZ, ELIZABETH J.
1986 Vertebrate Fauna from Locus 39, Puerto Real, Haiti. *Journal of Field Archaeology* 13(3):317–328.
1991 Animal Use and Culture Change in Spanish Florida. In *Animal Use and Culture Change,* Pamela J. Crabtree and K. Ryan, editors, pp. 62–77. University Museum Publications, Philadelphia, PA.
1992 The Spanish Colonial Experience and Domestic Animals. *Historical Archaeology* 26(1):84–91.

REITZ, ELIZABETH J., AND STEPHEN L. CUMBAA
1983 Diet and Foodways of Eighteenth-Century Spanish St. Augustine. In *Spanish St. Augustine: The Archaeology of a Colonial Creole Community,* Kathleen A. Deagan, editor, pp. 151–185. Academic Press, New York, NY.

REITZ, ELIZABETH J., AND C. MARGARET SCARRY
1985 *Reconstructing Historic Subsistence with an Example from Sixteenth-Century Spanish Florida.* Society for Historical Archaeology, Ann Arbor, MI.

RICE, PRUDENCE
1996 The Archaeology of Wine: The Wine and Brandy Haciendas of Moquegua, Peru. *Journal of Field Archaeology* 23(2):187–204.

RODRÍGUEZ-ALEGRÍA, ENRIQUE
2005 Eating Like an Indian: Negotiating Social Relations in the Spanish Colonies. *Current Anthropology* 46(4):551–574.

ROMERO, ANA A., FERNANDO HERNÁNDEZ, AND DANIEL O. BARBOZA
2002 Arqueofauna: Enfoques y Estudios en el Espacio Fundacional de Mendoza (Arqueofauna: Approaches and Studies in the Historic Core of Mendoza). In *Arqueología Histórica Argentina: Actas del 1er Congreso Nacional de Arqueología Histórica* (Argentine Historical Archaeology: Proceedings of the First National Conference of Historical Archaeology), Daniel Schávelzon, editor, pp. 153–161. Ediciones Corregidor, Buenos Aires, Argentina.

SALVUCCI, RICHARD J.
1987 *Textiles and Capitalism in Mexico: An Economic History of the Obrajes, 1539–1840.* Princeton University Press, Princeton, NJ.

SCHÁVELZON, DANIEL
2000 *The Historical Archaeology of Buenos Aires: A City at the End of the World.* Kluwer Academic/Plenum Publishers, New York, NY.

SCHÁVELZON, DANIEL (EDITOR)
2002 *Arqueología Histórica Argentina: Actas del 1er Congreso Nacional de Arqueología Histórica* (Argentine Historical Archaeology: Proceedings of the First National Conference of Historical Archaeology). Ediciones Corregidor, Buenos Aires, Argentina.

SILVEIRA, MARIO J.
1995 Análisis de Restos Faunísticos en Sitios Históricos de la Ciudad de Buenos Aires (Analysis of Faunal Remains from Historic Sites in the City of Buenos Aires). *Historical Archaeology in Latin America* 7:43–56.
1996 Casa Peña: Análisis de los Restos Óseos (The Peña House: Analysis of Osteological Remains). *Historical Archaeology in Latin America* 14:75–90.
2002 Zooarqueología de un Sitio Jesuítico-Guaraní del Siglo XVII: Reducción de Nuestra Señora de Itapuá, Plaza 9 de Julio, Posadas (Zooarchaeology of a Jesuit-Guarani Site from the Seventeenth Century: Reducción de Nuestra Señora de Itapuá). In *Arqueología Histórica Argentina: Actas del 1er Congreso Nacional de Arqueología Histórica* (Argentine Historical Archaeology: Proceedings of the First Conference of Historical Archaeology), Daniel Schávelzon, editor, pp. 789–798. Ediciones Corregidor, Buenos Aires, Argentina.
2003 El Convento de Santa Catalina (Buenos Aires): Sus Comidas Vistas por la Zooarqueología (The Santa Catalina Convent [Buenos Aires]: Its Foodstuffs as Seen through Zooarchaeology). In *Actas del IV Congreso Argentino de Americanistas del 2001* (Proceedings of the Fourth Arentine Conference of the Americanists, 2001), pp. 647–666. Ediciones Corregidor, Buenos Aires, Argentina.

Perspectives from *Historical Archaeology*

SILVEIRA, MARIO J., AND MATILDE M. LANZA
  1998 Zooarqueología de un Basurero Colonial: Convento
        de Santo Domingo (Fines del Siglo XVIII a Principios
        Siglo XIX) (Zooarchaeology of a Colonial Midden:
        Santo Domingo Monastery [End of the Eighteenth to
        the Beginning of the Nineteenth Centuries]). In *Actas
        del Segundo Congreso Argentino de Americanistas,
        Vol. 2* (Proceedings of the Second Argentine
        Conference of the Americanists, Vol. 2), pp. 531–552.
        Sociedad Argentina de Americanistas, Buenos Aires,
        Argentina.
  1999 Zooarqueología de un Sitio Histórico en la Ciudad
        de Buenos Aires: Michelangelo (Zooarchaeology
        of an Historic Site in the City of Buenos Aires:
        Michelangelo). In *Actas del XII Congreso Nacional
        de Arqueología de la Argentina, Tomo I* (Proceedings
        of the Twelfth National Conference of Argentine
        Archaeology, Vol. 1), pp. 515–522. Universidad
        Nacional de la Plata, Buenos Aires, Argentina.

SIMPSON, LESLEY BYRD
  1952 *Exploitation of Land in Central Mexico in the Sixteenth
        Century.* University of California Press, Berkeley,
        CA.

SLUYTER, ANDREW S.
  1996 The Ecological Origins and Consequences of
        Cattle Ranching in Sixteenth-Century New Spain.
        Geographical Review 86(2):161–177.

SMITH, GREG C.
  1991 *Heard It through the Grapevine: Andean and European
        Contributions to Spanish Colonial Culture and
        Viticulture in Moquegua, Peru.* Doctoral dissertation,
        Department of Anthropology, University of Florida
        at Gainesville. University Microfilms International,
        Ann Arbor, MI.
  1997 Hispanic, Andean, and African Influences in the
        Moquegua Valley of Southern Peru. *Historical
        Archaeology* 31(7):74–83.

SOASTI, GUADALUPE
  1994 Obrajeros y Comerciantes en Riobamba (Workers
        and Traders in Riobamba). *Procesos* 1:5–22. Quito,
        Ecuador.

STAHL, ANN BROWER
  2002 Colonial Entanglements and the Practices of Taste:
        An Alternative to Logocentric Approaches. *American
        Anthropologist* 104(3):827–845.

STAHL, PETER W.
  2003 Pre-Columbian Andean Animal Domesticates at the
        Edge of Empire. *World Archaeology* 34(3):470–483.

STAVIG, WARD
  2000 Ambiguous Visions: Nature, Law, and Culture in
        Indigenous-Spanish Land Relations in Colonial Peru.
        Hispanic American Historical Review 80(1):77–
        111.

STINER, MARY C.
  1994 *Honor among Thieves: A Zooarchaeological Study
        of Neandertal Ecology.* Princeton University Press,
        Princeton, NJ.

TARCAN, CARMEN G.
  2005 Analysis of Vertebrate Faunal Remains from
        Two Spanish Archaeological Contexts in Cuenca,
        Ecuador. Manuscript, Ross Jamieson, Department
        of Archaeology, Simon Fraser University, Burnaby,
        BC, Canada.

TYRER, ROBSON BRINES
  1988 *Historia Demográfica y Económica de la Audiencia
        de Quito: Población Indígena e Industria Textil,
        1600–1800* (Demographic and Economic History
        of the Audiencia de Quito: Indian Population and
        the Textile Industry, 1600–1800). Banco Central del
        Ecuador, Quito.

UNESCO
  1999 Historic Centre of Santa Ana de Los Ríos de Cuenca.
        World Heritage List, World Heritage Centre, United
        Nations Educational, Scientific, and Cultural
        Organization, Paris, France <http://whc.unesco.org/
        en/list/863>.

VAN BUREN, MARY
  1993 *Community and Empire in Southern Peru: The Site of
        Torata Alta under Spanish Rule.* Doctoral dissertation,
        Department of Anthropology, University of Arizona,
        Tucson. University Microfilms International, Ann
        Arbor, MI.

WHEELER, JANE C., A. J. F. RUSSEL, AND HILARY REDDEN
  1995 Llamas and Alpacas: Pre-Conquest Breeds and Post-
        Conquest Hybrids. *Journal of Archaeological Science*
        22(6):833–840.

WING, ELIZABETH S.
  1986 Domestication of Andean Mammals. In *High Altitude
        Tropical Biogeography.* François Vuilleumier and
        Maximina Monasterio, editors, pp. 246–264. Oxford
        University Press, Oxford, England, UK.

ROSS W. JAMIESON
DEPARTMENT OF ARCHAEOLOGY
SIMON FRASER UNIVERSITY
BURNABY, BC, CANADA V5A 1S6

REBECCA SAUNDERS

Mission-Period Settlement Structure: A Test of the Model at San Martín de Timucua

ABSTRACT

Beginning in 1968, the Florida Division of Historical Resources sponsored several small-scale testing programs of Spanish mission sites in northern Florida. A formal model of Mission-period settlement structure emerged from those excavations. However, more recent excavations involving large block exposures at a few mission compounds have shown settlement structure to be more complex, and less regular, than modeled. Such is the case at San Martín de Timucua. Recent excavations there have demonstrated that the imposition of the preexisting model on results from previous limited excavations has resulted in misinterpretations of structure architecture and function as well as site layout. These results demonstrate that long-term commitments to extensive excavations will be necessary to understand intrasite settlement patterns in Florida missions.

Introduction

From 1968 to 1972, the Florida Division of Historical Resources (then the Division of Archives, History, and Records Management) conducted a project designed to locate and excavate Spanish mission sites in the region of the Apalachee, in and around Tallahassee, Florida. Six missions were recorded, bringing the total of known mission sites in Apalachee at the time to nine. The project was extended east into the area of the western Timucua, where two additional missions were located. During the testing of these mission sites, an informal model of mission compound layout in western Florida was generated and applied to most sites. Jones and Shapiro (1990) later formalized the principal aspects of the model.

In view of the limited scope of the excavations on which it was based, the model should have been treated as a hypothesis to be tested. Instead, it was routinely imposed on further limited excavations, leading to the misidentification of structure function and a poor appreciation of the variability of intrasite settlement patterning in

general. Application to more recent excavations has had the same consequences. The following description of results from large-scale excavations at San Martín de Timucua (8CO1) indicates that the model as applied by a previous excavator (Weisman 1992) fails to describe accurately the complex, diachronic process of mission construction.

The Mission Model

While noting variability in mission layout and architecture, the Jones and Shapiro model emphasized consistency. Jones and Shapiro noted that a church complex, or mission compound, consisted of a minimum of two buildings, interpreted as the church and the *convento*, or friary. Without exception, a church function was assigned to the larger of the two buildings. The church was described as rectangular and the *convento* roughly square. Church length was said to range from 17.8 to 26 m, though widths were more consistent (11–12.6 m). *Convento* sizes varied widely, as did their orientation with respect to the church (Jones and Shapiro 1990:504). Several missions had a third building, usually identified as a kitchen. Where present, these three buildings formed a right triangle with a courtyard completing the quadrangle (Jones and Shapiro 1990:504). At the time the article was written, only one church, at Patale (8LE152), was described as having burials through the floor of the nave; cemetery burial was considered the norm. Though in at least two cases, Escambe (8LE120) and Ivitachuco (8JE100), areas defined as cemeteries often had postholes within and surrounding them, these were interpreted as the remains of *ramadas* (light awnings) or as cemetery markers (Jones and Shapiro 1990:496, 505–506).

With more extensive and intensive excavation at a few Apalachee, Timucuan, and Atlantic coastal Guale mission sites, increasing familiarity with the historical record, and knowledge of Mexican and Caribbean precedents, a number of the above generalities can be questioned. With more data, it is clear that structure function has been misconstrued in a number of cases, largely because of preconceptions about what a mission compound should look like (cf. Marrinan 1993). This is clear in the case of Patale, where a portion of the church was originally identified as a *convento* (Marrinan 1993:267). Functional misidentification or mismapping is probable for the structures identified as churches at Ayubale (8JE1) and Aspalaga (8JE2) (Saunders 1990:532). Large-scale excavations at Santa Catalina on St. Catherines Island, Georgia (Thomas 1993), Santa Catalina and Santa Maria on Amelia Island, Florida (Saunders 1993), San Luis (Shapiro and Vernon 1992; McEwan and Larsen 1995), Patale (Marrinan 1993), and now Fig Springs, discussed below, have demonstrated that burial within the church was the rule rather than the exception.

Mission Variability

This author previously noted (Saunders 1990:531–532) that while there probably was a desire for uniformity among the missions—and this is demonstrated for Mexican missions by documentary evidence (McAndrew 1965:124–125), there were at least six historical factors that would encourage variability between missions in *La Florida*. These included: 1) whether or not the mission was established in an extant town, 2) the time period of construction, 3) the size of the labor pool, 4) local and regional economics, 5) politics, and 6) the architectural and managerial expertise of the friar(s) involved. Another consideration is the length of time a mission was occupied. Missions were not static phenomena; structures could change to meet the needs of an expanding or contracting population. Finally, a more methodological factor could have been included—to wit, the amount of variability observed is indirectly associated with the amount of excavation. At present, it seems that the more that is known about a site, the less it resembles other sites and the less it resembles the settlement plan model applied to the limited excavations done at most of the mission sites in La Florida.

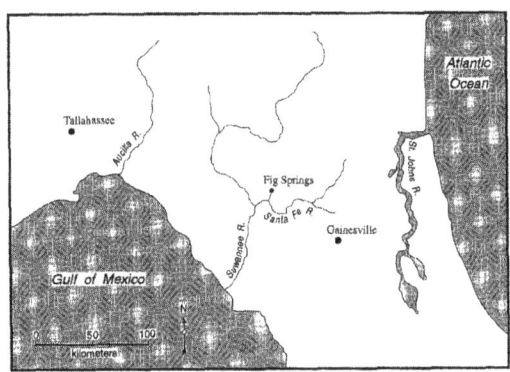

FIGURE 1. Site location.

San Martín de Timucua

These points are illustrated in the results of recent excavations at the Timucuan (Utinan) mission of San Martín de Timucua, the Fig Springs site (8CO1), located along the Ichetucknee River in north-central Florida (Figure 1). The site was originally recorded in 1949 by John Goggin (Weisman 1992:17). Goggin recognized Spanish pottery in a spring run at the base of a rise. The mission compound, up a steep slope from the spring, was not located until 1986. That year, Ken Johnson (1987, 1990) of the Florida Museum of Natural History (FLMNH) shovel-tested the site as part of a project to locate the route of Hernando de Soto through Florida. Johnson demonstrated the existence of human remains, Spanish artifacts, and a possible clay floor at the site. The Florida Division of Recreation and Parks sponsored three additional field seasons intended to gather architectural information.

The first two of these, directed by Brent Weisman of the Florida Division of Historical Resources in 1988, included a systematic auger survey conducted at 10-m intervals. Results of the survey indicated a concentration of Spanish artifacts in the northern area of the survey and of Native American artifacts in the southern portion. Based on artifact distributions, Weisman (1992:54–73) identified the locations of a church, *convento*, kitchen, and cemetery in

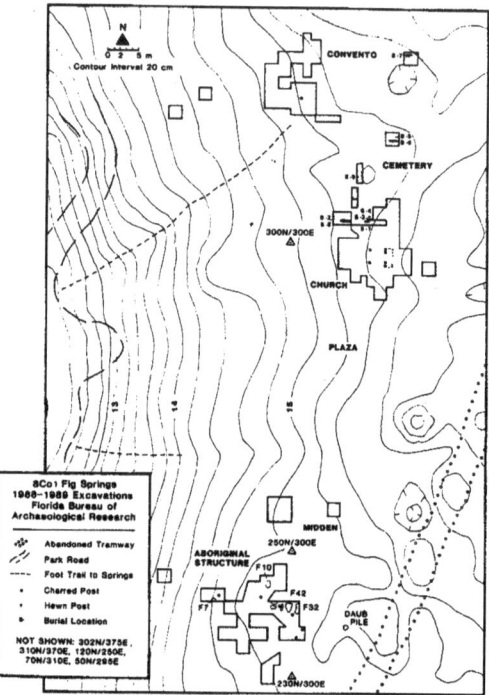

FIGURE 2. Map of excavations and features at Fig Springs as of 1989 (after Weisman 1992:55, Figure 21; courtesy of University Press of Florida, Gainesville).

locations conforming more or less with the Jones and Shapiro mission model (Figure 2). Weisman believed that subsequent tests and small block excavations (Figure 2) confirmed most of these initial identifications (Weisman 1992:164–165). The church was identified on the basis of several factors:

> the lack of internal features suggestive of domestic use . . . ; the special preparation of the building surface by the placement of construction fill, resulting in the structure being elevated above the surrounding grade; the shared alignment of building walls and floor plan with associated Christian Indian burials interred along the north wall of the building; and the general architectural similarity to other excavated mission structures that have been interpreted as churches (Weisman 1992:54).

In fact, while certain construction techniques were shared with other missions, the architecture as reported by Weisman is unique for missions in La Florida. Weisman described the structure as composed of three "rooms" built on a stripped, graded, and filled area (Figure 3). The

front of the structure was composed of an "L-shaped" room with a prepared clay floor. (This author believes that the L-shaped configuration could also be an artifact of excavation area and preservation/erosion. L-shaped *atrios* are known, however [Kubler 1946:318–319].) Roof supports of hewn pine were placed on clay support pads at the edge of the clay floor, creating a small façade. East of this façade, and at a higher elevation, was a wooden-floored room. The room, which was defined by in situ burned posts, the burned bases of vertical boards, and a sill plate, was enclosed by vertical board siding. Because double posts were found only for the eastern half of the structure, Weisman conjectured that only the eastern portion of the room had full-height partition boards. Weisman's third "room" was a portion of the sand fill area south of the enclosed room. Estimated dimensions of the building, based on covered floor area, were 10.5 m N–S and 8.5 m E–W.

An architectural reconstruction of the structure (Figure 3) is more easily apprehended. In fact, there was a single, small room fronted by a covered, clay floored, and partially eroded *atrio*. Such a structure conforms well with the definition of an open chapel, as Weisman (1992:63–64) noted. An open chapel was usually a small structure which served as "the sanctuary of a roofless nave" (McAndrew 1965:342). The structure was large enough only to provide shelter for the altar and its furnishings and a celebrant. If the furnishings, such as the altar stone, were kept in the open chapel, it probably had doors that locked. If the open chapel were in a *visita*, a converted village with no resident priest, however, it may not have had permanent altar furniture. Rather, for services, a friar traveled from a mission village with a portable altar service completely contained within a small chest (McAndrew 1965:354–355). Doors, then, probably were unnecessary in *visita* open chapels. The nave of the open chapel was the *atrio*, a cleared and leveled area extending in front of a chapel, or church; the *atrio* was sometimes surfaced with clay or plaster and/or fenced. Mass was said there, but the *atrio* was also used for religious instruction, baptism, processions and plays, and burial (Kubler 1946; McAndrew 1965).

Documentary evidence for Mexican missions indicates that the construction of open chapels was a customary part of the building program of a mission. Because of the necessity to safeguard the altar, they were the first structure erected in a mission compound—after large wooden crosses were raised (McAndrew 1965:247). The

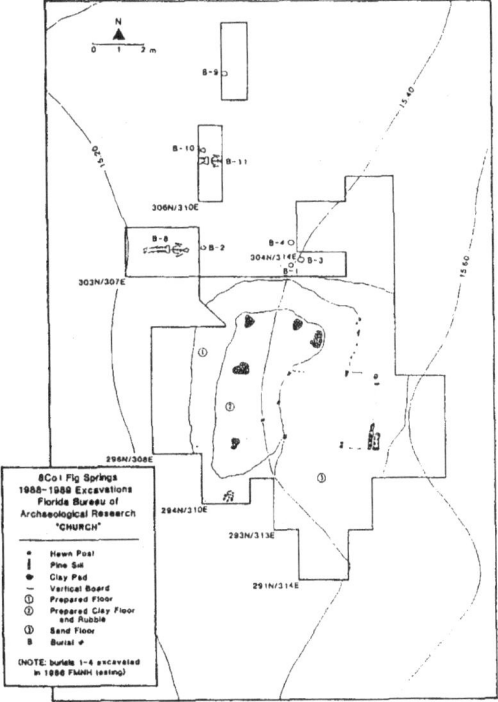

FIGURE 3. Plan map and architectural reconstruction of the Fig Springs open chapel (after Weisman 1992, Figures 24, 31; courtesy of University Press of Florida, Gainesville).

convento was built next. Only then was a more substantial church constructed. Sometimes the open chapel was abandoned at this point. In more Hispanicized areas, however, the church was reserved for Spanish use, and Native Americans continued to worship in the *atrio* of the open chapel. On the other hand, in poorer areas, for instance in the Yucatán and Tlaxcala, a church never supplanted the chapel, though the chapel could become increasingly complex. (It may be, as Hanson [1995] also noted, that the Yucatán provides a better analog for Florida mission construction than do areas with more complex traditional societies and/or which were better supported by the Crown.) Similarly, in Mexican *visitas*, with no resident friar, religious architecture was restricted to the open chapel and an *atrio*.

If the Fig Springs structure was an open chapel, it would be one of only two hypothesized for La Florida—though technically the term might apply to numerous rudimentary churches, for instance that proposed for Santa Catalina de Guale on Amelia Island (Saunders 1993). The other was excavated at the Baptizing Springs site (8SU65), perhaps the mission of San Juan de Guacara (Worth 1992:59; Loucks 1993:212, fn. 1). Subsurface integrity of the building, Structure B, was poor (Loucks 1979:8, 131). Excavation revealed "remains of packed red clay floor, some charred wood, five charred posts, and sections of two 'wall trenches' [defining] a structure roughly 10 m E–W by 8 m N–S" (Loucks 1979:130). Loucks suggested that Structure B was the church or a residence for a priest. However, the dimensions are quite close to the floor area of the open chapel at Fig Springs. The three-walled construction may also suggest that the structure was an open chapel (Saunders 1990:535).

Although these are the only two hypothetical open chapels known, given the prescribed method of mission construction in Mexico, most, if not all, Florida missions should have had an open chapel. At present, however, there are insufficient data to model the location of this structure with respect to coeval or later churches in any given Florida mission compound.

As noted above, burials were found aligned with the Fig Springs open chapel. These began some 1.5 m north of the clay pad. Based on the recovery of unidentified bone in an auger test and the burials exposed in Weisman's and Johnson's excavations, the size of the cemetery or *campo santo* was projected to be 8.5 m E–W and 36 m N–S (Weisman 1992:73).

The Fig Springs *convento* (Figure 2) was defined on the basis of a concentration of iron hardware, including 43 nails and spikes and an ornamental chest lock fragment (Weisman 1992:116, Table 8), glass beads and glass fragments, and the presence of a single burned post.

A substantial proportion of the nails and spikes (42%) came from the same unit as the burned post. Weisman (1992:66) noted that the "soils appeared heavily disturbed in the area as the result of erosion and redeposition."

In the summer of 1990, further excavations were undertaken in the cemetery area of the site by Jerald T. Milanich and Lisa Hoshower of FLMNH. Their objectives (Hoshower and Milanich 1993:217) were first to "determine the feasibility of on-site osteological analysis," with reburial of human remains following immediately, and second, to "gather bioanthropological data on the mission population." However, their

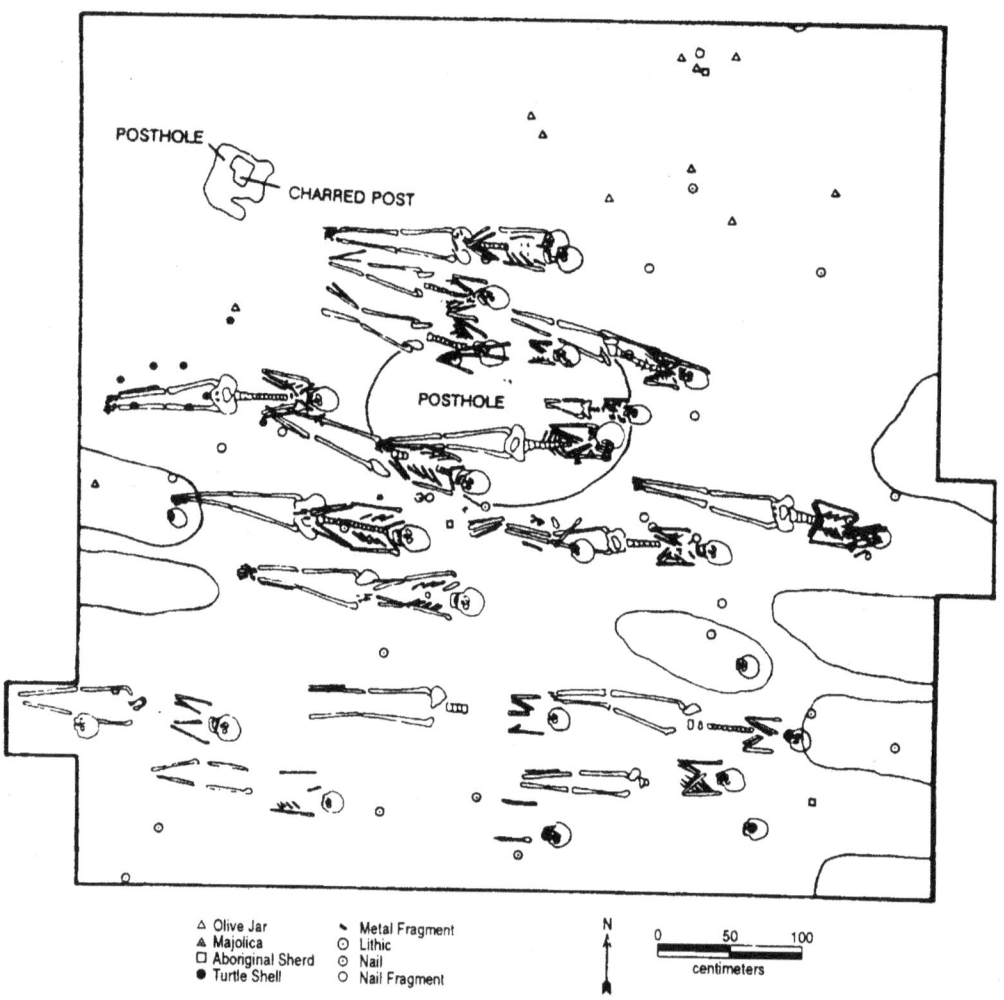

FIGURE 4. Burials and other features in block excavated in 1990 (after Hoshower and Milanich 1993:219, Figure 9.2; courtesy of University Press of Florida, Gainesville).

ca. 6-x-6-m block excavation in the *campo santo* revealed not only individual and multiple burials, but nails and spikes, a burned post at the same elevation as the *convento* post, and intermittent evidence of a clay floor—all suggestive of the presence of a structure (Figure 4). Differential preservation of burials also intimated the presence of a structure or floor covering the northern two-thirds of the block.

This author directed further investigations in 1991. Excavation was designed to accomplish two major objectives. The first objective was to gather more data on demography, nutrition, morbidity, and mortality of the population at San Martín through excavation of a larger sample of the cemetery. The second was to define better the extent of the burial area and to determine whether or not some or all burials were interred within a structure.

Initially a block excavation (Block 1) was placed north and east of the 1990 excavations (Figure 5). While stratigraphy and burials were studied in this area, a series of 1-m-wide trenches, with 2-m horizontal control, was completed. These tied together the various areas of the site investigated by Weisman. Trenches south and west of Block 1 were located to determine the extent of burials and the possible clay floor. In the *convento* area, Weisman's backfilled units were reexcavated and additional levels were removed. Other trenches explored the northern and southern boundaries of the mission compound and the eastern boundary of the cemetery/structure area. Once the extent of the burial area was better understood, two additional blocks (blocks 2 and 3) were excavated to provide a more representative sample of remains from more widely separated contexts within the cemetery.

What was uncovered in the postulated *campo santo* area appeared to be the remains of one or possibly two large church(es) (Figure 6). (Note that, in Figure 6, no human bone was found in the excavation unit laid over the location of the auger hole that had yielded unidentified bone.) Evidence for a clay floor for the structure was discontinuous. The only preserved floor in the 1990 excavations was a ca. 3-x-3-m expanse on the eastern edge of the structure, within 5 cm of the existing ground surface. All other areas within the church were lower in absolute elevation, and the floor had eroded away. However, evidence for a floor in these eroded areas was preserved in the worked orange clay found in some burial pit fill throughout the E–W extent of the proposed structure. To ensure that the burial area was continuous across this expanse, where burial pits were vague, excavation within the pit was continued until bone was exposed. The bone was reburied immediately after documentation in these instances.

The western side of the structure incorporated what had previously been defined as the *convento*. It was noted above that Weisman (1992:66) reported heavily disturbed soils in the *convento* area. In one unit reexcavated and taken below Weisman's final level, burial pit fill was recognized. A human humerus was exposed within this pitfill and immediately reburied (Figure 5). Two other reexcavated units contained huge postholes dug into the natural clay subsoil. These and other analogous features may account for the disturbed soils to which Weisman referred. In addition, throughout the western half of the site, profiles illustrated numerous erosional episodes delimited by thin lenses of watermarking, some as deep as 50 cm below surface (Figure 7). It is probable, therefore, that the artifact concentration in this area is from the "artifact creep"—increased frequencies of artifacts downslope—noted by Weisman (1993:179). Few of those artifacts are likely to have been in situ.

Nevertheless, these western units probably tested the sanctuary/altar end of the church, which would be expected to contain more artifacts than the nave. Two different lines of evidence support this idea. Burial orientation is one such datum. A number of researchers, including Marrinan (1993:284; cf. Larsen 1990), have suggested that feet were always placed towards the altar; heads were to the east and feet to the west at San Martín. Secondly, burial pit fill stops abruptly at the western end of the projected nave, whereas burials continue to the easternmost posts—the *atrio* area—on the east side

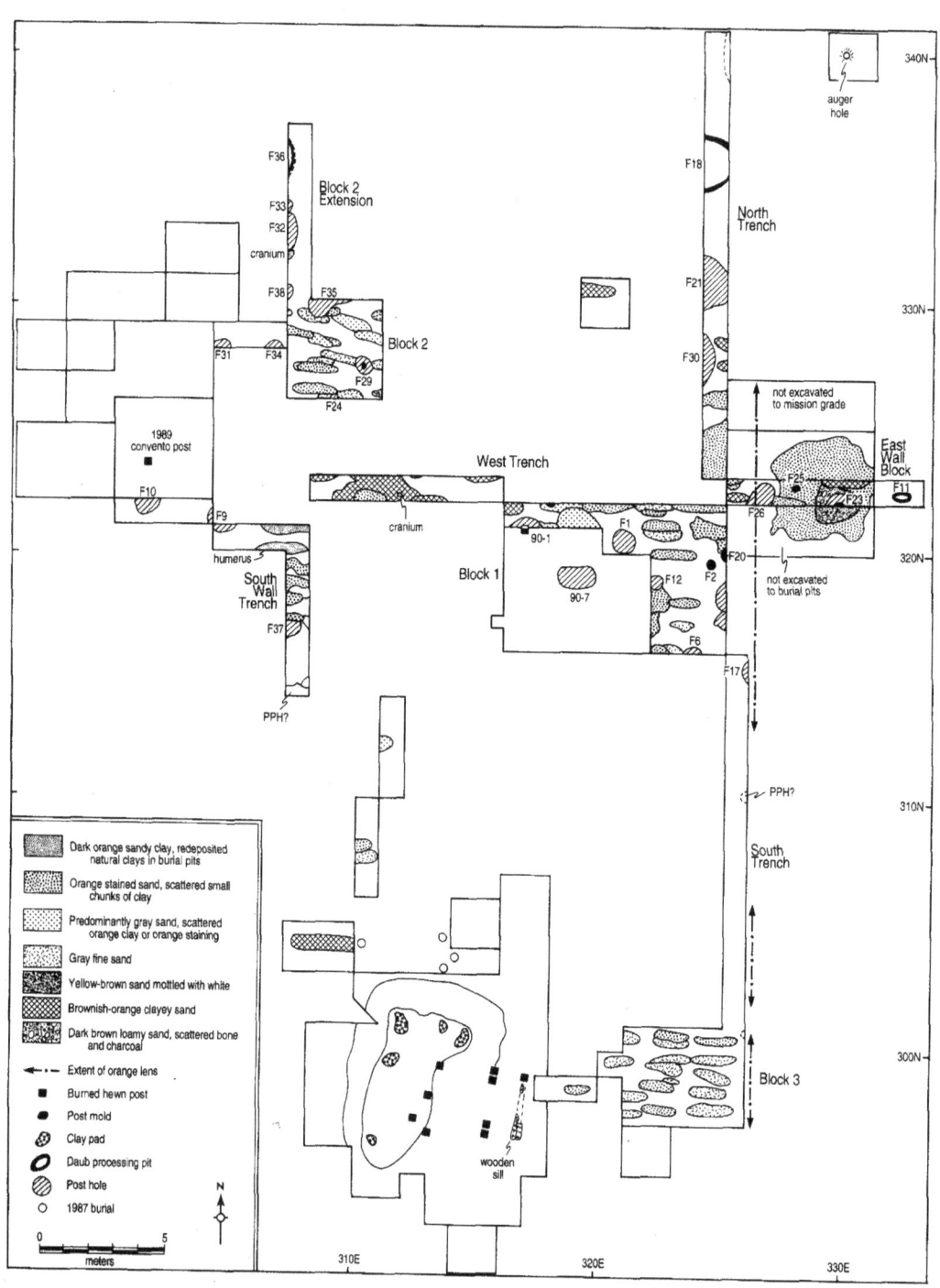

FIGURE 5. Results of excavations through 1991. Features prefaced with 90- were excavated by Johnson in 1990; all other numbered features were excavated in 1991.

Perspectives from *Historical Archaeology*

of the church. Though burials have been reported in reputed sanctuaries, it is unlikely that Native American burials occurred in this sacred space during the use-life of a church with a permanent altar. McEwan and Larsen (1995) and Marrinan (1993:267) consider evidence of sanctuaries with no burials.

Data on the construction materials used in the church are still ambiguous. As noted above, a large number of nails and spikes were recovered, in eroded sands, from the proposed sanctuary end of the church. A lesser concentration was present along the proposed southeast interior corner of the structure. These data may indicate that the entire structure was built of wood. On the other hand, several clay processing pits were uncovered. Most of these were quite small. However, one enormous (2.20 m diameter, 55 cm deep) clay-processing pit (Feature 18) was located outside the north wall of the church (Figure 5). These may imply clay walls in some locations, perhaps along the nave as in the mission church on St. Catherines Island (Thomas 1988:97). However, no daub—defined as burned clay with vermiculations representing combusted organic temper (cf. Ruhl 1987)—has been recovered at the site. It is likely that the smaller pits were used for working clay for chinking while the large pit may have been used to prepare clay for flooring.

No additional structural features were found in excavations near the open chapel. However, another burial area was located to the east of the structure. Like the burials previously identified immediately north of the structure, these extended right up to, but did not impinge on, the east wall of the chapel. This is good evidence that the two phenomena were contemporaneous. Vague discolorations along the eastern wall of Block 3 probably indicate that burials associated with the chapel extend further east. Reworked clay was found in some burial pits in this area, and a distinct stratum of light orange, slightly clayey sand was visible in the profiles in this cemetery area (Figure 5). This may indicate that the open chapel atrio extended north as far as the aforementioned stratum was mapped. Burials between the proposed northern end of the

open chapel atrio burials and the southern wall of the church could have been interred in unconsecrated ground between structures when priests were not supervising and/or within or between structures after the mission was abandoned. Several instances of post-abandonment interment were recorded at the presumed site of Santa Maria de Yamassee (8NA41) on Amelia Island (Saunders 1988:20–21).

Settlement History

The history of the settlement of San Martín may give some clues as to the relative chronology of the church and the open chapel. In July 1597, the brother of the cacique of Timucua traveled to St. Augustine to request a missionary. He was given tools, two iron axes and a hoe, and told to build a church and house for the prospective priest. In September of the same year, Fray Baltasar López spent three months in Timucua, probably at the village that became San Martín, and established a *visita* there. What kind of impact López had on the aboriginal population is unknown. However, after his return to San Pedro on Cumberland Island, there were insufficient friars to replace him until 1606. In 1607, Fray Martin Prieto traveled to Timucua "many times" and arrived at the village of the great cacique of Timucua "which is now called

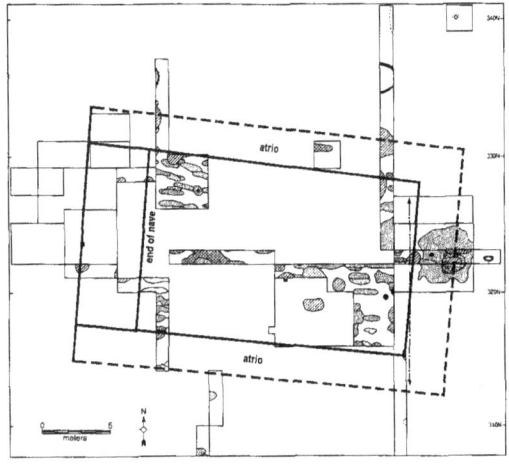

FIGURE 6. Site map with hypothetical single nave church superimposed.

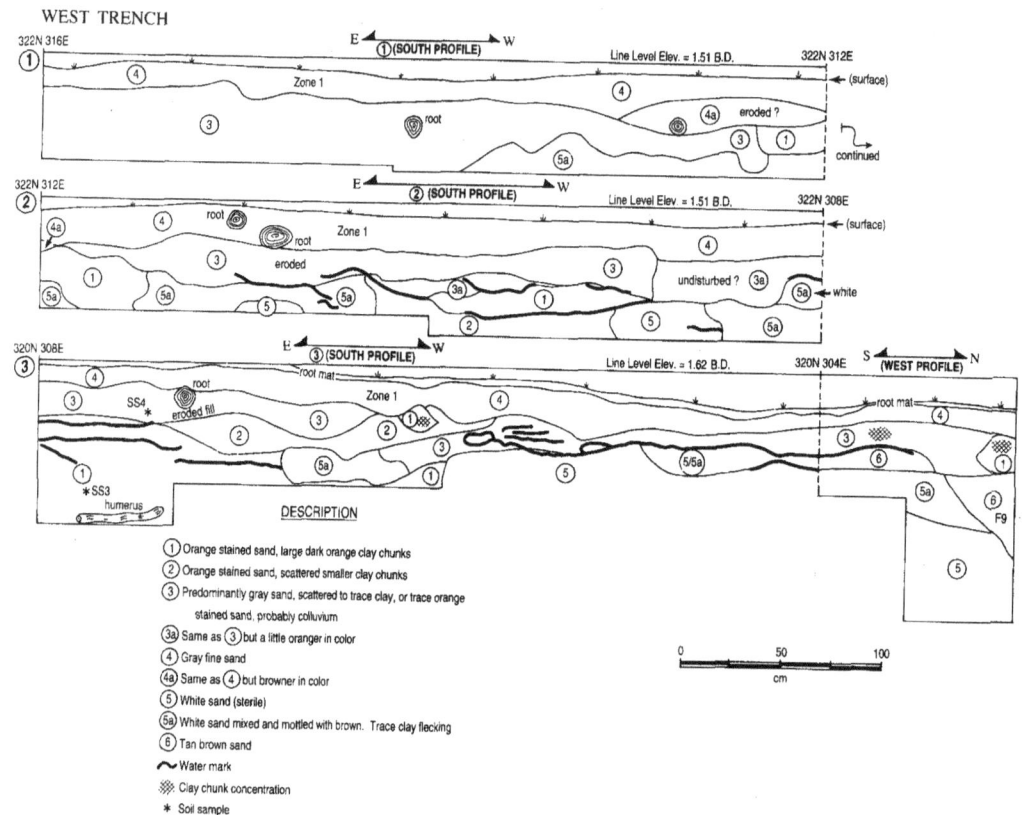

FIGURE 7. Profiles of test trenches 320N 304E (1 x 4 m; north profile) and 322N 308E (1 x 8 m; south profile).

San Martín" on 1 May 1608 (Oré 1936[1617]:114–115). At the cacique's behest, Prieto burned 12 "idols" that stood in the center of the plaza. Presumably Prieto used San Martín as his headquarters until mid-July, when he undertook the task of negotiating peace between the Timucua and Apalachee at Ivitachuco.

These data suggest at least two possible construction chronologies. First, it may be that no religious edifice was built prior to 1608, and the open chapel and church were built in relatively rapid succession after Prieto arrived. Conversely, the open chapel may have been constructed in 1597 and the church sometime in 1608 (cf. Milanich 1995:173–174). In any event, the community of San Martín functioned—probably at least some of the time without a resident friar—up to and after the Timucuan revolt (Worth 1992:291). At what

point in this history the open chapel was burned at what point . . . the open chapel was burned is unclear. Two church posts, the original *convento* post, and another discovered in Johnson's excavations (Figure 5, Feature 90-1) were also burned.

Intrasite Settlement Pattern: Unresolved Issues

Excavations in 1991 demonstrated the presence of a large church in addition to the open chapel at San Martin. In contrast to the specifications of the mission model, there does not appear to have been a Spanish-style convento at the mission, unless it has eroded away. In addition to these results, however, our excavations have raised the inevitable new questions. Many of these result from the fact that the mission compound was not a fixed entity, as suggested by the mission model, but an evolving settlement that responded to numerous socioenvironmental factors. For instance, one of the most problematic issues is the architecture of the church(es). As Figure 6 indicates, the (still limited) excavations within the San Martin church exposed a confounding number of architectural features. During and after excavation, a number of different hypotheses were forwarded to explain these features:

1) There may have been a large, single nave church encircled by a narrow covered walkway that functioned as an atrio (Figure 6; note that the north and south walls are not quite parallel). This church was originally unfloored and later floored, accounting for differences in burial pit fill–some of which contained evidence of clay flooring in the pitfill while others did not.

2) There may have been two smaller, single nave churches, one earlier and unfloored, the second clay floored, with the location shifted south (Figure 8). This accounts for differences in burial pit fill, the fact that it is difficult to square all conjectured walls, and the fact that some postholes intrude on burial pits. (Alternatively, burials may have been disturbed when posts were knocked down or otherwise removed).

3) Burials associated with the (earlier) open chapel extended as far north as the north wall of the church, and a clay floored structure was subsequently built over them.

Exhaustive explanations for the partial rejection of above hypotheses are present in Saunders (1994). Most damning, none of these hypotheses adequately account for the presence of large postholes throughout the interior of the structure. One possible explanation for those features, and one not usually considered by southeastern researchers (McEwan and Larsen 1995:4), is that the structure was an aisled church. In aisled churches, rows of columns were placed in the nave to support the roof (Figure 9). Though never as popular as the single nave church (Kubler 1946:307), aisled churches were constructed in the earlier days of the Mexican mission program, when "supplies of stone were in-

ferior to the abundant supplies of local timber" and/or before techniques for spanning large distances with arches had been mastered by the Native American builders (Kubler 1946:293). Both of these conditions pertained to San Martin. As Kubler noted for Mexico, the priests were under:

> evangelical obligation, in the service of Christianity, to impress the Indians by the size and magnificence of the new churches. . . Now although the magnificence of Indian building resides in the great mass of its pyramidal platforms, the magnificence of Christian church architecture is in the amplitude of its volumes. . . To the Europeans, it [the three-aisled church] was a sensible, simple, and thrifty solution, but to the Indians, it was a vast, splendid, and unprecedented treatment of space. Of this effect of their architecture upon the Indians, the colonists were surely aware (Kubler 1946:299–300).

In support of an aisled structure, at least four large postholes were identified *within* the structure (not including the interior member of the proposed walkway set). By definition, single nave churches should have no postholes in the nave area. Because these interior postholes were as large and as deep as the exterior wall postholes, they appeared to have been dug for major load-bearing supports.

The present working hypothesis is a combination of these theories. It is suggested that the

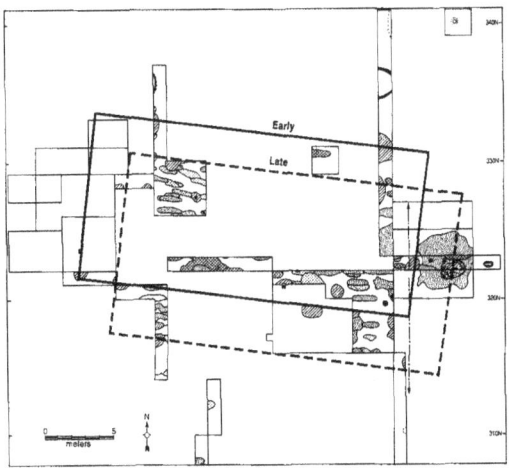

FIGURE 8. Site map with hypothetical early, unfloored church and later, clay floored church superimposed.

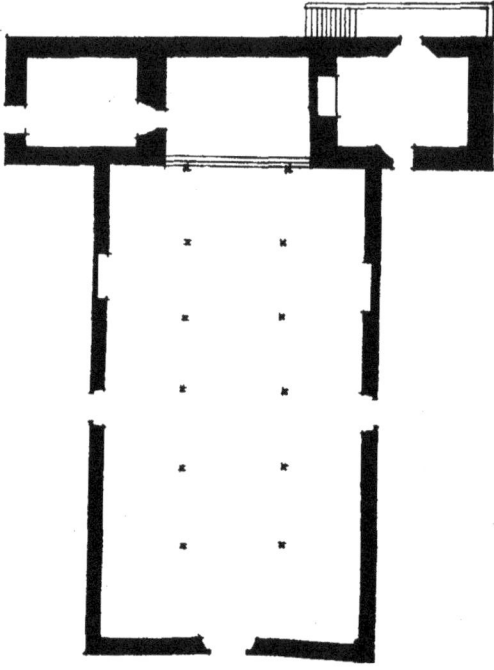

FIGURE 9. Example of an aisled church. The structure is a 16th-century, three-aisled structure from Muxupip, the Yucatán (after McAndrew 1965:521, Figure 265).

San Martín church had a nave composed of five aisles (Figure 10). The central aisle was somewhat wider than the two that flanked either side. The southernmost aisle remains poorly defined. The nave was at one time unfloored, and numerous burials occurred prior to clay flooring. Architectural characteristics of the sanctuary are unclear, but it may have been composed of a chancel and flanking chambers (e.g., Figure 9). There was a covered walkway around three sides of the church, including the eastern face or façade of the church. This walkway was treated as an *atrio*, and, for reasons which at present are unclear, burials were sometimes located in the *atrio* instead of the church. The *atrio* was floored at the façade end of the church. Postholes that intrude on burials within the nave represent either replacement posts or enlargement of the posthole during post extraction.

Conclusions

After five seasons at Fig Springs, it can be concluded that one, or possibly two, church(es) and an open chapel were present. Burials were associated with all structures—around the perimeter of the open chapel and clearly *within* either one or two successive churches. Chronological control over all these features is difficult. However, such control is critical to understanding the diachronic process of mission compound construction and elaboration, for which Native Americans provided all of the labor. More intensive and extensive excavation will be necessary to provide the information needed to resolve the problems of chronology and association. Here, it suffices to reiterate the thesis of this article as it pertains to Mission-period research. A number of the following points can be extended to archaeological research in general, however.

Preconceptions about what a mission should look like led to a number of misidentifications of structure function in the past. Jones and Shapiro's (1990) mission model incorporated these mistakes. In applying the model to his data, Weisman (1992, 1993) was not critical

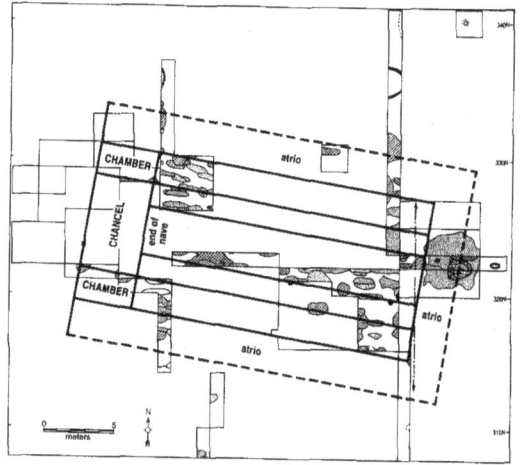

FIGURE 10. Hypothetical aisled church at Fig Springs.

enough of the inherent faults of the model; for instance, a lack of fit in his own data, in the necessity to base the presence of a *convento* on a single post and an artifact concentration, was glossed over.

The chain of events recounted above is not unusual in archaeology or any other scientific endeavor. Unfortunately, however, owing to the vagaries of archaeological research, further testing for substantiation of hypotheses often is not done. Subsequently, sites are destroyed, a few are "preserved" with no further excavation, and/or researchers and their interests go in other directions. Hypotheses are not tested, but they are repeated in the literature. And all too often, the uncertainty inherent in a hypotheses is forgotten and the hypothesis transmuted into fact, either in secondary resources or by the researcher. Indeed, some funding organizations might see "successful" results such as those of Weisman as reasons to deny support for future excavations. Researchers and, equally importantly, funding agencies need to understand that most archaeological results are hypotheses and that long-term commitments will be necessary to understand the complex site histories that missions, and other intensively-occupied archaeological sites, contain. Only after these histories are described can researchers begin to address the processes by which missions were incorporated into Native American villages and, through time, for better or for worse, into Native American lifeways.

ACKNOWLEDGMENTS

Thanks to Brent Weisman for sharing his data and ideas on the mission at Fig Springs. Thanks also to Bonnie McEwan for the update on San Luis. Most especially, thanks to Jerry Milanich for providing me with the opportunity to work at Fig Springs, among other things. A special acknowledgment should go to Keith Terry, a north Florida avocational archaeologist and my assistant site supervisor at Fig Springs. Keith's commitment to the archaeology of northern Florida has been of great benefit to the profession.

REFERENCES

DEAGAN, KATHLEEN
1972 Fig Springs: The Mid-Seventeenth Century in North-Central Florida. *Historical Archaeology* 6:23–46.

HANSON, CRAIG A.
1995 The Hispanic Horizon in Yucatán: A Model of Franciscan Missionization. *Ancient Mesoamerica* 6:15–28.

HOSHOWER, LISA
1992 Bioanthropological Analysis of a Seventeenth-Century Native American Spanish Mission Population: Biocultural Impacts on the Northern Utina. Unpublished Ph.D. dissertation, Department of Anthropology, University of Florida, Gainesville.

HOSHOWER, LISA, AND JERALD T. MILANICH
1993 Excavations in the Fig Springs Mission Burial Area. In *The Spanish Missions of La Florida*, edited by Bonnie G. McEwan, pp. 217–243. University Press of Florida, Gainesville.

JOHNSON, KENNETH W.
1987 The Search for Aquacaleyquen and Cali: Archaeological Survey of Portions of Alachua, Bradford, Citrus, Clay, Columbia, Marion, Sumber, and Union Counties, Florida. *Miscellaneous Project Report* 33. Department of Anthropology, Florida Museum of Natural History, Gainesville.
1990 The Discovery of a Seventeenth-Century Spanish Mission in Ichetucknee State Park, 1986. *Florida Journal of Anthropology* 15:39–46.

JONES, B. CALVIN, AND GARY SHAPIRO
1990 Nine Mission Sites in Apalachee. In *Columbian Consequences*. Vol. 2, *Archaeological and Historical Perspectives on the Spanish Borderlands East*, edited by David Hurst Thomas, pp. 491–510. Smithsonian Institution Press, Washington, DC.

KUBLER, GEORGE
1946 *Mexican Architecture of the Sixteenth Century*, Vol. 2. Yale University Press, New Haven, CT.

LARSEN, CLARK SPENCER
1990 Biological Interpretation and the Context for Contact. In The Archaeology of Mission Santa Catalina de Guale. Vol. 2, Biocultural Interpretations of a Population in Transition, edited by Clark Spencer Larsen. *Anthropological Papers of the American Museum of Natural History* 68. NY.

LOUCKS, LANA JILL

1979 Political and Economic Interactions Between Spaniards and Indians: Archaeological and Ethnohistorical Perspectives of the Mission System in Florida. Unpublished Ph.D. dissertation, Department of Anthropology, University of Florida, Gainesville.

1993 Spanish–Indian Interaction on the Florida Missions: The Archaeology of Baptizing Spring. In *The Spanish Missions of La Florida*, edited by Bonnie G. McEwan, pp. 193–216. University Press of Florida, Gainesville.

MARRINAN, ROCHELLE A.

1993 Archaeological Investigations at Mission Patale, 1984–1992. In *The Spanish Missions of La Florida*, edited by Bonnie G. McEwan, pp. 24–294. University Press of Florida, Gainesville.

MCANDREW, JOHN

1965 *The Open-Air Churches of Sixteenth-Century Mexico: Atrios, Posas, Open Chapels, and Other Studies.* Harvard University Press, Cambridge, MA.

MCEWAN, BONNIE G., AND CLARK SPENCER LARSEN

1995 Archaeological and Biocultural Investigations in the Church Complex at San Luis. *Interim Report to the National Endowment for the Humanities*, Grant # RK-20111-94. On file, San Luis de Talimali State Historical and Archaeological Site, Tallahassee, FL.

MILANICH, JERALD T.

1995 *Florida Indians and the Invasion from Europe.* University Press of Florida, Gainesville.

MORRELL, L. ROSS, AND B. CALVIN JONES

1970 San Juan de Aspalaga: A Preliminary Architectural Study. *Florida Bureau of Historic Sites and Properties Bulletin* 1:25–43.

ORÉ, LUÍS GERÓNIMO DE

1936 *The Martyrs of Florida (1513–1616)*, translated by M. Geiger. Reprint of 1617 edition. Joseph F. Wagner, NY.

RUHL, DONNA L.

1987 First Impressions in and on Daub: A Paleoethnobotanical and Ceramic Technological Analysis of Some Burned Clay from Three Mission Sites in *La Florida*. Paper presented at the 44th Annual Meeting of the Southeastern Archaeological Conference, Charleston, SC.

SAUNDERS, REBECCA

1988 Excavations at 8NA41: Two Mission-Period Sites on Amelia Island, Florida. *Miscellaneous Project Report* 35. Department of Anthropology, Florida State Museum, Gainesville.

1990 Ideal and Innovation: Spanish Mission Architecture in the Southeast. In *Columbian Consequences*. Vol. 2, *Archaeological and Historical Perspectives on the Spanish Borderlands East*, edited by David Hurst Thomas, pp. 527–542. Smithsonian Institution Press, Washington, DC.

1993 Architecture of the Missions Santa María and Santa Catalina de Amelia. In *The Spanish Missions of La Florida*, edited by Bonnie G. McEwan, pp. 35–61. University Press of Florida, Gainesville.

1994 Model Behavior: Examples from the Mission Period in La Florida. Paper presented at the Annual Meeting of the Society for American Archaeology, Los Angeles, CA.

SHAPIRO, GARY, AND RICHARD VERNON

1992 Archaeology at San Luis—Part Two: The Church Complex. *Florida Archaeology* 6:177–277.

SMITH, HALE G.

1951 A Spanish Mission Site in Jefferson County, Florida. In *Here They Once Stood*, by Mark F. Boyd, Hale G. Smith, and James W. Griffin, pp. 107–136. University Press of Florida, Gainesville.

THOMAS, DAVID HURST

1988 Saints and Soldiers at Santa Catalina: Hispanic Designs for Colonial America. In *The Recovery of Meaning in Historical Archaeology*, edited by Mark P. Leone and Parker B. Potter, Jr., pp. 73–140. Smithsonian Institution Press, Washington, DC.

1993 The Archaeology of Mission Santa Catalina de Guale: Our First 15 Years. In *The Spanish Missions of La Florida*, edited by Bonnie G. McEwan, pp. 1–34. University Press of Florida, Gainesville.

WEISMAN, BRENT R.

1992 *Excavations on the Franciscan Frontier: Archaeology at the Fig Springs Mission.* University Press of Florida, Gainesville.

1993 Archaeology of Fig Springs Mission, Ichetucknee Springs State Park. In *The Spanish Missions of La Florida*, edited by Bonnie G. McEwan, pp. 165–192. University Press of Florida, Gainesville.

WORTH, JOHN E.

1992 The Timucuan Missions of Spanish Florida and the Rebellion of 1656. Unpublished Ph.D. dissertation, Department of Anthropology, University of Florida, Gainesville.

REBECCA SAUNDERS
MUSEUM OF NATURAL SCIENCE
LOUISIANA STATE UNIVERSITY
BATON ROUGE, LA 70803-3216

Rebecca Allen

Rethinking Mission Land Use and the Archaeological Record in California: An Example from Santa Clara

ABSTRACT

Previous archaeology at California's missions has primarily focused on structures and the areas immediately adjacent to structures. Study of the documentary record tends to concentrate on annual reports (*informes*) and communication between mission fathers, with some attention paid to buildings and structures shown on historic maps. Recent construction activities on the Santa Clara University campus have triggered archaeological planning and research, and have shown the importance of open-area excavation for understanding land use between and among structures of Mission Santa Clara, as well as in more outlying areas. Focus on areas between buildings increases the likelihood of finding more ephemeral living and usage areas. Complementary study of historic drawings and descriptions also demonstrates that Native Americans used lands between and surrounding structures for living, agricultural, and food-processing areas.

Introduction

Exploration, construction, and expansion typifies the Spanish (1769–1821) and Mexican (1821–1848) periods in Alta California, that is, the northern part of California that now belongs to the United States (Figure 1). This era saw the founding of 21 mission sites overseen by Franciscans, and the Spanish and later Mexican governments. Many of these missions were constructed in several locations, as each went through a period of trial and error. The purpose of the missions was to solidify Spain's (and later Mexico's) political foothold in Alta California, as well as to transform the native population—called *neophytes* once they entered the mission system—into a "Spanish-speaking, revenue-generation population" (Barker et al. 1995:5). Spain and Mexico also maintained a military presence at several *presidios* (Voss 2008), and established several civil settlements at Los Angeles, Branciforte (Santa Cruz), and San José de Guadalupe.

Archaeological and documentary evidence has offered insights on life in Spanish and Mexican colonial Alta California (Barker et al. 1995; Hackel 2005; Lightfoot 2005; Lightfoot et al. 2005). Most of this work has focused on the structures that make up the central buildings of the mission—the church and associated quadrangle. Fewer studies have looked at structures and their associated archaeological components that represent living, agricultural, and industrial areas.

More than 15 years ago, David Hurst Thomas (1991:145–146) encouraged archaeologists to look beyond the main church and quadrangle. He also predicted that it would be studies undertaken as a result of cultural resource legislation that would test the boundaries of previous California mission-era archaeology:

> Many of California's missions exist today in urban settings, and historical archaeology has demonstrated time and time again that associational and architectural integrity may be present beneath streets, buildings, parking lots, and gardens. Although the church/mission quadrangle has often been heavily worked over, there is every reason to be optimistic that this new brand of off-site archaeology will divulge new insights into mission life, particularly hard-to-come-by data on economic, industrial, biocultural, and other ancillary activities. The preservation of this potential testifies to the importance of Cultural Resource Management legislation requiring compliance with current environmental regulations.

Recent excavations at Mission Santa Clara have demonstrated Thomas's prescient statement. Prompted by the legal requirements of the California Environmental Quality Act (CEQA), archaeological investigation has recovered data on mission-era Native American living and food-processing areas, found well outside the Mission Santa Clara church and quadrangle areas.

Previous Archaeology at California Mission Sites

Barker et al. (1995:14–17) discuss architectural, engineering, and archaeological studies that were carried out in Alta California from the 1920s to the early 1990s. Some of the earliest studies focused on evidence of vegetation in adobe bricks

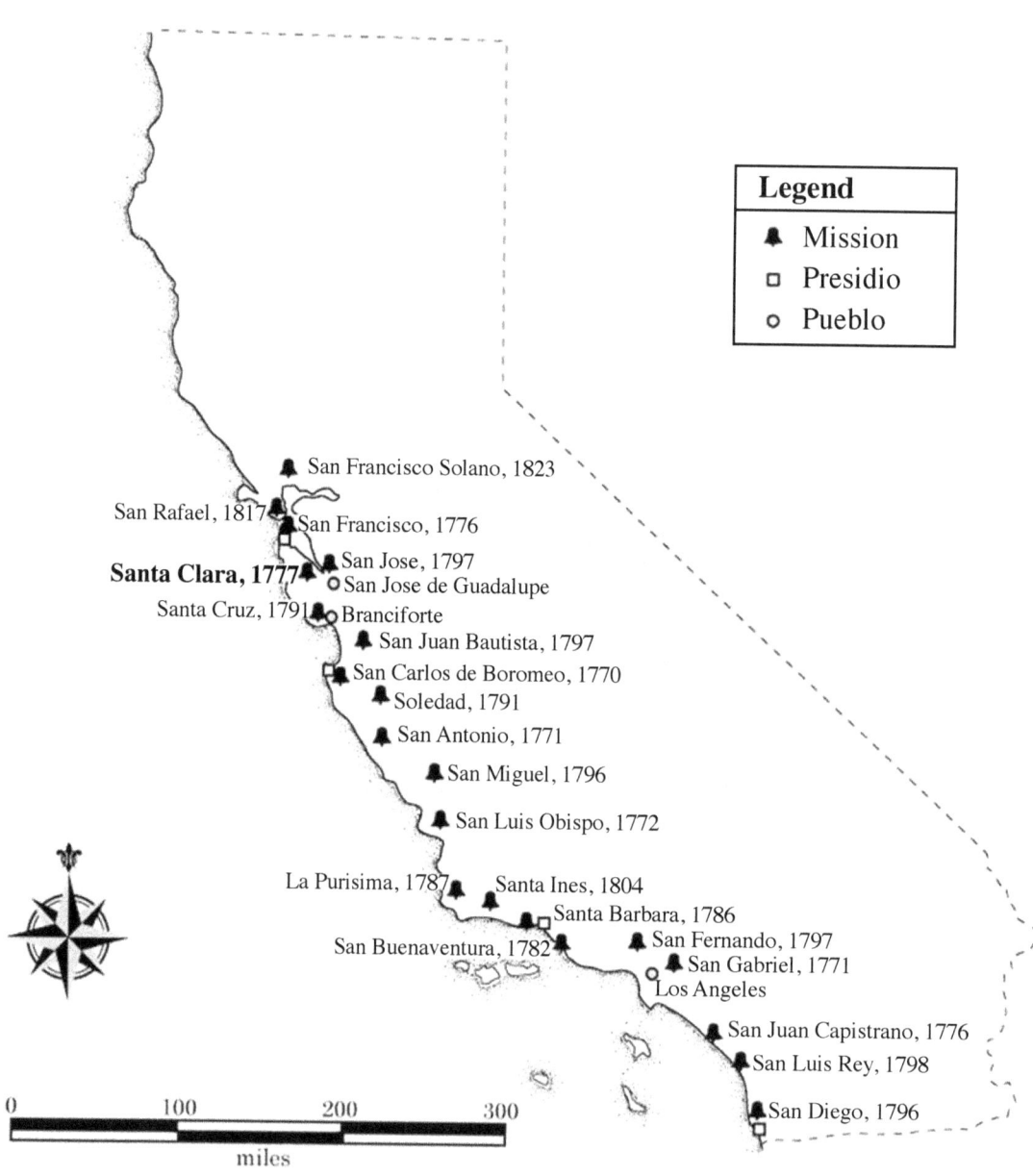

FIGURE 1. Missions, pueblos, and presidios founded during the Spanish and Mexican periods in Alta California, 1769–1834, highlighting Mission Santa Clara. (Drawing by Stella D'Oro, 2008.)

(Hendry and Kelly 1925; Hendry 1931). Numerous articles have since been written on the material artifacts of everyday life, including beads, buttons, ceramics, faunal material, and Native American lithics and groundstone, many summarized in Barker et al. (1995:19–20). Most of the archaeological reporting has been on buildings within the mission quadrangle, that is, the mission church and the adjacent (generally square) arrangement of rooms for mission priests' (padres') living quarters and eating area, workshops, and the convent (also called the *monjerio*, where young unmarried women lived in dormitory style). There are some studies of structures outside the quadrangle, such as soldiers' quarters and neophyte residences, but these are fewer in number.

Table 1 summarizes archaeological and relevant historical studies of buildings and structures

TABLE 1

MISSION ARCHAEOLOGICAL STUDIES IN CALIFORNIA, PRIMARILY FOCUSED
ON BUILDINGS AND STRUCTURES

Mission	Topic(s) of Archaeological Study	Reference(s)
Nuestra Señora de La Soledad	Padres' quarters, neophyte residence areas, aqueduct	Farnsworth 1987, 1992
La Purísima Concepcíon	Archaeological and historical studies, mostly tied to reconstruction efforts. Investigation of 18 buildings and features: church, padres' residence, workshops, water system, neophyte residences, blacksmith shop, warehouse, tallow and soap works, cemetery	Whitehead 1980
	Neophyte quarters	Gabel 1952; Deetz 1963
	Cemetery	Humphrey 1965
	Warehouse and granary	Farris 1997
	Study of original site—La Purísima Vieja	Costello 1993, 1994b
	Possible fulling mill	Hoover 2001
San Antonio de Padua	Aqueduct system	Smith 1932
	Neophyte quarters	Hoover and Costello 1985; Hoover 2002
	Soldiers' quarters, house of mission vineyardist, mission workshops	Bertrando 1997; ongoing work: field school California Polytechnic University, San Luis Obispo
	Aqueduct system	Jones et al. 1997
	Geophysical survey and summary of structures	Hoover et al. 2004; Hoover and Hoover 2008
San Buenaventura	Aqueduct system	Greenwood and Gessler 1968; Foster and Greenwood 1989
	Archaeological study of mission layout and history	Greenwood 1975, 1976
San Carlos Borromeo	Architectural history, assessment of ruins	Smith 1921; Broadbent 1955
San Diego de Alcalá	Dam and irrigation	Green 1933
	Multiple-year archaeological program, focusing on structures	Brandes et al. 1987
San Fernando	Granary, cooking hearth, "midden"	Abdo-Hintzman 2008
San Francisco Solano (Sonoma)	Study for restoration work	Bennyhoff and Elsasser 1954; Treganza 1956
San José	Residence areas	Dietz et al. 1983
	Neophyte quarters	Thompson et al. 2003

TABLE 1

MISSION ARCHAEOLOGICAL STUDIES IN CALIFORNIA, PRIMARILY FOCUSED
ON BUILDINGS AND STRUCTURES

Mission	Topic(s) of Archaeological Study	Reference(s)
Nuestra Señora de La Soledad	Padres' quarters, neophyte residence areas, aqueduct	Farnsworth 1987, 1992
La Purísima Concepcíon	Archaeological and historical studies, mostly tied to reconstruction efforts. Investigation of 18 buildings and features: church, padres' residence, workshops, water system, neophyte residences, blacksmith shop, warehouse, tallow and soap works, cemetery	Whitehead 1980
	Neophyte quarters	Gabel 1952; Deetz 1963
	Cemetery	Humphrey 1965
	Warehouse and granary	Farris 1997
	Study of original site—La Purísima Vieja	Costello 1993, 1994b
	Possible fulling mill	Hoover 2001
San Antonio de Padua	Aqueduct system	Smith 1932
	Neophyte quarters	Hoover and Costello 1985; Hoover 2002
	Soldiers' quarters, house of mission vineyardist, mission workshops	Bertrando 1997; ongoing work: field school California Polytechnic University, San Luis Obispo
	Aqueduct system	Jones et al. 1997
	Geophysical survey and summary of structures	Hoover et al. 2004; Hoover and Hoover 2008
San Buenaventura	Aqueduct system	Greenwood and Gessler 1968; Foster and Greenwood 1989
	Archaeological study of mission layout and history	Greenwood 1975, 1976
San Carlos Borromeo	Architectural history, assessment of ruins	Smith 1921; Broadbent 1955
San Diego de Alcalá	Dam and irrigation	Green 1933
	Multiple-year archaeological program, focusing on structures	Brandes et al. 1987
San Fernando	Granary, cooking hearth, "midden"	Abdo-Hintzman 2008
San Francisco Solano (Sonoma)	Study for restoration work	Bennyhoff and Elsasser 1954; Treganza 1956
San José	Residence areas	Dietz et al. 1983
	Neophyte quarters	Thompson et al. 2003

TABLE 1 (CONTINUED)

MISSION ARCHAEOLOGICAL STUDIES IN CALIFORNIA, PRIMARILY FOCUSED
ON BUILDINGS AND STRUCTURES

Mission	Topic(s) of Archaeological Study	Reference(s)
San Juan Bautista	Neophyte quarters	Clemmer 1961; Farris 1991
	Quadrangle, mission well	Field school, California State University, Monterey Bay, Mendoza 2002
	Faunal study, comparative assemblage from courtyard and neophyte quarters	St. Clair 2005
	Soldiers' quarters	Cannon 2005
San Juan Capistrano	Archaeological and historical studies	Magalousis 1989
	Restoration work, including archaeological studies	Summarized in Schafer and Loomis 2005
San Luis Rey	*Lavendarias* (laundry), aqueducts, orchards, kiln, soldiers' quarters	Soto 1961
	Sunken gardens	Cohen-Williams 2005
	Neophyte quarters	Williams and Williams 2007
San Miguel	Archaeological work during seismic retrofit of church	Greenwood 2009; Hoover 2009
Santa Barbara	Water storage and aqueduct system	Imwalle 1996; Allen and Felton 1998
	Mausoleum	Costello 1990
	National Historic Landmark study; overview of known architectural and archaeological features	Allen et al. 2000
	Neophyte village	Williams 2005
Santa Clara de Asís—see additional references in text	Third mission site	Lynch 1981; Huelsbeck 1985; Hylkema 1995
	Fourth, fifth mission church, cemetery	Skowronek and Wizorek 1997
	Butchering area (*matanza*)	Burson 1999
	Neophyte living areas, butchering area	Hylkema and Skowronek 2000; Garlinghouse 2007; Allen and Blount 2009; Allen et al. 2009; Hylkema and Allen 2009
Santa Cruz	Neophyte quarters	Felton 1987; Allen 1998; Allen et al. 2003
	Tanning vat	Dietz 1986
Santa Inés	Padres' quarters	Costello 1989
	Neophyte village associated with mission	Wilcoxon et al. 1989a, 1989b
	Tanning vat	Wilcoxon et al. 1992
	Threshing floor	Tremaine 1992
	Fulling mill	Hoover 1992
	National Historic Landmark study; overview of known architectural and archaeological features	Costello et al. 1997
	Possible soldiers' quarters	Hoover 2002

undertaken at each mission, listed alphabetically. Note that there have also been historic structure reports at many of California's missions that are not detailed here. Full consideration of all these excavations could easily prompt an article to update the discussion of the status of mission-period archaeology in California (Barker et al. 1995:15–17), which is not the intent of the current article. Citations in Table 1 are presented as background, and the text below considers only some of the implications of these many excavations.

Consideration of the Documentary Record

The documentary record of California's mission history is equally as rich. Original sources of information come from the mission fathers, military personnel, and foreign visitors. At each mission, the fathers compiled annual *informes* (reports) that detail each mission's baptisms, marriages, deaths, livestock counts, agricultural plantings and harvestings, building construction and repairs, and mission furnishings. The College of San Fernando in Mexico also required missionaries to produce biennial population reports. Typically, mission baptismal, marriage, and death registers are also extant with confirmation records up until about 1810 (and after 1833). Most of the mission fathers corresponded with their superiors, military personnel, and each other; the record of priests' letters is nearly overwhelming. Several libraries and repositories house these documents, including primarily the Santa Barbara Mission Archive-Library, the San Francisco Archdiocese Chancery Archive, and the Bancroft Library at the University of California, Berkeley. One of the most-cited pieces of documentary evidence is a questionnaire sent to all missionaries in 1812, and answered between 1813 and 1815. The priests responded to the inquiry about the natives of California and their progress within the mission system; fathers answered questions on native education, Spanish-speaking abilities, feelings regarding the fathers and military, virtues and vices, religion, social status, marriages, curing techniques, food sources, burial customs, and general conditions within the mission (Geiger and Meighan 1976).

Many foreign visitors and explorers visited California during the Spanish and Mexican periods. Especially interesting is a journal from a 1792 visit to California by two small ships searching for the Northwest Passage. The author of the journal is unknown, but is suspected to be José Cardero, a scribe and artist (Cutter 1990). Many foreign travelers, mostly associated with trading vessels, also passed through parts of California. Egenhoff (1952) provides original text and translations of these visitor accounts, as well of as many of the illustrations that various artists have left behind. Costello (1991) also presents the history of many of these traders and explorers, and their associated documents.

After the Mexican War of Independence in 1822, the secularization (turning over to civil authorities) of mission lands began, and large ranches were carved out of their expanses. Costello (1994a) gives the example of Mission San Antonio, and the kinds of documentary records of these land transactions that exist that can help reconstruct mission land use. During the American period (post-1848), the U.S. Land Commission began hearings in 1852 with the intent of segregating private land from public domain; as part of a U.S. District Court case maps were commissioned in order to settle mission land expanses and rights to that land. In 1854, John G. Cleal and George Black surveyed many of California's missions, and produced maps that provide much information about the layout of the missions. As a result, these maps focus on the main church and quadrangle, but show some areas of orchards, gardens, and vineyards, all of which was land in dispute. Several other post-1850 maps and photographs exist for each mission, and can be found in repositories and libraries throughout California, as well as on the Internet.

A small body of literature from the Native Americans whose lands were colonized adds nuance and depth to the records written by and for Europeans, government agents, and religious officials. Pablo Tac (1822–1841) was a Luiseño, born in Mission San Luis Rey, and the author of an account of California natives and their languages (Hewes and Hewes 1958; Kottman 2008). Only a few other documentary sources, in the form of oral histories, have been left behind by the native occupants of the missions. Lorenzo Asisara was born toward the end of the mission period (he was baptized in 1819), but offers recollections about life at Mission Santa Cruz from his own experience and that of his father (Mora-Torres 2005). Julio César was also born in

Mission San Luis Rey (around 1824), and was interviewed as part of the Bancroft history program. John P. Harrington interviewed Fernando Librado, a Chumash native, sometime around 1912–1915. Lightfoot (2005:91–96) discusses these texts and their implications for understanding the native experience within the mission system; he also discusses the importance of the ethnohistorical record to interpretation.

All of these sources can be mined for information about the layout, buildings, and structures of California's missions. Maps and photographs are perhaps the most useful, although many details can be surmised about mission land use from the other sources. Colonial and native attitudes towards the landscape and its uses can also be inferred. Barbara Voss (2000), for example, derives through study of the documentary and archaeological records some of the Native American attitudes towards the use of structured space within the mission system.

Documentary and Archaeological History at Mission Santa Clara

Many documentary lines of evidence that provide details of Mission Santa Clara history exist. Mission Santa Clara was founded on 18 January 1777, the eighth Franciscan mission in Alta California. It was secularized in 1836. Annual reports and priests' letters, many of which were recently translated and published, exist in the Santa Clara University campus archives (Skowronek et al. 2006). Like many missions, Santa Clara went through trial-and-error phases of construction, although it is somewhat unique in that the mission church was built in five different locations during the mission period (Skowronek and Wizorek 1997). Remnants of the third church and quadrangle, the fourth church, and the fifth church and quadrangle are found within the boundaries of the modern Santa Clara University campus. Several historic maps, although created long after the mission period, are particularly important for understanding the evolution of the mission complex.

In 1854, George Black produced a map of buildings that depicted the third and fifth iterations of the Mission Santa Clara complex (Figure 2). Drawings also provide evidence for structures and a general sense of the building layout and surrounding landscape. G. M. Waseurtz af San-

dels (1945), a Swedish traveler in California, sketched the fifth mission church of Santa Clara in 1842 (Figure 3). The drawing also shows the structure of the fourth church in the left foreground, portions of the third church complex in the lower right foreground, and rows of adobe residences for the Indian neophytes along the right edge. Historic photographs, mostly found at Santa Clara University, Santa Clara City Library, and San Jose Public Library show the evolution of the university campus and remnants of older buildings (Figure 4). Father Spearman (1958, 1963) used these and other sources to plot the mission-era features found within the boundaries of the university, including the third, fourth, and fifth church locations, as well as several agricultural features including a vineyard, orchard, cemeteries, *zanjas* (irrigation ditches), a swamp, and small pond area. More recently, Hylkema (1995:map 10) interpreted and updated this map, which proved invaluable for recording and locating recent and past archaeological finds on campus.

Construction activities have been the primary driver behind archaeological investigations at Santa Clara. Archaeological evidence came from inadvertent finds during utility replacement and installation, excavation prior to the rerouting of one of the main roads, and monitoring during construction of new buildings on campus. Excavations for a sewer line (1907), basements (1907), gas main (1911), water-pipe trench (1920), and additional gas mains (1924, 1928) found burials, third mission walls, and finds of beads, bones, and shell. In 1934, Father Spearman conducted excavations at the third mission site, and encountered a 36 in. wide adobe wall and scattered foundation stones. A water main laid in the 1960s encountered more burials. Mark Lynch (1981:12–14), Santa Clara University's first campus archaeologist, summarized these finds.

In 1981, the California Department of Transportation investigated the third mission site (designated CA-SCL-30) as part of an impact zone identified during the proposed realignment of Route 82 (also known as El Camino Real in this area). Mayfield et al. (1981) detailed the archaeological testing and excavation in the area of the third mission church, and noted the integrity of mission-era deposits found. Discoveries include foundation stones, adobe brick, roof tiles, floor tiles, ceramics, glass, and human bone.

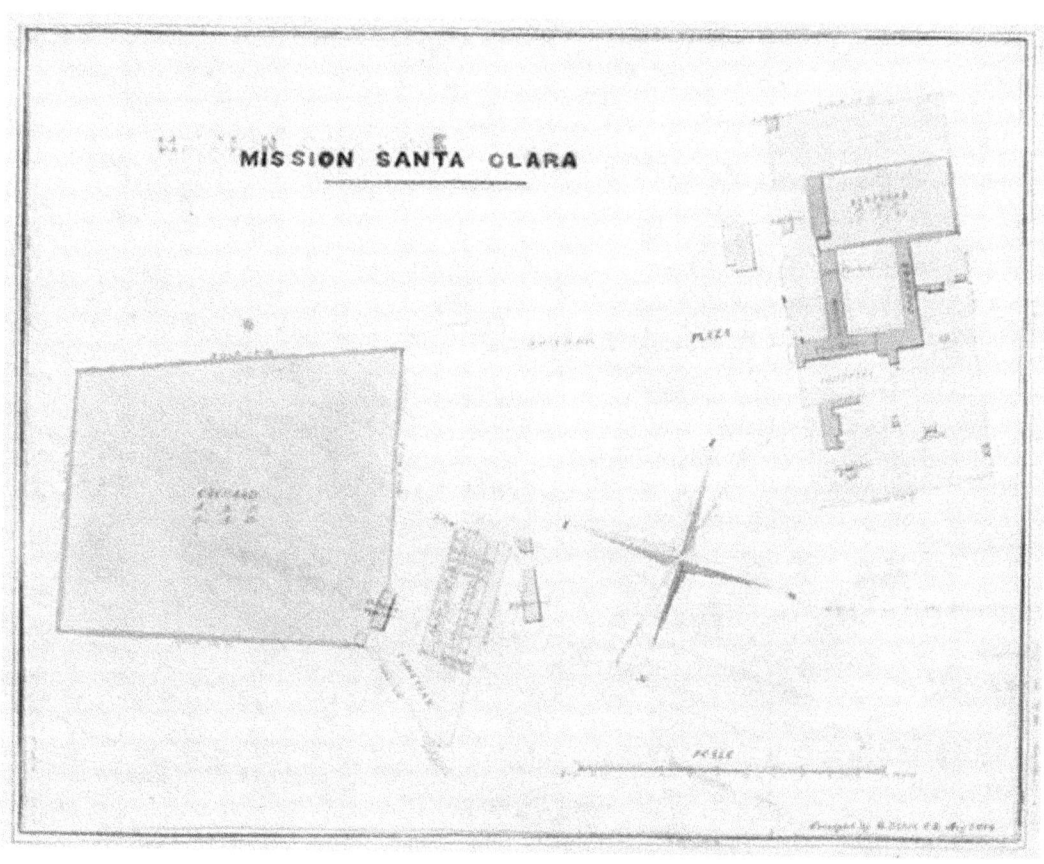

FIGURE 2. Mission Santa Clara, surveyed by George Black, C.E., August 1854. (Courtesy of the Bancroft Library, University of California, Berkeley, Landcase Maps Collection, Land Case Map D916R:17.)

FIGURE 3. Drawing by G. M. Waseurtz af Sandels of the fifth church at Santa Clara. Note the rows of neophyte adobe houses at the right edge. (Courtesy of Santa Clara University Archives and Special Collections.)

Perspectives from *Historical Archaeology*

FIGURE 4. Students near Old Adobe Wall, part of the fifth mission complex, 14 May 1911. (Photograph Courtesy of Santa Clara University Archives and Special Collections, Turrill-Miller Photograph Collection.)

still impact the archaeological record in the area. In 1989, construction activities related to a new entrance road into Santa Clara University included trenching for electrical and water lines. Archaeological monitoring during trenching noted that while the new entrance road was mostly constructed on fill near the third mission quadrangle, a trash pit and foundation stones were disturbed (Huelsbeck 1989; Hylkema 1995:56). After roadwork completion, the City of Santa Clara used imbedded pavers to mark the outline of the third mission church and portions of the complex (Figure 5). Unfortunately, the markers are slightly off in their interpretation (Hylkema 1995:100), and the university later added a wall that many mistake for a boundary of the archaeological preserve, although the site extends well beyond the wall's confines.

In 1982, Mark Lynch conducted further excavations at the third mission site (Hylkema 1995:44), and also investigated a portion of a wall associated with the quadrangle of the fifth mission church during renovations of the Faculty Club (Jenkins et al. 1998). In 1985 to 1987, under the direction of David Huelsbeck (then campus archaeologist and a Santa Clara University professor), additional excavations occurred at the third mission site. Huelsbeck (1985, 1988) verified the location and orientation of the quadrangle, although some of his assumptions were slightly off (Hylkema 1995:44). Huelsbeck also identified tanning vats, a portion of the *zanja* (ditch), and the location of the orchard-keeper's house. In 1987, in response to demolition proposed for several residential structures, he monitored the buildings' destruction and associated excavations, noting adobe blocks, foundation walls, adobe borrow pits, and mission-era trash pits, as well as later American-period finds.

Trenching for electrical conduits during the construction of the new El Camino Real route in 1988 encountered a tile-floor feature, as well as shell beads and cobbles (Hylkema 1995:51–54). In that same year an archaeological preserve was created at the site of the third mission, with the intent to prevent further disturbance of archaeological components. The boundaries of that preserve, CA-SCL-30/H, have not been fully determined, and intermittent disturbances

FIGURE 5. Paver outline of the third mission church, in the area of the archaeological preserve. (Photo by author, 2007.)

Russell Skowronek provided the impetus to create the Santa Clara Archaeology Research Lab in 1994, with the stated goals of providing on-campus archaeologists to supply cultural resource management expertise, establish a repository for materials, and to provide students with research opportunities (Hylkema and Skowronek 2000:2). A campuswide lighting and trenching program in 1995 prompted more archaeological monitoring (Skowronek and Wizorek 1997:74–75; Wizorek 1998). Campus archaeologists noted two parallel cobblestone foundations of the fourth mission church and associated mission-era artifacts, portions of the cemetery associated with the fifth mission church, floor tiles believed to be associated with the *mayordomo* (overseer's) residence, and foundations of other mission-period buildings, as well as adobe buildings from the immediate post-mission period. Additional monitoring during upgrades to utility lines and landscaping efforts in 1996, 1997, 2000, and 2001 found portions of the third mission, including the orchard wall, and remnants of roof tile, ceramics, and other mission-period artifacts. Archaeological reports and finds are summarized in Skowronek and Wizorek (1997) and in Allen et al. (2004:84–85).

The impending construction of a new communications, public policy, and applied ethics building prompted campus archaeologists to write a short treatment plan (Wizorek and Skowronek 1997). In 1998, during construction of a new parking structure, archaeological monitoring encountered an area of 24 × 52 m containing at least 1,625 animal carcasses. Burson (1999) identified this area as a *matanza*, a large area of animal slaughtering and butchering. Repair of a swimming pool in 2000 prompted the discovery of what was interpreted as a "large borrow pit for soil to make adobe blocks and secondarily filled with kitchen refuse from the nearby neophyte quarters" (Hylkema and Skowronek 2000:3). These last examples of archaeology on campus began to raise further questions about mission land use areas, and the need for a more programmatic approach to archaeological resources.

Campus-Wide Research Plan

During preparation of a 10-year capital plan (Santa Clara University 2003) for new and renovated buildings on the 106-acre area that makes up the campus, the university initiated a proactive research design and treatment plan for the avoidance and data recovery of archaeological resources prior to demolition of existing structures and construction of new facilities (Allen et al. 2004; Allen et al. 2009). The Archaeology Research Lab at Santa Clara, Albion Environmental, Inc., and Past Forward, Inc. teamed together to research the history and archaeology of the entire campus and surrounding areas, summarize previous archaeological investigations, and promote an active archaeological program that stressed avoidance whenever possible. In areas where avoidance was not possible, rather than simply monitoring, the treatment plan emphasized a program of data recovery and research that would occur well before demolition and construction activities. The treatment plan also recognized that historical land use is often quite site specific, and historical and archaeological information will improve over time. To remedy this, it was recommended that specific treatment plans and field excavation guidelines be written for each new construction project that requires ground disturbance, and that these shorter documents be appended to the original document.

Since 2004, archaeological investigations have occurred in areas designated for a new business school, library facilities, multiuse facility, residence for Jesuit professors and staff, green-building student commons, and the expansion of some existing structures such as parking lots. Construction plans for a new athletic facility, re-installation and upgrades of major utility lines, and re-alignment of existing roadways are on the horizon. To date, excavations that have occurred have encountered deposits associated with the mission era (1777–1836), Mexican period (1836–1848), American period (1848–1930s), and the Native American, colonial, and European American settlers of the area. Reporting is still underway; this article addresses only mission-era finds.

The research design and treatment plan prescribed archaeological methodologies that in addition to testing emphasize open-area excavation to the extent possible, coupled with stratigraphic recordation methods. Barker (1977:15) noted the re-emergence of excavation techniques that emphasized horizontal exposure. He also made a strong argument for excavating whole features (and sites where possible), rather than sampling (Barker 1977:54). Harris (1989:25) noted that while open-area excavation methods developed during the 1960s, this excavation did not always include recordation and analysis of the stratigraphy exposed by the excavation, and his creation and explanation of the Harris Matrix went a long way towards closing that informational gap. Lightfoot (1995:209) encouraged researchers to consider excavation methods and the complementary information provided by vertical and horizontal area excavation. Careful excavation of stratigraphic layers has been used with success at some California missions (Felton 1987; Costello 1989). Its use is not yet pervasive though, and for that matter, neither is the practice of open-area excavation. Both methodologies are critical to achieving Thomas's (1991:145–146) vision of realizing the potential for archaeology beneath the urban settings that currently surround most of California's missions. The Santa Clara treatment plan (Allen et al. 2004) stressed that while testing and trenching may provide presence-and-absence information as well as chronological placement of resources, only through open areas of excavation could historic land uses be fully understood.

Recent Archaeological Finds—
Between Known Mission Buildings

At Mission Santa Clara, previous investigations demonstrated that despite its urban setting and 19th- and 20th-century land uses, much of the archaeological record remains intact beneath parking lots, streets, landscaped areas, and structures. Unlike many earlier projects, most of the new proposed construction has occurred in areas between known buildings and structures noted on maps and shown in drawings and photographs. Based on previous findings, the overall treatment plan (and later supplements) predicted the archaeological presence of refuse pit features, sheet refuse (broad scatters of artifacts), building foundations, tiled floors, orchard walls, and possibly more ephemeral features such as gardens, post-holes, drainage systems, and orchards. Research themes highlighted missionization, culture contact, cultural adaptation, and environmental changes.

Santa Clara University slated the location of a parking lot west of the third mission church site for the construction of a new school of business. Before it had become a parking lot in 1994, this area was densely occupied by residences and businesses during the late 19th and most of the 20th century. Review of Sanborn insurance maps illustrated the intensity of American-period alterations to the block. An aerial view from 1975 showed that a commercial presence dominated the northern half of the block until Santa Clara University purchased the properties. The university demolished several of the residences in the late 1980s. During monitoring of house demolition, Huelsbeck (1987:3) noted two trash pits that he thought were mission period exposed in the cellar of one house. A decade later, monitoring during the demolition of a corner bar (Lord John's Inn), a large mission-period "adobe mixing

pit" (an area that was mined for soil and used to mix it with straw to make adobe blocks) was discovered in a section of the sidewalk. Fragments of *tejas* (roof tiles), *ladrillos* (floor tiles), and faunal remains of butchered animals filled the feature (Ginn et al. 2002). In 1996, a construction project extended walkways and landscaping, and included pavement removal and utility-line (water, sewer, electrical) excavation. Archaeological monitoring noted a deposit of poorly fired *tejas* and tile wasters. Archaeologists (Wizorek and Skowronek 1996:2) surmised that this deposit was part of a mission-period attempt to level the naturally sloping roadway. Also in 1996, utility trenching in a nearby street encountered a cobble feature west of the former location of the third mission. During 2001, archaeological monitoring for subsurface utility-related activities in the same area found many fragments of *tejas* (Bryne 2001).

Still, much of the mission-era archaeological record survived, although archaeologists were only seeing glimpses of the block's potential. Given these archaeological findings, and to assess the potential for remaining archaeological deposits in the block proposed for the new school of business building, Linda Hylkema, assistant campus archaeologist, and Albion Environmental, Inc. conducted an extensive trenching program (Peterson et al. 2002). This testing showed the presence of an abundance of mission-period artifacts and "features."

Past Forward, Inc. and Albion Environmental, Inc. undertook three extended sessions of fieldwork to excavate areas within this same block. Fieldwork sessions were staggered in order to accommodate university parking needs, but occurred well before demolition and construction activities began, and only after the campus-wide treatment plan and research design had been written and approved by the university and the City of Santa Clara. The primary and most substantial excavation occurred in August 2004; later excavations occurred in May 2006 and April 2007. Archaeologists directed the exploration of the area using mechanical equipment (a backhoe outfitted with a flat blade) to remove the overburden and expose as much of the area as possible. By creating large-area exposures, archaeologists were able to see that an overburden covered the site features. During the late American period, much fill had been brought into the project area, likely in an attempt to "even out" the mission-period topography, which would have been a more undulating terrain. This fill was probably brought from nearby areas on campus, and contained not only soil, but a mix of artifacts (out of their original context) from the mission and American periods. This history of fill showed one of the problems which would have been created by excavation of narrow trenches only.

The 2001 testing program (Peterson et al. 2002) was intended to demonstrate the presence/absence of intact archaeological deposits; this was an important step, because given the number of previous excavations and historic disturbance, university officials were skeptical of the possibility of finding more archaeological remains. Only narrow trenches were excavated, masking the extent and content of the refuse layer that was filled with mission-period refuse, but brought in from elsewhere and not in its primary context.

In several instances, archaeological monitors believed they were seeing features when in fact they were seeing segments of this introduced fill. This is not a criticism of this presence/absence exercise: its intent was to confirm the presence of a rich archaeological deposit in the area so that additional excavation efforts could be justified and approved. Rather, the current excavations and open-area excavation refined archaeological understanding of what the narrow trenching had encountered. Prescribed open-area excavation allowed for a much more comprehensive view of site stratigraphy and composition over horizontal expanses, as well as an understanding of vertical alterations and site layers. The purpose of the open-area excavation was to expose living surfaces and other more ephemeral elements of the historic landscape. This method resulted in the finding, identification, and interpretation of an archaeologically documented native-style residence that dates to the mission period in California, as well as other important features related to neophyte living areas.

Discovering Neophyte Living and Use Areas

Mission Santa Clara's historic records, especially marriage and death records, give evidence that several groups were brought into the mission system. Baptisms began at Mission Santa Clara in the year of its founding. In 1777, 69 baptisms of local Ohlone occurred (Milliken 2002:49). Not all of the newly "converted" neophytes lived at the mission—records noted the mission's native population as 13. The first native converts were Ohlone from nearby villages.

As with many colonized peoples in the New World, California Native Americans were particularly susceptible to diseases that the colonizers brought with them. Mayfield et al. (1981:30–33) undertook a study of the death records at Mission Santa Clara. In part, this was done to determine which cultural groups were represented in the cemetery associated with the third mission church complex. The authors noted that the majority of neophytes buried within the cemetery were Ohlone; in 1785, Ohlone deaths represented 94.4% of the buried population. Neophytes brought from other missions and a few non-native colonial individuals represent the remainder of the recorded deaths. Death from disease became commonplace, and periodic epidemics, such as one in 1802, further devastated the native population. As Milliken (2002:54) notes, by the end of the 18th century, "all autonomous native villages from the ocean shore to the eastside of the Santa Clara Valley were empty."

Within the mission, neophyte numbers reached more than 1,400 by 1806. Mission Santa Clara was only able to sustain and grow the native population, and thus the labor force, through a constant influx of new converts. After 1811, native groups east of Santa Clara, the majority of which spoke the Yokuts language, were brought into the mission to replace the dwindling numbers of Ohlone (Milliken 2002:57–60). By 1815, the cultural affiliations of individuals buried in the cemetery had markedly changed (Mayfield et al. 1981:30). Cultural affiliation was noted as 38.4% Ohlone, 26.5% Santa Clara Mission Indians (meaning those born at the mission), 22.2% Yokuts, 6% Miwok, 1.7% nonnative colonials, and 1.7% with no affiliation listed. During the next several decades, more than 1,800 Yokuts were incorporated into this mission system. After 1829 and a tribal revolt against the soldiers, fewer Yokuts were baptized, although the baptisms continued to the end of the mission period. Miwok were also brought into the mission, although in smaller numbers. Baptism of new Miwok converts continued until secularization; in 1835, 60 Miwok were baptized at Mission Santa Clara (Milliken 2002:57–60).

Native American response to this program

of indoctrination was varied. Milliken (1995) describes the imbalance of power once colonization began, and the policies that restricted neophyte actions and reactions. For example, mission fathers determined where neophyte populations lived, and directed construction of adobe buildings for use as native housing. Allen (1998:91) notes that despite limitations, some native patterns continued within the mission system, including construction of native-style houses. Construction of shelter was a necessity—native converts had to live somewhere and there were never enough adobe houses for everyone. Neophytes' tribal affiliations and thousands of years of cultural habit determined the styles of the houses, especially for the newly converted. Recent excavations uncovered evidence of these two kinds of housing for this neophyte population: connected rooms of adobe on a stone foundation, and a native-style housepit.

Documentary and Ethnographic Evidence for Housing

In 1777, when the Franciscan Fathers founded Mission Santa Clara, they noted nearby Ohlone villages, as well as their houses. Father Peña specifically noted more than 40 "rancherias" within a five-league distance. Spearman (1963:15) recounts that the fathers noted "willow and grass huts." According to a number of ethnographic sources, summarized by Allen (1998:23), and also Levy (1978) and Heizer and Elsasser (1980), the common Ohlone winter houses had a conical base structure. Tule matting or brush covered a framework of bent willow poles. Houses typically provided a residence for 6 to 20 people. Spring and summer dwellings were more informal, and often smaller. The Ohlone moved frequently during seasonal rounds; they abandoned and often burned their residences as they left them. This cycle of abandonment helped to control animal and insect infestation, as well as refuse.

Under the supervision of the Franciscan fathers, Indian neophytes constructed all of the buildings within a mission complex. Building programs at all mission sites began with the church, and then expanded to the structures surrounding the church, known as the mission quadrangle. The latter structures included quarters for the priests. Neophytes lived in the vicinity of these buildings, in their native-style houses. As the annual report for 1779 notes, "There are 11 families of married neophytes that live in the Missions in their tule houses" (Skowronek et al. 2006:49). By 1786, the annual report noted: "There are in the Mission 61 families of married neophytes who live in a village of straw houses and they go to church mornings and afternoons to pray the Christian doctrine together with the bachelors, and all together there are 557" (Skowronek et al. 2006:125). The following year, the father reported: "There remain 70 families of married neophytes, 507 individuals of both sexes and all ages, which add up to 647 persons who live communally in a village of straw huts" (Skowronek et al. 2006:133). The annual report for 1789 notes that "There are 84 families of married neophytes who live in the town made of straw huts, supporting themselves communally from the grain of their crops" (Skowronek et al. 2006:141).

Some adobe housing for neophyte families were eventually built at all missions. At Mission Santa Clara, the first neophyte adobe houses were built in 1792, some 15 years after the founding of the mission. Until that time, neophytes would have lived in their native-style houses. In 1792, during the construction phase of the third mission church and quadrangle complex, eight houses were built. Remarkably, one of these neophyte adobe houses still exists, and is owned by the Santa Clara Woman's Club (Figure 6). It is registered as California Historical Landmark No. 249, and dates to approximately 1792–1800 (Office of Historic Preservation 2008). Although none of these structures appears on historic mission maps, they appear in Sandel's drawing at the right edge. As he depicts (Figure 3), there were several rows of residences in this area. The 1792 annual report noted that they were "8 varas long and 5 varas wide, each one as a home for the Indians" (Skowronek et al. 2006:160). A vara is generally ascribed to be approximately 32.755 in. (Spearman 1963:n5,116), ostensibly making each room about 21.8 ft. long and 13.6 ft. wide. The Native American population numbered 1,001 individuals in 1792, certainly too many to house all in the new adobe structures.

During a voyage in the north Pacific, Captain George Vancouver visited Mission Santa Clara in 1792. The naturalist on the voyage (as dictated by one of the officers) noted the living conditions of the neophytes:

FIGURE 6. "Oldest Adobe House in Santa Clara, built by Mission Indians." Colorized postcard made from photograph taken by Alice Hare, ca. 1904. (Courtesy of the Santa Clara City Library.)

They saw a crouded [sic] Indian Village close to the Mission, composd [sic] of mean huts or wigwams similar in form and materials to those we have already described at the Mission of San Francisco and containing about the same number of Natives converted to the Christian Religion by the indefatigable and persuasive endeavours of these worthy Fathers. These Natives are usefully employed in the various occupations necessary for the support of the Settlement and their own subsistence. They were at this time building for themselves under the direction of the Fathers a long row of Houses similar to those of the Spaniards, with two snug Apartments in each, and when they once experience the comforts and conveniences of these dwellings, there is no doubt but they will be induced to continue a plan so laudable and which cannot fail to contribute greatly to their general welfare and happiness (Eastwood 1924:278–280; Skowronek et al. 2006:156–159).

In 1793, the annual report noted that "14 adobe houses with thatched roofs for the Indians were built. 2 houses of adobe measuring 10 varas [27.3 ft.] with a dirt loft and straw roof" (Skowronek et al. 2006:162). The distinction between the two kinds of construction is not clear, but the description implies that the latter two houses were of cruder construction. In 1794, nine more

houses "have been built adjacent to each other, for the Indians, and of the same style as last year" (Skowronek et al. 2006:165).

In 1800, President of the Missions Father Lasuén responded to charges regarding living conditions in the Alta California missions. He specifically noted the following about Mission Santa Clara, indicating that the neophytes were living in native-style houses as well as the adobe rows of rooms:

[Question:] "In what condition are the quarters of the Indians in general, and of the girls and single men in particular?"

Outwardly they do not differ from those of the Indians in general, for they are made of palisades and grass. They protect against the weather, but are not secure against fire. Until now it has not been possible to provide more convenient quarters, owing to the necessity of constructing the requisite buildings for the produce and other goods; but they are very decent and comfortable, round in shape. They are not as small and narrow as those of the pagans, inasmuch as they measure six yards in diameter, some even seven and eight yards. Adobe structures are being erected gradually and

Perspectives from *Historical Archaeology*

covered with tiles. The adobe houses are between six and seven yards [*varas*?] long and four and one-half yards wide. Each has a door and a window (Engelhardt 1915:2.574; Skowronek et al. 2006:180).

There is a hiatus in the annual reports between 1797 and 1809. Beginning in 1810, the annual reports regularly state that for the most part, existing buildings were reroofed. Although other structures are reported, no new neophyte adobe quarters are noted after this date. After 1811, and the influx of Yokuts-speaking natives into the mission, more native-style housing would have been required. Yokuts residences were similar in shape to their Ohlone counterparts (Latta 1949; Wallace 1978). An oval framework of light poles was placed over a circular depression and overlapping tule mats (made from vegetal materials found in abundant freshwater sources) were laid on top of the framework. Houses were generally placed on flat areas next to water sources, and were constructed and abandoned according to the dictates of seasonal rounds.

Captain Otto von Kotzebue of the Russian Imperial Navy visited Mission Santa Clara in 1824. He described the area, vegetation, livestock, and the mission complex itself:

> They consist of a large stone church, a spacious dwelling-house for the monks, a large magazine for the preservation of corn, and the Rancherios, or barracks, for the Indians, of which mention has already been made [of the Indians]. These are divided into long rows of houses, or rather stalls, where each family is allowed a space scarcely large enough to enable them to lie down to repose (von Kotzebue 1830; Skowronek et al. 2006:245).

Captain F. W. Beechey, during his voyage in the Pacific, visited Mission Santa Clara in 1826. He noted "five rows of buildings" for neophyte accommodation (Mayfield et al. 1981:35). Beechey also noted that these buildings were for a population of "1,400 Indians, who since Vancouver's visit, have been provided with comparatively comfortable dwellings, instead of occupying straw huts, which were always wet and miserable" (Skowronek et al. 2006:264).

The annual reports do not state how many rooms were in each row. Given the population of neophytes, which the 1826 report lists at 1,428 individuals (Skowronek et al. 2006:370), there were still simply not enough adobe houses for all neophytes, even considering that young girls of marriageable age were housed separately in the quadrangle building adjacent to the church, in the dormitory known as the *monjerio*. It seems very probable that some families continued to live in native houses. It is most likely that neophytes who had lived longest at the mission, and had gained the trust of the missionaries, would be housed in the adobe structures (Farris 1991:40; Allen 1998:51; Farris and Johnson 1999:8). Newer arrivals constructed their own native-style houses in which to live.

Contemporary drawings and travel accounts by seafaring Europeans also describe native-style houses within other missions. Auguste Bernard Duhaut-Cilly, a 19th-century explorer who visited California in 1827 to 1828, near the end of the mission period, depicted native houses at Mission San Luis Rey alongside temporary Spanish/Mexican-style palisade (*palisada*) buildings (Figure 7). In the drawing, the native houses are in an open area in front of the adobe church and quadrangle of Mission San Luis Rey (Egenhoff 1952:43). Alfred Robinson, traveling in 1829, produced a drawing of San Luis Rey with much the same perspective, although he did not depict either the temporary *palisada* or the native structures, perhaps in an effort to "clean up" the perspective. Interestingly, Robinson depicted native structures at Missions San Gabriel and San Buenaventura (Egenhoff 1952:48–50). He also described the native residences: "In many of the villages the residences consist of straw huts of an oval form, which, when decayed, the Indians set on fire and erect new ones" (Egenhoff 1952:48). José Cardero, visiting in 1792, also drew illustrations of Carmel Mission that show rows of native-style houses (Cutter 1990:83,130). At Mission Santa Inés as well, the number of neophytes required that the majority of them would have lived in traditional-style houses. Importantly, the area of the probable Indian village has been identified (Wilcoxon et al. 1989a:26–28). An artist's reconstruction was commissioned for the interpretation of archaeological investigations at Mission Vieja de la Purísima (the first location of this mission). Although not archaeologically confirmed, the illustration shows native-style huts that extend out behind and to the side of the south wing of the mission quadrangle (Costello 1994b:76).

Archaeological Evidence

Evidence of native-style housing had not been archaeologically encountered until the recent

FIGURE 7. "Vue de la Mission de San-Luis-Rey en Californie, Voyage Autour du Monde, 1834," by Auguste Bernard Duhaut-Cilly. (Courtesy of the Bancroft Library, University of California, Berkeley, G440.B48 Vault v.1opp.p.215; also reproduced in Egenhoff 1952:43.)

excavations at Santa Clara. The housepit that marked the location of the native house was circular in plan view, and measured 9.8 ft. (3 m) in diameter. First identified as an irregularly shaped stain in the bottom of an open-area excavation, a half circle became apparent as more overburden soil was mechanically removed (Figure 8). Hand excavation of the feature revealed the details of this remarkable find (Figure 9). The circular housepit was shaped like a shallow basin with sloping walls and a flat floor, and a slightly raised berm extending around the eastern half of the housepit, and likely continuing on the western edge. In the center of the housepit, archaeologists encountered an intact hearth filled with ash. A posthole was situated just south of the hearth. A second posthole, on the opposite side of the hearth, was truncated and expanded by the excavation of a pit that clearly had been dug into the abandoned and burned housepit at a later date. From the housepit, what was interpreted as an entryway extended westward. A small, shallow secondary hearth was found at the western extension of the entryway. This suggests that the entryway itself was not covered, but became hard packed with use. Another post-abandonment pit feature truncated the hard-packed entryway at its westernmost extension.

Soil in the section of the housepit clearly indicated that the house had been burned after abandonment, a typical pattern of native residential abandonment, and one indicated by Robinson and ethnographic information. Burned vegetal material covered the floor of the housepit, and was subject to pollen, phytolith, and macrofloral analyses (Cummings et al. 2008). Remains from the sunflower family (Asteraceae) dominated the pollen record, leading researchers to posit that evidence of this European-introduced plant was either from cooking fires built within the structure, used as part of the house frame, or a vegetal layer used to cover the dirt floor. Phytolith evidence showed the presence of cut straw, probably brought in on clothing, as there was not enough evidence to suggest that straw was used to cover the floor. Soil samples from the hearth and surrounding areas were also sent out for pollen and macrofloral study. The reports by G. James West and Eric Wogelmuth are in Allen et al. (2009). The macrofloral sample contained

296

FIGURE 8. Large spikes mark the row of pits, visible as stains after removal of overburden; archaeologist Dave Makar is in the foreground excavating one of these pits. The beginning of the housepit outline is just above the approximate center of the photograph. (Photo by author, August 2004.)

the feature. Hylkema and Allen (2009) summarize the number and kinds of *Olivella* shell disc beads recovered at Mission Santa Clara, and indicate that a bead type labeled as H1a is attributed to a temporal span described as early mission period, ca. A.D. 1770 to 1800. The edges of this type are ground smooth. A later type of similar *Olivella* disc bead is given the designation of H1b. These are similar in size and shape to H1a, but the degree of edge grinding diminished during the later mission period, ca. A.D. 1800 to 1816 (King 1974:91; Gibson 1976). A third kind of bead has been designated as H2; its edges are chipped only and not ground in any way. Like the H1b beads, H2 beads are from later mission periods (after 1800). From the living surface outside the housepit, a single H1b bead was recovered. From the post-abandonment fill, one medium-sized *Olivella* spire-lopped bead (A1b) was found, as well as an H2 bead. Two abalone beads, similar in shape and size to the *Olivella* ground beads were found. One bead showed signs of having its central hole drilled with a stone tip (H7a1), and the other with a needle (H7a2). Five clamshell beads (both stone-tip and needle-drilled varieties) were also found in the post-abandonment fill. Clamshell beads generally represent an economy that has been documented within late prehistoric and post-European contexts among Native Californian groups of the North Coast Ranges, South Coast Ranges, and interior San Joaquin Valley (Hylkema and Allen 2009). Their presence suggests Yokuts-speaking peoples. Overall, the shell beads, although few in number, suggest that the housepit feature dates after 1800.

A Desert Side-Notched projectile point was also recovered from the living surface associated with the housepit. The blade and tip of this Franciscan chert specimen was reworked; and it had also been exposed to heat (from the burning of the housepit?). From the post-abandonment fill, one Cottonwood triangular point was recovered. Hylkema (Allen et al. 2009:appendix I-D) notes the Cottonwood type is very common in late prehistoric and mission-period contexts in southern California. It is rarely found in Santa Clara Valley, but it was made of Franciscan red chert, a locally available material. While both of these projectile points are associated with mission-era deposits, further refinement of dates is not forthcoming. Their presence also suggests

elements of food remains (black walnuts, wheat, elderberries, and maize/corn), as well as evidence of tobacco use. Other vegetal elements were sunflower family members, manzanita, a goldenbush-type shrub, arrowweed, white oak, box elder, and willow/cottonwood. The woods may have formed part of the structure.

Evidence for dating the housepit comes from the presence of locally made roof tiles and ceramic vessels. According to Spearman (1963:49), ceramic roof- and floor-tile manufacturing began at Mission Santa Clara in 1795. Schuetz-Miller (1994:91) notes that in 1796, José Antonio Romero, a soldier at the San Francisco Presidio, was sent to missions San Francisco, Santa Clara, and Santa Cruz. The idea was that the artisan would teach neophytes the skills necessary to make ceramics of local clay.

Archaeologists also recovered a small number of shell beads from the housepit, providing additional information on the approximate date of

FIGURE 9. Clinton Blount photographing central hearth in housepit. (Photo by author, August 2004.)

a cultural affiliation with Yokuts groups to the south of Santa Clara.

The location of the housepit, west of the third mission church, suggests that this area was occupied after the rows of adobe neophyte housing were constructed, that is, also after about 1800. During that time, the neophyte population numbered more than 1,300. As noted above, after 1811 there was an influx of Yokuts-speaking natives into Mission Santa Clara. These new converts would have constructed native-style houses to live within the mission community.

Several other pit features were found in the vicinity of the housepit, and represent a neophyte living and use area that likely postdates the use of the housepit. One of these certainly did, as it was cut into the burned remnants of the native house and overlying strata. These pits are interpreted as caches, either for food or belongings, or both. They were filled with material similar to

that recovered in the housepit, that is, *tejas*, animal bones, ceramics, and chipped-stone artifacts. Most remarkable was the quantity of shell beads found (Hylkema and Allen 2009). The presence and content of the pits indicates that the area was used for neophyte housing for an extended period of time, and neophytes may have used these pits to store (or hide) food and potential trade items, as well as to provide a convenient place for later discard.

To the northeast of the housepit feature, archaeologists encountered a long, linear rock feature. A portion of this same foundation was identified in 1996 (Skowronek et al. 2006:147). Clearly a large structure, it does not appear on any historic maps. At this time it seems too outsized to be a foundation for a neophyte housing row, especially in comparison with the foundation of the Santa Clara Woman's Adobe, and was likely a granary building, but one that is not noted in the extant annual reports.

Perspectives from *Historical Archaeology*

To the north and further west of the business school area, four other similar mission-era pit features were found. Field methodologies in this area designated for a new Jesuit residence and parking also emphasized removal of the overburden and open areas of excavation. Archaeologists directed a backhoe as it stripped away pavement, fill, and other modern intrusions and exposed the historic ground surface(s). This process consisted of both vertical and horizontal excavation, usually accomplished with heavy equipment. Excavation depth did not generally exceed the vertical project impact unless it was necessary to excavate and expose features. If the tops of features were to be impacted by construction activities, then the entire feature was excavated. All features were hand excavated, and wet screening occurred concurrently with the field effort.

Great amounts of roof tile and animal bone filled the pit features. The pits seemed to be of two varieties. The first, roughly conical in shape, were excavated to about 3–4 ft. in depth. The second type combined two associated pits, with larger, deeper pits (up to 5 ft. in depth) dug adjacent to shallower "platform" pits (2–3 ft. in depth). These "platforms" would have allowed easier access to the deeper pits; one pit had hand- and footholds visible in the sidewalls. Given their larger size, the bigger pits may have originally been used as adobe borrow pits, similar to the one found several years earlier (Hylkema and Skowronek 2000). In addition to the roof tile and animal bone, all pits had domestic materials found within the fill, including chipped stone; clamshell, *Olivella*, and glass beads; imported and local ceramics; charcoal; fire-affected rock; and other cultural debris. Further reporting on these features is currently underway.

To the east of these pit features, and to the west of the Santa Clara Woman's Adobe (the neophyte structure), the foundation of another adobe neophyte residence was found. As the proposed disturbance in the area of this possible residence was limited to a light pole, only minimal excavation occurred. Recovered artifacts were few in number, but included faunal and shellfish remains, roof tile, adobe-block fragments, fire-affected rock, a single glass bead, and a single sherd of Mexican lead-glazed earthenware. The feature was protected and left in situ.

Archaeologists also encountered an area of butchering. Backhoe trenches were used to

FIGURE 10. Area exposure, used to determine depth and boundaries of Feature 1, a large butchering area. (Photo by author, 17 March 2005.)

determine the extent of this sizeable refuse feature. Shallow mechanical scrapes, stepped to help determine stratigraphy, revealed that the feature covered a very large area (Figure 10). A deeper trench on the east side of the feature illustrated a section of what was now recognized as a large mission-period animal-bone refuse scatter. Study of the section suggested that deposits within the refuse pit were not particularly variable, and that contexts exposed in the deeper trench were much the same as the shallower exposures. It also indicated that during the mission period there was a small hillock dipping to a drainage in the area. The animals seemed to have been butchered on the hill, and non-useable animal parts and other trash were "tossed" down the side. During the later American period, the area was filled and flattened, and remains so today.

In a preliminary report, Garlinghouse (2007) reported that approximately 8,210 fragments of faunal material were recovered from mission-era archaeological contexts. The vast majority of the bone was highly fragmented and/or burned, so that only undifferentiated mammal or vertebrate subphylum could be identified. As a result, only about 20% of the assemblage was identified, including domestic cattle (*Bos taurus*), sheep/goat (*Ovis/Capra*), rabbit/hare (lagomorphs), and other rodent. Cattle bone represented about a third of the identifiable material, and three types of butchering marks were found on these materials. Knives and axes were the main instruments used during the Spanish and Mexican periods for butchering cattle, leaving cut and hack marks typical of the mission period. Gust (1981) has described these patterns. There was also evidence of spiral fracturing—a smash and twist method—that represents a common technique for marrow extraction among prehistoric Native Americans. As Garlinghouse (2008) notes, "the implication then is that at least some traditional Native American butchering practices survived missionization, especially with regard to the processing of limb bones of large mammals." The feature is an interesting counterpoint to the *matanza* reported by Burson (1999). As with previous excavations, narrow trenching or smaller units would have masked the coverage and the content of this large butchering feature. Only broad expansive removal of overburden showed its extent and purpose.

Reconsidering Mission Land Use and the Archaeological Record

The author has conducted research at a few other mission sites in California. At Santa Cruz, research focused on a standing adobe neophyte residence similar to the building found at Santa Clara. California Department of Parks and Recreation archaeologists conducted excavations in support of restoration of the adobe building and the creation of public space (Felton 1987; Allen 1998). Excavations focused on the interior of the structure, and recovered construction materials, ceramics, glass, faunal remains, organic food and vegetal remains, metal, leather, shell and glass beads, and miscellaneous personal artifacts. Some artifacts were also recovered directly from adjacent yard areas and included some trash deposits. Governed by project constraints, archaeologists recognized that "[w]hile the archaeological assemblage recovered was rich, it was also limited in its ability to fully describe the past" and represented "only a small portion of neophyte everyday life" (Allen et al. 2003:11). In part this was a comment on the limits of the archaeological record, but it is also a commentary on the location of the excavation units. Neophytes did not constrain their activities to areas only *within* and *nearby* buildings; much of the land surrounding the surviving neophyte adobe remains an untapped archaeological resource for discovering other more temporary land use and residential areas. Recent excavations at Santa Clara make one wonder about the

impact of project constraints, and consequently what parts and evidence of neophyte daily life, from archival, ethnographic, and archaeological evidence, the author's dissertation research was not able to consider.

Similarly, as part of a team of researchers studying an update of the National Historic Landmark description and boundaries for Mission Santa Barbara, the author's attention focused primarily on standing buildings and structures (Allen and Felton 1998; Allen et al. 2000). In large part, this is due to the nature of the program and designation process. Identified contributing elements included the mission church, quadrangle, adjacent cemetery, fountain, laundry, filter house, reservoirs, visible aqueduct systems, and dams. Structures that had deteriorated but of which much was still visible were identified as contributing archaeological features: garden, pottery, tanning vats, grist mill, and a stone building of unidentified function. The text also noted that based on a study of historic maps and historians' reports (Webb 1952:103; Geiger 1963:12,70), many other buildings, structures, and landscaping elements were likely present in the archaeological record, including a corral, threshing floor, neophyte adobe residences, orchard walls, kilns, granary, gardener's house, soldiers' quarters, etc. Recent discoveries at Santa Clara make the author look at historic maps and historic drawings in an entirely new light, and realize that while structures may be a good place to begin archaeological investigation and plan for preservation whenever possible, envisioning the potential for archaeological features of everyday life and activity areas should not be so constrained.

Much of the historical and archaeological literature considers the impact of the mission on the Native American communities, and the transformation of cultural self-identities and practices. The same has to be true of the missionaries; interactions with the neophytes must have altered their worldview as well as their daily activities. Consideration of the archaeological record of everyday life, in the spaces where those activities occurred, is critical to understanding these cultural nuances and transformations. It also has important implications for the ecological and biological transformation of nearby lands that occurred along with the colonization. These kinds of studies will require investigations that stretch the planning for where excavations occur, in order to define or redefine known areas of land use, and move away from the structures. Findings also prompt reconsideration of documentary and ethnographic lines of data and evidence, expanding the historical and archaeological view of Alta California's mission past.

Acknowledgments

My thanks to those who made the archaeological recovery and interpretation possible at Santa Clara: Joe Sugg, Linda Hylkema, and students at Santa Clara University; Clinton Blount and his talented crew at Albion Environmental, Inc.; and my business partner and excellent field director R. Scott Baxter. Russ Skowronek's recent publications on Mission Santa Clara made many of the interpretations of data possible. I have also benefitted from excavations at Mission Santa Cruz undertaken by the California Department of Parks and Recreation, and a longstanding history of garnering invaluable criticisms and insights from Larry Felton. Mike Imwalle provided some important references from Mission Santa Inés. Margie Purser kindly herded this paper through the review process, and the paper's content and prose was greatly improved by the input of Glenn Farris, Minette Church, Barb Voss, and the Waselkovs. Finally, thanks to Maher Tleimat and Amanda Allen for helping me learn how to structure my time so that I could write down some of my thoughts.

References

ABDO-HINTZMAN, KHOLOOD
2008 Brand Park Community Center Project, Mission Hills, California. *Society for Historical Archaeology Newsletter* 41(4):36–37.

ALLEN, REBECCA
1998 *Native Americans at Mission Santa Cruz, 1791–1834, Interpreting the Archaeological Record.* Perspectives in California Archaeology, Vol. 5. Institute of Archaeology, University of California, Los Angeles.

ALLEN, REBECCA, R. SCOTT BAXTER, LINDA HYLKEMA, CLINTON BLOUNT, AND STELLA D'ORO
2009 Uncovering and Interpreting History and Archaeology at Mission Santa Clara. Report to Santa Clara University, Santa Clara, from Past Forward, Inc., Garden Valley, Albion Environmental, Inc., Santa Cruz, and Archaeology Research Lab, Santa Clara University, Santa Clara, CA.

ALLEN, REBECCA, ROMAN BECK, JAMES H. CLELAND, DAVID L. FELTON, TIM HAZELTINE, ROBERT HOOVER, AND JOHN R. JOHNSON
2000 Mission Santa Barbara, California, National Historic Landmark District. Report to National Historic Landmarks Survey, National Park Service, Washington, DC, from Past Forward, Richmond, CA.

ALLEN, REBECCA, AND CLINTON BLOUNT
2009 Preliminary Report on Recent Mission Era Findings at Santa Clara University. *Proceedings of the Society for California Archaeology* 21:21–27. Society for California Archaeology, Chico, CA.

ALLEN, REBECCA, GLENN J. FARRIS, DAVID L. FELTON, EDNA E. KIMBRO, AND KAREN HILDEBRAND
2003 Restoration Research at Santa Cruz Mission State Historic Park: A Retrospective. In Archaeological, Cultural and Historical Perspectives on Alta California, Rose Marie Beebe, editor, pp. 1–20. *Proceedings of the 20th Annual Conference of the California Mission Studies Association, Santa Cruz, California, February 14–16, 2003.* California Mission Studies Association, Bakersfield, CA.

ALLEN, REBECCA, AND DAVID L. FELTON
1998 The Water System at Mission Santa Barbara. *California Mission Studies Association Occasional Paper* 1. California Mission Studies Association, Bakersfield, CA.

ALLEN, REBECCA, TOM GARLINGHOUSE, JENNIFER FARQUHAR, CLINTON BLOUNT, LESLIE FRYMAN, AND DANA MCGOWAN
2004 Cultural Resources Treatment Plan for the Ten Year Capital Plan. Report to Santa Clara University, Santa Clara, from Past Forward, Inc., Garden Valley, Albion Environmental, Inc., Santa Cruz, and Jones and Stokes, Sacramento, CA.

BARKER, PHILIP
1977 *Techniques of Archaeological Excavation.* Universe Books, New York, NY.

BARKER, LEO R., REBECCA ALLEN, AND JULIA G. COSTELLO
1995 The Archaeology of Spanish and Mexican Alta California. In *The Archaeology of Spanish and Mexican Colonialism in the American Southwest,* James E. Ayres, editor, pp. 3–51. Guides to the Archaeological Literature of the Immigrant Experience in America, No. 3, Society for Historical Archaeology, Ann Arbor, MI.

BENNYHOFF, JAMES A., AND ALBERT B. ELSASSER
1954 *Sonoma Mission: An Historical and Archaeological Study of Primary Construction, 1823–1913.* Reports of the University of California Archaeological Survey, No. 27. University of California, Berkeley.

BERTRANDO, LUTHER
1997 Mission San Antonio de Padua Archaeological Field School Excavations of 1993, 1994, and 1996. *Pacific Coast Archaeological Society Quarterly* 33(4):57–93.

BRANDES, RAYMOND, JAMES R. MORIARTY III, TONI NAGLE, GREGORY NELSON CHASE, AND LOIS T. CAMPBELL
1987 Mission San Diego de Alcalá: The Archaeological Design and Fieldwork Conducted by the University of San Diego, 1966 to 1984. Manuscript, University of San Diego, San Diego, CA.

BROADBENT, SYLVIA M.
1955 Carmel Mission (Mnt-18): A Preliminary Report on Excavated Materials. Archaeological Research Facility, Department of Anthropology, University of California, Berkeley.

BRYNE, STEPHEN
2001 Archaeological Monitoring of the Field House Electrical Upgrade, Santa Clara University, Santa Clara County, California. Report to Archaeology Research Lab, Santa Clara University, Santa Clara, from Garcia and Associates, San Anselmo, CA.

BURSON, ELIZABETH
1999 Cow Pit—A Probable Matanzas Cattle Bone Deposit on the Santa Clara University Campus. Archaeology Research Lab, Santa Clara University, Santa Clara, CA.

CANNON, RENÉE
2005 Beneath the Plaza Hotel: In Search of the San Juan Bautista Mission Escolta. Master's thesis, Department of Anthropology, California State University, East Bay.

CLEMMER, JOHN S.
1961 The Archaeology of the Neophyte Indian Village at San Juan Bautista. Manuscript 115. California State Division of Beaches and Parks, Sacramento.

COHEN-WILLIAMS, ANITA G.
2005 Archaeological Investigations of the Sunken Gardens of Mission San Luis Rey. In Architecture, Physical Environment and Society in Alta California, Rose Marie Beebe and Robert M. Senkewicz, editors, pp.13–64. Proceedings of the 22nd Annual Conference of the California Mission Studies Association, Mission San Fernando Rey de España February 18–20, 2005. California Mission Studies Association, Bakersfield, CA.

COSTELLO, JULIA G.
1989 Santa Inés Mission Excavations: 1986–1988. California Historical Archaeology, Vol. 1. Coyote Press, Salinas, CA.
1990 Test Excavations at Santa Barbara Mission Mausoleum Addition, CA-SBA-25. Report to Dames and Moore, Goleta, from Foothill Resources, Mokelumne, CA.
1993 Mission Vieja de la Purísima, CA-SBA-521H, Report on the 1991–1992 Archaeological Investigations. Report to City of Lompoc, from Foothill Resources, Mokelumne, CA.
1994a The Ranches and Ranchos of Mission San Antonio de Padua. California Mission Studies Association Keepsake Volume. California Mission Studies Association, Bakersfield, CA.
1994b Putting Mission Vieja de la Purísima on the Map. Proceedings of the Society for California Archaeology 7:67–85.

COSTELLO, JULIA G. (EDITOR)
1991 Documentary Evidence for the Spanish Missions of Alta California. Garland Publishing, New York, NY.

COSTELLO, JULIA, EDNA KIMBRO, AND LARRY R. WILCOXON
1997 Mission Santa Inés, California, National Historic Landmark Nomination. Report to National Park Service, Washington, DC, from Foothill Resources, Mokelumne Hill, CA.

CUMMINGS, LINDA SCOTT, KATHRYN PUSEMAN, AND CHAD YOST
2008 Pollen, Phytolith, and Macrofloral Analysis of Samples from Feature 57 at the SCU-Leavey Site, Santa Clara, California. Report to Past Forward, Inc., Garden Valley, CA, from Paleo Research Institute, Golden, CO.

CUTTER, DONALD C.
1990 California in 1792: A Spanish Naval Visit. University of Oklahoma Press, Norman.

DEETZ, JAMES F.
1963 Final Summary Report of Investigations at La Purísima Mission, State Historical Monument. Manuscript 133, California State Division of Beaches and Parks, Sacramento.

DIETZ, STEPHEN A.
1986 Archaeological Investigations of a Mission Santa Cruz Tanning Vat Located at 126 Escalona Drive, Santa Cruz, California. Manuscript, Archaeological Consulting and Research Services, Santa Cruz, CA.

DIETZ, STEPHEN A., G. J. WEST, J. G. COSTELLO, H. H. NEEDLES, AND V. CASSMAN
1983 Final Report of Archaeological Investigations at Mission San Jose (CA-Ala-1). Report to Gilbert Arnold Sanchez, A.I.A., Santa Cruz, from Archaeological Consulting and Research Services, Santa Cruz, CA.

EASTWOOD, ALICE
1924 Archibald Menzies' Journal of the Vancouver Expedition. California Historical Quarterly 2(4):265–340.

EGENHOFF, ELISABETH L.
1952 Fabricas: A Collection of Pictures and Statements on the Mineral Materials Used in Building in California Prior to 1850. Supplement to the California Journal of Mines and Geology (April). State of California, Department of Natural Resources, Division of Mines, San Francisco.

ENGELHARDT, ZEPHYRIN
1915 The Missions and Missionaries in California, Vol. 2. James H. Barry, San Francisco, CA.

FARNSWORTH, PAUL
1987 The Economics of Acculturation in the California Missions: A Historical and Archaeological Study of Mission Nuestra Señora de La Soledad. Doctoral dissertation, Department of Anthropology, University of California, Los Angeles. University Microfilms International, Ann Arbor, MI.

1992 Missions, Indians, and Cultural Continuity. *Historical Archaeology* 26(1):21–36.

FARRIS, GLENN J.
1991 Archeological Testing in the Neophyte Family Housing Area at Mission San Juan Bautista, California. Manuscript, California Department of Parks and Recreation, Cultural Heritage Section, Sacramento.
1997 Archaeological Excavation of the "Old Warehouse" and Granary at La Purisima Mission State Historic Park. *Pacific Coast Archaeological Society Quarterly* 33(4):1–28.

FARRIS, GLENN J., AND JOHN R. JOHNSON
1999 Prominent Indian Families at Mission La Purisima Concepcion as Identified in Baptismal, Marriage, and Burial Records. *California Mission Studies Association Occasional Paper* 3. California Mission Studies Association, Bakersfield, CA.

FELTON, DAVID L.
1987 Santa Cruz Mission Historic Park: Architectural and Archeological Investigations, 1984–1985. Revision of 1985 edition. Manuscript, California Department of Parks and Recreation, Cultural Heritage Section, Sacramento.

FOSTER, JOHN M., AND ROBERTA S. GREENWOOD
1989 Examination of a Small Portion of the Mission San Buenaventura Aqueduct. Report to City of San Buenaventura, from Greenwood and Associates, Pacific Palisades, CA.

GABEL, NORMAN E.
1952 Report on Archaeological Research Project at La Purisima Mission State Historic Monument During 25 June to 4 August 1951. Manuscript 177, California State Division of Beaches and Parks, District 5 Office, Goleta.

GARLINGHOUSE, THOMAS S.
2007 Preliminary Analysis of Faunal Remains from Mission Period Features at Santa Clara. Paper presented at the 41st Conference on Historical Archaeology, San Jose, CA. Society for California Archaeology, Chico, CA

GEIGER, MAYNARD
1963 *A Pictorial History of the Physical Development of Mission Santa Barbara from Brush Hut to Institutional Greatness 1786–1963.* Franciscan Fathers of California, San Francisco.

GEIGER, MAYNARD, AND CLEMENT W. MEIGHAN
1976 *As the Padres Saw Them: California Indian Life and Customs as Reported by the Franciscan Missionaries, 1813–1815.* Santa Barbara Mission Archive-Library, Santa Barbara, CA.

GIBSON, ROBERT O.
1976 A Study of Beads and Ornaments from the San Buenaventura Mission Site (Ven-87). In The Changing Faces of Main Street: San Buenaventura Mission Plaza Project Archeological Report, Roberta S. Greenwood, editor, pp. 77–166. Report to the Redevelopment Agency, City of San Buenaventura, from Greenwood and Associates, Pacific Palisades, CA.

GINN, SARAH, LINDA HYLKEMA, AND RUSSELL SKOWRONEK
2002 Cultural Resources Evaluation for the Lord John's Excavation Project SCU-ARL Project No. 1996.3. Manuscript, Archaeology Research Lab, Santa Clara University, Santa Clara, CA.

GREEN, FRED E.
1933 The San Diego Old Mission Dam and Irrigation System. Manuscript, San Diego Historical Society Library, San Diego, CA.

GREENWOOD, ROBERTA S.
2009 Recent Archaeological Investigations at Mission San Miguel: Postcards as Windows of Change. Paper presented at the 26th Annual Conference of the California Mission Studies Association, Carmel Mission.

GREENWOOD, ROBERTA S. (EDITOR)
1975 3500 Years on a City Block: San Buenaventura Mission Plaza Project Archeological Report 1974. Report to the Redevelopment Agency, City of San Buenaventura, from Greenwood and Associates, Pacific Palisades, CA.
1976 The Changing Faces of Main Street: San Buenaventura Mission Plaza Project Archeological Report. Report to the Redevelopment Agency, City of San Buenaventura, from Greenwood and Associates, Pacific Palisades, CA.

GREENWOOD, ROBERTA S., AND N. GESSLER
1968 The Mission San Buenaventura Aqueduct with Particular Reference to Fragments at Weldon Canyon. *Pacific Coast Archaeological Society Quarterly* 4(4):61–86.

GUST, SHERRI
1981 The Cooper-Molera Adobe Mammal Bones: A Mexican California Fauna. Manuscript, Cultural Heritage Section, California Department of Parks and Recreation, Sacramento.

HACKEL, STEVEN W.
2005 *Children of Coyote, Missionaries of Saint Francis: Indian-Spanish Relations in Colonial California, 1769–1850.* University of North Carolina, Chapel Hill.

HARRIS, EDWARD C.
1989 *Principles of Archaeological Stratigraphy,* 2nd edition. Academic Press, London, UK.

HEIZER, ROBERT F., AND ALFRED B. ELSASSER
1980 *The Natural World of the California Indians.* University of California, Berkeley.

HENDRY, GEORGE W.
1931 The Adobe Brick as an Historical Source. *Agricultural History* 5(3):110–127.

HENDRY, GEORGE W., AND MARGARET P. KELLY
1925 The Plant Content of Adobe Bricks. *California Historical Society Quarterly* 4(4):360–373.

HEWES, GORDON, AND MINNA HEWES (EDITORS AND TRANSLATORS)
1958 *Indian Life and Customs in Mission San Luis Rey: A Record of California Mission Life by Pablo Tac, an Indian Neophyte*. Old Mission, San Luis Rey, CA.

HOOVER, DAVID N., AND ROBERT L. HOOVER
2008 Mission San Antonio de Padua, A Chronology of Building. *Boletín, The Journal of the California Mission Studies Association* 25(1):35–66.

HOOVER, ROBERT L.
1992 Excavations at the Santa Inés Mill Complex. *Pacific Coast Archaeological Society Quarterly* 28(2):48–66.
2001 Excavations at the Mystery Column: The Possible Remains of a Wind-Powered Wool Fulling Post Mill at La Purísima State Park. *Pacific Coast Archaeological Society Quarterly* 37(1):37–49.
2002 Excavations at Mission San Antonio and Mission Santa Ines, 2002. *California Mission Studies Association Boletín* 19(2):41–42.
2009 Archaeological Research During the Seismic Retrofit of Mission San Miguel. Paper presented at the 26th Annual Conference of the California Mission Studies Association, Carmel Mission.

HOOVER, ROBERT L., DAVID L. MAKI, AND LEWIS SUMMERS
2004 A Geophysical Survey of Mission San Antonio de Padua. In The Mission and the Community, Dan Krieger, editor, pp. 1–9, plus figures. *Proceedings of the 21st Annual Conference of the California Mission Studies Association, San Luis Obispo, California, February 14–15, 2004*. California Mission Studies Association, Bakersfield, CA.

HOOVER, ROBERT L., AND JULIA G. COSTELLO (EDITORS)
1985 *Excavations at Mission San Antonio: The First Three Seasons, 1976–1978*. University of California, Los Angeles, Institute of Archaeology Monograph 26.

HUELSBECK, DAVID R.
1985 Santa Clara Mission Dig, Summer 1985. Interim Report. Manuscript, Archaeology Research Lab, Santa Clara University, Santa Clara, CA.
1987 Archaeological Resources in the Santa Clara University Expansion Area: Monitoring Demolition. Manuscript, Archaeology Research Lab, Santa Clara University, Santa Clara, CA.
1988 Test Excavations in the Proposed Right-of-Way of SCU's New Entrance Road: A Preliminary Report. Manuscript, Archaeology Research Lab, Santa Clara University, Santa Clara, CA.
1989 Monitoring Construction of SCU's New Entrance Road: A Preliminary Report. Manuscript, Archaeology Research Lab, Santa Clara University, Santa Clara, CA.

HUMPHREY, RICHARD
1965 The La Purísima Mission Cemetery. *Annual Reports of the University of California Archeological Survey* 7:179–192. Los Angeles.

HYLKEMA, LINDA, AND RUSSELL SKOWRONEK
2000 Diving Into the Past. *California Mission Studies Association Newsletter* 17(2):2–5.

HYLKEMA, MARK G.
1995 Archaeological Investigations at the Third Location of Mission Santa Clara de Asís: The Murguía Mission, 1781–1818 (CA-SCL-30/H). Manuscript, California Department of Transportation, District 4, Environmental Planning, Oakland.

HYLKEMA, MARK G., AND REBECCA ALLEN
2009 Archaeological Investigations at the Third Mission Site, Santa Clara University, and a Comparison of Shell Bead Assemblages with Recent Mission-Era Findings. *Proceedings of the Society for California Archaeology* 21:28–35. Society for California Archaeology, Chico, CA.

IMWALLE, MICHAEL H.
1996 Mission Canyon Aqueduct (CA-SBA-1852H) Research Project. Report to Santa Barbara Botanic Gardens, Santa Barbara, CA.

JENKINS, ISABEL R., B. MARK LYNCH, AND RUSSELL K. SKOWRONEK
1998 The Adobe Lodge: A Review of Archaeological Excavation and Historical Background. Manuscript, Archaeology Research Lab, Santa Clara University, Santa Clara, CA.

JONES, TERRY L., JULIA CORLEY, EDNA KIMBRO, AND JOHN L. EDWARDS
1997 Historical and Archaeological Evaluation of the Mission San Antonio de Padua Water System, Fort Hunter Liggett, Monterey County, California. Report to U.S. Army Corps of Engineers, Sacramento, from Garcia and Associates, Tiburon, CA.

KING, CHESTER
1974 Northern Santa Clara County Ethnography. In Archaeological Element: San Felipe Water Distribution Environmental Impact Report, Thomas King and G. Berg, editors, Appendix. Report to Santa Clara Valley Water District, from Environmental Science Associates, Foster City, CA.

KOTTMAN, KARL A.
2008 Pablo Tac's Manuscript "Concerning the Californians." *Boletín, The Journal of the California Mission Studies Association* 25(1):67–79.

LATTA, FRANK
1949 *Handbook of Yokuts Indians*. Bear State Books, Oildale, CA.

LEVY, RICHARD
1978 Costanoan. In *Handbook of North American Indians*, Vol. 8, *California*, Robert F. Heizer, editor, pp. 485–495. Smithsonian Institution, Washington, DC.

LIGHTFOOT, KENT G.
1995 Culture Contact Studies: Redefining the Relationship Between Prehistoric and Historical Archaeology. *American Antiquity* 60(2):199–217.
2005 *Indians, Missionaries, and Merchants*. University of California Press, Berkeley.

LIGHTFOOT, KENT G., MALCOLM MARGOLIN, KEITH DOUGLASS WARNER, JOHN R. JOHNSON, AND JULIA COSTELLO
 2005 Symposium: Indians, Missionaries, and Merchants: The Legacy of Colonial Encounters on the California Frontiers. *Boletín, The Journal of the California Mission Studies Association* 22(1):62–86.

LYNCH, MARK
 1981 Mission Santa Clara, 1777–1822. Manuscript, Archaeology Research Lab, Santa Clara University, Santa Clara, CA.

MAGALOUSIS, NICHOLAS M. (EDITOR)
 1989 Ten Years of Interdisciplinary Studies at Mission San Juan Capistrano: A Round Table Discussion. In *Proceedings of the Conference of Orange County History 1988*, pp. 34–35. Chapman College, Orange, CA.

MAYFIELD, DAVID W., MARGARET BUSS, AND JEFFERY C. BINGHAM
 1981 Archaeological Survey Report for an Improvement/ Realignment of Route 82 in the City of Santa Clara, Santa Clara County. Report to California Department of Transportation, District 4, Oakland.

MENDOZA, RUBEN G.
 2002 This Old Mission: San Juan Bautista Archaeology and the Hispanic Tradition. *California Mission Studies Association Boletín* 19(2):35–40.

MILLIKEN, RANDALL
 1995 *A Time of Little Choice: The Disintegration of Tribal Culture in the San Francisco Bay Area, 1769–1810.* Ballena Press, Menlo Park, CA.
 2002 The Indians of Mission Santa Clara. In *Telling the Santa Clara Story: Sesquicentennial Voices*, Russell K. Skowronek, editor, pp. 45–63. Santa Clara University and City of Santa Clara, CA.

MORA-TORRES, GREGORIO (TRANSLATOR AND EDITOR)
 2005 *Californio Voices: The Oral Memoirs of Jose Maria Amador And Lorenzo Asisara.* University of North Texas Press, Denton.

OFFICE OF HISTORIC PRESERVATION
 2008 California Historical Landmarks, Santa Clara. Office of Historic Preservation, California State Parks, Sacramento <http://www.ohp.parks.ca.gov/default .asp?page_id=21522>.

PETERSON, CHER, ROBERT JOHNSON, AND CLINTON BLOUNT
 2002 Extended Archaeological Survey, Leavey School of Business, Santa Clara University. Report to Santa Clara University, Santa Clara, from Albion Environmental, Inc., Santa Cruz, CA.

SANDELS, G. M. WASEURTZ AF
 1945 *A Sojourn in California by the King's Orphan: The Travels and Sketches of G. M. Waseurtz af Sandels, A Swedish Gentleman Who Visited California in 1842–1843.* Grabhorn Press, San Francisco, CA.

SANTA CLARA UNIVERSITY
 2003 Ten Year Capital Plan. Final Environmental Impact Report. Manuscript, City of Santa Clara Planning Commission, Santa Clara, CA.

SCHAFER, ROBERT G., AND CHRISTOPHER LOOMIS
 2005 Preserving the Jewel of the Missions: San Juan Capistrano's Great Stone Church, 1806–2004. *Boletín, The Journal of the California Mission Studies Association* 22(1):3–8.

SCHUETZ-MILLER, MARDITH K.
 1994 *Buildings and Builders in Hispanic California, 1769–1850.* Southwest Mission Research Center, Tuscon, AZ, and Santa Barbara Trust for Historic Preservation, Santa Barbara, CA.

SKOWRONEK, RUSSELL K., ELIZABETH THOMPSON, AND VERONICA (LOCOCO) JOHNSON
 2006 *Situating Mission Santa Clara de Asís, 1776–1851, Documentary and Material Evidence of Life on the Alta California Frontier: A Timeline.* Academy of American Franciscan History, Berkeley, CA.

SKOWRONEK, RUSSELL K., AND JULIE C. WIZOREK
 1997 Archaeology at Santa Clara de Asís: the Slow Rediscovery of a Moveable Mission. *Pacific Coast Archaeological Society Quarterly* 33(3):54–92.

SMITH, FRANCES RAND
 1921 *Architectural History of Mission San Carlos Borromeo, California.* Publications of the California Historical Survey Commission, Sacramento.
 1932 *Mission San Antonio de Padua.* Stanford University Press, Stanford, CA.

SOTO, ANTHONY
 1961 Mission San Luis Rey, California: Excavations in the Sunken Gardens. *Kiva* 26(4):34–43.

SPEARMAN, ARTHUR D.
 1958 Sites of Temporary and Permanent Churches and Buildings, Orchard, Gardens, and Corral of Mission Santa Clara de Asis A.D. 1777–1851, 1912–1957. Map, Santa Clara University Archives, Santa Clara, CA.
 1963 *The Five Franciscan Churches of Mission Santa Clara, 1777 to 1825.* National Press, Palo Alto, CA.

ST. CLAIR, MICHELLE
 2005 Mission San Juan Bautista: Zooarchaeological Investigations at a California Mission. Master's Thesis, Department of Anthropology, College of William and Mary, Williamsburgh, VA.

THOMAS, DAVID HURST
 1991 Harvesting Ramona's Garden: Life in California's Mythical Mission Past. In *Columbian Consequences, The Spanish Borderlands in Pan-American Perspective, Volume 3*, David Hurst Thomas, editor, pp. 119–153. Smithsonian Institution, Washington DC.

THOMPSON, RICHARD, PHILLIP REID, AND ANDREW A. GALVAN
2003   Excavations at a Neophyte Indian Dormitory CA-Ala-1/H, Mission San Jose, Located at 155 Washington Boulevard, City of Fremont, Alameda County, California. Report to Montessori Schools of Fremont, from Archaeor, Archaeological Consultants, Fremont, CA.

TREGANZA, A. E.
1956   Sonoma Mission: An Archaeological Reconstruction of the Mission San Francisco de Solano Quadrangle. *Kroeber Anthropological Society Papers* 14:1–18.

TREMAINE, KIM J.
1992   Investigation of a Nineteenth-Century Threshing Floor at Mission Santa Inés (CA-SBA-518). *Pacific Coast Archaeological Society Quarterly* 28(2):35–47.

VON KOTZEBUE, OTTO
1830   *A New Voyage Around the World in the Years 1823, 24, 25, and 26.* Henry Colburn and Richard Bentley, London, UK.

VOSS, BARBARA L.
2000   Colonial Sex: Archaeology, Structured Space, and Sexuality in Alta California's Spanish-Colonial Missions. In *Archaeologies of Sexuality*, Robert A. Schmidt and Barbara L. Voss, editors, pp. 35–61. Routledge, London, UK.
2008   *The Archaeology of Ethnogenesis: Race and Sexuality in Colonial San Francisco.* University of California, Berkeley.

WALLACE, EDITH
1978   Sexual Status and Role Differences. In *Handbook of North American Indians*, Vol. 8, *California*, Robert F. Heizer, editor, pp. 683–689. Smithsonian Institution, Washington, DC.

WEBB, EDITH BUCKLAND
1952   *Indian Life at the Old Missions.* University of Nebraska Press, Lincoln.

WHITEHEAD, RICHARD S. (EDITOR)
1980   *An Archaeological and Restoration Study of Mission La Purísima Concepcíon: Reports Written for the National Park Service.* Santa Barbara Trust for Historic Preservation, A. H. Clark, Glendale, CA.

WILCOXON, LARRY R., BRIAN D. HALEY, AND JULIA G. COSTELLO
1989a   An Evaluation of Cultural Resources on the Duff Mesa Property Pursuant to the City of Solvang's Proposed Specific Plan EIR Scenarios. Report to INTERFACE Environmental and Planning Services, Santa Barbara, from Larry R. Wilcoxon Archaeological Consultants, Goleta, CA.

WILCOXON, LARRY R., BRIAN D. HALEY, AND JAMES M. HARMON
1989b   Results of a Subsurface Archaeological Boundary Definition Program for Archaeological Sites SBA-518 and SBA-548 on Duff Mesa, Solvang, California. Report to INTERFACE Environmental and Planning Services, Santa Barbara, from Larry R. Wilcoxon Archaeological Consultants, Goleta, CA.

WILCOXON, LARRY R., MICHAEL H. IMWALLE, AND JULIA G. COSTELLO
1992   Preliminary Results of Archaeological Excavations at the Santa Ines Mission Tanning Vats in Conjunction with the Alisal Ranch Public Golf Course Development Near the City of Solvang, Santa Barbara County, California. Report to U.S. Army Corps of Engineers, Los Angeles District, from Larry R. Wilcoxon Archaeological Consultants, Goleta, CA.

WILLIAMS, JACK S.
2005   An Archaeological Investigation of the Neophyte Village at Mission Santa Barbara. Manuscript, Center for Spanish Colonial Research, San Diego, CA.

WILLIAMS, JACK S., AND ANITA G. COHEN-WILLIAMS
2007   Some Observations on the Archaeological Evidence of the Later Indian Village at Mission San Luis Rey, California. In Mission San Francisco de Asís in the Ohlone Village of Chutchui, Rose Marie Beebe and Robert M. Senekewicz, editors, pp. 97–112. *Proceedings of the 24th Annual Conference of the California Mission Studies Association, Mission San Francisco de Asís, February 16–18, 2007.* California Mission Studies Association, Bakersfield, CA.

WIZOREK, JULIE C.
1998   Santa Clara University Campus Lighting Project 1995.2. Manuscript, Archaeology Research Lab, Santa Clara University, Santa Clara, CA.

WIZOREK, JULIE C., AND RUSSELL K. SKOWRONEK
1996   Archaeological Monitoring Report: Alameda Mall Project, 1996.6. Manuscript, Archaeology Research Lab, Santa Clara University, Santa Clara, CA.
1997   Archaeological Site Treatment Plan, Communication, Public Policy, and Applied Ethics Building Five Year Master Plan Use Permit (File U.2077). Manuscript, Archaeology Research Lab, Santa Clara University, Santa Clara, CA.

REBECCA ALLEN
PAST FORWARD, INC.
PO BOX 969
GARDEN VALLEY, CA 95633